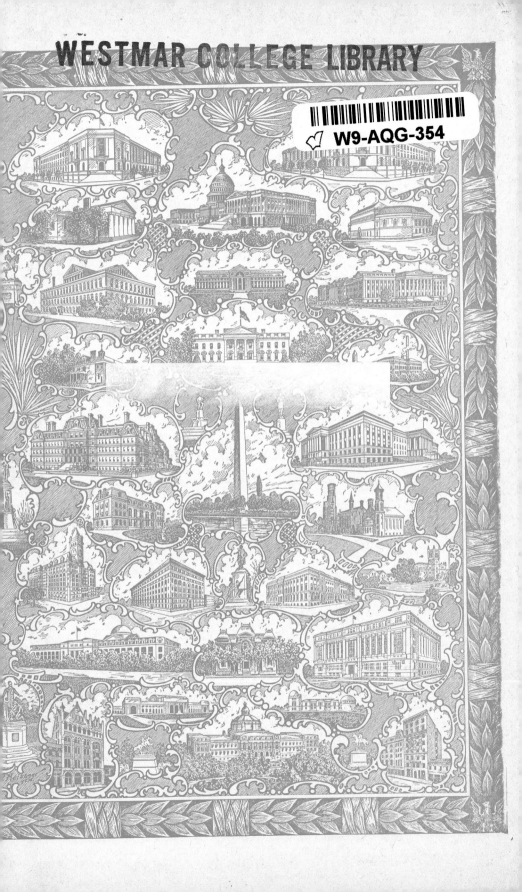

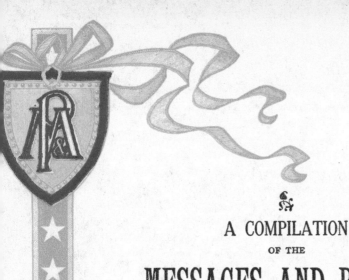

A COMPILATION

OF THE

MESSAGES AND PAPERS

OF THE

PRESIDENTS

Prepared Under the Direction of the Joint Committee
on Printing, of the House and Senate,
Pursuant to an Act of the Fifty-Second Congress
of the United States

(With Additions and Encyclopedic Index
by Private Enterprise)

VOLUME XI

PUBLISHED BY

BUREAU OF NATIONAL LITERATURE, Inc.
NEW YORK

Copyright, 1897

BY

JAMES D. RICHARDSON

Senate Chamber

ILLUSTRATIONS IN VOLUME ELEVEN

6th May, 1882, and 5th July, 1884. The hardship has in some cases been remedied by the action of the courts. In other cases, however, where the phraseology of the statutes has appeared to be conclusive against any discretion on the part of the officers charged with the execution of the law, Chinese persons expressly entitled to free admission under the treaty have been refused a landing and sent back to the country whence they came without being afforded any opportunity to show in the courts or otherwise their right to the privilege of free ingress and egress which it was the purpose of the treaty to secure.

In the language of one of the judicial determinations of the Supreme Court of the United States to which I have referred—

The supposition should not be indulged that Congress, while professing to faithfully execute the treaty stipulations and recognizing the fact that they secure to a certain class the right to go from and come to the United States, intended to make its protection depend upon the performance of conditions which it was physically impossible to perform. (112 U. S. Reports, p. 554, Chew Heong *vs.* United States.)

The act of July 5, 1884, imposes such an impossible condition in not providing for the admission, under proper certificate, of Chinese travelers of the exempted classes in the cases most likely to arise in ordinary commercial intercourse.

The treaty provisions governing the case are as follows:

ART. I. * * * The limitation or suspension shall be reasonable, and shall apply only to Chinese who may go to the United States as laborers, other classes not being included in the limitations. * * *

ART. II. Chinese subjects, whether proceeding to the United States as teachers, students, merchants, or from curiosity, together with their body and household servants, * * * shall be allowed to go and come of their own free will and accord, and shall be accorded all the rights, privileges, immunities, and exemptions which are accorded to the citizens and subjects of the most favored nation.

Section 6 of the amended Chinese immigration act of 1884 purports to secure this treaty right to the exempted classes named by means of prescribed certificates of their status, which certificates shall be the *prima facie* and the sole permissible evidence to establish a right of entry into the United States. But it provides in terms for the issuance of certificates in two cases only:

(*a*) Chinese subjects departing from a port of China; and

(*b*) Chinese persons (*i. e.*, of the Chinese race) who may at the time be subjects of some foreign government other than China, and who may depart for the United States from the ports of such other foreign government.

A statute is certainly most unusual which, purporting to execute the provisions of a treaty with China in respect of Chinese subjects, enacts strict formalities as regards the subjects of other governments than that of China.

It is sufficient that I should call the earnest attention of Congress to the circumstance that the statute makes no provision whatever for the somewhat numerous class of Chinese persons who, retaining their Chinese subjection in some countries other than China, desire to come from such countries to the United States.

Chinese merchants have trading operations of magnitude throughout the world. They do not become citizens or subjects of the country where they may temporarily reside and trade; they continue to be subjects of China, and to them the explicit exemption of the treaty applies. Yet if such a Chinese subject, the head of a mercantile house at Hongkong or Yokohama or Honolulu or Havana or Colon, desires to come from any of these places to the United States, he is met with the requirement that he must produce a certificate, in prescribed form and in the English tongue, issued by the Chinese Government. If there be at the foreign place of his residence no representative of the Chinese Government competent to issue a certificate in the prescribed form, he can obtain none, and is under the provisions of the present law unjustly debarred from entry into the United States. His usual Chinese passport will not suffice, for it is not in the form which the act prescribes shall be the sole permissible evidence of his right to land. And he can obtain no such certificate from the Government of his place of residence, because he is not a subject or citizen thereof "at the time," or at any time.

There being, therefore, no statutory provision prescribing the terms upon which Chinese persons resident in foreign countries but not subjects or citizens of such countries may prove their status and rights as members of the exempted classes in the absence of a Chinese representative in such country, the Secretary of the Treasury, in whom the execution of the act of July 5, 1884, was vested, undertook to remedy the omission by directing the revenue officers to recognize as lawful certificates those issued in favor of Chinese subjects by the Chinese consular and diplomatic officers at the foreign port of departure, when viséed by the United States representative thereat. This appears to be a just application of the spirit of the law, although enlarging its letter, and in adopting this rule he was controlled by the authority of high judicial decision as to what evidence is necessary to establish the fact that an individual Chinaman belongs to the exempted class.

He, however, went beyond the spirit of the act and the judicial decisions, by providing, in a circular dated January 14, 1885, for the original issuance of such a certificate by the United States consular officer at the port of departure, in the absence of a Chinese diplomatic or consular representative thereat; for it is clear that the act of Congress contemplated the intervention of the United States consul only in a supervisory capacity, his function being to check the proceeding and see that no abuse of the privilege followed. The power or duty of original certification is wholly distinct from that supervisory function. It either dispenses with the foreign certificate altogether, leaving the consular visé to stand alone and sufficient, or else it combines in one official act the distinct functions of certification and verification of the fact certified.

The official character attaching to the consular certification contemplated by the unamended circular of January 14, 1885, is to be borne in mind. It is not merely *prima facie* evidence of the status of the bearer, such as the courts may admit in their discretion; it was prescribed as an official attestation, on the strength of which the customs officers at the port of entry were to admit the bearer without further adjudication of his status unless question should arise as to the truth of the certificate itself.

It became, therefore, necessary to amend the circular of January 14, 1885, and this was done on the 13th of June following, by striking out the clause prescribing original certification of status by the United States consuls. The effect of this amendment is to deprive any certificate the United States consuls may issue of the value it purported to possess as sole permissible evidence under the statute when its issuance was prescribed by Treasury regulations. There is, however, nothing to prevent consuls giving certificates of facts within their knowledge to be received as evidence in the absence of statutory authentication.

The complaint of the Chinese minister in his note of March 24, 1886, is that the Chinese merchant Lay Sang, of the house of King Lee & Co., of San Francisco, having arrived at San Francisco from Hongkong and exhibited a certificate of the United States consul at Hongkong as to his status as a merchant, and consequently exempt under the treaty, was refused permission to land and was sent back to Hongkong by the steamer which brought him. While the certificate he bore was doubtless insufficient under the present law, it is to be remembered that there is at Hongkong no representative of the Government of China competent or authorized to issue the certificate required by the statute. The intent of Congress to legislate in execution of the treaty is thus defeated by a prohibition directly contrary to the treaty, and conditions are exacted which, in the words of the Supreme Court hereinbefore quoted, "it was physically impossible to perform."

This anomalous feature of the act should be reformed as speedily as possible, in order that the occurrence of such cases may be avoided and the imputation removed which would otherwise rest upon the good faith of the United States in the execution of their solemn treaty engagements.

GROVER CLEVELAND.

EXECUTIVE MANSION, *April 9, 1886.*

To the House of Representatives:

I transmit herewith a report of the Secretary of State, in relation to the mercantile marines of France, Germany, Great Britain, and Italy.

GROVER CLEVELAND.

EXECUTIVE MANSION, *April 14, 1886.*

To the House of Representatives:

In response to a resolution of the House of Representatives of the 17th ultimo, requesting the Secretary of State "to communicate to the House of Representatives, if not incompatible with the public interest, copies of the recent correspondence and dispatches between the Secretary of State and the minister of the United States at The Hague touching the subject of taxation of petroleum in Holland and in the Dutch colonies, and that of the export therefrom of leaf tobacco to the United States," I transmit herewith the report of the Secretary of State on the subject.

GROVER CLEVELAND.

EXECUTIVE MANSION, *April 14, 1886.*

To the House of Representatives:

In response to a resolution of the House of Representatives of the 6th instant, requesting the Secretary of State "to transmit, if not incompatible with the public interest, copies of all correspondence between his Department and the representatives of France, Germany, Austria, and any other European country which has partially or entirely restricted the importation of American pork," I transmit herewith the report of the Secretary of State on the subject.

GROVER CLEVELAND.

EXECUTIVE MANSION, *April 20, 1886.*

To the House of Representatives:

I transmit herewith a report of the Secretary of State on the manufacture of milk sugar in Switzerland.

GROVER CLEVELAND.

EXECUTIVE MANSION, *April 22, 1886.*

To the Senate and House of Representatives:

The Constitution imposes upon the President the duty of recommending to the consideration of Congress from time to time such measures as he shall judge necessary and expedient.

I am so deeply impressed with the importance of immediately and thoughtfully meeting the problem which recent events and a present condition have thrust upon us, involving the settlement of disputes arising between our laboring men and their employers, that I am constrained to recommend to Congress legislation upon this serious and pressing subject.

Under our form of government the value of labor as an element of national prosperity should be distinctly recognized, and the welfare of the laboring man should be regarded as especially entitled to legislative care. In a country which offers to all its citizens the highest attainment of social and political distinction its workingmen can not justly or safely be considered as irrevocably consigned to the limits of a class and entitled to no attention and allowed no protest against neglect.

The laboring man, bearing in his hand an indispensable contribution to our growth and progress, may well insist, with manly courage and as a right, upon the same recognition from those who make our laws as is accorded to any other citizen having a valuable interest in charge; and his reasonable demands should be met in such a spirit of appreciation and fairness as to induce a contented and patriotic cooperation in the achievement of a grand national destiny.

While the real interests of labor are not promoted by a resort to threats and violent manifestations, and while those who, under the pretext of an advocacy of the claims of labor, wantonly attack the rights of capital and for selfish purposes or the love of disorder sow seeds of violence and discontent should neither be encouraged nor conciliated, all legislation on the subject should be calmly and deliberately undertaken, with no purpose of satisfying unreasonable demands or gaining partisan advantage.

The present condition of the relations between labor and capital is far from satisfactory. The discontent of the employed is due in a large degree to the grasping and heedless exactions of employers and the alleged discrimination in favor of capital as an object of governmental attention. It must also be conceded that the laboring men are not always careful to avoid causeless and unjustifiable disturbance.

Though the importance of a better accord between these interests is apparent, it must be borne in mind that any effort in that direction by the Federal Government must be greatly limited by constitutional restrictions. There are many grievances which legislation by Congress can not redress, and many conditions which can not by such means be reformed.

I am satisfied, however, that something may be done under Federal authority to prevent the disturbances which so often arise from disputes between employers and the employed, and which at times seriously threaten the business interests of the country; and, in my opinion, the proper theory upon which to proceed is that of voluntary arbitration as the means of settling these difficulties.

But I suggest that instead of arbitrators chosen in the heat of conflicting claims, and after each dispute shall arise, for the purpose of determining the same, there be created a commission of labor, consisting of three members, who shall be regular officers of the Government, charged among other duties with the consideration and settlement, when possible, of all controversies between labor and capital.

A commission thus organized would have the advantage of being a stable body, and its members, as they gained experience, would constantly

improve in their ability to deal intelligently and usefully with the questions which might be submitted to them. If arbitrators are chosen for
temporary service as each case of dispute arises, experience and familiar-
ity with much that is involved in the question will be lacking, extreme
partisanship and bias will be the qualifications sought on either side, and
frequent complaints of unfairness and partiality will be inevitable. The
imposition upon a Federal court of a duty so foreign to the judicial function as the selection of an arbitrator in such cases is at least of doubtful
propriety.

The establishment by Federal authority of such a bureau would be a
just and sensible recognition of the value of labor and of its right to be
represented in the departments of the Government. So far as its concil-
iatory offices shall have relation to disturbances which interfere with
transit and commerce between the States, its existence would be justified under the provision of the Constitution which gives to Congress the
power "to regulate commerce with foreign nations and among the several States;" and in the frequent disputes between the laboring men and
their employers, of less extent, and the consequences of which are confined within State limits and threaten domestic violence, the interposition of such a commission might be tendered, upon the application of the
legislature or executive of a State, under the constitutional provision
which requires the General Government to "protect" each of the States
"against domestic violence."

If such a commission were fairly organized, the risk of a loss of popular
support and sympathy resulting from a refusal to submit to so peaceful
an instrumentality would constrain both parties to such disputes to invoke
its interference and abide by its decisions. There would also be good
reason to hope that the very existence of such an agency would invite
application to it for advice and counsel, frequently resulting in the avoid-
ance of contention and misunderstanding.

If the usefulness of such a commission is doubted because it might lack
power to enforce its decisions, much encouragement is derived from the
conceded good that has been accomplished by the railroad commissions
which have been organized in many of the States, which, having little
more than advisory power, have exerted a most salutary influence in the
settlement of disputes between conflicting interests.

In July, 1884, by a law of Congress, a Bureau of Labor was established
and placed in charge of a Commissioner of Labor, who is required to
"collect information upon the subject of labor, its relations to capital,
the hours of labor and the earnings of laboring men and women, and the
means of promoting their material, social, intellectual, and moral prosperity."

The commission which I suggest could easily be ingrafted upon the
bureau thus already organized by the addition of two more commissioners and by supplementing the duties now imposed upon it by such other

powers and functions as would permit the commissioners to act as arbitrators when necessary between labor and capital, under such limitations and upon such occasions as should be deemed proper and useful.

Power should also be distinctly conferred upon this bureau to investigate the causes of all disputes as they occur, whether submitted for arbitration or not, so that information may always be at hand to aid legislation on the subject when necessary and desirable.

GROVER CLEVELAND.

EXECUTIVE MANSION, *April 26, 1886.*

To the House of Representatives:

I transmit herewith a communication from the Secretary of State, accompanied by a report of Mr. Somerville P. Tuck, appointed to carry out certain provisions of section 5 of an act entitled "An act to provide for the ascertainment of claims of American citizens for spoliations committed by the French prior to the 31st day of July, 1801," approved January 20, 1885. GROVER CLEVELAND.

[The same message was sent to the Senate.]

EXECUTIVE MANSION, *May 5, 1886.*

To the Senate and House of Representatives:

I transmit herewith a communication of 1st instant from the Secretary of the Interior, submitting a draft of a bill recommended by the Commissioner of Indian Affairs, providing for the payment of improvements made by settlers on the lands of the Mescalero Indian Reservation in the Territory of New Mexico.

The subject is presented for the consideration and action of Congress.

GROVER CLEVELAND.

EXECUTIVE MANSION, *May 11, 1886.*

To the Senate and House of Representatives:

I herewith transmit a report from the Secretary of State, dated the 6th instant, touching the claims of Benjamin Weil and La Abra Silver Mining Company against the Government of Mexico.

GROVER CLEVELAND.

EXECUTIVE MANSION, *May 11, 1886.*

To the Senate and House of Representatives:

By a joint resolution of Congress approved March 3, 1877, the President was authorized and directed to accept the colossal statue of "Liberty Enlightening the World" when presented by the citizens of the French Republic, and to designate and set apart for the erection thereof a suitable site upon either Governors or Bedloes Island, in the harbor of New York, and upon the completion thereof to cause the statue "to be inaugurated with such ceremonies as will serve to testify the gratitude of our people for this expressive and felicitous memorial of the sympathy of the citizens of our sister Republic."

The President was further thereby "authorized to cause suitable regulations to be made for its future maintenance as a beacon and for the permanent care and preservation thereof as a monument of art and the continued good will of the great nation which aided us in our struggle for freedom."

Under the authority of this resolution, on the 4th day of July, 1884, the minister of the United States to the French Republic, by direction of the President of the United States, accepted the statue and received a deed of presentation from the Franco-American Union, which is now preserved in the archives of the Department of State.

I now transmit to Congress a letter to the Secretary of State from Joseph W. Drexel, esq., chairman of the executive committee of "the American committee on the pedestal of the great statue of 'Liberty Enlightening the World,'" dated the 27th of April, 1886, suggesting the propriety of the further execution by the President of the joint resolution referred to by prescribing the ceremonies of inauguration to be observed upon the complete erection of the statue upon its site on Bedloes Island, in the harbor of New York.

Thursday, the 3d of September, being the anniversary of the signing of the treaty of peace at Paris by which the independence of these United States was recognized and secured, has been suggested by this committee under whose auspices and agency the pedestal for the statue has been constructed as an appropriate day for the ceremonies of inauguration.

The international character which has been imprinted upon this work by the joint resolution of 1877 makes it incumbent upon Congress to provide means to carry their resolution into effect.

Therefore I recommend the appropriation of such sum of money as in the judgment of Congress shall be deemed adequate and proper to defray the cost of the inauguration of this statue.

I have been informed by the committee that certain expenses have been incurred in the care and custody of the statue since it was deposited on Bedloes Island, and the phraseology of the joint resolution providing for "the permanent care and preservation thereof as a monument of art" would seem to include the payment by the United States of the expense so incurred since the reception of the statue in this country.

The action of the French Government and people in relation to the presentation of this statue to the United States will, I hope, meet with hearty and responsive action upon the part of Congress, in which the Executive will be most happy to cooperate.

GROVER CLEVELAND.

EXECUTIVE MANSION, *May 11, 1886.*

To the Senate and House of Representatives:

The last general appropriation bill passed by the legislature of Utah was vetoed by the then governor of that Territory. It made an appropriation of money for the support of the district courts of the Territory, including the pay of reporters, jurors, and witnesses, and for the completion and maintenance of the Deseret University and the education of the deaf mutes therein. It also appropriated for the support of the Territorial insane asylum, as well as the salaries of Territorial officers, including that of the superintendent of the district schools, the auditor, the librarian, and the treasurer of the Territory. It also provided for internal improvements, such as roads and bridges.

The appropriation for the district courts, for the payment of witnesses and jurors in criminal cases, was $40,000; that for the Deseret University and the deaf mutes was $66,000, and for the insane asylum $25,000.

The board of regents of the Deseret University have borrowed money for the completion of the university buildings which were authorized by legislative action, and which is now due and no provision made for the payment. The act appropriating for the benefit of the Territorial insane asylum passed by the legislature was also vetoed. This included the sum of $13,000, which had been borrowed by the board of directors of the asylum for its completion and furnishing, and which now remains due and unpaid. It also included the sum of $3,548.85 for the care and maintenance of the indigent insane.

The legislature of the Territory, under existing law, will not again convene for nearly two years, there being no authority for a special session. In the meantime, under present conditions, the good order of society will be jeopardized, educational and charitable institutions will be paralyzed, and internal improvements stopped until the legislature meets and makes provision for their support.

A determination on the part of the General Government to suppress certain unlawful practices in this Territory demands neither the refusal of the means to support the local government nor the sacrifice of the interests of the community.

I therefore recommend the immediate enactment of such legislation as will authorize the assembling of the legislature of that Territory in special session at an early day, so that provision can be made to meet the difficulties herein suggested. GROVER CLEVELAND.

EXECUTIVE MANSION,
Washington, May 17, 1886.

To the Senate:

I transmit to the Senate, for its consideration with a view to ratification, a supplementary article, signed the 14th instant by the Secretary of State and the minister of Mexico here, extending until May 20, 1887, the time specified in Article VIII of the commercial reciprocity treaty of January 20, 1883, between the United States and Mexico, for the approval of the laws necessary to carry the said treaty into effect.

GROVER CLEVELAND.

EXECUTIVE MANSION,
Washington, May 17, 1886.

To the Senate:

In response to a resolution of the Senate of the 5th instant, inquiring as to the necessity for the continuance of the present charge for passports for American citizens desiring to visit foreign countries, I transmit herewith the report of the Secretary of State on the subject.

GROVER CLEVELAND.

EXECUTIVE MANSION,
Washington, May 17, 1886.

To the Senate and House of Representatives:

With reference to the paragraph in my annual message to Congress in which I called attention to the uncertainty that exists as to the location of the frontier line between Alaska and British Columbia as defined by the treaty of cession with Russia of March 30, 1867, I now transmit herewith, for the information and consideration of Congress, a report of the Secretary of State upon the subject, with accompanying papers.

In view of the importance of the subject, I recommend that provision be made by law for a preliminary survey of the boundary line in question by officers of the United States, in order that the information necessary for the basis of a treaty between this country and Great Britain for the establishment of a definite boundary line may be obtained; and I also recommend that the sum of $100,000, or so much thereof as may be necessary, be appropriated for the expenses of making such survey.

GROVER CLEVELAND.

EXECUTIVE MANSION,
Washington, May 21, 1886.

To the Senate of the United States:

I transmit herewith, for your consideration with a view to their ratification, the "convention concerning the international exchanges for official documents and literary publications" and the "convention for assuring the immediate exchange of the official journal as well as of the parliamentary annals and documents."

The first was signed at Brussels on the 15th of March, 1886, by the plenipotentiaries of the United States, Belgium, Brazil, Spain, Italy, Portugal, Servia, and Switzerland.

The second was signed at the same place and on the same date by the plenipotentiaries of the above-named powers, with the exception of Switzerland.

GROVER CLEVELAND.

EXECUTIVE MANSION, *May 21, 1886.*

To the Senate and House of Representatives:

I herewith transmit a report from the Secretary of State, dated the 19th instant, touching the necessity of legislation to carry into effect the provisions of Article II of the treaty between the United States and China of November 17, 1880, for the repression of the opium traffic, and recommend that appropriate legislation to fulfill that treaty promise of this Government be provided without further delay.

GROVER CLEVELAND.

EXECUTIVE MANSION, *May 28, 1886.*

To the House of Representatives:

I transmit herewith a report of the Secretary of State, accompanying the report of consuls of the United States on the trade and commerce of foreign countries.

GROVER CLEVELAND.

EXECUTIVE MANSION, *June 1, 1886.*

To the House of Representatives:

In response to a resolution of the House of Representatives of the 17th of March last, requesting the Secretary of State "to communicate to the House of Representatives, if not incompatible with the public interest, copies of recent correspondence and dispatches between the Secretary of State and the minister of the United States at The Hague touching the subject of taxation on petroleum in Holland and in the Dutch colonies, and that of the export therefrom of leaf tobacco to the United States," with reference to my message to the House of Representatives of the 14th ultimo [April], I now transmit a further report of the Secretary of State on the subject.

GROVER CLEVELAND.

EXECUTIVE MANSION, *June 2, 1886.*

To the House of Representatives:

In compliance with the request of the House of Representatives of this date, I return herewith House bill No. 6391, entitled "An act to authorize the Kansas City, Fort Scott and Gulf Railway Company to construct and operate a railway through the Indian Territory, and for other purposes."

GROVER CLEVELAND.

EXECUTIVE MANSION, *June 9, 1886.*

To the Senate and House of Representatives:

I herewith transmit a letter from the Secretary of State, with an accompanying paper, in relation to the distribution of the fund appropriated by the act of April 20, 1882, for the relief of the captain, owners, officers, and crew of the brig *General Armstrong*.

GROVER CLEVELAND.

EXECUTIVE MANSION,
Washington, *June 9, 1886.*

To the Senate of the United States:

I transmit herewith, for your consideration with a view to its ratification, a convention for the extradition of criminals, signed at Tokyo on the 29th day of April, 1886, by the plenipotentiaries of the United States and the Empire of Japan.

The negotiation which led to the conclusion of this convention was caused immediately by the case of a forger in San Francisco, who, having fled to Japan, was delivered up to the authorities of the State of California. It was not possible for this Government to ask his surrender, but the Japanese Government of its own motion caused his delivery as a friendly act. It then suggested the conclusion of an extradition convention between the two countries. The suggestion was favorably entertained by this Government, not only on account of the importance of such a treaty to the execution of the criminal laws of the United States, but also because of the support which its conclusion would give to Japan in her efforts toward judicial autonomy and complete sovereignty.

GROVER CLEVELAND.

EXECUTIVE MANSION, *June 15, 1886.*

To the House of Representatives:

I transmit herewith a report from the Secretary of State, concerning the claim of Benjamin Weil and La Abra Mining Company, of Mexico, agreeably to the resolution of the House of Representatives dated May 13, 1886.

GROVER CLEVELAND.

EXECUTIVE MANSION, *June 19, 1886.*

To the House of Representatives:

Upon an examination of a bill originating in the House of Representatives, No. 4838, entitled "An act to abolish certain fees for official services to American vessels, and to amend the laws relating to shipping commissioners, seamen, and owners of vessels, and for other purposes," I find that there is such a failure to adjust existing laws to the new departure proposed by the bill as to greatly endanger the public service if this bill should not be amended or at once supplemented by additional legislation.

The fees which are at present collected from vessels for services performed by the Bureau of Inspection, and which made up the fund from which certain expenses appurtenant to that Bureau were paid, are by the proposed bill abolished, but no provision has been substituted directing that such expenses shall be paid from the public Treasury or any other source.

The objects of the bill are in the main so useful and important that I have concluded to approve the same upon the assurance of those actively promoting its passage that another bill shall at once be introduced to cover the defect above referred to.

The necessity of such supplemental legislation is so obvious that I hope it will receive the immediate action of the Congress.

GROVER CLEVELAND

EXECUTIVE MANSION, *June 28, 1886.*

To the Senate and House of Representatives:

I herewith inclose a report from the Secretary of State, with its accompanying copies of papers, relative to the case of the American schooner *Ounalaska*, which was duly condemned by the Government of Salvador for having been employed in aid of an insurrection against that Republic, and was subsequently presented to the United States. It seems that an act of Congress accepting the gift on the part of this Government is necessary to complete the transfer, and I recommend that legislation in this sense be adopted. It further appears that one Isidore Gutte, of San Francisco, has sought to obtain possession of the condemned vessel, and I therefore suggest that a second provision to the law accepting her be made giving authority to the Court of Claims to hear and determine the question of title.

GROVER CLEVELAND.

EXECUTIVE MANSION, *June 28, 1886.*

To the Senate and House of Representatives:

I transmit herewith a communication, with an accompanying paper, from the Secretary of State, in relation to the distribution of the award of the late Mexican Claims Commission in the case of S. A. Belden & Co. against the Republic of Mexico.

GROVER CLEVELAND.

EXECUTIVE MANSION, *June 30, 1886.*

To the Senate:

In response to the resolution of the Senate of the 28th of April last, I transmit herewith a report of the Secretary of State in relation to the affairs of the independent State of the Kongo.

GROVER CLEVELAND.

EXECUTIVE MANSION, *July 6, 1886.*

To the House of Representatives:

In compliance with a concurrent resolution of this date, I return herewith House bill No. 3501, entitled "An act granting a pension to Daniel J. Bingham."

GROVER CLEVELAND.

EXECUTIVE MANSION,
Washington, July 8, 1886.

To the Senate of the United States:

I transmit herewith, for your consideration with a view to its ratification, a convention signed at London June 25, 1886, between the United States of America and Great Britain, concerning the extradition of persons charged with crime.

I also inclose a report from the Secretary of State and a copy of a dispatch from the United States minister at London dated June 26, 1886, in reference thereto.

The question of extradition has been discussed between the two countries by Secretaries Fish, Evarts, and Frelinghuysen, as well as by the present Secretary of State, and the method adopted by the inclosed convention, namely, that of amending and extending the provisions of the tenth article of the treaty of 1842, has seemed the most convenient and expeditious.

In view of the continued pendency of the question and its great importance owing to the contiguity of Her Majesty's territories with those of the United States, I respectfully urge the consideration of the convention by the Senate during the present session.

GROVER CLEVELAND.

EXECUTIVE MANSION, *July 9, 1886.*

To the Senate and House of Representatives:

I transmit herewith, for your information, a report from the Secretary of State, inclosing the correspondence which has been exchanged between the Department of State and the Governments of Switzerland and Italy on the subject of international copyright.

GROVER CLEVELAND.

EXECUTIVE MANSION, *July 12, 1886.*

To the Senate and House of Representatives:

I transmit herewith a communication of 3d instant, with inclosures, from the Secretary of the Interior, recommending legislative authority for the use of funds from appropriation, Sioux, etc., 1887, for the subsistence of certain Northern Cheyenne Indians who have gone or who may go from the Sioux Reservation in Dakota to the Tongue River Indian Agency or vicinity, in Montana.

The matter is presented for the favorable consideration of Congress.

GROVER CLEVELAND.

EXECUTIVE MANSION, *July 24, 1886.*

To the Senate of the United States:

In response to the resolutions of the Senate dated respectively May 10 and July 10, 1886, touching alleged seizures and detentions of vessels of the United States in British North American waters, I transmit herewith a report of the Secretary of State, with accompanying papers.

GROVER CLEVELAND.

EXECUTIVE MANSION, *July 27, 1886.*

To the House of Representatives:

I transmit herewith, in response to the House resolution of the 10th instant, a report from the Secretary of State, and accompanying papers, relating to the imprisonment in Ecuador and subsequent release of Julio R. Santos.

GROVER CLEVELAND.

EXECUTIVE MANSION, *July 29, 1886.*

To the House of Representatives:

I transmit herewith a report of the Secretary of State, in reply to the resolution of the House of Representatives of the 27th of May last, in relation to trust funds.

GROVER CLEVELAND.

EXECUTIVE MANSION, *July 29, 1886.*

To the Senate of the United States:

I transmit herewith reports from the heads of the several Executive Departments of the Government, in answer to a resolution of the Senate of June 18, 1886, which requested certain information regarding appointments in such Departments, and having relation to the civil-service law.

GROVER CLEVELAND.

EXECUTIVE MANSION, *July 30, 1886.*

To the Senate of the United States:

In further response to the Senate resolutions of the 10th of May and 10th of July, 1886, touching the seizure and detention of American vessels in Canadian waters, I transmit herewith a letter from the Secretary of State dated the 29th instant, accompanied by a report from the consul-general at Halifax relative to the subject.

GROVER CLEVELAND.

EXECUTIVE MANSION, *July 31, 1886.*

To the House of Representatives:

I have approved House bill No. 4335, entitled "An act making an appropriation to continue the construction of a public building at Clarksburg, W. Va., and changing the limit of cost thereof."

A law passed by the last Congress authorized the construction of this building and appropriated $50,000 for that purpose, which was declared to be the limit of its cost. A site has been purchased for said building, and, as is too often the case, it is now discovered that the sum appropriated is insufficient to meet the expense of such a building as is really needed.

The object of the bill which I have approved is to extend the limit of the cost to $80,000 and to make the additional appropriation to reach that sum. The first section fixes the limit above mentioned, but the second section appropriates $35,000, and thus, with the appropriation of $50,000 heretofore made, the aggregate appropriations exceed the sum to which the cost of the building is limited by $5,000.

Inasmuch as this latter sum can not properly be applied to the construction of the building, attention is called to the existence of this excess of appropriation and the suggestion made that it be returned to the Treasury.

GROVER CLEVELAND.

EXECUTIVE MANSION, *August 2, 1886.*

To the Senate of the United States:

In response to the resolution of your honorable body of the 26th ultimo, I transmit a report of the Secretary of State, with accompanying papers, communicating the information possessed by the Department of State "concerning the alleged illegal detention of A. K. Cutting, an American citizen, by the Mexican authorities at El Paso del Norte;" and as to the further inquiry contained in said resolution, "whether any additional United States troops have been recently ordered to Fort Bliss," I answer in the negative.

GROVER CLEVELAND.

EXECUTIVE MANSION, *August 2, 1886.*

To the House of Representatives:

In performance of the duty imposed upon me by the Constitution, I herewith transmit for your information (the same having heretofore been communicated to the Senate in response to a resolution of inquiry adopted by that body July 26, 1886) certain correspondence and accompanying documents in relation to the arrest and imprisonment at Paso del Norte by Mexican authority of A. K. Cutting, a citizen of the United States.

GROVER CLEVELAND.

EXECUTIVE MANSION, *August 2, 1886.*

To the House of Representatives:

I have this day approved a bill originating in the House of Representatives entitled "An act defining butter, also imposing a tax upon and regulating the manufacture, sale, importation, and exportation of oleomargarine."

This legislation has awakened much interest among the people of the country, and earnest argument has been addressed to the Executive for the purpose of influencing his action thereupon. Many in opposition have urged its dangerous character as tending to break down the boundaries between the proper exercise of legislative power by Federal and State authority; many in favor of the enactment have represented that it promised great advantages to a large portion of our population who sadly need relief; and those on both sides of the question whose advocacy or opposition is based upon no broader foundation than local or personal interest have outnumbered all the others.

This upon its face and in its main features is a revenue bill, and was first introduced in the House of Representatives, wherein the Constitution declares that all bills for raising revenue shall originate.

The Constitution has invested Congress with a very wide legislative discretion both as to the necessity of taxation and the selection of the objects of its burdens; and though if the question was presented to me as an original proposition I might doubt the present need of increased taxation, I deem it my duty in this instance to defer to the judgment of the legislative branch of the Government, which has been so emphatically announced in both Houses of Congress upon the passage of this bill.

Moreover, those who desire to see removed the weight of taxation now pressing upon the people from other directions may well be justified in the hope and expectation that the selection of an additional subject of internal taxation so well able to bear it will in consistency be followed by legislation relieving our citizens from other revenue burdens, rendered by the passage of this bill even more than heretofore unnecessary and needlessly oppressive.

It has been urged as an objection to this measure that while purporting to be legislation for revenue its real purpose is to destroy, by the use of the taxing power, one industry of our people for the protection and benefit of another.

If entitled to indulge in such a suspicion as a basis of official action in this case, and if entirely satisfied that the consequences indicated would ensue, I should doubtless feel constrained to interpose Executive dissent.

But I do not feel called upon to interpret the motives of Congress otherwise than by the apparent character of the bill which has been presented to me, and I am convinced that the taxes which it creates can not possibly destroy the open and legitimate manufacture and sale of the thing upon which it is levied. If this article has the merit which its friends claim for it, and if the people of the land, with full knowledge of its real character, desire to purchase and use it, the taxes exacted by this bill will permit a fair profit to both manufacturer and dealer. If the existence of the commodity taxed and the profits of its manufacture and sale depend upon disposing of it to the people for something else which it deceitfully imitates, the entire enterprise is a fraud and not an industry; and if it can not endure the exhibition of its real character which will be effected by the inspection, supervision, and stamping which this bill directs, the sooner it is destroyed the better in the interest of fair dealing.

Such a result would not furnish the first instance in the history of legislation in which a revenue bill produced a benefit which was merely incidental to its main purpose.

There is certainly no industry better entitled to the incidental advantages which may follow this legislation than our farming and dairy interests, and to none of our people should they be less begrudged than our farmers and dairymen. The present depression of their occupations, the hard, steady, and often unremunerative toil which such occupations exact, and the burdens of taxation which our agriculturists necessarily bear entitle them to every legitimate consideration.

Nor should there be opposition to the incidental effect of this legislation on the part of those who profess to be engaged honestly and fairly in the manufacture and sale of a wholesome and valuable article of food which by its provisions may be subject to taxation. As long as their business is carried on under cover and by false pretenses such men have bad companions in those whose manufactures, however vile and harmful, take their place without challenge with the better sort in a common crusade of deceit against the public. But if this occupation and its methods are forced into the light and all these manufactures must thus either stand upon their merits or fall, the good and bad must soon part company and the fittest only will survive.

Not the least important incident related to this legislation is the defense afforded to the consumer against the fraudulent substitution and sale of an imitation for a genuine article of food of very general household use. Notwithstanding the immense quantity of the article described in this bill which is sold to the people for their consumption as food, and notwithstanding the claim made that its manufacture supplies a cheap substitute for butter, I venture to say that hardly a pound ever entered a poor man's house under its real name and in its true character.

While in its relation to an article of this description there should be no governmental regulation of what the citizen shall eat, it is certainly not a cause of regret if by legislation of this character he is afforded a means by which he may better protect himself against imposition in meeting the needs and wants of his daily life.

Having entered upon this legislation, it is manifestly a duty to render it as effective as possible in the accomplishment of all the good which should legitimately follow in its train.

This leads to the suggestion that the article proposed to be taxed and the circumstances which subject it thereto should be clearly and with great distinctness defined in the statute. It seems to me that this object has not been completely attained in the phraseology of the second section of the bill, and that question may well arise as to the precise condition the article to be taxed must assume in order to be regarded as "made in imitation or semblance of butter, or, when so made, calculated or intended to be sold as butter or for butter."

The fourteenth and fifteenth sections of the bill, in my opinion, are in danger of being construed as an interference with the police powers of the States. Not being entirely satisfied of the unconstitutionality of these provisions, and regarding them as not being so connected and interwoven with the other sections as, if found invalid, to vitiate the entire measure, I have determined to commend them to the attention of the House with a view to an immediate amendment of the bill if it should be deemed necessary and if it is practicable at this late day in the session of Congress.

The fact, too, that the bill does not take effect by its terms until ninety days have elapsed after its approval, thus leaving it but one month in operation before the next session of Congress, when, if time does not now permit, the safety and efficiency of the measure may be abundantly protected by remedial legislative action, and the desire to see realized the beneficial results which it is expected will immediately follow the inauguration of this legislation, have had their influence in determining my official action.

The considerations which have been referred to will, I hope, justify this communication and the suggestions which it contains.

GROVER CLEVELAND.

EXECUTIVE MANSION, *August 4, 1886.*

To the House of Representatives:

In compliance with a resolution of the House of Representatives of the 3d instant (the Senate concurring), I return herewith Senate bill No. 2056, entitled "An act to amend the pension laws by increasing the pensions of soldiers and sailors who have lost an arm or leg in the service."

GROVER CLEVELAND.

VETO MESSAGES.

EXECUTIVE MANSION, *March 10, 1886.*

To the Senate of the United States:

I have carefully considered Senate bill No. 193, entitled "An act for the relief of John Hollins McBlair," and hereby return the same without approval to the Senate, where it originated, with my objections to the same.

The object of this bill is to suspend the provisions of law regulating appointments in the Army by promotion so far as they affect John Hollins McBlair, and to authorize the President to nominate and, by and with the advice and consent of the Senate, appoint said McBlair a first lieutenant in the Army and to place him upon the retired list as of the date of April 8, 1864, with the pay of his rank from April 30, 1884.

The beneficiary named in this bill was appointed a first lieutenant in the Army, from civil life, in June, 1861, with rank from May 14, 1861.

It appears from his own testimony, afterwards taken before a retiring board, that at the time he was commissioned he was but 17 years of age.

In October, 1861, he was in the field for five days with his regiment, within which time he participated in no battle, skirmish, or engagement of any kind.

After five days spent in marching and camping he was taken sick, and after remaining in camp six or seven weeks, his illness still continuing, he was granted sick leave and came to Washington.

In June, 1862, he was put on duty in the Commissary Department at Washington and remained there until August, 1863, when he was summoned before a retiring board convened for the purpose of retiring disabled officers.

From testimony before this board it appears that the illness which caused him to leave his regiment was one not uncommon in the Army, and yielded to treatment, so that in April or May, 1862, he was completely cured.

About this time, however, he was attacked with convulsions, which were pronounced by the physicians examined before the board to be a form of epilepsy, and for this cause he was found to be incapacitated for active service.

The medical testimony, while it suggested various causes for this epileptic condition, negatives entirely any claim that these attacks were at all related to the illness which obliged this officer to abandon service with his regiment. He testified himself that he had been told he had one or two convulsions in childhood, but there is no direct testimony that he was subject to epileptic attacks before he entered the Army.

The retiring board determined upon the proof that this incapacity did not result from any incident of military service, and therefore Lieutenant McBlair was in October, 1863, retired wholly from the service with one year's pay and allowances, which is the usual action in such cases, and which was approved by the President.

But in April, 1864, the President, in a review of the case, made an order that instead of this officer being wholly retired he should be placed upon the retired list as of the date when the action of the retiring board was originally approved.

For about twenty years, and up to April 30, 1884, he remained upon the retired list and received the pay to which this position entitled him.

Quite recently, in consequence of a claim of additional pay which he made upon the Government, his status was examined by the Court of Claims, which decided that the action of the President in April, 1864, by which he sought to change the original disposition of the case upon the findings of the retiring board, was nugatory, and that ever since October, 1863, this officer had not been connected with the Army and had been receiving from the Government money to which he was not entitled.

If the bill herewith returned becomes a law, it makes valid all payments made, and if its purpose is carried out causes such payments to be resumed.

The finding of the retiring board seems so satisfactory and the merits of this case so slight in the light of the large sum already paid to the applicant, while the claims of thousands of wounded and disabled soldiers wait for justice at the hands of the Government, that I am constrained to interpose an objection to a measure which proposes to suspend general and wholesome laws for the purpose of granting what appears to me to be an undeserved gratuity.

GROVER CLEVELAND.

EXECUTIVE MANSION, *March 11, 1886.*

To the Senate of the United States:

I return herewith without approval, and with a statement of my objections thereto, Senate bill No. 150, entitled "An act to quiet title of settlers on the Des Moines River lands in the State of Iowa, and for other purposes."

This proposed legislation grows out of a grant of land made to the Territory of Iowa in the year 1846 to aid in the improvement of the navigation of the Des Moines River.

The language of this grant was such that it gave rise to conflicting decisions on the part of the Government Departments as to its extent, and it was not until 1860 that this question was authoritatively and finally settled by the Supreme Court of the United States. Its decision diminished the extent of the grant to a quantity much less than had been insisted on by certain interested parties and rendered invalid the titles of parties who held, under the Territory or State of Iowa, lands beyond the limit of the grant fixed by the decision of the court.

For the purpose of validating such titles and to settle all disputes so far as the General Government was concerned, the Congress, in the year 1861, by a joint resolution, transferred to the State of Iowa all the title then retained by the United States to the lands within the larger limits which had been claimed, and then held by *bona fide* purchasers from the State; and in 1862 an act of Congress was passed for the same general purpose.

Without detailing the exact language of this resolution and statute, it certainly seems to be such a transfer and relinquishment of all interests in the land mentioned on the part of the United States as to relieve the Government from any further concern therein.

The questions unfortunately growing out of this grant and the legislation relating thereto have been passed upon by the United States Supreme Court in numerous cases, and as late as 1883 that court, referring to its many previous decisions, adjudged that "the act of 1862 (12 U. S. Statutes at Large, ch. 161, p. 543) transferred the title from the United States and vested it in the State of Iowa for the use of its grantees under the river grant."

Bills similar to this have been before Congress for a number of years and have failed of passage; and at least on one occasion the Committee on the Judiciary of the Senate reported adversely upon a measure covering the same ground.

I have carefully examined the legislation upon the subject of this grant, and studied the decisions of the court upon the numerous and complicated questions which have arisen from such legislation, and the positions of the parties claiming an interest in the land covered by said grant, and I can not but think that every possible question that can be raised, or at least that ought to be raised, in any suit relating to these lands has been determined by the highest judicial authority in the land; and if any substantial point remains yet unsettled, I believe there is no difficulty in presenting it to the proper tribunal.

This bill declares that certain lands which nearly twenty-four years ago the United States entirely relinquished are still public lands, and directs the Attorney-General to begin suits to assert and protect the title of the United States in such lands.

If it be true that these are public lands, the declaration that they are so by enactment is entirely unnecessary; and if they are wrongfully withheld from the Government, the duty and authority of the Attorney-General are not aided by the proposed legislation. If they are not public lands because the United States have conveyed them to others, the bill is subject to grave objections as an attempt to destroy vested rights and disturb interests which have long since become fixed.

If a law of Congress could, in the manner contemplated by the bill, change, under the Constitution, the existing rights of any of the parties claiming interests in these lands, it hardly seems that any new questions could be presented to the courts which would do more than raise false hopes and renew useless and bitter strife and litigation.

It seems to me that all controversies which can hereafter arise between those claiming these lands have been fairly remitted to the State of Iowa, and that there they can be properly and safely left; and the Government, through its Attorney-General, should not be called upon to litigate the rights of private parties.

It is not pleasant to contemplate loss threatened to any party acting in good faith, caused by uncertainty in the language of laws or their conflicting interpretation; and if there are persons occupying these lands who labor under such disabilities as prevent them from appealing to the courts for a redress of their wrongs, a plain statute, directed simply to a remedy for such disabilities, would not be objectionable.

Should there be meritorious cases of hardship and loss, caused by an invitation on the part of the Government to settle upon lands apparently public, but to which no right or lawful possession can be secured, it would be better, rather than to attempt a disturbance of titles already settled, to ascertain such losses and do equity by compensating the proper parties through an appropriation for that purpose.

A law to accomplish this very object was passed by Congress in the year 1873.

Valuable proof is thus furnished, by the only law ever passed upon the subject, of the manner in which it was thought proper by the Congress at that time to meet the difficulties suggested by the bill now under consideration.

Notwithstanding the fact that there may be parties in the occupancy of these lands who suffer hardship by the application of strict legal principles to their claims, safety lies in noninterference by Congress with matters which should be left to judicial cognizance; and I am unwilling to concur in legislation which, if not an encroachment upon judicial power, trenches so closely thereon as to be of doubtful expediency, and which at the same time increases the elements of litigation that have heretofore existed and endangers vested rights.

GROVER CLEVELAND.

EXECUTIVE MANSION, *April 26, 1886.*

To the Senate of the United States:

I herewith return Senate bill No. 349, entitled "An act for the promotion of anatomical science and to prevent the desecration of graves," without my approval.

The purpose of this bill is to permit the delivery of certain dead bodies to the medical colleges located in the District of Columbia for dissection.

Such disposition of the bodies of unknown and pauper dead is only excused by the necessity of acquiring by this means proper and useful anatomical knowledge, and the laws by which it is permitted should, in deference to a decent and universal sentiment, carefully guard against abuse and needless offense.

The measure under consideration does not with sufficient care specify and limit the officers and the parties who it is proposed to invest with discretion in the disposition of dead bodies remaining in the institutions and places mentioned in the bill. The second section indicates an intention to prevent the use of said bodies for any other purpose than the promotion of anatomical and surgical knowledge within the District of Columbia, and to secure after such use the decent burial of the remains. It declares that a bond shall be given providing for the performance of these conditions. But instead of exacting the bond from the medical colleges, to which alone, by the terms of the first section, the bodies are to be delivered, such bond is required of "every physician or surgeon before receiving such dead body."

The bill also provides that a relative by blood or marriage, or a friend, may, within forty-eight hours after death, demand that any body be buried, upon satisfying "the authorities" of the relationship claimed to the deceased.

The "authorities" to be thus satisfied should be clearly defined, and the determination of a question so important should be left with those only who will perform this duty with proper care and consideration.

GROVER CLEVELAND.

EXECUTIVE MANSION,
Washington, April 30, 1886.

To the Senate of the United States:

I herewith return without my approval Senate bill No. 141, entitled "An act to extend the provisions of the act of June 10, 1880, entitled 'An act to amend the statutes in relation to immediate transportation of dutiable goods, and for other purposes,' to the port of Omaha, in the State of Nebraska."

The statute, which was passed June 10, 1880, referred to in the title of this bill permitted certain merchandise imported at specified ports, but which was consigned to certain other ports which were mentioned by name in the seventh section of said act, to be shipped immediately after entry at the port of arrival to such destination.

The seventh section of said act contained the names of more than seventy ports or places to which imported merchandise might be thus immediately shipped. One of the places thus named is "Omaha, in Nebraska."

But it was declared in a proviso which was made a part of this section that the privilege of immediate transportation contemplated by the act should "not extend to any place at which there are not the necessary officers for the appraisement of merchandise and the collection of duties."

Because there were no such officers at Omaha the privilege mentioned was withheld from that place by the Treasury Department.

The bill submitted to me for approval provides that these privileges conferred by the act of June 10, 1880, be "extended to the port of Omaha, in the State of Nebraska, as provided for as to the ports mentioned in section 7 of said act."

I can not see that anything is gained by this legislation.

If the circumstances should warrant such a course, the authority which withholds such privileges from any of the places mentioned in the law of 1880 can confer the same without the aid of a new statute. This position is sustained by an opinion of the Attorney-General, dated in February, 1885.

If the legislation now proposed should become operative, the privileges extended to the city of Omaha would still be subject to the proviso attached to the seventh section of the law of 1880, and such newly granted privileges would be liable to immediate withdrawal by the Secretary of the Treasury.

Thus, if the design of this bill is to restore to the city named the privileges permitted by the law of 1880, it seems to be entirely unnecessary, since the power of such restoration is now fully vested in the Treasury Department. If the object sought is to bestow such privileges entirely free from the operation of the proviso above recited, the language of the bill does not accomplish that result.

I understand that the Government has not now at Omaha "the necessary officers for the appraisement of merchandise and the collection of duties," which by such proviso are necessary in order to secure to any place the advantages of immediate transportation. In the absence of such officers the proposed legislation would be nugatory and inoperative.

                                        GROVER CLEVELAND.

EXECUTIVE MANSION, *May 8, 1886.*

To the House of Representatives:

I herewith return without approval a bill numbered 3019, entitled "An act to increase the pension of Abigail Smith," which bill originated in the House of Representatives.

This proposed legislation does injustice to a very worthy pensioner who was on the pension roll at the time of the passage of the law which took effect on the 19th day of March last, and by virtue of which all pensions of her class were increased from $8 to $12 per month. Under this law she became entitled to her increased pension from the date of its passage. The bill now returned allows her the same amount, but if it became a law I suppose it would supersede her claim under the previous statute and postpone the receipt by her of the increase to the date of the passage of the new law.

She would thus lose for nearly two months the increase of pension already secured to her.   GROVER CLEVELAND.

EXECUTIVE MANSION, *May 8, 1886.*

To the House of Representatives:

I return without my approval House bill No. 1471, entitled "An act increasing the pension of Andrew J. Hill."

This bill doubles the pension which the person named therein has been receiving for a number of years. It appears from the report of the committee to which the bill was referred that a claim made by him for increased pension has been lately rejected by the Pension Bureau "on the ground that the claimant is now receiving a pension commensurate with the degree of disability found to exist."

The policy of frequently reversing by special enactment the decisions of the Bureau invested by law with the examination of pension claims, fully equipped for such examination, and which ought not to be suspected of any lack of liberality to our veteran soldiers, is exceedingly questionable. It may well be doubted if a committee of Congress has a better opportunity than such an agency to judge of the merits of these claims. If, however, there is any lack of power in the Pension Bureau for a full investigation, it should be supplied; if the system adopted is inadequate to do full justice to claimants, it should be corrected, and if there is a want of sympathy and consideration for the defenders of our Government the Bureau should be reorganized.

The disposition to concede the most generous treatment to the disabled, aged, and needy among our veterans ought not to be restrained; and it must be admitted that in some cases justice and equity can not be done nor the charitable tendencies of the Government in favor of worthy objects of its care indulged under fixed rules. These conditions sometimes justify a resort to special legislation, but I am convinced that the interposition by special enactment in the granting of pensions should be rare and exceptional. In the nature of things if this is lightly done and upon slight occasion, an invitation is offered for the presentation of claims to Congress which upon their merits could not survive the test of an examination by the Pension Bureau, and whose only hope of success depends upon sympathy, often misdirected, instead of right and justice. The instrumentality organized by law for the determination of pension claims is thus often overruled and discredited, and there is danger that in the end popular prejudice will be created against those who are worthily entitled to the bounty of the Government.

There has lately been presented to me, on the same day, for approval, nearly 240 special bills granting and increasing pensions and restoring to the pension list the names of parties which for cause have been dropped. To aid Executive duty they were referred to the Pension Bureau for examination and report. After a delay absolutely necessary they have been returned to me within a few hours of the limit constitutionally permitted for Executive action. Two hundred and thirty-two of these bills are thus classified:

Eighty-one cover cases in which favorable action by the Pension Bureau was denied by reason of the insufficiency of the testimony filed to prove the facts alleged.

These bills I have approved on the assumption that the claims were meritorious and that by the passage of the bills the Government has waived full proof of the facts.

Twenty-six of the bills cover claims rejected by the Pension Bureau because the evidence produced tended to prove that the alleged disability existed before the claimant's enlistment; 21 cover claims which have been denied by such Bureau because the evidence tended to show that the disability, though contracted in the service, was not incurred in the line of duty; 33 cover claims which have been denied because the evidence tended to establish that the disability originated after the soldier's discharge from the Army; 47 cover claims which have been denied because the general pension laws contain no provisions under which they could be allowed, and 24 of the claims have never been presented to the Pension Bureau.

I estimate the expenditure involved in these bills at more than $35,000 annually.

Though my conception of public duty leads me to the conclusion, upon the slight examination which I have been able to give such of these bills as are not comprised in the first class above mentioned, that many of them should be disapproved, I am utterly unable to submit within the time allowed me for that purpose my objections to the same.

They will therefore become operative without my approval.

A sufficient reason for the return of the particular bill now under consideration is found in the fact that it provides that the name of Andrew J. Hill be placed upon the pension roll, while the records of the Pension Bureau, as well as a medical certificate made a part of the committee's report, disclose that the correct name of the intended beneficiary is Alfred J. Hill.

GROVER CLEVELAND.

EXECUTIVE MANSION, *May 17, 1886.*

To the Senate of the United States:

I return without approval Senate bill No. 1397, entitled "An act to establish a port of delivery at Springfield, in the State of Massachusetts."

It appears that the best reasons urged for the passage of this bill are that Springfield has a population of about 40,000, that the imports to the section of country where the city is located for the last year amounted in value to nearly $3,000,000, and that the importers at this point labored under a disadvantage in being obliged to go to New York and Boston to clear their goods, which are frequently greatly delayed.

The Government is now subjected to great loss of revenue through the intricacies of the present system relating to the collection of customs dues, and through the frauds and evasions which that system permits and invites. It is also the cause of much of the delay and vexation to which the honest importer is subjected.

I am of the opinion that the reforms of present methods which have been lately earnestly pressed upon Congress should be inaugurated, instead of increasing the number of ports where present evils may be further extended.

The bill now under consideration provides that a surveyor of customs shall be appointed to reside at said port, who shall receive a salary not to exceed $1,000 per annum.

It is quite obvious that an experienced force of employees at the ports where goods for Springfield are entered would be much better qualified to adjust the duties upon the same than the person thus proposed to be added to the vast army of Federal officials.

There are many cities in the different States having larger populations than Springfield, and fully as much entitled, upon every ground presented, to the advantages sought by this bill; and yet it is clear that the following of the precedent which the proposed legislation would establish could not fail to produce confusion and uncertainty in the adjustment of customs dues, leading to irritating discriminations and probable loss to the Government.

GROVER CLEVELAND.

EXECUTIVE MANSION, *May 24, 1886.*

To the Senate of the United States:

I herewith return without approval Senate bill No. 2186, entitled "An act granting a pension to Louis Melcher."

This claimant enlisted on the 25th day of May, 1861, and was discharged for disability on the 16th day of August, 1861, having been in the service less than three months.

The certificate of the surgeon of his regiment, made at the time of his discharge, stated his disability to be "lameness, caused by previous repeated and extensive ulcerations of his legs, extending deeply among the muscles and impairing their powers and action by cicatrices, all existing before enlistment and not mentioned to the mustering officers at the time."

Upon this certificate, given at the time of the claimant's discharge and while he was actually under the surgeon's observation, an application for a pension was rejected by the Pension Bureau.

In the absence of anything impeaching the ability and integrity of the surgeon of the regiment, his certificate should, in my opinion, be regarded as a true statement of the condition of the claimant at the time of his discharge, though the committee's report suggests that the surgeon's skill may have been at fault when he declared that the ulcers existed before enlistment. The cicatrices showing beyond a doubt the previous existence of this difficulty would be plainly apparent upon an examination by a surgeon, and their origin could hardly be mistaken. The term of the claimant's service was not sufficiently long to have developed and healed, even imperfectly, in a location previously healthy, ulcers of the kind mentioned in the claimant's application.

My approval of this bill is therefore withheld upon the ground that I find nothing in my examination of the facts connected with the case which impeaches the value of the surgeon's certificate upon which the adverse action of the Pension Bureau was predicated.

GROVER CLEVELAND.

EXECUTIVE MANSION, *May 24, 1886.*

To the Senate of the United States:

A bill which originated in the Senate, entitled "An act granting a pension to Edward Ayers," and numbered 363, is herewith returned without approval.

The person named in this bill enlisted October 3, 1861, in an Indiana regiment and was mustered out of the service December 13, 1865. He represents that he was injured in the hip at the battle of Days Gap, April 30, 1863, and for this a pension is provided for him by the bill under consideration. His application for pension has been rejected by the Pension Bureau on the ground that it was proved on a special examination of the case that the claimant was injured by a fall when a boy, and that the injury complained of existed prior to his enlistment.

There is not a particle of proof or a fact stated either in the committee's report or the records in the Pension Bureau, so far as they are brought to my notice, tending to show that the claimant was in hospital or under medical care a single day during the whole term of his enlistment.

The report of the committee contains the following statement:

> The record evidence proves that he was in this engagement, but there is no proof from this source that he was wounded. By numerous comrades who were present it is proven that he was hurt by the explosion of a shell as claimed. It is also shown that he has been disabled ever since; and the examining surgeon specifically describes the wound, and twice verifies that he is permanently disabled. From the fact that a man was exceedingly liable to injury under the circumstances in which he was placed, and from the evidence of eyewitnesses, the committee are of opinion that he was wounded as alleged.

A wound from a shell causing the person injured to be "disabled ever since" usually results in hospital or medical treatment. Not only is there no such claim made in this case, but, on the contrary, it appears that the claimant served in his regiment two years and nearly eight months after the alleged injury, and until he was mustered out.

It is represented to me by a report from the Pension Bureau that after his alleged wound, and in May or June, 1863, the claimant deserted, and in July of that year was arrested in the State of Indiana and returned to duty without trial. If this report is correct, the party now seeking a pension at the hands of the Government for disability incurred in the service seems to have been capable of considerable physical exertion, though not very creditable, within a few weeks after he claims to have received the injury upon which his application is based.

GROVER CLEVELAND.

EXECUTIVE MANSION, *May 24, 1886.*

To the Senate of the United States:

I return without approval Senate bill No. 1630, entitled "An act granting a pension to James C. Chandler."

It appears from the report of the committee to whom this bill was referred and from an examination of the official records that the proposed beneficiary first enlisted on the 27th day of August, 1861, and about nine months thereafter, on the 1st day of June, 1862, was discharged on account of disability arising from chronic bronchitis.

Notwithstanding the chronic character of his alleged disability, he enlisted again on the 3d day of January, 1864, seventeen months after such discharge.

No statement is presented of the bounty received by him upon either enlistment.

He was finally mustered out on the 19th day of September, 1865.

He first applied for a pension under the general law in May, 1869, alleging that in April, 1862, he was run over by a wagon and injured in his ankle. This accident occurred during his first enlistment; but instead of the injury having been then regarded a disability, he was discharged from such enlistment less than two months thereafter on account of chronic bronchitis.

It appears from the committee's report that his application was rejected and that another was afterwards made, alleging that the claimant had been afflicted with typhoid fever contracted in May, 1862, resulting in "rheumatism and disease of the back in region of kidneys."

This application was also rejected, on the ground that any disability that might have arisen from the cause alleged "had not existed in a pensionable degree since the date of filing the claim therefor," which was February 10, 1885.

There still remained an appeal to Congress, and probably there were not wanting those who found their interests in advising such an appeal and who had at hand Congressional precedents which promised a favorable result. That the parties interested did not miscalculate the chances of success is demonstrated by the bill now before me, which, in direct opposition to the action of the Pension Bureau, grants a pension to a man who, though discharged from enlistment for a certain alleged disability, made two applications for a pension based upon two distinct causes, both claimed to exist within two months prior to such discharge, and both different from the one upon which he accepted the same, and notwithstanding the fact that the proposed beneficiary, after all these disabilities had occurred, passed an examination as to his physical fitness for reenlistment, actually did reenlist, and served till finally mustered out at the close of the war.

If any money is to be given this man from the public Treasury, it should not be done under the guise of a pension.

GROVER CLEVELAND.

EXECUTIVE MANSION, *May 24, 1886.*
To the Senate of the United States:

I hereby return without approval Senate bill No. 857, entitled "An act granting a pension to Dudley B. Branch."

This claim is based upon the allegation, as appears by the committee's report, that the person named in the bill has a hernia, and that on the 9th day of June, 1862, while in the military service and in the line of duty, "in getting over a fence he fell heavily, striking a stone or hard substance, and received the hernia in his left side."

In December, 1875, thirteen and a half years thereafter, he filed an application for a pension, which was rejected by the Pension Bureau on the ground that there was no record of the alleged hernia, and the claimant was unable to furnish satisfactory evidence of its origin in the service.

The fact is stated in the committee's report that late in the year 1863 this soldier was transferred to the Invalid Corps, and the records show that he was thus transferred for a disability entirely different from that upon which he now bases his claim. He was mustered out in September, 1864, at the end of his term of service.

I am convinced that the rejection of this claim by the Pension Bureau was correct, and think its action should not be reversed.

I suppose an injury of the description claimed, if caused by violence directly applied, is quite palpable, its effect usually immediate, and its existence easily proved. The long time which elapsed between the injury and the claimant's application for a pension may be fairly considered as bearing upon the merits of such application, while the fact that the claimant was transferred to the Invalid Corps more than a year after he alleges the injury occurred, for an entirely different disability, can not be overlooked. In the committee's report the statement is found that the beneficiary named in the bill was in two different hospitals during the year 1863, and yet it is not claimed that the history of his hospital treatment furnishes any proof of the injury upon which his claim is now based.

GROVER CLEVELAND.

EXECUTIVE MANSION, *May 25, 1886.*
To the Senate of the United States:

I return without approval Senate bill No. 1998, entitled "An act for the relief of John D. Ham," which grants a pension to the party named.

The claimant alleges that he enrolled in the Army in January, 1862, and was "sworn in at his own home;" that the next day he started on horseback to go to the regiment he was to join, and that on the way his horse fell upon his left ankle, whereby he sustained an injury which entitles him to a pension.

His name is not borne upon any of the rolls of the regiment he alleges ne was on his way to join.

He filed his application for pension in the Pension Bureau October 17, 1879 (seventeen years after his alleged injury), which was rejected apparently on the ground that he was not in the military service when the disability claimed was incurred.

He was drafted in 1863 and served until he was mustered out in 1865.

It is entirely clear that this claimant was not in the military service at the time he claims to have been injured; and his conduct in remaining at home until he was drafted, nearly two years afterwards, furnishes proof that he did not regard himself as in the meantime owing any military duty. These considerations, and the further facts that upon being drafted he was accepted as physically qualified for service, that he actually thereafter served a year and eight months, and that he waited seventeen years before claiming pension for his injury, in my mind present a case upon which the claimant is entitled to no relief even if charity instead of just liberality is invoked.

GROVER CLEVELAND.

EXECUTIVE MANSION, *May 25, 1886.*

To the Senate of the United States:

I herewith return without approval Senate bill No. 1290, entitled "An act granting a pension to David W. Hamilton."

A claim for pension filed by him in November, 1879, was rejected by the Pension Bureau on the ground that his alleged disability existed prior to his enlistment.

An examination of the records in the Adjutant-General's Office and a statement from the Pension Bureau derived from the claimant's application there for pension, with a reference to the report of the committee to whom this bill was referred, disclose the following facts:

The claimant was mustered in the service as first lieutenant in September, 1861, and as captain June 12, 1862. He is reported as present with his company until the 30th of that month. For the six months immediately following the latter date he is reported as "absent sick," and for the ten months next succeeding, and until October 27, 1863, as "absent on detached service." On the day last mentioned he tendered his resignation at Camp Morton, in the State of Indiana, to enable him to accept an appointment as captain in the Invalid Corps. He was thereupon so appointed upon account of "chronic enlargement of the spermatic cord of several years' standing, consequent upon hydrocele." He remained in the Invalid Corps until July 12, 1864, when, upon the tender of his resignation, he was discharged.

HAWAIIAN SCENES

HAWAII

" During the greater part of the nineteenth century the islands formed an independent kingdom. January 17, 1893, Queen Liliuokalani was deposed and a provisional government was formed, with Sanford B. Dole at the head; and annexation to the United States asked. A treaty of annexation was concluded with President Harrison, but before it could be ratified by the Senate President Cleveland was inaugurated; he, at once, withdrew it and sent James H. Blount as special commissioner to investigate the affairs of the islands. The restoration of the Queen was attempted, but failed mainly because she refused to grant an amnesty. On July 4, 1894, a Republic was proclaimed with Mr. Dole as its president. During President McKinley's first term, another treaty of annexation was sent to the Senate, but, pending its consideration, a joint resolution passed Congress annexing the islands. The resolution was approved on July 7, 1898, and the formal annexation occurred on August 12th of the same year."

Quoted from the article entitled "Hawaii" in the Encyclopedic Index, which carries the narrative from the discovery of the island down to the last census.

Less than four months afterwards, and on the 6th day of November, 1864, he was mustered in the service as a captain in another regiment of volunteers, and on the 17th day of November, 1865, again tendered his resignation, and was finally discharged.

Upon his application for pension under the general law, fourteen years thereafter, he admitted that he suffered from hydrocele as early as 1856, but claimed that an operation then performed for the same had given him permanent relief.

It will be seen that the claimant's term of service was liberally interspersed with sick leave, detached service, resignations, and membership in the Invalid Corps. He admits having the trouble which would naturally result in his alleged disability long before he entered the service. The surgeon upon whose certificate he was appointed to the Invalid Corps must have stated to him the character of his difficulty and that it was chronic. No application for pension was made until fourteen years after his discharge and just prior to the expiration of the time within which large arrearages might have been claimed. There is no hint of any medical testimony at all contradicting the certificate of the army surgeon made in 1863, but it is stated in the report of the committee that he can not procure medical testimony as to his soundness before entering the service because his family physician is dead. If he had filed his application earlier, it would have appeared in better faith, and it may be that he could have secured the evidence of his family physician if it was of the character he desired.

After the Pension Bureau has been in operation for a score of years since the late civil war, equipped with thousands of employees charged with no other duty except the ascertainment and adjustment of the claims of our discharged soldiers and their surviving relatives, it seems to me that a stronger case than this should be presented to justify the passage of a special act, twenty-three years after an alleged disability, granting a pension which has been refused by the Bureau especially organized for the purpose of allowing the same under just and liberal laws.

I am by no means insensible to that influence which leads the judgment toward the allowance of every claim alleged to be founded upon patriotic service in the nation's cause; and yet I neither believe it to be a duty nor a kindness to the worthy citizens for whose benefit our scheme of pensions was provided to permit the diversion of the nation's bounty to objects not within its scope and purpose.

GROVER CLEVELAND.

EXECUTIVE MANSION, *May 28, 1886.*

To the Senate:

I hereby return without approval Senate bill No. 1850, entitled "An act granting a pension to Mrs. Annie C. Owen."

The husband of the claimant was mustered into the service as second lieutenant December 14, 1861, and discharged October 16, 1862. It appears that he died in 1876 from neuralgia of the heart. In 1883 the present claimant filed her application for pension, alleging that her husband received two shell wounds, one in the calf of his left leg and one in his left side, on the 1st day of July, 1862, and claiming that they were in some way connected with the cause of his death.

On the records of his command there is no mention made of either wound, but it does appear that on the 8th day of July, seven days after the date of the alleged wounds, he was granted a leave of absence for thirty days on account, as stated in a medical certificate, of "remittent fever and diarrhea." A medical certificate dated August 5, 1862, while absent on leave, represents him to be at that time suffering from "chronic bronchitis and acute dysentery."

The application made for pension by the widow was rejected by the Pension Bureau February 1, 1886.

There is nothing before me showing that the husband of the claimant ever filed an application for pension, though he lived nearly fourteen years after his discharge; and his widow's claim was not made until twenty-one years after the alleged wounds and seven years after her husband's death.

If the information furnished concerning this soldier's service is correct, this claim for pension must be based upon a mistake. It is hardly possible that wounds such as are alleged should be received in battle by a second lieutenant and no record made of them; that he should seven days thereafter receive a leave of absence for other sickness, with no mention of these wounds, and that a medical certificate should be made (probably with a view of prolonging his leave) stating still other ailments, but silent as to wounds. The further facts that he made no claim for pension and that the claim of his widow was long delayed are worthy of consideration. And if the wounds were received as described there is certainly no necessary connection between them and death fourteen years afterwards from neuralgia of the heart.

GROVER CLEVELAND.

EXECUTIVE MANSION, *May 28, 1886.*

To the House of Representatives:

I return without approval a bill originating in the House of Representatives, numbered 2145, and entitled "An act for the relief of Rebecca Eldridge."

This bill provides for the payment of a pension to the claimant as the widow of Wilber H. Eldridge, who was mustered into the service on the 24th day of July, 1862, and discharged June 21, 1865. He was pensioned at the rate of $2 per month for a slight wound in the calf of the left leg, received on the 25th day of March, 1865. There is no pretense that this wound was at all serious, and a surgeon who examined it in 1880 reported that in his opinion the wounded man "was not incapacitated from obtaining his subsistence by manual labor;" that the ball passed "rather superficially through the muscles," and that the party examined said there was no lameness "unless after long standing or walking a good deal."

On the 28th of January, 1881, while working about a building, he fell backward from a ladder and fractured his skull, from which he died the same day.

Without a particle of proof and with no fact established which connects the fatal accident in the remotest degree with the wound referred to, it is proposed to grant a pension to the widow of $12 per month.

It is not a pleasant thing to interfere in such a case; but we are dealing with pensions, and not with gratuities.

GROVER CLEVELAND.

EXECUTIVE MANSION, *May 28, 1886.*

To the Senate:

I hereby return without approval Senate bill No. 1253, entitled "An act granting a pension to J. D. Haworth."

It is proposed by this bill to grant a pension to the claimant for the alleged loss of sight in one eye and the impairment of the vision of the other.

From the information furnished me I am convinced that the difficulty alleged by this applicant had its origin in causes existing prior to his enlistment, and that his present condition of disability is not the result of his service in the Army.

GROVER CLEVELAND.

EXECUTIVE MANSION, *May 28, 1886.*

To the House of Representatives:

I hereby return without approval a bill which originated in the House of Representatives, numbered 1582, and entitled "An act for the relief of Eleanor C. Bangham."

The claimant in this case is the widow of John S. Bangham, who was mustered into the service of the United States as a private on the 26th day of March, 1864, and was discharged by general order June 23, 1865.

It appears that during his fifteen months of service he was sick a considerable part of the time, and the records in two of the hospitals to which he was admitted show that his sickness was epilepsy. There are no records showing the character of his illness in other hospitals.

His widow, the present claimant, filed an application for pension March 12, 1878, alleging that her husband committed suicide September 10, 1873, from the effects of chronic diarrhea and general debility contracted in the service. Upon the evidence then produced her claim was allowed at the rate of $8 a month. She remained upon the rolls until July, 1885, when a special examination of the case was made, upon which it was developed and admitted by the pensioner that the deceased soldier had suffered from epilepsy from early childhood, and that during a despondent mood following an epileptic fit he committed suicide.

Upon these facts it was determined by the Pension Bureau that the pension should not have been granted, and it was withdrawn. It was so satisfactorily proven that the disease which indirectly caused the death of the claimant's husband was not contracted in the service that, in my opinion, the conclusion arrived at on such examination should stand.

GROVER CLEVELAND.

EXECUTIVE MANSION, *May 28, 1886.*

To the House of Representatives:

I hereby return without approval bill No. 1406, which originated in the House of Representatives and is entitled "An act granting a pension to Simmons W. Harden."

The claimant mentioned in this bill enlisted as a private December 30, 1863, and was discharged May 17, 1865.

He filed an application for pension in 1866, in which he alleged that he was injured in the left side by a fall from a wagon while in the service.

In 1880 he filed another application, in which he claimed that he was afflicted with an enlargement of the lungs and heart from overexertion at a review. His record in the Army makes no mention of either of these troubles, but does show that he had at some time during his service dyspepsia and intermittent fever.

The fact that fourteen years elapsed after he claimed to have been injured by a fall from a wagon before he discovered that enlargement of the lungs and heart was his real difficulty is calculated to at least raise a doubt as to the validity of his claim.

The evidence as to his condition at the time of enlistment, as well as since, seems quite contradictory and unsatisfactory. The committee to which the bill was referred report that "the only question in the case is as to his condition at time of enlistment, and the evidence is so flatly contradictory on that point that it is impossible to decide that question."

Notwithstanding this declaration, it is proposed to allow him a pension of $16 a month, though he has survived all his ailments long enough to reach the age of 72 years.

I think upon the case presented the action of the Pension Bureau overruling his claim should not be reversed.

GROVER CLEVELAND.

EXECUTIVE MANSION, *June 1, 1886.*

To the Senate:

I return herewith Senate bill No. 1441, entitled "An act granting a pension to M. Romahn."

The beneficiary named in this bill enlisted September 13, 1862, and was discharged May 24, 1865.

He filed his claim in the Pension Bureau December 5, 1882, alleging that in the winter of 1862, from being put on duty—standing guard excessively—he became afflicted with varicose veins. His army record shows no disability of any kind, though he served more than two years after the date at which he alleges his injury was incurred. His application was rejected on the ground that no record of his disability appeared and that the evidence of the same filed upon such application was insufficient.

The claim now made to Congress for relief is the same as that made to the Pension Bureau, with the allegation added that in May, 1865, his breast and shoulder were injured by a railroad accident while he was on detail duty.

If the latter-described injury really existed, it is exceeding strange that it found no place in his claim before the Pension Bureau, while the account given of the cause of his alleged varicose veins must surprise those who are at all familiar with the character of that difficulty and the routine of army service. His continued performance of military duty after he incurred this infirmity, the fact that he made no claim for pension on that account until twenty years had passed, and the unsatisfactory evidence now produced to support his allegation tend to induce the suspicion that the decision of the Pension Bureau was entirely just and that this bill is not based upon substantial merits.

GROVER CLEVELAND.

EXECUTIVE MANSION, *June 2, 1886.*
To the Senate:

Senate bill No. 789, entitled "An act granting a pension to John S. Williams," is herewith returned without approval.

This claimant enlisted in 1861. He alleges that his shoulder was dislocated in 1862 while ferrying troops across a river. The records of the War Department fail to furnish any information as to the alleged injury. He served afterwards until 1865 and was discharged. His claim for pension was rejected by the Pension Bureau in 1882, twenty years after the time he fixes as the date of his injury; and after such long delay he states as an excuse for the unsatisfactory nature of his proof that the doctors, surgeons, and officers who knew him are dead.

Considering that the injury complained of is merely a dislocation of the shoulder, and in view of the other facts developed in the case, I think the Pension Bureau arrived at a correct conclusion when this claim was rejected.

GROVER CLEVELAND.

EXECUTIVE MANSION, *June 2, 1886.*
To the Senate:

I return without approval Senate bill No. 327, entitled "An act granting a pension to James E. O'Shea."

From the report of the committee to whom this bill was referred I learn that the claimant enlisted in April, 1861, and was discharged in October, 1864.

He filed a claim in the Pension Bureau alleging that he received a saber wound in the head March 7, 1862, and a gunshot wound in the left leg in the autumn of the same year.

It appears upon examination of his military record that there is no mention of either disability, and that he served two years after the time he claims to have received these injuries. So far from being disabled, it is reported as an incident of his army life that in the year 1864 this soldier was found guilty of desertion and sentenced to forfeit all pay and allowances for the time he was absent.

The report of the committee, in apparent explanation of the lack of any official mention of the injuries alleged, declares that "the fact that the records of the War Department are often imperfect works great hardship to men who apply for pensions;" and his conviction of desertion and the lack of proof to sustain his allegations as to his injuries are disposed of as follows in the committee's report:

The Adjutant-General's report shows that the man was under discipline for some irregularities, but notwithstanding this and the lack of the required proof that he was wounded in the line of duty the committee are of the opinion that, situated as he was, he was very liable to and very probably did receive the wound from which he has suffered and is still suffering.

I am convinced that there exists serious difficulty on the part of the claimant instead of in the record of the War Department; that the kind of irregularity for which he was under discipline is calculated to produce a lack of confidence in his merits as a pensioner, and that the fact of his situation being such as to render him liable to receive a wound is hardly sufficient to establish his right to a soldier's pension, which is only justified by injuries actually received and affirmatively proven.

GROVER CLEVELAND.

To the Senate: EXECUTIVE MANSION, *June 2, 1886.*

I return herewith without approval Senate bill No. 1726, entitled "An act granting a pension to Augustus Field Stevens."

It appears that this claimant enlisted August 21, 1861, and was discharged on the 3d day of October, 1861, after a service of less than two months, upon a medical certificate of disability which represented him as "incapable of performing the duties of a soldier because of general debility, advanced age, unfit for service before entering."

His claim is not based upon any wound or injury, but he alleges that he contracted chronic diarrhea or dysentery while in the service. The committee to whom the bill was referred by the Senate admit that "there is a quantity of contradictory testimony, biased in about equal proportion for and against the claimant."

His claim was rejected by the Pension Bureau in 1882 and again in 1885, after a special examination concerning the facts, on the ground that the claimant had failed to show any pensionable disability contracted while he was in the service.

The medical certificate upon which he was discharged makes no mention of the disorders of which the applicant for pension now complains, but contains other statements which demonstrate that no allowance should be made to him by way of pension, unless such pension is to be openly and confessedly regarded as a mere charity, or unless the medical certificate made at the time of discharge, with the patient under observation, is to be, without any allegation to that effect, impeached.

I am not prepared either to gratuitously set at naught two determinations of the Pension Bureau, one very lately made after a special examination, and especially when the evidence produced before the committee to reverse the Bureau's action is admitted to be "contradictory" and "biased in about equal proportion for and against the claimant."

GROVER CLEVELAND.

EXECUTIVE MANSION, *June 19, 1886.*

To the Senate:

I return herewith Senate bill No. 226, entitled "An act granting a pension to Margaret D. Marchand," without approval.

The beneficiary named in this bill is the widow of John B. Marchand, who entered the United States Navy in 1828, who was promoted to the rank of commodore in 1866, and who was placed upon the retired list in 1870. He died in August, 1875, of heart disease.

His widow filed an application for pension in 1883, claiming that his fatal disease was caused by exposure and exertion in the service during the War of the Rebellion. The application was rejected because of the inability to furnish evidence to prove that the death had any relation to the naval service of the deceased.

I am unable to see how any other conclusion could have been reached. The information furnished by the report of the committee to whom this bill was referred and derived from other data before me absolutely fails to connect the death of Commodore Marchand with any incident of his naval service.

This officer was undoubtedly brave and efficient, rendering his country valuable service; but it does not appear to have been of so distinguished a character, nor are the circumstances of his widow alleged to be such, as to render a gratuity justifiable.

GROVER CLEVELAND.

EXECUTIVE MANSION, *June 19, 1886.*

To the Senate:

I hereby return without my approval Senate bill No. 183, entitled "An act for the relief of Thomas S. Hopkins, late of Company C, Sixteenth Maine Volunteers."

This soldier was enrolled in the Army June 2, 1862, and discharged June 30, 1865. He was sent to the Government hospital September 20, 1863, and thereupon transferred to the Invalid Corps.

He filed his declaration for a pension in November, 1880, alleging that while in the service he contracted malarial fever and chronic diarrhea, and was seized with convulsions, suffering from great general debility.

A pension of $50 a month was granted to him in June, 1881, dating from the time of filing his application, which sum he has been receiving up to the present time.

This bill proposes to remove the limitation fixed by the law of 1879 prescribing the date prior to which an application for pension must be filed in order to entitle the claimant to draw the pension allowed from the time of his discharge from the service.

If this bill should become a law, it would entitle the claimant to about $9,000 of back pension. This is claimed upon the ground that the soldier was so sick from the time of the passage of the act creating the limitation up to the date allowed him to avail himself of the privileges of the act that he could not file his claim.

I think the limitation thus fixed a very wise one, and that it should not, in fairness to other claimants, be relaxed for causes not mentioned in the statute; nor should the door be opened to applications of this kind.

The beneficiary named in this bill had fifteen years after the accruing of his claim, and before it is alleged that he was incapacitated, within which he might have filed his application and entitled himself to the back pension now applied for.

The facts here presented come so far short of furnishing a satisfactory excuse for his delay that, in my judgment, the discrimination asked in his favor should not be granted.

                                   GROVER CLEVELAND.

To the Senate: EXECUTIVE MANSION, *June 19, 1886.*

I return without approval Senate bill No. 763, entitled "An act for the erection of a public building at Sioux City, Iowa."

The report of the committee of the House of Representatives to whom this bill was referred states that by the census of 1880 the population of Sioux City was nearly 8,000, and that by other enumerations since made its population would seem to exceed 23,000. It is further stated in the report that for the accommodation of this population the city contains 393 brick and 2,984 frame buildings.

It seems to me that in the consideration of the merits of this bill the necessities of the Government should control the question, and that it should be decided as a business proposition, depending upon the needs of a Government building at the point proposed in order to do the Government work.

This greatly reduces the value of statistics showing population, extent of business, prospective growth, and matters of that kind, which, though exceedingly interesting, do not always demonstrate the necessity of the expenditure of a large sum of money for a public building.

I find upon examination that United States courts are sometimes held at Sioux City, but that they have been thus far held in the county courthouse without serious inconvenience and without any expense to the Government. There are actually no other Federal officers there for whom the Government in any view should provide accommodations except the postmaster. The post-office is now located in a building rented by the Government until the 1st day of January, 1889, at the rate of $2,200 per annum.

By the last report of the Supervising Architect it appears that on October 1, 1885, there were 80 new public buildings in course of construction, and that the amount expended thereon during the preceding year was nearly $2,500,000, while large appropriations are asked to be expended on these buildings during the current year.

In my judgment the number of public buildings should not at this time be increased unless a greater public necessity exists therefor than is apparent in this case.   GROVER CLEVELAND.

EXECUTIVE MANSION, *June 19, 1886.*

To the Senate:

I return without approval Senate bill No. 206, entitled "An act to provide for the erection of a public building in the city of Zanesville, Ohio."

No Federal courts are held at Zanesville, and there are no Government officers located there who should be provided for at the public expense except the postmaster.

So far as I am informed the patrons of the post-office are fairly well accommodated in a building which is rented by the Government at the rate of $800 per annum; and though the postmaster naturally certifies that he and his fourteen employees require much more spacious surroundings, I have no doubt he and they can be induced to continue to serve the Government in its present quarters.

The public buildings now in process of construction, numbering 80, involving constant supervision, are all the building projects which the Government ought to have on hand at one time, unless a very palpable necessity exists for an increase in the number. The multiplication of these structures involves not only the appropriations made for their completion, but great expense in their care and preservation thereafter.

While a fine Government building is a desirable ornament to any town or city, and while the securing of an appropriation therefor is often considered as an illustration of zeal and activity in the interest of a constituency, I am of the opinion that the expenditure of public money for such a purpose should depend upon the necessity of such a building for public uses.

In the case under consideration I have no doubt the Government can be well accommodated for some time to come in all its business relations with the people of Zanesville by renting quarters, at less expense than the annual cost of maintaining the proposed new building after its completion.

GROVER CLEVELAND.

EXECUTIVE MANSION, *June 19, 1886.*
To the House of Representatives:

I hereby return without approval House bill No. 1990, entitled "An act granting a pension to John Hunter."

The claimant was enrolled July 20, 1864, and was discharged by expiration of his term of service July 13, 1865.

During four months of the twelve while he remained in the service he is reported as "absent sick." His hospital record shows that he was treated for intermittent fever and rheumatism. In 1879, fourteen years after his discharge, he filed his claim for a pension, alleging that in May, 1864, he received a gunshot wound in the right leg while in a skirmish. The month of May, 1864, is included in the time during which, by the record, he appears to have been absent sick and undergoing treatment for fever and rheumatism. His claim was rejected in December, 1884, on the ground that there was no record of the alleged wound and the claimant was unable, though aided by the Bureau, to prove that the injury claimed was due to the service.

The evidence recited in the report of the Congressional committee to whom this bill was referred, though it tends to show, if reliable, that when the soldier returned from his service his leg was affected, fails to show a continuous disability from that cause. It is stated that about five years ago, while the claimant was gathering dandelions, in stepping across a ditch his leg broke. The doctor who attended him states that the leg was about four weeks longer in uniting than is usual, but he is not represented as giving an opinion that the fracture had anything to do with his patient's military service.

I find no reference to his condition since his recovery from the fracture of his leg, and there seems to be no allegation of present disability either from army service or the injury sustained while gathering dandelions.

GROVER CLEVELAND.

EXECUTIVE MANSION, *June 19, 1886.*
To the House of Representatives:

I return without my approval House bill No. 4002, entitled "An act granting a pension to Carter W. Tiller."

The records of the War Department show that George W. Tiller, the son of the claimant, enlisted in a Kentucky regiment on the 8th day of October, 1861, and that he deserted on the 20th day of September, 1863; that he was captured by the Confederates afterwards, but the time and circumstances are not given. On the 21st day of July, 1864, he was admitted to the Andersonville hospital, and died the same day of scorbutus.

The father filed his claim for a pension in 1877, alleging his dependence upon the deceased soldier. It is probably true that the son while in the Army sent money to the claimant, though he appears to have been employed as a policeman in the city of Louisville ever since his son's death, at a fair salary.

The claim thus made was rejected by the Pension Bureau on the ground that the claimant was not dependent upon his son.

I am entirely satisfied of the correctness of this determination, and if the records presented to me are reliable I think the fact which appears therefrom, that the death of the soldier occurred ten months after desertion and had no apparent relation to any service in the Union Army, is conclusive against the claim now made.

GROVER CLEVELAND.

EXECUTIVE MANSION, *June 19, 1886.*

To the House of Representatives:

I return without approval House bill No. 3826, entitled "An act for the relief of John Taylor."

By this bill it is proposed to increase the pension of the beneficiary named to $16 a month. He has been receiving a pension under the general law, dating from his discharge in 1865. His pension has been twice already increased, once by the Pension Bureau and once by a special act passed in 1882. His wound is not such as to cause his disability to become aggravated by time. The increase allowed by this bill, when applied for at the Pension Bureau in 1885, was denied on the ground that "the rate he was receiving was commensurate with the degree of his disability, a board of surgeons having reported that he was receiving a liberal rating."

I can discover no just ground for reversing this determination and making a further discrimination in favor of this pensioner.

GROVER CLEVELAND.

EXECUTIVE MANSION, *June 19, 1886.*

To the House of Representatives:

I return without approval House bill No. 5997, entitled "An act granting a pension to Elizabeth Luce."

The claimant named in this bill is the widow of John W. Luce, who entered the Army in August, 1861, and who was discharged in January,

1864, for a disability declared at the time in the surgeon's certificate to arise from "organic stricture of the urethra," which, from his statement, existed at the time of his enlistment.

Notwithstanding the admission which thus appears to have been made by him at the time of his discharge, he soon afterwards made an application for a pension, alleging that his difficulty arose from his being thrown forward on the pommel of his saddle when in the service.

Upon an examination of this claim by a special examiner, it is stated that no one could be found who had any knowledge of such an injury, and the claim was rejected.

In 1883, twenty years after the soldier alleged he was injured in the manner stated, he died, and the cause of his death was declared to be "chronic gastritis, complicated with kidney difficulty."

It is alleged that the examinations made by the Pension Bureau developed the fact that the deceased soldier was a man of quite intemperate habits.

The theory upon which this widow should be pensioned can only be that the death of her husband resulted from a disability or injury contracted or received in the military service. It seems to me that however satisfactorily the injury which he described may be established, and though every suspicion as to his habits be dismissed, there can hardly possibly be any connection between such an injury and the causes to which his death is attributed.

                                                    GROVER CLEVELAND.

EXECUTIVE MANSION, *June 19, 1886.*
To the House of Representatives:

I return without approval House bill No. 4058, entitled "An act for the relief of Joel D. Monroe."

The claimant mentioned in this bill enlisted in August, 1864, and was discharged with his regiment June 4, 1865.

The record of his short military service exhibits no mention of any injury or disability; but in June, 1880, fifteen years after his discharge, he filed in the Pension Bureau a claim for a pension based upon the allegation that in December, 1864, he was injured by the falling of a tree, which struck him on his head, affecting both of his eyes. He added to this allegation the further complaint that he contracted rheumatism while in the service.

The application for a pension was rejected by the Pension Bureau because there was no record of the disabilities claimed, nor was satisfactory proof furnished that any such disabilities originated in the service.

I am so entirely satisfied with this determination of the Pension Bureau that I am constrained to withhold my approval of this bill.

                                                    GROVER CLEVELAND.

EXECUTIVE MANSION, *June 21, 1886.*

To the House of Representatives:

I return without approval House bill No. 3624, entitled "An act grant-ing a pension to Fred. J. Leese."

This claimant enlisted September 7, 1864, and was discharged June 4, 1865. During his short term of service there does not appear on the records any evidence of disability.

But in November, 1883, eighteen years after his discharge, he filed his application for a pension, alleging that in November, 1864, he contracted chronic diarrhea from exposure and severe work.

His claim has not yet been fully passed upon by the Pension Bureau, which, in my opinion, is sufficient reason why this bill should not become a law. I am also thoroughly convinced, from examination of the case, that the claimant should not be pensioned.

GROVER CLEVELAND.

EXECUTIVE MANSION, *June 21, 1886.*

To the House of Representatives:

I herewith return without approval House bill No. 6897, entitled "An act granting a pension to Henry Hipple, jr."

This claimant entered the Army as a drummer August 6, 1862, and was discharged May 29, 1863.

In 1879, sixteen years after his discharge, he appears to have discov-ered that during his short term of military service in the inhospitable climate of Port Tobacco, within the State of Maryland, he contracted rheumatism to such an extent as to entitle him to pension, for which he then applied.

It is conceded that he received no medical treatment while in the Army for this complaint, nor does he seem to have been attended by a physician since his discharge.

Without commenting further upon the features of this case which tend to discredit it, I deem myself obliged to disapprove this bill on the ground that there is an almost complete failure to state any facts that should entitle the claimant to a pension.

GROVER CLEVELAND.

EXECUTIVE MANSION, *June 21, 1886.*

To the House of Representatives:

I hereby return without approval a bill originating in the House of Representatives, entitled "An act granting an increase of pension to John W. Farris," which bill is numbered 6136.

The claimant mentioned in this bill enlisted in the month of October, 1861, and was mustered out of the service in August, 1865.

In 1881, sixteen years after his discharge, he filed an application for a pension, alleging that he was afflicted with chronic diarrhea contracted in the Army, and in 1885 his claim was allowed, and he was granted a pension for that cause.

In September of the same year, and after this pension was granted, he filed an application for an increase of his rate, alleging that in 1884 his eyes became affected in consequence of his previous ailments and the debility consequent thereupon.

The ingenuity developed in the constant and persistent attacks upon the public Treasury by those claiming pensions, and the increase of those already granted, is exhibited in bold relief by this attempt to include sore eyes among the results of diarrhea.

I am entirely satisfied with the opinion of the medical referee, who, after examining this case in October, 1885, reported that "the disease of the eyes can not be admitted to be a result of chronic diarrhea."

On all grounds it seems to me that this claimant should be contented with the pension which has been already allowed him.

GROVER CLEVELAND.

EXECUTIVE MANSION, *June 21, 1886.*
To the House of Representatives:

I hereby return without approval House bill No. 1707, entitled "An act granting a pension to Elijah P. Hensley."

The records of the War Department show that this claimant was mustered into the Third North Carolina Regiment, but on the muster-out roll of his company he is reported to have deserted April 3, 1865, and there is no record of any discharge or disability.

In September, 1866, an order was issued from his department headquarters removing the charge of desertion against him. Thirteen days afterwards, and on the 25th day of September, 1866, he filed an application for pension, which in 1868 was granted. He drew such pension dating from 1865 until 1877, when, upon evidence that the injury for which he was pensioned was not received in the line of duty, his name was dropped from the rolls.

The pensioner appealed from this determination of the Pension Bureau to the Secretary of the Interior, who, as lately as May, 1885, rendered a decision sustaining the action of the Bureau.

I find nothing in the facts presented to me which, in my opinion, justifies the reversal of the judgment of the Bureau and the Secretary of the Interior.

GROVER CLEVELAND.

To the Senate: EXECUTIVE MANSION, *June 21, 1886.*

I return without approval Senate bill No. 2223, entitled "An act granting a pension to Elizabeth S. De Krafft."

My objection to this bill is that it is of no possible advantage to the beneficiary therein mentioned. It directs that her name be placed upon the pension roll, subject to the provisions and limitations of the pension laws. The effect of such legislation would be to permit Mrs. De Krafft to draw a pension at the rate of $30 each month from the date of the approval of the bill.

On the 26th day of February, 1886, under the provisions of the general pension law, she was allowed a pension of this exact sum, but the payments were to date from November 10, 1885.

I am so thoroughly tired of disapproving gifts of public money to individuals who in my view have no right or claim to the same, notwithstanding apparent Congressional sanction, that I interpose with a feeling of relief a veto in a case where I find it unnecessary to determine the merits of the application. In speaking of the promiscuous and ill-advised grants of pensions which have lately been presented to me for approval, I have spoken of their "apparent Congressional sanction" in recognition of the fact that a large proportion of these bills have never been submitted to a majority of either branch of Congress, but are the result of nominal sessions held for the express purpose of their consideration and attended by a small minority of the members of the respective Houses of the legislative branch of Government.

Thus in considering these bills I have not felt that I was aided by the deliberate judgment of the Congress; and when I have deemed it my duty to disapprove many of the bills presented, I have hardly regarded my action as a dissent from the conclusions of the people's representatives.

I have not been insensible to the suggestions which should influence every citizen, either in private station or official place, to exhibit not only a just but a generous appreciation of the services of our country's defenders. In reviewing the pension legislation presented to me many bills have been approved upon the theory that every doubt should be resolved in favor of the proposed beneficiary. I have not, however, been able to entirely divest myself of the idea that the public money appropriated for pensions is the soldiers' fund, which should be devoted to the indemnification of those who in the defense of the Union and in the nation's service have worthily suffered, and who in the day of their dependence resulting from such suffering are entitled to the benefactions of their Government. This reflection lends to the bestowal of pensions a kind of sacredness which invites the adoption of such principles and regulations as will exclude perversion as well as insure a liberal and generous application of grateful and benevolent designs. Heedlessness and a disregard of the principle which underlies the granting of pensions is unfair to the wounded, crippled soldier who is honored in the just recognition of his Government. Such a man should never find himself side by side on the pension roll with those who have been tempted to attribute the natural ills to which humanity is heir to service in the Army. Every relaxation of principle in the granting of pensions invites applications without merit and encourages those who for gain urge honest men to become dishonest. Thus is the demoralizing lesson taught the people that as against the public Treasury the most questionable expedients are allowable.

During the present session of Congress 493 special pension bills have been submitted to me, and I am advised that 111 more have received the favorable action of both Houses of Congress and will be presented within a day or two, making over 600 of these bills which have been passed up to this time during the present session, nearly three times the number passed at any entire session since the year 1861. With the Pension Bureau, fully equipped and regulated by the most liberal rules, in active operation, supplemented in its work by constant special legislation, it certainly is not unreasonable to suppose that in all the years that have elapsed since the close of the war a majority of the meritorious claims for pensions have been presented and determined.

I have now more than 130 of these bills before me awaiting Executive action. It will be impossible to bestow upon them the examination they deserve, and many will probably become operative which should be rejected.

In the meantime I venture to suggest the significance of the startling increase in this kind of legislation and the consequences involved in its continuance.

GROVER CLEVELAND.

To the Senate: EXECUTIVE MANSION, *June 21, 1886.*

I hereby return without approval Senate bill No. 1584, entitled "An act for the relief of Cornelia R. Schenck."

It is proposed by this bill to grant a pension to Mrs. Schenck as the widow of Daniel F. Schenck, who entered the military service of the United States in August, 1861, and was mustered out October 21, 1864.

The record of his service contains no mention of any disability. He died in December, 1875, of a disease called gastroenteritis, which, being interpreted, seems to denote "inflammation of the stomach and small intestines." So far as the facts are made to appear, the soldier, neither during the term of his service nor during the eleven years he lived after his discharge, made any claim of any disability.

The claim of his widow was filed in the Pension Bureau in 1885, ten years after her husband's death, and is still undetermined.

The fact that her application is still pending in that Bureau is sufficient reason why this bill should not become a law.

A better reason is based upon the entire lack of any facts shown to exist which entitle the beneficiary named to a pension.

GROVER CLEVELAND.

EXECUTIVE MANSION, *June 22, 1886.*

To the Senate:

I return herewith without approval Senate bill No. 1192, entitled "An act granting a pension to Alfred Denny."

It appears that the claimant entered the United States military service as captain and assistant quartermaster of volunteers on the 12th day of June, 1863. After remaining in such position for less than a year he resigned to accept a civil position.

The short record of his military service discloses no mention of any accident or disability. But twenty years after his resignation, and on the 12th day of March, 1884, he reappears as an applicant for a pension, and alleges in his declaration filed in the Pension Bureau that in August, 1863, while in the line of duty, he was, by a sudden movement of the horse he was riding, thrown forward upon the horn of his saddle and thereby received a rupture in his right side, which at some time and in a manner wholly unexplained subsequently caused a rupture in his left side also.

The number of instances in which those of our soldiers who rode horses during the war were injured by being thrown forward upon their saddles indicate that those saddles were very dangerous contrivances.

I am satisfied there is not a particle of merit in this claim, and no facts are presented to me which entitle it to charitable consideration.

GROVER CLEVELAND.

EXECUTIVE MANSION, *June 22, 1886.*

To the Senate:

I hereby return without approval Senate bill No. 1400, entitled "An act granting a pension to William H. Beck."

This claimant enlisted in 1861. He reenlisted as a veteran volunteer January 1, 1864, and was finally mustered out April 20, 1866. In all this time of service his record shows no medical treatment or claim of disability. Indeed, an abstract of his reenlistment January 1, 1864, shows a medical examination and perfect soundness.

Notwithstanding all this, he filed his declaration on the 4th day of April, 1879, nearly thirteen years after his discharge, alleging that in June, 1863, he incurred epilepsy, to which he has been subject since, and that his fits have been from one to ten days apart. To connect this in some way with his military service he stated that the doctor at a hospital said his epilepsy was caused "by jar to the head from heavy firing."

Six months after this alleged "jar" and his consequent epilepsy he reenlisted upon a medical certificate of perfect soundness and served more than two years thereafter.

Every conceded fact in the case negatives the allegations of his declaration, and the rejection of his claim necessarily followed.

If this disease can be caused in the manner here detailed, its manifestations are such as to leave no doubt of its existence, and it seems to me simply impossible under the circumstances detailed that there should be any lack of evidence to support the claim upon which this bill is predicated.

GROVER CLEVELAND.

To the Senate: EXECUTIVE MANSION, *June 22, 1886.*

I hereby return without approval Senate bill No. 2005, entitled "An act granting a pension to Mary J. Nottage."

The beneficiary named in this bill is the widow of Thomas Nottage, who enlisted in August, 1861, and was discharged for disability September 17, 1862. The assistant surgeon of his regiment, upon his discharge, certified the cause to be "disease of the urinary organs," which had troubled him several years.

He died of consumption January 8, 1879, nearly seventeen years after his discharge, without ever having made any application for a pension.

In 1880 his widow made an application for pension, alleging that he contracted in the service "malarial poisoning, causing remittent fever, piles, general debility, consumption, and death," and that he left two children, both born after his discharge, one in 1866 and the other in 1874.

The only medical testimony which has been brought to my attention touching his condition since his discharge is that of a single physician to the effect that he attended him from the year 1873 to the time of his death in 1879. He states that the patient had during that time "repeated attacks of remittent fever and irritability of the bladder, with organic deposits;" that "in the spring of 1878 he had sore throat and cough, which resulted in consumption, of which he died."

The claim of the widow was rejected in July, 1885, on the ground that "the soldier's death was not the result of his service."

I am satisfied that this conclusion of the Pension Bureau was correct.

GROVER CLEVELAND.

To the Senate: EXECUTIVE MANSION, *June 22, 1886.*

I return herewith without approval Senate bill No. 342, entitled "*An* act granting a pension to Marrilla Parsons, of Detroit, Mich."

No claim has ever been made for a pension in this case to the Pension Bureau, probably for the reason that there is no pretext that the beneficiary named is entitled to a pension under any general law.

Daniel P. Parsons was her stepson, who enlisted in 1861 and died of consumption on the 13th day of August, 1864.

There are no special circumstances to distinguish this case from many others whose claims might be made by stepparents, and there are no facts stated in support of the conclusion embodied in the committee's report that the soldier was taken sick from exposure incident to the service.

To depart from all rules regulating the granting of pensions by such an enactment as is proposed would establish a precedent which could not fail to cause embarrassment and perplexity.

GROVER CLEVELAND.

EXECUTIVE MANSION, *June 22, 1886.*

To the Senate:

I return without approval Senate bill No. 1383, entitled "An act granting a pension to Harriet Welch."

The beneficiary named in this bill asks for a pension as the widow of Syreannous Welch, who was wounded in 1864 while in the service, and was pensioned therefor in 1867. In 1876 his rate of pension was increased. In 1877 he appears to have applied to have his pension again increased. It is alleged that upon such application he was directed to appear before an examining board or a surgeon at Green Bay, Wis., for examination, and in returning to his home from that place on the 7th day of September, 1877, he fell from the cars and was killed, his remains having been found on the track the next morning.

No one appears to have seen the accident, but it is claimed that he could not depend upon his wounded leg, and that it "gave way many times and caused him to fall." From this statement the inference seems to have been indulged that his death was attributable to the wound he had received thirteen years before.

The widow's claim based upon this state of facts was rejected by the Pension Bureau on the ground that the accident resulting in death was not the result of his military service, and on an appeal taken to the Secretary of the Interior from that determination the same was sustained.

Though this widow admits that prior to her marriage with the deceased soldier she had married another man whom she could only say she believed to be dead, I believe her case to be a pitiable one and wish that I could join in her relief; but, unfortunately, official duty can not always be well done when directed solely by sympathy and charity.

GROVER CLEVELAND.

EXECUTIVE MANSION, *June 22, 1886.*

To the Senate:

I return without approval Senate bill No. 1288, entitled "An act granting a pension to Robert Holsey."

This claimant enlisted in 1862, and though he appears to have been sick on two occasions during his term of service, he remained with his company until it was mustered out in 1865.

This soldier was really sick during the time he remained in the Army, and in this respect his claim for a pension has a better origin than many that are presented. But the fact must be recognized, I suppose, that every army ailment does not necessarily result in death or disability.

In 1882, seventeen years after his discharge, this soldier filed his declaration for a pension, alleging that in 1863 he contracted intermittent fever, affecting his lungs, kidneys, and stomach.

A board of surgeons, upon an examination made in 1882, find disease of kidneys, but no indication of lung and stomach trouble; and a medical referee reported in 1885 that there had been no disease of the stomach and lungs since the filing of the claim, and that the difficulty affecting the kidneys had no relation to the sickness for which the claimant had been treated while in the Army.

I am of the opinion that a correct conclusion was reached when the application for pension in this case was denied by the Pension Bureau.

GROVER CLEVELAND.

EXECUTIVE MANSION, *June 22, 1886.*

To the House of Representatives:

I return herewith without approval House bill No. 7979, entitled "An act granting a pension to Jackson Steward."

This claimant's application for pension is now pending in the Pension Bureau, and has been sent to a special examiner for the purpose of taking additional proof.

This I deem sufficient reason why the proposed bill should not now become a law.

GROVER CLEVELAND.

EXECUTIVE MANSION, *June 22, 1886.*

To the Senate:

I hereby return without approval Senate bill No. 2025, entitled "An act granting a pension to James Butler."

This claimant was enrolled as a private in a New Hampshire regiment August 23, 1864, but on the organization of his company, on the 12th day of September, 1864, he was discharged on account of a fracture of his leg, which happened on the 11th day of September, 1864.

It appears that before the organization of the company to which he was attached, and on the 10th day of September, he obtained permission to leave the place of rendezvous for the purpose of visiting his family, and was to return the next day. At a very early hour in the morning, either while preparing to return or actually on his way, he fell into a new cellar and broke his leg. It is said that the leg fractured is now shorter than the other.

His claim for pension was rejected in December, 1864, by the Pension Bureau, and its action was affirmed in 1871 upon the ground that the injury was received while the claimant was on an individual furlough, and therefore not in the line of duty.

Considering the fact that neither his regiment nor his company had at the time of his accident been organized, and that he was in no sense in the military service of the United States, and that his injury was received while on a visit, and not in the performance of duty, I can see no pretext for allowing a pension in this case.

GROVER CLEVELAND.

EXECUTIVE MANSION, *June 23, 1886.*

To the House of Representatives:

I hereby return without approval House bill No. 6688, entitled "An act for the relief of William Bishop."

This claimant was enrolled as a substitute on the 25th day of March, 1865. He was admitted to a post hospital at Indianapolis on the 3d day of April, 1865, with the measles; was removed to the City General Hospital, in Indianapolis, on the 5th day of May, 1865; was returned to duty May 8, 1865, and was mustered out with a detachment of unassigned men on the 11th day of May, 1865.

This is the military record of this soldier, who remained in the Army one month and seventeen days, having entered it as a substitute at a time when high bounties were paid.

Fifteen years after this brilliant service and this terrific encounter with the measles, and on the 28th day of June, 1880, the claimant discovered that his attack of the measles had some relation to his army enrollment and that this disease had "settled in his eyes, also affecting his spinal column."

This claim was rejected by the Pension Bureau, and I have no doubt of the correctness of its determination.

GROVER CLEVELAND.

EXECUTIVE MANSION, *June 23, 1886.*

To the House of Representatives:

I herewith return without approval House bill No. 6266, entitled "An act granting a pension to Philip Arner."

It is conceded in the application for a pension made by this claimant that he was perfectly well prior to his enlistment, during his service, and for a year thereafter. He was discharged in July, 1864, and the proof is that he was taken seriously ill in the fall of 1865, since which time he has been troubled with lung difficulty.

He filed his application for pension in 1883. This was rejected on the ground that the sickness which produced his disability having occurred more than a year after his discharge from the Army, it can not be accepted as a result of his military service.

There is absolutely no allegation of any incident of his service which it is claimed is at all related to his sickness and disability.

GROVER CLEVELAND.

EXECUTIVE MANSION, *June 23, 1886.*

To the House of Representatives:

I herewith return without approval House bill No. 6170, entitled "**An** act granting a pension to Mary A. Van Etten."

In her declaration for a pension, filed July 28, 1885, this claimant alleges that her husband was drowned upon attempting to cross Braddocks Bay, near his residence, in the State of New York, on the 16th day of July, 1875.

It is claimed that in an effort to drive across that bay in a buggy with his young son the buggy was overturned and both were drowned. The application for pension was based upon the theory that during his military service the deceased soldier contracted rheumatism, which so interfered with his ability to save himself by swimming that his death may be fairly traced to a disability incurred in the service.

He does not appear to have been treated while in the Army for rheumatism, though some evidence is presented of his complaining of rheumatic symptoms.

He was mustered out in 1863, and though he lived twelve years thereafter it does not appear that he ever applied for a pension; and though he was drowned in 1875, his widow apparently did not connect his military service with his death until ten years thereafter.

It seems to me that there is such an entire absence of direct and tangible evidence that the death of this soldier resulted from any incident of his service that the granting of a pension upon such a theory is not justified.

GROVER CLEVELAND.

EXECUTIVE MANSION, *June 23, 1886.*

To the House of Representatives:

I return herewith without approval House bill No. 6117, entitled "An act granting a pension to James D. Cotton."

The claim for a pension in this case is on behalf of the father of Thomas Cotton, who was killed at Pittsburg Landing April 6, 1862.

The application of this claimant still remains in the Pension Bureau undetermined. The doubt in the case appears to relate to the dependence of the father upon his son at the time of his death.

This is a question which the Bureau is so well fitted to investigate and justly determine that it is, in my opinion, best to permit the same to be there fully examined.

GROVER CLEVELAND.

EXECUTIVE MANSION, *June 23, 1886.*

To the House of Representatives:

I return herewith without approval House bill No. 6753, entitled "**An act** granting a pension to Mrs. Alice E. Travers."

The husband of the beneficiary, John T. Travers, enlisted August 25, 1864, and was discharged June 11, 1866.

He died January 6, 1881, from the effects of an overdose of morphine which he administered himself. He was a druggist, and when suffering severely was in the habit of taking opiates for relief and sleep.

The disease from which it is said he suffered was lung difficulty, claimed to have been caused by a severe cold contracted in the service.

It does not appear that he ever applied for a pension, and the widow's claim seems to have been properly rejected by the Pension Bureau on the ground that the soldier's death was not due to his military service.

GROVER CLEVELAND.

EXECUTIVE MANSION, *June 23, 1886.*

To the House of Representatives:

I return herewith without approval House bill No. 1816, entitled "An act granting a pension to Mary Ann Miller."

Hamilton Miller, the husband of the claimant, enlisted April 22, 1861, and was sent with his regiment to Camp Dennison, in the suburbs of Cincinnati.

While thus in camp, apparently before he had ever been to the front, and on the 3d of June, 1861, he obtained permission to go to the city of Cincinnati, and was there killed by a blow received from some person who appears to be unknown; but undoubtedly the injury occurred in a fight or as the result of an altercation.

It is very clear to me that the Pension Bureau properly rejected the widow's claim for pension, for the reason that the soldier was not in the line of duty at the date of his death. It is also impossible to connect the death with any incident of the soldier's military service.

GROVER CLEVELAND.

EXECUTIVE MANSION, *June 23, 1886.*

To the House of Representatives:

I return herewith without approval House bill No. 7436, entitled "An act to grant a pension to Mary Anderson."

This claimant is the widow of Richard Anderson, who at the time of his death was receiving a pension on account of chronic diarrhea contracted in the service.

On the 7th day of February, 1882, the deceased pensioner went to Sparta, in the State of Wisconsin, to be examined for an increase of his pension. He called on the surgeon and was examined, and the next morning was found beheaded on the railroad track under such circumstances as indicated suicide.

The claim of the widow was rejected by the Pension Bureau on the ground that the cause of the death of her husband was in no way connected with his military service.

His wife and family present pitiable objects for sympathy, but I am unable to see how they have any claim to a pension.

GROVER CLEVELAND.

EXECUTIVE MANSION, *June 23, 1886.*
To the House of Representatives:

I hereby return without approval House bill 576, entitled "An act for the relief of Louisa C. Beezeley."

By this bill it is proposed to grant a pension to the beneficiary named, as the widow of Nathaniel Beezeley, who was enrolled in an Indiana regiment as a farrier in September, 1861. He was discharged July 17, 1862, after having been in the hospital considerable of the short time he was connected with the Army. The surgeon's certificate on his discharge stated that it was granted by reason of "old age," he then being 60 years old.

He never made any claim for pension, but in 1877 his widow filed her declaration, stating that her husband died in 1875 from disease contracted in the service.

I am convinced that the Pension Bureau acted upon entirely satisfactory evidence when this claim was rejected upon the ground that the cause of death originated subsequent to the soldier's discharge.

GROVER CLEVELAND.

EXECUTIVE MANSION, *June 23, 1886.*
To the House of Representatives:

I return herewith without approval House bill No. 6895, entitled "An act granting a pension to Sarah Harbaugh."

The husband of this claimant enlisted August 1, 1861, and was discharged September 7, 1864. He received a gunshot wound in the left ankle in May, 1863, and died suddenly of disease of the heart October 4, 1881. He was insane before his death, but in my opinion any connection between his injury and his service in the Army is next to impossible.

GROVER CLEVELAND.

EXECUTIVE MANSION, *June 23, 1886.*
To the House of Representatives:

I hereby return without approval House bill No. 7167, entitled "An act for the relief of Mrs. Maria Hunter."

The beneficiary named in this bill, to whom it is therein proposed to grant a pension at the rate of $50 a month, on the 23d day of March, 1886, filed her application for a pension in the Pension Bureau, where it is still pending undetermined.

Although the deceased soldier held a high rank, I have no doubt his widow will receive ample justice through the instrumentality organized for the purpose of dispensing the nation's grateful acknowledgment of military service in its defense.　　　GROVER CLEVELAND.

EXECUTIVE MANSION, *June 23, 1886.*

To the House of Representatives:

I return herewith without approval House bill No. 3205, entitled "An act granting a pension to George W. Guyse."

The claimant filed his declaration for a pension in 1878, alleging that about the 25th day of December, 1863, he received a gunshot wound in his left knee while engaged in a skirmish.

There has been much testimony taken in this case, and a great deal of it is exceedingly contradictory. Three of the claimant's comrades, who originally testified to the receipt of the injury by him, afterwards denied that he was wounded in the service, and a portion of the evidence taken by the Bureau tends to establish the fact that the claimant cut his left knee with a knife shortly after his discharge.

An examining surgeon in November, 1884, reports that he finds "no indication of a gunshot wound, there being no physical or rational signs to sustain claimant in his application for pension."

He further reports that there "seems to be an imperfect scar near the knee, so imperfect as to render its origin uncertain, but in no respect resembling a gunshot wound."

I think upon all the facts presented the Pension Bureau properly rejected this claim, because there was no record of the injury and no satisfactory evidence produced showing that it was incurred in service and in line of duty, "all sources of information having been exhausted."

GROVER CLEVELAND.

EXECUTIVE MANSION, *June 23, 1886.*

To the House of Representatives:

I return without approval House bill No. 7401, entitled "An act granting a pension to Samuel Miller."

This man was discharged from one enlistment June 16, 1864, and enlisted again in August of that year. He was finally discharged July 1, 1865.

In 1880 he filed an application for a pension, alleging that in May, 1862, he contracted in the service "kidney disease and weakness of the back."

A board of surgeons in 1881 reported that they failed to "discover any evidence of disease of kidneys."

It will be observed that since the date when it is claimed his disabilities visited him Mr. Miller not only served out his first term of enlistment, but reenlisted, and necessarily must have passed a medical examination.

I am entirely satisfied with the rejection of this claim by the Pension Bureau.

GROVER CLEVELAND.

EXECUTIVE MANSION, *June 23, 1886.*
To the House of Representatives:

I return herewith without approval House bill No. 424, entitled "An act to pension Giles C. Hawley."

This claimant enlisted August 5, 1861, and was discharged November 14, 1861, upon a surgeon's certificate, in which he stated: "I deem him unfit to stay in the service on account of deafness. He can not hear an ordinary command."

Seventeen years after his discharge from a military service of a little more than three months' duration, and in the year 1878, the claimant filed an application for pension, in which he alleged that "from exposure and excessive duty in the service his hearing was seriously affected."

There is no doubt that his disability existed to quite an extent at least before his enlistment, and there was plenty of opportunity for its increase between the time of discharge and of his application for pension.

I am entirely satisfied that it should not be altogether charged to the three months he spent in the service.

GROVER CLEVELAND.

EXECUTIVE MANSION, *June 23, 1886.*
To the House of Representatives:

I return herewith without approval House bill No. 7222, entitled "An act granting a pension to Callie West."

I base my action upon the opinion, derived from an examination of the circumstances attending the death of the claimant's husband, that his fatal disease did not have its origin in his military service and was entirely disconnected therewith.

GROVER CLEVELAND.

EXECUTIVE MANSION, *June 23, 1886.*
To the House of Representatives:

I return without approval House bill No. 6257, entitled "An act for the relief of Julia Connelly."

It is proposed by this bill to grant a pension to the beneficiary named as the widow of Thomas Connelly.

This man was mustered into the service October 26, 1861. He never did a day's service so far as his name appears, and the muster-out roll of his company reports him as having deserted at Camp Cameron, Pa., November 14, 1861.

He visited his family about the 1st day of December, 1861, and was found December 30, 1861, drowned in a canal about 6 miles from his home.

Those who prosecute claims for pensions have grown very bold when cases of this description are presented for consideration.

GROVER CLEVELAND.

EXECUTIVE MANSION, *June 23, 1886.*

To the House of Representatives:

I herewith return without approval House bill No. 6774, entitled "An act granting a pension to Bruno Schultz."

The application of this claimant for a pension, which was filed a number of years ago, though at one time rejected, has been since opened for reexamination, and is now awaiting additional evidence.

In this condition of this case I think this bill should not be approved.

GROVER CLEVELAND.

EXECUTIVE MANSION, *June 23, 1886.*

To the House of Representatives:

I hereby return without approval House bill No. 7298, entitled "An act for the relief of Charles Schuler."

It is proposed by this bill to grant a pension to the person above named, who was discharged from the military service in December, 1864. He filed a declaration for a pension in the Pension Bureau in January, 1883. This application is still pending. Without referring to the merits of the case, I am of the opinion that the matter should be determined by the Bureau to which it has properly been presented before special legislation should be invoked.

GROVER CLEVELAND.

EXECUTIVE MANSION, *June 23, 1886.*

To the House of Representatives:

I return herewith without approval House bill No. 7073, entitled "An act granting a pension to Mary S. Woodson."

Henry Woodson, the husband of the beneficiary named, enlisted in September, 1861, and was discharged in October, 1863, on account of valvular disease of the heart.

The application for pension on behalf of his widow was filed August 5, 1881.

She concedes that she is unable to furnish any evidence of the date or the cause of her husband's death.

It appears that he left home in March, 1874, for the purpose of finding work, and neither she nor her friends have ever heard from him since. His death may naturally be presumed, and the condition of his family is such that it would be a positive gratification to aid them in the manner proposed; but the entire and conceded absence of any presumption, however weak, that he died from any cause connected with his military service seems to render it improper to place the widow's name upon the pension rolls.

GROVER CLEVELAND.

EXECUTIVE MANSION, *June 23, 1886.*
To the House of Representatives:

I return without approval House bill No. 7108, entitled "An act granting a pension to Andrew J. Wilson."

It appears that this man was drafted and entered the service in February, 1865, and was discharged in September of the same year on account of "chronic nephritis and deafness."

In 1882 he filed his application for a pension, alleging that in June, 1865, from exposure, he contracted rheumatism. Afterwards he described his trouble as inflammation of the muscles of the back, with pain in the kidneys. In another statement, filed in December, 1884, he alleges that while in the service he contracted diarrhea and was injured in one of his testicles, producing a rupture.

Whatever else may be said of this claimant's achievements during his short military career, it must be conceded that he accumulated a great deal of disability.

There is no doubt in my mind that whatever ailments he may honestly lay claim to, his title to the same was complete before he entered the Army.

GROVER CLEVELAND.

EXECUTIVE MANSION, *June 23, 1886.*
To the House of Representatives:

I return herewith without approval House bill No. 7703, entitled "An act granting a pension to Anna A. Probert."

The husband of this beneficiary was pensioned in 1864. He was a druggist and apothecary at Norwalk, in the State of Ohio. Shortly before his death, in 1878, he went to Memphis for the purpose of giving his professional assistance to those suffering from yellow fever at that place. He was himself attacked by that disease, and died on the 28th day of October, 1878.

His widow has never herself applied for a pension, but a power of attorney has been filed, authorizing the prosecution of her claim by another.

That she has employed an ingenious attorney or agent is demonstrated by the fact that the bill now before me seems to be based upon the theory that Mr. Probert might have recovered from his attack of yellow fever if he had been free from the ailments for which he had been pensioned fourteen years before.

If such speculations and presumptions as this are to be indulged, we shall find ourselves surrounded and hedged in by the rule that all men entering an army were free from disease or the liability to disease before their enlistment, and every infirmity which is visited upon them thereafter is the consequence of army service.

GROVER CLEVELAND.

EXECUTIVE MANSION, *June 23, 1886.*
To the House of Representatives:

I return without approval House bill No. 7162, entitled "An act granting a pension to Martha McIlwain."

R. J. McIlwain, the husband of the claimant, enlisted in 1861, and was discharged in 1862 because of the loss of his right leg by a gunshot wound. He was pensioned for this disability. He died May 15, 1883, from an overdose of morphia. It is claimed by the widow that her husband was in the habit of taking morphia to alleviate the pain he endured from his stump, and that he accidentally took too much.

The case was investigated by a special examiner upon the widow's application for pension, and his report shows that the deceased had been in the habit of taking morphia and knew how to use it; that he had been in the habit of buying 6 grains at a time, and that his death was caused by his taking one entire purchase of 6 grains while under the influence of liquor.

In any event it is quite clear that the taking of morphia in any quantity was not the natural result of military service or injury received therein.

I concur in the judgment of the Pension Bureau, which rejected the widow's claim for pension on the ground that "the death of the soldier was not due to his military service."

GROVER CLEVELAND.

EXECUTIVE MANSION, *June 23, 1886.*
To the House of Representatives:

I hereby return without approval House bill No. 7931, entitled "An act increasing the pension of Clark Boon."

This claimant filed his declaration for pension February 3, 1874, in which he states that he lost his health while a prisoner at Tyler, Tex.

On the 19th day of October, 1874, he filed an affidavit claiming that he contracted diseases of the heart and head while in the service. In a further application, filed January 16, 1878, he abandoned his allegations as to disease, and asks for a pension on account of a gunshot wound in the left ankle. Medical testimony was produced on his behalf tending to show not only a gunshot wound, but a disease of the eyes.

A small pension was at last granted him upon the theory advanced by a board of surgeons in 1880 that it was "possible that applicant was entitled to a small rating for weakness of ankle."

A declaration was filed June 4, 1885, by which this claimant insists upon an increase of pension on account of the wound and also for disease of eyes and rheumatism.

I am entirely satisfied that all has been done in this case that the most liberal treatment demands.

GROVER CLEVELAND.

EXECUTIVE MANSION, *June 23, 1886.*
To the House of Representatives:

I hereby return without approval House bill No. 7257, entitled "An act granting a pension to James H. Darling."

This man enlisted in November, 1861, and was reported as having deserted March 5, 1862. The charge of desertion was, however, removed, and it is stated that he went to his home in Ohio at the date stated, by proper authority, where he remained sick till December, 1862, when he was discharged for disability caused "by a disease of the kidneys known as Bright's disease," from which, the physician making the certificate thought, "there was no reasonable prospect of his recovery."

The claimant filed his application for pension, alleging that in January, 1862, he contracted rheumatism.

The claim was investigated by a special examiner and rejected on the ground that the evidence produced failed to show the alleged disability was contracted in the service and in the line of duty.

A medical examination made in 1877 showed that the claimant was "a well-nourished man, 65 years old; height, 5 feet 8 inches; weight, 165 pounds." No disability was discovered, "but a general stiffness of joints, especially of legs, which he says is much aggravated in stormy, cold weather."

Another examination in 1882 found this victim of war disability with "the appearance of a hale, hearty old man—no disease that was discoverable by examination (without chemical test), except some lameness from rheumatism." His weight upon this examination is stated to be 186 pounds.

It is evident to me that this man ought not to be pensioned.

GROVER CLEVELAND.

EXECUTIVE MANSION, *June 23, 1886.*

To the House of Representatives:

I return herewith without my approval House bill No. 6372, entitled "An act to pension Charles A. Chase."

This claimant was enrolled September 6, 1864, and mustered out with his detachment June 1, 1865. His brief service contains no record of disability.

But in 1880 he filed a declaration for pension, in which he claims that by reason of exposure suffered in the service about the 20th of October, 1864, he contracted disease of the liver and kidneys.

The application for pension was denied January 9, 1884, because there was no record of the alleged diseases, and no satisfactory proof of their contraction in the Army was produced, and because of the meager and unconvincing evidence of disability found by the surgeon on an actual examination of the claimant.

I adopt these as the reasons for my action in withholding my approval of this bill.

GROVER CLEVELAND.

EXECUTIVE MANSION, *June 23, 1886.*

To the House of Representatives:

I return herewith without approval House bill No. 6192, entitled "An act granting a pension to Mary Norman."

The husband of this claimant was enrolled May 22, 1863, and was mustered out of the service June 1, 1866.

He was wounded in the head February 20, 1864; was treated for the same, and returned to duty September 3, 1864.

In her declaration for pension, filed in February, 1880, the claimant claims a pension because of his wound and deafness consequent therefrom, and that he died after he left the service.

In a letter, however, dated October 13, 1880, she states that her husband was drowned while trying to cross Roanoke River in December, 1868.

Her claim was rejected in 1881 on the ground that the cause of the soldier's death was accidental drowning, and was not due to his military service.

In an attempt to meet this objection it was claimed as lately as 1885, on behalf of the widow, that her husband's wound caused deafness to such an extent that at the time he was drowned he was unable to hear the ferryman, with whom he was crossing the river, call out that the boat was sinking.

How he could have saved his life if he had heard the warning is not stated.

It seems very clear to me that this is not a proper case for the granting of a pension.

GROVER CLEVELAND.

EXECUTIVE MANSION, *June 23, 1886.*

To the House of Representatives:

I return herewith without my approval House bill No. 7614, entitled "An act granting an increase of pension to Hezekiah Tillman."

This claimant, in his declaration for pension, filed in 1866, alleges that he received a gunshot wound in his right leg November 25, 1862. He was mustered out with his company September 22, 1864.

He was pensioned for the wound which he claimed to have received as his only injury.

In another declaration, filed in 1872, he alleged that in December, 1862, he was struck in his left eye by some hard substance, which destroyed the vision of that organ.

In a subsequent declaration, filed in 1878, he claimed that he received a shell wound in his left knee in November, 1863.

This latter claim has not been finally acted upon by the Pension Bureau, and I am of the opinion that with the diverse claims for injuries which have been there presented on behalf of the beneficiary named justice will be done in the case.

GROVER CLEVELAND.

EXECUTIVE MANSION, *June 23, 1886.*

To the House of Representatives:

I return without approval House bill No. 6718, entitled "An act granting a pension to William H. Starr."

An application made by this claimant to the Pension Bureau is still pending there, and additional evidence has been called for, which the claim is awaiting before final decision.

I am of the opinion that the investigation there should be fully completed before special legislation is resorted to.

GROVER CLEVELAND.

EXECUTIVE MANSION, *June 23, 1886.*

To the House of Representatives:

I return without approval House bill No. 7109, entitled "An act granting a pension to Joseph Tuttle."

This man claims a pension as the dependent father of Charles Tuttle, who enlisted in 1861 and was killed in action May 31, 1862.

The claimant, being, as he says, poor, took his son Charles, at the age of 9 years, and placed him in charge of an uncle living in Ohio. An arrangement was afterwards made by which the boy should live with a stranger named Betts. Upon the death of this gentleman the lad was transferred to one Captain Hill, with whom he remained until his enlistment in 1861.

It is stated that during the time he remained with Mr. Hill he sent his father $5; but the fatherly care and interest of the claimant in his son is exhibited by his statement that though the son was killed in 1862 his father was not aware of it until the year 1864.

After the exhibition of heartlessness and abandonment on the part of a father which is a prominent feature in this case, I should be sorry to be a party to a scheme permitting him to profit by the death of his patriotic son. The claimant relinquished the care of his son, and should be held to have relinquished all claim to his assistance and the benefits so indecently claimed as the result of his death.

GROVER CLEVELAND.

EXECUTIVE MANSION, *June 23, 1886.*

To the House of Representatives:

I return herewith without approval House bill No. 5995, entitled "An act granting a pension to David T. Elderkin."

This claimant enlisted August 5, 1862. From his record it appears that he was dishonorably discharged the service, to date from June 11, 1863, with a loss of all pay, bounty, and allowances.

He filed a declaration for a pension in 1882, claiming that he was wounded in the head by a shell January 1, 1863, which cut his cheek close to his right ear, causing almost total deafness.

There is conflicting evidence as to the claimant's freedom from deafness prior to enlistment, and on a special examination it was shown that he was slightly hard of hearing before enlistment. Indeed the claimant himself stated to the special examiner and also to the board of surgeons that he had been somewhat deaf from childhood.

In 1882 an examining surgeon reports that he finds no scar or evidence of wound, but his hearing is very much impaired.

The claim was rejected in 1885 on the ground that deafness existed prior to enlistment, and also because of no ratable disability by reason of alleged wound in the cheek.

I think, considering the manner of the soldier's discharge and the facts developed, that the claimant should not be pensioned.

GROVER CLEVELAND.

EXECUTIVE MANSION, *June 29, 1886.*

To the Senate:

I hereby return Senate bill No. 1797, entitled "An act granting a pension to John S. Kirkpatrick."

This claimant appears to have enlisted December 10, 1861, and to have been discharged December 20, 1864. He is borne upon the rolls of his company as present up to June, 1862; in July and August, 1862, as on detached service as hospital attendant, and so reported February 28, 1863. In March and April, 1863, he is reported as present, and in May

161

and June, 1863, as on detached service. There is nowhere in his service any record of disability.

He filed his application for a pension in 1880, in which he alleged that from hardship and exposure on a long march in New Mexico in the month of December, 1862, he contracted varicose veins in his legs.

As I understand the record given above, this claimant was on detached service from July, 1862, to February, 1863.

It will be observed that his claim is that he contracted his disability within that time, and in December, 1862. He appears also to have served for two years after the date of his alleged injury, and that he did not file his application for pension till about sixteen years afterwards.

His claim is still pending, undetermined, in the Pension Bureau, and if there is merit in it there is no doubt that he will be able to make it apparent.   GROVER CLEVELAND.

To the Senate: EXECUTIVE MANSION, *June 29, 1886.*

I hereby return without approval Senate bill No. 1077, entitled "An act granting a pension to Newcomb Parker."

This claimant filed an application for a pension in the year 1880.

Before the passage of the bill herewith returned the Commissioner of Pensions, in ignorance of the action of Congress, allowed his claim under the general law. As this decision of the Pension Bureau entitles the beneficiary named to draw a pension from the date of filing his application, which, under the provisions of the special bill in his favor, would only accrue from the time of its passage, I am unwilling that one found worthy to be placed upon the pension rolls by the Bureau, to which he properly applied, should be an actual loser by reason of a special interposition of Congress in his behalf.   GROVER CLEVELAND.

EXECUTIVE MANSION, *July 2, 1886.*
To the House of Representatives:

I return without approval House bill No. 473, entitled "An act granting a pension to William Boone."

There is not the slightest room for doubt as to the facts involved in this case.

No application for pension was ever made to the Pension Bureau by the beneficiary named in this bill. He enlisted in August, 1862; was in action November, 1862, and taken prisoner and at once paroled. During his parole, and at Aurora, in the State of Illinois, he took part in the celebration of the 4th day of July, 1863, and while so engaged was terribly injured by the discharge of a cannon. He is poor, and has a wife and a number of children.

These facts are derived from the report of the committee in Congress to whom the bill was referred, and from a letter written by the soldier since favorable action was had upon said bill by both Houses of Congress, which letter is now before me. In this letter he says: "I never thought of trying getting a pension until my old comrades urged me to do so."

This declaration does not in the least, I think, militate against the present application for pension, but it tends to show the ideas that have become quite prevalent concerning the facts necessary to be established in order to procure a pension by special act of Congress.

Let it be conceded that during the three months which elapsed between the soldier's enlistment and his capture and parole he was constantly in the field and bravely did his duty. The case presented is that of a brave soldier, not injured in any engagement with the enemy, but honorably captured, and by his parole placed in a condition which prevented for the time being his further active military service. He proceeded to his home or to his friends and took his place among noncombatants. Eight months afterwards he joined the citizens of the place of his sojourn and the citizens of every town and hamlet in the loyal States in the usual and creditable celebration of our national holiday. Among the casualties which unfortunately always result from such celebrations there occurred a premature discharge of a cannon, which the present claimant for pension was assisting other citizens to discharge and manage.

Whether any of those thus engaged with him were injured is not disclosed, but it is certain that the paroled soldier was very badly hurt.

I am utterly unable to discover any relation between this accident and the military service, or any reason why, if a pension is granted as proposed by this bill, there should not also be a pension granted to any of the companions of the claimant who chanced to be injured at the same time.

A disabled man and a wife and family in need are objects which appeal to the sympathy and charitable feelings of any decent man; but it seems to me that it by no means follows that those intrusted with the people's business and the expenditure of the people's money are justified in so executing the pension laws as that they shall furnish a means of relief in every case of distress or hardship. GROVER CLEVELAND.

EXECUTIVE MANSION, *July 3, 1886.*

To the Senate:

I hereby return without approval Senate bill No. 365, entitled "An act for the relief of Martin L. Bundy."

By this bill it is proposed to allow in the settlement by the United States with Mr. Bundy, who was lately a paymaster in the Army, the sum of $719.47 for the forage of two horses to which he claims he was entitled while in the service, and which has never been drawn by him. The time during which it is alleged this forage was due is stated to be between July 17, 1862, and April 15, 1866.

This claimant was mustered out as paymaster on the last-mentioned date, and in 1872 a certificate was issued that, his accounts having been adjusted, they exhibited no indebtedness on his part to the United States.

Subsequently, however, and in or about the year 1879, it was discovered that by reason of a duplicate credit, which had been allowed him by mistake, he was actually indebted to the Government in the sum of $528.72.

After the fact had been made known to him the claim embodied in this bill was suggested to or invented by him, which, if allowed, will not only extinguish his indebtedness to the Government, but leave a balance due to him.

By the law and the Army Regulations the forage upon which this claim is based is or should be only allowed to those in the service who actually have and use horses in the performance of their duties.

And when thus entitled to forage it was necessary to draw it in kind or in the specific articles permitted every month, and if not thus drawn it could not afterwards be claimed. There seems to be no such thing as commutation of forage in such cases.

There is no suggestion that the claimant named in this bill had or used any horses while in the service. If he did and paid for their maintenance and at the time of the settlement of his accounts made no claim for reimbursement, he presents a case of incredible ignorance of his rights or a wonderful lack of that disposition to gain every possible advantage which is usually found among those who deal with the Government.

It is quite apparent that the claim is not valid, and the fact that it is made long after the discovery of his deficit leads to the suspicion that it is insisted on merely for the purpose of paying his debt.

Though in this particular case it would do but little more than to extinguish an indebtedness to the Government, the allowance of this claim would set a precedent which could hardly be ignored, and which, if followed, would furnish another means of attack upon the public Treasury quite as effective as many which are now in active operation.

GROVER CLEVELAND.

EXECUTIVE MANSION, *July 5, 1886.*
To the House of Representatives:

I herewith return without approval House bill No. 7018, entitled "An act granting a pension to Aretus F. Loomis."

The Commissioner of Pensions, before he became aware of the passage of this bill, directed favorable action upon the application of the claimant pending in the Pension Bureau. A certificate has been issued for the payment of a pension to him, dating from September 30, 1882.

In the interest of the claimant I therefore withhold my signature from the bill, as the pension granted by special act would only date from the time of its passage.

GROVER CLEVELAND.

EXECUTIVE MANSION, *July 5, 1886.*

To the House of Representatives:

I herewith return without approval House bill No. 1818, entitled "An act granting a pension to H. L. Kyler."

A pension was granted to the person named in this bill, dating from September, 1864, for neuralgia and disease of the eyes.

He was mustered into the service, to serve one hundred days, May 14, 1864, and mustered out September 8, 1864.

In 1880 information reached the Pension Bureau that the pensioner was treated for neuralgia and disease of the eyes at various times between the years 1859 and 1864, and this fact appearing to the satisfaction of the Bureau upon the examination which followed, the pensioner's name was dropped from the roll.

Afterwards another thorough examination of the case was made, when the pensioner was permitted to confront the witnesses against him and produce evidence in his own behalf.

It is claimed that a Dr. Saunders, who testified to treating the pensioner before his enlistment, was exceedingly unfriendly; but he was corroborated by his son and by entries on his books. Another physician, apparently disinterested, also testified to his treatment of the pensioner in 1860 for difficulties with his eyes and ears. The pensioner himself admitted that he had trouble with one of his eyes in 1860, but that he entirely recovered. Six other witnesses testified to the existence of disease of the pensioner's eyes before enlistment.

Though twelve neighbors of the pensioner testified that he was free from neuralgia and disease of the eyes before enlistment, I am of the opinion that the evidence against the pension was quite satisfactory, and that it should not be restored, as the bill before me proposes.

GROVER CLEVELAND.

EXECUTIVE MANSION, *July 5, 1886.*

To the House of Representatives:

I return herewith without approval House bill No. 3640, entitled "An act granting a pension to James T. Irwin."

This claimant enlisted in February, 1864, and was mustered out June 10, 1865. He is reported as absent sick from August 20, 1864, until mustered out. He seems to have been treated for remittent fever, chronic diarrhea, general debility, and palpitation of the heart.

In 1876 he filed a declaration for pension, alleging that at Petersburg, July 1, 1864, he contracted fever and inflammation of the eyes.

He filed an affidavit in January, 1877, in which he states that his diseased eyes resulted from diseased nerves, caused by a wound received June 18, 1864, at Petersburg, and from a consequent abscess on the back of the neck.

In an affidavit filed in July, 1878, he states that in June, 1864, in front of Petersburg, he had his gun smashed in front of his face and his eyes injured, and afterwards he had an abscess on the back of his neck, typhoid fever, and disease of the left lung.

His claim founded upon these various allegations of injury was rejected in February, 1879.

In September, 1884, a declaration was filed for a pension, alleging disease of the heart contracted at Petersburg June 16, 1864.

The claimant was examined once in 1882 and twice in 1884 by United States examining surgeons and boards, and it is stated that these examinations failed to reveal any disease or disability except disease of the eyes and an irritable heart, the result of indigestion.

An oculist who made an examination in 1884 reported that the unnatural condition of claimant's eyes was congenital and in no manner the result of injury or disease.

Upon a consideration of the very short time that the claimant was in actual service, the different claims he has made touching his alleged disability, and the positive results of medical examinations, I am satisfied this pension should not be allowed.

GROVER CLEVELAND.

EXECUTIVE MANSION, *July 5, 1886.*
To the House of Representatives:

I return herewith without my approval House bill No. 5306, entitled "An act granting a pension to Roxana V. Rowley."

The beneficiary named in this bill is the widow of Franklin Rowley, who enlisted February 8, 1865, was promoted to first lieutenant March 13, 1865, and was discharged May 22, 1865, having tendered his resignation, as it is stated, on account of incompetency. His tender of resignation was indorsed by the commanding officer of his regiment as follows: "This man is wholly unfit for an officer."

It will be seen that he was in the service a little more than three months.

In 1880, fifteen years after his discharge, he applied for a pension, alleging that he contracted disease of the liver while in the service.

Upon an examination of the claim his attending physician before enlistment stated that as early as 1854 the claimant was afflicted with dyspepsia and functional disease of the liver; that he regarded him as incurable, so far as being restored to sound health was concerned, and that if he had been at home at the time when he enlisted he would have advised against it.

The testimony of this physician as to the claimant's condition after his discharge is referred to in the report of the Committee of the House to whom this bill was referred, and I do not understand that he is at all impeached. He certainly is better informed than any other person regarding the condition of the man who was his patient.

The soldier died in 1881, sixteen years after his discharge, and his widow filed her claim for pension in 1882, alleging that the death of her husband was caused by a disease of the liver contracted in the service.

Her claim was rejected in 1883 upon the ground that the disease of which her husband died existed prior to his enlistment.

I can not avoid the conclusion, upon all the facts presented, that his death was not chargeable to any incident of his brief military service.

GROVER CLEVELAND.

EXECUTIVE MANSION, *July 5, 1886.*

To the House of Representatives:

I herewith return without approval House bill No. 5021, entitled "An act granting a pension to Mrs. Margaret A. Jacoby."

A pension has been allowed on account of the disability of the claimant's husband, dating from his discharge in 1864.

The beneficiary named in this bill applied for pension in 1885, alleging that she married the soldier in 1864; that he incurred deafness and chronic diarrhea while in the service, from the combined effect of which he partially lost his mind; that on the 7th day of September, 1875, he disappeared, and that after diligent search and inquiry she is unable to learn anything of him since that time.

His disability from army service should be conceded and his death at some time and in some manner may well be presumed; but the fact that he died from any cause related to his disability or his service in the Army has no presumption and not a single particle of proof to rest upon.

With proper diligence something should be discovered to throw a little light upon this subject. GROVER CLEVELAND.

EXECUTIVE MANSION, *July 5, 1886.*

To the House of Representatives:

I return without approval House bill No. 3304, entitled "An act to restore the name of Abner Morehead to the pension roll."

The person mentioned in this bill was pensioned in November, 1867, upon the claim made by him that in 1863, from hardship and exposure incident to camp life and field duty, he contracted a fever which settled in his eyes, almost wholly destroying his sight. Afterwards his pension was increased to $15 a month, dating from December, 1867, and arrears at the rate of $8 a month from February, 1864. In 1876 the case was put in the hands of a special agent of the Pension Bureau for examination, and upon his report, showing that the claimant's disease of the eyes existed prior to enlistment, his name was dropped from the rolls.

An application for restoration was made in 1879, and a thorough examination was made by a special examiner in 1885, who reported that the testimony taken conclusively established the fact that the claimant had

disease of the eyes prior to the time of enlistment, the result of a disorder
which he specifically mentions, and that he was treated for the same more
than a year subsequently to 1860.   He adds:

> There is no merit whatever in this case, and it is evident that he obtained a large
> sum as pension to which he must have known he was not entitled.

The results of these examinations, instituted for the express purpose
of developing the facts, and with nothing apparent to impeach them,
should, I think, control as against the statements of neighbors and comrades based upon mere general observation, and not necessarily covering
the period which is important to the controversy.

GROVER CLEVELAND.

Executive Mansion, July 5, 1886.

To the House of Representatives:

I herewith return without approval House bill No. 4782, entitled "An
act granting a pension to Elizabeth McKay."

The beneficiary named is the widow of Rowley S. McKay, who in 1862
seems to have been employed as pilot on the ram *Switzerland*.   He seems
to have been upon the rolls of two other vessels of the United States, the
Covington and *General Price*, but was discharged by Admiral Porter in
June, 1864, with loss of all pay and emoluments.

He filed an application for pension in 1870, alleging that while on duty
as pilot and in action with the rebel ram *Arkansas* his hearing became
affected by heavy firing.   He also claimed that in February, 1863, while
on the vessel *Queen of the West*, she grounded, and to escape capture he
got off and floated down the river on a cotton bale, and, being in the
water about three hours, the exposure caused a disease of the urinary
organs; and that a few days after, while coming up the river on a transport, the boat was fired into and several balls passed through his left
thigh.   It seems that this claim was not definitely passed upon, but it is
stated that the records failed to show that McKay was in the service of
the United States at the time he alleged the contraction of disease of the
urinary organs and was wounded in the thigh.

The beneficiary named in this bill never made application for pension
to the Pension Bureau, but it appears that she bases her claims to consideration by Congress upon the allegation that in 1862, while her husband was acting as pilot of the ram or gunboat *Switzerland*, he contracted
chronic diarrhea, from which he never recovered, and that he died from
the effects of said disease in May, 1874.

It will be observed that among the various causes which the soldier
or sailor himself alleged as the grounds of his application for pension
chronic diarrhea is not mentioned.

There does not appear to be any medical testimony to support the
claim thus made by the widow, and the cause of death is not definitely
stated.

Taking all together, it has the appearance of a case, by no means rare, where chronic diarrhea or rheumatism are appealed to as a basis for a pension claim in the absence of something more substantial and definite.

The fact that the claim of the beneficiary has never been presented to the Pension Bureau influences in some degree my action in withholding my approval of this bill. GROVER CLEVELAND.

EXECUTIVE MANSION, *July 5, 1886.*

To the House of Representatives:

I return herewith without approval House bill No. 3623, entitled "An act granting a pension to William H. Nevil."

This bill directs that the name of the claimant be placed upon the pension roll "subject to the provisions and limitations of the pension laws."

This very thing was done on the 22d day of June, 1865, and the claimant is in the receipt at the present time of the full amount of pension allowed by our pension laws as administered by the Pension Bureau.

I suppose the intention of the bill was to increase this pension, but it is not framed in such a way as to accomplish that object or to benefit the claimant in any way whatever. GROVER CLEVELAND.

EXECUTIVE MANSION, *July 5, 1886.*

To the House of Representatives:

I herewith return without approval House bill No. 1505, entitled "An act granting a pension to William Dermody."

By the records of the War Department which have been furnished me it appears that this claimant enlisted August 19, 1861; that he deserted August 29, 1862; in November and December, 1862, he is reported as present in confinement in regimental guardhouse, to forfeit one month's pay by sentence of regimental court-martial; he is reported as having deserted again in December, 1863, but as present for duty in January and February, 1864; he reenlisted in the latter month, and was mustered out July 17, 1865, and with his company was paid up to and including July 21, 1865.

He filed a declaration for pension in 1879, alleging that he received a gunshot wound in the thigh at Trenton, N. J., July 21, 1865, and that the wound was inflicted by a member of the Invalid Corps, who was whipping a drummer boy, and the claimant interfered in behalf of the boy.

It is quite certain that the transaction took place July 23.

An examining board, in 1880, found pistol shot in thigh, but refused to give the claimant a rating, because, as they report, "from the evidence before the board there is reason to suppose that he was deserting from the barracks at Trenton July 23, 1865, and was shot by the guard."

This may not be a just suspicion or finding, but he surely was not in the service nor in the performance of any military duty at the time of the injury, nor was he engaged in such manner as to entitle him to indemnification at the hands of the Government.

GROVER CLEVELAND.

EXECUTIVE MANSION, *July 5, 1886.*

To the House of Representatives:

I herewith return without approval House bill No. 1059, entitled "An act to grant a pension to Joseph Komiser."

The Pension Bureau reports that the records of the office fail to show that an application has been filed in favor of this claimant, though it is stated in the report of the House committee that such a claim was made and rejected on the ground that the claimant was not at the time of injury in the service of the United States.

It certainly appears from the report of the committee that the beneficiary named in this bill was not in the service of the Government at such a time, and also that he had not been mustered into the service of any State military organization. It is stated that he belonged to Captain Frank Mason's company of volunteers, of Frostburg, in the State of Maryland.

Whether this company was organized for the purpose of cooperating at any time with the Union or State forces is not alleged, and it may well have been existing merely for the purpose of neighborhood protection.

Such as it was, the company was ordered in June, 1861, to proceed to Cumberland to repel a threatened attack of Confederate forces. Upon arriving at that place the men were ordered to uncap their muskets. In doing this, and through the negligence of another member of the company, whose musket was discharged, the claimant was wounded.

It does not seem to me that the facts in this case, so far as they have been developed, justify the passage of this act.

GROVER CLEVELAND.

EXECUTIVE MANSION, *July 5, 1886.*

To the House of Representatives:

I herewith return without approval House bill No. 4226, entitled "An act granting a pension to Fannie E. Evans."

The beneficiary named in this bill is the widow of George S. Evans. He was a soldier in the Mexican War, and entered the Union Army in the War of the Rebellion, on the 16th day of October, 1861, as major of a California regiment. He became a colonel in February, 1863, and resigned in April of that year, to take effect on the 31st of May ensuing.

His resignation seems to have been tendered on account of private matters and no mention was then made of any disability. It is stated in the committee's report to the House that in 1864 he accepted the office of adjutant-general of the State of California, which he held for nearly four years.

He died in 1883 from cerebral apoplexy.

In March, 1884, his widow filed an application for pension, based upon the allegation that from active and severe service in a battle with the Indians at Spanish Fort in 1863 her husband incurred a hernia, which incapacitated him for active service.

There appears to be evidence to justify this statement, notwithstanding the fact that the deceased during the twenty years that followed before his death made no claim for such disability.

But it seems to me that the effort to attribute his death by apoplexy to the existence of hernia ought not to be successful.

GROVER CLEVELAND.

EXECUTIVE MANSION, *July 5, 1886.*

To the House of Representatives:

I herewith return without approval House bill No. 2971, entitled "An act granting a pension to Francis Deming."

This claimant entered the service in August, 1861, and was discharged September 15, 1865.

His hospital record shows that during his service he was treated for various temporary ailments, among which rheumatism is not included.

He filed an application for pension in September, 1884, alleging that in August, 1864, he contracted rheumatism, which had resulted in blindness.

On an examination of his case in November, 1884, he stated that his eyesight began to fail in 1882.

There seems to be no testimony showing his condition from the time of his discharge to 1880, a period of fifteen years.

The claim that his present condition of blindness is the result of his army service is not insisted upon as a reason for granting him relief as strongly as his sad and helpless condition. The committee of the House to which this bill was referred, after detailing his situation, close their report with these words: "He served well his country in its dire need; his necessities now appeal for relief."

We have here presented the case of a soldier who did his duty during his army service, and who was discharged in 1865 without any record of having suffered with rheumatism and without any claim of disability arising from the same. He returned to his place as a citizen, and in peaceful pursuits, with chances certainly not impaired by the circumstance that he had served his country, he appears to have held his place in the race of life for fifteen years or more. Then, like many another, he was subjected to loss of sight, one of the saddest afflictions known to human life.

Thereupon, and after nineteen years had elapsed since his discharge from the Army, a pension is claimed for him upon a very shadowy allegation of the incurrence of rheumatism while in the service, coupled with the startling proposition that this rheumatism resulted, just previous to his application, in blindness. Upon medical examination it appeared that his blindness was caused by amaurosis, which is generally accepted as an affection of the optic nerve.

I am satisfied that a fair examination of the facts in this case justifies the statement that the bill under consideration can rest only upon the grounds that aid should be furnished to this ex-soldier because he served in the Army and because he a long time thereafter became blind, disabled, and dependent.

The question is whether we are prepared to adopt this principle and establish this precedent.

None of us are entitled to credit for extreme tenderness and consideration toward those who fought their country's battles. These are sentiments common to all good citizens. They lead to the most benevolent care on the part of the Government and deeds of charity and mercy in private life. The blatant and noisy self-assertion of those who, from motives that may well be suspected, declare themselves above all others friends of the soldier can not discredit nor belittle the calm, steady, and affectionate regard of a grateful nation.

An appropriation has just been passed setting apart $76,000,000 of the public money for distribution as pensions, under laws liberally constructed, with a view of meeting every meritorious case. More than $1,000,000 was added to maintain the Pension Bureau, which is charged with the duty of a fair, just, and liberal apportionment of this fund.

Legislation has been at the present session of Congress perfected considerably increasing the rate of pension in certain cases. Appropriations have also been made of large sums for the support of national homes where sick, disabled, or needy soldiers are cared for, and within a few days a liberal sum has been appropriated for the enlargement and increased accommodation and convenience of these institutions.

All this is no more than should be done.

But with all this, and with the hundreds of special acts which have been passed granting pensions in cases where, for my part, I am willing to confess that sympathy rather than judgment has often led to the discovery of a relation between injury or death and military service, I am constrained by a sense of public duty to interpose against establishing a principle and setting a precedent which must result in unregulated, partial, and unjust gifts of public money under the pretext of indemnifying those who suffered in their means of support as an incident of military service.

GROVER CLEVELAND.

EXECUTIVE MANSION, *July 6, 1886.*

To the House of Representatives:

I herewith return without approval House bill No. 4642, entitled "An act granting a pension to James Carroll."

The claimant alleges that he was wounded while in the service as a member of Company B, Third Regiment North Carolina Mounted Volunteers, while securing recruits for the regiment at Watauga, N. C., January 25, 1865.

The records of the War Department develop the fact that the name of this man is not borne upon any roll of the company to which he claims to belong.

He stated in his application that he was sworn in by one George W. Perkins, who, it appears, was a private in said company, and that Perkins was with him at the time he was shot.

This is undoubtedly true, and that the claimant was injured by a gunshot is also probably true. He was not, however, at the time regularly in the United States service, but this objection might in some circumstances be regarded as technical. The difficulty is that the fact that he was creditably employed in a service of benefit to the country is not satisfactorily shown. He gives two accounts of the business in which he was engaged, and Mr. Perkins's explanation of the manner in which the two were occupied is somewhat different still.

Carroll's claim, presented to the Pension Bureau, was rejected upon the ground that there was no record of his service on file; but in his testimony he stated that Perkins was wounded on the same occasion as himself, and that he (Perkins) was then a pensioner on account thereof.

The records of the Pension Bureau show that Perkins was pensioned in 1873 on account of three wounds received at the time and place of Carroll's injury.

It also appears that his name was dropped from the rolls in 1877 on the ground that his wounds were not received in the line of duty.

After an investigation made at that time by a special examiner, he reported that Perkins and Carroll had collected a number of men together, who made their headquarters at the home of Carroll's mother and were engaged in plundering the neighborhood, and that on account of their depredations they were hunted down by home guards and shot at the time they stated.

If this report is accepted as reliable, it should of course lead to the rejection of the claim for pension on the part of Mr. Carroll.

GROVER CLEVELAND.

EXECUTIVE MANSION, *July 6, 1886.*

To the House of Representatives:

I herewith return without approval House bill No. 3043, entitled "An act granting a pension to Lewis W. Scanland."

The claimant filed his declaration for a pension in 1884, alleging that he contracted chronic diarrhea while serving in a company of mounted Illinois volunteers in the Black Hawk War.

The records show that he served from April 18, 1832, to May 28, in the same year.

He was examined by a board of surgeons in 1884, when he was said to be 75 years old. In his examination he did not claim to have diarrhea for a good many years. On the contrary, he claimed to be affected with constipation, and said he had never had diarrhea of late years, except at times when he had taken medicine for constipation.

I am inclined to think it would have been a fortunate thing if in this case it could have been demonstrated that a man could thrive so well with the chronic diarrhea for fifty-two years as its existence in the case of this good old gentleman would prove. We should then, perhaps, have less of it in claims for pensions.

The fact is, in this case there is no disability which can be traced to the forty days' military service of fifty-four years ago, and I think little, if any, more infirmity than is usually found in men of the age of the claimant.

Entertaining this belief, I am constrained to withhold my signature from this bill.

GROVER CLEVELAND.

EXECUTIVE MANSION, *July 6, 1886.*
To the House of Representatives:

I return herewith without approval House bill No. 5414, entitled "An act granting a pension to Maria Cunningham."

The husband of the beneficiary named in this bill enlisted January 29, 1862, and was discharged January 20, 1865.

He applied for a pension in 1876, alleging a shell wound in the head. His claim was rejected on the ground that there appeared to be no disability from that cause. No other injury or disability was ever claimed by him, but at the time of his examination in 1876 he was found to be sickly, feeble, and emaciated, and suffering from an advanced stage of saccharine diabetes.

His widow filed an application for a pension in 1879, alleging that her husband died in December, 1877, of spinal disease and diabetes, contracted in the service.

Her claim was rejected because evidence was not furnished that the cause of the soldier's death had its origin in the military service.

There seems to be an entire absence of proof of this important fact.

GROVER CLEVELAND.

EXECUTIVE MANSION, *July 6, 1886*
To the House of Representatives:

I herewith return without approval House bill No. 4797, entitled "An act granting a pension to Robert H. Stapleton."

This claimant filed an application for pension in the Pension Bureau in 1883, alleging that while acting as lieutenant-colonel of a New Mexico regiment, on February 21, 1862, the tongue of a caisson struck him, injuring his left side. A medical examination made in 1882 showed a fracture of the ninth, tenth, and eleventh ribs of the left side.

If these fractures were the result of the injury alleged, they were immediately apparent, and the delay of twenty-one years in presenting the claim for pension certainly needs explanation.

Claims of this description, by a wise provision of law, must, to be valid, be prosecuted to a successful issue prior to the 4th day of July, 1874.

The rank which this claimant held presupposes such intelligence as admits of no excuse on the ground of ignorance of the law for his failure to present his application within the time fixed by law.

The evidence of disability from the cause alleged is weak, to say the most of it, and I can not think that such a wholesome provision of law as that above referred to, which limits the time for the adjustment of such claims, should be modified upon the facts presented in this case.

GROVER CLEVELAND.

EXECUTIVE MANSION, *July 6, 1886.*
To the House of Representatives:

I herewith return without approval House bill No. 5550, entitled "An act to provide for the erection of a public building at Duluth, Minn."

After quite a careful examination of the public needs at the point mentioned I am entirely satisfied that the public building provided for in this bill is not immediately necessary.

Not a little legislation has lately been perfected, and very likely more will be necessary, to increase miscalculated appropriations for and correct blunders in the construction of many of the public buildings now in process of erection.

While this does not furnish a good reason for disapproving the erection of other buildings where actually necessary, it induces close scrutiny and gives rise to the earnest wish that new projects for public buildings shall for the present be limited to such as are required by the most pressing necessities of the Government's business.

GROVER CLEVELAND.

EXECUTIVE MANSION, *July 6, 1886.*
To the House of Representatives:

I return herewith without approval House bill No. 2043, entitled "An act to place Mary Karstetter on the pension roll."

The husband of this beneficiary, Jacob Karstetter, was enrolled June 30, 1864, as a substitute in a Pennsylvania regiment, and was discharged for disability June 20, 1865, caused by a gunshot wound in the left hand.

A declaration for pension was filed by him in 1865, based upon this wound, and the same was granted, dating from June in that year, which he drew till the time of his death, August 21, 1874.

In 1882 his widow filed her application for pension, alleging that he died of wounds received in battle. The claim was made that he was injured while in the Army by a horse running over him.

There is little or no evidence of such an injury having been received; and if this was presented there would be no necessary connection between that and the cause of the soldier's death, which was certified by the attending physician to be gastritis and congestion of the kidneys.

I can hardly see how the Pension Bureau could arrive at any conclusion except that the death of the soldier was not due to his military service, and the acceptance of this finding, after an examination of the facts, leads me to disapprove this bill.

GROVER CLEVELAND.

EXECUTIVE MANSION, *July 6, 1886.*
To the House of Representatives:

I herewith return without approval House bill No. 5394, entitled "An act granting a pension to Sallie Ann Bradley."

The husband of this proposed beneficiary was discharged from the military service in 1865, after a long service, and was afterwards pensioned for gunshot wound.

He died in 1882. The widow appears to have never filed a claim for pension in her own right.

No cause is given of the soldier's death, but it is not claimed that it resulted from his military service, her pension being asked for entirely because of her needs and the faithful service of her husband and her sons.

This presents the question whether a gift in such a case is a proper disposition of money appropriated for the purpose of paying pensions.

The passage of this law would, in my opinion, establish a precedent so far-reaching and open the door to such a vast multitude of claims not on principle within our present pension laws that I am constrained to disapprove the bill under consideration.

GROVER CLEVELAND.

EXECUTIVE MANSION, *July 6, 1886.*
To the House of Representatives:

I return herewith without approval House bill No. 5603, entitled "An act granting a pension to Mrs. Catherine McCarty."

The beneficiary is the widow of John McCarty, of the First Missouri Regiment of State Militia Volunteers, who died at Clinton, Mo., April 8, 1864.

The widow filed her claim in 1866, alleging that her husband died while in the service from an overdose of colchicum.

The evidence shows without dispute that on the day previous to the death of the soldier a comrade procured some medicine from the regimental surgeon and asked McCarty to smell and taste it; that he did so, and shortly afterwards became very sick and died the next morning.

It is quite evident that the deceased soldier did more than taste this medicine.

Although it would be pleasant to aid the widow in this case, it is hardly fair to ask the Government to grant a pension for the freak or gross heedlessness and recklessness of this soldier.

GROVER CLEVELAND.

EXECUTIVE MANSION, *July 6, 1886.*

To the House of Representatives:

I herewith return without my approval House bill No. 6648, entitled "An act for the relief of Edward M. Harrington."

It appears that this claimant was enrolled as a recruit December 31, 1863, and mustered in at Dunkirk, N. Y. He remained at the barracks there until March, 1864, when he was received at the Elmira rendezvous. From there he was sent to his regiment on the 7th day of April, 1864.

He was discharged June 15, 1864, upon a surgeon's certificate of disability, declaring the cause of discharge to be epilepsy, produced by blows of violence over the hypochondrial region while in the service, producing a deformity of sternum.

The claimant filed an application for pension in June, 1879, and in that and subsequent affidavits he alleged that while in barracks at Dunkirk, N. Y., and about the 9th day of January, 1864, and in the line of duty, he was attacked by one Patrick Burnes, who struck him upon the head and stamped upon and kicked him, breaking his collar bone and a number of ribs, causing internal injury and fits, the latter recurring every two weeks.

It is hardly worth while considering the character of these alleged injuries or their connection with the fits with which the claimant is afflicted.

I am entirely unable to see how the injuries are related to the claimant's army service.

The Government ought not to be called upon to insure against the quarrelsome propensities of its individual soldiers, nor to compensate one who is worsted in a fight, or even in an unprovoked attack, when the cause of injury is in no way connected with or related to any requirement or incident of military service.

GROVER CLEVELAND.

EXECUTIVE MANSION, *July 7, 1886.*

To the Senate of the United States:

I return without approval Senate bill No. 2281, entitled "An act grant-ing to railroads the right of way through the Indian reservation in north-ern Montana."

The reservation referred to stretches across the extreme northern part of Montana Territory, with British America for its northern boundary. It contains an area of over 30,000 square miles. It is dedicated to Indian occupancy by treaty of October 17, 1855, and act of Congress of April 15, 1874. No railroads are within immediate approach to its boundaries, and only one, as shown on recent maps, is under construction in the neighborhood leading in its direction. The surrounding country is sparsely settled, and I have been unable to ascertain that the necessities of commerce or any public exigencies demand this legislation, which would affect so seriously the rights and interests of the Indians occupy-ing the reservation.

The bill is in the nature of a general right of way for railroads through this Indian reservation. The Indian occupants have not given their con-sent to it, neither have they been consulted regarding it, nor is there any provision in it for securing their consent or agreement to the location or construction of railroads upon their lands. No routes are described, and no general directions on which the line of any railroad will be constructed are given.

No particular organized railway company engaged in constructing a railroad toward the reservation and ready or desirous to build its road through the Indian lands to meet the needs and requirements of trade and commerce is named. The bill gives the right to any railroad in the country, duly organized under the laws of any Territory, of any State, or of the United States, except those of the District of Columbia, to enter this Indian country, prospect for routes of travel, survey them, and con-struct routes of travel wherever it may please, with no check save possible disapproval by the Secretary of the Interior of its maps of location, and no limitation upon its acts except such rules and regulations as he may prescribe.

This power vested in the Secretary of the Interior might itself be im-providently exercised and subject to abuse.

No limit of time is fixed within which the construction of railroads should begin or be completed. Without such limitations speculating corporations would be enabled to seek out and secure the right of way over the natural and most feasible routes, with no present intention of constructing railroads along such lines, but with the view of holding their advantageous easements for disposal at some future time to some other corporation for a valuable consideration. In this way the construc-tion of needed railroad facilities in that country could be hereafter greatly obstructed and retarded.

If the United States must exercise its right of eminent domain over the Indian Territories for the general welfare of the whole country, it should be done cautiously, with due regard for the interests of the Indians, and to no greater extent than the exigencies of the public service require.

Bills tending somewhat in the direction of this general character of legislation, affecting the rights of the Indians reserved to them by treaty stipulations, have been presented to me during the present session of Congress. They have received my reluctant approval, though I am by no means certain that a mistake has not been made in passing such laws without providing for the consent to such grants by the Indian occupants and otherwise more closely guarding their rights and interests; and I hoped that each of those bills as it received my approval would be the last of the kind presented. They, however, designated particular railroad companies, laid down general routes over which the respective roads should be constructed through the Indian lands, and specified their direction and termini, so that I was enabled to reasonably satisfy myself that the exigencies of the public service and the interests of commerce probably demanded the construction of the roads, and that by their construction and operation the Indians would not be too seriously affected.

The bill now before me is much more general in its terms than those which have preceded it. It is a new and wide departure from the general tenor of legislation affecting Indian reservations. It ignores the right of the Indians to be consulted as to the disposition of their lands, opens wide the door to any railroad corporation to do what, under the treaty covering the greater portion of the reservation, is reserved to the United States alone; it gives the right to enter upon Indian lands to a class of corporations carrying with them many individuals not known for any scrupulous regard for the interest or welfare of the Indians; it invites a general invasion of the Indian country, and brings into contact and intercourse with the Indians a class of whites and others who are independent of the orders, regulations, and control of the resident agents.

Corporations operating railroads through Indian lands are strongly tempted to infringe at will upon the reserved rights and the property of Indians, and thus are apt to become so arbitrary in their dealings and domineering in their conduct toward them that the Indians become disquieted, often threatening outbreaks and periling the lives of frontier settlers and others.

I am impressed with the belief that the bill under consideration does not sufficiently guard against an invasion of the rights and a disturbance of the peace and quiet of the Indians on the reservation mentioned; nor am I satisfied that the legislation proposed is demanded by any exigency of the public welfare.

GROVER CLEVELAND.

EXECUTIVE MANSION, *July 9, 1886.*

To the House of Representatives:

I return herewith without approval House bill No. 524, entitled "An act granting a pension to Daniel H. Ross."

An application for pension was filed in the Pension Bureau by the beneficiary named in this bill, and considerable testimony was filed in support of the same. I do not understand that the claim has been finally rejected. But however that may be, the claimant died, as I am advised, on the 1st day of February last. This, of course, renders the proposed legislation entirely inoperative, if it would not actually prejudice the claim of his surviving widow. She has already been advised of the evidence necessary to complete the claim of her husband, and it is not at all improbable that she will be able to prosecute the same to a successful issue for her benefit.

At any rate, her rights should not be in the least jeopardized by the completion of the legislation proposed in this bill.

GROVER CLEVELAND.

EXECUTIVE MANSION, *July 9, 1886.*

To the Senate:

I herewith return without approval Senate bill No. 856, entitled "An act to provide for the erection of a public building in the city of Dayton, Ohio."

It is not claimed that the Government has any public department or business which it should quarter at Dayton except its post-office and internal-revenue office. The former is represented as employing ten clerks, sixteen regular and two substitute letter carriers, and two special-delivery employees, who, I suppose, are boys, only occasionally in actual service. I do not understand that the present post-office quarters are either insufficient or inconvenient. By a statement prepared by the present postmaster it appears that they are rented by the Government for a period of ten years from the 15th day of October, 1883, at an annual rent of $2,950, which includes the cost of heating the same.

The office of the internal-revenue collector is claimed to be inadequate, but I am led to believe that this officer is fairly accommodated at an annual rental of $900. It is not impossible that a suggestion to change the area of this revenue district may be adopted, which would relieve any complaint of inadequacy of office room.

With only these two offices to provide for, I am not satisfied that the expenditure of $150,000 for their accommodation, as proposed by this bill, is in accordance with sound business principles or consistent with that economy in public affairs which has been promised to the people.

GROVER CLEVELAND.

EXECUTIVE MANSION, *July 10, 1886.*

To the House of Representatives:

I herewith return without approval House bill No. 5546, entitled "An act for the erection of a public building at Asheville, N. C."

If the needs of the Government are alone considered, the proposed building is only necessary for the accommodation of two terms of the United States court in each year and to provide an office for the clerk of that court and more commodious quarters for the post-office.

The terms of the court are now held in the county court room at Asheville at an expense to the Government of $50 for each term; the clerk of the court occupies a room for which an annual rent of $150 is paid, and the rent paid for the rooms occupied by the post-office is $180 each year.

The postmaster reports that four employees are regularly engaged in his office, which is now rated as third class.

I have no doubt that the court could be much more conveniently provided for in a new building if one should be erected; but it is represented to me that the regular terms held at Asheville last only two or three weeks each, though special terms are ordered at times to clear the docket. It is difficult to see from any facts presented in support of this bill why the United States court does not find accommodations which fairly answer its needs in the rooms now occupied by it. The floor space furnished for the terms of the Federal court is stated to be 75 by 100 feet, which, it must be admitted, provides a very respectable court room.

It is submitted that the necessity to the Government of a proper place to hold its courts is the only consideration which should have any weight in determining upon the propriety of expending the money which will be necessary to erect the proposed new building.

The limit of its cost is fixed in the bill under consideration at the sum of $80,000, but the history of such projects justifies the expectation that this limit will certainly be exceeded.

I am satisfied that the present necessity for this building is not urgent, and that something may be gained by a delay which will demonstrate more fully the public needs, and thus better suggest the style and size of the building to be erected. GROVER CLEVELAND.

EXECUTIVE MANSION, *July 20, 1886.*

To the Senate:

I return without approval Senate bill No. 63, entitled "An act to authorize the construction of a highway bridge across that part of the waters of Lake Champlain lying between the towns of North Hero and Alburg, in the State of Vermont."

On the 20th day of June, 1884, a bill was approved and became a law having the same title and containing precisely the same provisions and in the exact words of the bill herewith returned.

The records of the War Department indicate that nothing has been done toward building the bridge permitted by such prior act. It is hardly possible that the bill now before me is intended to authorize an additional bridge between the two towns named, and I have been unable to discover any excuse or necessity for new legislation on the subject.

I conclude, therefore, that Congress in passing this bill acted in ignorance of the fact that a law providing for its objects and purposes was already on the statute book.

My approval of the bill is withheld for this reason and in order to prevent an unnecessary and confusing multiplicity of laws.

                                                    GROVER CLEVELAND.

                                        EXECUTIVE MANSION, *July 30, 1886.*
To the House of Representatives:

I hereby return without my approval House bill No. 1391, entitled "An act to provide for the erection of a public building at Springfield, Mo."

It appears from the report of the committee of the House of Representatives to which this bill was referred that the city of Springfield is in a thriving condition, with stores, banks, and manufactories, and having, with North Springfield, which is an adjoining town, about 20,000 inhabitants.

No Federal courts are held at this place, and apparently the only quarters which the Government should provide are such as are necessary for the accommodation of the post-office and the land-office located there.

The postmaster reports that six employees are engaged in his office.

The rooms used as a post-office are now furnished the Government free of expense, and the rent paid for the quarters occupied as a land-office amounts to $300 annually.

Upon the facts presented I am satisfied that the business of the Government at this point can be well transacted for the present without the construction of the proposed building.

                                                    GROVER CLEVELAND.

To the Senate: EXECUTIVE MANSION, *July 31, 1886.*

I return without approval Senate bill No. 2160, entitled "A bill granting a pension to Mary J. Hagerman."

The husband of this proposed beneficiary enlisted in 1861 and was wounded by a gunshot, which seriously injured his left forearm. In 1864 he was discharged; was afterwards pensioned for his wound, and died in August, 1884.

Dr. Hageman, who attended the deceased in his last illness, testifies that he was called to attend him in August, 1884; that he was sick with typhomalarial fever, and that upon inquiry he (the physician) found that it was caused by hard work or overexertion and exposure. He was ill for about ten days.

The application of his widow for pension was rejected in 1885 on the ground that the fatal disease was not due to military service.

I am unable to discover how any different determination could have been reached.

To grant a pension in this case would clearly contravene the present policy of the Government, and either establish a precedent which, if followed, would allow a pension to the widow of every soldier wounded or disabled in the war, without regard to the cause of death, or would unjustly discriminate in favor of the few thus receiving the bounty of the Government against many whose cases were equally meritorious.

GROVER CLEVELAND.

To the Senate. EXECUTIVE MANSION, *July 31, 1886.*

I herewith return without my approval Senate bill No. 1421, entitled "An act granting a pension to William H. Weaver."

The claimant named in this bill enlisted August 12, 1862, and was mustered out of service June 12, 1865. During his service he was treated in hospital for diarrhea and lumbago, and in the reports for May and June, as well as July and August, 1864, he is reported as absent sick.

He filed his application for pension in November, 1877, alleging that in March, 1863, he contracted measles, and in May, 1864, remittent fever, and that as a result of the two attacks he was afflicted with weakness in the limbs and eyes. He made statements afterwards in support of his application that he was also troubled in the service with rheumatism and diarrhea.

The case was examined by several special examiners, from which, as reported to me, it appeared from the claimant's admission that he had sore eyes previous to his enlistment, though he claimed they were sound when he entered the Army.

A surgeon who made an examination in March, 1881, reported that he could not find any evidence whatever of disease of the eyes, and nothing to corroborate the claimant's assertion that he was suffering from rheumatism, piles, or diarrhea.

Another surgeon, who examined the claimant in 1879, reported that he found the eyelids slightly granulated, producing some irritation of the eyeball and rendering the eyes a little weak, and that he found no other disability.

In 1882 a surgeon who made an examination reported that he discovered indications that the claimant had suffered at some time with chronic ophthalmia, but that in his opinion his eyes did not disable him in the least, and that the claimant was well nourished and in good health.

The report of the committee to whom this bill was referred in the Senate states that six special examinations have been made in the case and that two of them were favorable to the claim.

The trouble and expense incurred by the Pension Bureau to ascertain the truth and to deal fairly by this claimant, and the entire absence of any suspicion of bias against the claim in that Bureau, ought to give weight to its determination.

The claim was rejected by the Pension Bureau in July, 1885, upon the ground that disease of the eyes existed prior to enlistment and that the evidence failed to show that there had existed a pensionable degree of disability, since discharge, from diarrhea or rheumatism.

It will be observed that this is not a case where there was a lack of the technical proof required by the Pension Bureau, but that its judgment was based upon the merits of the application and affected the very foundation of the claim.

I think it should be sustained; and its correctness is somewhat strengthened by the fact that the claimant continued in active service for more than a year after his alleged sickness, that after filing his claim he added thereto allegations of additional disabilities, and that he made no application for pension until more than twelve years after his discharge.

GROVER CLEVELAND.

EXECUTIVE MANSION, *July 31, 1886.*

To the House of Representatives:

I herewith return without approval House bill No. 3363, entitled "An act granting a pension to Jennette Dow."

The husband of the claimant enlisted August 7, 1862; received a gunshot wound in his left knee in September, 1863, and was mustered out with his company June 10, 1865. He was pensioned for his wound in 1878 at the rate of $4 per month, dating from the time of his discharge, which amount was increased to $8 per month from June 4, 1880. The pensioned soldier died December 17, 1882, and in 1883 his widow, the claimant, filed an application for pension, alleging that her husband's death resulted from his wound. Her claim was rejected in 1885 upon the ground that death was not caused by the wound.

The physician who was present at the time of the death certifies that the same resulted from apoplexy in twelve hours after the deceased was attacked.

It also appears from the statement of this physician that the deceased was employed for years after his discharge from the Army as a railroad conductor, and that at the time of his death he had with difficulty reached his home. He then describes as following the attack the usual manifestations of apoplexy, and adds that he regards the case as one of "hemiplegia, the outgrowth primarily of nerve injury, aggravated by the life's calling, and eventuating in apoplexy as stated."

Evidence is filed in the Pension Bureau showing that after his discharge he was more or less troubled with his wound, though one witness testifies that he railroaded with him for fifteen years after his injury. I find no medical testimony referred to which with any distinctness charges death to the wound, and it would be hardly credible if such evidence was found.

I am sure that in no case except in an application for pension would an attempt be made in the circumstances here developed to attribute death from apoplexy to a wound in the knee received nineteen years before the apoplectic attack.

GROVER CLEVELAND.

EXECUTIVE MANSION, *July 31, 1886.*

To the House of Representatives:

I return without approval House bill No. 9106, entitled "An act granting a pension to Rachel Barnes."

William Barnes, the husband of the beneficiary named in this bill, enlisted in the United States infantry in February, 1838, and was discharged February 24, 1841.

In 1880 he applied for a pension, alleging that while serving in Florida in 1840 and 1841 he contracted disease of the eyes. He procured considerable evidence in support of his claim, but in 1882, and while still endeavoring to furnish further proof, he committed suicide by hanging.

The inference that his death thus occasioned was the result of despondency and despair brought on by his failure to procure a pension, while it adds a sad feature to the case, does not aid in connecting his death with his military service.

That this was the view of the committee of the House to whom the bill was referred is evidenced by the conclusion of their report in these words:

And while your committee do not feel justified under the law as at present existing in recommending that the name of the widow be placed upon the pension roll for the purpose of a pension in her own right as widow of the deceased soldier and by reason of the soldier's death, they do think that she should be allowed such pension as, had her husband's claim been favorably determined on the day of his decease, he would have received.

And yet the bill under consideration directs the Secretary of the Interior to place this widow's name on the pension roll and to "pay her a pension as such widow from and after the passage of this act, subject to the provisions and limitations of the pension laws."

GROVER CLEVELAND.

EXECUTIVE MANSION, *July 31, 1886.*

To the House of Representatives:

I return herewith without approval House bill No. 8336, entitled "An act granting an increase of pension to Duncan Forbes."

The beneficiary named in this bill enlisted, under the name of Alexander Sheret, January 7, 1862, in the Regular Army, and was discharged January 8, 1865.

He applied for a pension in 1879, alleging that he was wounded in his right breast December 31, 1862, and in his right ankle September 20, 1863. He was pensioned in 1883, dating from January 9, 1865, for the ankle wound, but that part of his claim based upon the wound in his breast was rejected upon the ground that there was no record of the same and the testimony failed to show that such a wound had its origin in the service.

Though the lack of such a record is sufficiently accounted for, I am convinced that, conceding both the wounds alleged were received, this pensioner has been fairly and justly treated.

It appears from the allegations of his application to the Pension Bureau that after the wound in his breast, in December, 1862, he continued his service till September, 1863, when he was wounded again in the ankle, and that with both wounds he served until his discharge in January, 1865. It also appears from the records that after his discharge from the Army, and on the 3d day of February, 1865, he enlisted as landsman in the United States Navy, and served in that branch of the service for three years.

A medical examination in May, 1885, disclosed the appearance of a gunshot wound in the right breast, which is thus described:

The missile struck the seventh rib of right side and glanced off, leaving a horizontal scar 2¼ inches long and one-half inch wide, deeply depressed and firmly adherent.

I credit this claimant with being a good soldier, and I am willing to believe that his insistence upon a greater pension than that already allowed by the Pension Bureau, under liberal general laws, enacted for the benefit of himself and all his comrades, is the result of the demoralization produced by ill-advised special legislation on the subject.

GROVER CLEVELAND.

EXECUTIVE MANSION, *August 4, 1886.*

To the House of Representatives:

I return without approval House bill No. 5389, entitled "An act granting a pension to Ann Kinney."

This beneficiary applied for a pension in 1877 as the widow of Edward Kinney, alleging that he died September 5, 1875, from the effects of a wound received in the Army. He enlisted November 4, 1861, and was discharged July 28, 1862, on account of a gunshot wound in his left elbow, for which wound he was pensioned in the year 1865.

A physician testifies that the pensioned soldier's death was, in his opinion, brought on indirectly by the intemperate use of intoxicating liquors, and that he died from congestion of the brain.

The marshal of the city where he resided states that on the day of the soldier's death he was called to remove him from a house in which he was making a disturbance, and that finding him intoxicated he arrested him and took him to the lockup and placed him in a cell. In a short time, not exceeding an hour, thereafter he was found dead. He further states that he was addicted to periodical sprees.

Another statement is made that the soldier was an intemperate man, and died very suddenly in the city lockup, where he had been taken by an officer while on a drunken spree.

This is not a pleasant recital, and as against the widow I should be glad to avoid its effect. But the most favorable phase of the case does not aid her, since her claim rests upon the allegation that her husband was subject to epileptic fits and died from congestion of the brain while in one of these fits. Even upon this showing the connection between the fits and the wound in the elbow is not made apparent.

GROVER CLEVELAND.

EXECUTIVE MANSION, *August 4, 1886.*

To the House of Representatives:

I herewith return without approval House bill No. 8556, entitled "An act granting a pension to Abraham Points."

This soldier enlisted August 11, 1864, and was mustered out June 28, 1865.

He was treated during his short term of service for "catarrhal," "constipation," "diarrhea," "jaundice," and "colic."

He filed an application for pension in 1878, alleging that some of his comrades in a joke twisted his arm in such a manner that the elbow joint became stiffened and anchylosed, and that his eyes became sore and have continued to grow worse ever since. There is no record of either of these disabilities.

The application was denied upon the ground, as stated in the report from the Pension Bureau, that the claim "was specially examined, and it was shown conclusively, from the evidence of neighbors and acquaintances of good repute and standing, that the alleged disabilities existed at and prior to claimant's enlistment."

I am satisfied from an examination of the facts submitted to me that this determination was correct.

GROVER CLEVELAND.

EXECUTIVE MANSION, *August 4, 1886.*

To the House of Representatives:

I herewith return without approval House bill No. 3551, entitled "An act granting a pension to George W. Cutler, late a private in Company B, Ninth New Hampshire Volunteers."

This claimant enlisted July 12, 1862, and was discharged June 22, 1863, for disability resulting from "scrofulous ulceration of the tibia and fibula of right leg; loss of sight of left eye."

He made a claim for pension in 1865, alleging an injury while loading commissary stores, resulting in spitting of blood, injury to lungs, and heart disease.

This claim was rejected August 31, 1865.

In 1867 he again enlisted in the United States infantry, and was discharged from that enlistment March 29, 1869, for disability, the certificate stating that—

He is unfit for military service by reason of being subject to bleeding of the lungs. He was wounded, while in the line of his duty in the United States Army, at Fredericksburg, Va., December 13, 1862. Said wound is not the cause of his disability.

Afterwards, and in the year 1879, he filed affidavits claiming that he was wounded by a minie ball at the battle of Fredericksburg, December 13, 1862, and was injured by falling down an embankment.

In 1883 he filed an affidavit in which he stated that the disability for which he claims a pension arose from injuries received in falling down a bank at Fredericksburg and being tramped on by troops, causing a complication of diseases resulting in general debility.

The statement in the certificate of discharge from his second enlistment as to the wound he received by a minie ball at Fredericksburg was of course derived from his own statement, as it was related to a prior term of service.

The records of the Adjutant-General's Office furnish no evidence of wounds or injury at Fredericksburg.

The injury alleged at first as a consequence of loading commissary stores seems to have been abandoned by the claimant for the adoption of a wound at Fredericksburg, which in its turn seems to have been abandoned and a fall down a bank and trampling upon by troops substituted.

Whatever injuries he may have suffered during his first enlistment, and to whatever cause he chooses at last to attribute them, they did not prevent his reenlistment and passing the physical examination necessary before acceptance.

The surgeon of the Ninth New Hampshire Volunteers, in which he first enlisted, states that he remembers the claimant well; that he was mustered and accepted as a recruit in spite of his (the surgeon's) protest; that he was physically unfit for duty; that he had the appearance of impaired health, and that his face and neck were marked by one or more deep scars, the result, as the claimant himself alleged, of scrofulous abscesses in early youth. He expresses the opinion that he is attempting to palm off these old scars as evidence of wounds received, and that if he had been wounded as he claimed he (the surgeon) would have known it and remembered it.

It is true that whenever in this case a wound is described it is located in the jaw, while some of the medical testimony negatives the existence of any wound.

The contrariety of the claimant's statements and the testimony and circumstances tend so strongly to impeach his claim that I do not think the decision of the Pension Bureau should be reversed and the claimant pensioned.

GROVER CLEVELAND.

EXECUTIVE MANSION, *August 4, 1886.*

To the House of Representatives:

I herewith return without my approval House bill No. 7234, entitled "An act granting a pension to Susan Hawes."

The beneficiary named in this bill is the mother of Jeremiah Hawes, who enlisted in February, 1861, in the United States artillery, and was discharged in February, 1864. He filed a claim for pension in 1881, alleging that in 1862, by the premature discharge of a cannon, he sustained paralysis of his right arm and side. In 1883, while his claim was still pending, he died.

He does not appear to have made his home with his mother altogether, if at all. For some years prior to his death and at the time of its occurrence he was an inmate, or had been an inmate, of a soldiers' home in Ohio.

But whatever may be said of the character of any injuries he may have received in the service or of his relations to his mother, the cause of his death, it seems to me, can not possibly upon any reasonable theory be attributable to any incident of his military service.

It appears that in July, 1883, while the deceased was on his way from Buffalo, where he had been in a hospital, to the soldiers' home in Ohio, he attempted to step on a slowly moving freight train, and making a misstep a wheel of the car passed over his foot, injuring it so badly that it was deemed necessary by two physicians who were called to amputate the foot. An anæsthetic was administered preparatory to the operation, but before it was entered upon the injured man died, having survived the accident but two hours.

The physicians who were present stated that in their opinion death was due to heart disease.

The above account of the death of the soldier is derived from a report furnished by the Pension Bureau, and differs somewhat from the statement contained in the report of the House Committee on Invalid Pensions as related to the intention of the physicians to amputate the injured foot and their administration of an anæsthetic. But the accident and the death two hours thereafter under the treatment of the physicians are conceded facts.

GROVER CLEVELAND.

EXECUTIVE MANSION, *August 4, 1886.*

To the House of Representatives:

I herewith return without approval House bill No. 1584, entitled "An act for the relief of Mrs. Aurelia C. Richardson."

Albert H. Fillmore, the son of the beneficiary mentioned in this bill, enlisted in August, 1862, and died in the service, of smallpox, May 20, 1865.

His father having died some time prior to the soldier's enlistment, his mother in 1858 married Lorenzo D. Richardson. It is stated in the report upon this case from the Pension Bureau that the deceased did not live with his mother after her marriage to Richardson, and that there is no competent evidence that he contributed to her support after that event.

At the time of the soldier's death his stepfather was a blacksmith, earning at about that time, as it is represented, not less than $70 a month, and owning considerable property, a part of which still remains to him.

While in ordinary cases of this kind I am by no means inclined to distinguish very closely between dependence at the date of the soldier's death and the date of proposed aid to a needy mother, I think the circumstances here presented, especially the fact of nonresidence by the son with his mother since her second marriage, do not call for a departure from the law governing claims based upon dependence.

GROVER CLEVELAND.

POCKET VETOES.

EXECUTIVE MANSION,
Washington, August 17, 1886.

Hon. THOS. F. BAYARD,
Secretary of State.

DEAR SIR: The President directs me to transmit to you the accompanying bills and joint resolutions, which failed to become laws at the close of the late session of Congress, being unsigned and not having been presented to him ten days prior to adjournment.

I may add that the printed copy of memorandum (without signature) is by the President, and is attached to each bill and resolution by his direction.

Very respectfully,

O. L. PRUDEN,
Assistant Secretary.

["An act for the relief of Francis W. Haldeman."—Received July 28, 1886.]

This bill appropriates $200 to the party named therein "as compensation for services performed and money expended for the benefit of the United States Army." It appears from a report of the House Committee on War Claims that in the fall of 1863 Haldeman, a lad 12 years of age, purchased a uniform and armed himself and attached himself to various Ohio regiments, and, as is said, performed various duties connected with the army service until the end of the year 1864, and for this it is proposed to give him $200.

Of course he never enlisted and never was regularly attached to any regiment. What kind of arms this boy 12 years of age armed himself with is not stated, and it is quite evident that his military service could not have amounted to much more than the indulgence of a boyish freak and his being made a pet of the soldiers with whom he was associated. There is a pleasant sentiment connected with this display of patriotism and childish military ardor, and it is not a matter of surprise that he should, as stated by the committee, have "received honorable mention by name in the history of his regiment;" but when it is proposed twenty-two years after his one year's experience with troops to pay him a sum nearly if not quite equal to the pay of a soldier who fought and suffered all the dangers and privations of a soldier's life, I am constrained to dissent.

["An act for the relief of R. D. Beckley and Leon Howard."—Received July 28, 1886.]

These two men were employed by the Doorkeeper of the Forty-eighth Congress as laborers at the rate of $720 per annum.

They claim that in both sessions of that Congress they not only performed the duties appertaining to their positions as laborers, but also performed the full duties of messengers. Having received their pay as laborers, this bill proposes to appropriate for them the difference between their compensation as laborers and $1,200, the pay allowed messengers.

Congress, in appropriation bills covering the period in which these men claim to have performed these dual duties, provided for a certain specified number of messengers and a fixed number of laborers. They both accepted the latter position. If they actually performed the duties of both places, their ability to do so is evidence that the labor of either place was very light. In any case they owed their time and services to the Government, and while they were performing the duties of messengers they were not engaged in the harder tasks which might have been required of them as laborers. They ought not to complain if they have received the amount for which they agreed to work, and which was allowed for as the wages of a place which they were glad enough to secure. If they really did the work of both places, I don't see why they should not be paid both compensations. This proposition of course would not be entertained for a moment.

I am of the opinion that claims for extra compensation such as these should be firmly discountenanced, and I am sure no injustice will be done by my declining to approve this bill.

["An act for the relief of Thomas P. Morgan, jr."—Received July 31, 1886.—Memorandum.]

Thomas P. Morgan, jr., in the year 1881 entered into a contract with the Government to do certain excavating in the harbor of Norfolk.

He performed considerable of the work, but though the time limited by the contract for the completion was extended by the Government, he failed to complete the work, which necessitated other arrangements, to the damage of the Government in quite a large sum. His contract was forfeited by the Government because the progress he made was so slow and unsatisfactory. It seems that a certain percentage of the money earned by him in the progress of the work was, under the terms of the contract, retained by the Government to insure its completion, and when work was terminated the sum thus retained amounted to $4,898.04, which sum was justly forfeited to the Government.

The object of this bill is to waive this forfeiture and pay this sum to the derelict contractor.

Inasmuch as I am unable to see any equities in this case that should overcome the fact that the amount of loss to the Government through the contract is greater than the sum thus sought to be released to him, I am not willing to agree to his release from the consequence of his failure to perform his contract.

["An act for the relief of Charles F. Bowers."—Received August 2, 1886.]

It appears that Charles F. Bowers, while acting as regimental quartermaster in 1862, received of John Weeks, assistant quartermaster of volunteers, the sum of $230, for which he gave a receipt. On the settlement of his accounts he was unable to account for said sum, for the reason, as he alleges, that certain of his papers were lost and destroyed. Thus in the statement of his account he is represented as a debtor of the Government in that amount.

This bill directs that a credit be allowed to him of the said sum of $230. But since his account was adjusted as above stated, showing him in debt to the Government in the amount last stated, he has paid the sum of $75 and been allowed a credit of $125 for the value of a horse; so that whatever may be said of the merits of his claim that he should not be charged with the sum of $230, if he should now be credited with that sum the Government would owe him upon its books the sum of $30.

The bill is therefore not approved.

["An act to provide for the erection of a public building in the city of Annapolis, Md."—Received August 3, 1886.—Memorandum.]

The post-office at Annapolis is now accommodated in quarters for which the Government pays rent at the rate of $500 per annum, and the office occupied by the collector of customs is rented for $75 per annum.

The Government has no other use for a public building at Annapolis than is above indicated, and the chief argument urged why a building should be constructed there is based upon the fact that this city is the capital of the State of Maryland and should have a Government building because most if not all the other capitals of the States have such edifices.

There seems to be so little necessity for the building proposed for the transaction of Government business, and if there is anything in the argument last referred to it seems so well answered by the maintenance of the Naval Academy at Annapolis, this bill is allowed to remain inoperative.

["An act for the relief of J. A. Henry and others."—Received August 3, 1886.—Memorandum.]

This bill appropriates various sums to the parties named therein, being claims of rent of quarters occupied during the war by the Quartermaster's Department of the Army.

Among the appropriations there proposed to be made is one of the sum of $51 to L. F. Green. This account has been once paid, a special act directing such payment having been approved February 12, 1885. The fact of this payment and important information bearing upon the validity of some of the other claims mentioned in the bill could have been easily obtained by application to the Third Auditor.

["An act for the relief of William H. Wheeler."—Received August 3, 1886.]

This bill directs the payment of the sum of $633.50 to William H. Wheeler for quartermaster's stores furnished the Army in the year 1862.

From the data furnished me by the Quartermaster-General I am quite certain that this claim has been once paid. The circumstances presented to prove this are so strong that they should be explained before the relief provided by this bill is afforded the claimant.

["An act granting a pension to Margaret D. Marchand."—Received August 5, 1886.—Memorandum.]

A bill presented to me for approval, granting a pension of $50 per month to the beneficiary named, was disapproved upon the ground that the death of her husband did not appear to be in any way related to any incident of his military service.

This bill differs from the prior one simply in granting a pension subject to the provisions and limitations of the pension laws instead of fixing the rate of pension at a specified sum. I am still unable to see how the objection to the first bill has been obviated.

["Joint resolution providing for the distribution of the Official Register of the United States."—Received August 5, 1886.—Memorandum.]

This resolution reached me five minutes after the adjournment of the two Houses of Congress, and is the only enactment of the session which came to me too late for official action.

I do not understand this resolution nor the purposes sought to be accomplished by its passage, and while in that frame of mind should have been constrained to withhold my approval from the same even if it had reached me in time for consideration.

["Joint resolution directing payment of the surplus in the Treasury on the public debt."—Received
August 5, 1886.—Memorandum.]

This resolution involves so much and is of such serious import that I do not deem it best to discuss it at this time. It is not approved because I believe it to be unnecessary and because I am by no means convinced that its mere passage and approval at this time may not endanger and embarrass the successful and useful operations of the Treasury Department and impair the confidence which the people should have in the management of the finances of the Government.

PROCLAMATIONS.

BY THE PRESIDENT OF THE UNITED STATES OF AMERICA.
A PROCLAMATION.

Whereas it is represented to me by the governor of the Territory of Washington that domestic violence exists within the said Territory, and that by reason of unlawful obstructions and combinations and the assemblage of evil-disposed persons it has become impracticable to enforce by the ordinary course of judicial proceedings the laws of the United States at Seattle and at other points and places within said Territory, whereby life and property are there threatened and endangered; and

Whereas, in the judgment of the President, an emergency has arisen and a case is now presented which justifies and requires, under the Constitution and laws of the United States, the employment of military force to suppress domestic violence and enforce the faithful execution of the laws of the United States if the command and warning of this proclamation be disobeyed and disregarded:

Now, therefore, I, Grover Cleveland, President of the United States of America, do hereby command and warn all insurgents and all persons who have assembled at any point within the said Territory of Washington for the unlawful purposes aforesaid to desist therefrom and to disperse and retire peaceably to their respective abodes on or before 6 o'clock in the afternoon of the 10th day of February instant.

And I do admonish all good citizens of the United States and all persons within the limits and jurisdiction thereof against aiding, abetting, countenancing, or taking any part in such unlawful acts or assemblages.

In witness whereof I have set my hand and caused the seal of the United States to be hereunto affixed.

[SEAL.] Done at the city of Washington, this 9th day of February, A. D. 1886, and of the Independence of the United States the one hundred and tenth. GROVER CLEVELAND.

By the President:
T. F. BAYARD, *Secretary of State.*

By the President of the United States of America.

A PROCLAMATION.

Whereas by a proclamation of the President of the United States dated the 14th day of February, in the year 1884,* upon evidence then appearing satisfactory to him that the Government of Spain had abolished the discriminating customs duty theretofore imposed upon the products of and articles proceeding from the United States of America imported into the islands of Cuba and Puerto Rico, such abolition to take effect on and after the 1st day of March of said year 1884, and, by virtue of the authority vested in him by section 4228 of the Revised Statutes of the United States, the President did thereby declare and proclaim that on and after the said 1st day of March, 1884, so long as the products of and articles proceeding from the United States imported into the islands of Cuba and Puerto Rico should be exempt from discriminating customs duties, any such duties on the products of and articles proceeding from Cuba and Puerto Rico under the Spanish flag should be suspended and discontinued; and

Whereas by Article I of the commercial agreement signed at Madrid the 13th day of February, 1884, it was stipulated and provided that "the duties of the third column of the customs tariffs of Cuba and Puerto Rico, which implies the suppression of the differential flag duty," should at once be applied to the products of and articles proceeding from the United States of America; and

Whereas the complete suppression of the differential flag duty in respect of all vessels of the United States and their cargoes entering the ports of Cuba and Puerto Rico is by the terms of the said agreement expressly made the consideration for the exercise of the authority conferred upon the President in respect of the suspension of the collection of foreign discriminating duties of tonnage and imposts upon merchandise brought within the United States from Cuba and Puerto Rico in Spanish vessels by said section 4228 of the Revised Statutes, which section reads as follows:

SEC. 4228. Upon satisfactory proof being given to the President by the government of any foreign nation that no discriminating duties of tonnage or imposts are imposed or levied in the ports of such nation upon vessels wholly belonging to citizens of the United States, or upon the produce, manufactures, or merchandise imported in the same from the United States or from any foreign country, the President may issue his proclamation declaring that the foreign discriminating duties of tonnage and impost within the United States are suspended and discontinued so far as respects the vessels of such foreign nation, and the produce, manufactures, or merchandise imported into the United States from such foreign nation or from any other foreign country; the suspension to take effect from the time of such notification being given to the President, and to continue so long as the reciprocal exemption of vessels belonging to citizens of the United States and their cargoes, shall be continued, and no longer.

*See pp. 4810-4811.

And whereas proof is given to me that such complete suppression of the differential flag duty in respect of vessels of the United States and their cargoes entering the ports of Cuba and Puerto Rico has not in fact been secured, but that, notwithstanding the said agreement dated at Madrid, February 13, 1884, and in contravention thereof, as well as of the provisions of the said section 4228 of the Revised Statutes, higher and discriminating duties continue to be imposed and levied in said ports upon certain produce, manufactures, or merchandise imported into said ports from the United States or from any foreign country in vessels of the United States than is imposed and levied on the like produce, manufactures, or merchandise carried to said ports in Spanish vessels:

Now, therefore, I, Grover Cleveland, President of the United States of America, in execution of the aforesaid section 4228 of the Revised Statutes, do hereby revoke the suspension of the discriminating customs imposed and levied in the ports of the United States on the products of and articles proceeding under the Spanish flag from Cuba and Puerto Rico, which is set forth and contained in the aforesaid proclamation dated the 14th day of February, 1884; this revocation of said proclamation to take effect on and after the 25th day of October instant.

In witness whereof I have hereunto set my hand and caused the seal of the United States to be affixed.

[SEAL.]   Done at the city of Washington, this 13th day of October, A. D. 1886, and of the Independence of the United States the one hundred and eleventh.

GROVER CLEVELAND.

By the President:

T. F. BAYARD,
Secretary of State.

BY THE PRESIDENT OF THE UNITED STATES OF AMERICA.

A PROCLAMATION.

Whereas satisfactory proof has been given to me by the Government of Spain that no discriminating duties of tonnage or imposts are imposed or levied in the islands of Cuba and Puerto Rico upon vessels wholly belonging to citizens of the United States, or upon the produce, manufactures, or merchandise imported in the same from the United States or from any foreign country; and

Whereas notification of such abolition of discriminating duties of tonnage and imposts as aforesaid has been given to me by a memorandum of agreement signed this day in the city of Washington between the Secretary of State of the United States and the envoy extraordinary and minister plenipotentiary of Her Majesty the Queen Regent of Spain accredited to the Government of the United States of America:

Now, therefore, I, Grover Cleveland, President of the United States of

America, by virtue of the authority vested in me by section 4228 of the Revised Statutes of the United States, do hereby declare and proclaim that from and after the date of this my proclamation, being also the date of the notification received as aforesaid, the foreign discriminating duties of tonnage and impost within the United States are suspended and discontinued so far as respects the vessels of Spain and the produce, manufactures, or merchandise imported in said vessels into the United States from the islands of Cuba and Puerto Rico or from any other foreign country; such suspension to continue so long as the reciprocal exemption of vessels belonging to citizens of the United States, and their cargoes, shall be continued in the said islands of Cuba and Puerto Rico, and no longer.

In witness whereof I have hereunto set my hand and caused the seal of the United States to be affixed.

[SEAL.] Done at the city of Washington, this 27th day of October, A. D. 1886, and of the Independence of the United States the one hundred and eleventh.

GROVER CLEVELAND.

By the President:

T. F. BAYARD,
Secretary of State.

A PROCLAMATION

BY THE PRESIDENT OF THE UNITED STATES.

It has long been the custom of the people of the United States, on a day in each year especially set apart for that purpose by their Chief Executive, to acknowledge the goodness and mercy of God and to invoke His continued care and protection.

In observance of such custom I, Grover Cleveland, President of the United States, do hereby designate and set apart Thursday, the 25th day of November instant, to be observed and kept as a day of thanksgiving and prayer.

On that day let all our people forego their accustomed employments and assemble in their usual places of worship to give thanks to the Ruler of the Universe for our continued enjoyment of the blessings of a free government, for a renewal of business prosperity throughout our land, for the return which has rewarded the labor of those who till the soil, and for our progress as a people in all that makes a nation great.

And while we contemplate the infinite power of God in earthquake, flood, and storm let the grateful hearts of those who have been shielded from harm through His mercy be turned in sympathy and kindness toward those who have suffered through His visitations.

Let us also in the midst of our thanksgiving remember the poor and needy with cheerful gifts and alms so that our service may by deeds of charity be made acceptable in the sight of the Lord.

In witness whereof I have hereunto set my hand and caused the seal of the United States to be affixed.

[SEAL.]   Done at the city of Washington, this 1st day of November, A. D. 1886, and of the Independence of the United States of America the one hundred and eleventh.

GROVER CLEVELAND.

By the President:

T. F. BAYARD, *Secretary of State.*

EXECUTIVE ORDERS.

Whereas in an Executive order dated the 21st day of July, 1875, directing the distribution of the fund of 400,000 pesetas received from the Spanish Government in satisfaction of the reclamation of the United States arising from the capture of the *Virginius*, it was provided "that should any further order or direction be required the same will hereafter be made in addition hereto;" and

Whereas a further order or direction is deemed necessary:

Now, therefore, I, Grover Cleveland, President of the United States, do hereby direct that all persons entitled to the benefit of any of the aforesaid fund of 400,000 pesetas who have not yet presented their claims thereto shall formulate and present their claims to the Secretary of State of the United States within six months from the date of this order, or be held as forever barred from the benefits of said fund.

And I hereby further direct that the balance of the fund which shall remain unclaimed at the expiration of the aforesaid period of six months shall be distributed *pro rata* among the beneficiaries under the original distribution, provided they or their heirs or representatives shall within the six months next succeeding the said former period present to the Secretary of State of the United States petitions for their shares of said balance.

And to these ends the Secretary of State is requested to cause public notice to be given of the above direction.

In witness whereof I have hereunto set my hand, at the city of Washington, this 12th day of December, A. D. 1885, and of the Independence of the United States of America the one hundred and tenth.

GROVER CLEVELAND.

EXECUTIVE MANSION,
Washington, February 9, 1886—4 o'clock p. m.

Tidings of the death of Winfield Scott Hancock, the senior major-general of the Army of the United States, have just been received.

A patriotic and valiant defender of his country, an able and heroic soldier, a spotless and accomplished gentleman, crowned alike with the laurels of military renown and the highest tribute of his fellow-countrymen to his worth as a citizen, he has gone to his reward.

It is fitting that every mark of public respect should be paid to his memory.

Therefore it is now ordered by the President that the national flag be displayed at half-mast upon all the buildings of the Executive Departments in this city until after his funeral shall have taken place.

By direction of the President:

DANIEL S. LAMONT,
Private Secretary.

In the exercise of the power vested in the President by the Constitution, and by virtue of the seventeen hundred and fifty-third section of the Revised Statutes and of the civil-service act approved January 16, 1883, the following rule for the regulation and improvement of the executive civil service is hereby amended and promulgated, as follows:

RULE XXII.

Any person in the classified departmental service may be transferred and appointed to any other place therein upon the following conditions:

1. That he is not debarred by clause 2 of Rule XXI.

2. That the head of a Department has, in a written statement to be filed with the Commission, requested such transfer to a place in said Department, to be designated in the statement.

3. That said person is shown in the statement or by other evidence satisfactory to the Commission to have been during six consecutive months in such service since January 16, 1883.

4. That such person has passed at the required grade one or more examinations under the Commission which are together equal to that required for the place to which the transfer is to be made.

But any person who has for three years last preceding served as a clerk in the office of the President of the United States may be transferred or appointed to any place in the classified service without examination.

Approved, April 12, 1886.   GROVER CLEVELAND.

EXECUTIVE MANSION, *May 20, 1886.*

Under the provisions of section 4 of the act approved March 3, 1883, it is hereby ordered that the several Executive Departments, the Department of Agriculture, and the Government Printing Office be closed on Monday, the 31st instant, to enable the employees to participate in the decoration of the graves of the soldiers who fell during the rebellion.

GROVER CLEVELAND.

EXECUTIVE MANSION, *July 3, 1886.*

To Heads of the Government Departments:

Inasmuch as the 4th of July of the present year falls upon Sunday and the celebration of Independence Day is to be generally observed upon Monday, July 5, it is hereby ordered that the several Executive Departments, the Department of Agriculture, and the Government Printing Office be closed on Monday the 5th instant.

GROVER CLEVELAND.

EXECUTIVE MANSION,
Washington, July 14, 1886.

To the Heads of Departments in the Service of the General Government:

I deem this a proper time to especially warn all subordinates in the several Departments and all officeholders under the General Government against the use of their official positions in attempts to control political movements in their localities.

Officeholders are the agents of the people, not their masters. Not only is their time and labor due to the Government, but they should scrupulously avoid in their political action, as well as in the discharge of their official duty, offending by a display of obtrusive partisanship their neighbors who have relations with them as public officials.

They should also constantly remember that their party friends from whom they have received preferment have not invested them with the power of arbitrarily managing their political affairs. They have no right as officeholders to dictate the political action of their party associates or to throttle freedom of action within party lines by methods and practices which pervert every useful and justifiable purpose of party organization.

The influence of Federal officeholders should not be felt in the manipulation of political primary meetings and nominating conventions. The use by these officials of their positions to compass their selection as delegates to political conventions is indecent and unfair; and proper regard for the proprieties and requirements of official place will also prevent their assuming the active conduct of political campaigns.

Individual interest and activity in political affairs are by no means condemned. Officeholders are neither disfranchised nor forbidden the exercise of political privileges, but their privileges are not enlarged nor is their duty to party increased to pernicious activity by officeholding.

A just discrimination in this regard between the things a citizen may properly do and the purposes for which a public office should not be used is easy in the light of a correct appreciation of the relation between the people and those intrusted with official place and a consideration of the necessity under our form of government of political action free from official coercion.

You are requested to communicate the substance, of these views to those for whose guidance they are intended.

GROVER CLEVELAND.

In the exercise of the power vested in the President by the Constitution, and by virtue of the seventeen hundred and fifty-third section of the Revised Statutes and of the civil-service act approved January 16, 1883, the following rule for the regulation and improvement of the executive civil service is hereby amended and promulgated, as follows:

RULE IX.

All applications for regular competitive examinations for admission to the classified civil service must be made on blank forms to be prescribed by the Commission.

Requests for blank forms of application for competitive examination for admission to the classified civil service and all regular applications for such examination shall be made—

1. If for the classified departmental service, to the United States Civil Service Commission at Washington, D. C.

2. If for the classified customs service, to the civil-service board of examiners for the customs district in which the person desiring to be examined wishes to enter the customs service.

3. If for the classified postal service, to the civil-service board of examiners for the post-office at which the person desiring to be examined wishes to enter the postal service.

Requests for blank forms of application to customs and postal boards of examiners must be made in writing by the persons desiring examination, and such blank forms shall not be furnished to any other persons.

Approved, August 13, 1886.

GROVER CLEVELAND.

EXECUTIVE MANSION,
Washington, November 16, 1886.

Hon. DANIEL MANNING,
Secretary of the Treasury.

DEAR SIR: In pursuance of a joint resolution of the Congress approved March 3, 1877, authorizing the President to cause suitable regulations to be made for the maintenance of the statue of "Liberty Enlightening the World," now located on Bedloes Island, in the harbor of New York, as a beacon, I hereby direct that said statue be at once placed under the care and superintendence of the Light-House Board, and that it be from henceforth maintained by said board as a beacon, and that it be so maintained, lighted, and tended in accordance with such rules and regulations as now exist applicable thereto, or such other and different rules and regulations as said board may deem necessary to carry out the design of said joint resolution and this order.

GROVER CLEVELAND.

GENERAL ORDERS, NO. 84.

HEADQUARTERS OF THE ARMY,
ADJUTANT-GENERAL'S OFFICE,
Washington, November 18, 1886.

I. The following proclamation [order] has been received from the President:

EXECUTIVE MANSION,
Washington, D. C., November 18, 1886.

To the People of the United States:

It is my painful duty to announce the death of Chester Alan Arthur, lately the President of the United States, which occurred, after an illness of long duration, at an early hour this morning at his residence in the city of New York.

Mr. Arthur was called to the chair of the Chief Magistracy of the nation by a tragedy which cast its shadow over the entire Government.

His assumption of the grave duties was marked by an evident and conscientious sense of his responsibilities and an earnest desire to meet them in a patriotic and benevolent spirit.

With dignity and ability he sustained the important duties of his station, and the reputation of his personal worth, conspicuous graciousness, and patriotic fidelity will long be cherished by his fellow-countrymen.

In token of respect to the memory of the deceased it is ordered that the Executive Mansion and the several departmental buildings be draped in mourning for a period of thirty days and that on the day of the funeral all public business in the departments be suspended.

The Secretaries of War and of the Navy will cause orders to be issued for appropriate military and naval honors to be rendered on that day.

Done at the city of Washington this 18th day of November, A. D. 1886, [SEAL.] and of the Independence of the United States of America the one hundred and eleventh.

GROVER CLEVELAND.

By the President:

THOMAS F. BAYARD,
Secretary of State.

II. In compliance with the instructions of the President, on the day of the funeral, at each military post, the troops and cadets will be paraded and this order read to them, after which all labors for the day will cease.

The national flag will be displayed at half-staff.

At dawn of day thirteen guns will be fired, and afterwards at intervals of thirty minutes between the rising and setting of the sun a single gun, and at the close of the day a national salute of thirty-eight guns.

The officers of the Army will wear crape on the left arm and on their swords and the colors of the Battalion of Engineers, of the several regiments, and of the United States Corps of Cadets will be put in mourning for the period of six months.

The date and hour of the funeral will be communicated to department commanders by telegraph, and by them to their subordinate commanders. By command of Lieutenant-General Sheridan:

R. C. DRUM, *Adjutant-General.*

NAVY DEPARTMENT,
Washington, November 18, 1886.

The President of the United States announces the death of ex-President Chester Alan Arthur in the following proclamation [order]:

[For order see preceding page.]

It is hereby directed, in pursuance of the instructions of the President, that on the day of the funeral, where this order may be received in time, otherwise on the day after its receipt, the ensign at each naval station and of each of the vessels of the United States Navy in commission be hoisted at half-mast from sunrise to sunset, and that also, at each naval station and on board of flagships and vessels acting singly, a gun be fired at intervals of every half hour from sunrise to sunset.

The officers of the Navy and Marine Corps will wear the usual badge of mourning attached to the sword hilt and on the left arm for a period of thirty days.

WILLIAM C. WHITNEY,
Secretary of the Navy.

EXECUTIVE MANSION,
Washington, November 20, 1886.

It is hereby ordered, That the Department of Agriculture, the Government Printing Office, and all other Government offices in the District of Columbia be closed on Monday, the 22d instant, the day of the funeral of the late Chester Alan Arthur, ex-President of the United States.

GROVER CLEVELAND.

SECOND ANNUAL MESSAGE.

WASHINGTON, *December 6, 1886.*
To the Congress of the United States:

In discharge of a constitutional duty, and following a well-established precedent in the Executive office, I herewith transmit to the Congress at its reassembling certain information concerning the state of the Union, together with such recommendations for legislative consideration as appear necessary and expedient.

Our Government has consistently maintained its relations of friendship toward all other powers and of neighborly interest toward those whose possessions are contiguous to our own. Few questions have arisen during the past year with other governments, and none of those are beyond the reach of settlement in friendly counsel.

We are as yet without provision for the settlement of claims of citizens of the United States against Chile for injustice during the late war with Peru and Bolivia. The mixed commissions organized under claims conventions concluded by the Chilean Government with certain European States have developed an amount of friction which we trust can be avoided in the convention which our representative at Santiago is authorized to negotiate.

The cruel treatment of inoffensive Chinese has, I regret to say, been repeated in some of the far Western States and Territories, and acts of violence against those people, beyond the power of the local constituted authorities to prevent and difficult to punish, are reported even in distant Alaska. Much of this violence can be traced to race prejudice and competition of labor, which can not, however, justify the oppression of strangers whose safety is guaranteed by our treaty with China equally with the most favored nations.

In opening our vast domain to alien elements the purpose of our lawgivers was to invite assimilation, and not to provide an arena for endless antagonism. The paramount duty of maintaining public order and defending the interests of our own people may require the adoption of measures of restriction, but they should not tolerate the oppression of individuals of a special race. I am not without assurance that the Government of China, whose friendly disposition toward us I am most happy to recognize, will meet us halfway in devising a comprehensive remedy by which an effective limitation of Chinese emigration, joined to protection of those Chinese subjects who remain in this country, may be secured.

Legislation is needed to execute the provisions of our Chinese convention of 1880 touching the opium traffic.

While the good will of the Colombian Government toward our country is manifest, the situation of American interests on the Isthmus of Panama has at times excited concern and invited friendly action looking to the performance of the engagements of the two nations concerning the territory embraced in the interoceanic transit. With the subsidence of the Isthmian disturbances and the erection of the State of Panama into a federal district under the direct government of the constitutional administration at Bogota, a new order of things has been inaugurated, which, although as yet somewhat experimental and affording scope for arbitrary exercise of power by the delegates of the national authority, promises much improvement.

The sympathy between the people of the United States and France, born during our colonial struggle for independence and continuing today, has received a fresh impulse in the successful completion and dedication of the colossal statue of "Liberty Enlightening the World" in New York Harbor—the gift of Frenchmen to Americans.

A convention between the United States and certain other powers for the protection of submarine cables was signed at Paris on March 14, 1884, and has been duly ratified and proclaimed by this Government. By agreement between the high contracting parties this convention is to go into effect on the 1st of January next, but the legislation required for its execution in the United States has not yet been adopted. I earnestly recommend its enactment.

Cases have continued to occur in Germany giving rise to much correspondence in relation to the privilege of sojourn of our naturalized citizens of German origin revisiting the land of their birth, yet I am happy to state that our relations with that country have lost none of their accustomed cordiality.

The claims for interest upon the amount of tonnage dues illegally exacted from certain German steamship lines were favorably reported in both Houses of Congress at the last session, and I trust will receive final and favorable action at an early day.

The recommendations contained in my last annual message in relation to a mode of settlement of the fishery rights in the waters of British North America, so long a subject of anxious difference between the United States and Great Britain, was met by an adverse vote of the Senate on April 13 last, and thereupon negotiations were instituted to obtain an agreement with Her Britannic Majesty's Government for the promulgation of such joint interpretation and definition of the article of the convention of 1818 relating to the territorial waters and inshore fisheries of the British Provinces as should secure the Canadian rights from encroachment by the United States fishermen and at the same time insure the enjoyment by the latter of the privileges guaranteed to them by such convention.

The questions involved are of long standing, of grave consequence, and from time to time for nearly three-quarters of a century have given rise to earnest international discussions, not unaccompanied by irritation.

Temporary arrangements by treaties have served to allay friction, which, however, has revived as each treaty was terminated. The last arrangement, under the treaty of 1871, was abrogated after due notice by the United States on June 30, 1885, but I was enabled to obtain for our fishermen for the remainder of that season enjoyment of the full privileges accorded by the terminated treaty.

The joint high commission by whom the treaty had been negotiated, although invested with plenary power to make a permanent settlement, were content with a temporary arrangement, after the termination of which the question was relegated to the stipulations of the treaty of 1818, as to the first article of which no construction satisfactory to both countries has ever been agreed upon.

The progress of civilization and growth of population in the British Provinces to which the fisheries in question are contiguous and the expansion of commercial intercourse between them and the United States present to-day a condition of affairs scarcely realizable at the date of the negotiations of 1818.

New and vast interests have been brought into existence; modes of intercourse between the respective countries have been invented and multiplied; the methods of conducting the fisheries have been wholly changed; and all this is necessarily entitled to candid and careful consideration in the adjustment of the terms and conditions of intercourse and commerce between the United States and their neighbors along a frontier of over 3,500 miles.

This propinquity, community of language and occupation, and similarity of political and social institutions indicate the practicability and obvious wisdom of maintaining mutually beneficial and friendly relations.

Whilst I am unfeignedly desirous that such relations should exist between us and the inhabitants of Canada, yet the action of their officials during the past season toward our fishermen has been such as to seriously threaten their continuance.

Although disappointed in my efforts to secure a satisfactory settlement of the fishery question, negotiations are still pending, with reasonable hope that before the close of the present session of Congress announcement may be made that an acceptable conclusion has been reached.

As at an early day there may be laid before Congress the correspondence of the Department of State in relation to this important subject, so that the history of the past fishing season may be fully disclosed and the action and the attitude of the Administration clearly comprehended, a more extended reference is not deemed necessary in this communication.

The recommendation submitted last year that provision be made for a preliminary reconnoissance of the conventional boundary line between Alaska and British Columbia is renewed.

I express my unhesitating conviction that the intimacy of our relations with Hawaii should be emphasized. As a result of the reciprocity treaty of 1875, those islands, on the highway of Oriental and Australasian traffic, are virtually an outpost of American commerce and a stepping-stone to the growing trade of the Pacific. The Polynesian Island groups have been so absorbed by other and more powerful governments that the Hawaiian Islands are left almost alone in the enjoyment of their autonomy, which it is important for us should be preserved. Our treaty is now terminable on one year's notice, but propositions to abrogate it would be, in my judgment, most ill advised. The paramount influence we have there acquired, once relinquished, could only with difficulty be regained, and a valuable ground of vantage for ourselves might be converted into a stronghold for our commercial competitors. I earnestly recommend that the existing treaty stipulations be extended for a further term of seven years. A recently signed treaty to this end is now before the Senate.

The importance of telegraphic communication between those islands and the United States should not be overlooked.

The question of a general revision of the treaties of Japan is again under discussion at Tokyo. As the first to open relations with that Empire, and as the nation in most direct commercial relations with Japan, the United States have lost no opportunity to testify their consistent friendship by supporting the just claims of Japan to autonomy and independence among nations.

A treaty of extradition between the United States and Japan, the first concluded by that Empire, has been lately proclaimed.

The weakness of Liberia and the difficulty of maintaining effective sovereignty over its outlying districts have exposed that Republic to encroachment. It can not be forgotten that this distant community is an offshoot of our own system, owing its origin to the associated benevolence of American citizens, whose praiseworthy efforts to create a nucleus of civilization in the Dark Continent have commanded respect and sympathy everywhere, especially in this country. Although a formal protectorate over Liberia is contrary to our traditional policy, the moral right and duty of the United States to assist in all proper ways in the maintenance of its integrity is obvious, and has been consistently announced during nearly half a century. I recommend that in the reorganization of our Navy a small vessel, no longer found adequate to our needs, be presented to Liberia, to be employed by it in the protection of its coastwise revenues.

The encouraging development of beneficial and intimate relations between the United States and Mexico, which has been so marked within the past few years, is at once the occasion of congratulation and of friendly solicitude. I urgently renew my former representation of the need of speedy legislation by Congress to carry into effect the reciprocity commercial convention of January 20, 1883.

Our commercial treaty of 1831 with Mexico was terminated, according to its provisions, in 1881, upon notification given by Mexico in pursuance of her announced policy of recasting all her commercial treaties. Mexico has since concluded with several foreign governments new treaties of commerce and navigation, defining alien rights of trade, property, and residence, treatment of shipping, consular privileges, and the like. Our yet unexecuted reciprocity convention of 1883 covers none of these points, the settlement of which is so necessary to good relationship. I propose to initiate with Mexico negotiations for a new and enlarged treaty of commerce and navigation.

In compliance with a resolution of the Senate, I communicated to that body on August 2 last, and also to the House of Representatives,* the

* See p. 4991.

correspondence in the case of A. K. Cutting, an American citizen, then imprisoned in Mexico, charged with the commission of a penal offense in Texas, of which a Mexican citizen was the object.

After demand had been made for his release the charge against him was amended so as to include a violation of Mexican law within Mexican territory.

This joinder of alleged offenses, one within and the other exterior to Mexico, induced me to order a special investigation of the case, pending which Mr. Cutting was released.

The incident has, however, disclosed a claim of jurisdiction by Mexico novel in our history, whereby any offense committed anywhere by a foreigner, penal in the place of its commission, and of which a Mexican is the object, may, if the offender be found in Mexico, be there tried and punished in conformity with Mexican laws.

This jurisdiction was sustained by the courts of Mexico in the Cutting case, and approved by the executive branch of that Government, upon the authority of a Mexican statute. The appellate court in releasing Mr. Cutting decided that the abandonment of the complaint by the Mexican citizen aggrieved by the alleged crime (a libelous publication) removed the basis of further prosecution, and also declared justice to have been satisfied by the enforcement of a small part of the original sentence.

The admission of such a pretension would be attended with serious results, invasive of the jurisdiction of this Government and highly dangerous to our citizens in foreign lands. Therefore I have denied it and protested against its attempted exercise as unwarranted by the principles of law and international usages.

A sovereign has jurisdiction of offenses which take effect within his territory, although concocted or commenced outside of it; but the right is denied of any foreign sovereign to punish a citizen of the United States for an offense consummated on our soil in violation of our laws, even though the offense be against a subject or citizen of such sovereign. The Mexican statute in question makes the claim broadly, and the principle, if conceded, would create a dual responsibility in the citizen and lead to inextricable confusion, destructive of that certainty in the law which is an essential of liberty.

When citizens of the United States voluntarily go into a foreign country, they must abide by the laws there in force, and will not be protected by their own Government from the consequences of an offense against those laws committed in such foreign country; but watchful care and interest of this Government over its citizens are not relinquished because they have gone abroad, and if charged with crime committed in the foreign land a fair and open trial, conducted with decent regard for justice and humanity, will be demanded for them. With less than that this Government will not be content when the life or liberty of its citizens is at stake.

Whatever the degree to which extraterritorial criminal jurisdiction may have been formerly allowed by consent and reciprocal agreement among certain of the European States, no such doctrine or practice was ever known to the laws of this country or of that from which our institutions have mainly been derived.

In the case of Mexico there are reasons especially strong for perfect harmony in the mutual exercise of jurisdiction. Nature has made us irrevocably neighbors, and wisdom and kind feeling should make us friends.

The overflow of capital and enterprise from the United States is a potent factor in assisting the development of the resources of Mexico and in building up the prosperity of both countries.

To assist this good work all grounds of apprehension for the security of person and property should be removed; and I trust that in the interests of good neighborhood the statute referred to will be so modified as to eliminate the present possibilities of danger to the peace of the two countries.

The Government of the Netherlands has exhibited concern in relation to certain features of our tariff laws, which are supposed by them to be aimed at a class of tobacco produced in the Dutch East Indies. Comment would seem unnecessary upon the unwisdom of legislation appearing to have a special national discrimination for its object, which, although unintentional, may give rise to injurious retaliation.

The establishment, less than four years ago, of a legation at Teheran is bearing fruit in the interest exhibited by the Shah's Government in the industrial activity of the United States and the opportunities of beneficial interchanges.

Stable government is now happily restored in Peru by the election of a constitutional President, and a period of rehabilitation is entered upon; but the recovery is necessarily slow from the exhaustion caused by the late war and civil disturbances. A convention to adjust by arbitration claims of our citizens has been proposed and is under consideration.

The naval officer who bore to Siberia the testimonials bestowed by Congress in recognition of the aid given to the *Jeannette* survivors has successfully accomplished his mission. His interesting report will be submitted. It is pleasant to know that this mark of appreciation has been welcomed by the Russian Government and people as befits the traditional friendship of the two countries.

Civil perturbations in the Samoan Islands have during the past few years been a source of considerable embarrassment to the three Governments—Germany, Great Britain, and the United States—whose relations and extraterritorial rights in that important group are guaranteed by treaties. The weakness of the native administration and the conflict of opposing interests in the islands have led King Malietoa to seek alliance or protection in some one quarter, regardless of the distinct engagements whereby no one of the three treaty powers may acquire any paramount or exclusive interest. In May last Malietoa offered to place Samoa under the protection of the United States, and the late consul, without authority, assumed to grant it. The proceeding was promptly disavowed and the overzealous official recalled. Special agents of the three Governments have been deputed to examine the situation in the islands. With a change in the representation of all three powers and a harmonious understanding between them, the peace, prosperity, autonomous administration, and neutrality of Samoa can hardly fail to be secured.

It appearing that the Government of Spain did not extend to the flag of the United States in the Antilles the full measure of reciprocity requisite under our statute for the continuance of the suspension of discriminations against the Spanish flag in our ports, I was constrained in October last* to rescind my predecessor's proclamation of February 14, 1884,† permitting such suspension. An arrangement was, however, speedily reached, and upon notification from the Government of Spain that all differential treatment of our vessels and their cargoes, from the United States or from any foreign country, had been completely and absolutely relinquished, I availed myself of the discretion conferred by law and issued on the 27th of October my proclamation‡ declaring reciprocal suspension in the United States. It is most gratifying to bear testimony to the earnest spirit in which the Government of the Queen Regent has met our efforts to avert the initiation of commercial discriminations and reprisals, which are ever disastrous to the material interests and the political good will of the countries they may affect.

The profitable development of the large commercial exchanges between the United States and the Spanish Antilles is naturally an object of solicitude. Lying close at our doors, and finding here their main markets of supply and demand, the welfare of Cuba and Puerto Rico and their production and trade are scarcely less important to us than to Spain. Their commercial and financial movements are so naturally a part of our system that no obstacle to fuller and freer intercourse should be permitted to exist. The standing instructions of our representatives at Madrid and Havana have for years been to leave no effort unessayed to further these ends, and at no time has the equal good desire of Spain been more hopefully manifested than now.

The Government of Spain, by removing the consular tonnage fees on cargoes shipped to the Antilles and by reducing passport fees, has shown its recognition of the needs of less trammeled intercourse.

An effort has been made during the past year to remove the hindrances to the proclamation of the treaty of naturalization with the Sublime Porte, signed in 1874, which has remained inoperative owing to a disagreement of interpretation of the clauses relative to the effects of the return to and sojourn of a naturalized citizen in the land of origin. I trust soon to be able to announce a favorable settlement of the differences as to this interpretation.

It has been highly satisfactory to note the improved treatment of American missionaries in Turkey, as has been attested by their acknowledgments to our late minister to that Government of his successful exertions in their behalf.

The exchange of ratifications of the convention of December 5, 1885, with Venezuela, for the reopening of the awards of the Caracas Commission under the claims convention of 1866, has not yet been effected, owing to the delay of the Executive of that Republic in ratifying the measure. I trust that this postponement will be brief; but should it much longer continue, the delay may well be regarded as a rescission of the compact and a failure on the part of Venezuela to complete an arrangement so persistently sought by her during many years and assented to by this Government in a spirit of international fairness, although to the detriment of holders of *bona fide* awards of the impugned commission.

I renew the recommendation of my last annual message that existing legislation concerning citizenship and naturalization be revised. We have treaties with many states providing for the renunciation of citizenship by naturalized aliens, but no statute is found to give effect to such engagements, nor any which provides a needed central bureau for the registration of naturalized citizens.

Experience suggests that our statutes regulating extradition might be advantageously amended by a provision for the transit across our territory, now a convenient thoroughfare of travel from one foreign country to another, of fugitives surrendered by a foreign government to a third state. Such provisions are not unusual in the legislation of other countries, and tend to prevent the miscarriage of justice. It is also desirable, in order to remove present uncertainties, that authority should be conferred on the Secretary of State to issue a certificate, in case of an arrest for the purpose of extradition, to the officer before whom the proceeding is pending, showing that a requisition for the surrender of the person charged has been duly made. Such a certificate, if required to be received before the prisoner's examination, would prevent a long and expensive judicial inquiry into a charge which the foreign government might not desire to press. I also recommend that express provision be made for the immediate discharge from custody of persons committed for extradition where the President is of opinion that surrender should not be made.

The drift of sentiment in civilized communities toward full recognition of the rights of property in the creations of the human intellect has brought about the adoption by many important nations of an international copyright convention, which was signed at Berne on the 18th of September, 1885.

Inasmuch as the Constitution gives to the Congress the power "to promote the progress of science and useful arts by securing for limited times to authors and inventors the exclusive right to their respective writings and discoveries," this Government did not feel warranted in becoming a signatory pending the action of Congress upon measures of international copyright now before it; but the right of adhesion to the Berne convention hereafter has been reserved. I trust the subject will receive at your hands the attention it deserves, and that the just claims of authors, so urgently pressed, will be duly heeded.

Representations continue to be made to me of the injurious effect upon American artists studying abroad and having free access to the art collections of foreign countries of maintaining a discriminating duty against the introduction of the works of their brother artists of other countries, and I am induced to repeat my recommendation for the abolition of that tax.

Pursuant to a provision of the diplomatic and consular appropriation act approved July 1, 1886, the estimates submitted by the Secretary of State for the maintenance of the consular service have been recast on the basis of salaries for all officers to whom such allowance is deemed advisable. Advantage has been taken of this to redistribute the salaries of the offices now appropriated for, in accordance with the work performed, the importance of the representative duties of the incumbent, and the cost of living at each post. The last consideration has been too often lost sight of in the allowances heretofore made. The compensation which may suffice for the decent maintenance of a worthy and capable officer in a position of onerous and representative trust at a post readily accessible, and where the necessaries of life are abundant and cheap, may prove an inadequate pittance in distant lands, where the better part of a year's pay is consumed in reaching the post of duty, and where the comforts of ordinary civilized existence can only be obtained with difficulty and at exorbitant cost. I trust that in considering the submitted schedules no mistaken theory of economy will perpetuate a system which in the past has virtually closed to deserving talent many offices where capacity and attainments of a high order are indispensable, and in not a few instances has brought discredit on our national character and entailed embarrassment and even suffering on those deputed to uphold our dignity and interests abroad.

In connection with this subject I earnestly reiterate the practical necessity of supplying some mode of trustworthy inspection and report of the manner in which the consulates are conducted. In the absence of such reliable information efficiency can scarcely be rewarded or its opposite corrected.

Increasing competition in trade has directed attention to the value of the consular reports printed by the Department of State, and the efforts of the Government to extend the practical usefulness of these reports have created a wider demand for them at home and a spirit of emulation abroad. Constituting a record of the changes occurring in trade and of the progress of the arts and invention in foreign countries, they are much sought for by all interested in the subjects which they embrace.

The report of the Secretary of the Treasury exhibits in detail the condition of the public finances and of the several branches of the Government related to his Department. I especially direct the attention of the Congress to the recommendations contained in this and the last preceding report of the Secretary touching the simplification and amendment of the laws relating to the collection of our revenues, and in the interest of economy and justice to the Government I hope they may be adopted by appropriate legislation.

The ordinary receipts of the Government for the fiscal year ended June 30, 1886, were $336,439,727.06. Of this amount $192,905,023.41 was received from customs and $116,805,936.48 from internal revenue. The total receipts, as here stated, were $13,749,020.68 greater than for the previous year, but the increase from customs was $11,434,084.10 and from internal revenue $4,407,210.94, making a gain in these items for the last year of $15,841,295.04, a falling off in other resources reducing the total increase to the smaller amount mentioned.

The expense at the different custom-houses of collecting this increased customs revenue was less than the expense attending the collection of such revenue for the preceding year by $490,608, and the increased receipts of internal revenue were collected at a cost to the Internal-Revenue Bureau $155,944.99 less than the expense of such collection for the previous year.

The total ordinary expenses of the Government for the fiscal year ended June 30, 1886, were $242,483,138.50, being less by $17,788,797 than such expenditures for the year preceding, and leaving a surplus in the Treasury at the close of the last fiscal year of $93,956,588.56, as against $63,463,771.27 at the close of the previous year, being an increase in such surplus of $30,492,817.29.

The expenditures are compared with those of the preceding fiscal year and classified as follows:

	Year ending June 30, 1886.	Year ending June 30, 1885.
For civil expenses	$21,955,604.04	$23,826,942.11
For foreign intercourse	1,332,320.88	5,439,609.11
For Indians	6,099,158.17	6,552,494.63
For pensions	63,404,864.03	56,102,267.49
For the military, including river and harbor improvements and arsenals	34,324,152.74	42,670,578.47
For the Navy, including vessels, machinery, and improvement of navy-yards	13,907,887.74	16,021,079.69
For interest on public debt	50,580,145.97	51,386,256.47
For the District of Columbia	2,892,321.89	3,499,650.95
Miscellaneous expenditures, including public buildings, light-houses, and collecting the revenue	47,986,683.04	54,728,056.21

For the current year to end June 30, 1887, the ascertained receipts up to October 1, 1886, with such receipts estimated for the remainder of the year, amount to $356,000,000.

The expenditures ascertained and estimated for the same period are $266,000,000, indicating an anticipated surplus at the close of the year of $90,000,000.

The total value of the exports from the United States to foreign countries during the fiscal year is stated and compared with the preceding year as follows:

	For the year ending June 30, 1886.	For the year ending June 30, 1885.
Domestic merchandise	$665,964,529	$726,682,946
Foreign merchandise	13,560,301	15,506,809
Gold	42,952,191	8,477,892
Silver	29,511,219	33,753,633

The value of some of our leading exports during the last fiscal year, as compared with the value of the same for the year immediately preceding, is here given, and furnishes information both interesting and suggestive:

	For the year ending June 30, 1886.	For the year ending June 30, 1885.
Cotton and cotton manufactures	$219,045,576	$213,799,049
Tobacco and its manufactures	30,424,908	24,767,305
Breadstuffs	125,846,558	160,370,821
Provisions	90,625,216	107,332,456

Our imports during the last fiscal year, as compared with the previous year, were as follows:

	1886.	1885.
Merchandise	$635,436,136.00	$579,580,053.80
Gold	20,743,349.00	26,691,696.00
Silver	17,850,307.00	16,550,627.00

In my last annual message to the Congress attention was directed to the fact that the revenues of the Government exceeded its actual needs, and it was suggested that legislative action should be taken to relieve the people from the unnecessary burden of taxation thus made apparent.

In view of the pressing importance of the subject I deem it my duty to again urge its consideration.

The income of the Government, by its increased volume and through economies in its collection, is now more than ever in excess of public necessities. The application of the surplus to the payment of such portion of the public debt as is now at our option subject to extinguishment, if continued at the rate which has lately prevailed, would retire that class of indebtedness within less than one year from this date. Thus a continuation of our present revenue system would soon result in the receipt of an annual income much greater than necessary to meet Government expenses, with no indebtedness upon which it could be applied. We should then be confronted with a vast quantity of money, the circulating medium of the people, hoarded in the Treasury when it should be in their hands, or we should be drawn into wasteful public extravagance, with all the corrupting national demoralization which follows in its train.

But it is not the simple existence of this surplus and its threatened attendant evils which furnish the strongest argument against our present scale of Federal taxation. Its worst phase is the exaction of such a surplus through a perversion of the relations between the people and their Government and a dangerous departure from the rules which limit the right of Federal taxation.

Good government, and especially the government of which every American citizen boasts, has for its objects the protection of every person within its care in the greatest liberty consistent with the good order of society and his perfect security in the enjoyment of his earnings with the least possible diminution for public needs. When more of the people's substance is exacted through the form of taxation than is necessary to meet the just obligations of the Government and the expense of its economical administration, such exaction becomes ruthless extortion and a violation of the fundamental principles of a free government.

The indirect manner in which these exactions are made has a tendency to conceal their true character and their extent. But we have arrived at a stage of superfluous revenue which has aroused the people to a realization of the fact that the amount raised professedly for the support of the Government is paid by them as absolutely if added to the price of the things which supply their daily wants as if it was paid at fixed periods into the hand of the taxgatherer.

Those who toil for daily wages are beginning to understand that capital, though sometimes vaunting its importance and clamoring for the protection and favor of the Government, is dull and sluggish till, touched by the magical hand of labor, it springs into activity, furnishing an occasion for Federal taxation and gaining the value which enables it to bear its burden. And the laboring man is thoughtfully inquiring whether in these circumstances, and considering the tribute he constantly pays into the public Treasury as he supplies his daily wants, he receives his fair share of advantages.

There is also a suspicion abroad that the surplus of our revenues indicates abnormal and exceptional business profits, which, under the system which produces such surplus, increase without corresponding benefit to the people at large the vast accumulations of a few among our citizens, whose fortunes, rivaling the wealth of the most favored in antidemocratic nations, are not the natural growth of a steady, plain, and industrious republic.

Our farmers, too, and those engaged directly and indirectly in supplying the products of agriculture, see that day by day, and as often as the daily wants of their households recur, they are forced to pay excessive and needless taxation, while their products struggle in foreign markets with the competition of nations, which, by allowing a freer exchange of productions than we permit, enable their people to sell for prices which distress the American farmer.

As every patriotic citizen rejoices in the constantly increasing pride of our people in American citizenship and in the glory of our national achievements and progress, a sentiment prevails that the leading strings useful to a nation in its infancy may well be to a great extent discarded in the present stage of American ingenuity, courage, and fearless self-reliance; and for the privilege of indulging this sentiment with true American enthusiasm our citizens are quite willing to forego an idle surplus in the public Treasury.

And all the people know that the average rate of Federal taxation upon imports is to-day, in time of peace, but little less, while upon some articles of necessary consumption it is actually more, than was imposed by the grievous burden willingly borne at a time when the Government needed millions to maintain by war the safety and integrity of the Union.

It has been the policy of the Government to collect the principal part of its revenues by a tax upon imports, and no change in this policy is desirable. But the present condition of affairs constrains our people to demand that by a revision of our revenue laws the receipts of the Government shall be reduced to the necessary expense of its economical administration; and this demand should be recognized and obeyed by the people's representatives in the legislative branch of the Government.

In readjusting the burdens of Federal taxation a sound public policy requires that such of our citizens as have built up large and important industries under present conditions should not be suddenly and to their injury deprived of advantages to which they have adapted their business; but if the public good requires it they should be content with such consideration as shall deal fairly and cautiously with their interests, while the just demand of the people for relief from needless taxation is honestly answered.

A reasonable and timely submission to such a demand should certainly be possible without disastrous shock to any interest; and a cheerful concession sometimes averts abrupt and heedless action, often the outgrowth of impatience and delayed justice.

Due regard should be also accorded in any proposed readjustment to the interests of American labor so far as they are involved. We congratulate ourselves that there is among us no laboring class fixed within unyielding bounds and doomed under all conditions to the inexorable fate of daily toil. We recognize in labor a chief factor in the wealth of the Republic, and we treat those who have it in their keeping as citizens entitled to the most careful regard and thoughtful attention. This regard and attention should be awarded them, not only because labor is the capital of our workingmen, justly entitled to its share of Government favor, but for the further and not less important reason that the laboring man, surrounded by his family in his humble home, as a consumer is vitally interested in all that cheapens the cost of living and enables him to bring within his domestic circle additional comforts and advantages.

This relation of the workingman to the revenue laws of the country and the manner in which it palpably influences the question of wages should not be forgotten in the justifiable prominence given to the proper maintenance of the supply and protection of well-paid labor. And these considerations suggest such an arrangement of Government revenues as shall reduce the expense of living, while it does not curtail the opportunity for work nor reduce the compensation of American labor and injuriously affect its condition and the dignified place it holds in the estimation of our people.

But our farmers and agriculturists—those who from the soil produce the things consumed by all—are perhaps more directly and plainly concerned than any other of our citizens in a just and careful system of Federal taxation. Those actually engaged in and more remotely connected with this kind of work number nearly one-half of our population. None labor harder or more continuously than they. No enactments limit their hours of toil and no interposition of the Government enhances to any great extent the value of their products. And yet for many of the necessaries and comforts of life, which the most scrupulous economy enables them to bring into their homes, and for their implements of husbandry, they are obliged to pay a price largely increased by an unnatural profit, which by the action of the Government is given to the more favored manufacturer.

I recommend that, keeping in view all these considerations, the increasing and unnecessary surplus of national income annually accumulating be released to the people by an amendment to our revenue laws which shall cheapen the price of the necessaries of life and give freer entrance to such imported materials as by American labor may be manufactured into marketable commodities.

Nothing can be accomplished, however, in the direction of this much-needed reform unless the subject is approached in a patriotic spirit of devotion to the interests of the entire country and with a willingness to yield something for the public good.

The sum paid upon the public debt during the fiscal year ended June 30, 1886, was $44,551,043.36.

During the twelve months ended October 31, 1886, 3 per cent bonds were called for redemption amounting to $127,283,100, of which $80,643,200 was so called to answer the requirements of the law relating to the sinking fund and $46,639,900 for the purpose of reducing the public debt by application of a part of the surplus in the Treasury to that object. Of the bonds thus called $102,269,450 became subject under such calls to redemption prior to November 1, 1886. The remainder, amounting to $25,013,650, matured under the calls after that date.

In addition to the amount subject to payment and cancellation prior to November 1, there were also paid before that day certain of these bonds, with the interest thereon, amounting to $5,072,350, which were anticipated as to their maturity, of which $2,664,850 had not been called. Thus $107,341,800 had been actually applied prior to the 1st of November, 1886, to the extinguishment of our bonded and interest-bearing debt, leaving on that day still outstanding the sum of $1,153,443,112. Of this amount $86,848,700 were still represented by 3 per cent bonds. They, however, have been since November 1, or will at once be, further reduced by $22,606,150, being bonds which have been called, as already stated, but not redeemed and canceled before the latter date.

During the fiscal year ended June 30, 1886, there were coined, under the compulsory silver-coinage act of 1878, 29,838,905 silver dollars, and the cost of the silver used in such coinage was $23,448,960.01. There had been coined up to the close of the previous fiscal year under the provisions of the law 203,882,554 silver dollars, and on the 1st day of December, 1886, the total amount of such coinage was $247,131,549.

The Director of the Mint reports that at the time of the passage of the law of 1878 directing this coinage the intrinsic value of the dollars thus coined was $94\frac{1}{4}$ cents each, and that on the 31st day of July, 1886, the price of silver reached the lowest stage ever known, so that the intrinsic or bullion price of our standard silver dollar at that date was less than 72 cents. The price of silver on the 30th day of November last was such as to make these dollars intrinsically worth 78 cents each.

These differences in value of the coins represent the fluctuations in the price of silver, and they certainly do not indicate that compulsory coinage by the Government enhances the price of that commodity or secures uniformity in its value.

Every fair and legal effort has been made by the Treasury Department to distribute this currency among the people. The withdrawal of United States Treasury notes of small denominations and the issuing of small silver certificates have been resorted to in the endeavor to accomplish this result, in obedience to the will and sentiments of the representatives of the people in the Congress. On the 27th day of November, 1886, the people held of these coins, or certificates representing them, the nominal sum of $166,873,041, and we still had $79,464,345 in the Treasury as against about $142,894,055 so in the hands of the people and $72,865,376 remaining in the Treasury one year ago. The Director of the Mint again urges the necessity of more vault room for the purpose of storing these silver dollars which are not needed for circulation by the people.

I have seen no reason to change the views expressed in my last annual message on the subject of this compulsory coinage, and I again urge its suspension on all the grounds contained in my former recommendation, reenforced by the significant increase of our gold exportations during the last year, as appears by the comparative statement herewith presented, and for the further reasons that the more this currency is distributed among the people the greater becomes our duty to protect it from disaster, that we now have abundance for all our needs, and that there seems but little propriety in building vaults to store such currency when the only pretense for its coinage is the necessity of its use by the people as a circulating medium.

The great number of suits now pending in the United States courts for the southern district of New York growing out of the collection of customs revenue at the port of New York and the number of such suits that are almost daily instituted are certainly worthy the attention of the Congress. These legal controversies, based upon conflicting views by importers and the collector as to the interpretation of our present complex and indefinite revenue laws, might be largely obviated by an amendment of those laws.

But pending such amendment the present condition of this litigation should be relieved. There are now pending about 2,500 of these suits. More than 1,100 have been commenced within the past eighteen months, and many of the others have been at issue for more than twenty-five years. These delays subject the Government to loss of evidence and prevent the preparation necessary to defeat unjust and fictitious claims, while constantly accruing interest threatens to double the demands involved.

In the present condition of the dockets of the courts, well filled with private suits, and of the force allowed the district attorney, no greater than is necessary for the ordinary and current business of his office, these revenue litigations can not be considered.

In default of the adoption by the Congress of a plan for the general reorganization of the Federal courts, as has been heretofore recommended, I urge the propriety of passing a law permitting the appointment of an additional Federal judge in the district where these Government suits have accumulated, so that by continuous sessions of the courts devoted to the trial of these cases they may be determined.

It is entirely plain that a great saving to the Government would be accomplished by such a remedy, and the suitors who have honest claims would not be denied justice through delay.

The report of the Secretary of War gives a detailed account of the administration of his Department and contains sundry recommendations for the improvement of the service, which I fully approve.

The Army consisted at the date of the last consolidated return of 2,103 officers and 24,946 enlisted men.

The expenses of the Department for the last fiscal year were $36,990,903.38, including $6,294,305.43 for public works and river and harbor improvements.

I especially direct the attention of the Congress to the recommendation that officers be required to submit to an examination as a preliminary to their promotion. I see no objection, but many advantages, in adopting this feature, which has operated so beneficially in our Navy Department, as well as in some branches of the Army.

The subject of coast defenses and fortifications has been fully and carefully treated by the Board on Fortifications, whose report was submitted at the last session of Congress; but no construction work of the kind recommended by the board has been possible during the last year from the lack of appropriations for such purpose.

The defenseless condition of our seacoast and lake frontier is perfectly palpable. The examinations made must convince us all that certain of our cities named in the report of the board should be fortified and that work on the most important of these fortifications should be commenced at once. The work has been thoroughly considered and laid out, the Secretary of War reports, but all is delayed in default of Congressional action.

The absolute necessity, judged by all standards of prudence and foresight, of our preparation for an effectual resistance against the armored ships and steel guns and mortars of modern construction which may threaten the cities on our coasts is so apparent that I hope effective steps will be taken in that direction immediately.

The valuable and suggestive treatment of this question by the Secretary of War is earnestly commended to the consideration of the Congress

In September and October last the hostile Apaches who, under the leadership of Geronimo, had for eighteen months been on the war path, and during that time had committed many murders and been the cause of constant terror to the settlers of Arizona, surrendered to General Miles, the military commander who succeeded General Crook in the management and direction of their pursuit.

Under the terms of their surrender as then reported, and in view of the understanding which these murderous savages seemed to entertain of the assurances given them, it was considered best to imprison them in such manner as to prevent their ever engaging in such outrages again, instead of trying them for murder. Fort Pickens having been selected as a safe place of confinement, all the adult males were sent thither and will be closely guarded as prisoners. In the meantime the residue of the band, who, though still remaining upon the reservation, were regarded as unsafe and suspected of furnishing aid to those on the war path, had been removed to Fort Marion. The women and larger children of the hostiles were also taken there, and arrangements have been made for putting the children of proper age in Indian schools.

The report of the Secretary of the Navy contains a detailed exhibit of the condition of his Department, with such a statement of the action needed to improve the same as should challenge the earnest attention of the Congress.

The present Navy of the United States, aside from the ships in course of construction, consists of—

First. Fourteen single-turreted monitors, none of which are in commission nor at the present time serviceable. The batteries of these ships are obsolete, and they can only be relied upon as auxiliary ships in harbor defense, and then after such an expenditure upon them as might not be deemed justifiable.

Second. Five fourth-rate vessels of small tonnage, only one of which was designed as a war vessel, and all of which are auxiliary merely.

Third. Twenty-seven cruising ships, three of which are built of iron, of small tonnage, and twenty-four of wood. Of these wooden vessels it is estimated by the Chief Constructor of the Navy that only three will be serviceable beyond a period of six years, at which time it may be said that of the present naval force nothing worthy the name will remain.

All the vessels heretofore authorized are under contract or in course of construction except the armored ships, the torpedo and dynamite boats, and one cruiser. As to the last of these, the bids were in excess of the limit fixed by Congress. The production in the United States of armor and gun steel is a question which it seems necessary to settle at an early day if the armored war vessels are to be completed with those materials of home manufacture. This has been the subject of investigation by two boards and by two special committees of Congress within the last three years. The report of the Gun Foundry Board in 1884, of the Board on Fortifications made in January last, and the reports of the select committees of the two Houses made at the last session of Congress have entirely exhausted the subject, so far as preliminary investigation is involved, and in their recommendations they are substantially agreed.

In the event that the present invitation of the Department for bids to furnish such of this material as is now authorized shall fail to induce domestic manufacturers to undertake the large expenditures required to prepare for this new manufacture, and no other steps are taken by Congress at its coming session, the Secretary contemplates with dissatisfaction the necessity of obtaining abroad the armor and the gun steel for the authorized ships. It would seem desirable that the wants of the Army and the Navy in this regard should be reasonably met, and that by uniting their contracts such inducement might be offered as would result in securing the domestication of these important interests.

The affairs of the postal service show marked and gratifying improvement during the past year. A particular account of its transactions and condition is given in the report of the Postmaster-General, which will be laid before you.

The reduction of the rate of letter postage in 1883, rendering the postal revenues inadequate to sustain the expenditures, and business depression also contributing, resulted in an excess of cost for the fiscal year ended June 30, 1885, of eight and one-third millions of dollars. An additional check upon receipts by doubling the measure of weight in rating sealed correspondence and diminishing one-half the charge for newspaper carriage was imposed by legislation which took effect with the beginning of the past fiscal year, while the constant demand of our territorial development and growing population for the extension and increase of mail facilities and machinery necessitates steady annual advance in outlay, and the careful estimate of a year ago upon the rates of expenditure then existing contemplated the unavoidable augmentation of the deficiency in the last fiscal year by nearly $2,000,000. The anticipated revenue for the last year failed of realization by about $64,000, but proper measures of economy have so satisfactorily limited the growth of expenditure that the total deficiency in fact fell below that of 1885, and at this time the increase of revenue is in a gaining ratio over the increase of cost, demonstrating the sufficiency of the present rates of postage ultimately to sustain the service. This is the more pleasing because our people enjoy now both cheaper postage proportionably to distances and a vaster and more costly service than any other upon the globe.

Retrenchment has been effected in the cost of supplies, some expenditures unwarranted by law have ceased, and the outlays for mail carriage have been subjected to beneficial scrutiny. At the close of the last fiscal year the expense of transportation on star routes stood at an annual rate of cost less by over $560,000 than at the close of the previous year and steamboat and mail-messenger service at nearly $200,000 less.

The service has been in the meantime enlarged and extended by the establishment of new offices, increase of routes of carriage, expansion of carrier-delivery conveniences, and additions to the railway mail facilities, in accordance with the growing exigencies of the country and the long-established policy of the Government.

The Postmaster-General calls attention to the existing law for compensating railroads and expresses the opinion that a method may be devised which will prove more just to the carriers and beneficial to the Government; and the subject appears worthy of your early consideration.

The differences which arose during the year with certain of the ocean steamship companies have terminated by the acquiescence of all in the policy of the Government approved by the Congress in the postal appropriation at its last session, and the Department now enjoys the utmost service afforded by all vessels which sail from our ports upon either ocean—a service generally adequate to the needs of our intercourse. Petitions have, however, been presented to the Department by numerous merchants and manufacturers for the establishment of a direct service to the Argentine Republic and for semimonthly dispatches to the Empire of Brazil, and the subject is commended to your consideration. It is an obvious duty to provide the means of postal communication which our commerce requires, and with prudent forecast of results the wise extension of it may lead to stimulating intercourse and become the harbinger of a profitable traffic which will open new avenues for the disposition of the products of our industry. The circumstances of the countries at the far south of our continent are such as to invite our enterprise and afford the promise of sufficient advantages to justify an unusual effort to bring about the closer relations which greater freedom of communication would tend to establish.

I suggest that, as distinguished from a grant or subsidy for the mere benefit of any line of trade or travel, whatever outlay may be required to secure additional postal service, necessary and proper and not otherwise attainable, should be regarded as within the limit of legitimate compensation for such service.

The extension of the free-delivery service as suggested by the Postmaster-General has heretofore received my sanction, and it is to be hoped a suitable enactment may soon be agreed upon.

The request for an appropriation sufficient to enable the general inspection of fourth-class offices has my approbation.

I renew my approval of the recommendation of the Postmaster-General that another assistant be provided for the Post-Office Department, and I invite your attention to the several other recommendations in his report.

The conduct of the Department of Justice for the last fiscal year is fully detailed in the report of the Attorney-General, and I invite the earnest attention of the Congress to the same and due consideration of the recommendations therein contained.

In the report submitted by this officer to the last session of the Congress he strongly recommended the erection of a penitentiary for the confinement of prisoners convicted and sentenced in the United States courts, and he repeats the recommendation in his report for the last year.

This is a matter of very great importance and should at once receive Congressional action. United States prisoners are now confined in more than thirty different State prisons and penitentiaries scattered in every part of the country. They are subjected to nearly as many different modes of treatment and discipline and are far too much removed from the control and regulation of the Government. So far as they are entitled to humane treatment and an opportunity for improvement and reformation, the Government is responsible to them and society that these things are forthcoming. But this duty can scarcely be discharged without more absolute control and direction than is possible under the present system.

Many of our good citizens have interested themselves, with the most beneficial results, in the question of prison reform. The General Government should be in a situation, since there must be United States prisoners, to furnish important aid in this movement, and should be able to illustrate what may be practically done in the direction of this reform and to present an example in the treatment and improvement of its prisoners worthy of imitation.

With prisons under its own control the Government could deal with the somewhat vexed question of convict labor, so far as its convicts were concerned, according to a plan of its own adoption, and with due regard to the rights and interests of our laboring citizens, instead of sometimes aiding in the operation of a system which causes among them irritation and discontent.

Upon consideration of this subject it might be thought wise to erect more than one of these institutions, located in such places as would best subserve the purposes of convenience and economy in transportation. The considerable cost of maintaining these convicts as at present, in State institutions, would be saved by the adoption of the plan proposed, and by employing them in the manufacture of such articles as were needed for use by the Government quite a large pecuniary benefit would be realized in partial return for our outlay.

I again urge a change in the Federal judicial system to meet the wants of the people and obviate the delays necessarily attending the present condition of affairs in our courts. All are agreed that something should be done, and much favor is shown by those well able to advise to the plan suggested by the Attorney-General at the last session of the Congress and recommended in my last annual message. This recommendation is here renewed, together with another made at the same time, touching a change in the manner of compensating district attorneys and marshals; and the latter subject is commended to the Congress for its action in the interest of economy to the Government, and humanity, fairness, and justice to our people.

The report of the Secretary of the Interior presents a comprehensive summary of the work of the various branches of the public service connected with his Department, and the suggestions and recommendations which it contains for the improvement of the service should receive your careful consideration.

The exhibit made of the condition of our Indian population and the progress of the work for their enlightenment, notwithstanding the many embarrassments which hinder the better administration of this important branch of the service, is a gratifying and hopeful one.

The funds appropriated for the Indian service for the fiscal year just passed, with the available income from Indian land and trust moneys, amounting in all to $7,850,775.12, were ample for the service under the conditions and restrictions of laws regulating their expenditure. There

THE CUSTER MONUMENT

CUSTER MONUMENT.

For the event which this monument commemorates, see the article Custer's Massacre in the Encyclopedic Index. The Indians held Custer himself in so high esteem that his was the only body found unmutilated when the main division of the army came upon the scene where Custer's little detachment had been outnumbered and slain. It is hence peculiarly appropriate that the preceding picture should show an Indian chieftain by the monument of the brave white leader whom the Indians venerated even in death.

remained a balance on hand on June 30, 1886, of $1,660,023.30, of which $1,337,768.21 are permanent funds for fulfillment of treaties and other like purposes, and the remainder, $322,255.09, is subject to be carried to the surplus fund as required by law.

The estimates presented for appropriations for the ensuing fiscal year amount to $5,608,873.64, or $442,386.20 less than those laid before the Congress last year.

The present system of agencies, while absolutely necessary and well adapted for the management of our Indian affairs and for the ends in view when it was adopted, is in the present stage of Indian management inadequate, standing alone, for the accomplishment of an object which has become pressing in its importance—the more rapid transition from tribal organizations to citizenship of such portions of the Indians as are capable of civilized life.

When the existing system was adopted, the Indian race was outside of the limits of organized States and Territories and beyond the immediate reach and operation of civilization, and all efforts were mainly directed to the maintenance of friendly relations and the preservation of peace and quiet on the frontier. All this is now changed. There is no such thing as the Indian frontier. Civilization, with the busy hum of industry and the influences of Christianity, surrounds these people at every point. None of the tribes are outside of the bounds of organized government and society, except that the Territorial system has not been extended over that portion of the country known as the Indian Territory. As a race the Indians are no longer hostile, but may be considered as submissive to the control of the Government. Few of them only are troublesome. Except the fragments of several bands, all are now gathered upon reservations.

It is no longer possible for them to subsist by the chase and the spontaneous productions of the earth.

With an abundance of land, if furnished with the means and implements for profitable husbandry, their life of entire dependence upon Government rations from day to day is no longer defensible. Their inclination, long fostered by a defective system of control, is to cling to the habits and customs of their ancestors and struggle with persistence against the change of life which their altered circumstances press upon them. But barbarism and civilization can not live together. It is impossible that such incongruous conditions should coexist on the same soil.

They are a portion of our people, are under the authority of our Government, and have a peculiar claim upon and are entitled to the fostering care and protection of the nation. The Government can not relieve itself of this responsibility until they are so far trained and civilized as to be able wholly to manage and care for themselves. The paths in which they should walk must be clearly marked out for them, and they

163

must be led or guided until they are familiar with the way and competent to assume the duties and responsibilities of our citizenship.

Progress in this great work will continue only at the present slow pace and at great expense unless the system and methods of management are improved to meet the changed conditions and urgent demands of the service.

The agents, having general charge and supervision in many cases of more than 5,000 Indians, scattered over large reservations, and burdened with the details of accountability for funds and supplies, have time to look after the industrial training and improvement of a few Indians only. The many are neglected and remain idle and dependent, conditions not favorable for progress and civilization.

The compensation allowed these agents and the conditions of the service are not calculated to secure for the work men who are fitted by ability and skill to properly plan and intelligently direct the methods best adapted to produce the most speedy results and permanent benefits.

Hence the necessity for a supplemental agency or system directed to the end of promoting the general and more rapid transition of the tribes from habits and customs of barbarism to the ways of civilization.

With an anxious desire to devise some plan of operation by which to secure the welfare of the Indians and to relieve the Treasury as far as possible from the support of an idle and dependent population, I recommended in my previous annual message the passage of a law authorizing the appointment of a commission as an instrumentality auxiliary to those already established for the care of the Indians. It was designed that this commission should be composed of six intelligent and capable persons—three to be detailed from the Army—having practical ideas upon the subject of the treatment of Indians and interested in their welfare, and that it should be charged, under the direction of the Secretary of the Interior, with the management of such matters of detail as can not with the present organization be properly and successfully conducted, and which present different phases, as the Indians themselves differ in their progress, needs, disposition, and capacity for improvement or immediate self-support.

· By the aid of such a commission much unwise and useless expenditure of money, waste of materials, and unavailing efforts might be avoided; and it is hoped that this or some measure which the wisdom of Congress may better devise to supply the deficiency of the present system may receive your consideration and the appropriate legislation be provided.

The time is ripe for the work of such an agency.

There is less opposition to the education and training of the Indian youth, as shown by the increased attendance upon the schools, and there is a yielding tendency for the individual holding of lands. Development and advancement in these directions are essential, and should have every encouragement. As the rising generation are taught the language of civilization and trained in habits of industry they should assume the duties, privileges, and responsibilities of citizenship.

No obstacle should hinder the location and settlement of any Indian willing to take land in severalty; on the contrary, the inclination to do so should be stimulated at all times when proper and expedient. But there is no authority of law for making allotments on some of the reservations, and on others the allotments provided for are so small that the Indians, though ready and desiring to settle down, are not willing to accept such small areas when their reservations contain ample lands to afford them homesteads of sufficient size to meet their present and future needs.

These inequalities of existing special laws and treaties should be corrected and some general legislation on the subject should be provided, so that the more progressive members of the different tribes may be settled upon homesteads, and by their example lead others to follow, breaking away from tribal customs and substituting therefor the love of home, the interest of the family, and the rule of the state.

The Indian character and nature are such that they are not easily led while brooding over unadjusted wrongs. This is especially so regarding their lands. Matters arising from the construction and operation of railroads across some of the reservations, and claims of title and right of occupancy set up by white persons to some of the best land within other reservations require legislation for their final adjustment.

The settlement of these matters will remove many embarrassments to progress in the work of leading the Indians to the adoption of our institutions and bringing them under the operation, the influence, and the protection of the universal laws of our country.

The recommendations of the Secretary of the Interior and the Commissioner of the General Land Office looking to the better protection of public lands and of the public surveys, the preservation of national forests, the adjudication of grants to States and corporations and of private land claims, and the increased efficiency of the public-land service are commended to the attention of Congress. To secure the widest distribution of public lands in limited quantities among settlers for residence and cultivation, and thus make the greatest number of individual homes, was the primary object of the public-land legislation in the early days of the Republic. This system was a simple one. It commenced with an admirable scheme of public surveys, by which the humblest citizen could identify the tract upon which he wished to establish his home. The price of lands was placed within the reach of all the enterprising, industrious, and honest pioneer citizens of the country. It was soon, however, found that the object of the laws was perverted, under the system of cash sales, from a distribution of land among the people to an accumulation of land capital by wealthy and speculative persons. To check this tendency a preference right of purchase was given to settlers on the land, a plan which culminated in the general preemption act of 1841. The foundation of this system was actual residence and cultivation. Twenty years later the homestead law was devised to more surely place actual homes in the possession of actual cultivators of the soil. The land was given without price, the sole conditions being residence, improvement, and cultivation. Other laws have followed, each designed to encourage the acquirement and use of land in limited individual quantities. But in later years these laws, through vicious administrative methods and under changed conditions of communication and transportation, have been so evaded and violated that their beneficent purpose is threatened with entire defeat. The methods of such evasions and violations are set forth in detail in the reports of the Secretary of the Interior and Commissioner of the General Land Office. The rapid appropriation of our public lands without *bona fide* settlements or cultivation, and not only without intention of residence, but for the purpose of their aggregation in large holdings, in many cases in the hands of foreigners, invites the serious and immediate attention of the Congress.

The energies of the Land Department have been devoted during the present Administration to remedy defects and correct abuses in the public-land service. The results of these efforts are so largely in the nature of reforms in the processes and methods of our land system as to prevent adequate estimate; but it appears by a compilation from the reports of the Commissioner of the General Land Office that the immediate effect in leading cases which have come to a final termination has been the restoration to the mass of public lands of 2,750,000 acres; that 2,370,000 acres are embraced in investigations now pending before the Department or the courts, and that the action of Congress has been asked to effect the restoration of 2,790,000 acres additional; besides which 4,000,000 acres have been withheld from reservation and the rights of entry thereon maintained.

I recommend the repeal of the preemption and timber-culture acts, and that the homestead laws be so amended as to better secure compliance with their requirements of residence, improvement, and cultivation for the period of five years from date of entry, without commutation or provision for speculative relinquishment. I also recommend the repeal of the desert-land laws unless it shall be the pleasure of the Congress to so amend these laws as to render them less liable to abuses. As the chief motive for an evasion of the laws and the principal cause of their result in land accumulation instead of land distribution is the facility with which transfers are made of the right intended to be secured to settlers, it may be deemed advisable to provide by legislation some guards and checks upon the alienation of homestead rights and lands covered thereby until patents issue.

Last year an Executive proclamation* was issued directing the removal of fences which inclosed the public domain. Many of these have

* See pp. 4893-4894.

been removed in obedience to such order, but much of the public land still remains within the lines of these unlawful fences. The ingenious methods resorted to in order to continue these trespasses and the hardihood of the pretenses by which in some cases such inclosures are justified are fully detailed in the report of the Secretary of the Interior.

The removal of the fences still remaining which inclose public lands will be enforced with all the authority and means with which the executive branch of the Government is or shall be invested by the Congress for that purpose.

The report of the Commissioner of Pensions contains a detailed and most satisfactory exhibit of the operations of the Pension Bureau during the last fiscal year. The amount of work done was the largest in any year since the organization of the Bureau, and it has been done at less cost than during the previous year in every division.

On the 30th day of June, 1886, there were 365,783 pensioners on the rolls of the Bureau.

Since 1861 there have been 1,018,735 applications for pensions filed, of which 78,834 were based upon service in the War of 1812. There were 621,754 of these applications allowed, including 60,178 to the soldiers of 1812 and their widows.

The total amount paid for pensions since 1861 is $808,624,811.57.

The number of new pensions allowed during the year ended June 30, 1886, is 40,857, a larger number than has been allowed in any year save one since 1861. The names of 2,229 pensioners which had been previously dropped from the rolls were restored during the year, and after deducting those dropped within the same time for various causes a net increase remains for the year of 20,658 names.

From January 1, 1861, to December 1, 1885, 1,967 private pension acts had been passed. Since the last-mentioned date, and during the last session of the Congress, 644 such acts became laws.

It seems to me that no one can examine our pension establishment and its operations without being convinced that through its instrumentality justice can be very nearly done to all who are entitled under present laws to the pension bounty of the Government.

But it is undeniable that cases exist, well entitled to relief, in which the Pension Bureau is powerless to aid. The really worthy cases of this class are such as only lack by misfortune the kind or quantity of proof which the law and regulations of the Bureau require, or which, though their merit is apparent, for some other reason can not be justly dealt with through general laws. These conditions fully justify application to the Congress and special enactments. But resort to the Congress for a special pension act to overrule the deliberate and careful determination of the Pension Bureau on the merits or to secure favorable action when it could not be expected under the most liberal execution of general laws, it must be admitted opens the door to the allowance of questionable claims and presents to the legislative and executive branches of the Government applications concededly not within the law and plainly devoid of merit, but so surrounded by sentiment and patriotic feeling that they are hard to resist.   I suppose it will not be denied that many claims for pension are made without merit and that many have been allowed upon fraudulent representations.   This has been declared from the Pension Bureau, not only in this but in prior Administrations.

The usefulness and the justice of any system for the distribution of pensions depend upon the equality and uniformity of its operation.

It will be seen from the report of the Commissioner that there are now paid by the Government 131 different rates of pension.

He estimates from the best information he can obtain that 9,000 of those who have served in the Army and Navy of the United States are now supported, in whole or in part, from public funds or by organized charities, exclusive of those in soldiers' homes under the direction and control of the Government.   Only 13 per cent of these are pensioners, while of the entire number of men furnished for the late war something like 20 per cent, including their widows and relatives, have been or now are in receipt of pensions.

The American people, with a patriotic and grateful regard for our ex-soldiers, too broad and too sacred to be monopolized by any special advocates, are not only willing but anxious that equal and exact justice should be done to all honest claimants for pensions.   In their sight the friendless and destitute soldier, dependent on public charity, if otherwise entitled, has precisely the same right to share in the provision made for those who fought their country's battles as those better able, through friends and influence, to push their claims.   Every pension that is granted under our present plan upon any other grounds than actual service and injury or disease incurred in such service, and every instance of the many in which pensions are increased on other grounds than the merits of the claim, work an injustice to the brave and crippled, but poor and friendless, soldier, who is entirely neglected or who must be content with the smallest sum allowed under general laws.

There are far too many neighborhoods in which are found glaring cases of inequality of treatment in the matter of pensions, and they are largely due to a yielding in the Pension Bureau to importunity on the part of those, other than the pensioner, who are especially interested, or they arise from special acts passed for the benefit of individuals.

The men who fought side by side should stand side by side when they participate in a grateful nation's kind remembrance.

Every consideration of fairness and justice to our ex-soldiers and the protection of the patriotic instinct of our citizens from perversion and violation point to the adoption of a pension system broad and comprehensive enough to cover every contingency, and which shall make unnecessary an objectionable volume of special legislation.

As long as we adhere to the principle of granting pensions for service, and disability as the result of the service, the allowance of pensions should be restricted to cases presenting these features.

Every patriotic heart responds to a tender consideration for those who, having served their country long and well, are reduced to destitution and dependence, not as an incident of their service, but with advancing age or through sickness or misfortune. We are all tempted by the contemplation of such a condition to supply relief, and are often impatient of the limitations of public duty. Yielding to no one in the desire to indulge this feeling of consideration, I can not rid myself of the conviction that if these ex-soldiers are to be relieved they and their cause are entitled to the benefit of an enactment under which relief may be claimed as a right, and that such relief should be granted under the sanction of law, not in evasion of it; nor should such worthy objects of care, all equally entitled, be remitted to the unequal operation of sympathy or the tender mercies of social and political influence, with their unjust discriminations.

The discharged soldiers and sailors of the country are our fellow-citizens, and interested with us in the passage and faithful execution of wholesome laws. They can not be swerved from their duty of citizenship by artful appeals to their spirit of brotherhood born of common peril and suffering, nor will they exact as a test of devotion to their welfare a willingness to neglect public duty in their behalf.

On the 4th of March, 1885, the current business of the Patent Office was, on an average, five and a half months in arrears, and in several divisions more than twelve months behind. At the close of the last fiscal year such current work was but three months in arrears, and it is asserted and believed that in the next few months the delay in obtaining an examination of an application for a patent will be but nominal.

The number of applications for patents during the last fiscal year, including reissues, designs, trade-marks, and labels, equals 40,678, which is considerably in excess of the number received during any preceding year.

The receipts of the Patent Office during the year aggregate $1,205,-167.80, enabling the office to turn into the Treasury a surplus revenue, over and above all expenditures, of about $163,710.30.

The number of patents granted during the last fiscal year, including reissues, trade-marks, designs, and labels, was 25,619, a number also quite largely in excess of that of any preceding year.

The report of the Commissioner shows the office to be in a prosperous condition and constantly increasing in its business. No increase of force is asked for.

The amount estimated for the fiscal year ending June 30, 1886, was $890,760. The amount estimated for the year ending June 30, 1887, was $853,960. The amount estimated for the fiscal year ending June 30, 1888, is $778,770.

The Secretary of the Interior suggests a change in the plan for the payment of the indebtedness of the Pacific subsidized roads to the Government. His suggestion has the unanimous indorsement of the persons selected by the Government to act as directors of these roads and protect the interests of the United States in the board of direction. In considering the plan proposed the sole matters which should be taken into account, in my opinion, are the situation of the Government as a creditor and the surest way to secure the payment of the principal and interest of its debt.

By a recent decision of the Supreme Court of the United States it has been adjudged that the laws of the several States are inoperative to regulate rates of transportation upon railroads if such regulation interferes with the rate of carriage from one State into another. This important field of control and regulation having been thus left entirely unoccupied, the expediency of Federal action upon the subject is worthy of consideration.

The relations of labor to capital and of laboring men to their employers are of the utmost concern to every patriotic citizen. When these are strained and distorted, unjustifiable claims are apt to be insisted upon by both interests, and in the controversy which results the welfare of all and the prosperity of the country are jeopardized. Any intervention of the General Government, within the limits of its constitutional authority, to avert such a condition should be willingly accorded.

In a special message* transmitted to the Congress at its last session I suggested the enlargement of our present Labor Bureau and adding to its present functions the power of arbitration in cases where differences arise between employer and employed. When these differences reach such a stage as to result in the interruption of commerce between the States, the application of this remedy by the General Government might be regarded as entirely within its constitutional powers. And I think we might reasonably hope that such arbitrators, if carefully selected and if entitled to the confidence of the parties to be affected, would be voluntarily called to the settlement of controversies of less extent and not necessarily within the domain of Federal regulation.

I am of the opinion that this suggestion is worthy the attention of the Congress.

But after all has been done by the passage of laws, either Federal or State, to relieve a situation full of solicitude, much more remains to be accomplished by the reinstatement and cultivation of a true American sentiment which recognizes the equality of American citizenship. This, in the light of our traditions and in loyalty to the spirit of our institutions, would teach that a hearty cooperation on the part of all interests is the surest path to national greatness and the happiness of all our people; that capital should, in recognition of the brotherhood of our citizenship and in a spirit of American fairness, generously accord to labor its just compensation and consideration, and that contented labor is capital's

* See pp. 4974-4982.

best protection and faithful ally. It would teach, too, that the diverse situations of our people are inseparable from our civilization; that every citizen should in his sphere be a contributor to the general good; that capital does not necessarily tend to the oppression of labor, and that violent disturbances and disorders alienate from their promoters true American sympathy and kindly feeling.

The Department of Agriculture, representing the oldest and largest of our national industries, is subserving well the purposes of its organization. By the introduction of new subjects of farming enterprise and by opening new sources of agricultural wealth and the dissemination of early information concerning production and prices it has contributed largely to the country's prosperity. Through this agency advanced thought and investigation touching the subjects it has in charge should, among other things, be practically applied to the home production at a low cost of articles of food which are now imported from abroad. Such an innovation will necessarily, of course, in the beginning be within the domain of intelligent experiment, and the subject in every stage should receive all possible encouragement from the Government.

The interests of millions of our citizens engaged in agriculture are involved in an enlargement and improvement of the results of their labor, and a zealous regard for their welfare should be a willing tribute to those whose productive returns are a main source of our progess and power.

The existence of pleuro-pneumonia among the cattle of various States has led to burdensome and in some cases disastrous restrictions in an important branch of our commerce, threatening to affect the quantity and quality of our food supply. This is a matter of such importance and of such far-reaching consequences that I hope it will engage the serious attention of the Congress, to the end that such a remedy may be applied as the limits of a constitutional delegation of power to the General Government will permit.

I commend to the consideration of the Congress the report of the Commissioner and his suggestions concerning the interest intrusted to his care.

The continued operation of the law relating to our civil service has added the most convincing proofs of its necessity and usefulness. It is a fact worthy of note that every public officer who has a just idea of his duty to the people testifies to the value of this reform. Its staunchest friends are found among those who understand it best, and its warmest supporters are those who are restrained and protected by its requirements.

The meaning of such restraint and protection is not appreciated by those who want places under the Government regardless of merit and efficiency, nor by those who insist that the selection of such places should rest upon a proper credential showing active partisan work. They mean to public officers, if not their lives, the only opportunity afforded them to attend to public business, and they mean to the good people of the country the better performance of the work of their Government.

It is exceedingly strange that the scope and nature of this reform are so little understood and that so many things not included within its plan are called by its name. When cavil yields more fully to examination, the system will have large additions to the number of its friends.

Our civil-service reform may be imperfect in some of its details; it may be misunderstood and opposed; it may not always be faithfully applied; its designs may sometimes miscarry through mistake or willful intent; it may sometimes tremble under the assaults of its enemies or languish under the misguided zeal of impracticable friends; but if the people of this country ever submit to the banishment of its underlying principle from the operation of their Government they will abandon the surest guaranty of the safety and success of American institutions.

I invoke for this reform the cheerful and ungrudging support of the Congress. I renew my recommendation made last year that the salaries of the Commissioners be made equal to other officers of the Government having like duties and responsibilities, and I hope that such reasonable appropriations may be made as will enable them to increase the usefulness of the cause they have in charge.

I desire to call the attention of the Congress to a plain duty which the Government owes to the depositors in the Freedman's Savings and Trust Company.

This company was chartered by the Congress for the benefit of the most illiterate and humble of our people, and with the intention of encouraging in them industry and thrift. Most of its branches were presided over by officers holding the commissions and clothed in the uniform of the United States. These and other circumstances reasonably, I think, led these simple people to suppose that the invitation to deposit their hard-earned savings in this institution implied an undertaking on the part of their Government that their money should be safely kept for them.

When this company failed, it was liable in the sum of $2,939,925.22 to 61,131 depositors. Dividends amounting in the aggregate to 62 per cent have been declared, and the sum called for and paid of such dividends seems to be $1,648,181.72. This sum deducted from the entire amount of deposits leaves $1,291,744.50 still unpaid. Past experience has shown that quite a large part of this sum will not be called for. There are assets still on hand amounting to the estimated sum of $16,000.

I think the remaining 38 per cent of such of these deposits as have claimants should be paid by the Government, upon principles of equity and fairness.

The report of the commissioner, soon to be laid before Congress, will give more satisfactory details on this subject.

The control of the affairs of the District of Columbia having been placed in the hands of purely executive officers, while the Congress still retains all legislative authority relating to its government, it becomes my duty to make known the most pressing needs of the District and recommend their consideration.

The laws of the District appear to be in an uncertain and unsatisfactory condition, and their codification or revision is much needed.

During the past year one of the bridges leading from the District to the State of Virginia became unfit for use, and travel upon it was forbidden. This leads me to suggest that the improvement of all the bridges crossing the Potomac and its branches from the city of Washington is worthy the attention of Congress.

The Commissioners of the District represent that the laws regulating the sale of liquor and granting licenses therefor should be at once amended, and that legislation is needed to consolidate, define, and enlarge the scope and powers of charitable and penal institutions within the District.

I suggest that the Commissioners be clothed with the power to make, within fixed limitations, police regulations. I believe this power granted and carefully guarded would tend to subserve the good order of the municipality.

It seems that trouble still exists growing out of the occupation of the streets and avenues by certain railroads having their termini in the city. It is very important that such laws should be enacted upon this subject as will secure to the railroads all the facilities they require for the transaction of their business and at the same time protect citizens from injury to their persons or property.

The Commissioners again complain that the accommodations afforded them for the necessary offices for District business and for the safe-keeping of valuable books and papers are entirely insufficient. I recommend that this condition of affairs be remedied by the Congress, and that suitable quarters be furnished for the needs of the District government.

In conclusion I earnestly invoke such wise action on the part of the people's legislators as will subserve the public good and demonstrate during the remaining days of the Congress as at present organized its ability and inclination to so meet the people's needs that it shall be gratefully remembered by an expectant constituency.

GROVER CLEVELAND.

SPECIAL MESSAGES.

EXECUTIVE MANSION, *December 8, 1886.*
To the Senate and House of Representatives of the United States:

I transmit herewith a letter from the Secretary of State, which is accompanied by the correspondence in relation to the rights of American fishermen in the British North American waters, and commend to your favorable consideration the suggestion that a commission be authorized by law to take perpetuating proofs of the losses sustained during the past year by American fishermen owing to their unfriendly and unwarranted treatment by the local authorities of the maritime provinces of the Dominion of Canada.

I may have occasion hereafter to make further recommendations during the present session for such remedial legislation as may become necessary for the protection of the rights of our citizens engaged in the open-sea fisheries in the North Atlantic waters.

GROVER CLEVELAND.

EXECUTIVE MANSION, *December 13, 1886.*
To the Senate and House of Representatives:

I transmit herewith a communication of the 8th instant from the Secretary of the Interior, submitting, with accompanying papers, an estimate of appropriation in the sum of $22,000, prepared in the Office of Indian Affairs, to provide for the payment to the Eel River band of Miami Indians of a principal sum in lieu of all annuities now received by them under existing treaty stipulations.

The matter is presented for the consideration of Congress.

GROVER CLEVELAND.

EXECUTIVE MANSION,
Washington, December 13, 1886.
To the Senate of the United States:

I transmit herewith, with a view to their ratification, an additional article, signed June 23, 1884, to the treaty of friendship, commerce, and navigation of July 27, 1853, between the United States and the Argentine Confederation; also an additional clause to the said additional article, signed June 25, 1885.

The report of the Secretary of State of even date and the papers inclosed therewith set forth the reasons which have, in my opinion, rendered it advisable to again transmit for ratification the additional article above mentioned, which was withdrawn from the Senate at my request on April 2, 1885.

GROVER CLEVELAND.

EXECUTIVE MANSION, *December 15, 1886.*
To the Senate and House of Representatives:

I transmit herewith, for your information, a report from the Secretary of State, inclosing the correspondence which has passed between the Department of State and the Governments of Switzerland and France on the subject of international copyright since the date of my message of July 9, 1886, on this question.

GROVER CLEVELAND.

EXECUTIVE MANSION, *December 20, 1886.*

To the Senate and House of Representatives:

I transmit herewith a report from the Secretary of State, in relation to the invitation from Her Britannic Majesty to this Government to participate in an international exhibition which is to be held at Adelaide, South Australia, in 1887.

GROVER CLEVELAND.

EXECUTIVE MANSION, *December 21, 1886.*

To the Senate of the United States:

I nominate James C. Matthews, of New York, to be recorder of deeds in the District of Columbia, in the place of Frederick Douglass, resigned.

This nomination was submitted to the Senate at its last session, upon the retirement of the previous incumbent, who for a number of years had held the office to which it refers. In the last days of the session the Senate declined to confirm the nomination.

Opposition to the appointment of Mr. Matthews to the office for which he was named was developed among the citizens of the District of Columbia, ostensibly upon the ground that the nominee was not a resident of the District; and it is supposed that such opposition, to some extent at least, influenced the determination of the question of his confirmation.

Mr. Matthews has now been in occupancy of the office to which he was nominated for more than four months, and he has in the performance of the duties thereof won the approval of all those having business to transact with such office, and has rendered important service in rescuing the records of the District from loss and illegibility.

I am informed that his management of this office has removed much of the opposition to his appointment which heretofore existed.

I have ventured, therefore, in view of the demonstrated fitness of this nominee, and with the understanding that the objections heretofore urged against his selection have to a great extent subsided, and confessing a desire to cooperate in tendering to our colored fellow-citizens just recognition and the utmost good faith, to again submit this nomination to the Senate for confirmation, at the same time disclaiming any intention to question its previous action in the premises.

GROVER CLEVELAND.

EXECUTIVE MANSION, *January 5, 1887.*

To the Senate and House of Representatives:

Referring to my message of the 12th of January last,* transmitting the final report of the commissioners appointed under the act of July 7, 1884, to visit the States of Central and South America, I have now to submit

* See p. 4955.

a special report by Commissioner Thomas C. Reynolds on the condition and commerce of Nicaragua, Honduras, and Salvador.

GROVER CLEVELAND.

EXECUTIVE MANSION, *January 5, 1887.*

To the House of Representatives:

I transmit herewith a letter from the Secretary of State, inclosing statement of customs duties levied by foreign nations upon the produce and manufactures of the United States.

GROVER CLEVELAND.

EXECUTIVE MANSION, *January 10, 1887.*

To the Senate and House of Representatives:

I transmit herewith a communication of 22d ultimo from the Secretary of the Interior, submitting, with accompanying papers, a draft of proposed legislation, prepared in the Office of Indian Affairs, providing for the per capita payment to the Delaware Indians resident in the Cherokee Nation, in Indian Territory, of the amount of their trust fund, principal and interest, held by the Government of the United States by virtue of the several treaties with the said Delaware Indians.

The matter is presented for the consideration and action of Congress.

GROVER CLEVELAND

EXECUTIVE MANSION, *January 11, 1887.*

To the Senate and House of Representatives of the United States:

I transmit herewith a report from the Secretary of State, in relation to an invitation which has been extended to this Government to appoint a delegate or delegates to the Fourth International Prison Congress, to meet at St. Petersburg in the year 1890, and commend its suggestions to the favorable attention of Congress.

GROVER CLEVELAND.

EXECUTIVE MANSION,
Washington, January 13, 1887.

To the Senate of the United States:

I transmit to the Senate, for its consideration with a view to ratification, a declaration of the late international conference at Paris, explanatory of the convention of March 14, 1884, for the protection of submarine cables, made between the United States of America and Germany, Argentine Confederation, Austria-Hungary, Belgium, Brazil, Costa Rica, Denmark, Dominican Republic, Spain, United States of Colombia, France, Great Britain, Guatemala, Greece, Italy, Turkey, Netherlands, Persia,

Portugal, Roumania, Russia, Salvador, Servia, Sweden and Norway, and Uruguay.

The declaration has been generally accepted by the signatory powers, and Mr. McLane, the representative of the United States at the conference, has been instructed to sign it, subject to the approval of the Senate.

GROVER CLEVELAND.

EXECUTIVE MANSION, *January 17, 1887.*

To the Senate and House of Representatives:

I transmit herewith a communication of the 11th instant from the Secretary of the Interior, submitting, with accompanying papers, a copy of an agreement duly made under the provisions of the act of May 15, 1886 (24 U. S. Statutes at Large, p. 44), with the Indians residing upon the Fort Berthold Reservation, in Dakota, for the cession of a portion of their reservation in said Territory, and for other purposes.

The agreement, together with the recommendations of the Department, is presented for the action of Congress.

GROVER CLEVELAND.

EXECUTIVE MANSION,
Washington, January 18, 1887.

To the Senate of the United States:

Referring to the message of the President of the United States dated February 2, 1885,* I transmit herewith, for your consideration, a report from the Secretary of State, inclosing a translation of the convention for the protection of industrial property, of the *protocole de clôture* of said convention, and of a protocol proposed by the conference of 1886 for ratification by the Governments which have adhered to the convention.

GROVER CLEVELAND.

EXECUTIVE MANSION, *January 18, 1887.*

To the Senate and House of Representatives:

As a matter of national interest, and one solely within the discretion and control of Congress, I transmit the accompanying memorial of the executive committee of the subconstitutional centennial commission, proposing to celebrate on the 17th of September, in the city of Philadelphia, as the day upon which and the place where the convention that framed the Federal Constitution concluded their labors and submitted the results for ratification to the thirteen States then composing the United States.

The epoch was one of the deepest interest and the events well worthy of commemoration.

*See p. 4857.

I am aware that as each State acted independently in giving its adhesion to the new Constitution the dates and anniversaries of their several ratifications are not coincident. Some action looking to a national expression in relation to the celebration of the close of the first century of popular government under a written constitution has already been suggested, and whilst stating the great interest I share in the renewed examination by the American people of the historical foundations of their Government, I do not feel warranted in discriminating in favor or against the propositions to select one day or place in preference to all others, and therefore content myself with conveying to Congress these expressions of popular feeling and interest upon the subject, hoping that in a spirit of patriotic cooperation, rather than of local competition, fitting measures may be enacted by Congress which will give the amplest opportunity all over these United States for the manifestation of the affection and confidence of a free and mighty nation in the institutions of a Government of which they are the fortunate inheritors and under which unexampled prosperity has been enjoyed by all classes and conditions in our social system.

GROVER CLEVELAND.

EXECUTIVE MANSION, *January 18, 1887.*
To the Senate and House of Representatives:

I transmit herewith a communication of the 7th ultimo from the Secretary of the Interior, submitting, with accompanying papers, a draft of a bill "for the relief of Hiatt & Co., late traders for the Osage tribe of Indians, and for other purposes."

The matter is presented for the consideration of Congress.

GROVER CLEVELAND.

EXECUTIVE MANSION,
Washington, January 20, 1887.
To the Senate of the United States:

I transmit herewith, with a view to its ratification, a draft of declaration explanatory of Articles II and IV of the convention for the protection of submarine cables, which has been proposed by the conference of 1886 for ratification by the Governments adhering to the said convention.

GROVER CLEVELAND.

EXECUTIVE MANSION, *January 20, 1887.*
To the Senate and House of Representatives:

I herewith transmit a communication addressed to me by Mr. Samuel C. Reid, who offers to the United States the battle sword (now in my custody) of his father, Captain Samuel Chester Reid, who commanded the

United States private armed brig *General Armstrong* at the battle of Fayal, in September, 1814.

I respectfully recommend that appropriate action be taken by Congress for the acceptance of this gift.

GROVER CLEVELAND.

EXECUTIVE MANSION, *January 20, 1887.*

To the Senate of the United States:

I have the honor to transmit to the Senate herewith a report of the Secretary of State, in answer to the resolution of the Senate of the 11th instant, requesting "estimates for the contingent fund of each bureau" in the Department of State.

GROVER CLEVELAND.

EXECUTIVE MANSION, *January 20, 1887.*

To the Senate:

I transmit herewith a report of the Secretary of State, in answer to the resolution of the Senate of December 8, 1886, relative to the claims of Antonio Pelletier and A. H. Lazare against the Republic of Hayti.

GROVER CLEVELAND.

EXECUTIVE MANSION, *January 25, 1887.*

To the Senate of the United States:

In response to the resolution of the Senate of the 21st ultimo, calling for certain correspondence touching the construction of a ship canal through Nicaragua, I transmit herewith a report from the Secretary of State on the subject, with accompanying papers.

GROVER CLEVELAND.

EXECUTIVE MANSION, *February 1, 1887.*

To the Senate and House of Representatives:

I transmit herewith a letter from the Secretary of State, together with a copy of the report, which it incloses, of Lieutenant William H. Schuetze, United States Navy, who was designated by the Secretary of the Navy, in pursuance of the act of Congress of March 3, 1885, making appropriations for the sundry civil expenses of the Government for the year ending June 30, 1886, to distribute the testimonials of the Government to subjects of Russia who extended aid to the survivors of the *Jeannette* exploring expedition and to the parties dispatched by this Government to aid the said survivors.

The report is interesting alike to the people of the United States and to the subjects of Russia, and will be gratifying to all who appreciate the generous and humane action of Congress in providing for the testimonials.

GROVER CLEVELAND.

EXECUTIVE MANSION, *February 1, 1887.*
To the House of Representatives of the United States:

In response to the resolution of the House of Representatives adopted on the 22d ultimo, calling upon me for a "copy of the treaty or convention proposed to the Senate and ratified by that body between the United States and the Government of the Hawaiian Islands," I transmit herewith a report of the Secretary of State, with accompanying papers.

It is proper to remark in this relation that no convention whatever has been "agreed to and ratified" by "the President and Senate," as is recited in the preamble to the said resolution of the House of Representatives, but that the documents referred to, exhibiting the action of the Executive and the Senate, respectively, are communicated in compliance with the request of the resolution.

GROVER CLEVELAND.

EXECUTIVE MANSION, *February 8, 1887.*
To the House of Representatives of the United States:

I transmit herewith, in response to a resolution of the House of the 24th ultimo, a report of the Secretary of State, with accompanying copies of correspondence between the Governments of the United States and Great Britain concerning the rights of American fishermen in the waters of British North America, supplemental to the correspondence already communicated to Congress with my message of December 8, 1886.*

GROVER CLEVELAND.

EXECUTIVE MANSION, *February 10, 1887.*
To the Senate and House of Representatives:

I transmit herewith a letter from the Secretary of State, accompanying reports by consular officers of the United States on the extent and character of the emigration from and immigration into their respective districts.

GROVER CLEVELAND.

EXECUTIVE MANSION,
Washington, February 14, 1887.
To the Senate of the United States:

I transmit herewith, with a view to its ratification, a treaty of amity, commerce, and navigation, concluded October 2, 1886, in the harbor of Nukualofa, Tongatabu, between the United States of America and the King of Tonga.

I also transmit, for your information, a report from the Secretary of State, inclosing copies of the treaties of friendship concluded between the Kingdom of Tonga and Germany and Great Britain.

GROVER CLEVELAND.

* See pp. 5114–5115.

EXECUTIVE MANSION, *February 14, 1887.*

To the Senate of the United States:

I transmit herewith a report furnished by the Secretary of State in response to a resolution of the Senate of January 31 ultimo, calling for particulars of the investment and distribution of the indemnity received in 1875 from Spain, and known as the "*Virginius* fund."

GROVER CLEVELAND.

EXECUTIVE MANSION, *February 15, 1887.*

To the House of Representatives:

In compliance with the resolution of the Senate of the 12th instant (the House of Representatives concurring), I return herewith the bill (H. R. 5652) for the relief of James W. Goodrich.

GROVER CLEVELAND.

EXECUTIVE MANSION, *February 16, 1887.*

To the Senate and House of Representatives:

I transmit herewith a letter from the Secretary of State, accompanying the annual reports of the consuls of the United States on the trade and industries of foreign countries.

GROVER CLEVELAND.

EXECUTIVE MANSION, *February 19, 1887.*

To the House of Representatives of the United States:

I transmit herewith to the House of Representatives a report from the Secretary of State, in response to a resolution of that body of the 16th instant, inquiring as to the action of this Department to protect the interests of American citizens whose property was destroyed by fire caused by insurgents at Aspinwall in 1885.

GROVER CLEVELAND.

EXECUTIVE MANSION, *February 23, 1887.*

To the Senate:

In answer to the resolution of the Senate of the 14th instant, relating to the arrest, trial, and discharge of A. K. Cutting, a citizen of the United States, by the authorities of Mexico, I transmit herewith a letter from the Secretary of State of this date, with its accompaniment.

GROVER CLEVELAND.

EXECUTIVE MANSION, *February 25, 1887.*

To the House of Representatives:

In compliance with the resolution of the House of Representatives (the Senate concurring), I return herewith the bill (H. R. 367) to amend section 536 of the Revised Statutes of the United States, relating to the division of the State of Illinois into judicial districts, and to provide for holding terms of court of the northern district at the city of Peoria.

GROVER CLEVELAND.

EXECUTIVE MANSION,
Washington, February 25, 1887.

To the Senate of the United States:

I transmit herewith, with a view to its ratification, an additional article to the treaty of extradition concluded October 11, 1870, between the United States of America and the Republic of Guatemala.

GROVER CLEVELAND.

To the Senate: EXECUTIVE MANSION, *February 26, 1887.*

I transmit herewith, in reply to a resolution of the Senate of the 21st ultimo, a report from the Secretary of State, relative to the seizure and sale of the American schooner *Rebecca* at Tampico and the resignation of Henry R. Jackson, esq., as minister of the United States to Mexico. It is not thought compatible with the public interests to publish the correspondence in either case at the present time.

GROVER CLEVELAND.

EXECUTIVE MANSION, *February 28, 1887.*
To the Senate and House of Representatives:

I transmit herewith a communication of 17th instant from the Secretary of the Interior, submitting, with accompanying papers, two agreements made with Chippewa Indians in the State of Minnesota under the provisions of the act of May 15, 1886 (24 U. S. Statutes at Large, p. 44).

The papers are presented for the consideration and action of Congress.

GROVER CLEVELAND.

EXECUTIVE MANSION,
Washington, March 1, 1887.
To the Senate of the United States:

In answer to the resolution of the Senate of the 22d ultimo, requesting copies of certain letters, dated June 8, 1886, and September 20, 1886, addressed by the counsel of A. H. Lazare to the Secretary of State, in regard to the award against the Republic of Hayti in favor of A. H. Lazare under the protocol signed by the Secretary of State and the minister of Hayti on May 24, 1884, I transmit a report from the Secretary of State upon the subject.

GROVER CLEVELAND.

EXECUTIVE MANSION,
Washington, March 1, 1887.

To the House of Representatives:

In compliance with the resolution of the House of Representatives of the 28th ultimo (the Senate concurring), I return herewith the bill of the House (H. R. 7310) granting a pension to Mrs. Arlanta T. Taylor.

GROVER CLEVELAND.

EXECUTIVE MANSION, *March 2, 1887.*

To the Senate of the United States:

In response to the resolution of the Senate of the 14th ultimo, requesting information concerning the service rendered by Count Casimir Pulaski, a brigadier-general of the Army of the United States in the years 1777, 1778, and 1779, and also respecting his pay and compensation, I transmit herewith reports upon the subject from the Secretary of State, the Secretary of the Treasury, and the Secretary of War.

GROVER CLEVELAND.

EXECUTIVE MANSION,
Washington, March 2, 1887.

To the Senate of the United States:

I transmit herewith a report of the Secretary of State, with accompanying papers, furnished in response to the resolution of the Senate of the 26th ultimo, calling for information touching the conditions under which certain transatlantic telegraph companies have been permitted to land their cables in the United States, and touching contracts of such companies with each other or with other cable or telegraph companies.

GROVER CLEVELAND.

VETO MESSAGES.

EXECUTIVE MANSION, *January 19, 1887.*

To the Senate:

I return without approval Senate bill No. 2269, entitled "An act granting a pension to William Dickens."

The beneficiary named in this bill filed his application for pension in the Pension Bureau in 1880, and in December, 1886, the same was granted, taking effect from the 15th day of October, 1864.

If the bill herewith returned should become a law, it would permit the payment of a pension only from the date of its approval. Thus, if it did not result in loss to the claimant by superseding the action of the Pension Bureau, it is plain that it would be a useless enactment.

GROVER CLEVELAND.

EXECUTIVE MANSION, *January 27, 1887.*
To the Senate:

I hereby return without approval Senate bill No. 2173, entitled "An act granting a pension to Benjamin Obekiah."

This bill directs that the beneficiary named therein be placed upon the pension roll, "subject to the provisions and limitations of the pension laws."

In July, 1886, the person named in this bill was placed upon the pension roll at a rate determined upon by the Pension Bureau, pursuant to the provisions and limitations of the pension laws; and it is entirely certain that the special act now presented to me would give the claimant no new rights or additional benefits.

GROVER CLEVELAND.

EXECUTIVE MANSION, *January 27, 1887.*
To the Senate:

I herewith return without approval Senate bill No. 127, entitled "An act for the relief of H. K. Belding."

This bill directs the sum of $1,566 to be paid to the said H. K. Belding "for carrying the mails of the United States between the years 1858 and 1862."

In April, 1858, a contract was awarded to the said Belding for carrying the mails from Brownsville, Minn., to Carimona, in the same State, a distance of 63 miles, and return, three times a week, for the sum of $1,800 per annum, said service to begin on the 1st day of July, 1858, and to terminate on the 30th day of June, 1862. This contract contained a provision that the Post-Office Department might discontinue the service in whole or in part, allowing to the contractor one month's extra pay therefor.

On May 9, 1859, in consequence of a failure on the part of the Congress to make the necessary appropriation, a general reduction of mail service was ordered, and the service under the contract with the claimant was reduced to two trips per week from May 10, 1859, instead of three, as stipulated in the contract, and a deduction of one-third of the annual sum to be paid by the contract was made for such reduced service; and thereupon one month's extra pay was allowed and paid the contractor on account of said reduction.

It is conceded that payment was made in full according to the terms of the contract up to the 10th day of May, 1859, but it is claimed that notwithstanding the reduction of the service to two trips per week and the receipt by the contractor of one month's extra pay by reason thereof, he continued to perform the full service of three trips per week from the 10th day of May, 1859, to the 30th day of September, 1860, being seventeen months.

Of the sum directed to be paid to him in the bill under consideration, $850 is allowed him on account of this service, he having been paid for the period stated at the rate of $1,200 per annum. The contractor claims that this full service was performed after the reduction by the Post-Office Department because he had received an intimation from the Postmaster-General that if the full service was continued after such reduction there was no doubt that the Congress would at its next session make provision for the payment of the sum deducted.

Of course no legal claim in favor of the contractor can be predicated upon the facts which he alleges; and if he did continue full service under the circumstances stated, it must be conceded that his conduct was hardly in accordance with the rules which regulate transactions of this kind.

But a thorough search of the correspondence and records in the Post-Office Department fails to disclose any letter, document, or record giving the least support to the allegation that any such intimation or assurance as is claimed was given; nor is there the least evidence in the Department that the full service was actually performed. There is, however, on the files of the Department a letter from the claimant, dated August 25, 1860, containing the following statement:

When I received official information of the curtailing service, the reasons why, I wrote to the Department that I would, if allowed, continue service three times a week and take certificates, if I could be allowed to connect with La Crosse at *pro rata* rates. That letter was never answered and I continued service three times a week till 3d of September following, then run twice a week.

Thus it appears that this contractor, who in August, 1860, claimed that he continued full service upon the invitation of his own unanswered letter for less than four months, insists twenty-seven years after the date of the alleged service that he performed such service for seventeen months, and up to October, 1860. Not only has he himself in this manner almost conclusively shown that the claim now made and allowed is exorbitant, but the evidence gives rise to a strong presumption that it is entirely fictitious.

The remainder of the amount allowed to the claimant in this bill is based upon an alleged performance by the contractor of the same mail service which has been referred to from October 1, 1860, to February 14, 1861, a period of four months and fourteen days.

Prior to October 1, 1860, the claimant's contract was annulled and a new or more extended route established, entirely covering that upon which he had carried the mails. Thereupon a month's extra pay was allowed to him, and new contractors undertook the service and were paid therefor by the Government for the period covered by the claimant's alleged service. From the 14th day of February, 1861, Mr. Belding's contract with the Government was reinstated; but if he performed the service alleged during the period of four months and fourteen days immediately prior to that date, it is quite clear that he did so under an arrangement with the new contractors, and not under circumstances creating any legal or equit-able claim against the Government.

GROVER CLEVELAND.

Executive Mansion, *January 31, 1887.*

To the Senate:

I hereby return without approval Senate bill No. 2167, entitled "An act granting a pension to Mrs. Margaret Dunlap."

By this bill it is proposed to grant a pension to the beneficiary therein named as the mother of James F. Dunlap, who enlisted in the Seventh Missouri State Militia Cavalry in 1862 and died in July, 1864, of wounds received at the hand of a comrade.

The favorable action of the Senate upon this bill appears to be based, so far as the cause of death is concerned, upon an affidavit contained in the report of the committee to which the bill was referred, made by one G. Will Houts, second lieutenant in the company to which the deceased soldier belonged, in which the affiant deposes that some of the comrades of the deceased being engaged in an affray he attempted to separate the combatants, whereupon one of them, without cause or provocation, stabbed the deceased in the breast, from which, in a few days thereafter, he died; to which affidavit is added the finding of a court-martial that the party inflicting the wound was found guilty of manslaughter and sentenced to five years' imprisonment.

Upon this showing it might be difficult to spell out the facts that the injury to the soldier was received in the line of duty or that any theory of granting pensions covered the case.

But the weak features of this application are not alluded to in the committee's report.

The record of the soldier's death states that he was "killed by one of his comrades in a difficulty."

The same Lieutenant Houts who in 1872 made oath that the soldier was wounded while attempting to separate comrades who were fighting testified in 1864 before the court-martial upon the trial of the man who did the wounding, and whose name was Capehart, that Dunlap, the deceased, stated to him "that he was more to blame than Capehart, and that they had been scuffling, at first good-naturedly, and then both got angry; that he was rougher with Capehart than he ought to have been."

Another witness testified that the affray took place between Dunlap and Capehart; that Dunlap handled Capehart very roughly, kicking him, etc., and that finally Capehart stabbed Dunlap, upon which the latter attempted to get his gun, but was prevented from doing so by the witness.

Of course there can be no pretense of any kind of claim against the Government arising from these facts.

It is quite evident that the affidavit presented to the Senate committee was contrived to deceive, and it is to be feared that it is but a sample of many that are made in support of claims for pensions.

GROVER CLEVELAND.

EXECUTIVE MANSION, *February 3, 1887.*

To the House of Representatives:

I return without approval House bill No. 6443, entitled "An act granting a pension to Alexander Falconer." •

This claimant filed his application for pension in 1879, alleging that in 1837, being then an enlisted man in the United States Army, he received a gunshot wound in his right leg below the knee at the battle of Okeechobee Lake, Florida.

The records disclose the fact that this soldier enlisted in 1834, and was almost continuously in the service and attached to the same company until 1846.

It further appears that he is reported sick during the month in which the battle was fought. The list of casualties does not contain his name among the wounded.

He reenlisted in 1846 and again in 1847, and was finally discharged in 1848. These latter enlistments were for service in the Mexican War.

His claim for pension was denied in 1885 on the ground that no disability existed in a pensionable degree from the alleged gunshot wound in his leg.

It is perfectly clear that the only pretexts for giving this claimant a pension are military service, old age, and poverty.

Inasmuch as he was a soldier in the Mexican War, his case is undoubtedly provided for by a general law approved within the last few days.

Under this bill the amount to be paid him is fixed, while if the bill herewith returned were approved the sum to be paid him would depend upon the determination of the Pension Bureau as to the extent of his disability as the result of his wound. As that Bureau has quite lately determined that there was no disability, it is evident that this old soldier can better rely upon the general law referred to.

GROVER CLEVELAND.

EXECUTIVE MANSION, *February 3, 1887.*

To the House of Representatives:

I herewith return without approval House bill No. 6132, entitled "An act granting a pension to William Lynch."

The claimant mentioned in this bill enlisted in the Fifth Regiment United States Infantry in 1849, and was discharged, after a reenlistment September 8, 1859.

He filed a claim for pension more than twenty-four years afterwards in April, 1884, claiming that he contracted rheumatism of the right hip and leg in the winter of 1857–58, while serving in Utah. He admitted that he was not under treatment while in the service and that he never consulted a physician in regard to his disability until he commenced proceedings for a pension.

The evidence disclosed to me falls far short of establishing this claim for pension upon its merits.

The application made to the Pension Bureau is still pending and awaiting answer to inquiries made by the Bureau in January, 1886.

I do not understand that the Congress intends to pass special acts in cases thus situated.

GROVER CLEVELAND.

EXECUTIVE MANSION, *February 4, 1887.*

To the House of Representatives:

I hereby return without approval House bill No. 7698, entitled "An act granting a pension to Robert K. Bennett."

The beneficiary named in this bill enlisted in September, 1862, and it appears that very soon after that he was detailed to the cook shop. This seems to be the only military service he rendered, and on February 7, 1863, five months after enlistment, he was received into the marine hospital at New Orleans for varicocele. He was discharged from the service February 22, 1863, and the cause of discharge is stated to be "varicocele, to which he was subject four years before enlistment."

Seventeen years thereafter, and in June, 1880, this claimant filed an application for pension in the Pension Bureau, alleging that about the 10th day of February, 1863, in unloading a barrel it fell upon him, producing a hernia, shortly after which he was affected by piles.

It will be seen that he fixes this injury as occurring three days after his admission to the hospital, but he might well be honestly mistaken as to this date. If the injury, however, was such as he stated, it is difficult to see why no mention was made of it in the hospital records.

He persisted at all times, as I understand the case, until the rejection of his claim in 1883, that his disability arose from hernia and piles. The reason of this rejection is stated to be that varicocele existed prior to enlistment and that there was no evidence of the existence of piles in the service or at discharge. From a medical examination made in December, 1882, it appears that there was "no evidence or symptoms of disability resulting from piles or hernia."

Subsequent to the rejection of this claim some proof was filed tending to show that the disability was in the right leg, but it is of such a nature, in the light of the claimant's own previous allegations, that I think the Pension Bureau did entirely right in informing his attorney that the additional evidence did not change the status of the case.

GROVER CLEVELAND.

EXECUTIVE MANSION, *February 4, 1887.*

To the House of Representatives:

I hereby return without approval House bill No. 7540, entitled "An act to increase the pension of Franklin Sweet."

This soldier was pensioned in 1863 as sergeant, though before that time he had been acting as captain, and was in command of his company when he was wounded. He is entitled in equity, and, I think, upon the theory of an act very recently approved, in law, to be treated in regard to his pension as a captain; and the Pension Bureau has within the last few days ordered a certificate for pension to issue to him as captain as of the date of his discharge.

I fully approve this action of the Bureau, and as this is much more favorable to a deserving soldier than his remedy under this bill, I am not willing that the action so lately and so justly taken in his behalf under the general law should be superseded by the approval of this act.

GROVER CLEVELAND.

EXECUTIVE MANSION, *February 4, 1887.*

To the House of Representatives:

I herewith return without approval House bill No. 8834, entitled "An act granting a pension to Abraham P. Griggs."

The claimant mentioned in this bill enlisted in a New Jersey regiment August 14, 1861, and was discharged for disability November 17, 1863.

He entered hospital January 2, 1863, and was transferred to general hospital at Newark, N. J., March 28, 1863, with "debility."

He was discharged from that hospital and from the service in November, 1863, as above stated, and the following statement from his certificate of discharge, if trustworthy, sheds some light upon the kind of debility with which he was afflicted:

This man has been in this hospital for the past eight months. We do not believe him sick, or that he has been sick, but completely worthless. He is obese and a malingerer to such an extent that he is almost an imbecile—worthlessness, obesity, and imbecility and laziness. He is totally unfit for the Invalid Corps or for any other military duty.

I do not regard it at all strange that this claimant, encouraged by the ease with which special acts are passed, seeks relief through such means, after his application, filed in the Pension Bureau nearly twenty years after his discharge, had been rejected.

Of the four comrades who make affidavit in support of his claim, two of them are recorded as deserters.

His claim is predicated upon rheumatism. He alleges that after his discharge from his enlistment he was drafted and served in the Third New York Cavalry, but the Adjutant-General reports that his name does not appear on the rolls of the company to which he says he was attached.

The board of United States examining surgeons at Trenton, N. J., report as the result of an examination as late as May 27, 1885, that they found "no disease of heart or lungs, no thickening or wasting of any of the joints of the body, no evidence of any rheumatic diathesis, no rupture or hemorrhoids, no disease of his spleen or kidney; hands are hard and indicate an ability to work."

I can not think that the official statements referred to, and which militate so strongly against the merits of the claimant, should be impeached or set aside by any of the other testimony which has been brought to my attention.

GROVER CLEVELAND.

EXECUTIVE MANSION, *February 4, 1887.*
To the House of Representatives:

I hereby return without approval House bill No. 927, entitled "An act granting a pension to Cudbert Stone."

The report of the committee of the House of Representatives to whom this bill was referred states that the claimant enlisted October 3, 1861, in Company H, Fourteenth Kentucky Volunteers, and was honorably discharged on the 31st day of January, 1865; that he filed his claim for pension July 20, 1881, more than sixteen years thereafter, alleging that he contracted piles while in the service, from exposure while in the line of duty, and that his claim was rejected in October, 1884, on the ground that the allegation of the claimant shows that his disability originated while undergoing the sentence of a court-martial, and therefore not in the line of duty.

The report of the committee closes with the statement that—

In view of the long and faithful service and high character of the claimant and the well-established facts that claimant was a stout and able-bodied man, free from any and all disease when he enlisted, and that by reason of his faithful service to his country and the great suffering and hardship through which he passed while in said service his health was permanently destroyed, the committee earnestly recommend the passage of the bill.

The records of the War Department show that the claimant enlisted October 25, 1861, and that on the muster-in roll of his company dated December 10, 1861, he is reported as present; that on the roll dated December 31, 1861, he is reported as absent without leave; that on the roll for January and February, 1862, he is reported as deserted; that he is not borne on subsequent rolls until that for November, 1864, when he is reported as gained from desertion; he was mustered out with his company January 31, 1865, and the records offered no evidence of disability; that in his claim for pension, filed in 1881, he alleges that he contracted piles in the winter of 1863.

In a subsequent statement he alleges that this date is erroneous, and that his disability was contracted in October, 1864, and that he believes it was the result of his having diarrhea for about twelve months prior to that date, contracted while he was being carried from place to place as a prisoner, he having been tried by a court-martial in May, 1862, for desertion and sentenced to imprisonment until the expiration of his term of enlistment.

Thus it quite plainly appears that this claimant spent the most of his term of enlistment in desertion or in imprisonment as a punishment of that offense; and thus is exhibited the "long and faithful service and the high character of the claimant" mentioned as entitling him to consideration by the committee who reported favorably upon this bill.

I withhold my assent from this bill because, if the facts before me, derived from the army records and the statements of the claimant are true, the allowance of this claim would, in my opinion, be a travesty upon our whole scheme of pensions and an insult to every decent veteran soldier.

GROVER CLEVELAND.

EXECUTIVE MANSION, *February 4, 1887.*

To the House of Representatives:

I return herewith without approval House bill No. 8150, entitled "An act granting a pension to Jesse Campbell."

The claim for a pension made by the beneficiary named in this bill to the Pension Bureau, and rejected in 1881, was reopened upon further proof in January, 1887, and the claimant was ordered before a board of examining surgeons, upon which a report has not yet been made.

Inasmuch as the only ground for the rejection of his claim was the nonexistence of pensionable disability from the cause he alleged, and in view of the fact that he now alleges a different disability, which the new evidence seems to support, there is no doubt that justice will be done the claimant under the general law.

This bill if passed would only place the name of the beneficiary upon the pension roll, "subject to the restrictions and limitations of the pension laws." Whether any sum was allowed him or not would still depend upon the existence of a disability; and if this is found upon the examination lately ordered, he will undoubtedly be put upon the pension roll, under existing law, in accordance with his supplementary claim.

GROVER CLEVELAND.

EXECUTIVE MANSION, *February 4, 1887.*

To the House of Representatives:

I hereby return without approval House bill No. 6832, entitled "An act granting a pension to Mrs. Catharine Sattler."

The beneficiary named in this bill claims a pension as the surviving widow of Julius Sattler, who enlisted in Company A, Seventh New York

Volunteers, and was in the service from March 10, 1864, to March 22, 1865, when he was discharged because of the amputation of his left forearm in consequence of a wound received in the battle of Deep Bottom, Virginia, on the 14th day of August, 1864. He was pensioned in 1865 at the rate of $8 per month, which was afterwards increased to $15 per month, dating from June 6, 1866.

In October, 1867, he was employed as a watchman in the United States bonded warehouse in the city of New York, and on the 31st day of that month he received his monthly pay of $50. He disappeared on that day, and on the 13th day of November, 1867, his body was found in the North River, at the foot of West Thirteenth street, in the city of New York without his hat, coat, watch, or money.

These facts, with the further statement that he was a strong and healthy man at the time of his death, constitute the case on the part of the widow, who filed her application for a pension July 8, 1884, nearly seventeen years after her husband's death, alleging that she was married to the deceased in 1865, after the amputation of his arm.

Her claim was rejected in November, 1884, upon the ground that the soldier's death was not due to his military service.

This rejection was clearly right, unless the Government is to be held as an insurer against every fatal casualty incurred by those who have served in the Army, without regard to the manner of its occurrence.

GROVER CLEVELAND.

EXECUTIVE MANSION, *February 4, 1887*.

To the House of Representatives:

I herewith return without approval House bill No. 6825, entitled "An act granting a pension to James R. Baylor."

The claim of the beneficiary named in this bill is based upon an injury to his left ankle in 1862.

A medical examination in 1877 showed no appearance of there ever having been a fracture of the left ankle, as alleged by the claimant, and it was determined that there was no disability. A later examination in the same year was had with the same result. Still another medical examination was had in June, 1884, which, although nearly agreeing with the previous ones, and giving rise to some suspicion that the claimant was inclined to exaggerate and prevent a free and fair examination, still does not absolutely exclude a very slight disability.

Upon the report of this last examination the case has been reopened for further proof of disability since discharge, which if found will entitle the claimant to a pension under general laws. On the question to be determined he would have no advantage under a special act, inasmuch as there must be a ratable disability to entitle him to any payment in pursuance of its provisions.

GROVER CLEVELAND.

EXECUTIVE MANSION, *February 11, 1887.*

To the House of Representatives:

I herewith return without my approval House bill No. 10457, entitled "An act for the relief of dependent parents and honorably discharged soldiers and sailors who are now disabled and dependent upon their own labor for support."

This is the first general bill that has been sanctioned by the Congress since the close of the late civil war permitting a pension to the soldiers and sailors who served in that war upon the ground of service and present disability alone, and in the entire absence of any injuries received by the casualties or incidents of such service.

While by almost constant legislation since the close of this war there has been compensation awarded for every possible injury received as a result of military service in the Union Army, and while a great number of laws passed for that purpose have been administered with great liberality and have been supplemented by numerous private acts to reach special cases, there has not until now been an avowed departure from the principle thus far adhered to respecting Union soldiers, that the bounty of the Government in the way of pensions is generously bestowed when granted to those who, in this military service and in the line of military duty, have to a greater or less extent been disabled.

But it is a mistake to suppose that service pensions, such as are permitted by the second section of the bill under consideration, are new to our legislation. In 1818, thirty-five years after the close of the Revolutionary War, they were granted to the soldiers engaged in that struggle, conditional upon service until the end of the war or for a term not less than nine months, and requiring every beneficiary under the act to be one "who is, or hereafter by reason of his reduced circumstances in life shall be, in need of assistance from his country for support." Another law of a like character was passed in 1828, requiring service until the close of the Revolutionary War; and still another, passed in 1832, provided for those persons not included in the previous statute, but who served two years at some time during the war, and giving a proportionate sum to those who had served not less than six months.

A service-pension law was passed for the benefit of the soldiers of 1812 in the year 1871, fifty-six years after the close of that war, which required only sixty days' service; and another was passed in 1878, sixty-three years after the war, requiring only fourteen days' service.

The service-pension bill passed at this session of Congress, thirty-nine years after the close of the Mexican War, for the benefit of the soldiers of that war, requires either some degree of disability or dependency or that the claimant under its provisions should be 62 years of age, and in either case that he should have served sixty days or been actually engaged in a battle.

It will be seen that the bill of 1818 and the Mexican pension bill, being thus passed nearer the close of the wars in which its beneficiaries were engaged than the others—one thirty-five years and the other thirty-nine years after the termination of such wars—embraced persons who were quite advanced in age, assumed to be comparatively few in number, and whose circumstances, dependence, and disabilities were clearly defined and could be quite easily fixed.

The other laws referred to appear to have been passed at a time so remote from the military service of the persons which they embraced that their extreme age alone was deemed to supply a presumption of dependency and need.

The number of enlistments in the Revolutionary War is stated to be 309,791, and in the War of 1812 576,622; but it is estimated that on account of repeated reenlistments the number of individuals engaged in these wars did not exceed one-half of the number represented by these figures. In the war with Mexico the number of enlistments is reported to be 112,230, which represents a greater proportion of individuals engaged than the reported enlistments in the two previous wars.

The number of pensions granted under all laws to soldiers of the Revolution is given at 62,069; to the soldiers of the War of 1812 and their widows, 60,178; and to soldiers of the Mexican War and their widows, up to June 30, 1885, 7,619. The latter pensions were granted to the soldiers of a war involving much hardship for disabilities incurred as a result of such service; and it was not till within the last month that the few remaining survivors were awarded a service pension.

The war of the Rebellion terminated nearly twenty-two years ago; the number of men furnished for its prosecution is stated to be 2,772,408. No corresponding number of statutes have ever been passed to cover every kind of injury or disability incurred in the military service of any war. Under these statutes 561,571 pensions have been granted from the year 1861 to June 30, 1886, and more than 2,600 pensioners have been added to the rolls by private acts passed to meet cases, many of them of questionable merit, which the general laws did not cover.

On ths 1st day of July, 1886, 365,763 pensioners of all classes were upon the pension rolls, of whom 305,605 were survivors of the War of the Rebellion and their widows and dependents. For the year ending June 30, 1887, $75,000,000 have been appropriated for the payment of pensions, and the amount expended for that purpose from 1861 to July 1, 1886, is $808,624,811.51.

While annually paying out such a vast sum for pensions already granted, it is now proposed by the bill under consideration to award a service pension to the soldiers of all wars in which the United States has been engaged, including of course the War of the Rebellion, and to pay those entitled to the benefits of the act the sum of $12 per month.

So far as it relates to the soldiers of the late civil war, the bounty it affords them is given thirteen years earlier than it has been furnished the

DEBRIS AFTER THE JOHNSTOWN FLOOD

THE JOHNSTOWN FLOOD

The Mississippi River floods have been a constant source of anxiety and expense to the Federal Government as well as to the States bordering it. Of the score of inundations which, owing to their devastating effect, have been judged worthy of record, that of Johnstown is most widely remembered. It occurred May 31, 1889. The swelling by rain of the Conemaugh River in Pennsylvania broke a dam 18 miles above Johnstown and in seven minutes the deluge was upon them. Two thousand one hundred and forty-two lives were lost; $9,674,105 in property was destroyed. The charity of the country came to the rescue nobly with a $3,000,000 fund.

soldiers of any other war, and before a large majority of its beneficiaries have advanced in age beyond the strength and vigor of the prime of life.

It exacts only a military or naval service of three months, without any requirement of actual engagement with an enemy in battle, and without a subjection to any of the actual dangers of war.

The pension it awards is allowed to enlisted men who have not suffered the least injury, disability, loss, or damage of any kind, incurred in or in any degree referable to their military service, including those who never reached the front at all and those discharged from rendezvous at the close of the war, if discharged three months after enlistment. Unde the last call of the President for troops, in December, 1864, 11,303 men were furnished who were thus discharged.

The section allowing this pension does, however, require, besides a service of three months and an honorable discharge, that those seeking the benefit of the act shall be such as "are now or may hereafter be suffering from mental or physical disability, not the result of their own vicious habits or gross carelessness, which incapacitates them for the performance of labor in such a degree as to render them unable to earn a support, and who are dependent upon their daily labor for support."

It provides further that such persons shall, upon making proof of the fact, "be placed on the list of invalid pensioners of the United States, and be entitled to receive for such total inability to procure their subsistence by daily labor $12 per month; and such pension shall commence from the date of the filing of the application in the Pension Office, upon proof that the disability then existed, and continue during the existence of the same in the degree herein provided: *Provided*, That persons who are now receiving pensions under existing laws, or whose claims are pending in the Pension Office, may, by application to the Commissioner of Pensions, in such form as he may prescribe, receive the benefit of this act."

It is manifestly of the utmost importance that statutes which, like pension laws, should be liberally administered as measures of benevolence in behalf of worthy beneficiaries should admit of no uncertainty as to their general objects and consequences.

Upon a careful consideration of the language of the section of this bill above given it seems to me to be so uncertain and liable to such conflicting constructions and to be subject to such unjust and mischievous application as to alone furnish sufficient ground for disapproving the proposed legislation.

Persons seeking to obtain the pension provided by this section must be now or hereafter—

1. "Suffering from mental or physical disability."

2. Such disability must not be "the result of their own vicious habits or gross carelessness."

3. Such disability must be such as "incapacitates them for the performance of labor in such a degree as to render them unable to earn a support."

4. They must be "dependent upon their daily labor for support."

5. Upon proof of these conditions they shall "be placed on the lists of invalid pensioners of the United States, and be entitled to receive for such total inability to procure their subsistence by daily labor $12 per month."

It is not probable that the words last quoted, "such total inability to procure their subsistence by daily labor," at all qualify the conditions prescribed in the preceding language of the section. The "total inability" spoken of must be "such" inability—that is, the inability already described and constituted by the conditions already detailed in the previous parts of the section.

It thus becomes important to consider the meaning and the scope of these last-mentioned conditions.

The mental and physical disability spoken of has a distinct meaning in the practice of the Pension Bureau and includes every impairment of bodily or mental strength and vigor. For such disabilities there are now paid 131 different rates of pension, ranging from $1 to $100 per month.

This disability must not be the result of the applicant's "vicious habits or gross carelessness." Practically this provision is not important. The attempt of the Government to escape the payment of a pension on such a plea would of course in a very large majority of instances, and regardless of the merits of the case, prove a failure. There would be that strange but nearly universal willingness to help the individual as between him and the public Treasury which goes very far to insure a state of proof in favor of the claimant.

The disability of applicants must be such as to "incapacitate them for the performance of labor in such a degree as to render them unable to earn a support."

It will be observed that there is no limitation or definition of the incapacitating injury or ailment itself. It need only be such a degree of disability from any cause as renders the claimant unable to earn a support by labor. It seems to me that the "support" here mentioned as one which can not be earned is a complete and entire support, with no diminution on account of the least impairment of physical or mental condition. If it had been intended to embrace only those who by disease or injury were totally unable to labor, it would have been very easy to express that idea, instead of recognizing, as is done, a "degree" of such inability.

What is a support? Who is to determine whether a man earns it, or has it, or has it not? Is the Government to enter the homes of claimants for pension and after an examination of their surroundings and circumstances settle those questions? Shall the Government say to one man that his manner of subsistence by his earnings is a support and to another that the things his earnings furnish are not a support? Any attempt, however honest, to administer this law in such a manner would necessarily produce more unfairness and unjust discrimination and give more scope for partisan partiality, and would result in more perversion of the Government's benevolent intentions, than the execution of any statute ought to permit.

If in the effort to carry out the proposed law the degree of disability as related to earnings be considered for the purpose of discovering if in any way it curtails the support which the applicant, if entirely sound, would earn, and to which he is entitled, we enter the broad field long occupied by the Pension Bureau, and we recognize as the only difference between the proposed legislation and previous laws passed for the benefit of the surviving soldiers of the Civil War the incurrence in one case of disabilities in military service and in the other disabilities existing, but in no way connected with or resulting from such service.

It must be borne in mind that in no case is there any grading of this proposed pension. Under the operation of the rule first suggested, if there is a lack in any degree, great or small, of the ability to earn such a support as the Government determines the claimant should have, and, by the application of the rule secondly suggested, if there is a reduction in any degree of the support which he might earn if sound, he is entitled to a pension of $12.

In the latter case, and under the proviso of the proposed bill permitting persons now receiving pensions to be admitted to the benefits of the act, I do not see how those now on the pension roll for disabilities incurred in the service, and which diminish their earning capacity, can be denied the pension provided in this bill.

Of course none will apply who are now receiving $12 or more per month. But on the 30th day of June, 1886, there were on the pension rolls 202,621 persons who were receiving fifty-eight different rates of pension from $1 to $11.75 per month. Of these, 28,142 were receiving $2 per month; 63,116, $4 per month; 37,254, $6 per month, and 50,274, whose disabilities were rated as total, $8 per month.

As to the meaning of the section of the bill under consideration there appears to have been quite a difference of opinion among its advocates in the Congress. The chairman of the Committee on Pensions in the House of Representatives, who reported the bill, declared that there was in it no provision for pensioning anyone who has a less disability than a total inability to labor, and that it was a charity measure. The chairman of the Committee on Pensions in the Senate, having charge of the bill in that body, dissented from the construction of the bill announced in the House of Representatives, and declared that it not only embraced all soldiers totally disabled, but, in his judgment, all who are disabled to any considerable extent; and such a construction was substantially given to the bill by another distinguished Senator, who, as a former Secretary of the Interior, had imposed upon him the duty of executing pension laws and determining their intent and meaning.

Another condition required of claimants under this act is that they shall be "dependent upon their daily labor for support."

This language, which may be said to assume that there exists within the reach of the persons mentioned "labor," or the ability in some degree to work, is more aptly used in a statute describing those not wholly deprived of this ability than in one which deals with those utterly unable to work.

I am of the opinion that it may fairly be contended that under the provisions of this section any soldier whose faculties of mind or body have become impaired by accident, disease, or age, irrespective of his service in the Army as a cause, and who by his labor only is left incapable of gaining the fair support he might with unimpaired powers have provided for himself, and who is not so well endowed with this world's goods as to live without work, may claim to participate in its bounty; that it is not required that he should be without property, but only that labor should be necessary to his support in some degree; nor is *it* required that he should be now receiving support from others.

Believing this to be the proper interpretation of the bill, I can not but remember that the soldiers of our Civil War in their pay and bounty received such compensation for military service as has never been received by soldiers before since mankind first went to war; that never before on behalf of any soldiery have so many and such generous laws been passed to relieve against the incidents of war; that statutes have been passed giving them a preference in all public employments; that the really needy and homeless Union soldiers of the rebellion have been to a large extent provided for at soldiers' homes, instituted and supported by the Government, where they are maintained together, free from the sense of degradation which attaches to the usual support of charity; and that never before in the history of the country has it been proposed to render Government aid toward the support of any of its soldiers based alone upon a military service so recent, and where age and circumstances appeared so little to demand such aid.

Hitherto such relief has been granted to surviving soldiers few in number, venerable in age, after a long lapse of time since their military service, and as a parting benefaction tendered by a grateful people.

I can not believe that the vast peaceful army of Union soldiers, who, having contentedly resumed their places in the ordinary avocations of life, cherish as sacred the memory of patriotic service, or who, having been disabled by the casualties of war, justly regard the present pension roll on which appear their names as a roll of honor, desire at this time and in the present exigency to be confounded with those who through such a bill as this are willing to be objects of simple charity and to gain a place upon the pension roll through alleged dependence.

Recent personal observation and experience constrain me to refer to another result which will inevitably follow the passage of this bill. It is sad, but nevertheless true, that already in the matter of procuring pensions there exists a widespread disregard of truth and good faith, stimulated by those who as agents undertake to establish claims for pensions heedlessly entered upon by the expectant beneficiary, and encouraged, or at least not condemned, by those unwilling to obstruct a neighbor's plans.

In the execution of this proposed law under any interpretation a wide field of inquiry would be opened for the establishment of facts largely within the knowledge of the claimants alone, and there can be no doubt that the race after the pensions offered by this bill would not only stimulate weakness and pretended incapacity for labor, but put a further premium on dishonesty and mendacity.

The effect of new invitations to apply for pensions or of new advantages added to causes for pensions already existing is sometimes startling.

Thus in March, 1879, large arrearages of pensions were allowed to be added to all claims filed prior to July 1, 1880. For the year from July 1, 1879, to July 1, 1880, there were filed 110,673 claims, though in the year immediately previous there were but 36,832 filed, and in the year following but 18,455.

While cost should not be set against a patriotic duty or the recognition of a right, still when a measure proposed is based upon generosity or motives of charity it is not amiss to meditate somewhat upon the expense which it involves. Experience has demonstrated, I believe, that all estimates concerning the probable future cost of a pension list are uncertain and unreliable and always fall far below act ial realization.

The chairman of the House Committee on Pensions calculates that the number of pensioners under this bill would be 33,105 and the increased cost $4,767,120. This is upon the theory that only those who are entirely unable to work would be its beneficiaries. Such was the principle of the Revolutionary pension law of 1818, much more clearly stated, it seems to me, than in this bill. When the law of 1818 was upon its passage in Congress, the number of pensioners to be benefitted thereby was thought to be 374, but the number of applicants under the act was 22,297, and the number of pensions actually allowed 20,485, costing, it is reported, for the first year, $1,847,900, instead of $40,000, the estimated expense for that period.

A law was passed in 1853 for the benefit of the surviving widows of Revolutionary soldiers who were married after January 1, 1800. It was estimated that they numbered 300 at the time of the passage of the act; but the number of pensions allowed was 3,742, and the amount paid for such pensions during the first year of the operation of the act was $180,000, instead of $24,000, as had been estimated.

I have made no search for other illustrations, and the above, being at hand, are given as tending to show that estimates can not be relied upon in such cases.

If none should be pensioned under this bill except those utterly unable to work, I am satisfied that the cost stated in the estimate referred to would be many times multiplied, and with a constant increase from year to year; and if those partially unable to earn their support should be admitted to the privileges of this bill, the probable increase of expense would be almost appalling.

I think it may be said that at the close of the War of the Rebellion every Northern State and a great majority of Northern counties and cities were burdened with taxation on account of the large bounties paid our soldiers; and the bonded debt thereby created still constitutes a large item in the account of the taxgatherer against the people. Federal taxation, no less borne by the people than that directly levied upon their property, is still maintained at the rate made necessary by the exigencies of war. If this bill should become a law, with its tremendous addition to our pension obligation, I am thoroughly convinced that further efforts to reduce the Federal revenue and restore some part of it to our people will, and perhaps should, be seriously questioned.

It has constantly been a cause of pride and congratulation to the American citizen that his country is not put to the charge of maintaining a large standing army in time of peace. Yet we are now living under a war tax which has been tolerated in peaceful times to meet the obligations incurred in war. But for years past, in all parts of the country, the demand for the reduction of the burdens of taxation upon our labor and production has increased in volume and urgency.

I am not willing to approve a measure presenting the objections to which this bill is subject, and which, moreover, will have the effect of disappointing the expectation of the people and their desire and hope for relief from war taxation in time of peace.

In my last annual message the following language was used:

Every patriotic heart responds to a tender consideration for those who, having served their country long and well, are reduced to destitution and dependence, not as an incident of their service, but with advancing age or through sickness or misfortune. We are all tempted by the contemplation of such a condition to supply relief, and are often impatient of the limitations of public duty. Yielding to no one in the desire to indulge this feeling of consideration, I can not rid myself of the conviction that if these ex-soldiers are to be relieved they and their cause are entitled to the benefit of an enactment under which relief may be claimed as a right, and that such relief should be granted under the sanction of law, not in evasion of it; nor should such worthy objects of care, all equally entitled, be remitted to the unequal operation of sympathy or the tender mercies of social and political influence, with their unjust discriminations.

I do not think that the objects, the conditions, and the limitations thus suggested are contained in the bill under consideration.

I adhere to the sentiments thus heretofore expressed. But the evil threatened by this bill is, in my opinion, such that, charged with a great responsibility in behalf of the people, I can not do otherwise than to bring to the consideration of this measure my best efforts of thought and judgment and perform my constitutional duty in relation thereto, regardless of all consequences except such as appear to me to be related to the best and highest interests of the country.

GROVER CLEVELAND.

EXECUTIVE MANSION, *February 16, 1887.*

To the House of Representatives:

I return without my approval House bill No. 10203, entitled "An act to enable the Commissioner of Agriculture to make a special distribution of seeds in the drought-stricken counties of Texas, and making an appropriation therefor."

It is represented that a long-continued and extensive drought has existed in certain portions of the State of Texas, resulting in a failure of crops and consequent distress and destitution.

Though there has been some difference in statements concerning the extent of the people's needs in the localities thus affected, there seems to be no doubt that there has existed a condition calling for relief; and I am willing to believe that, notwithstanding the aid already furnished, a donation of seed grain to the farmers located in this region, to enable them to put in new crops, would serve to avert a continuance or return of an unfortunate blight.

And yet I feel obliged to withhold my approval of the plan, as proposed by this bill, to indulge a benevolent and charitable sentiment through the appropriation of public funds for that purpose.

I can find no warrant for such an appropriation in the Constitution, and I do not believe that the power and duty of the General Government ought to be extended to the relief of individual suffering which is in no manner properly related to the public service or benefit. A prevalent tendency to disregard the limited mission of this power and duty should, I think, be steadfastly resisted, to the end that the lesson should be constantly enforced that though the people support the Government the Government should not support the people.

The friendliness and charity of our countrymen can always be relied upon to relieve their fellow-citizens in misfortune. This has been repeatedly and quite lately demonstrated. Federal aid in such cases encourages the expectation of paternal care on the part of the Government and weakens the sturdiness of our national character, while it prevents the indulgence among our people of that kindly sentiment and conduct which strengthens the bonds of a common brotherhood.

It is within my personal knowledge that individual aid has to some extent already been extended to the sufferers mentioned in this bill. The failure of the proposed appropriation of $10,000 additional to meet their remaining wants will not necessarily result in continued distress if the emergency is fully made known to the people of the country.

It is here suggested that the Commissioner of Agriculture is annually directed to expend a large sum of money for the purchase, propagation, and distribution of seeds and other things of this description, two-thirds of which are, upon the request of Senators, Representatives, and Delegates in Congress, supplied to them for distribution among their constituents.

The appropriation of the current year for this purpose is $100,000, and it will probably be no less in the appropriation for the ensuing year. I understand that a large quantity of grain is furnished for such distribution, and it is supposed that this free apportionment among their neighbors is a privilege which may be waived by our Senators and Representatives.

If sufficient of them should request the Commissioner of Agriculture to send their shares of the grain thus allowed them to the suffering farmers of Texas, they might be enabled to sow their crops, the constituents for whom in theory this grain is intended could well bear the temporary deprivation, and the donors would experience the satisfaction attending deeds of charity.

GROVER CLEVELAND.

EXECUTIVE MANSION, *February 19, 1887.*

To the Senate :

I herewith return without approval Senate bill No. 859, entitled "An act granting a pension to Charlotte O'Neal."

This bill proposes to grant a pension to the beneficiary therein named as the widow of Richard O'Neal, late colonel of the Twenty-sixth Regiment Indiana Volunteers.

In the report of the committee in the Senate to whom this bill was referred it is stated that the deceased soldier was the first colonel of the regiment named ; that he resigned from the Army, and was by order of the governor of Indiana put in charge of the United States camps at Indianapolis. A military order is made part of the report, announcing that the funeral of Lieutenant-Colonel Richard O'Neal will take place January 6, 1863, and reciting the fact that the deceased had charge of the camps near Indianapolis for the preceding four months.

It is distinctly alleged in the report that the beneficiary did not apply to the Pension Bureau for relief because the disease of which her husband died was incurred after his resignation.

The records of the War Department fail to show that there was a colonel of the Twenty-sixth Indiana Regiment named Richard O'Neal, but it does appear that Richard Neal was lieutenant-colonel of said regiment; that he was mustered in August 31, 1861, and resigned June 30, 1862.

If this is the officer whose widow is named in the bill, the proposition is to pension a widow of a soldier who, after a ten months' service, resigned, and who seven months after his resignation died of disease which was in no manner related to his military service.

There is besides such a discrepancy between the name given in the bill and the name of the officer who served as lieutenant-colonel in the regiment mentioned that if the merits were with the widow the bill would need further Congressional consideration.

GROVER CLEVELAND.

EXECUTIVE MANSION, *February 19, 1887.*

To the Senate:

I herewith return without approval Senate bill No. 1626, entitled "An act granting a pension to John Reed, sr."

The report of the Senate Committee on Pensions merely states that the mother of John Reed was granted a pension, commencing the 5th day of December, 1862; that she has since died, and that the proposed bill is to secure a pension to John Reed, sr., the aged and dependent father of the deceased soldier.

The records show that the beneficiary named in this bill filed an application for a pension in 1877, alleging that he was the father of John Reed, who died in the service, and that his wife, the mother of the deceased soldier, died May 10, 1872, and that he, the father, was mainly dependent upon his son for support. He filed evidence of the mother's death, and one witness alleged that he was present at her death and attended her funeral.

In 1864 Martha Reed, the mother of the soldier, filed her application for pension, in which she at first claimed to be the widow of John Reed. She afterwards, however, alleged that her husband, John Reed, abandoned his family in 1859 and had not thereafter contributed to their support, and that the soldier was her main support after such abandonment. She was allowed a pension as dependent mother, which commenced in 1862, the date of her son's death, and seems to have terminated July 22, 1884, when she died.

The claim of the father was rejected in 1883 for the reason that the mother, who had a prior right, was still living, and when his claim was again pressed in 1886 he was informed that his abandonment of his family in 1859 precluded the idea that he was entitled to a pension as being dependent upon the soldier for support.

Of course these decisions were correct in law, in equity, and in morals.

This case demonstrates the means employed in attempts to cheat the Government in applications for pensions—too often successful.

The allegation in 1877 of the man who now poses as the aged and dependent father of a dead soldier that the mother died in 1872, when at that time her claim was pending for pension largely based upon his abandonment; the affidavit of the man who testified that he saw her die in 1872; the effrontery of this unworthy father renewing his claim after the detection of his fraud and the actual death of the mother, and the allegation of the mother that she was a widow when in fact she was an abandoned wife, show the processes which enter into these claims for pensions and the boldness with which plans are sometimes concocted to rob the Government by actually trafficking in death and imposing upon the sacred sentiments of patriotism and national gratitude.

GROVER CLEVELAND.

To the Senate: EXECUTIVE MANSION, *February 21, 1887.*

I herewith return without approval Senate bill No. 2452, entitled "An act granting a pension to Rachel Ann Pierpont."

At the time this bill was introduced and passed an application for pension on behalf of the beneficiary named was pending in the Pension Bureau. This application was filed in December, 1879. Within the last few days, and on the 17th day of February, 1887, a pension was granted upon said application and a certificate issued at precisely the same rate which the bill herewith returned authorizes.

But the pension under the general laws dates from the time of filing the application in 1879, while under a special act it would date only from the time of its passage.

In the interest of the beneficiary and for her advantage the special bill is therefore disapproved.

GROVER CLEVELAND.

To the Senate: EXECUTIVE MANSION, *Washington, February 21, 1887.*

I return herewith without approval Senate bill No. 2111, entitled "An act granting a pension to Jacob Smith."

The beneficiary named in this bill filed his claim for a pension November 11, 1882. He seems upon the facts presented to be justly entitled to it, and since this bill has been in my hands the Commissioner of Pensions has reported to me that a certificate therefor would at once be issued.

Under such a certificate this disabled soldier's pension will commence November 11, 1882. Under this bill, if approved, it would date only from the time of its approval. I suppose his certificate has already been issued, and I am unwilling to jeopardize the advantages he has gained thereunder, as might be done if the bill herewith returned became a law.

GROVER CLEVELAND.

To the Senate: EXECUTIVE MANSION, *February 21, 1887.*

I herewith return without approval Senate bill No. 1768, entitled "An act granting a pension to John D. Fincher."

The beneficiary named in this bill enlisted August 6, 1862, and was discharged for disability February 24, 1863.

The surgeon's certificate of disability given at the time of the soldier's discharge recites "general debility, which will disable him from performing the duties of a soldier for a good period of time. The disease was contracted by exposure and fatigue while performing the duties of a soldier."

The claimant filed his application for pension in September, 1882, nearly twenty years after his discharge, alleging that in November, 1862, he was attacked with bilious fever, followed by chronic diarrhea and lung trouble.

In support of his application an affidavit of a comrade was filed, setting forth the fact that the claimant was taken sick, as he alleged, in the fall of 1862, and that he was sent to the hospital on that account. The affidavit further expresses the belief that the claimant still suffers from the effects of his sickness and exposure.

So far as I am informed, and so far as the committee's report discloses, this is the only proof furnished of any continuance of disability at the time of filing the application for pension, and this proof, if it may be so regarded, is the mere expression of an opinion or belief, not necessarily based upon any personal knowledge, and which might have been honestly expressed if derived from representations of the claimant himself.

In this condition of the case the claimant was examined by a surgeon in 1882, whose report seems to negative all ailments except as one may be found in the fact alleged therein that he had pneumonia in 1868, and that there might be some pleuritic adhesions, plainly inferring that if such adhesions existed they were the result of the sickness to which he refers.

In February, 1885, the claimant was again examined by a board of surgeons. This examination seems to have been very carefully and thoroughly made, and as a result of the same the board reported that there was no disability. On this ground the claim was rejected.

There is no doubt as to the sickness of the claimant during his service and his disability at the time of his discharge, but unless the report of the board of surgeons is to be impeached without apparent reason there is as little doubt of the claimant's complete recovery.

No case has been presented to me in which the evidence afforded of a continuance of disability seems so inconclusive. In these circumstances the report of the board of surgeons appears to be upon the evidence before me almost uncontradicted.

GROVER CLEVELAND.

EXECUTIVE MANSION, *February 23, 1887.*

To the House of Representatives:

I herewith return without approval House bill No. 7327, entitled "An act granting a pension to Anthony McRobertson."

The beneficiary named in this bill was badly wounded in a battle which occurred about the 17th day of November, 1863.

He applied for pension in 1874, and the same was granted in November, 1886, to date from the time of his disability, November 17, 1863.

He is now receiving the highest rate allowed under the general law for cases such as his, and he would be entitled to no more under the special act.

It could not, therefore, by any possibility be of the least benefit to him, but, on the other hand, might jeopardize his advantages already gained.

GROVER CLEVELAND.

EXECUTIVE MANSION, *February 23, 1887.*

To the House of Representatives:

I herewith return without approval House bill No. 8002, entitled "An act to increase the pension of Loren Burritt."

The beneficiary named in this bill enlisted in October, 1863, and in December of that year was mustered in as major of the Eighth Regiment United States Colored Troops; was promoted to lieutenant-colonel and very badly wounded in February, 1864, and was mustered out with his regiment November 10, 1865.

His condition at the present time is most pitiable, and his helplessness is such that he needs the constant care and assistance of others. He was obliged to give up business about the year 1873.

In 1866 he was pensioned for his wound, which was in the right leg; and such pension has been increased from time to time until he is now in the receipt of $72 per month, the highest pension allowed under general laws. This rate was awarded him under a law passed in 1880, increasing from $50 to $72 per month the pensions of those who were rendered permanently and totally helpless, so that they required the regular and personal attendance of another.

On the 30th day of June, 1886, there were 1,009 persons on the rolls receiving this rate of pension.

This bill was reported upon adversely by the House Committee on Pensions, and they, while fully acknowledging the distressing circumstances surrounding the case, felt constrained to adverse action on the ground, as stated in the language of their report, that "there are many cases just as helpless and requiring as much attention as this one, and were the relief asked for granted in this instance it might reasonably be looked for in all."

No man can check, if he would, the feeling of sympathy and pity aroused by the contemplation of utter helplessness as the result of patriotic and faithful military service; but in the midst of all this I can not put out of mind the soldiers in this condition who were privates in the ranks, who sustained the utmost hardships of war, but who, because they were privates and in the humble walks of life, are not so apt to share in special favors of Congressional action. I find no reason why this beneficiary should be singled out from his class, except it be that he was a lieutenant-colonel instead of a private.

I am aware of a precedent for the legislation proposed, which is furnished by an enactment of the last session of Congress, to which I assented, as I think improvidently; but I am certain that exact equality and fairness in the treatment of our veterans is, after all, more just, beneficent, and useful than unfair discrimination in favor of officers or the special benefit born of sympathy in individual cases.

I am constrained, therefore, to agree with the House Committee on Pensions in their views of this bill.

GROVER CLEVELAND.

EXECUTIVE MANSION, *February 23, 1887.*

To the House of Representatives:

I herewith return without approval House bill No. 10082, entitled "An act to increase the pension of Margaret R. Jones."

The beneficiary mentioned in this bill is now receiving the highest rate of pension allowed in cases such as hers under the general law.

All the information which is available to me fails to furnish any reason why this pension should be specially increased, except the general statement in the claimant's petition that she is in necessitous circumstances and that the rate now allowed her is insufficient for her support.

The further statement in the petition that her husband's death "was caused prematurely by his endeavor to comply with unusual, disrespectful, and indefinite orders" to go to League Island Navy-Yard certainly does not in all its bearings furnish conclusive proof that his widow's pension should be increased beyond that furnished others in her situation.

GROVER CLEVELAND.

EXECUTIVE MANSION, *February 23, 1887.*

To the House of Representatives:

I return without approval House bill No. 5877, entitled "An act for the relief of William H. Morhiser."

This beneficiary, though apparently not regularly enlisted in the military service of the country during the time covered by this bill for his relief, performed military duty, was captured and imprisoned. No technicality should be interposed in considering this bill to prevent the receipt by him of the same pay and allowances awarded under like circumstances to soldiers regularly enlisted.

But this bill proposes to appropriate for the benefit of this claimant such sum as pay and allowances as would be allowed a private of cavalry from November 30, 1863, to January 1, 1865. It appears from the records of the War Department that he has already been paid for at least two months of that time.

The bill also provides that there shall also be allowed to the claimant such additional pay and allowances, as commutation of rations and so forth, as were allowed prisoners of war, from July 30, 1864, to January 1, 1865. The records disclose the fact that he has been allowed commutation of rations from July 30, 1864, to December 11, 1864.

As the purpose of this bill, as gathered from the report of the committee to whom it was referred, appears to be to secure for the claimant therein named compensation "at the rate at which other soldiers in the same situation were paid," and as he seems already to have received a considerable part of the compensation provided for in the bill, I am led to suppose that a mistake has been made in framing the same.

GROVER CLEVELAND.

EXECUTIVE MANSION, *February 24, 1887.*

To the House of Representatives:

I herewith return without approval House bill No. 7648, entitled "An act for the relief of the estate of the late John How, Indian agent, and his sureties."

John How was appointed Indian agent in July, 1878, and upon such appointment gave a bond to the Government in the penal sum of $10,000 conditioned for the faithful performance of his duties as such agent and to protect the Government from loss by mismanagement or malfeasance in his official conduct. The parties named in the bill were his sureties on said bond.

On the 23d day of December, 1881, upon a report of inspectors connected with the Indian Bureau suggesting frauds and mismanagement in the conduct of this agency, Mr. How was suspended from his office, which suspension was approved by the President in January, 1882.

After such suspension the accounts of the agent were examined and various explanations offered by him in relation thereto. It is stated, however, in a report from the Indian Office now before me, that such explanations were deemed by that office sufficient to remove only a small part of the items in the accounts which were questioned. The matter was thereupon referred to the Treasury Department for further examination and adjustment.

The Second Comptroller reports that the final settlement of this agent's accounts was pending before the accounting officers for upward of eighteen months, affording ample opportunity for any explanation which might be deemed necessary and proper, and that on the 21st day of July, 1885, a final adjustment was made of the said accounts, by which a sum very much in excess of the penalty of his bond was found due from said agent to the Government.

A suit was afterwards instituted against the agent and his sureties to recover the amount thus found due, so far as the bond covered the same. This suit is still pending.

The object of the bill now under consideration is to wholly release and discharge these sureties from any liability upon said bond.

It seems to be the opinion of all the officers of the Government who have examined the matter at all that a debt exists in favor of the Government upon this bond. It is reported that a large amount of evidence has been taken, and that in the opinion of these officers the amount due the Government can not be reduced to a less amount than the penalty of the bond.

The Second Comptroller states, as results of examinations made in his office and by the Second Auditor, that it appears that many of the vouchers presented by the agent were fictitious, the persons in whose names they were given testifying that services and supplies therein mentioned were never rendered or furnished; that in other cases parties denied the genuineness of vouchers purporting to be made by them; that a large voucher apparently given for cattle was actually given for money loaned, and that supplies bought with Government funds were appropriated for the agent's personal benefit.

I do not suppose that it was intended by the Congress to entirely relieve these sureties if a condition exists such as is above set out, which results in an indebtedness to the Government. The proposed legislation, judging from the report of the House Committee on Claims, seems rather to proceed upon the theory that no sum is due the Government in the premises.

I think it will hardly be claimed that the patient investigation of the accounting officers should be lightly discredited in this case; and it seems to me that justness to the Government and fairness to the sureties seeking relief will presumably be secured by the further prosecution of the suit already instituted, in which the truth of all matters involved can be thoroughly tested.

GROVER CLEVELAND.

EXECUTIVE MANSION, *February 25, 1887.*

To the Senate:

I herewith return without approval Senate bill No. 1162, entitled "An act for the erection of a post-office building at Lynn, Mass."

The title of this bill sufficiently indicates its purpose.

Congressional action in its favor appears to be based, as usual in such cases, upon representations concerning the population of the town in which it is proposed to erect the building, and the increase in such population, the number of railroad trains arriving and departing daily, and various other items calculated to demonstrate the importance of the city selected for Federal decoration.

These statements are supplemented by a report from the postmaster setting forth that his postal receipts are increasing, giving the number of square feet now occupied by his office, the amount of rent paid, and the number of his employees.

This bill, unlike others of its class which seek to provide a place for a number of Federal offices, simply authorizes the construction of a building for the accommodation of the post-office alone.

The report of the postmaster differs also in this case from those which are usually furnished, inasmuch as it is therein distinctly stated that the space now furnished for his office is sufficient for its present operations. He adds, however, that from present indications there will be a large increase in the business of the office during the next ten years.

It is quite apparent that there is no necessity for the expenditure of $100,000, the amount limited in this bill, or any other sum, for the construction of the proposed building to meet the wants of the Government, and for this reason I am constrained to disapprove the proposed legislation.

GROVER CLEVELAND.

To the Senate: EXECUTIVE MANSION, *February 26, 1887.*

I herewith return without approval Senate bill No. 2045, entitled "An act granting a pension to Mrs. Sarah Hamilton."

Thomas Hamilton, the husband of the beneficiary named in this bill, enlisted September 2, 1862. Upon the records he is reported present to April 30, 1863; deserted May 27, 1863. His name is dropped from subsequent rolls to February 29, 1864, when he is reported as a deserter in arrest. He is not borne upon the rolls for March and April, 1864; for May and June, 1864, he is reported absent in arrest; for July and August, present under arrest; and for September and October, present for duty. He was mustered out with his company May 24, 1865.

He applied for a pension in 1872, alleging that he received an injury to his left leg about February 15, 1863, at St. Louis, by falling from a ladder, causing varicose veins and stiffening of the leg.

He was granted a pension January 29, 1881, to commence May 25, 1865.

He subsequently applied for an increase of pension, claiming that his eyes had become affected as a result of his varicose veins. This application was rejected upon the ground that the disability for which he was pensioned had not increased and that the disease of his eyes was not a result of such disability.

The pensioner died April 22, 1883, twenty years after his alleged injury, of cerebral apoplexy; and a physician states it as his judgment that the varicosed condition of the venous system was primarily the cause of his disabilities and death.

His widow filed an application for pension October 31, 1883, which was rejected upon the ground that the soldier's death was not the result of his military service.

Notwithstanding the record of the deceased soldier, stained as it is with the charge of desertion, and the entire absence of any record proof of sickness and injury, I should consider myself, in favor of his widow, bound by the act of the Pension Bureau in allowing him a pension, and should cheerfully aid her attempt to procure a pension for herself in her needy condition, if I was not thoroughly convinced that her husband's death had no relation to his military service or any injury for which he was pensioned.

To the ordinary mind it seems impossible that apoplexy could result from such a varicosed condition as is described in this case. I do not understand that the physician who gives a contrary opinion bases his judgment upon actual observation at the time the soldier died. The last medical examination by the Pension Bureau before the soldier's death was in October, 1882, and resulted in the following report of the examining surgeon:

Weight, 180 pounds; age, 69 years; has varicose veins of left leg, but not to such an extent as to increase the size of the leg or result in marked disability; he is entirely blind in both eyes from glaucoma, which does not in any degree, in my opinion, depend upon the pensioned disability—varicose veins.

It appears that the benefit proposed by this bill can neither be properly regarded as a gratuity, based upon the honorable service and record of the soldier, nor predicated on his death resulting from a disability incurred in such service. GROVER CLEVELAND.

EXECUTIVE MANSION, *February 26, 1887.*
To the Senate:

I herewith return without approval Senate bill No. 2210, entitled "An act granting a pension to Anna Wright."

The beneficiary named in this bill was granted a pension on the 17th day of November, 1886, dating from May 25, 1863, and is now under the general law receiving precisely the pension which she would receive under the bill herewith returned if the same should be approved.

GROVER CLEVELAND.

EXECUTIVE MANSION,
Washington, February 26, 1887.
To the House of Representatives:

I herewith return without approval House bill No. 6976, entitled "An act to erect a public building at Portsmouth, Ohio."

It is represented in support of this bill that Portsmouth by its last census had a population of 11,321, and that it contains at present not less than 15,000 inhabitants; that it is a place of considerable manufacturing and commercial importance, and that there is no public building for the transaction of the business of the General Government nearer than Columbus or Cincinnati, both about 100 miles distant.

It is further stated in a communication from the promoter of this bill that—

There is not a Federal public building in the State of Ohio east of the line drawn on the accompanying map from Cleveland through Columbus to Cincinnati; and when wealth and population and the needs of the public service are considered, the distribution of public buildings in the State is an unfair one.

Here is disclosed a theory of expenditure for public buildings which I can hardly think should be adopted. If an application for the erection of such a building is to be determined by the distance between its proposed location and another public building, or upon the allegation that a certain division of a State is without a Government building, or that the distribution of these buildings in a particular State is unfair, we shall rapidly be led to an entire disregard of the considerations of necessity and public need which it seems to me should alone justify the expenditure of public funds for such a purpose.

The care and protection which the Government owes to the people do not embrace the grant of public buildings to decorate thriving and prosperous cities and villages, nor should such buildings be erected upon any principle of fair distribution among localities.

The Government is not an almoner of gifts among the people, but an instrumentality by which the people's affairs should be conducted upon business principles, regulated by the public needs.

Applying these principles to the case embraced in the bill under consideration, we find that at Portsmouth there is a post-office and an internal-revenue collector's office for which the Government should provide.

It is represented that the quarters now furnished for these offices are inadequate and that more spacious rooms are desirable. In the post-office there are six employees, and the collector of internal revenue has five assistants. The annual rent paid for both these offices is $600.

Upon these facts the proposition is to expend $60,000 for a building to accommodate these offices, entailing after its completion quite a large sum annually for its care and superintendence.

Though the sum of $60,000 is the limit fixed for the cost of this building, if it should be completed for this sum it would be an exception to the rule in such cases; and if it is absolutely impossible to do the public business in the quarters now occupied by these offices, which does not appear to be claimed, there can be no difficulty in securing in this enterprising city adequate accommodations at a rent not largely in excess of that at present paid.

Upon the whole it does not appear, as a business proposition, that the building proposed should be undertaken.

GROVER CLEVELAND.

EXECUTIVE MANSION,
Washington, February 28, 1887.

To the Senate:

I herewith return without approval Senate bill No. 531, entitled "An act to provide for the erection of a public building at Lafayette, Ind."

This bill appropriates $50,000 for the purpose indicated in its title.

It is represented that a deputy internal-revenue collector is located at Lafayette, but no information is furnished that he has an office there which is or ought to be furnished by the Government. It is not claimed that the Federal business at this point requires other accommodation except for the post-office located there.

As usual in such cases, the postmaster reports, in reply to inquiries, that his present quarters are inadequate, and, as usual, it appears that the postal business is increasing. The rent paid for the rooms or building in which the post-office is kept is $1,100 per annum.

I have been informed since this bill has been in my hands that last spring a building was erected at Lafayette with special reference to its use for the post-office, and that a part of it was leased by the Government for that purpose for the term of five years. Upon the faith of such lease the premises thus rented were fitted up and furnished by the owner of the building in a manner especially adapted to postal uses, and an account of such fitting up and furnishing is before me, showing the expense of the same to have been more than $2,500.

In view of such new and recent arrangements made by the Government for the transaction of its postal business at this place, it seems that the proposed expenditure for the erection of a building for that purpose is hardly necessary or justifiable. GROVER CLEVELAND.

PROCLAMATIONS.

BY THE PRESIDENT OF THE UNITED STATES OF AMERICA.
A PROCLAMATION.

Whereas satisfactory proof has been given to me by the Government of the Netherlands that no light-house and light dues, tonnage dues, or beacon and buoy dues are imposed in the ports of the Kingdom of the Netherlands; that no other equivalent tax of any kind is imposed upon vessels in said ports, under whatever flag they may sail; that vessels belonging to the United States of America and their cargoes are not required in the Netherlands to pay any fee or due of any kind or nature, or any import due higher or other than is payable by vessels of the Netherlands or their cargoes; that no export duties are imposed in the Netherlands: and that in the free ports of the Dutch East Indies, to wit, Riouw (in the island of Riouw), Pabean, Sangrit, Loloan, and

Tamboekoes (in the island of Bali), Koepang (in the island of Timor), Makassar, Menado, Kema, and Gorontalo (in the island of Celebes), Amboina, Saparoa, Banda, Ternate, and Kajeli (in the Moluccas), Olehleh and Bengkalis (in the island of Sumatra), vessels are subjected to no fiscal tax, and no import or export duties are there levied:

Now, therefore, I, Grover Cleveland, President of the United States of America, by virtue of the authority vested in me by section 11 of the act of Congress entitled "An act to abolish certain fees for official services to American vessels, and to amend the laws relating to shipping commissioners, seamen, and owners of vessels, and for other purposes," approved June 19, 1886, do hereby declare and proclaim that from and after the date of this my proclamation shall be suspended the collection of the whole of the duty of 6 cents per ton, not to exceed 30 cents per ton per annum (which is imposed by said section of said act), upon vessels entered in the ports of the United States from any of the ports of the Kingdom of the Netherlands in Europe, or from any of the above-named free ports of the Dutch East Indies.

Provided, That there shall be excluded from the benefits of the suspension hereby declared and proclaimed the vessels of any foreign country in whose ports the fees or dues of any kind or nature imposed on vessels of the United States, or the import or export duties on their cargoes, are in excess of the fees, dues, or duties imposed on the vessels of such foreign country or their cargoes, or of the fees, dues, or duties imposed on the vessels of the country in which are the ports mentioned in this proclamation, or the cargoes of such vessels.

And the suspension hereby declared and proclaimed shall continue so long as the reciprocal exemption of vessels belonging to citizens of the United States and their cargoes shall be continued in the said ports of the Kingdom of the Netherlands in Europe and the said free ports of the Dutch East Indies, and no longer.

In witness whereof I have hereunto set my hand and caused the seal of the United States to be affixed.

[SEAL.]   Done at the city of Washington, this 22d day of April, A. D. 1887, and of the Independence of the United States the one hundred and eleventh.

GROVER CLEVELAND.

By the President:
   T. F. BAYARD, *Secretary of State*.

BY THE PRESIDENT OF THE UNITED STATES OF AMERICA.
A PROCLAMATION.

Whereas satisfactory proof has been given to me by the Government of Spain that no discriminating duties of tonnage or imposts are imposed or levied in the islands of Cuba, Puerto Rico, and the Philippines, and all countries belonging to the Crown of Spain, upon vessels wholly belonging to citizens of the United States, or upon the produce, manufactures, or merchandise imported in the same from the United States or from any foreign country; and

Whereas notification of such abolition of discriminating duties of tonnage and imposts as aforesaid has been given to me by a memorandum of agreement signed this day at the city of Washington between the Secretary of State of the United States and the envoy extraordinary and minister plenipotentiary of Her Majesty the Queen Regent of Spain accredited to the Government of the United States of America:

Now, therefore, I, Grover Cleveland, President of the United States of America, by virtue of the authority vested in me by section 4228 of the Revised Statutes of the United States, do hereby declare and proclaim that from and after the date of this my proclamation, being also the date of the notification received as aforesaid, the foreign discriminating duties of tonnage and imposts within the United States are suspended and discontinued so far as respects the vessels of Spain and the produce, manufactures, or merchandise imported in said vessels into the United States from the islands of Cuba and Puerto Rico, the Philippines, and all other countries belonging to the Crown of Spain, or from any other foreign country; such suspension to continue so long as the reciprocal exemption of vessels belonging to citizens of the United States and their cargoes shall be continued in the said islands of Cuba and Puerto Rico, and the Philippines, and all other Spanish possessions, and no longer.

In witness whereof I have hereunto set my hand and caused the seal of the United States to be affixed.

[SEAL.] Done at the city of Washington this 21st day of September, A. D. 1887, and of the Independence of the United States the one hundred and twelfth.

GROVER CLEVELAND.

By the President:

T. F. BAYARD, *Secretary of State.*

A PROCLAMATION

BY THE PRESIDENT OF THE UNITED STATES.

The goodness and the mercy of God, which have followed the American people during all the days of the past year, claim their grateful recognition and humble acknowledgment. By His omnipotent power He has protected us from war and pestilence and from every national calamity; by His gracious favor the earth has yielded a generous return to the labor of the husbandman, and every path of honest toil has led to comfort and contentment; by His loving kindness the hearts of our people have been replenished with fraternal sentiment and patriotic endeavor, and by His unerring guidance we have been directed in the way of national prosperity.

To the end that we may with one accord testify our gratitude for all these blessings, I, Grover Cleveland, President of the United States, do hereby designate and set apart Thursday, the 24th day of November next, as a day of thanksgiving and prayer, to be observed by all the people of the land.

On that day let all secular work and employment be suspended, and let our people assemble in their accustomed places of worship and with prayer and songs of praise give thanks to our Heavenly Father for all that He has done for us, while we humbly implore the forgiveness of our sins and a continuance of His mercy.

Let families and kindred be reunited on that day, and let their hearts, filled with kindly cheer and affectionate reminiscence, be turned in thankfulness to the source of all their pleasures and the giver of all that makes the day glad and joyous.

And in the midst of our worship and our happiness let us remember the poor, the needy, and the unfortunate, and by our gifts of charity and ready benevolence let us increase the number of those who with grateful hearts shall join in our thanksgiving.

In witness whereof I have set my hand and caused the seal of the United States to be hereunto affixed.

[SEAL.]   Done at the city of Washington, this 25th day of October, A. D. 1887, and of the Independence of the United States the one hundred and twelfth.

By the President.   GROVER CLEVELAND.

T. F. BAYARD, *Secretary of State.*

EXECUTIVE ORDERS.

JANUARY 4, 1887.

In the exercise of the power vested in the President by the Constitution, and by virtue of the seventeen hundred and fifty-third section of the Revised Statutes and of the civil-service act approved January 16, 1883, the following regulations governing promotions in the customs service at the city of New York are hereby approved and promulgated:

REGULATION I.

The board of examiners at the New York customs district may at any time, with the approval of the Civil Service Commission, order an examination for promotion, and at least five days before the examination is to take place shall cause a notice to be posted conspicuously in the office for which such examination is to be held, and shall state in said notice the class or classes to test fitness for promotion to which the examination is to be held and the time and place of examination. Promotions shall be from class to class, and the examination of persons in one class shall be to test their fitness for promotion to the next higher class: *Provided, however,* That if in any examination for promotion the competitors in the next lower class shall not exceed three in number, the board may, at its discretion, open the competition to one or more of the classes below the class in which there are not more than three competitors. All persons in the class immediately below the class for which promotions are to be made, and who have been in said class at least six months, must be examined for promotion.

REGULATION 2.

The examination must be held upon such subjects as in the opinion of the board of examiners, with the approval of the Commission, the general nature of the business of the office and the special nature of the positions to be filled may require. In grading the competitors due weight must be given to the efficiency with which the several competitors shall have performed their duties in the office; but none who shall fail to attain a minimum standard of 75 per cent in the written examination shall be certified for promotion.

REGULATION 3.

The whole list of eligibles from which the promotion is to be made shall be certified to the nominating officer.

REGULATION 4.

Any person employed in any of the offices to which these regulations apply may be transferred without examination, after service of six months consecutively since January 16, 1883, from one office to a class no higher in another office, upon certification by the board of examiners that he has passed an examination for the class in which he is doing duty, and with the consent of the heads of the respective offices and the approval of the Secretary of the Treasury.

REGULATION 5.

The Civil Service Commission may at any time amend these regulations or substitute other regulations therefor.

The foregoing regulations are adopted and approved.

GROVER CLEVELAND.

In the exercise of the power vested in the President by the Constitution, and by virtue of the seventeen hundred and fifty-third section of the Revised Statutes and of the civil-service act approved January 16, 1883, the following rule for the regulation and improvement of the executive civil service is hereby amended and promulgated, as follows:

RULE IV.

1. The Civil Service Commission shall have authority to appoint the following-named boards of civil-service examiners:

The central board.—This board shall be composed of seven members, who shall be detailed from the Departments in which they may be serving at the time of appointment for continuous service at the office of the Civil Service Commission. Under the supervision of the Commission, the central board shall examine and mark the papers of all examinations for entrance to the departmental service, and also such of the papers of examinations for entrance to either the customs or the postal service as shall be submitted to it by the Commission. The Commission shall have authority to require any customs or postal board to send the papers of any examination conducted by said board to be examined and marked by the central board. The persons composing this board shall be in the departmental service.

Special boards.—These boards shall mark the papers of special examinations for the classified departmental service, and shall be composed of persons in the public service.

Supplementary boards.—These boards shall mark the papers of supplementary examinations for the classified departmental service, and shall be composed of persons in the public service.

Local departmental boards.—These boards shall be organized at one or more places in each State and Territory where examinations for the departmental service are to be held, and shall each be composed of persons in the public service residing in the State or Territory in which the board is to act.

Customs boards.—One for each classified customs district, to be composed of persons in the customs service in the district for which the board is to act. These boards shall conduct examinations for entrance to and promotion in the classified customs service.

Postal boards.—One for each classified post-office, to be composed of persons in the postal service at the post-office for which said board is to act. These boards shall conduct examinations for entrance to and promotions in the postal service.

2. No person shall be appointed a member of any board of examiners named herein until after consultation by the Civil Service Commission with the head of the Department or office in which the person whom it desires to appoint is serving.

3. It shall be the duty of the head of any classified customs office or classified post-office to promptly inform the Civil Service Commission, in writing, of the removal or resignation from the public service, or of the death, of any member of a board of examiners appointed from his office; and upon request of the Commission such officer shall state to the Commission which of the persons employed in his office he regards as most competent to fill the vacancy thus occasioned, or any vacancy which may otherwise occur; and in making this statement the officer shall mention generally the qualifications of each of the persons named therein by him.

4. The duties of a member of a special, supplementary, local, departmental, customs, or postal board of examiners shall be regarded as a part of the public duties of such examiner, and each examiner shall be allowed time during office hours to perform the duties required of him.

5. The Civil Service Commission shall have authority to adopt regulations which shall (1) prescribe the manner of organizing the several boards of civil-service examiners herein named, (2) more particularly state the powers of each of said boards, and (3) specifically define the duties of the members thereof.

6. The Civil Service Commission shall have authority to change at any time the membership of any of the above-named boards of civil-service examiners.

Approved, January 15, 1887.
GROVER CLEVELAND.

REGULATIONS FOR THE DISTRIBUTION OF ARMS, ORDNANCE STORES, QUARTERMASTER'S STORES, AND CAMP EQUIPAGE TO THE TERRITORIES AND THE DISTRICT OF COLUMBIA, PRESCRIBED BY THE PRESIDENT OF THE UNITED STATES IN CONFORMITY WITH THE SECOND SECTION OF THE ACT ENTITLED "AN ACT TO AMEND SECTION 1661, REVISED STATUTES, MAKING AN ANNUAL APPROPRIATION TO PROVIDE ARMS AND EQUIPMENTS FOR THE MILITIA."

EXECUTIVE MANSION, *April 22, 1887.*

1. Each Territory shall, if included within the provisions of said act, annually receive arms, ordnance stores, quartermaster's stores, and camp equipage equivalent to the quota of a State having the least representation in Congress, and the District of Columbia shall annually receive

arms, ordnance stores, quartermaster's stores, and camp equipage not exceeding double the quota of a State having the least representation in Congress.

2. Arms, ordnance stores, quartermaster's stores, and camp equipage shall be issued to the Territories on requisitions of the governors thereof and to the District of Columbia on requisitions approved by the senior general of the District Militia present for duty. Returns shall be made annually by the senior general of the District Militia in the manner as required by sections 3 and 4 of the act above referred to in the case of States and Territories.

3. It is forbidden to make issues to States and Territories in excess of the amount to their credit under the provisions of section 1161, Revised Statutes, as amended by the above act.

4. The regulations established by President Pierce April 30, 1855, under the act approved March 30, 1855, are hereby revoked.

GROVER CLEVELAND.

In the exercise of the power vested in the President by the Constitution, and by virtue of the seventeen hundred and fifty-third section of the Revised Statutes and of the civil-service act approved January 16, 1883, Rules IV, VI, XIX, XXI of the rules for the regulation and improvement of the executive civil service are hereby amended and promulgated as follows:

RULE IV.

1. The Commission may appoint boards of examiners as follows:

The central board.—A board composed of seven members, who shall be detailed from the Departments in which they are serving when appointed for continuous service at the office of the Commission. This board shall mark such papers of examinations for admission to the departmental, customs, and postal services as the Commission may direct.

Departmental special boards.—These boards shall mark such papers of special examinations for the departmental service as the Commission may direct, and shall be composed of persons in the public service.

Departmental supplementary boards.—These boards shall mark the papers of such supplementary examinations for the departmental service as the Commission may direct, and shall be composed of persons in the public service.

Departmental promotion boards.—One for each of the Executive Departments, of three members, and one auxiliary member for each bureau of the Department for which the board is to act.

Departmental local boards.—These boards shall be organized at one or more places in each State and Territory where examinations for the departmental service are to be held, and shall each be composed of persons in the public service residing in the State or Territory in which the board is to act.

Customs boards.—One for each classified customs district, to be composed of persons in the customs service in the district for which said board is to act. These boards shall conduct examinations for entrance to and promotions in the classified customs service, and shall mark such of the examination papers for that service as the Commission shall direct. They shall also conduct such departmental examinations as the Commission may direct.

Postal boards.—One for each classified post-office, to be composed of persons in the postal service at the post-office in which said board is to act. These boards shall conduct examinations for entrance to and promotions in the postal service, and shall mark such of the examination papers for that service as the Commission may direct. They shall also conduct such departmental examinations as the Commission may direct.

2. No person shall be appointed an examiner until after consultation by the Commission with the head of the Department or office in which the person whom it desires to appoint is serving.

3. It shall be the duty of the head of any classified customs office or post-office to promptly give written information to the Commission of the removal or resignation from the public service, or of the inability or refusal to act, of any examiner in his office; and on request of the Commission such officer shall state which of the persons in his office he regards as most competent to fill the vacancy, and shall mention generally the qualifications of each person named by him.

4. The duties of an examiner shall be regarded as a part of his public duties, and each examiner shall be allowed time during office hours to perform the duties required of him.

5. The Commission may adopt regulations which shall prescribe (1) the manner of organizing the boards of examiners, (2) the powers of each board, and (3) the duties of the members thereof.

6. The Commission may create additional boards of examiners and may change the membership of any board; and boards of examiners shall perform such other appropriate duties as the Commission may impose upon them.

RULE VI.

1. There shall be open competitive examinations for testing the fitness of applicants for admission to the service. Such examinations shall be practical in their character, and so far as may be shall relate to those matters which will fairly test the relative capacity and fitness of the persons examined to discharge the duties of the branch of the service which they seek to enter.

2. And for the purpose of establishing in the classified service the principle of compulsory competitive examination for promotion there shall be, so far as practicable and useful, such examinations of a suitable character to test the fitness of persons for promotion in the service, and the Commission may make regulations applying them to any classified Department, customs office, or post-office, under which regulations examinations for promotion shall be conducted and all promotions made; but until regulations made by the Commission in accordance herewith have been applied to a classified Department, customs office, or post-office, promotions therein may be made upon any test of fitness determined upon by the promoting officer. And in any classified Department, customs office, or post-office in which promotions are made under examinations as herein provided the Commission may, in special session, if the exigencies of the service require such action, provide noncompetitive examinations for promotion.

RULE XIX.

There are excepted from examination the following: (1) The confidential clerk or secretary of any head of a Department or office; (2) cashiers of collectors; (3) cashiers of postmasters; (4) superintendents of money-order divisions in post-offices; (5) the direct custodians of money for whose fidelity another officer is under official bond, and disbursing officers having the custody of money, who give bonds; but these exceptions shall not extend to any official below the grade of assistant cashier or teller; (6) persons employed exclusively in the secret service of the Government, or as translators or interpreters or stenographers; (7) persons whose employment is exclusively professional, but medical examiners are not included among such persons; (8) chief clerks, deputy collectors, deputy naval officers, deputy surveyors of customs, and superintendents or chiefs of divisions or bureaus. But no person so excepted shall be either transferred, appointed, or promoted, unless to some excepted place, without an examination under the Commission, which examination shall not take place within six months after entering the service.

RULE XXI.

1. No person, unless excepted under Rule XIX, shall be admitted into the classified civil service from any place not within said service without an examination and certification under the rules, with this exception, that any person who shall have been an officer for one year or more last preceding in any Department or office in a grade above the classified service thereof may be transferred or appointed to any place in the service of the same without examination.

2. No person who has passed only a limited examination under clause 4 of Rule VII for the lower classes or grades in the departmental or customs service shall be appointed or be promoted within two years after appointment to any position giving a salary of $1,000 or upward without first passing an examination under clause 1 of said rule; and such examination shall not be allowed within the first year after appointment.

3. But a person who has passed the examination under said clause 1 and has accepted a position giving a salary of $900 or less shall have the same right of promotion as if originally appointed to a position giving a salary of $1,000 or more.

4. The Commission may at any time certify for a $900 or any lower place in the classified service any person upon the register who has passed the examination under clause 1 of Rule VII, if such person does not object before such certification is made.

5. The provisions of this rule relating to promotions shall cease to be operative in any classified Department, customs office, or post-office when regulations for promotions have been applied thereto by the Commission under the authority conferred by clause 2 of Rule VI.

Approved, May 5, 1887. GROVER CLEVELAND.

EXECUTIVE MANSION,
Washington, May 9, 1887.

The executive offices and Departments at the seat of Government, including the public printing establishment, will be closed at noon on Thursday, the 12th instant, to enable persons employed therein to attend the exercises at the unveiling of the statue of the late President Garfield.

And employees in such offices and Departments who desire to accompany any organization to which they belong in the parade or other exercises preceding on that day the unveiling ceremonies may, by permission of the heads of their respective offices or Departments, also be granted such leave of absence as may be necessary for that purpose.

Members of the Society of the Army of the Cumberland desiring to attend any meeting of such society on Wednesday, the 11th instant, may, by special permission of the respective heads of Departments and offices, be excused from duty during the hours on that day as said meetings may be held. GROVER CLEVELAND.

WAR DEPARTMENT, ADJUTANT-GENERAL'S OFFICE,
Washington, April 30, 1887.

Hon. WILLIAM C. ENDICOTT,
        Secretary of War.

SIR: I have the honor to state that there are now in this office, stored in one of the attic rooms of the building, a number of Union flags captured in action, but recovered on the fall of the Confederacy and forwarded to the War Department for safe-keeping, together with a number of Confederate flags which the fortunes of war placed in our hands during the late Civil War.

While in the past favorable action has been taken on applications properly supported for the return of Union flags to organizations representing survivors of the military regiments in the service of the Government, I beg to submit that it would be a graceful act to anticipate future requests of this nature, and venture to suggest the propriety of returning all the flags (Union and Confederate) to the authorities of the respective States in which the regiments which bore these colors were organized, for such final disposition as they may determine.

While in all the civilized nations of the world trophies taken in war against foreign enemies have been carefully preserved and exhibited as proud mementos of the nation's military glories, wise and obvious reasons have always excepted from the rule evidences of past internecine troubles which by appeals to the arbitrament of the sword have disturbed the peaceful march of a people to its destiny.

Over twenty years have elapsed since the termination of the late Civil War. Many of the prominent leaders, civil and military, of the late Confederate States are now honored representatives of the people in the national councils, or in other eminent positions lend the aid of their talents to the wise administration of affairs of the whole country; and the people of the several States composing the Union are now united, treading the broader road to a glorious future.

Impressed with these views, I have the honor to submit the suggestion made in this letter for the careful consideration it will receive at your hands.

        Very truly, yours,

                                R. C. DRUM,
                                        Adjutant-General.

                        [Indorsement.]

                                WAR DEPARTMENT, *May 26, 1887.*

The within recommendation approved by the President, and the Adjutant-General will prepare letters to governors of those States whose troops carried the colors and flags now in this Department, with the offer to return them as herein proposed. The history of each flag and the circumstances of its capture or recapture should be given.

                                WILLIAM C. ENDICOTT,
                                        Secretary of War.

                WAR DEPARTMENT, ADJUTANT-GENERAL'S OFFICE,
                                Washington, June 7, 1887.

Honorable GOVERNOR OF ——.

SIR: The President of the United States having approved the recommendation that all the flags in the custody of the War Department be returned to the authorities of the respective States in which the regiments which bore them were organized, for such final disposition as they may determine, I am instructed by the honorable Secretary of War to make you, in the name of the War Department, a tender of the flags now in this office belonging to the late volunteer organizations of the State of ——.

In discharging this pleasant duty I beg you will please advise me of your wishes in this matter. It is the intention in returning each flag to give its history as far as it is possible to do so, stating the circumstances of its capture and recovery.

I have the honor to be, very respectfully, your obedient servant,

R. C. DRUM, *Adjutant-General.*

EXECUTIVE MANSION,
Washington, June 16, 1887.

The SECRETARY OF WAR:

I have to-day considered with more care than when the subject was orally presented me the action of your Department directing letters to be addressed to the governors of all the States offering to return, if desired, to the loyal States the Union flags captured in the War of the Rebellion by the Confederate forces and afterwards recovered by Government troops, and to the Confederate States the flags captured by the Union forces, all of which for many years have been packed in boxes and stored in the cellar and attic of the War Department.

I am of the opinion that the return of these flags in the manner thus contemplated is not authorized by existing law nor justified as an executive act.

I request, therefore, that no further steps be taken in the matter except to examine and inventory these flags and adopt proper measures for their preservation. Any direction as to the final disposition of them should originate with Congress.

Yours, truly, GROVER CLEVELAND.

WAR DEPARTMENT, ADJUTANT-GENERAL'S OFFICE,
Washington, June —, 1887.

Hon. —— ——,
Governor of ——.

SIR: Referring to the letter from this office dated June —, 1887, on the subject of the return to the respective States of the flags now in the custody of the War Department, I am instructed by the Secretary of War to inform you of the withdrawal of the offer made therein, as on a more careful consideration of the legal points involved in the proposed action the President of the United States is of the opinion that the return of these flags is not authorized by existing law nor justified as an executive act, and that any direction as to their final disposition should originate with Congress.

I have the honor to be, very respectfully, your obedient servant,

—— ——, *Adjutant-General.*

EXECUTIVE MANSION,
Washington, August 25, 1887.

It appearing to me that the promoters of the International Military Encampment to be held in Chicago in October proximo, in commemoration of the fiftieth anniversary of the settlement of that city, have extended to the militia organizations of foreign countries, in behalf of the citizen soldiers of the State of Illinois, an invitation to take part in said encampment as the guests of the city of Chicago, and that representatives of the soldiery of certain foreign countries have accepted such invitation and are about to arrive in the United States:

I hereby direct the Secretary of the Treasury to instruct the collectors of customs at the several ports of entry that upon being satisfied that such visitors come as guests, in pursuance of the aforesaid invitation, they shall permit the entrance of such foreign soldiers into the United States, with their personal baggage, uniforms, arms, and equipments, without payment of customs duties thereon, and without other formality than such as may be necessary to insure the reexportation of said uniforms, baggage, arms, and equipments.

GROVER CLEVELAND.

DEPARTMENT OF STATE,
Washington, October 24, 1887.

By direction of the President the undersigned is charged with the sad duty of announcing the death, on the 22d instant, at 4 o'clock p. m., at his residence, Chicago, Ill., of Elihu B. Washburne, an illustrious citizen, formerly Secretary of State of the United States.

Mr. Washburne rendered great service to the people of the United States in many and important capacities. As a Representative from the State of Illinois in the National Legislature, and subsequently as envoy extraordinary and minister plenipotentiary of the United States to France, his career was marked by eminent usefulness, in which abilities of a high order were applied with unsparing devotion and fidelity in the performance of the trusts of public power.

His private life was unstained, his public service unquestionably great, and his memory will be cherished with affection and respect by his grateful countrymen.

On the day of his funeral this Department will be closed for all public business, and be draped in mourning for ten days thereafter.

The diplomatic and consular officers of the United States in foreign countries will be directed to make proper expression of the public sorrow experienced by the death of Mr. Washburne.

T. F. BAYARD, *Secretary of State.*

THIRD ANNUAL MESSAGE.

WASHINGTON, *December 6, 1887.*

To the Congress of the United States:

You are confronted at the threshold of your legislative duties with a condition of the national finances which imperatively demands immediate and careful consideration.

The amount of money annually exacted, through the operation of present laws, from the industries and necessities of the people largely exceeds the sum necessary to meet the expenses of the Government.

When we consider that the theory of our institutions guarantees to every citizen the full enjoyment of all the fruits of his industry and enterprise, with only such deduction as may be his share toward the careful and economical maintenance of the Government which protects him, it is plain that the exaction of more than this is indefensible extortion and a culpable betrayal of American fairness and justice. This wrong inflicted upon those who bear the burden of national taxation, like other wrongs, multiplies a brood of evil consequences. The public Treasury, which should only exist as a conduit conveying the people's tribute to its legitimate objects of expenditure, becomes a hoarding place for money needlessly withdrawn from trade and the people's use, thus crippling our national energies, suspending our country's development, preventing investment in productive enterprise, threatening financial disturbance, and inviting schemes of public plunder.

This condition of our Treasury is not altogether new, and it has more than once of late been submitted to the people's representatives in the Congress, who alone can apply a remedy. And yet the situation still continues, with aggravated incidents, more than ever presaging financial convulsion and widespread disaster.

It will not do to neglect this situation because its dangers are not now palpably imminent and apparent. They exist none the less certainly, and await the unforeseen and unexpected occasion when suddenly they will be precipitated upon us.

On the 30th day of June, 1885, the excess of revenues over public expenditures, after complying with the annual requirement of the sinking-fund act, was $17,859,735.84; during the year ended June 30, 1886, such excess amounted to $49,405,545.20, and during the year ended June 30, 1887, it reached the sum of $55,567,849.54.

The annual contributions to the sinking fund during the three years above specified, amounting in the aggregate to $138,058,320.94, and deducted from the surplus as stated, were made by calling in for that purpose outstanding 3 per cent bonds of the Government. During the six months prior to June 30, 1887, the surplus revenue had grown so large by repeated accumulations, and it was feared the withdrawal of this great sum of money needed by the people would so affect the business of the country, that the sum of $79,864,100 of such surplus was applied to the payment of the principal and interest of the 3 per cent bonds still outstanding, and which were then payable at the option of the Government. The precarious condition of financial affairs among the people still needing relief, immediately after the 30th day of June, 1887, the remainder of the 3 per cent bonds then outstanding, amounting with principal and interest to the sum of $18,877,500, were called in and applied to the sinking-fund contribution for the current fiscal year. Notwithstanding these operations of the Treasury Department, representations of distress in business circles not only continued, but increased, and absolute peril seemed at hand. In these circumstances the contribution to the sinking fund for the current fiscal year was at once completed by the expenditure of $27,684,283.55 in the purchase of Government bonds not yet due bearing 4 and 4½ per cent interest, the premium paid thereon averaging about 24 per cent for the former and 8 per cent for the latter. In addition to this, the interest accruing during the current year upon the outstanding bonded indebtedness of the Government was to some extent anticipated, and banks selected as depositories of public money were permitted to somewhat increase their deposits.

While the expedients thus employed to release to the people the money lying idle in the Treasury served to avert immediate danger, our surplus revenues have continued to accumulate, the excess for the present year amounting on the 1st day of December to $55,258,701.19, and estimated to reach the sum of $113,000,000 on the 30th of June next, at which date it is expected that this sum, added to prior accumulations, will swell the surplus in the Treasury to $140,000,000.

There seems to be no assurance that, with such a withdrawal from use of the people's circulating medium, our business community may not in the near future be subjected to the same distress which was quite lately produced from the same cause. And while the functions of our National Treasury should be few and simple, and while its best condition would be reached, I believe, by its entire disconnection with private business interests, yet when, by a perversion of its purposes, it idly holds money uselessly subtracted from the channels of trade, there seems to be reason for the claim that some legitimate means should be devised by the Government to restore in an emergency, without waste or extravagance, such money to its place among the people.

If such an emergency arises, there now exists no clear and undoubted executive power of relief. Heretofore the redemption of 3 per cent bonds, which were payable at the option of the Government, has afforded a means for the disbursement of the excess of our revenues; but these bonds have all been retired, and there are no bonds outstanding the payment of which we have a right to insist upon. The contribution to the sinking fund which furnishes the occasion for expenditure in the purchase of bonds has been already made for the current year, so that there is no outlet in that direction.

In the present state of legislation the only pretense of any existing executive power to restore at this time any part of our surplus revenues to the people by its expenditure consists in the supposition that the Secretary of the Treasury may enter the market and purchase the bonds of the Government not yet due, at a rate of premium to be agreed upon. The only provision of law from which such a power could be derived is found in an appropriation bill passed a number of years ago, and it is subject to the suspicion that it was intended as temporary and limited in its application, instead of conferring a continuing discretion and authority. No condition ought to exist which would justify the grant of power to a single official, upon his judgment of its necessity, to withhold from or release to the business of the people, in an unusual manner, money held in the Treasury, and thus affect at his will the financial situation of the country; and if it is deemed wise to lodge in the Secretary of the Treasury the authority in the present juncture to purchase bonds, it should be plainly vested, and provided, as far as possible, with such checks and limitations as will define this official's right and discretion and at the same time relieve him from undue responsibility.

In considering the question of purchasing bonds as a means of restoring to circulation the surplus money accumulating in the Treasury, it should be borne in mind that premiums must of course be paid upon such purchase, that there may be a large part of these bonds held as investments which can not be purchased at any price, and that combinations among holders who are willing to sell may unreasonably enhance the cost of such bonds to the Government.

It has been suggested that the present bonded debt might be refunded at a less rate of interest and the difference between the old and new security paid in cash, thus finding use for the surplus in the Treasury. The success of this plan, it is apparent, must depend upon the volition of the holders of the present bonds; and it is not entirely certain that the inducement which must be offered them would result in more financial benefit to the Government than the purchase of bonds, while the latter proposition would reduce the principal of the debt by actual payment instead of extending it.

The proposition to deposit the money held by the Government in banks throughout the country for use by the people is, it seems to me, exceedingly objectionable in principle, as establishing too close a relationship between the operations of the Government Treasury and the business of the country and too extensive a commingling of their money, thus fostering an unnatural reliance in private business upon public funds. If this scheme should be adopted, it should only be done as a temporary expedient to meet an urgent necessity. Legislative and executive effort should generally be in the opposite direction, and should have a tendency to divorce, as much and as fast as can be safely done, the Treasury Department from private enterprise.

Of course it is not expected that unnecessary and extravagant appropriations will be made for the purpose of avoiding the accumulation of an excess of revenue. Such expenditure, besides the demoralization of all just conceptions of public duty which it entails, stimulates a habit of reckless improvidence not in the least consistent with the mission of our people or the high and beneficent purposes of our Government.

I have deemed it my duty to thus bring to the knowledge of my

165

countrymen, as well as to the attention of their representatives charged with the responsibility of legislative relief, the gravity of our financial situation. The failure of the Congress heretofore to provide against the dangers which it was quite evident the very nature of the difficulty must necessarily produce caused a condition of financial distress and apprehension since your last adjournment which taxed to the utmost all the authority and expedients within executive control; and these appear now to be exhausted. If disaster results from the continued inaction of Congress, the responsibility must rest where it belongs.

Though the situation thus far considered is fraught with danger which should be fully realized, and though it presents features of wrong to the people as well as peril to the country, it is but a result growing out of a perfectly palpable and apparent cause, constantly reproducing the same alarming circumstances—a congested National Treasury and a depleted monetary condition in the business of the country. It need hardly be stated that while the present situation demands a remedy, we can only be saved from a like predicament in the future by the removal of its cause.

Our scheme of taxation, by means of which this needless surplus is taken from the people and put into the public Treasury, consists of a tariff or duty levied upon importations from abroad and internal-revenue taxes levied upon the consumption of tobacco and spirituous and malt liquors. It must be conceded that none of the things subjected to internal-revenue taxation are, strictly speaking, necessaries. There appears to be no just complaint of this taxation by the consumers of these articles, and there seems to be nothing so well able to bear the burden without hardship to any portion of the people.

But our present tariff laws, the vicious, inequitable, and illogical source of unnecessary taxation, ought to be at once revised and amended. These laws, as their primary and plain effect, raise the price to consumers of all articles imported and subject to duty by precisely the sum paid for such duties. Thus the amount of the duty measures the tax paid by those who purchase for use these imported articles. Many of these things, however, are raised or manufactured in our own country, and the duties now levied upon foreign goods and products are called protection to these home manufactures, because they render it possible for those of our people who are manufacturers to make these taxed articles and sell them for a price equal to that demanded for the imported goods that have paid customs duty. So it happens that while comparatively a few use the imported articles, millions of our people, who never used and never saw any of the foreign products, purchase and use things of the same kind made in this country, and pay therefor nearly or quite the same enhanced price which the duty adds to the imported articles. Those who buy imports pay the duty charged thereon into the public Treasury, but the great majority of our citizens, who buy domestic articles of the same class, pay a sum at least approximately equal to this duty to the home manufacturer. This reference to the operation of our tariff laws is not made by way of instruction, but in order that we may be constantly reminded of the manner in which they impose a burden upon those who consume domestic products as well as those who consume imported articles, and thus create a tax upon all our people.

It is not proposed to entirely relieve the country of this taxation. It must be extensively continued as the source of the Government's income; and in a readjustment of our tariff the interests of American labor engaged in manufacture should be carefully considered, as well as the preservation of our manufacturers. It may be called protection or by any other name, but relief from the hardships and dangers of our present tariff laws should be devised with especial precaution against imperiling the existence of our manufacturing interests. But this existence should not mean a condition which, without regard to the public welfare or a national exigency, must always insure the realization of immense profits instead of moderately profitable returns. As the volume and diversity of our national activities increase, new recruits are added to those who desire a continuation of the advantages which they conceive the present system of tariff taxation directly affords them. So stubbornly have all efforts to reform the present condition been resisted by those of our fellow-citizens thus engaged that they can hardly complain of the suspicion, entertained to a certain extent, that there exists an organized combination all along the line to maintain their advantage.

We are in the midst of centennial celebrations, and with becoming pride we rejoice in American skill and ingenuity, in American energy and enterprise, and in the wonderful natural advantages and resources developed by a century's national growth. Yet when an attempt is made to justify a scheme which permits a tax to be laid upon every consumer in the land for the benefit of our manufacturers, quite beyond a reasonable demand for governmental regard, it suits the purposes of advocacy to call our manufactures infant industries still needing the highest and greatest degree of favor and fostering care that can be wrung from Federal legislation.

It is also said that the increase in the price of domestic manufactures resulting from the present tariff is necessary in order that higher wages may be paid to our workingmen employed in manufactories than are paid for what is called the pauper labor of Europe. All will acknowledge the force of an argument which involves the welfare and liberal compensation of our laboring people. Our labor is honorable in the eyes of every American citizen; and as it lies at the foundation of our development and progress, it is entitled, without affectation or hypocrisy, to the utmost regard. The standard of our laborers' life should not be measured by that of any other country less favored, and they are entitled to their full share of all our advantages.

By the last census it is made to appear that of the 17,392,099 of our population engaged in all kinds of industries 7,670,493 are employed in agriculture, 4,074,238 in professional and personal service (2,934,876 of whom are domestic servants and laborers), while 1,810,256 are employed in trade and transportation and 3,837,112 are classed as employed in manufacturing and mining.

For present purposes, however, the last number given should be considerably reduced. Without attempting to enumerate all, it will be conceded that there should be deducted from those which it includes 375,143 carpenters and joiners, 285,401 milliners, dressmakers, and seamstresses, 172,726 blacksmiths, 133,756 tailors and tailoresses, 102,473 masons, 76,241 butchers, 41,309 bakers, 22,083 plasterers, and 4,891 engaged in manufacturing agricultural implements, amounting in the aggregate to 1,214,023, leaving 2,623,089 persons employed in such manufacturing industries as are claimed to be benefited by a high tariff.

To these the appeal is made to save their employment and maintain their wages by resisting a change. There should be no disposition to answer such suggestions by the allegation that they are in a minority among those who labor, and therefore should forego an advantage in the interest of low prices for the majority. Their compensation, as it may be affected by the operation of tariff laws, should at all times be scrupulously kept in view; and yet with slight reflection they will not overlook the fact that they are consumers with the rest; that they too have their own wants and those of their families to supply from their earnings, and that the price of the necessaries of life, as well as the amount of their wages, will regulate the measure of their welfare and comfort.

But the reduction of taxation demanded should be so measured as not to necessitate or justify either the loss of employment by the workingman or the lessening of his wages; and the profits still remaining to the manufacturer after a necessary readjustment should furnish no excuse for the sacrifice of the interests of his employees, either in their opportunity to work or in the diminution of their compensation. Nor can the worker in manufactures fail to understand that while a high tariff is claimed to be necessary to allow the payment of remunerative wages, it certainly results in a very large increase in the price of nearly all sorts of manufactures, which, in almost countless forms, he needs for the use of himself and his family. He receives at the desk of his employer his wages, and perhaps before he reaches his home is obliged, in a purchase for family use of an article which embraces his own labor, to return in the payment of the increase in price which the tariff permits the hard-earned compensation of many days of toil.

The farmer and the agriculturist, who manufacture nothing, but who pay the increased price which the tariff imposes upon every agricultural implement, upon all he wears, and upon all he uses and owns, except the increase of his flocks and herds and such things as his husbandry produces from the soil, is invited to aid in maintaining the present situation; and he is told that a high duty on imported wool is necessary for the benefit of those who have sheep to shear, in order that the price of their wool may be increased. They, of course, are not reminded that the farmer who has no sheep is by this scheme obliged, in his purchases of clothing and woolen goods, to pay a tribute to his fellow-farmer as well as to the manufacturer and merchant, nor is any mention made of the fact that the sheep owners themselves and their households must wear clothing and use other articles manufactured from the wool they sell at tariff prices, and thus as consumers must return their share of this increased price to the tradesman.

I think it may be fairly assumed that a large proportion of the sheep owned by the farmers throughout the country are found in small flocks, numbering from twenty-five to fifty. The duty on the grade of imported wool which these sheep yield is 10 cents each pound if of the value of 30 cents or less and 12 cents if of the value of more than 30 cents. If the liberal estimate of 6 pounds be allowed for each fleece, the duty thereon would be 60 or 72 cents; and this may be taken as the utmost enhancement of its price to the farmer by reason of this duty. Eighteen dollars would thus represent the increased price of the wool from twenty-five sheep and $36 that from the wool of fifty sheep; and at present values this addition would amount to about one-third of its price. If upon its sale the farmer receives this or a less tariff profit, the wool leaves his hands charged with precisely that sum, which in all its changes will adhere to it until it reaches the consumer. When manufactured into cloth and other goods and material for use, its cost is not only increased to the extent of the farmer's tariff profit, but a further sum has been added for the benefit of the manufacturer under the operation of other tariff laws. In the meantime the day arrives when the farmer finds it necessary to purchase woolen goods and material to clothe himself and family for the winter. When he faces the tradesman for that purpose, he discovers that he is obliged not only to return in the way of increased prices his tariff profit on the wool he sold, and which then perhaps lies before him in manufactured form, but that he must add a considerable sum thereto to meet a further increase in cost caused by a tariff duty on the manufacture. Thus in the end he is aroused to the fact that he has paid upon a moderate purchase, as a result of the tariff scheme, which when he sold his wool seemed so profitable, an increase in price more than sufficient to sweep away all the tariff profit he received upon the wool he produced and sold.

When the number of farmers engaged in wool raising is compared with all the farmers in the country and the small proportion they bear to our population is considered; when it is made apparent that in the case of a large part of those who own sheep the benefit of the present tariff on wool is illusory; and, above all, when it must be conceded that the increase of the cost of living caused by such tariff becomes a burden upon those with moderate means and the poor, the employed and unemployed, the sick and well, and the young and old, and that it constitutes a tax which with relentless grasp is fastened upon the clothing of every man, woman, and child in the land, reasons are suggested why the removal or reduction of this duty should be included in a revision of our tariff laws.

In speaking of the increased cost to the consumer of our home manufactures resulting from a duty laid upon imported articles of the same description, the fact is not overlooked that competition among our domestic producers sometimes has the effect of keeping the price of their products below the highest limit allowed by such duty. But it is notorious that this competition is too often strangled by combinations quite prevalent at this time, and frequently called trusts, which have for their object the regulation of the supply and price of commodities made and sold by members of the combination. The people can hardly hope for any consideration in the operation of these selfish schemes.

If, however, in the absence of such combination, a healthy and free competition reduces the price of any particular dutiable article of home production below the limit which it might otherwise reach under our tariff laws, and if with such reduced price its manufacture continues to thrive, it is entirely evident that one thing has been discovered which should be carefully scrutinized in an effort to reduce taxation.

The necessity of combination to maintain the price of any commodity to the tariff point furnishes proof that someone is willing to accept lower prices for such commodity and that such prices are remunerative; and lower prices produced by competition prove the same thing. Thus where either of these conditions exists a case would seem to be presented for an easy reduction of taxation.

The considerations which have been presented touching our tariff laws are intended only to enforce an earnest recommendation that the surplus revenues of the Government be prevented by the reduction of our customs duties, and at the same time to emphasize a suggestion that in accomplishing this purpose we may discharge a double duty to our people by granting to them a measure of relief from tariff taxation in quarters where it is most needed and from sources where it can be most fairly and justly accorded.

Nor can the presentation made of such considerations be with any degree of fairness regarded as evidence of unfriendliness toward our manufacturing interests or of any lack of appreciation of their value and importance.

These interests constitute a leading and most substantial element of our national greatness and furnish the proud proof of our country's progress. But if in the emergency that presses upon us our manufacturers are asked to surrender something for the public good and to avert disaster, their patriotism, as well as a grateful recognition of advantages already afforded, should lead them to willing cooperation. No demand is made that they shall forego all the benefits of governmental regard; but they can not fail to be admonished of their duty, as well as their enlightened self-interest and safety, when they are reminded of the fact that financial panic and collapse, to which the present condition tends, afford no greater shelter or protection to our manufactures than to other important enterprises. Opportunity for safe, careful, and deliberate reform is now offered; and none of us should be unmindful of a time when an abused and irritated people, heedless of those who have resisted timely and reasonable relief, may insist upon a radical and sweeping rectification of their wrongs.

The difficulty attending a wise and fair revision of our tariff laws is not underestimated. It will require on the part of the Congress great labor and care, and especially a broad and national contemplation of the subject and a patriotic disregard of such local and selfish claims as are unreasonable and reckless of the welfare of the entire country.

Under our present laws more than 4,000 articles are subject to duty. Many of these do not in any way compete with our own manufactures, and many are hardly worth attention as subjects of revenue. A considerable reduction can be made in the aggregate by adding them to the free list. The taxation of luxuries presents no features of hardship; but the necessaries of life used and consumed by all the people, the duty upon which adds to the cost of living in every home, should be greatly cheapened.

The radical reduction of the duties imposed upon raw material used in manufactures, or its free importation, is of course an important factor in any effort to reduce the price of these necessaries. It would not only relieve them from the increased cost caused by the tariff on such material, but the manufactured product being thus cheapened that part of the tariff now laid upon such product, as a compensation to our manufacturers for the present price of raw material, could be accordingly modified. Such reduction or free importation would serve besides to largely reduce the revenue. It is not apparent how such a change can have any injurious effect upon our manufacturers. On the contrary, it would appear to give them a better chance in foreign markets with the manufacturers of other countries, who cheapen their wares by free material. Thus our people might have the opportunity of extending their sales beyond the limits of home consumption, saving them from the depression, interruption in business, and loss caused by a glutted domestic market and affording their employees more certain and steady labor, with its resulting quiet and contentment.

The question thus imperatively presented for solution should be approached in a spirit higher than partisanship and considered in the light of that regard for patriotic duty which should characterize the action of those intrusted with the weal of a confiding people. But the obligation to declared party policy and principle is not wanting to urge prompt and effective action. Both of the great political parties now represented in the Government have by repeated and authoritative declarations condemned the condition of our laws which permit the collection from the people of unnecessary revenue, and have in the most solemn manner promised its correction; and neither as citizens nor partisans are our countrymen in a mood to condone the deliberate violation of these pledges.

Our progress toward a wise conclusion will not be improved by dwelling upon the theories of protection and free trade. This savors too much of bandying epithets. It is a *condition* which confronts us, not a theory. Relief from this condition may involve a slight reduction of the advantages which we award our home productions, but the entire withdrawal of such advantages should not be contemplated. The question of free trade is absolutely irrelevant, and the persistent claim made in certain quarters that all the efforts to relieve the people from unjust and unnecessary taxation are schemes of so-called free traders is mischievous and far removed from any consideration for the public good.

The simple and plain duty which we owe the people is to reduce taxation to the necessary expenses of an economical operation of the Government and to restore to the business of the country the money which we hold in the Treasury through the perversion of governmental powers. These things can and should be done with safety to all our industries, without danger to the opportunity for remunerative labor which our workingmen need, and with benefit to them and all our people by cheapening their means of subsistence and increasing the measure of their comforts.

The Constitution provides that the President "shall from time to time give to the Congress information of the state of the Union." It has been the custom of the Executive, in compliance with this provision, to annually exhibit to the Congress, at the opening of its session, the general condition of the country, and to detail with some particularity the operations of the different Executive Departments. It would be especially agreeable to follow this course at the present time and to call attention to the valuable accomplishments of these Departments during the last fiscal year; but I am so much impressed with the paramount importance of the subject to which this communication has thus far been devoted that I shall forego the addition of any other topic, and only urge upon your immediate consideration the "state of the Union" as shown in the present condition of our Treasury and our general fiscal situation, upon which every element of our safety and prosperity depends.

The reports of the heads of Departments, which will be submitted, contain full and explicit information touching the transaction of the business intrusted to them and such recommendations relating to legislation in the public interest as they deem advisable. I ask for these reports and recommendations the deliberate examination and action of the legislative branch of the Government.

There are other subjects not embraced in the departmental reports demanding legislative consideration, and which I should be glad to submit. Some of them, however, have been earnestly presented in previous messages, and as to them I beg leave to repeat prior recommendations.

As the law makes no provision for any report from the Department of State, a brief history of the transactions of that important Department, together with other matters which it may hereafter be deemed essential to commend to the attention of the Congress, may furnish the occasion for a future communication. GROVER CLEVELAND.

SPECIAL MESSAGES.

EXECUTIVE MANSION,
Washington, December 14, 1887.

To the Senate of the United States:

I transmit herewith, with a view to its ratification, a final protocol, signed at Paris on the 7th day of July, 1887, by the plenipotentiaries of the United States and of the other powers parties to the convention of March 14, 1884, for the protection of submarine cables, fixing the 1st day of May, 1888, as the date on which the said convention of March 14, 1884, shall take effect, provided that those of the contracting Governments that have not adopted the measures provided for by article 12 of the said convention shall have conformed to that stipulation.

GROVER CLEVELAND.

EXECUTIVE MANSION,
Washington, December 14, 1887.

To the Senate of the United States:

I transmit herewith, with a view to its ratification, a convention between the United States and the Kingdom of the Netherlands for the extradition of criminals, signed at Washington on the 2d day of June, 1887.

GROVER CLEVELAND.

EXECUTIVE MANSION, *December 19, 1887.*
To the Senate and House of Representatives:

I transmit herewith a report from the Secretary of State, in relation to the invitation from Her Britannic Majesty to this Government to participate in the international exhibition which is to be held at Melbourne in 1888 to celebrate the centenary of the founding of New South Wales, the first Australian colony. GROVER CLEVELAND.

EXECUTIVE MANSION, *December 19, 1887.*

To the Senate and House of Representatives:

I transmit herewith a report from the Secretary of State, in relation to an invitation which has been extended to this Government to appoint a delegate or delegates to the International Exposition of Labor to be held in April, 1888, at Barcelona, Spain, and commend its suggestions to the favorable attention of Congress.

GROVER CLEVELAND.

EXECUTIVE MANSION,
Washington, December 20, 1887.

To the Senate and House of Representatives:

I transmit herewith a communication from the Secretary of State, accompanied by the report of Mr. Edward Atkinson, of Massachusetts, who was specially designated by me, under the provisions of successive acts of Congress in that behalf, to visit the financial centers of Europe in order to ascertain the feasibility of establishing by international arrangement a fixity of rates between the two precious metals in free coinage of both.

GROVER CLEVELAND.

EXECUTIVE MANSION, *January 4, 1888.*

To the Senate and House of Representatives:

I transmit herewith a communication of 23d ultimo from the Secretary of the Interior, submitting, with accompanying papers, a draft of a bill to amend section 2148 of the Revised Statutes of the United States, relating to trespasses upon Indian lands.

GROVER CLEVELAND.

EXECUTIVE MANSION, *January 4, 1888.*

To the Senate and House of Representatives:

I transmit herewith a communication of 23d ultimo from the Secretary of the Interior, submitting, with accompanying papers, a draft of a bill granting a right of way to the Jamestown and Northern Railroad Company through the Devils Lake Indian Reservation, in the Territory of Dakota.

GROVER CLEVELAND.

EXECUTIVE MANSION, *January 4, 1888.*

To the Senate and House of Representatives:

I transmit herewith a communication of the 22d ultimo from the Secretary of the Interior, submitting, with accompanying papers, a draft of a bill to amend section 5388 of the Revised Statutes of the United States, relating to timber trespasses upon the public lands, so as to include Indian lands.

GROVER CLEVELAND.

EXECUTIVE MANSION, *January 4, 1888.*

To the Senate and House of Representatives:

I transmit herewith a communication of 27th December, 1887, from the Secretary of the Interior, submitting, with accompanying papers, draft of a bill "to authorize the Secretary of the Interior to fix the amount of compensation to be paid for the right of way for railroads through Indian reservations in certain contingencies."

The matter is commended to the consideration of Congress.

GROVER CLEVELAND.

EXECUTIVE MANSION, *January 4, 1888.*

To the Senate and House of Representatives:

I transmit herewith a communication of 22d ultimo from the Secretary of the Interior, submitting, with accompanying papers, a draft of a bill to accept and ratify an agreement made with the Indians of the Yakima Reservation, in Washington Territory, for the right of way of the Northern Pacific Railroad across said reservation, etc.

The matter is presented for the consideration and action of Congress.

GROVER CLEVELAND.

EXECUTIVE MANSION, *January 4, 1888.*

To the Senate and House of Representatives:

I transmit herewith a communication of 24th ultimo from the Secretary of the Interior, submitting, with accompanying papers, a draft of a bill to accept and ratify an agreement made by the Pi-Ute Indians, and granting a right of way to the Carson and Colorado Railroad Company through the Walker River Reservation, in Nevada.

GROVER CLEVELAND.

EXECUTIVE MANSION, *January 4, 1888.*

To the Senate and House of Representatives:

I transmit herewith a communication of the 24th ultimo from the Secretary of the Interior, submitting, with accompanying papers, a draft of a bill to accept and ratify an agreement made with the Sisseton and Wahpeton Indians, and to grant a right of way for the Chicago, Milwaukee and St. Paul Railway through the Lake Traverse Indian Reservation, in Dakota.

The matter is presented for the consideration and action of Congress.

GROVER CLEVELAND.

EXECUTIVE MANSION, *January 5, 1888.*

To the Senate and House of Representatives:

I transmit herewith a communication of the 23d ultimo from the Secretary of the Interior, submitting a draft of a bill "to provide for the reduction of the Round Valley Indian Reservation, in the State of California, and for other purposes," with accompanying papers relating thereto. The documents thus submitted exhibit extensive and entirely unjustifiable encroachments upon lands set apart for Indian occupancy and disclose a disregard of Indian rights so long continued that the Government can not further temporize without positive dishonor. Efforts to dislodge trespassers upon these lands have in some cases been resisted upon the ground that certain moneys due from the Government for improvements have not been paid. So far as this claim is well founded the sum necessary to extinguish the same should be at once appropriated and paid. In other cases the position of these intruders is one of simple and barefaced wrongdoing, plainly questioning the inclination of the Government to protect its dependent Indian wards and its ability to maintain itself in the guaranty of such protection.

These intruders should forthwith feel the weight of the Government's power. I earnestly commend the situation and the wrongs of the Indians occupying the reservation named to the early attention of the Congress, and ask for the bill herewith transmitted careful and prompt attention.

GROVER CLEVELAND.

EXECUTIVE MANSION, *January 5, 1888.*

To the Senate:

In answer to the resolution of the Senate of the 28th of February last, requesting the President of the United States to obtain certain information from the Government of Great Britain relative to the proceedings of the authorities of New Zealand concerning the titles to lands in that colony claimed by American citizens, I transmit a report of the Secretary of State, together with the accompanying documents.

GROVER CLEVELAND.

EXECUTIVE MANSION,
Washington, January 5, 1888.

To the Senate of the United States:

I transmit herewith, with a view to its ratification, a treaty of friendship, commerce, and navigation between the United States and the Republic of Peru, signed at Lima on the 31st day of August, 1887.

GROVER CLEVELAND.

EXECUTIVE MANSION.
Washington, January 5, 1888.

To the Senate of the United States:

I transmit, with a view to its ratification, an additional article, signed October 22, 1887, to the treaty for the extradition of criminals concluded October 11, 1870, between the United States and the Republic of Guatemala, and, for the reasons suggested by the Secretary of State in his report, request the return of the additional article to the above-mentioned treaty signed February 4, 1887, and transmitted to the Senate on February 24 [25] of the same year.*   GROVER CLEVELAND.

EXECUTIVE MANSION, *January 9, 1888.*

To the Senate and House of Representatives:

I transmit herewith a communication of 30th of December, 1887, from the Secretary of the Interior, submitting, with accompanying papers, two additional reports from the commission appointed to conduct negotiations with certain tribes and bands of Indians for reduction of reservations, etc., under the provisions of the act of May 15, 1886 (24 U. S. Statutes at Large, p. 44), providing therefor.   GROVER CLEVELAND.

EXECUTIVE MANSION, *January 9, 1888.*

To the Senate and House of Representatives:

I transmit herewith a communication from the Secretary of State, relative to the requests which have been received from various maritime associations and chambers of commerce of this country asking that measures be taken to convoke an international conference at Washington of representatives of all maritime nations to devise measures for the greater security of life and property at sea.

I commend this important subject to the favorable consideration of Congress.   GROVER CLEVELAND.

EXECUTIVE MANSION, *January 9, 1888.*

To the Senate and House of Representatives:

I transmit herewith a report from the Secretary of State, recommending that this Government take action to approve the resolutions of the Washington International Meridian Conference, held in October, 1884, in favor of fixing a prime meridian and a universal day, and to invite the powers with whom this country has diplomatic relations to accede to the same.

                    GROVER CLEVELAND.

EXECUTIVE MANSION, *January 9, 1888.*

To the Senate and House of Representatives:

I transmit herewith a report of the Secretary of State, relative to the legislation required to carry into effect the international convention of March 14, 1884, for the protection of submarine cables, to which this country is a party.   GROVER CLEVELAND.

* See p. 5123.

EXECUTIVE MANSION, *January 12, 1888.*
To the Senate and House of Representatives:

I transmit herewith a report from the Secretary of State, in relation to the invitation from the Government of France to this Government to participate in the international exhibition which is to be held at Paris in 1889.

GROVER CLEVELAND.

EXECUTIVE MANSION,
Washington, January 16, 1888.
To the Senate of the United States:

I transmit herewith, in response to a resolution of the Senate of the 21st ultimo, a report of the Secretary of State touching correspondence of this Government with that of Hawaii, or of any foreign country, concerning any change or proposed change in the Government of the Hawaiian Islands.

GROVER CLEVELAND.

EXECUTIVE MANSION, *January 17, 1888.*
To the Senate and House of Representatives:

On the 3d day of March last an act was passed authorizing the appointment of three commissioners who should investigate the affairs of such railroads as have received aid from the United States Government. Among other things, the contemplated investigation included a history of the construction of these roads, their relations and indebtedness to the Government, and the question whether in the interest of the United States any extension of the time for the performance of the obligations of said roads to the Government should be granted; and if so, the said commissioners were directed to submit a scheme for such extension.

The commissioners were further directed by said act to report in full to the President upon all the matters submitted to them, and he was by said act required to forward said report to Congress with such recommendations or comments as he should see fit to make in the premises.

The commissioners immediately after their selection entered upon the discharge of their duties, and have prosecuted their inquiries with commendable industry, intelligence, and thoroughness. A large amount of testimony has been taken, and all the facts have been developed which appear to be necessary for the consideration of the questions arising from the condition of these aided railroads and their relations to the Government.

The commissioners have, however, been unable to agree upon the manner in which these railroads should be treated respecting their indebtedness to the United States, or to unite upon the plan best calculated to secure the payment of such indebtedness.

This disagreement has resulted in the preparation of two reports, both of which are herewith submitted to the Congress.

These reports exhibit such transactions and schemes connected with the construction of the aided roads and their management, and suggest the invention of such devices on the part of those having them in charge, for the apparent purpose of defeating any chance for the Government's reimbursement, that any adjustment or plan of settlement should be predicated upon the substantial interests of the Government rather than any forbearance or generosity deserved by the companies.

The wide publication which has already been given to the substance of the commissioners' reports obviates the necessity of detailing in this communication the facts found upon the investigation.

The majority report, while condemning the methods adopted by those who formerly had charge of the Union Pacific Railroad, declares that since its present management was inaugurated, in 1884, its affairs have been fairly and prudently conducted, and that the present administration "has devoted itself honestly and intelligently to the herculean task of rescuing the Union Pacific Railway from the insolvency which seriously threatened it at the inception of its work;" that it "has devoted itself, by rigid economy, by intelligent management, and by an application of every dollar of the earning capacity of the system to its improvement and betterment, to place that company on a sound and enduring financial foundation."

The condition of the present management of the Union Pacific Company has an important bearing upon its ability to comply with the terms of any settlement of its indebtedness which may be offered by the Government.

The majority of the commission are in favor of an extension of the time for the payment of the Government indebtedness of these companies, upon certain conditions; but the chairman of the commission, presenting the minority report, recommends, both upon principle and policy, the institution of proceedings for the forfeiture of the charters of the corporations and the winding up of their affairs.

I have been furnished with a statement or argument in defense of the transactions connected with the construction of the Central Pacific road and its branch lines, from which it may not be amiss to quote for the purpose of showing how some of the operations of the directors of such road, strongly condemned by the commissioners, are defended by the directors themselves. After speaking of a contract for the construction of one of these branch lines by a corporation called the Contract and Finance Company, owned by certain directors of the Central Pacific Railroad, this language is used:

It may be said of this contract, as of many others that were let to the different construction companies in which the directors of the Central Pacific have been stockholders, that they built the road with the moneys furnished by themselves and had the road for their outlay. In other words, they paid to the construction company the bonds and stock of the railroad so constructed, and waited until such time as they could develop sufficient business on the road built to induce the public to buy the bonds or the stock. If the country through which the railroad ran developed sufficient business, then the project was a success; if it did not, then the operation was a loss. These gentlemen took all the responsibility; any loss occurring was necessarily theirs, and of right the profit belonged to them.

But it is said that they violated a well-known rule of equity in dealing with themselves; that they were trustees, and that they were representing both sides of the contract.

The answer is that they did not find anybody else to deal with. They could not find anyone who would take the chances of building a road through what was then an almost uninhabited country and accept the bonds and stock of the road in payment. And when it is said that they were trustees, if they did occupy such relation it was merely technical, for they represented only their own interests on both sides, there being no one else concerned in the transaction. They became the incorporators of the company that was to build the road subscribed for its stock, and were the only subscribers; therefore it is difficult to see how anyone was wronged by their action. The rule of equity invoked, which has its origin in the injunction "No man can serve two masters," certainly did not apply to them, because they were acting in their own interests and were not charged with the duty of caring for others' rights, there being no other persons interested in the subject-matter.

In view of this statement and the facts developed in the commissioners' reports, it seems proper to recall the grants and benefits derived from the General Government by both the Union and Central Pacific companies for the purpose of aiding the construction of their roads.

By an act passed in 1862 it was provided that there should be advanced to said companies by the United States, to aid in such construction, the bonds of the Government amounting to $16,000 for every mile constructed, as often as a section of 40 miles of said roads should be built; that there should also be granted to said companies, upon the completion of every said section of 40 miles of road, five entire sections of public land for each mile so built; that the entire charges earned by said roads on account of transportation and service for the Government should be applied to the reimbursement of the bonds advanced by the United States and the interest thereon, and that to secure the repayment of the bonds so advanced, and interest, the issue and delivery to said companies of said bonds should constitute a first mortgage on the whole line of their roads and on their rolling stock, fixtures, and property of every kind and description.

The liberal donations, advances, and privileges provided for in this law were granted by the General Government for the purpose of securing the construction of these roads, which would complete the connection between our eastern and western coasts; and they were based upon a consideration of the public benefits which would accrue to the entire country from such consideration.

But the projectors of these roads were not content, and the sentiment which then seemed to pervade the Congress had not reached the limit of its generosity. Two years after the passage of this law it was supplemented and amended in various important particulars in favor of these companies by an act which provided, among other things, that the bonds, at the rate already specified, should be delivered upon the completion of sections of 20 miles in length instead of 40; that the lands to be conveyed to said companies on the completion of each section of said road should be ten sections per mile instead of five; that only half of the charges for transportation and service due from time to time from the United States should be retained and applied to the advances made to said companies by the Government, thus obliging immediate payment to its debtor of the other half of said charges, and that the lien of the United States to secure the reimbursement of the amount advanced to said companies in bonds, which lien was declared by the law of 1862 to constitute a first mortgage upon all the property of said companies, should become a junior lien and be subordinated to a mortgage which the companies were by the amendatory act authorized to execute to secure bonds which they might from time to time issue in sums not exceeding the amount of the United States bonds which should be advanced to them.

The immense advantages to the companies of this amendatory act are apparent; and in these days we may well wonder that even the anticipated public importance of the construction of these roads induced what must now appear to be a rather reckless and unguarded appropriation of the public funds and the public domain.

Under the operation of these laws the principal of the bonds which have been advanced is $64,023,512, as given in the reports of the commissioners; the interest to November 1, 1887, is calculated to be $76,-024,206.58, making an aggregate at the date named of $140,047,718.58. The interest calculated to the maturity of the bonds added to the principal produces an aggregate of $178,884,759.50. Against these amounts there has been repaid by the companies the sum of $30,955,039.61.

It is almost needless to state that the companies have availed themselves to the utmost extent of the permission given them to issue their bonds and to mortgage their property to secure the payment of the same, by an incumbrance having preference to the Government's lien and precisely equal to it in amount.

It will be seen that there was available for the building of each mile of these roads $16,000 of United States bonds, due in thirty years, with 6 per cent interest; $16,000 in bonds of the companies, secured by a first mortgage on all their property, and ten sections of Government land, to say nothing of the stock of the companies.

When the relations created between the Government and these companies by the legislation referred to is considered, it is astonishing that the claim should be made that the directors of these roads owed no duty except to themselves in their construction; that they need regard no interests but their own, and that they were justified in contracting with themselves and making such bargains as resulted in conveying to their pockets all the assets of the companies. As a lienor the Government was vitally interested in the amount of the mortgage to which its security had been subordinated, and it had the right to insist that none of the bonds secured by this prior mortgage should be issued fraudulently or for the purpose of division among these stockholders without consideration.

The doctrine of complete independence on the part of the directors of these companies and their freedom from any obligation to care for other interests than their own in the construction of these roads seems to have developed the natural consequences of its application, portrayed as follows in the majority report of the commissioners:

> The result is that those who have controlled and directed the construction and development of these companies have become possessed of their surplus assets through issues of bonds, stocks, and payment of dividends voted by themselves, while the great creditor, the United States, finds itself substantially without adequate security for the repayment of its loans.

The laws enacted in aid of these roads, while they illustrated a profuse liberality and a generous surrender of the Government's advantages, which it is hoped experience has corrected, were nevertheless passed upon the theory that the roads should be constructed according to the common rules of business, fairness, and duty, and that their value and their ability to pay their debts should not be impaired by unfair manipulations; and when the Government subordinated its lien to another it was in the expectation that the prior lien would represent in its amount only such bonds as should be necessarily issued by the companies for the construction of their roads at fair prices, agreed upon in an honest way between real and substantial parties. For the purpose of saving or improving the security afforded by its junior lien the Government should have the right now to purge this paramount lien of all that is fraudulent, fictitious, or unconscionable. If the transfer to innocent hands of bonds of this character secured by such first mortgage prevents their cancellation, it might be well to seek a remedy against those who issued and transferred them. If legislation is needed to secure such a remedy, the Congress can readily supply it.

I desire to call attention also to the fact that if all that was to be done on the part of the Government to fully vest in these companies the grants and advantages contemplated by the acts passed in their interest has not yet been perfected, and if the failure of such companies to perform in good faith their part of the contract justifies such a course, the power rests with the Congress to withhold further performance on the part of the Government. If donated lands are not yet granted to these companies, and if their violation of contract and of duty are such as in justice and morals forfeit their rights to such lands, Congressional action should intervene to prevent further consummation. Executive power must be exercised according to existing laws, and Executive discretion is probably not broad enough to reach such difficulties.

The California and Oregon Railroad is now a part of the Central Pacific system, and is a land-grant road. Its construction has been carried on with the same features and incidents which have characterized the other constructions of this system, as is made apparent on pages 78,

79, and 80 of the report of the majority of the commissioners. I have in my hands for approval the report of the commissioners appointed to examine two completed sections of this road. Upon such approval the company or the Central Pacific Company will be entitled to patents for a large quantity of public lands. I especially commend to the attention of Congress this condition of affairs, in order that it may determine whether or not it should intervene to save these lands for settlers, if such a course is justifiable.

It is quite time that the troublesome complications surrounding this entire subject, which has been transmitted to us as a legacy from former days, should be adjusted and settled.

No one, I think, expects that these railroad companies will be able to pay their immense indebtedness to the Government at its maturity.

Any proceeding or arrangement that would result now, or at any other time, in putting these roads, or any portion of them, in the possession and control of the Government is, in my opinion, to be rejected, certainly as long as there is the least chance for indemnification through any other means.

I suppose we are hardly justified in indulging the irritation and indignation naturally arising from a contemplation of malfeasance to such an extent as to lead to the useless destruction of these roads or loss of the advances made by the Government. I believe that our efforts should be in a more practical direction, and should tend, with no condonation of wrongdoing, to the collection by the Government, on behalf of the people, of the public money now in jeopardy.

While the plan presented by a majority of the commission appears to be well devised and gives at least partial promise of the results sought, the fact will not escape attention that its success depends upon its acceptance by the companies and their ability to perform its conditions after acceptance. It is exceedingly important that any adjustment now made should be final and effective. These considerations suggest the possibility that the remedy proposed in the majority report might well be applied to a part only of these aided railroad companies.

The settlement and determination of the questions involved are peculiarly within the province of the Congress. The subject has been made quite a familiar one by Congressional discussion. This is now supplemented in a valuable manner by the facts presented in the reports herewith submitted.

The public interest urges prompt and efficient action.

GROVER CLEVELAND.

EXECUTIVE MANSION, *January 23, 1888.*

To the Senate and House of Representatives:

I transmit herewith the first report of the board of control created by the act of Congress approved August 4, 1886 (24 U. S. Statutes at Large, p. 252), for the management of an industrial home in the Territory of

Utah, containing a statement of the action of the board in establishing the home and an account of expenditures from the appropriation made for that purpose in the act above mentioned.

GROVER CLEVELAND.

EXECUTIVE MANSION,
Washington, January 30, 1888.

To the Senate:

I transmit herewith, in response to the resolution of the Senate of the 21st of December last, a report from the Secretary of State, in relation to Midway Island.

GROVER CLEVELAND.

EXECUTIVE MANSION,
Washington, February 7, 1888.

To the Senate of the United States:

I transmit, with a view to its ratification, a declaration, signed December 1, 1886, and March 23, 1887, for Germany, by the delegates of the powers signatories of the convention of March 14, 1884, for the protection of submarine cables, defining the sense of articles 2 and 4 of the said convention.

GROVER CLEVELAND.

EXECUTIVE MANSION, *February 7, 1888.*

To the Senate and House of Representatives:

I transmit herewith a communication of 4th instant from the Secretary of the Interior, submitting, with other papers, a draft of a bill to accept and ratify an agreement made with the Shoshone and Bannock Indians for the surrender and relinquishment to the United States of a portion of the Fort Hall Reservation, in the Territory of Idaho, for the purposes of a town site, and for the grant of a right of way through said reservation to the Utah and Northern Railway Company, and for other purposes.

The matter is presented for the consideration of the Congress.

GROVER CLEVELAND.

EXECUTIVE MANSION, *February 20, 1888.*

To the Senate of the United States:

I transmit herewith a report furnished by the Secretary of State in response to a resolution of the Senate of the 2d instant, making inquiry respecting the present condition of the *Virginius* indemnity fund.

GROVER CLEVELAND.

EXECUTIVE MANSION, *February 20, 1888.*

To the Senate and House of Representatives:

I transmit herewith and commend to your favorable consideration a report from the Secretary of State, in relation to an invitation which this

Government has received from the Belgian Government to participate in an international exhibition of sciences and industry which will open at Brussels in the month of May next.

GROVER CLEVELAND.

EXECUTIVE MANSION, *February 20, 1888.*

To the Senate of the United States:

In my annual message transmitted to the Congress in December, 1886, it was stated that negotiations were then pending for the settlement of the questions growing out of the rights claimed by American fishermen in British North American waters.

As a result of such negotiations a treaty has been agreed upon between Her Britannic Majesty and the United States, concluded and signed in this capital, under my direction and authority, on the 15th of February instant, and which I now have the honor to submit to the Senate with the recommendation that it shall receive the consent of that body, as provided in the Constitution, in order that the ratifications thereof may be duly exchanged and the treaty be carried into effect.

Shortly after Congress had adjourned in March last, and in continuation of my efforts to arrive at such an agreement between the Governments of Great Britain and the United States as would secure to the citizens of the respective countries the unmolested enjoyment of their just rights under existing treaties and international comity in the territorial waters of Canada and of Newfoundland, I availed myself of opportune occurrences indicative of a desire to make without delay an amicable and final settlement of a long-standing controversy, productive of much irritation and misunderstanding between the two nations, to send through our minister in London proposals that a conference should take place on the subject at this capital.

The experience of the past two years had demonstrated the dilatory and unsatisfactory consequences of our indirect transaction of business through the foreign office in London, in which the views and wishes of the government of the Dominion of Canada were practically predominant, but were only to find expression at second hand.

To obviate this inconvenience and obstruction to prompt and well-defined settlement, it was considered advisable that the negotiations should be conducted in this city and that the interests of Canada and Newfoundland should be directly represented therein.

The terms of reference having been duly agreed upon between the two Governments and the conference arranged to be held here, by virtue of the power in me vested by the Constitution I duly authorized Thomas F. Bayard, the Secretary of State of the United States, William L. Putnam, a citizen of the State of Maine, and James B. Angell, a citizen of the State of Michigan, for and in the name of the United States, to meet and confer with the plenipotentiaries representing the Government of Her Britannic

Majesty, for the purpose of considering and adjusting in a friendly spirit all or any questions relating to rights of fishery in the seas adjacent to British North America and Newfoundland which were in dispute between the Government of the United States and that of Her Britannic Majesty, and jointly and severally to conclude and sign any treaty or treaties touching the premises; and I herewith transmit for your information full copies of the power so given by me.

In execution of the powers so conveyed the said Thomas F. Bayard, William L. Putnam, and James B. Angell, in the month of November last, met in this city the plenipotentiaries of Her Britannic Majesty and proceeded in the negotiation of a treaty as above authorized. After many conferences and protracted efforts an agreement has at length been arrived at, which is embodied in the treaty which I now lay before you.

The treaty meets my approval, because I believe that it supplies a satisfactory, practical, and final adjustment, upon a basis honorable and just to both parties, of the difficult and vexed question to which it relates.

A review of the history of this question will show that all former attempts to arrive at a common interpretation, satisfactory to both parties, of the first article of the treaty of October 20, 1818, have been unsuccessful, and with the lapse of time the difficulty and obscurity have only increased.

The negotiations in 1854 and again in 1871 ended in both cases in temporary reciprocal arrangements of the tariffs of Canada and Newfoundland and of the United States, and the payment of a money award by the United States, under which the real questions in difference remained unsettled, in abeyance, and ready to present themselves anew just so soon as the conventional arrangements were abrogated.

The situation, therefore, remained unimproved by the results of the treaty of 1871, and a grave condition of affairs, presenting almost identically the same features and causes of complaint by the United States against Canadian action and British default in its correction, confronted us in May, 1886, and has continued until the present time.

The greater part of the correspondence which has taken place between the two Governments has heretofore been communicated to Congress, and at as early a day as possible I shall transmit the remaining portion to this date, accompanying it with the joint protocols of the conferences which resulted in the conclusion of the treaty now submitted to you.

You will thus be fully possessed of the record and history of the case since the termination on June 30, 1885, of the fishery articles of the treaty of Washington of 1871, whereby we were relegated to the provisions of the treaty of October 20, 1818.

As the documents and papers referred to will supply full information of the positions taken under my Administration by the representatives of the United States, as well as those occupied by the representatives of the Government of Great Britain, it is not considered necessary or expedient to repeat them in this message. But I believe the treaty will be found to contain a just, honorable, and therefore satisfactory solution of the difficulties which have clouded our relations with our neighbors on our northern border.

Especially satisfactory do I believe the proposed arrangement will be found by those of our citizens who are engaged in the open-sea fisheries adjacent to the Canadian coast, and resorting to those ports and harbors under treaty provisions and rules of international law.

The proposed delimitation of the lines of the exclusive fisheries from the common fisheries will give certainty and security as to the area of their legitimate field. The headland theory of imaginary lines is abandoned by Great Britain, and the specification in the treaty of certain named bays especially provided for gives satisfaction to the inhabitants of the shores, without subtracting materially from the value or convenience of the fishery rights of Americans.

The uninterrupted navigation of the Strait of Canso is expressly and for the first time affirmed, and the four purposes for which our fishermen under the treaty of 1818 were allowed to enter the bays and harbors of Canada and Newfoundland within the belt of 3 marine miles are placed under a fair and liberal construction, and their enjoyment secured without such conditions and restrictions as in the past have embarrassed and obstructed them so seriously.

The enforcement of penalties for unlawfully fishing or preparing to fish within the inshore and exclusive waters of Canada and Newfoundland is to be accomplished under safeguards against oppressive or arbitrary action, thus protecting the defendant fishermen from punishment in advance of trial, delays, and inconvenience and unnecessary expense.

The history of events in the last two years shows that no feature of Canadian administration was more harassing and injurious than the compulsion upon our fishing vessels to make formal entry and clearance on every occasion of temporarily seeking shelter in Canadian ports and harbors.

Such inconvenience is provided against in the proposed treaty, and this most frequent and just cause of complaint is removed.

The articles permitting our fishermen to obtain provisions and the ordinary supplies of trading vessels on their homeward voyages, and under which they are accorded the further and even more important privilege on all occasions of purchasing such casual or needful provisions and supplies as are ordinarily granted to trading vessels, are of great importance and value.

The licenses, which are to be granted without charge and on application, in order to enable our fishermen to enjoy these privileges, are reasonable and proper checks in the hands of the local authorities to identify the recipients and prevent abuse, and can form no impediment to those who intend to use them fairly.

The hospitality secured for our vessels in all cases of actual distress, with liberty to unload and sell and transship their cargoes, is full and liberal.

These provisions will secure the substantial enjoyment of the treaty rights for our fishermen under the treaty of 1818, for which contention has been steadily made in the correspondence of the Department of State and our minister at London and by the American negotiators of the present treaty.

The right of our fishermen under the treaty of 1818 did not extend to the procurement of distinctive fishery supplies in Canadian ports and harbors, and one item supposed to be essential—to wit, bait—was plainly denied them by the explicit and definite words of the treaty of 1818, emphasized by the course of the negotiation and express decisions which preceded the conclusion of that treaty.

The treaty now submitted contains no provision affecting tariff duties, and, independently of the position assumed upon the part of the United States that no alteration in our tariff or other domestic legislation could be made as the price or consideration of obtaining the rights of our citizens secured by treaty, it was considered more expedient to allow any change in the revenue laws of the United States to be made by the ordinary exercise of legislative will and in the promotion of the public interests. Therefore the addition to the free list of fish, fish oil, whale and seal oil, etc., recited in the last article of the treaty, is wholly left to the action of Congress; and in connection therewith the Canadian and Newfoundland right to regulate sales of bait and other fishing supplies within their own jurisdiction is recognized, and the right of our fishermen to freely purchase these things is made contingent by this treaty upon the action of Congress in the modification of our tariff laws.

Our social and commercial intercourse with those populations who have been placed upon our borders and made forever our neighbors is made apparent by a list of United States common carriers, marine and inland, connecting their lines with Canada, which was returned by the Secretary of the Treasury to the Senate on the 7th day of February, 1888, in answer to a resolution of that body; and this is instructive as to the great volume of mutually profitable interchanges which has come into existence during the last half century.

This intercourse is still but partially developed, and if the amicable enterprise and wholesome rivalry between the two populations be not obstructed the promise of the future is full of the fruits of an unbounded prosperity on both sides of the border.

The treaty now submitted to you has been framed in a spirit of liberal equity and reciprocal benefits, in the conviction that mutual advantage and convenience are the only permanent foundation of peace and friendship between States, and that with the adoption of the agreement now placed before the Senate a beneficial and satisfactory intercourse between the two countries will be established so as to secure perpetual peace and harmony.

In connection with the treaty herewith submitted I deem it also my duty to transmit to the Senate a written offer or arrangement, in the nature of a *modus vivendi*, tendered after the conclusion of the treaty on the part of the British plenipotentiaries, to secure kindly and peaceful relations during the period that may be required for the consideration of the treaty by the respective Governments and for the enactment of the necessary legislation to carry its provisions into effect if approved.

This paper, freely and on their own motion signed by the British conferees, not only extends advantages to our fishermen pending the ratification of the treaty, but appears to have been dictated by a friendly and amicable spirit.

I am given to understand that the other Governments concerned in this treaty will within a few days, in accordance with their methods of conducting public business, submit said treaty to their respective legislatures, when it will be at once published to the world. In view of such action it appears to be advisable that by publication here early and full knowledge of all that has been done in the premises should be afforded to our people.

It would also seem to be useful to inform the popular mind concerning the history of the long-continued disputes growing out of the subject embraced in the treaty and to satisfy the public interests touching the same, as well as to acquaint our people with the present status of the questions involved, and to give them the exact terms of the proposed adjustment, in place of the exaggerated and imaginative statements which will otherwise reach them.

I therefore beg leave respectfully to suggest that said treaty and all such correspondence, messages, and documents relating to the same as may be deemed important to accomplish those purposes be at once made public by the order of your honorable body.

GROVER CLEVELAND.

EXECUTIVE MANSION, *February 20, 1888.*

To the Senate and House of Representatives:

I transmit herewith a report from the Secretary of State, relative to an invitation from the Imperial German Government to the Government of the United States to become a party to the International Geodetic Association.

GROVER CLEVELAND.

EXECUTIVE MANSION, *February 27, 1888.*

To the Senate of the United States:

I transmit herewith a report furnished by the Secretary of State in response to a resolution of the Senate of January 12, 1888, making various inquiries respecting the awards of the late Spanish and American

Claims Commission and the disposition of moneys received in satisfaction thereof.

GROVER CLEVELAND.

EXECUTIVE MANSION, *March 5, 1888.*

To the Senate and House of Representatives of the United States of America:

I transmit herewith, for the information and consideration of Congress, a report of the Secretary of State, with accompanying correspondence, touching the action of the Government of Venezuela in conveying to that country for interment the remains of the distinguished Venezuelan soldier and statesman, General José Antonio Paez, and take pleasure in expressing my concurrence in the suggestion therein referred to, that the employment of a national vessel of war for the transportation of General Paez's remains from New York to La Guayra be authorized and provided for by Congress.

GROVER CLEVELAND.

EXECUTIVE MANSION, *March 5, 1888.*

To the Senate and House of Representatives:

I transmit herewith a report from the Secretary of State, relative to an invitation which the Royal Bavarian Government has extended to this Government to participate in the Third International Exhibition of the Fine Arts, which is to be held at Munich, Bavaria, during the present year.

GROVER CLEVELAND.

EXECUTIVE MANSION, *March 5, 1888.*

To the Senate and House of Representatives:

I herewith transmit a letter from the Secretary of State, accompanied by documents and correspondence, in relation to the recent negotiations with Great Britain concerning American fishing interests in British North American waters.

GROVER CLEVELAND.

To the Senate: EXECUTIVE MANSION, *March 5, 1888.*

I transmit herewith a report from the Secretary of State, with its inclosures, in response to the resolution of the Senate of the 21st of December, 1887, and the 16th of January, 1888, touching the awards of the late Mexican Claims Commission, and especially those in favor of Benjamin Weil and La Abra Silver Mining Company.

It will be seen that the report concludes with a suggestion that these claims be referred to the Court of Claims, or such other court as may be deemed proper, in order that the charges of fraud made in relation to said claims may be fully investigated.

If for any reason this proceeding be considered inadvisable, I respectfully ask that some final and definite action be taken directing the executive department of the Government what course to pursue in the premises.

In view of the long delay that has already occurred in these cases, it would seem but just to all parties concerned that the Congress should speedily signify its final judgment upon the awards referred to and make the direction contemplated by the act of 1878, in default of which the money now on hand applicable to such awards now remains undistributed.

GROVER CLEVELAND.

EXECUTIVE MANSION, *March 7, 1888.*

To the Senate:

In compliance with the resolution of the Senate of the 24th of February, 1888, calling for information as to whether the Government of France has prohibited the importation into the country of any American products, and, if so, what products of the United States are affected thereby, and also as to whether any correspondence upon said subject has passed between the Governments of the United States and France, I transmit herewith a report from the Secretary of State on the subject, with the accompanying correspondence.

GROVER CLEVELAND.

EXECUTIVE MANSION, *March 8, 1888.*

To the Senate:

A copy of the following resolution, passed by the Senate on the 1st day of the present month, was delivered to me on the 3d instant:

Resolved, That in view of the difficulties and embarrassments that have attended the regulation of the immigration of Chinese laborers to the United States under the limitations of our treaties with China, the President of the United States be requested to negotiate a treaty with the Emperor of China containing a provision that no Chinese laborer shall enter the United States.

The importance of the subject referred to in this resolution has by no means been overlooked by the executive branch of the Government, charged under the Constitution with the formulation of treaties with foreign countries.

Negotiation with the Emperor of China for a treaty such as is mentioned in said resolution was commenced many months ago and has been since continued. The progress of the negotiation thus inaugurated has heretofore been freely communicated to such members of the Senate and of its Committee on Foreign Relations as sought information concerning the same. It is, however, with much gratification that I deem myself now justified in expressing to the Senate, in response to its resolution, the hope and expectation that a treaty will soon be concluded concerning the immigration of Chinese laborers which will meet the wants of our people and the approbation of the body to which it will be submitted for confirmation.

GROVER CLEVELAND.

EXECUTIVE MANSION,
Washington, March 12, 1888.

To the Senate of the United States:

I transmit herewith, with a view to its ratification, a treaty between the United States of America and Zanzibar, concluded July 3, 1886, enlarging and defining the stipulations of the treaty of September 21, 1833, between the United States of America and His Majesty Seyed Syed bin Sultan of Muscat and Sovereign of Zanzibar, which treaty has continued in force as to Zanzibar and its dependencies after the separation of Zanzibar from Muscat, and has been accepted, ratified, and confirmed by the Sultan of Zanzibar on October 20, 1879.

GROVER CLEVELAND.

EXECUTIVE MANSION,
Washington, March 16, 1888.

To the Senate:

I have the honor to transmit herewith and recommend for your constitutional approval a convention signed and concluded in this city on the 12th instant, under my direction, between the United States and China, for the exclusion hereafter of Chinese laborers from coming into this country.

This treaty is accompanied by a letter from the Secretary of State in recital of its provisions and explanatory of the reasons for its negotiation, and with it are transmitted sundry documents giving the history of events connected with the presence and treatment of Chinese subjects in the United States.

In view of the public interest which has for a long time been manifested in relation to the question of Chinese immigration, it would seem advisable that the full text of this treaty should be made public, and I respectfully recommend that an order to that effect be made by your honorable body.

GROVER CLEVELAND.

EXECUTIVE MANSION, *March 16, 1888.*

To the Senate of the United States:

I herewith transmit, in compliance with the resolution of the Senate of the 16th ultimo, a report from the Secretary of State, accompanied by certain correspondence in regard to the Mexican *zona libre.*

GROVER CLEVELAND.

EXECUTIVE MANSION, *March 20, 1888.*

To the Senate and House of Representatives:

I transmit herewith a communication of the 13th instant from the Secretary of the Interior, with accompanying papers, and submitting the draft of a proposed bill to forfeit lands granted to the State of Oregon for the construction of certain wagon roads, and for other purposes.

The presentation of facts by the Secretary of the Interior herewith transmitted is the result of an examination made under his direction, which has developed, as it seems to me, the most unblushing frauds upon the Government, which, if remaining unchallenged, will divert several hundred thousand acres of land from the public domain and from the reach of honest settlers to those who have attempted to prevent and prostitute the beneficent designs of the Government. The Government sought by the promise of generous donations of land to promote the building of wagon roads for public convenience and for the purpose of encouraging settlement upon the public lands. The roads have not been built, and yet an attempt is made to claim the lands under a title which depends for its validity entirely upon the construction of these roads.

The evidence which has been collected by the Secretary of the Interior, plainly establishing this attempt to defraud the Government and exclude the settlers who are willing to avail themselves of the liberal policy adopted for the settlement of the public lands, is herewith submitted to the Congress, with the recommendation that the bill which has been prepared, and which is herewith transmitted, may become a law, and with the earnest hope that the opportunity thus presented to demonstrate a sincere desire to preserve the public domain for settlers and to frustrate unlawful attempts to appropriate the same may not be neglected.

GROVER CLEVELAND.

EXECUTIVE MANSION,
Washington, March 22, 1888.

To the Senate:

I transmit herewith, for your advice and consent to the ratification thereof, a convention between the United States and Venezuela, signed the 15th instant, supplementary to the convention between the same powers for the settlement of claims signed December 5, 1885.

I transmit also a report of the Secretary of State thereon and copies of correspondence had with the diplomatic representative of Venezuela at this capital in relation thereto. GROVER CLEVELAND.

EXECUTIVE MANSION, *March 22, 1888.*

To the Senate:

In response to the resolution adopted by your honorable body on the 16th instant, as follows—

Resolved, That the President of the United States be requested, if in his judgment not incompatible with the public interest, to transmit to the Senate copies of the minutes and daily protocols of the meetings of the commissioners who negotiated the treaty with Great Britain submitted by the President to the Senate on the 20th of February, 1888—

I submit herewith a report of the Secretary of State, which I hope will satisfactorily meet the request for information embraced in said resolution.

GROVER CLEVELAND.

EXECUTIVE MANSION, *March 27, 1888.*

To the Senate and House of Representatives:

I transmit herewith a report from Hon. George H. Pendleton, our minister to Germany, dated January 30, 1888, from which it appears that trichinosis prevails to a considerable extent in certain parts of Germany and that a number of persons have already died from the effects of eating the meat of diseased hogs which were grown in that country.

I also transmit a report from our consul at Marseilles, dated February 4, 1888, representing that for a number of months a highly contagious and fatal disease has prevailed among the swine of a large section of France, which disease is thought to be very similar to hog cholera by the Commissioner of Agriculture, whose statement is herewith submitted.

It is extremely doubtful if the law passed April 29, 1878, entitled "An act to prevent the introduction of contagious or infectious diseases into the United States," meets cases of this description.

In view of the danger to the health and lives of our people and the contagion that may be spread to the live stock of the country by the importation of swine or hog products from either of the countries named, I recommend the passage of a law prohibiting such importation, with proper regulations as to the continuance of such prohibition, and permitting such further prohibitions in other future cases of a like character as safety and prudence may require.

GROVER CLEVELAND.

EXECUTIVE MANSION,
Washington, April 2, 1888.

To the House of Representatives:

I transmit herewith a report from the Secretary of State, with its inclosures, in response to the resolution of the House of Representatives of the 8th ultimo, in relation to affairs in Samoa.

GROVER CLEVELAND.

[A similar message was sent to the Senate in answer to a resolution of that body of December 21, 1887.]

EXECUTIVE MANSION, *April 5, 1888.*

To the Senate and House of Representatives:

I transmit herewith a communication of the 3d instant from the Secretary of the Interior, submitting, with accompanying papers, a draft of a bill to provide for the revocation of the withdrawal of lands made for the benefit of certain railroads, and for other purposes.

GROVER CLEVELAND.

EXECUTIVE MANSION, *April 9, 1888.*

To the Senate and House of Representatives:

I transmit herewith a communication of the 6th instant from the Secretary of the Interior, submitting, with accompanying papers, a draft of proposed legislation, prepared in the Office of Indian Affairs, to authorize the use of certain funds therein specified in the purchase of lands in the State of Florida upon which to locate the Seminole Indians in that State. The matter is presented for the favorable consideration of Congress.

GROVER CLEVELAND.

EXECUTIVE MANSION, *April 12, 1888.*

To the Senate and House of Representatives:

I transmit herewith and commend to your favorable consideration a letter from the Secretary of State, outlining a plan for publishing the important collections of historical manuscripts now deposited in the Department of State.

GROVER CLEVELAND.

EXECUTIVE MANSION, *April 12, 1888.*

To the Senate of the United States:

In response to the resolution of the Senate dated March 8, calling for the correspondence respecting the seizure of the American steamships *Hero*, *San Fernando*, and *Nutrias*, the property of the Venezuela Steam Transportation Company of New York, and the imprisonment of their officers by the authorities in Venezuela, I transmit herewith the report of the Secretary of State on the subject, together with the accompanying documents.

GROVER CLEVELAND.

EXECUTIVE MANSION, *April 18, 1888.*

To the Senate of the United States:

In answer to the resolution of the Senate of the 5th of March last, calling upon the Secretary of State for copies of the correspondence relating to the claim of William H. Frear against the Government of France for money due him for provisions furnished in March, 1871, for revictualing Paris, I transmit a report from that officer, together with the correspondence called for by the resolution.

GROVER CLEVELAND.

EXECUTIVE MANSION,
Washington, April 23, 1888.

To the Senate:

I transmit herewith a report from the Secretary of State and accompanying papers, in response to the resolution of the Senate of the 25th of January last, requesting correspondence and other information in relation to the claims convention of December 5, 1885, between the United States and Venezuela.

This resolution was adopted in open session; but in view of the change of circumstances since its adoption, by the signature on the 15th ultimo of the convention which I transmitted to the Senate with my message of the 22d ultimo,* and which is now under consideration there in executive session, I transmit the accompanying report as a confidential document also.

GROVER CLEVELAND.

EXECUTIVE MANSION,
Washington, May 8, 1888.

To the Senate of the United States:

I retransmit herewith a convention for the surrender of criminals between the United States and the Republic of Guatemala, concluded October 11, 1870, and ratified by the President of the United States, as amended by the Senate, on April 11, 1871, calling attention to the accompanying report of the Secretary of State as explanatory of my action.

GROVER CLEVELAND.

EXECUTIVE MANSION, *May 8, 1888.*

To the Senate of the United States:

In answer to the resolution of the Senate of April 12, directing the Secretary of State to transmit to the Senate a copy of the correspondence in his Department in regard to the case of John Fruchier, an American citizen who has been impressed into the military service of France, I transmit herewith a report in relation thereto from the Secretary of State, together with the accompanying papers, not considering their communication to be incompatible with the public interests.

GROVER CLEVELAND

EXECUTIVE MANSION,
Washington, May 14, 1888.

To the Senate and House of Representatives:

I transmit herewith a report from the Secretary of State, relative to the claim of Mr. Rudolph Lobsiger, a Swiss citizen, against the United States, and recommend that provision be made by law for referring the matter to the Court of Claims for examination on its merits.

GROVER CLEVELAND.

EXECUTIVE MANSION,
Washington, May 14, 1888.

To the Senate and House of Representatives:

I transmit herewith a communication from the Secretary of State, accompanied by a report of Mr. Somerville P. Tuck, appointed to carry out

* See p. 5106.

certain provisions of section 5 of an act entitled "An act to provide for the ascertainment of claims of American citizens for spoliations committed by the French prior to the 31st day of July, 1801," approved January 20, 1885.   GROVER CLEVELAND.

EXECUTIVE MANSION, *May 15, 1888.*
To the House of Representatives:

In compliance with a resolution originating in the House of Representatives and concurred in by the Senate, I return herewith the bill (H. R. 2699) entitled "An act for the relief of the heirs of the late Solomon Spitzer."   GROVER CLEVELAND.

EXECUTIVE MANSION,
Washington, June 14, 1888.
To the Senate of the United States:

I transmit herewith, in response to a resolution of the Senate of the 11th instant, a report of the Secretary of State, to whom said resolution was addressed, together with a copy of the letter addressed by William H. Seward, Secretary of State, to the governors of certain States of the Union, under date of October 14, 1861, as described in said resolution.
                    GROVER CLEVELAND.

EXECUTIVE MANSION, *June 26, 1888.*
To the Senate and House of Representatives:

I transmit herewith a report from the Secretary of State, accompanied with selected correspondence relating to foreign affairs for the year 1887.
                    GROVER CLEVELAND.

EXECUTIVE MANSION,
Washington, July 5, 1888.
To the Senate:

I transmit herewith, with a view to its ratification, a convention for the extradition of criminals between the United States of America and the Republic of Colombia, signed at Bogota on the 7th of May, 1888, and I at the same time call attention to the accompanying report of the Secretary of State, suggesting certain amendments to the convention.
                    GROVER CLEVELAND.

EXECUTIVE MANSION,
Washington, July 18, 1888.
To the Senate:

I transmit, with a view to its ratification, a convention between the United States and Mexico, signed July 11, 1888, regulating the crossing and recrossing of the frontier between the two countries by pasturing estray or stolen cattle, and I at the same time call attention to the report of the Secretary of State and accompanying papers, relating to the convention in question.

GROVER CLEVELAND.

EXECUTIVE MANSION, *July 18, 1888.*
To the Senate and House of Representatives:

I transmit herewith a communication from the Secretary of State, submitting a series of reports on taxation, prepared by the consular officers of the United States.

GROVER CLEVELAND.

EXECUTIVE MANSION, *July 18, 1888.*
To the Senate and House of Representatives:

I transmit herewith a letter from the Secretary of State, accompanying the annual reports of the consuls of the United States on the trade and industries of foreign countries.

GROVER CLEVELAND.

EXECUTIVE MANSION, *July 18, 1888.*
To the Senate and House of Representatives:

I transmit herewith a letter from the Acting Secretary of State and accompanying documents, being reports from the consuls of the United States on the production of and trade in coffee among the Central and South American States.

GROVER CLEVELAND.

EXECUTIVE MANSION, *July 23, 1888.*
To the Congress of the United States:

Pursuant to the second section of chapter 27 of the laws of 1883, entitled "An act to regulate and improve the civil service of the United States," I herewith transmit the fourth report of the United States Civil Service Commission, covering the period between the 16th day of January, 1886, and the 1st day of July, 1887.

While this report has especial reference to the operations of the Commission during the period above mentioned, it contains, with its accompanying appendixes, much valuable information concerning the inception of civil-service reform and its growth and progress which can not fail to be interesting and instructive to all who desire improvement in administrative methods.

During the time covered by the report 15,852 persons were examined for admission in the classified civil service of the Government in all its branches, of whom 10,746 passed the examination and 5,106 failed. Of those who passed the examination 2,977 were applicants for admission to the departmental service at Washington, 2,547 were examined for admission to the customs service, and 5,222 for admission to the postal service. During the same period 547 appointments were made from the eligible lists to the departmental service, 641 to the customs service, and 3,254 to the postal service.

Concerning separations from the classified service, the report only informs us of such as have occurred among employees in the public service who had been appointed from eligible lists under civil-service rules. When these rules took effect, they did not apply to the persons then in the service, comprising a full complement of employees, who obtained their positions independently of the new law. The Commission has no record of the separations in this numerous class. And the discrepancy apparent in the report between the number of appointments made in the respective branches of the service from the lists of the Commission and the small number of separations mentioned is to a great extent accounted for by vacancies, of which no report was made to the Commission, occurring among those who held their places without examination and certification, which vacancies were filled by appointment from the eligible lists.

In the departmental service there occurred between the 16th day of January, 1886, and the 30th day of June, 1887, among the employees appointed from the eligible lists under civil-service rules, 17 removals, 36 resignations, and 5 deaths. This does not include 14 separations in the grade of special pension examiners—4 by removal, 5 by resignation, and 5 by death.

In the classified customs and postal services the number of separations among those who received absolute appointments under civil-service rules is given for the period between the 1st day of January, 1886, and the 30th day of June, 1887. It appears that such separations in the customs service for the time mentioned embraced 21 removals, 5 deaths, and 18 resignations, and in the postal service 256 removals, 23 deaths, and 469 resignations.

More than a year has passed since the expiration of the period covered by the report of the Commission. Within the time which has thus elapsed many important changes have taken place in furtherance of a reform in our civil service. The rules and regulations governing the execution of the law upon the subject have been completely remodeled in such manner as to render the enforcement of the statute more effective and greatly increase its usefulness.

Among other things, the scope of the examinations prescribed for those who seek to enter the classified service has been better defined and made more practical, the number of names to be certified from the eligible lists to the appointing officers from which a selection is made has been reduced from four to three, the maximum limitation of the age of persons seeking entrance to the classified service to 45 years has been changed, and reasonable provision has been made for the transfer of employ es from one Department to another in proper cases. A plan has also been devised providing for the examination of applicants for promotion in the service, which, when in full operation, will eliminate all chance of favoritism in the advancement of employees, by making promotion a reward of merit and faithful discharge of duty.

Until within a few weeks there was no uniform classification of employees in the different Executive Departments of the Government. As a result of this condition, in some of the Departments positions could be obtained without civil-service examination, because they were not within the classification of such Department, while in other Departments an examination and certification were necessary to obtain positions of the same grade, because such positions were embraced in the classifications applicable to those Departments.

The exception of laborers, watchmen, and messengers from examination and classification gave opportunity, in the absence of any rule guarding against it, for the employment, free from civil-service restrictions, of persons under these designations, who were immediately detailed to do clerical work.

All this has been obviated by the application to all the Departments of an extended and uniform classification embracing grades of employees not theretofore included, and by the adoption of a rule prohibiting the detail of laborers, watchmen, or messengers to clerical duty.

The path of civil-service reform has not at all times been pleasant nor easy. The scope and purpose of the reform have been much misapprehended; and this has not only given rise to strong opposition, but has led to its invocation by its friends to compass objects not in the least related to it. Thus partisans of the patronage system have naturally condemned it. Those who do not understand its meaning either mistrust it or, when disappointed because in its present stage it is not applied to every real or imaginary ill, accuse those charged with its enforcement with faithlessness to civil-service reform. Its importance has frequently been underestimated, and the support of good men has thus been lost by their lack of interest in its success. Besides all these difficulties, those responsible for the administration of the Government in its executive branches have been and still are often annoyed and irritated by the disloyalty to the service and the insolence of employees who remain in place as the beneficiaries and the relics and reminders of the vicious system of appointment which civil-service reform was intended to displace.

And yet these are but the incidents of an advance movement which is radical and far-reaching. The people are, notwithstanding, to be congratulated upon the progress which has been made and upon the firm, practical, and sensible foundation upon which this reform now rests.

With a continuation of the intelligent fidelity which has hitherto characterized the work of the Commission; with a continuation and increase of the favor and liberality which have lately been evinced by the Congress in the proper equipment of the Commission for its work; with a firm but conservative and reasonable support of the reform by all its friends, and with the disappearance of opposition which must inevitably follow its better understanding, the execution of the civil-service law can not fail to ultimately answer the hopes in which it had its origin.

GROVER CLEVELAND.

EXECUTIVE MANSION, *July 26, 1888.*
To the Senate of the United States:

I transmit herewith, in response to a resolution of the Senate of 11th April last, a report of the Secretary of State, with accompanying correspondence, relating to the pending dispute between the Government of Venezuela and the Government of Great Britain concerning the boundaries between British Guiana and Venezuela.

GROVER CLEVELAND.

EXECUTIVE MANSION, *August 6, 1888.*
To the Senate and House of Representatives:

It becomes my painful duty to announce to the Congress and to the people of the United States the death of Philip H. Sheridan, General of the Army, which occurred at a late hour last night at his summer home in the State of Massachusetts.

The death of this valiant soldier and patriotic son of the Republic, though his long illness has been regarded with anxiety, has nevertheless shocked the country and caused universal grief.

He had established for himself a stronghold in the hearts of his fellow-countrymen, who soon caught the true meaning and purpose of his soldierly devotion and heroic temper.

His intrepid courage, his steadfast patriotism, and the generosity of his nature inspired with peculiar warmth the admiration of all the people.

Above his grave affection for the man and pride in his achievements will struggle for mastery, and too much honor can not be accorded to one who was so richly endowed with all the qualities which make his death a national loss.

GROVER CLEVELAND.

EXECUTIVE MANSION, *August 7, 1888.*
To the Senate:

In compliance with a resolution of the Senate of the 3d instant (the House of Representatives concurring), I return herewith the enrolled bill (S. 3303) amendatory of "An act relating to postal crimes and amendatory of the statutes therein mentioned," approved June 18, 1888.

GROVER CLEVELAND.

EXECUTIVE MANSION, *August 10, 1888.*

To the Senate and House of Representatives:

I transmit herewith a communication from the Secretary of State, accompanied by a report of the delegate on the part of the United States to the Fourth International Conference of the Red Cross Association, held at Carlsruhe, in the Grand Duchy of Baden, in September last.

GROVER CLEVELAND.

EXECUTIVE MANSION, *August 23, 1888.*

To the Congress:

The rejection by the Senate of the treaty lately negotiated for the settlement and adjustment of the differences existing between the United States and Great Britain concerning the rights and privileges of American fishermen in the ports and waters of British North America seems to justify a survey of the condition to which the pending question is thus remitted.

The treaty upon this subject concluded in 1818, through disagreements as to the meaning of its terms, has been a fruitful source of irritation and trouble. Our citizens engaged in fishing enterprises in waters adjacent to Canada have been subjected to numerous vexatious interferences and annoyances; their vessels have been seized upon pretexts which appeared to be entirely inadmissible, and they have been otherwise treated by the Canadian authorities and officials in a manner inexcusably harsh and oppressive.

This conduct has been justified by Great Britain and Canada by the claim that the treaty of 1818 permitted it and upon the ground that it was necessary to the proper protection of Canadian interests. We deny that treaty agreements justify these acts, and we further maintain that aside from any treaty restraints of disputed interpretation the relative positions of the United States and Canada as near neighbors, the growth of our joint commerce, the development and prosperity of both countries, which amicable relations surely guarantee, and, above all, the liberality always extended by the United States to the people of Canada furnished motives for kindness and consideration higher and better than treaty covenants.

While keenly sensitive to all that was exasperating in the condition and by no means indisposed to support the just complaints of our injured citizens, I still deemed it my duty, for the preservation of important American interests which were directly involved, and in view of all the details of the situation, to attempt by negotiation to remedy existing wrongs and to finally terminate by a fair and just treaty these ever-recurring causes of difficulty.

I fully believe that the treaty just rejected by the Senate was well suited to the exigency, and that its provisions were adequate for our security in the future from vexatious incidents and for the promotion of friendly neighborhood and intimacy, without sacrificing in the least our national pride or dignity.

I am quite conscious that neither my opinion of the value of the rejected treaty nor the motives which prompted its negotiation are of importance in the light of the judgment of the Senate thereupon. But it is of importance to note that this treaty has been rejected without any apparent disposition on the part of the Senate to alter or amend its provisions, and with the evident intention, not wanting expression, that no negotiation should at present be concluded touching the matter at issue.

The cooperation necessary for the adjustment of the long-standing national differences with which we have to deal by methods of conference and agreement having thus been declined, I am by no means disposed to abandon the interests and the rights of our people in the premises or to neglect their grievances; and I therefore turn to the contemplation of a plan of retaliation as a mode which still remains of treating the situation.

I am not unmindful of the gravity of the responsibility assumed in adopting this line of conduct, nor do I fail in the least to appreciate its serious consequences. It will be impossible to injure our Canadian neighbors by retaliatory measures without inflicting some damage upon our own citizens. This results from our proximity, our community of interests, and the inevitable commingling of the business enterprises which have been developed by mutual activity.

Plainly stated, the policy of national retaliation manifestly embraces the infliction of the greatest harm upon those who have injured us, with the least possible damage to ourselves. There is also an evident propriety, as well as an invitation to moral support, found in visiting upon the offending party the same measure or kind of treatment of which we complain, and as far as possible within the same lines. And above all things, the plan of retaliation, if entered upon, should be thorough and vigorous.

These considerations lead me at this time to invoke the aid and counsel of the Congress and its support in such a further grant of power as seems to me necessary and desirable to render effective the policy I have indicated.

The Congress has already passed a law, which received Executive assent on the 3d day of March, 1887, providing that in case American fishing vessels, being or visiting in the waters or at any of the ports of the British dominions of North America, should be or lately had been deprived of the rights to which they were entitled by treaty or law, or if they were denied certain other privileges therein specified or vexed and harassed in the enjoyment of the same, the President might deny to vessels and their masters and crews of the British dominions of North America any entrance into the waters, ports, or harbors of the United States, and also deny entry into any port or place of the United States of any product of said dominions or other goods coming from said dominions to the United States.

While I shall not hesitate upon proper occasion to enforce this act, it would seem to be unnecessary to suggest that if such enforcement is limited in such a manner as shall result in the least possible injury to our own people the effect would probably be entirely inadequate to the accomplishment of the purpose desired.

I deem it my duty, therefore, to call the attention of the Congress to certain particulars in the action of the authorities of the Dominion of Canada, in addition to the general allegations already made, which appear to be in such marked contrast to the liberal and friendly disposition of our country as in my opinion to call for such legislation as will, upon the principles already stated, properly supplement the power to inaugurate retaliation already vested in the Executive.

Actuated by the generous and neighborly spirit which has characterized our legislation, our tariff laws have since 1866 been so far waived in favor of Canada as to allow free of duty the transit across the territory of the United States of property arriving at our ports and destined to Canada, or exported from Canada to other foreign countries.

When the treaty of Washington was negotiated, in 1871, between the United States and Great Britain, having for its object very largely the modification of the treaty of 1818, the privileges above referred to were made reciprocal and given in return by Canada to the United States in the following language, contained in the twenty-ninth article of said treaty:

It is agreed that for the term of years mentioned in Article XXXIII of this treaty goods, wares, or merchandise arriving at the ports of New York, Boston, and Portland, and any other ports in the United States which have been or may from time to time be specially designated by the President of the United States, and destined for Her Britannic Majesty's possessions in North America, may be entered at the proper custom-house and conveyed in transit, without the payment of duties, through the territory of the United States, under such rules, regulations, and conditions for the protection of the revenue as the Government of the United States may from time to time prescribe; and, under like rules, regulations, and conditions, goods, wares, or merchandise may be conveyed in transit, without the payment of duties, from such possessions through the territory of the United States, for export from the said ports of the United States.

It is further agreed that for the like period goods, wares, or merchandise arriving at any of the ports of Her Britannic Majesty's possessions in North America, and destined for the United States, may be entered at the proper custom-house and conveyed in transit, without the payment of duties, through the said possessions, under such rules and regulations and conditions for the protection of the revenue as the governments of the said possessions may from time to time prescribe; and, under like rules, regulations, and conditions, goods, wares, or merchandise may be conveyed in transit, without payment of duties, from the United States through the said possessions to other places in the United States, or for export from ports in the said possessions.

In the year 1886 notice was received by the representatives of our

Government that our fishermen would no longer be allowed to ship their fish in bond and free of duty through Canadian territory to this country, and ever since that time such shipment has been denied.

The privilege of such shipment, which had been extended to our fishermen, was a most important one, allowing them to spend the time upon the fishing grounds which would otherwise be devoted to a voyage home with their catch, and doubling their opportunities for profitably prosecuting their vocation.

In forbidding the transit of the catch of our fishermen over their territory in bond and free of duty the Canadian authorities deprived us of the only facility dependent upon their concession and for which we could supply no substitute.

The value to the Dominion of Canada of the privilege of transit for their exports and imports across our territory and to and from our ports, though great in every aspect, will be better appreciated when it is remembered that for a considerable portion of each year the St. Lawrence River, which constitutes the direct avenue of foreign commerce leading to Canada, is closed by ice.

During the last six years the imports and exports of British Canadian Provinces carried across our territory under the privileges granted by our laws amounted in value to about $270,000,000, nearly all of which were goods dutiable under our tariff laws, by far the larger part of this traffic consisting of exchanges of goods between Great Britain and her American Provinces brought to and carried from our ports in their own vessels.

The treaty stipulation entered into by our Government was in harmony with laws which were then on our statute book and are still in force.

I recommend immediate legislative action conferring upon the Executive the power to suspend by proclamation the operation of all laws and regulations permitting the transit of goods, wares, and merchandise in bond across or over the territory of the United States to or from Canada.

There need be no hesitation in suspending these laws arising from the supposition that their continuation is secured by treaty obligations, for it seems quite plain that Article XXIX of the treaty of 1871, which was the only article incorporating such laws, terminated the 1st day of July, 1885.

The article itself declares that its provisions shall be in force "for the term of years mentioned in Article XXXIII of this treaty." Turning to Article XXXIII, we find no mention of the twenty-ninth article, but only a provision that Articles XVIII to XXV, inclusive, and Article XXX shall take effect as soon as the laws required to carry them into operation shall be passed by the legislative bodies of the different countries concerned, and that "they shall remain in force for the period of ten years from the date at which they may come into operation, and, further, until the expiration of two years after either of the high contracting parties shall have given notice to the other of its wish to terminate the same.''

I am of the opinion that the ''term of years mentioned in Article XXXIII,'' referred to in Article XXIX as the limit of its duration, means the period during which Articles XVIII to XXV, inclusive, and Article XXX, commonly called the ''fishery articles,'' should continue in force under the language of said Article XXXIII.

That the joint high commissioners who negotiated the treaty so understood and intended the phrase is certain, for in a statement containing an account of their negotiations, prepared under their supervision and approved by them, we find the following entry on the subject:

The transit question was discussed, and it was agreed that any settlement that might be made should include a reciprocal arrangement in that respect for the period for which the fishery articles should be in force.

In addition to this very satisfactory evidence supporting this construction of the language of Article XXIX, it will be found that the law passed by Congress to carry the treaty into effect furnishes conclusive proof of the correctness of such construction.

This law was passed March 1, 1873, and is entitled ''An act to carry into effect the provisions of the treaty between the United States and Great Britain signed in the city of Washington the 8th day of May, 1871, relating to the fisheries.'' After providing in its first and second sections for putting in operation Articles XVIII to XXV, inclusive, and Article XXX of the treaty, the third section is devoted to Article XXIX, as follows:

SEC. 3. That from the date of the President's proclamation authorized by the first section of this act, and so long as the articles eighteenth to twenty-fifth, inclusive, and article thirtieth of said treaty shall remain in force according to the terms and conditions of article thirty-third of said treaty, all goods, wares, and merchandise, arriving—

etc., etc., following in the remainder of the section the precise words of the stipulation on the part of the United States as contained in Article XXIX, which I have already fully quoted.

Here, then, is a distinct enactment of the Congress limiting the duration of this article of the treaty to the time that Articles XVIII to XXV, inclusive, and Article XXX should continue in force. That in fixing such limitation it but gave the meaning of the treaty itself is indicated by the fact that its purpose is declared to be to carry into effect the provisions of the treaty, and by the further fact that this law appears to have been submitted before the promulgation of the treaty to certain members of the joint high commission representing both countries, and met with no objection or dissent.

There appearing to be no conflict or inconsistency between the treaty and the act of the Congress last cited, it is not necessary to invoke the well-settled principle that in case of such conflict the statute governs the question.

In any event, and whether the law of 1873 construes the treaty or governs it, section 29 of such treaty, I have no doubt, terminated with the proceedings taken by our Government to terminate Articles XVIII to XXV, inclusive, and Article XXX of the treaty. These proceedings had their inception in a joint resolution of Congress passed May 3, 1883, declaring that in the judgment of Congress these articles ought to be terminated, and directing the President to give the notice to the Government of Great Britain provided for in Article XXXIII of the treaty. Such notice having been given two years prior to the 1st day of July, 1885, the articles mentioned were absolutely terminated on the last-named day, and with them Article XXIX was also terminated.

If by any language used in the joint resolution it was intended to relieve section 3 of the act of 1873, embodying Article XXIX of the treaty, from its own limitations, or to save the article itself, I am entirely satisfied that the intention miscarried.

But statutes granting to the people of Canada the valuable privileges of transit for their goods from our ports and over our soil, which had been passed prior to the making of the treaty of 1871 and independently of it, remained in force; and ever since the abrogation of the treaty, and notwithstanding the refusal of Canada to permit our fishermen to send their fish to their home market through her territory in bond, the people of that Dominion have enjoyed without diminution the advantages of our liberal and generous laws.

Without basing our complaint upon a violation of treaty obligations, it is nevertheless true that such refusal of transit and the other injurious acts which have been recited constitute a provoking insistence upon rights neither mitigated by the amenities of national intercourse nor modified by the recognition of our liberality and generous considerations.

The history of events connected with this subject makes it manifest that the Canadian government can, if so disposed administer its laws and protect the interests of its people without manifestation of unfriendliness and without the unneighborly treatment of our fishing vessels of which we have justly complained, and whatever is done on our part should be done in the hope that the disposition of the Canadian government may remove the occasion of a resort to the additional executive power now sought through legislative action.

I am satisfied that upon the principles which should govern retaliation our intercourse and relations with the Dominion of Canada furnish no better opportunity for its application than is suggested by the conditions herein presented, and that it could not be more effectively inaugurated than under the power of suspension recommended.

While I have expressed my clear conviction upon the question of the continuance of section 29 of the treaty of 1871, I of course fully concede the power and the duty of the Congress, in contemplating legislative action, to construe the terms of any treaty stipulation which might upon any possible consideration of good faith limit such action, and likewise the peculiar propriety in the case here presented of its interpretation of its own language, as contained in the laws of 1873 putting in operation said treaty and of 1883 directing the termination thereof; and if in the deliberate judgment of Congress any restraint to the proposed legislation exists, it is to be hoped that the expediency of its early removal will be recognized.

I desire also to call the attention of the Congress to another subject involving such wrongs and unfair treatment to our citizens as, in my opinion, require prompt action.

The navigation of the Great Lakes and the immense business and carrying trade growing out of the same have been treated broadly and liberally by the United States Government and made free to all mankind, while Canadian railroads and navigation companies share in our country's transportation upon terms as favorable as are accorded to our own citizens.

The canals and other public works built and maintained by the Government along the line of the lakes are made free to all.

In contrast to this condition, and evincing a narrow and ungenerous commercial spirit, every lock and canal which is a public work of the Dominion of Canada is subject to tolls and charges.

By Article XXVII of the treaty of 1871 provision was made to secure to the citizens of the United States the use of the Welland, St. Lawrence, and other canals in the Dominion of Canada on terms of equality with the inhabitants of the Dominion, and to also secure to the subjects of Great Britain the use of the St. Clair Flats Canal on terms of equality with the inhabitants of the United States.

The equality with the inhabitants of the Dominion which we were promised in the use of the canals of Canada did not secure to us freedom from tolls in their navigation, but we had a right to expect that we, being Americans and interested in American commerce, would be no more burdened in regard to the same than Canadians engaged in their own trade; and the whole spirit of the concession made was, or should have been, that merchandise and property transported to an American market through these canals should not be enhanced in its cost by tolls many times higher than such as were carried to an adjoining Canadian market. All our citizens, producers and consumers as well as vessel owners, were to enjoy the equality promised.

And yet evidence has for some time been before the Congress, furnished by the Secretary of the Treasury, showing that while the tolls charged in the first instance are the same to all, such vessels and cargoes as are destined to certain Canadian ports are allowed a refund of nearly the entire tolls, while those bound for American ports are not allowed any such advantage.

To promise equality, and then in practice make it conditional upon our vessels doing Canadian business instead of their own, is to fulfill a promise with the shadow of performance.

I recommend that such legislative action be taken as will give Canadian vessels navigating our canals, and their cargoes, precisely the advantages granted to our vessels and cargoes upon Canadian canals, and that the same be measured by exactly the same rule of discrimination.

The course which I have outlined and the recommendations made relate to the honor and dignity of our country and the protection and preservation of the rights and interests of all our people. A government does but half its duty when it protects its citizens at home and permits them to be imposed upon and humiliated by the unfair and overreaching disposition of other nations. If we invite our people to rely upon arrangements made for their benefit abroad, we should see to it that they are not deceived; and if we are generous and liberal to a neighboring country, our people should reap the advantage of it by a return of liberality and generosity.

These are subjects which partisanship should not disturb or confuse. Let us survey the ground calmly and moderately; and having put aside other means of settlement, if we enter upon the policy of retaliation let us pursue it firmly, with a determination only to subserve the interests of our people and maintain the high standard and the becoming pride of American citizenship.   GROVER CLEVELAND.

EXECUTIVE MANSION, *August 27, 1888.*

To the House of Representatives:

In compliance with a resolution of the House of Representatives of the 27th instant (the Senate concurring), I return herewith House bill No. 10060, entitled "An act prescribing the times for sales and for notice of sales of property in the District of Columbia for overdue taxes."

GROVER CLEVELAND.

EXECUTIVE MANSION, *September 7, 1888.*

To the Senate of the United States:

In reply to the resolution of the Senate in the words following—

IN THE SENATE OF THE UNITED STATES,
September 5, 1888.

Resolved, That the President is requested, if not incompatible with the public interests, to inform the Senate whether the recent treaty with China and the amendments adopted by the Senate have been ratified by the Emperor of China—

I have to communicate the annexed copies of dispatches from our minister to China, giving the only official information at hand in relation to the matter to which reference is had.

GROVER CLEVELAND.

To the Senate: EXECUTIVE MANSION, *September 12, 1888.*

Responding to the inquiries contained in the subjoined resolution of the Senate of the 28th ultimo, I have the honor to state in reply to the subject first therein mentioned, calling upon the Executive for "copies of all communications, if any, addressed by his direction to the Government of Great Britain, remonstrating with that Government against the wrongs and unfair treatment to our citizens by the action of the Canadian Government in refunding to vessels and cargoes which pass through the Welland and other Canadian canals nearly the entire tolls if they are destined to Canadian ports, while those bound for American ports are not allowed any such advantage, and the breach of the engagement contained in the treaty of 1871 whereby Great Britain promised to the United States equality in the matter of such canal transportation; also copies of any demand made by his direction upon Great Britain for the redress of such wrongs, and the replies of Great Britain to such communication and demand," that I herewith transmit copies of all communications between the Department of State and the United States consul at Ottawa, which are accompanied by copies of the orders of the Canadian officials in relation to the subject inquired of; also correspondence between the Department of State and the British minister at this capital, with copies of the documents therein referred to.

I also inclose, as connected therewith, a copy of Executive Document No. 406, House of Representatives, Fiftieth Congress, first session, containing the answer of the Acting Secretary of the Treasury, dated July 23, 1888, in reply to a resolution of the House of Representatives relating to the navigation of the Welland Canal, and the documents thus transmitted comprise the entire correspondence in relation to the subjects referred to in that portion of the resolution of inquiry which is above quoted.

The second branch of inquiry is in the words following:

And also that there be communicated to the Senate copies of all papers, correspondence, and information touching the matter of the refusal of the British Government, or that of any of her North American dominions, to allow the entry at Dominion seaports of American fish or other cargoes for transportation in bond to the United States since the 1st day of July, 1885.

It will be remembered that though the fishing articles of the treaty of 1871 expired on the said 1st day of July, 1885, a temporary arrangement was made whereby the privileges accorded to our fishermen under said articles were continued during the remainder of that year's fishing season.

No instance of refusal by the Canadian authorities since July 1, 1885, up to the present time to allow the entry at Dominion seaports of American cargoes other than fish for transportation in bond across the territory of Canada to the United States has been made known to the Department of State.

The case of the fishing steamer *Novelty*, involving, among other things, a refusal, on July 1, 1886, of the right to permit the transshipment of fish in bond at the port of Pictou, Nova Scotia, was duly communicated to Congress in my message of December 8, 1886, a copy of which I herewith transmit. (Ex. Doc. No. 19, Forty-ninth Congress, second session, p. 1.)

On page 16 of this document will be found a copy of a communication addressed by the Secretary of State to the British minister, dated June 14, 1886, on the subject of the refusal of transshipment of fish in bond. At page 24 of the same publication will be found the protest of the Secretary of State in the case of the *Novelty*, and at pages 49–50 are the response of the British minister and report of the Canadian privy council.

On the 26th of January, 1887, a revised list of cases of alleged ill treatment of our fishing vessels in Canadian waters was furnished by the Secretary of State to the Committee on Foreign Relations of the Senate, in which the above case is included, a copy of which, being Senate Executive Document No. 55 of the second session Forty-ninth Congress, is herewith inclosed; and in the report by Mr. Edmunds, from the Committee on Foreign Relations (No. 1683 of the same session), the case referred to was again published. And, as relating to the subject of the resolution now before me, the following pertinent passage, taken from the said report, may be of interest:

As regards commercial and other friendly business intercourse between ports and places in the Dominion and the United States, it is, of course, of much importance that regulations affecting the same should be mutually reasonable and fairly administered. If an American vessel should happen to have caught a cargo of fish at sea 100 miles distant from some Canadian port, from which there is railway communication to the United States, and should be denied the privilege of landing and shipping its cargo therefrom to the United States, as the Canadians do, it would be, of course, a serious disadvantage; and there is, it is thought, nothing in the treaty of 1818 which would warrant such an exclusion. But the Dominion laws may make such a distinction, and it is understood that in fact the privilege of so shipping fish from American vessels has been refused during the last year.

I also respectfully refer to Senate Miscellaneous Document No. 54, Forty-ninth Congress, second session, being a communication from the Commissioner of Fish and Fisheries to Hon. George F. Edmunds, chairman of the Committee on Foreign Relations, dated February 5, 1887, which is accompanied by a partial list of vessels injuriously treated by the Canadian authorities, based upon information furnished to the United States Commissioner of Fish and Fisheries.

This list is stated to be supplementary to the revised list which had been transmitted to the committee by the Secretary of State January 26, 1887.

Of the sixty-eight vessels comprised in this list it is stated that six, to wit, the *Nellie M. Snow, Andrew Burnham, Harry G. French, Col. J. H. French, W. H. Wellington,* and *Ralph Hodgdon,* were refused permission to transship fish. None of these cases, however, were ever reported to the Department of State by the parties interested, or were accompanied by affidavit; nor does it appear the facts ever were investigated in any of the cases by the parties making the reports, which were obtained by circulars issued by order of the Commissioner of Fish and Fisheries.

The concluding inquiry is as follows:

And also that he communicate to the Senate what instances have occurred since the 3d of March, 1887, of wrongs to American fishing vessels or other American vessels in the ports or waters of British North America, and what steps, if any, have been taken in respect thereto.

Soon after the passage of the act of March 3, 1887, the negotiation which had been proceeding for several months previously progressed actively, and the proposed conference and the presence at this capital of the plenipotentiaries of the two Governments, out of which the since rejected treaty of February 7, 1888, eventuated, had their natural influence in repressing causes of complaint in relation to the fisheries. Therefore since March 3, 1887, no case has been reported to the Department of State wherein complaint was made of unfriendly or unlawful treatment of American fishing vessels on the part of the Canadian authorities in which reparation was not promptly and satisfactorily obtained by the United States consul-general at Halifax.

A single case of alleged unjust treatment of an American merchant vessel, not engaged in fishing, has been reported since March 3, 1887. This was the ship *Bridgewater*, which was first brought to the attention of the Department of State by the claimant by petition filed June 1, 1888.

On June 18, 1888, legal counsel, who appeared and desired to be heard, filed their formal authority and the claim was at once duly investigated, and on June 22, 1888, a communication was addressed by the Secretary of State to the British minister, which sets forth the history of the claim, and a copy of which is herewith transmitted; and of this formal acknowledgment was made, but no further reply has been received.

GROVER CLEVELAND.

To the Senate: EXECUTIVE MANSION, *September 18, 1888.*

I herewith transmit, in reply to the resolution of the Senate of the 11th instant, a copy of a report from the Secretary of State, with accompanying documents, relative to the pending treaty with China.

GROVER CLEVELAND.

To the Congress: EXECUTIVE MANSION, *October 1, 1888.*

I have this day approved House bill No. 11336, supplementary to an act entitled "An act to execute certain treaty stipulations relating to Chinese," approved the 6th day of May, 1882.

It seems to me that some suggestions and recommendations may properly accompany my approval of this bill.

Its object is to more effectually accomplish by legislation the exclusion from this country of Chinese laborers.

The experiment of blending the social habits and mutual race idiosyncrasies of the Chinese laboring classes with those of the great body of the people of the United States has been proved by the experience of twenty years, and ever since the Burlingame treaty of 1868, to be in every sense unwise, impolitic, and injurious to both nations. With the lapse of time the necessity for its abandonment has grown in force, until those having in charge the Government of the respective countries have resolved to modify and sufficiently abrogate all those features of prior conventional arrangements which permitted the coming of Chinese laborers to the United States.

In modification of prior conventions the treaty of November 17, 1880, was concluded, whereby, in the first article thereof, it was agreed that the United States should at will regulate, limit, or suspend the coming of Chinese laborers to the United States, but not absolutely prohibit it; and under this article an act of Congress, approved on May 6, 1882 (see 22 U. S. Statutes at Large, p. 58), and amended July 5, 1884 (23 U. S. Statutes at Large, p. 115), suspended for ten years the coming of Chinese laborers to the United States, and regulated the going and coming of such Chinese laborers as were at that time in the United States.

It was, however, soon made evident that the mercenary greed of the parties who were trading in the labor of this class of the Chinese population was proving too strong for the just execution of the law, and that the virtual defeat of the object and intent of both law and treaty was being fraudulently accomplished by false pretense and perjury, contrary to the expressed will of both Governments.

To such an extent has the successful violation of the treaty and the laws enacted for its execution progressed that the courts in the Pacific States have been for some time past overwhelmed by the examination of cases of Chinese laborers who are charged with having entered our ports under fraudulent certificates of return or seek to establish by perjury the claim of prior residence.

Such demonstration of the inoperative and inefficient condition of the treaty and law has produced deep-seated and increasing discontent among the people of the United States, and especially with those resident on the Pacific Coast. This has induced me to omit no effort to find an effectual remedy for the evils complained of and to answer the earnest popular demand for the absolute exclusion of Chinese laborers having objects and purposes unlike our own and wholly disconnected with American citizenship.

Aided by the presence in this country of able and intelligent diplomatic and consular officers of the Chinese Government, and the representations made from time to time by our minister in China under the instructions of the Department of State, the actual condition of public sentiment and the status of affairs in the United States have been fully made known to the Government of China.

The necessity for remedy has been fully appreciated by that Government, and in August, 1886, our minister at Peking received from the Chinese foreign office a communication announcing that China, of her own accord, proposed to establish a system of strict and absolute prohibition of her laborers, under heavy penalties, from coming to the United States, and likewise to prohibit the return to the United States of any Chinese laborer who had at any time gone back to China, "in order" (in the words of the communication) "that the Chinese laborers may gradually be reduced in number and causes of danger averted and lives preserved."

This view of the Chinese Government, so completely in harmony with that of the United States, was by my direction speedily formulated in a treaty draft between the two nations, embodying the propositions so presented by the Chinese foreign office.

The deliberations, frequent oral discussions, and correspondence on the general questions that ensued have been fully communicated by me to the Senate at the present session, and, as contained in Senate Executive Document O, parts 1 and 2, and in Senate Executive Document No. 272, may be properly referred to as containing a complete history of the transaction.

It is thus easy to learn how the joint desires and unequivocal mutual understanding of the two Governments were brought into articulated form in the treaty, which, after a mutual exhibition of plenary powers from the respective Governments, was signed and concluded by the plenipotentiaries of the United States and China at this capital on March 12 last.

Being submitted for the advice and consent of the Senate, its confirmation, on the 7th day of May last, was accompanied by two amendments which that body ingrafted upon it.

On the 12th day of the same month the Chinese minister, who was the plenipotentiary of his Government in the negotiation and the conclusion of the treaty, in a note to the Secretary of State gave his approval to these amendments, "as they did not alter the terms of the treaty," and the amendments were at once telegraphed to China, whither the original treaty had previously been sent immediately after its signature on March 12.

On the 13th day of last month I approved Senate bill No. 3304, "to prohibit the coming of Chinese laborers to the United States." This bill was intended to supplement the treaty, and was approved in the confident anticipation of an early exchange of ratifications of the treaty and its amendments and the proclamation of the same, upon which event the legislation so approved was by its terms to take effect.

No information of any definite action upon the treaty by the Chinese Government was received until the 21st ultimo—the day the bill which I have just approved was presented to me—when a telegram from our minister at Peking to the Secretary of State announced the refusal of the Chinese Government to exchange ratifications of the treaty unless further discussion should be had with a view to shorten the period stipulated in the treaty for the exclusion of Chinese laborers and to change the conditions agreed on, which should entitle any Chinese laborer who might go back to China to return again to the United States.

By a note from the chargé d'affaires *ad interim* of China to the Secretary of State, received on the evening of the 25th ultimo (a copy of which is herewith transmitted, together with the reply thereto), a third amendment is proposed, whereby the certificate under which any departing Chinese laborer alleging the possession of property in the United States would be enabled to return to this country should be granted by the Chinese consul instead of the United States collector, as had been provided in the treaty.

The obvious and necessary effect of this last proposition would be practically to place the execution of the treaty beyond the control of the United States.

Article I of the treaty proposed to be so materially altered had in the course of the negotiations been settled in acquiescence with the request of the Chinese plenipotentiary and to his expressed satisfaction.

In 1886, as appears in the documents heretofore referred to, the Chinese foreign office had formally proposed to our minister strict exclusion of Chinese laborers from the United States without limitation, and had otherwise and more definitely stated that no term whatever for exclusion was necessary, for the reason that China would of itself take steps to prevent its laborers from coming to the United States.

In the course of the negotiations that followed suggestions from the same quarter led to the insertion in behalf of the United States of a term of "thirty years," and this term, upon the representations of the Chinese plenipotentiary, was reduced to "twenty years," and finally so agreed upon.

Article II was wholly of Chinese origination, and to that alone owes its presence in the treaty.

And it is here pertinent to remark that everywhere in the United States laws for the collection of debts are equally available to all creditors without respect to race, sex, nationality, or place of residence, and equally with the citizens or subjects of the most favored nations and with the citizens of the United States recovery can be had in any court of justice in the United States by a subject of China, whether of the laboring or any other class.

No disability accrues from nonresidence of a plaintiff, whose claim can be enforced in the usual way by him or his assignee or attorney in our courts of justice.

In this respect it can not be alleged that there exists the slightest discrimination against Chinese subjects, and it is a notable fact that large trading firms and companies and individual merchants and traders of that nation are profitably established at numerous points throughout the Union, in whose hands every claim transmitted by an absent Chinaman of a just and lawful nature could be completely enforced.

The admitted and paramount right and duty of every government to exclude from its borders all elements of foreign population which for any reason retard its prosperity or are detrimental to the moral and physical health of its people must be regarded as a recognized canon of international law and intercourse. China herself has not dissented from this doctrine, but has, by the expressions to which I have referred, led us confidently to rely upon such action on her part in cooperation with us as would enforce the exclusion of Chinese laborers from our country.

This cooperation has not, however, been accorded us. Thus from the unexpected and disappointing refusal of the Chinese Government to confirm the acts of its authorized agent and to carry into effect an international agreement, the main feature of which was voluntarily presented by that Government for our acceptance, and which had been the subject of long and careful deliberation, an emergency has arisen, in which the Government of the United States is called upon to act in self-defense by the exercise of its legislative power. I can not but regard the expressed demand on the part of China for a reexamination and renewed discussion of the topics so completely covered by mutual treaty stipulations as an indefinite postponement and practical abandonment of the objects we have in view, to which the Government of China may justly be considered as pledged.

The facts and circumstances which I have narrated lead me, in the performance of what seems to me to be my official duty, to join the Congress in dealing legislatively with the question of the exclusion of Chinese laborers, in lieu of further attempts to adjust it by international agreement.

But while thus exercising our undoubted right in the interest of our people and for the general welfare of our country, justice and fairness seem to require that some provision should be made by act or joint resolution under which such Chinese laborers as shall actually have embarked on their return to the United States before the passage of the law this day approved, and are now on their way, may be permitted to land, provided they have duly and lawfully obtained and shall present certificates heretofore issued permitting them to return in accordance with the provisions of existing law.

Nor should our recourse to legislative measures of exclusion cause us to retire from the offer we have made to indemnify such Chinese subjects as have suffered damage through violence in the remote and comparatively unsettled portions of our country at the hands of lawless men. Therefore I recommend that, without acknowledging legal liability therefor, but because it was stipulated in the treaty which has failed to take effect, and in a spirit of humanity befitting our nation, there be appropriated the sum of $276,619.75, payable to the Chinese minister at this capital on behalf of his Government, as full indemnity for all losses and injuries sustained by Chinese subjects in the manner and under the circumstances mentioned.   GROVER CLEVELAND.

EXECUTIVE MANSION,
Washington, October 12, 1888.

To the Senate:

I transmit, with a view to its ratification, a convention between the United States of America and Venezuela to further extend the period for the exchange of ratifications of the claims convention of December 5, 1885, between the said contracting parties and to extend the period for the exchange of ratifications of the convention of March 15, 1888, between the same contracting parties, also relating to claims.

I invite attention to the accompanying report of the Secretary of State and the papers inclosed therein.   GROVER CLEVELAND.

VETO MESSAGES.

EXECUTIVE MANSION,
Washington, April 4, 1888.

To the House of Representatives:

I return herewith without approval House bill 2477, entitled "An act for the relief of Nathaniel McKay and the executors of Donald McKay."

It is proposed by this bill to allow the beneficiaries named therein to present to the Court of Claims for determination certain demands made by them against the Government on account of the construction of two ironclad monitors called the *Squando* and the *Nauset* and a side-wheel steamer called the *Ashuelot.*

The contracts for building these vessels were made early in 1863. It was agreed that they should be completed within six or eight months. It was also provided in these contracts that the Government "should have the privilege of making alterations and additions to the plans and specifications at any time during the progress of the work, as it may deem necessary and proper," and that if said alterations and additions should cause extra expense to the contractors the Government would "pay for the same at fair and reasonable rates."

It thus appears that the time allowed for the completion of these vessels was with the assent of the contractors made exceedingly short; that notwithstanding this fact they consented to permit such alterations of plans as must almost necessarily prolong the time, fixing no limit to such extension, and that in the same breath they fix their measure of compensation for such alterations and an extended time consequent thereon at "a fair and reasonable rate" for the extra expense caused thereby.

Almost immediately upon the beginning of their work alterations and changes were made in the original plans for these vessels, and they were repeated and continued to such a degree that the completion of the vessels was delayed many months.

In the latter part of the year 1864 and early in the year 1865 payments in excess of the contract price were made by the Navy Department to the contractors under the provisions of the contract above recited. The contract price for the *Squando* was $395,000. The contractors claimed extra compensation amounting to $337,329.46, and there was allowed $194,-525.70. The contract price of the *Nauset* was $386,000, the extra compensation claimed was $314,768.93, and the amount allowed $192,110.98. The contract price of the side-wheel steamer *Ashuelot* was $275,000, the extra compensation claimed was $81,447.50, and the amount allowed was $22,415 92. The different sums as thus adjusted were received by the contractors in settlement of their claims for extra expense, and receipts in full were given by them to the Government.

A number of other contractors had done like work for the Government and claimed to have demands growing out of the same for extra compensation.

Evidently with the view of investigating and settling these claims, on the 9th day of March, 1865, the Senate passed the following resolution:

Resolved, That the Secretary of the Navy be requested to organize a board of not less than three persons, whose duty it shall be to inquire into and determine how much the vessels of war and steam machinery contracted for by the Department in the years 1862 and 1863 cost the contractors over and above the contract price and allowance for extra work, and report the same to the Senate at its next session; none but those that have given satisfaction to the Department to be considered.

This board was appointed by the Secretary of the Navy on the 25th day of May, 1865, and consisted of a commodore, a chief engineer, and a paymaster in the Navy. Its powers were broad and liberal, and comprehended an inquiry touching all things that made up "the cost to the contractors" of their work in excess of the contract price and allowances for extra work.

The board convened on the 6th day of June, 1865, and sat continuously until the 23d day of December following, and made numerous awards to contractors. The parties mentioned in the bill now under consideration were notified on the 9th and 15th days of June, 1865, to prepare and submit testimony to the board in support of their claims, and they repeatedly signified their intention to do so.

Donald McKay was the contractor for the construction of the monitor *Nauset* and the steamer *Ashuelot*. The proceedings of the board show that on the 11th day of August, 1865, he notified the board that the only claim he made for loss was on the hull, boiler, and machinery of the *Ashuelot*, which he would be prepared to present in about six weeks.

Neither of these parties presented any statement to the board, and no claim of theirs was passed upon.

On the 2d day of March, 1867, an act was passed directing the Secretary of the Navy to investigate the claims of all contractors for building vessels of war and steam machinery for the same under contracts made after May 1, 1861, and before January 1, 1864. He was by said act required "to ascertain the additional cost which was necessarily incurred by each contractor in the completion of his work by reason of any changes or alterations in the plans and specifications required and delays in the prosecution of the work occasioned by the Government which were not provided for in the original contract." It was further provided that there should be reported to Congress a tabular statement of each case, which should contain "the name of the contractor, a description of the work, the contract price, the whole increased cost of the work over the contract price, and the amount of such increased cost caused by the delay and action of the Government as aforesaid, and the amount already paid the contractor over and above the contract price."

Under this act Commodore J. A. Marchand, Chief Engineer J. W. King, and Paymaster Edward Foster, of the Navy, were designated by the Secretary of the Navy to make the investigation required. These officers on the 26th day of November, 1867, made a report of their proceedings, which was submitted to the Senate with a tabulated statement of all the claims examined by them and their findings thereon.

It appears by this report that the claims of the beneficiaries mentioned in the bill herewith returned were examined by the board, and that nothing was found due thereon under the terms of the law directing their examination.

These claims have frequently been before Congress since that time. They have been favorably reported and acted upon a number of times, and have also been more than once strongly condemned by committees to whom they were referred.

A resolution was passed in 1871 by the Congress referring these and other claims of a like character to the Court of Claims for adjudication, but it was vetoed by the President for reasons not necessarily affecting the merits of the claims.

The case of Chouteau *vs.* The United States, reported in Fifth Otto, page 61, which arose out of the contract to build a vessel called the *Etlah*, appears to present the same features that belong to the claims here considered. It is stated in the report of the House committee on this bill that "the *Squando* and *Nauset* were identical in the original plans and the changes and alterations thereon with the *Etlah* and *Shiloh*, built in St. Louis;" and yet the Supreme Court of the United States distinctly decided in the *Etlah* case that the only pretext for further compensation should be sought for in the contract, where the contractor had evidently been content to provide for all the remedy he desired.

It seems, then, that the contractors mentioned in this bill, after entering into contracts plainly indicating that changes of plans and consequent delay in their work were in their contemplation, availed themselves of the remedy which they themselves had provided, and thereupon received about 50 per cent in the case of two of these vessels of the contract price for extra work, giving the Government a receipt in full. When soon thereafter opportunity was offered them to make further claim of as broad a nature as they could desire, they failed to do so, and one of them disclaimed any right to recover on account of one of the vessels, though all are now included in the present bill. In 1867 the claims were fully examined under a law of Congress and rejected, and the Supreme Court in an exactly similar case finds neither law nor equity supporting them.

If it be claimed that no compensation has been yet allowed solely for the increase in the price of labor and material caused by delay in construction, it is no hardship to say that as the contractors made provision for change of plans and delay they must be held to have taken the risk of such rise in price and be satisfied with the provision they have made against it. Besides, much of the increase in the price of labor and material is included in the extra cost which has already been reimbursed to them.

But the bill does not provide that these contractors shall be limited in the Court of Claims to a recovery solely for loss occasioned by increase of the cost of labor and material during the delay caused by the Government. By the terms of the proposed act the court is directed to ascertain the additional cost necessarily incurred in building the vessels by reason of any changes or alterations in the plans and specifications and delays in the prosecution of the work. This, it seems to me, would enable these contractors to open the whole question of compensation for extra work.

It hardly seems fair to the Government to permit these claims to be presented after a lapse of twenty-three years since a settlement in full was made and receipts given, after the opportunity which has been offered for establishing further claims if they existed, and when, as a consequence of the contractor's neglect, the Government would labor under great disadvantages in its defense.

I am of the opinion, in view of the history of these claims and the suspicion naturally excited as to their merit, that no injustice will be done if they are laid at rest instead of being given new life and vigor in the Court of Claims.

GROVER CLEVELAND.

EXECUTIVE MANSION, *April 16, 1888.*

To the House of Representatives:

I return herewith without approval House bill No. 445, entitled "An act granting a pension to Laura A. Wright."

The beneficiary named in this bill is the widow of Charles H. Wright, who was pensioned for a gunshot wound received in the military service of the United States on the 19th day of September, 1864. He continued in the receipt of such pension until June 25, 1884, when he committed suicide by hanging.

It is alleged on behalf of his widow that the pain caused by his wound was so great that it caused temporary insanity, under the influence of which he destroyed himself.

There is not a particle of proof that I can discover tending to show an unsound mind, unless it be the fact of his suicide. He suffered much pain at intervals. He was a farmer in comfortable circumstances, and according to the testimony of one of the physicians, filed in support of the widow's claim, his health was good up to the time of his death, except for the wound and its results. The day before his death he was engaged in work connected with his farming occupation, though he complained of pain from his wound. Early the next morning, still complaining, as it is alleged, of his wound, he went out, declaring he was going out to milk, and not returning in due time, upon search his body was found and his self-destruction discovered. This was nearly twenty years after the deceased received his wound, and there is not a suggestion of any act or word of his in all that time indicating insanity. It seems to me it can hardly be assumed in such circumstances that the insanity and death of the soldier resulted from pain arising from his wound, merely because no other explanation can be given. In numerous cases of suicide no cause or motive for self-destruction is discovered.

We have within our borders thousands of widows living in poverty, and some of them in need, whose dead husbands fought bravely and well in defense of the Government, but whose deaths were not occasioned by any incident of military service. In these cases the wife's long vigil at the bed of wasting disease, the poverty that came before the death, and the distressing doubt and uncertainty which darkened the future have not secured to such widows the aid of our pension laws.

With these in sight the bounty of the Government may without injustice be withheld from one whose soldier husband received a pension for nearly twenty years, though all that time able to labor, and who, having reached a stage of comfortable living, made his wife a widow by destroying his own life.

GROVER CLEVELAND.

EXECUTIVE MANSION, *April 16, 1888.*

To the Senate:

I return herewith without approval Senate bill No. 809, entitled "An act granting a pension to Betsey Mannsfield."

It is proposed to grant a pension to the beneficiary named in this bill as the mother of Franklin J. Mannsfield, who enlisted as a private April

27, 1861, and died in camp of disease on the 14th day of November, in the same year. His mother filed an application for pension in June, 1882.

The testimony filed in the Pension Bureau discloses the following facts:

At the time of the death of the soldier the family, besides himself, consisted of three persons—his father and mother and an unmarried sister. They owned and resided upon a homestead in Wisconsin comprising 293 acres, 20 of which were cleared, the balance being in timber, all unencumbered. The assessed valuation was $1,170, the real value being considerably more. The father was a farmer and blacksmith, healthy and able-bodied, and furnishing a comfortable support, but shortly after the soldier's death he began to drink and his health began to fail. Upon the marriage of the daughter he deeded her 50 acres of the land. He became indebted, and from time to time sold portions of his homestead to pay debts; but in 1882, at the time the mother's application for pension was filed, there still remained 110 acres of land, valued at about $3,300, 40 acres of which was mortgaged in 1880 for $600. Since 1879 the farm had been rented, except 8 or 10 acres reserved for a residence for the family. They owned two cows, and the rent averaged about $125 a year.

This was the condition of affairs as late as 1886, when the claim of the mother for a pension was, after investigation, rejected by the Pension Bureau, and it is supposed to be substantially the same now.

It also appears that a son, born since the soldier's death, and upward of 18 years of age, resides with his parents and furnishes them some assistance.

The claimant certainly was not dependent in the least degree upon the soldier at the time of his death, and she did not file her claim for pension until nearly twenty-one years thereafter.

Though the lack of dependence at the date of the soldier's death is sufficient to defeat a parent's claim for pension under our laws, I believe that in proper cases a relaxation of rules and a charitable liberality should be shown to parents old and in absolute need through default of the help which, it may be presumed, a son would have furnished if his life had not been sacrificed in his country's service.

But it seems to me the case presented here can not be reached by any theory of pensions which has yet been suggested.

GROVER CLEVELAND.

To the Senate: EXECUTIVE MANSION, *April 16, 1888.*

I return herewith without approval Senate bill No. 549, entitled ''An act granting a pension to Hannah R. Langdon.''

The husband of the beneficiary named in this bill entered the military service of the United States as assistant surgeon in a Vermont regiment

on the 7th day of October, 1862, and less than six months thereafter tendered his resignation, based upon a surgeon's certificate of disability on
account of chronic hepatitis (inflammation of the liver) and diarrhea.

On the 12th day of June, 1880, more than seventeen years after his
discharge, he filed a claim for pension, alleging chronic diarrhea and
resulting piles. He was allowed a pension in January, 1881, and died of
consumption on the 24th day of September, in the same year.

Prior to the allowance of his claim for pension he wrote to the Bureau
of Pensions a full history of his disability as resulting from chronic diarrhea and piles, and in that letter he made the following statement:

I have had no other disease, except last September (1880) I had pleurisy and congestion of my left lung.

From other sources the Bureau derived the information that the deceased had suffered an attack of pleuro-pneumonia on his left side, and
that his recovery had been partial.

In December, 1880, he was examined by two members of the board of
surgeons at Burlington, Vt., of which board he was also a member, and
the following facts were certified:

For the past fifteen years claimant has practiced his profession in this city, and
has up to within a year or a year and a half of this date shown a vigor and power of
endurance quite equal to the labor imposed upon him by the popular demand for his
services. About a year ago he evinced symptoms of breaking down, cough, emaciation, and debility.

These results—"breaking down, cough, emaciation, and debility"—
are the natural effects of such an attack as the deceased himself reported,
though not made by him any ground of a claim for pension, and it seems
quite clear that his death in September, 1881, must be chargeable to the
same cause.

His widow, the beneficiary named in this bill, filed her claim for pension December 5, 1881, based upon the ground that her husband's death
from consumption was due to the chronic diarrhea for which he was
pensioned. Upon such application the testimony of Dr. H. H. Atwater
was filed, to the effect that about 1879 he began to treat the deceased
regularly for pleuro-pneumonia, followed by abscesses and degeneration
of lung tissue, which finally resulted in death, and that these diseased
conditions were complicated with digestive affections, such as diarrhea,
dyspepsia, and indigestion. Another affidavit of Dr. Atwater, made in
1886, will be found in the report upon this bill made by the House Committee on Invalid Pensions.

The claimant's application for a pension was rejected by the Pension
Bureau on the ground that the cause of her husband's death was not
shown to have been connected in any degree with the disease on account
of which he was pensioned or with his military service.

I am entirely satisfied that this determination was correct.

I am constrained to disapprove the bill under consideration, because it is thus far our settled and avowed policy to grant pensions only to widows whose husbands have died from causes related to military service, and because the proposed legislation would, in my opinion, result in a discrimination in favor of this claimant unfair and unjust toward thousands of poor widows who are equally entitled to our sympathy and benevolence.

GROVER CLEVELAND.

EXECUTIVE MANSION, *April 18, 1888.*

To the Senate:

I return without approval Senate bill No. 258, entitled "An act for the relief of Major Daniel N. Bash, paymaster, United States Army."

The object of this bill is to release Paymaster Bash from all liability to the Government for the loss by theft of $7,350.93, which was intrusted to him for the payment of United States troops at various posts, one of which was Fort McKinney, in Wyoming Territory.

He started from Cheyenne Depot, accompanied by his clerk, D. F. Bash. Before starting he attempted to procure an iron safe in which he could deposit the money which he should have in his possession during his absence, but was unable to do so. It is alleged that it is customary for paymasters in such cases to be furnished with safes by the Government.

On the 17th day of March, 1887, Major Bash arrived at Douglas, Wyoming Territory, having in his possession $350.93, which was a balance left in his hands after making previous payments on the way. At Douglas he received by express $7,000, $250 of which were in silver. He was met here by an escort consisting of a sergeant and private soldier, who had been sent from Fort McKinney, and who were under orders to report to the paymaster at Douglas and to act as guard from that place to Fort McKinney.

Another unsuccessful attempt having been made at Douglas to obtain a safe or treasure box in which to carry the money, the same was put in a leather valise as the best thing that could be done in the circumstances. The money was first handed by the paymaster to his clerk, and by the clerk put in the valise and handed to the sergeant of the escort. There is evidence that the sergeant was told not to permit it to be out of his sight. Immediately after supper at Douglas the entire party entered the stage and proceeded upon their journey, the sergeant carrying the valise. Major Bash asserts that he said to the sergeant, "You must take good care of the valise; it contains the money."

The next morning, on the 18th day of March, the party arrived at Dry Cheyenne. When the paymaster went in to breakfast at that place, he found all the party at the breakfast table. After breakfast he walked out to the stage, the sergeant going at the same time. He asked him what he had done with the valise, and received the reply that it was in the stage. He then said to the sergeant, "You ought to have brought it in with you; you should take better care of that valise." The valise was then examined and the money was found untouched.

Pursuing their journey, the party arrived at Antelope Springs, Wyoming Territory, at half past 10 o'clock the same morning. The paymaster alleges that he asked the sergeant if he should take dinner there, and that, being answered in the negative, he remarked to him that he might then stay at the stage; that he then went to the stage station, leaving the two soldiers and the clerk at the stage; that he remained at the station warming himself a short time, finding there three citizens, one of whom he afterwards learned was Parker, the thief; that he left the room in which he had been warming himself and went to the dining room, passing along the front of the house, and as he did so noticed the stage standing there with no one near it except a stock tender; that on reaching the dining room he found his entire party at the table; that he looked "pretty sharp" at the sergeant, as he was surprised to see him there, but as he was just eating his pie he (the paymaster) said nothing to him; that not more than a minute after that the sergeant and driver got up and went out; that three or four minutes after they went out they rushed back and said that the valise had been taken.

It was found that the valise and money had been taken by Parker, who had mounted a horse and ridden away. He was pursued so closely that revolver shots were exchanged between the sergeant, who was badly mounted, and the thief. The sergeant alleged that he could have shot Parker if he had been provided with a gun instead of a revolver.

The facts in relation to this subject were developed upon a court of inquiry called for that purpose; and much of the above recited is derived from the evidence of Major Bash himself, taken upon such inquiry.

The following is the finding of the court concerning the conduct of the paymaster in the premises:

That Major Daniel N. Bash, paymaster, United States Army, did not give such direct and detailed orders to the members of the escort as to the manner in which they should guard the public money in his (Bash's) possession while en route to Fort McKinney as the importance of the matter required, and that he did not take the proper and necessary pains to see that any orders which he had given on this subject were duly obeyed.

This finding defines a case of negligence which renders the paymaster liable for the loss of these funds. But a number of army officers, including the members of the court of inquiry, suggest that the paymaster thus found at fault should be relieved from responsibility. This is much the fashion in these days.

It is said that a safe should have been provided; that the paymaster had the right to rely upon the fidelity and efficiency of the escort, and that the two men furnished him as an escort were unintelligent and negligent; that they should have been armed with guns instead of pistols, and that the instructions given to the escort by the paymaster were sufficient to acquit him of culpable neglect.

It seems to me that the omissions of care on the part of this officer are of such a nature as to render much that is urged in his favor irrelevant. He had the charge of this money. It was his care, vigilance, and intelligence which were the safeguards of its protection. If he had as full an appreciation as he indicates of the importance of having a safe, he must have known that in its absence additional care and watchfulness on his part were necessary, whatever his escort or his clerk might do.

But notwithstanding all this he seemed quite content to leave this large sum of money in the hands of those sent to him, not to have the custody of his funds, but to guard him from violence and robbery. On the very morning of the day the theft was committed he had found fault with the sergeant for leaving the money in the stage while he took breakfast, and had said to him that he (the sergeant) ought to have brought it in with him. He here furnishes his own definition of the kind of care which should have been taken of the money—the sergeant "ought to have brought it in with him;" and this suggests the idea that it would have been quite consistent with his duty, and perhaps not much beneath his dignity, if he had taken it in himself. (Chief Paymaster Terrell, in a letter favoring leniency, states that the coin could not have weighed less than 15 pounds.)

It must certainly be conceded that what then took place plainly warned him that to insure the safety of this money he must either take personal charge of it or he must at least be sure that those to whom he surrendered it were watchful and vigilant. And yet when, a few hours later, on the same day, upon arriving at Antelope Springs, he was informed by the sergeant that he did not propose to take dinner there, the paymaster almost casually said to him, "Then you stay at the stage," and he himself went to a room at the station to warm himself. When, as he went from there to the dining room, he passed the stage and saw no one near it except a stock tender, a very conservative idea of duty and care would have induced him to stop at the stage and ascertain the condition of affairs. If he had done so, he probably would have found the money there, and could have taken it in with him or watched it until some of his party came out from dinner. Instead of doing this, he himself went to the dining room, and indicated his surprise at seeing the sergeant there by looking at him sharply. However, as he was just eating his pie, nothing was said.

It is not improbable that the thief waited for the clerk and escort, and lastly the paymaster himself, to enter the dining room before venturing to take, entirely unmolested, the valise containing the money. When it is considered that after finishing his pie the sergeant came out to the stage so nearly the exact moment of the theft that, though badly mounted, he was able to approach near enough in pursuit of the fleeing chief to exchange revolver shots with him, it is quite apparent that the loss might have been prevented if the paymaster had remained a short time by the stage when he saw it unprotected, or had taken the valise in with him, or promptly diverted the attention of the sergeant from his pie to the money which all had abandoned.

When, therefore, it is said that this loss can be charged in any degree to the neglect or default of the Government, it is answered that the direct and immediate cause of the loss was the omission on the part of this pay-master of the Government, in whose custody these funds were placed, of the plainest and simplest acts of prudence and care.

The temptation is very strong to yield assent to the proposition for the relief of a citizen from liability to the Government arising from conduct not absolutely criminal; but the bonds and the security wisely exacted by the Government from its officers to insure proper discharge of public duty will be of very limited value if everything is to be excused except actual dishonesty.

I am thoroughly convinced that the interests of the public would be better protected if fewer private bills were passed relieving officials, upon slight and sentimental grounds, from their pecuniary responsibilities; and the readiness with which army officers join in applications for the condo-nation of negligence on the part of their army comrades does not tend, in my opinion, to maintain that regard for discipline and that scrupu-lous observance of duty which should characterize those belonging to their honorable profession.

I can not satisfy myself that the negligence made apparent in this case should be overlooked. GROVER CLEVELAND.

EXECUTIVE MANSION, *April 21, 1888.*

To the House of Representatives:

I return without approval House bill No. 823, entitled "An act grant-ing a pension to Hannah C. De Witt."

An act the precise duplicate of this was passed at the present session of the Congress, and received Executive approval on the 10th day of March, 1888. Pursuant to said act the name of the beneficiary men-tioned in the bill herewith returned has been placed upon the pension rolls. The second enactment is of course entirely useless, and was evi-dently passed by mistake. GROVER CLEVELAND.

EXECUTIVE MANSION, *April 21, 1888.*

To the House of Representatives:

I return without approval House bill No. 418, entitled "An act grant-ing a pension to William H. Brokenshaw."

The history of the military service of the beneficiary mentioned in this bill, as derived from the records of the War Department, shows that he was received at draft rendezvous at Jackson, Mich., on the 25th day of March, 1865; that he was sent to the Twenty-fourth Regiment of Michigan Volunteers on the 29th day of the same month, and that he was present with his command, without any record of disability, from that date until the 30th day of June, 1865, when he was mustered out with his company. It will thus be seen that he was in the service a few days more than three months, just at the close of the war. It is not alleged that he did any actual fighting.

In 1883 he filed an application for pension, alleging that on the evening of the 25th of March, 1865, being the day he was received at rendezvous, he was injured in his ribs while getting into his bunk by three other recruits, who were scuffling in the room and who jumped upon him or crushed him against the side of his bunk.

An examination upon such application made in 1884 tended to show an injury to his ribs, but the claim was rejected upon the ground that no injury was incurred in the line of duty. It must be conceded that upon the claimant's own showing he was not injured as an incident to military service.

Aside from this objection, it is hardly possible that an injury of this kind, producing the consequences which it is alleged followed its infliction, could have been sustained by this soldier and not in the least interrupted the performance of his military service, though such service was very short and probably not severe. When with this it is considered that eighteen years elapsed between the date of the alleged injury and the soldier's application for pension, I am satisfied that no injustice will be done if the disposition made of this case by the Pension Bureau is allowed to stand.

GROVER CLEVELAND.

EXECUTIVE MANSION, *April 21, 1888.*

To the House of Representatives:

I return without approval House bill No. 4633, entitled "An act granting a pension to Morris T. Mantor."

The records in this case show that the beneficiary named in this bill enlisted on the 25th day of February, 1864, and that he was mustered out July 18, 1865.

It is also shown that though he was reported sick a considerable part of his period of service there is no mention of any trouble with his eyes.

In the year 1880 he filed an application for pension, alleging dropsy and disease of his eyes, caused by an explosion of ammunition.

The case was examined in 1882 and 1883, and was again specially examined very thoroughly and critically in 1885.

The evidence thus secured seemed to establish the fact that the claimant's eyes were sore for many years before enlistment, and that their

WORLD'S FAIR, CHICAGO

WORLD'S FAIR.

The World's Fair was held in Chicago in 1893 to commemorate the four hundredth anniversary of the discovery of America by Columbus. The Fair was a comprehensive exhibit of the arts, industries, manufactures and natural products of the United States. The exhibits covered more than a square mile of land on Chicago's famous Lake Shore. Despite the financial depression, the attendance at the Fair was enormous, and students of American life assert that by no means the least valuable service of the exhibit was its unifying effect upon the country as a whole. (See World's Columbian Exposition in Encyclopedic Index.)

condition before that date, during his service, and after his discharge did not materially differ. It also appeared that no pensionable disability from dropsy had existed since the filing of his application.

On these grounds the application was rejected, and I am convinced such action was entirely justified.

The reported conduct of the claimant on the last examination and his attempts to influence witnesses in their testimony add weight to the proposition, quite well established by the proof, that his claim to a pension lacks merit.

GROVER CLEVELAND.

Executive Mansion, *April 24, 1888.*

To the House of Representatives:

I return without approval House bill No. 5247, entitled "An act granting a pension to William H. Brimmer."

The beneficiary named in this bill enlisted September 5, 1864, as a wagon master, and was discharged on the 30th day of May, 1865. There is no record of any disability during his short service.

In February, 1888, nearly twenty-three years after his discharge, he filed an application for a pension, alleging that in the fall of 1864 he was made to carry sacks of corn, which produced a weakness of the walls of the abdomen, resulting in rupture. In an affidavit filed upon said application the claimant testifies that he said nothing about his injury or disability to anyone while in the service and can furnish no evidence except his own statement.

The first and only medical evidence presented touching this claim is that of Dr. Reynolds, who examined him in 1880 or 1881, who then came to the conclusion that the claimant was suffering from an incomplete hernia, which a few months thereafter developed in the right groin. From this examination and testimony no hint is furnished that the injury was due to military service, nor any intimation that it might be.

In February, 1888, a medical examination was made under direction of the Pension Bureau, when it was found that the claimant had the general appearance of being healthy and well nourished, but that he had a small uncomplicated inguinal hernia on the right side, which was easily retained.

I can not believe upon the facts presented that an injury of the character alleged could have been sustained in the service and still permitted the performance of all the duties of wagon master for months thereafter, remaining undeveloped for so many years, and that there should now be such a lack of testimony connecting it with any incident of military service.

I believe the rejection of this claim was right and just upon its merits.

GROVER CLEVELAND.

EXECUTIVE MANSION, *April 24, 1888.*

To the House of Representatives:

I return without approval House bill 6908, entitled "An act granting a pension to William P. Witt."

The beneficiary named in the bill was enrolled for one hundred days' service on the 13th day of July, 1864, and was mustered out on the 16th day of November, in the same year. The record shows that he was reported present on all rolls until he was mustered out.

He filed a claim for pension in 1884, alleging that he incurred chronic diarrhea, liver disease, rheumatism, and a disease of the head affecting his hearing during his military service. Two comrades testify to his being sick and being in the hospital to such an extent as to wholly discredit his presence with his company. A physician testifies that he prescribed for him some time in the month of November, 1864, for liver disease and jaundice, to which rheumatism supervened, confining him six weeks or more.

There seems to be a complete hiatus of any medical or other evidence concerning his physical condition from that time until nearly twenty years thereafter, in July, 1884, when he was examined, and it was found that he had impaired hearing in both ears, but no symptoms of rheumatism, and that his liver was normal.

Without further detailing particulars, the entire complexion of this case satisfies me that the claimant contracted no pensionable disability during his one hundred days of service.

GROVER CLEVELAND.

EXECUTIVE MANSION, *April 24, 1888.*

To the House of Representatives:

I return without approval House bill No. 4550, entitled "An act granting a pension to Chloe Quiggle, widow of Phillip Quiggle."

The husband of the beneficiary named enlisted February 11, 1865, and was discharged September 27, 1865. The records show that he was reported August 31, 1865, as "absent, confined in post prison at Chattanooga since August 18, 1865."

He filed a claim for pension June 25, 1880, alleging that after a march from Chattanooga to a point 1½ miles distant and back he upon his return drank some water, which produced diarrhea, since which time he had been troubled also with disease of kidneys and rheumatism.

He died in September, 1882, and the claim then pending on his behalf was completed by his widow. After a special examination the claim for diarrhea was, on the 21st day of April, 1887, allowed from September 28, 1865, to January 1, 1870, when it was shown that any disability from this cause ceased. The claim for disease of kidneys and rheumatism was rejected upon the ground that no such disabilities were shown to be due to military service.

The widow filed a claim on her own behalf August 27, 1883, alleging the death of the soldier from the results of prostration by heat while marching near Nashville, Tenn., and also from disease of kidneys, rheumatism, and chronic diarrhea.

It is reported to me that the evidence taken during a special examination of this case established that before and after enlistment the soldier was addicted to the excessive use of intoxicating liquors.

One physician stated to the examiner that shortly after the soldier's discharge he found him suffering from disease of kidneys and from rheumatism and diarrhea, but that he concluded the disease of the kidneys had been coming on for a year; that it could not have been caused by a sunstroke a few weeks previously, and that the diseases were of longer standing than that.

Another physician who attended the soldier during his last illness testified that he did not know that he suffered from any disease until the summer of 1882; that he found him suffering from retention of urine, and that the difficulty rapidly developed into an acute attack of Bright's disease; that no indications of rheumatism were found, but that the disease progressed steadily and was a well-marked case of Bright's disease of the kidneys. He also testified that the origin of the disease was no doubt recent, though possibly it might have existed in a low form for some years.

A medical examination in May, 1882, developed no disease of the kidneys.

It seems to me that all the reliable testimony in the case tends to show beyond a doubt that the soldier's death was not due to any incident of his military service. I do not find that the medical testimony given by his neighbors makes a suggestion that it was, and upon all the facts I am of the opinion that the pension which has been already allowed was a liberal disposition of the case.

The beneficiary named in this bill is aged, and it would certainly be a gratification to grant her relief; but the question is whether we do well to establish a precedent for the allowance of claims of this character in the distribution of pension funds.   GROVER CLEVELAND.

EXECUTIVE MANSION, *April 30, 1888.*
To the Senate:

I return without approval Senate bill No. 465, entitled "An act granting a pension to William Sackman, sr."

The beneficiary named in this bill served from December 24, 1861, to February 29, 1864, in the Fifth Regiment of the Missouri Militia Cavalry.

He was discharged on the day last named for disability. His certificate of discharge states his disability as follows:

Palpitation of the heart and defective lungs, the disability caused by falling off his horse near Fredericktown, Mo., while intoxicated, on detached service, in the month of September, 1862. Not having done any duty since, a discharge would benefit the Government and himself.

It appears that a claim for pension was filed in the year 1881, in which the claimant alleged that—

At Fredericktown, Mo., about the 10th or 12th of April, 1863, he had three ribs broken by falling from his horse while surrounded by guerrillas.

It will be seen that while the certificate of discharge mentions a fall in September, 1862, no allusion is made to any fracture of ribs, while the claimant alleges such an injury occurred in April, 1863.

In 1885 the surgeon who made the medical certificate attached to the discharge, in answer to an inquiry made by the Commissioner of Pensions, says:

I have to state that I remember the case very distinctly. I made the examination in person, and was thoroughly acquainted with the case. I read the statement on which the application for discharge was based to the man, and he consen⸱ ·d to have the papers forwarded as they read. The application for pension is frauulent and should not be allowed.

I have omitted references made to the habits of the soldier by this medical officer.

Of course much reliance should be placed upon these statements made by an officer whose business it was to know the exact facts, and who made his certificate at a time when such facts were fresh in his mind. There is no intimation that the surgeon who made the statement referred to was inimical to the soldier or influenced by any unjust motive.

The attempt to impeach the record thus made is based upon affidavits made by a number of the soldier's comrades, who testify to his character and habits, and only three of whom speak of an injury to the soldier caused by falling from his horse. Two of these affiants allege that they were with the claimant on detached duty when his horse took fright and ran away with him, injuring him so that he could not rise and get on his horse without assistance. So far as these affidavits are before me, no date of this occurrence is given, nothing is said as to the character of the injuries, and no reference is made to the condition of the soldier at the time. The third affiant, who speaks of an injury, says that it occurred while on duty on the march from Pilot Knob to Cape Girardeau, in the year 1862 or 1863, and that it was caused by the soldier's being thrown from his horse. He says further that the soldier was not intoxicated at that time.

No mention is made that I can discover of any fracture of the ribs except in the claimant's application for pension made in 1881, seventeen years after his discharge, and in a report of an examining surgeon made in 1882.

With no denial of the soldier's condition, as stated by the surgeon, on the part of the only parties who claim to have been present at the time of the injury, I can not satisfy myself, in view of the other circumstances surrounding this case, that the allegations contained in the claimant's discharge are discredited.

GROVER CLEVELAND.

EXECUTIVE MANSION, *April 30, 1888.*

To the Senate:

I return without approval Senate bill No. 838, entitled "An act granting a pension to Mary Sullivan."

On the 1st day of July, 1886, an act was approved which is an exact copy of the one herewith returned. In pursuance of that act the beneficiary's name was placed upon the pension rolls.

A second law for the same purpose is of course unnecessary.

GROVER CLEVELAND.

EXECUTIVE MANSION, *May 1, 1888.*

To the House of Representatives:

I return without approval House bill No. 19, entitled "An act for the relief of H. B. Wilson, administrator of the estate of William Tinder, deceased."

The purpose of this bill is to refund to the estate of William Tinder the sum of $5,000, which was paid to the Government by his administrator in June, 1880, upon the following facts:

In 1876 two indictments were found against one Evans, charging him with passing counterfeit money. In May, 1878, he was tried upon one of said indictments and the jury failed to agree. Thereupon the prisoner entered into two recognizances in the sum of $5,000 each, with W. R. Evans and William Tinder as sureties, conditioned for the appearance of the prisoner Evans at the next term of the court, in November, 1878, for trial upon said indictment. Before that date, however, the prisoner fled the country and failed to appear according to the condition of his bond. In the meantime William Tinder died and H. B. Wilson was appointed his administrator.

Suits were brought upon the two bail bonds, and, the liability of the sureties not being admitted, the suits were tried in March, 1880, resulting in two judgments in favor of the United States and against the surety Evans and the estate of Tinder for $5,000 each and the costs.

Soon thereafter an application was made by the administrator of the estate of William Tinder for relief, and an offer was made by him to pay $5,000 and the costs in compromise and settlement of the liability of said estate upon said two judgments.

These judgments were a preferred claim against the estate, which was represented to be worth sixteen or eighteen thousand dollars. The other surety, Evans, was alleged to be worthless, and it was claimed that neither the administrator of the Tinder estate nor his attorneys had known the whereabouts of the indicted party since his flight, and that some time would elapse before certain litigation in which the estate was involved could be settled and the claims against it paid.

It was considered best by the officers of the Government to accept the proposition of the administrator, which was done in June, 1880. The sum of $5,099.06, the amount of one of said judgments, with interest and costs, was paid into the United States Treasury, and the estate of Tinder was in consideration thereof released and discharged from all liability upon both of said judgments.

Thus was the transaction closed, in exact accordance with the wishes and the prayer of the representative of this estate and by the favor and indulgence of the Government upon his application. There was, so far as I can learn, no condition attached, and no understanding or agreement that any future occurrence would affect the finality of the compromise by which the Government had accepted one-half of its claim in full settlement.

It appears that in 1881 the party indicted was arrested and brought to trial, which resulted in his conviction; and apparently for this reason alone it is proposed by the bill under consideration to open the settlement made at the request of the administrator and refund to him the sum which he paid on such settlement pursuant to his own offer.

I can see no fairness or justice to the Government in such a proposition. I do not find any statement that the administrator delivered the prisoner to the United States authorities for trial. On the contrary, it appears from an examination made in the First Comptroller's Office that he was arrested by the marshal on the 25th day of May, 1881, who charged and was paid his fees therefor. And if the administrator had surrendered the prisoner to justice it would not entitle him to the repayment of the money he has paid to compromise the two judgments against him.

The temptation to relieve from contracts with the Government upon plausible application is, in my opinion, not sufficiently resisted; but to refund money paid into the public Treasury upon such a liberal compromise as is exhibited in this case seems like a departure from all business principles and an unsafe concession that the interests of the Government are to be easily surrendered.

GROVER CLEVELAND.

EXECUTIVE MANSION, *May 3, 1888.*

To the House of Representatives:

I return without approval House bill No. 4534, entitled "An act for the relief of Emily G. Mills."

The object of this bill is to provide a pension for the beneficiary named therein as the widow of Oscar B. Mills, late a second assistant engineer, retired, in the United States Navy. The deceased was appointed an acting third assistant engineer in October, 1862, and in 1864 he was promoted to the place of second assistant engineer.

It is supposed that while in active service he did his full duty, though I am not informed of any distinguished acts of bravery or heroism. In February, 1871, he was before a naval retiring board, which found that he was incapacitated for active service on account of malarious fever, contracted in 1868, and recommended that he be allowed six months' leave of absence to recover his health.

In December, 1871, he was again examined for retirement, and the board found that he was not in any way incapacitated from performing the duties of his office. The next year, in 1872, another retiring board, upon an examination of his case, found that he was "laboring under general debility, the effect of intermittent fever acting upon an originally delicate constitution," and he was thereupon placed upon the retired list of the Navy.

On the 10th day of August, 1873, he was accidentally shot and killed by a neighbor, who was attempting to shoot an owl.

As long as there is the least pretense of limiting the bestowal of pensions to disability or death in some way related to the incidents of military and naval service, claims of this description can not consistently be allowed.

GROVER CLEVELAND.

EXECUTIVE MANSION, *May 7, 1888.*

To the House of Representatives:

I return without approval House bill No. 1406, entitled "An act to provide for the sale of certain New York Indian lands in Kansas."

Prior to the year 1838 a number of bands and tribes of New York Indians had obtained 500,000 acres of land in the State of Wisconsin, upon which they proposed to reside. In the year above named a treaty was entered into between the United States and these Indians whereby they relinquished to the Government these Wisconsin lands. In consideration thereof, and, as the treaty declares, "in order to manifest the deep interest of the United States in the future peace and prosperity of the New York Indians," it was agreed there should be set apart as a permanent home for all the New York Indians then residing in the State of New York, or in Wisconsin, or elsewhere in the United States, who had no permanent home, a tract of land amounting to 1,824,000 acres, directly west of the State of Missouri, and now included in the State of Kansas—being 320 acres for each Indian, as their number was then computed—"to have and to hold the same in fee simple to the said tribes or nations of Indians by patent from the President of the United States."

Full power and authority was also given to said Indians "to divide said lands among the different tribes, nations, or bands in severalty," with the right to sell and convey to and from each other under such rules and regulations as should be adopted by said Indians in their respective tribes or in general council.

The treaty further provided that such of the tribes of these Indians as did not accept said treaty and agree to remove to the country set apart for their new homes within five years or such other time as the President might from time to time appoint should forfeit all interest in the land so set apart to the United States; and the Government guaranteed to protect and defend them in the peaceable possession and enjoyment of their new homes.

I have no positive information that any considerable number of these Indians removed to the lands provided for them within the five years limited by the treaty. Their omission to do so may have been owing to the failure of the Government to appropriate the money to pay the expense of such removal, as it agreed to do in the treaty.

It is, however, stated in a letter of the Secretary of the Interior dated April 6, 1878, contained in the report of the Senate committee to whom the bill under consideration was referred, that in the year 1842 some of these Indians settled upon the lands described in the treaty; and it is further alleged in said report that in 1846 about two hundred more of them were removed to said lands.

The letter of the Secretary of the Interior above referred to contains the following statement concerning these Indian occupants:

From death and the hostility of the settlers, who were drawn in that direction by the fertility of the soil and other advantages, all of the Indians gradually relinquished their selections, until of the Indians who had removed thither from the State of New York only thirty-two remained in 1860.

And the following further statement is made:

The files of the Indian Office show abundant proof that they did not voluntarily relinquish their occupation.

The proof thus referred to is indeed abundant, and is found in official reports and affidavits made as late as the year 1859. By these it appears that during that year, in repeated instances, Indian men and widows of deceased Indians were driven from their homes by the threats of armed men; that in one case at least the habitation of an Indian woman was burned, and that the kind of outrages were resorted to which too often follow the cupidity of whites and the possession of fertile lands by defenseless and unprotected Indians.

An agent, in an official letter dated August 9, 1859, after detailing the cruel treatment of these occupants of the lands which the Government had given them, writes:

Since these Indians have been placed under my charge, which was, I think, in 1855, I have endeavored to protect them; but complaint after complaint has reached me, and I have reported their situation again and again; and I hope that it will not be long when the Indians who are entitled to land under the decision of the Indian Office shall have it set apart to them.

The same agent, under date of January 18, 1860, referring to these Indians, declares:

These Indians have been driven off their land and claims upon the New York tract by the whites, and they are now very much scattered and many of them are very destitute.

It was found in 1860 that of all the Indians who had prior to that date selected and occupied part of these lands but thirty-two remained, and it seems to have been deemed but justice to them to confirm their selections by some kind of governmental grant or declaration, though it does not appear that any of them had been able to maintain actual possession of all their selected lands against white intrusion. Thus certain special commissioners appointed to examine this subject, under date of May 29, 1860, make the following statement:

In this connection it may be proper to remark that many of the tracts so selected were claimed by lawless men who had compelled the Indians to abandon them under threats of violence; but we are confident that no serious injury will be done to anyone, as the improvements are of but little value.

On the 14th day of September, 1860, certificates were issued to the thirty-two Indians who had made selections of lands and who still survived, with a view of securing to them such selections and at the same time granting to them the number of acres which it was provided they should have by the treaty of 1838. These certificates were made by the Commissioner of Indian Affairs, and declared that in conformity with the provisions of the treaty of 1838 there had been assigned and allotted to the person named therein 320 acres of the land designated in said treaty, which land was particularly described in said certificates, which concluded as follows:

And the selection of said tract for the exclusive use and benefit of said reserve, having been approved by the Secretary of the Interior, is not subject to be alienated in fee, leased, or otherwise disposed of except to the United States.

In a letter dated September 13, 1860, from the Indian Commissioner to the agent in the neighborhood of these lands reference is made to the conduct of white intruders upon the same, and the following instructions were given to said agent:

In view of these representations and the fact that these white persons who are in possession of the land are intruders, I have to direct that you will visit the New York Reserve in Kansas at your earliest convenience, accompanied by those Indians living among the Osages to whom said lands have been allotted, with a view to place them in possession of the lands to which they are entitled; and if you should meet with any forcible resistance from white settlers you will report their names to this office, in order that appropriate action may be taken in the premises, and you will inform them that if they do not immediately abandon said lands they will be removed by force. When you shall have given the thirty-two Indians peaceable possession of their lands, or attempted to do so and have been prevented by forcible resistance, you will make a report of your action to this Bureau.

The records of the Indian Bureau do not disclose that any report was ever made by the agent to whom these instructions were given.

In 1861 and 1862 mention was made by the agents of the destitute condition of these Indians and of their being deprived of their lands, and in these years petitions were presented in their behalf asking that justice be done them on account of the failure of the Government to provide them with homes.

In the meantime, and in December, 1860, the remainder of the reserve not allotted to the thirty-two survivors was thrown open to settlement by Executive proclamation. Of course this was followed by increased conflict between the settlers and the Indians. It is presumed that it became dangerous for those to whom lands had been allotted to attempt to gain possession of them. On the 4th day of December, 1865, Agent Snow returned twenty-seven of the certificates of allotment which had not been delivered, and wrote as follows to the Indian Bureau:

A few of these Indians were at one time put in possession of their lands. They were driven off by the whites; one Indian was killed, others wounded, and their houses burned. White men at this time have possession of these lands, and have valuable improvements on them. The Indians are deterred even asking for possession. I would earnestly ask, as agent for these wronged and destitute people, that some measure be adopted by the Government to give these Indians their rights.

An official report made to the Secretary of the Interior dated February 16, 1871, gives the history of these lands, and concludes as follows:

These lands are now all or nearly all occupied by white persons who have driven the Indians from their homes—in some instances with violence. There is great necessity that some relief should be afforded to them by legislation of Congress, authorizing the issue of patents to the allottees or giving them power to sell and convey.

In this way they will be enabled to realize something from the land, and the occupants can secure titles for their homes.

Apparently in the line of this recommendation, and in an attempt to remedy the condition of affairs then existing, an act was passed on the 19th day of February, 1873, permitting heads of families and single persons over 21 years of age who had made settlements and improvements upon and were *bona fide* claimants and occupants of the lands for which the thirty-two certificates of allotments were issued to enter and purchase at the proper land office such lands so occupied by them, not exceeding 160 acres, upon paying therefor the appraised value of said tracts respectively, to be ascertained by three disinterested and competent appraisers, to be appointed by the Secretary of the Interior, who should report the value of such lands, exclusive of improvements, but that no sale should be made under said act for less than $3.75 per acre.

It was further provided that the entries allowed should be made within twelve months after the promulgation by the Secretary of the Interior of regulations to carry said act into effect, and that the money arising upon such sales should be paid into the Treasury of the United States in trust for and to be paid to the Indians respectively to whom such certificates of allotment had been issued, or to their heirs, upon satisfactory proof of their identity, at any time within five years from the passage of the act, and that in default of such proof the money should become a part of the public moneys of the United States.

It was also further provided that any Indian to whom any certificate of allotment had been issued, and who was then occupying the land allotted thereby, should be entitled to receive a patent therefor.

Pursuant to this statute these lands were appraised. The lowest value per acre fixed by the appraisers was $3.75, and the highest was $10, making the average for the whole $4.90 per acre.

It is reported that only eight pieces, containing 879.76 acres of land taken from six of these Indian allotments, were sold under this statute to the settlers thereon, producing the sum of $4,058.06, and that the price paid in no case was less than $4.50 per acre.

It is proposed by the bill under consideration to sell the remainder of this allotted land to those who failed to avail themselves of the law of 1873 for the sum of $2.50 per acre.

Whatever may be said of the effect of the action of the Indian Bureau in issuing certificates of allotment to individual Indians as it relates to the title of the lands described therein, it was the only way that the Government could perform its treaty obligation to furnish homes for any number of Indians less than a tribe or band; and if these allotments did not vest a title in these individual Indians they secured to them such rights to the lands as the Government was bound to protect and which it could not refuse to confirm if it became necessary by the issuance of patents therefor.

These rights are fully recognized by the statute of 1873, as well as by the bill under consideration.

The right and power of the Government to divest these allottees of their interests under their certificates is so questionable that perhaps it could only be done under the plan proposed, through an estoppel arising from the acceptance of the price for which their allotted lands were sold.

But whatever the effect of a compliance with the provisions of this bill would be upon the title of the settlers to these lands, I can see no fairness or justice in permitting them to enter and purchase such lands at a sum much less than their appraised value in 1873 and for hardly one-half the price paid by their neighbors under the law passed in that year.

The occupancy upon these lands of the settlers seeking relief, and of their grantors, is based upon wrong, violence, and oppression. A continuation of the wrongful exclusion of these Indians from their lands should not inure to the benefit of the wrongdoers. The opportunities afforded by the law of 1873 were neglected, perhaps, in the hope and belief that death would remove the Indians who by their appeals for justice annoyed those who had driven them from their homes, and perhaps in the expectation that the heedlessness of the Government concerning its obligations to the Indians would supply easier terms. The idea is too prevalent that, as against those who by emigration and settlement upon our frontier extend our civilization and prosperity, the rights of the Indians are of but little consequence. But it must be absolutely true that no development is genuine or valuable based upon the violence and cruelty of individuals or the faithlessness of a government.

While it might not result in exact justice or precisely rectify the wrong committed, it may well be that in existing circumstances the interests of the allottees or their heirs demand an adjustment of the kind now proposed. But their lands certainly are worth much more than they were in 1873, and the settlers, if they are not subjected to a reappraisement, should at least pay the price at which the lands were appraised in that year.

If the holders of the interests of the allottees have such a title as will give them a standing in the courts of Kansas, I do not think they need fear defeat by being charged with improvements under the occupying claimants' act, for it has been decided in a case to be found in the twentieth volume of Kansas Reports, at page 374, that—

Neither the title nor possession of the Indian owner, secured by treaty with the United States Government, can be disturbed by State legislation; and the occupying claimants' act has no application in this case.

And yet the delay, uncertainty, and expense of legal contests should be considered.

I suggest that any bill which is passed to adjust the rights of these Indians by such a general plan as is embodied in the bill herewith returned should provide for the payment by the settlers within a reasonable time of an appraised value, and that in case the same is not paid by the respective occupants that the lands be sold at public auction for a price not less than the appraisement.

GROVER CLEVELAND.

EXECUTIVE MANSION, *May 9, 1888.*

To the House of Representatives:

I return without approval House bill No. 4357, entitled "An act to erect a public building at Allentown, Pa."

The accommodation of the postal business is the only public purpose for which the Government can be called on to provide, which is suggested as a pretext for the erection of this building. It is proposed to expend $100,000 for a structure to be used as a post-office. It is said that a deputy collector of internal revenue and a board of pension examiners are located at Allentown, but I do not understand that the Government is obliged to provide quarters for these officers.

The usual statement is made in support of this bill setting forth the growth of the city where it is proposed to locate the building and the amount and variety of the business which is there transacted; and the postmaster in stereotyped phrase represents the desirability of increased accommodation for the transaction of the business under his charge.

But I am thoroughly convinced that there is no present necessity for the expenditure of $100,000 for any purpose connected with the public business at this place.

The annual rent now paid for the post-office is $1,300.

The interest, at 3 per cent, upon the amount now asked for this new building is $3,000. As soon as it is undertaken the pay of a superintendent of its construction will begin, and after its completion the compensation of janitors and other expenses of its maintenance will follow.

The plan now pursued for the erection of public buildings is, in my opinion, very objectionable. They are often built where they are not needed, of dimensions and at a cost entirely disproportionate to any public use to which they can be applied, and as a consequence they frequently serve more to demonstrate the activity and pertinacity of those who represent localities desiring this kind of decoration at public expense than to meet any necessity of the Government.

GROVER CLEVELAND.

EXECUTIVE MANSION, *May 10, 1888.*

To the House of Representatives:

I return without approval House bill No. 7715, entitled "An act for the relief of Georgia A. Stricklett."

By the terms of this bill a pension is allowed to the beneficiary above named, whose husband died on the 21st day of July, 1873. It appears from the records that he was mustered into the service to date from October 10, 1863, to serve for one year. It is alleged in the report of the committee of the House who reported this bill that he was wounded with buckshot in the face and head by bushwhackers, when on recruiting service, on the 23d day of July, 1863. If these dates are correct, he was wounded before he entered the service; but this fact is not made the basis of the disapproval of the widow's application for relief. There seems, however, to be no mention of any such injury during his term of service, though he is reported sick much of the time when present with his regiment, and is reported as once in hospital for a disease which, to say the least of it, can not be recognized as related to the service.

The soldier himself made no application for pension.

A physician testifies that he was present on the 21st day of July, 1873, when the soldier died; that he examined the body after death, and to the best of his knowledge such death was caused partially by epilepsy, and that the epilepsy was the result of "wounds about the face and head received during his service during the war."

Another physician testifies that the soldier applied to him for treatment in 1868, and that his disability was the development of confirmed epilepsy, and he expresses the opinion that this was due to a wound from a buckshot. This physician, while not giving epilepsy as the cause of death, says that "had he lived to die a natural death he certainly would have died an insane epileptic."

The report speaks of his death by "an accidental shot."

The truth appears to be that he was killed by a pistol shot in an altercation with another man.

Unless it shall be assumed that the epilepsy was caused by the buckshot wound spoken of, and unless a pension should be allowed because, if the soldier had not been killed in an altercation, he might have soon died from such epilepsy, this bill is entirely devoid of merit.

Surely no one will seriously propose that a claim for pension should rest upon a conjecture as to what would have caused death if it had not occurred in an entirely different way.

The testimony of the physician who testified in this case that death was caused partially by epilepsy suggests the extreme recklessness which may characterize medical testimony in applications for pension.

GROVER CLEVELAND.

EXECUTIVE MANSION, *May 18, 1888.*

To the House of Representatives:

I return without approval House bill No. 2282, entitled "An act to pension Mrs. Theodora M. Piatt."

The deceased husband of the beneficiary named in this bill served faithfully and well in the volunteer service, and after his discharge as major entered the Regular Army and was on the retired list at the time of his death, which occurred on the 17th day of April, 1885. At that time he seems to have been engaged in the practice of the law at Covington, Ky.

He does not appear to have contracted any distinct and definite disability in his army service, though his health and strength were doubtless somewhat impaired by hardship and exposure.

It is conceded that he committed suicide by shooting himself with a pistol.

A coroner's inquest was held and the following verdict was returned:

Benjamin M. Piatt came to his death from a pistol bullet through the brain, fired from a pistol in his own hand, with suicidal intent, while laboring under a fit of temporary insanity, caused by morbid sensitiveness of wasted opportunities and constantly brooding over imaginary troubles and financial difficulties.

It is said in support of his widow's claim for pension that, being lame as a result, in part at least, of his military service, he, by reason of such lameness, fell from a staircase a few months before his death, the injury from which affected his mind, causing insanity, which in its turn resulted in his suicide.

Much interest is manifested in this case, based upon former friendship and intimacy with the deceased and kind feeling and sympathy for his widow. I should be glad to respond to these sentiments to the extent of approving this bill, but it is one of the misfortunes of public life and official responsibility that a sense of duty frequently stands between a conception of right and a sympathetic inclination.

The verdict returned upon the coroner's inquest, founded upon a friendly examination of all the facts surrounding the melancholy death of this soldier, made at the time of death and in the midst of his neighbors and friends, both by what it contains and by what is omitted, together with the other facts developed, leads me to the conclusion that if a pension is granted in this case no soldier's widow's application based upon suicide can be consistently rejected.

GROVER CLEVELAND.

EXECUTIVE MANSION, *May 18, 1888.*

To the House of Representatives:

I return without approval House bill No. 5545, entitled "An act granting a pension to Nancy F. Jennings."

William Jennings, the husband of the beneficiary named in this bill, enlisted in October, 1861, and was discharged June 24, 1862, upon a surgeon's certificate of disability, the cause of disability being therein stated as "hemorrhoids."

He never applied for a pension, and died in 1877 of apoplexy.

In the report of the committee which reported this bill the allegation is made that the deceased came home from the Army with chronic diarrhea and suffered from the same to the date of his death.

The widow filed a claim for pension in 1878, which was rejected on the ground that the fatal disease (apoplexy) was not due to military service nor the result of either of the complaints mentioned.

If we are to adhere to the rule that in order to entitle the widow of a soldier to a pension the death of her husband must be in some way related to his military service, there can be no doubt that upon its merits this case was properly disposed of by the Pension Bureau.

GROVER CLEVELAND.

EXECUTIVE MANSION, *May 18, 1888.*

To the House of Representatives:

I return without approval a joint resolution, which originated in the House of Representatives, "authorizing the use and improvement of Castle Island, in Boston Harbor."

This island is separated from the mainland of the city of Boston by a channel over one-half mile wide. Fort Independence is located on the island, and it is regarded by our military authorities as quite important to the defense of the city.

The proposition contained in the joint resolution is to permit the city of Boston, through its park commissioners, to improve and beautify this island in connection with a public park to be laid out in the city, with the intention of joining the mainland and the island by the construction of a viaduct or causeway across the water now separating the same.

It is quite plain that the occupancy of this island as a place of pleasure and recreation, as contemplated under this resolution, would be entirely inconsistent with military or defensive uses. I do not regard the control reserved in the resolution to the Secretary of War over such excavations, fillings, and structures upon the island as may be proposed as of much importance. When a park is established there, the island is no longer a defense in time of need.

This scheme, or one of the same character, was broached more than four years ago, and met the disapproval of the Secretary of War and the Engineer Department.

I am now advised by the Secretary of War, the Chief of Engineers, and the Lieutenant-General of the Army, in quite positive terms, that the resolution under consideration should not, for reasons fully stated by them, become operative.

I deem the opinions of these officers abundant justification for my disapproval of the resolution without further statement of objections.

GROVER CLEVELAND.

EXECUTIVE MANSION, *May 18, 1888.*

To the Senate.

I return without approval Senate bill No. 1064, entitled "An act for the relief of L. J. Worden."

This bill directs the Postmaster-General to allow to L. J. Worden, recently the postmaster at Lawrence, Kans., the sum of $625 paid out by him as such postmaster for clerk hire during the period from July 1, 1882, to June 30, 1883.

The allowances to these officers for clerk hire and other like expenses are fixed in each case by the Post-Office Department and are paid out of an appropriation made in gross to cover them all. The excess of receipts for box rents and commissions over and above the salary of the postmaster is adopted by law as the maximum amount of such allowances in each case, and within that limit the amount appropriated is apportioned by the Post-Office Department to the different offices according to their needs.

The allowances to the Lawrence post-office for the year ending June

30, 1883, was $3,100. This was fully its proportion of the appropriation made by Congress for that year, and as much as was in most cases given to other offices of the same grade. In September, 1882, during the first quarter of the year in question, the postmaster made application for an increase of his allowances, which was declined, and a similar application in December of the same year was also declined. The reason given for noncompliance with this request in both cases was a lack of funds. It is the rule to make only such allowances in any year as can be paid from the appropriation made for that period.

No further application for increase of allowances was made by Mr. Worden until March, 1884, when the same were increased $300 for the year, to date from the 1st day of January preceding.

It was found at that time, after a full and fair investigation by the Department, which had in hand abundant funds for an increase of these allowances, that notwithstanding the increase of business at this post-office, $300 added to the allowances for the year from July 1, 1882, to June 30, 1883, was sufficient; and yet more than twice that sum is added by the bill under consideration to the allowances for the year last named.

Forty-four postmasters have submitted vouchers, amounting to nearly $9,000, for clerk hire during that year in excess of allowances; but they were all rejected, and I understand have not been insisted upon.

I assume that the Post-Office Department in 1884 dealt justly and fairly by the postmaster at Lawrence, and upon this theory, if he should be re-imbursed any expenditure for a previous year, the demand he now makes is excessive.

But the cases should be exceedingly rare in which postmasters are awarded any more than the allowances made by the Department officers. They have the very best means of ascertaining the amount necessary to meet the demands of the service in any particular case, and it certainly may be assumed that they desire to properly accommodate the public in the matter of postal facilities. When the appropriation is sufficient, the decision of the Department should be final; and when the money in hand does not admit of adequate allowances, postmasters should only be reim-bursed money voluntarily expended by them when recommended by the Postmaster-General.

Any other course leads to the expenditure of money by postmasters for work which they should do themselves and to the employment of clerks which are unnecessary. The least encouragement that they may be repaid such expenditure by a special appropriation would dangerously tend to the substitution of their judgment for that of the Department and to the relaxation of wholesome discipline.

I think, when the application of Mr. Worden for an increase in his allowances was twice declined for any cause during the year covering his present demand, that if he made personal expenditures for clerk hire, and especially if he did so without the encouragement of the Department, they were made at his own risk. It appears, too, that the amount of his claim is larger than can be justified in any event.

GROVER CLEVELAND.

The time allowed the Executive by the Constitution for the examination of bills presented to him by Congress for his action expired in the case of the bill herewith returned on Saturday, May 19. The Senate adjourned or took a recess on Thursday afternoon, May 17, until to-day, the 21st of May.

On the day of said recess or adjournment the above message, disapproving said bill and accompanying its return to the Senate, where it originated, was drawn, and on May 18 was engrossed and signed. On Saturday, the 19th of May, the Senate not being in session, the message and the bill were tendered to the Secretary of the Senate, who declined to receive them, and thereupon they were on the same day tendered to the President of the Senate, who also declined to receive the same, both of these officials claiming that the return of said bill and the delivery of said message could only properly be made to the Senate when in actual session.

They are therefore transmitted as soon as the Senate reconvenes after its recess, with this explanation.

GROVER CLEVELAND.

[May 22 the Senate proceeded, as the Constitution prescribes, to reconsider the said bill returned by the President of the United States with his objections, pending which it was ordered that the said bill and message be referred to the Committee on Privileges and Elections. No action was taken.]

EXECUTIVE MANSION, *May 19, 1888.*
To the House of Representatives:

I return without approval House bill No. 88, entitled "An act granting a pension to Sally A. Randall."

Antipas Taber enlisted in the War of 1812 and was discharged in the year 1814. There is no claim made that he received any injury in the Army or that his death, which happened long after his discharge, was in the slightest degree related to his military service. It does not appear that he ever made any application for a pension or was ever upon the pension rolls. He died at Trinidad, in the island of Cuba, April 11, 1831, leaving as his widow the beneficiary mentioned in this bill. About twenty-two years after his death, and in February, 1853, she married Albert Randall, and twenty years thereafter, in October, 1873, Randall died, leaving her again a widow.

It is alleged in the report of the committee in the House to which this bill was referred that Mrs. Randall is a worthy woman, 75 years of age, in needy circumstances, with health much impaired, and that the petition for her relief was signed by prominent citizens of Norwich, Conn., where she now resides.

All this certainly commends her case to the kindness and benevolence of the citizens mentioned, and the State of Connecticut ought not to allow her to be in needy circumstances.

It seems to me, however, that it would establish a bad precedent to provide for her from the Federal Treasury. From the statement of her present age she must have been born during the time of her first husband's enlistment. She knew nothing of his military service except as the same may have been detailed to her. Her first widowhood had no connection with any incident or condition of health traceable to such service, and her second husband, with whom she lived for twenty years, never entered the military service of the Government.

I do not see how the relief proposed can be granted in this case without an unjustifiable departure from the rules under which applications for pension should be determined.

GROVER CLEVELAND.

EXECUTIVE MANSION, *May 19, 1888.*

To the House of Representatives:

I return without approval House bill No. 879, entitled "An act granting a pension to Royal J. Hiar."

The beneficiary named in this bill enlisted November 11, 1861, in the First Regiment of Michigan Engineers and Mechanics. He is reported as absent without proper authority from May 24, 1862, to January 15, 1863, when he was discharged by reason of varicose veins of the left leg and thigh, claimed to have existed before enlistment.

He filed a claim for pension August 30, 1876, alleging disease of the right side and hip, due to typhoid pneumonia, contracted while repairing a hospital tent in March, 1862.

There is no record of this disease. The proof he furnishes of the same is extremely slight, though he was furnished ample opportunity. The disability of which he complains has no natural relation to the sickness he claims to have had during his service, but is quite a natural result of "an injury while logging," to which some of the witnesses examined in a special examination of the case attribute it.

GROVER CLEVELAND.

EXECUTIVE MANSION, *May 19, 1888.*

To the House of Representatives:

I return without approval House bill No. 5234, entitled "An act granting a pension to Cyrenius G. Stryker."

The beneficiary named in this bill enlisted for nine months in September, 1862, and was discharged June 27, 1863.

His enlistment was in Company A, Thirtieth New Jersey Regiment. The bill proposes to pension him as "a private in Company A, Thirtieth Regiment New York Volunteers."

He alleges that he was pushed or fell from the platform of a car in which he was transported to Washington after enlistment and injured his spine. On the claim which he presented to the Pension Bureau in June, 1879, repeated medical examinations failed to reveal any disability from the cause alleged, and after a special examination his claim was rejected because, with the assistance of such special examination, the claimant did not prove the origin of alleged injury in service and the line of duty or a pensionable degree of disability therefrom since discharge.

The evidence now offered in support of this claim appears to have reference to a time long anterior to its rejection by the Pension Bureau in 1886, and does not impeach the finding of the Bureau that at the latter date there existed no pensionable disability.

GROVER CLEVELAND.

EXECUTIVE MANSION. *May 19, 1888.*

To the House of Representatives:

I return without approval House bill No. 3579, entitled "An act granting a pension to Ellen Shea."

This beneficiary is an old lady and a widow. Her son, Michael Shea, enlisted in January, 1862. The records show that he was sick on one or two occasions during his service. He is also reported as a deserter and absent without leave and in arrest and confinement fully as often as he was sick. He was discharged January 20, 1865.

No application for a pension has been made on his behalf. The mother filed a claim for pension in July, 1884, alleging that her son contracted a fever in the service which resulted in insanity, which was the cause of his death on the 10th day of March, 1884.

He was killed by a snow slide in the State of Colorado. The only hint that his death was in any way connected with the service is the suggestion that not having the proper use of his mind he wandered away and was killed.

His mother now lives in Chicago and, I suppose, lived there at the time of her son's death. There is very little evidence offered of any unsoundness of mind, and his death occurring at Woodstock, Colo., it is hardly to be supposed that he wandered that far. And as tending to show that unsoundness of mind had nothing to do with his death it may be mentioned that an attorney having the mother's application for pension in charge withdrew from the case in October, 1884, for the reason that, having made inquiries at the place where the soldier was killed, he found that his death was caused by a snow slide, and that he was informed that a number of other persons lost their lives at the same time.

GROVER CLEVELAND.

EXECUTIVE MANSION, *May 19, 1888.*

To the House of Representatives:

I return without approval House bill No. 8164, entitled "An act granting a pension to William H. Hester."

It is claimed that the beneficiary named in this bill was injured by sand blowing in his eyes during a sand storm while in the service in the year 1869, resulting in nearly if not quite total blindness.

It is conceded in the report of the committee to which this bill was referred in the House that the claim for pension made by this man to the Pension Bureau was largely supported by perjury and forgery; but the criminality of these methods is made to rest upon three rogues and scoundrels who undertook to obtain a pension for the soldier, and it is stated by the committee as their opinion that the claimant himself was innocent of any complicity in the crimes committed and attempted.

I have quite a full report of the papers filed and proceedings taken in relation to the claim presented to the Pension Bureau, and I am sorry that I can not agree with the committee of the House as to the merits of the application now made or the good faith and honesty of the beneficiary named in the bill herewith returned.

Among the facts presented I shall refer to but one or two touching the conduct of the claimant himself.

Upon his examination, under oath, by a special examiner, he stated that he was brought to Washington to further his claim by a man named Miller, one of the rascally attorneys spoken of in the committee's report; that Miller was to pay his expenses while in Washington, and was to receive one-third of the money paid upon the claim.

This is not the conduct of a man claiming in good faith a pension from the Government.

He further stated under oath that his eyes became affected about January 15, 1869, by reason of a sand storm; that the sand blew into them and cut them all to pieces; that he was thereafter hardly able to see or get around and wait on himself, and that Edward N. Baldwin took care of him in his tent.

This Mr. Baldwin was found by the special examiner and testified that he knew the claimant and served in same regiment and bunked with him; that he never knew of the sand storm spoken of by Hester; that he never knew that he had sore eyes in the service; that he (Baldwin) did not take care of him when he was suffering with sore eyes, and that he never knew of Hester being sick but once, and that was when he had eaten too much. He was shown an affidavit purporting to be made by him and declared the entire thing to be false and a forgery.

I believe this claim for pension to be a fraud from beginning to end, and the effrontery with which it has been pushed shows the necessity of a careful examination of these cases.

GROVER CLEVELAND.

EXECUTIVE MANSION, *May 19, 1888.*
To the House of Representatives:

I return without approval House bill No. 6609, entitled "An act for the relief of Sarah E. McCaleb."

The husband of the beneficiary named in this bill was wounded in the head at the battle of Fort Donelson on the 15th day of February, 1862. He served thereafter and was promoted, and was discharged June 30, 1865.

He died by suicide in 1878.

He never applied for a pension.

The suggestion is made that the wound in his head predisposed him to mental unsoundness, but it does not appear to be claimed that he was insane.

I can not believe that his suicide had any connection with his army service.

GROVER CLEVELAND.

EXECUTIVE MANSION, *May 19, 1888.*
To the House of Representatives:

I return without approval House bill No. 4580, entitled "An act granting a pension to Farnaren Ball."

In the report of the committee to which this bill was referred the name of this beneficiary is given as "Farnasen Ball," and in a report from the Pension Bureau it is insisted that the correct name is "Tamezen Ball."

Her son, Augustus F. Coldecott, was pensioned for disease of the lungs up to the time of his death, which occurred June 2, 1872.

The cause of his death was an overdose of laudanum, and whether it was taken by mistake or design is uncertain.

The mother is not entirely destitute, deriving an income, though small, from the interest upon a mortgage given to her upon a sale of some real estate.

The proofs with which I have been furnished fail to satisfy me that the Government should grant a pension on account of death produced by a self-administered narcotic in the circumstances which surround this case.

As a general proposition I see nothing unjust or unfair in holding that if a pensioner is sick and through ignorance or design takes laudanum without the direction or regulation of a physician the Government should not be held responsible for the consequences.

GROVER CLEVELAND.

EXECUTIVE MANSION, *May 26, 1888.*
To the House of Representatives:

I return without approval House bill No. 339, entitled "An act for the relief of J. E. Pilcher."

This bill authorizes the Secretary of the Treasury to pay to the party named therein the sum of $905, being the amount of one bond of $100 and $805 in paper money of the Republic of Texas.

It is directed, however, that this money be paid out of the Texas indemnity fund.

This fund was created under a law passed on the 28th day of February, 1855, appropriating the sum of $7,750,000 to pay certain claims against the Republic of Texas. By the terms of said law a certain time was fixed within which such claims were to be presented to the Treasury Department.

Between the passage of said act and the year 1870 the sum of $7,648,-786.73 was paid upon said claims, leaving of the money appropriated an unexpended balance of $101,213.27.

This balance was on the 30th day of June, 1877, carried to the surplus fund and covered into the Treasury, pursuant to section 5 of chapter 328 of the laws of 1874.

Thus since that date it seems there has been no Texas indemnity fund, nor is there any such fund now from which the money mentioned in the bill herewith returned can be paid.

In this condition of affairs the proposed law could not be executed and would be of no possible use.

If the claims mentioned are such as should be paid by the United States, there appears to be no difficulty in making an appropriation for their payment from the general funds of the Government. I notice an item to meet a similar claim was inserted in a deficiency bill passed on the 7th day of July, 1884.

GROVER CLEVELAND.

EXECUTIVE MANSION, *May 28, 1888.*

To the Senate:

I return without approval Senate bill No. 347, entitled "An act to provide for the erection of a public building in the city of Youngstown, Ohio."

By the census of 1880 the population of Youngstown appears to be 15,435. It is claimed by those urging the erection of a public building there that its population has nearly doubled since that date. The amount appropriated in the bill herewith returned is $75,000. There does not seem to be any governmental purpose to which such a building could be properly devoted except the accommodation of the post-office.

I have listened to an unusual amount of personal representation in favor of this bill from parties whose desires I should be glad to meet on this or any other question; but none of them have insisted that there is any present governmental need of the proposed new building even for postal purposes. On the contrary, I am informed that the post-office is at present well accommodated in quarters held under a lease which does not expire, I believe, until 1892. A letter addressed to the postmaster at Youngstown containing certain questions bearing upon the necessity of a new building failed to elicit a reply. This fact is very unusual and extraordinary, for the postmaster can almost always be relied upon to make an exhibit of the great necessity of larger quarters when a new public building is in prospect.

The fact was communicated to me early in the present session of the Congress that the aggregate sum of the appropriations contained in bills for the erection and extension of public buildings which had up to that time been referred to the House Committee on Public Buildings and Grounds was about $37,000,000.

Of course this fact would have no particular relevancy if all the buildings asked for were necessary for the transaction of public business, as long as we have the money to pay for them; but inasmuch as a large number of the buildings proposed are unnecessary and their erection would be wasteful and extravagant, besides furnishing precedents for further and more extended reckless expenditures of a like character, it seems to me that applications for new and expensive public buildings should be carefully scrutinized.

I am satisfied that the appropriation of $75,000 for a building at Youngstown is at present not justified.

GROVER CLEVELAND.

To the Senate: EXECUTIVE MANSION, *May 28, 1888.*

I return without approval Senate bill No. 1237, entitled ''An act granting a pension to Anna Mertz.''

The beneficiary named in this bill is the widow of Charles A. Mertz, who served in the Army as captain from April, 1862, to June, 1863, when he resigned on account of impaired health. It is stated in the committee's report that after his return from the Army he worked occasionally at his trade, though subject to attacks of very severe diarrhea, accompanied with acute catarrhal pains in the head and face, which he constantly attributed to his army service.

It is alleged that he had several times taken morphine, under medical advice, to allay pain caused by these attacks.

He did not apply for a pension.

On the 1st day of December, 1884, more than twenty-one years after his discharge from the Army, he died from an overdose of morphine self-administered, for the purpose, it is claimed, of alleviating his suffering.

I do not think that in this case the death of the soldier was so related to his military service as to entitle his widow to a pension.

GROVER CLEVELAND.

To the Senate: EXECUTIVE MANSION, *May 28, 1888.*

I return without approval Senate bill No. 820, entitled ''An act granting a pension to David A. Servis.''

The beneficiary named in this bill enlisted August 14, 1862, and was discharged June 8, 1865.

It is alleged that about the month of January, 1863, a comrade, by way of a joke, put powder into a pipe which the beneficiary was accustomed to smoke and covered it with tobacco, so that when he lighted it the powder exploded and injured his eyes. The report of the Senate committee states that it does not appear that "any notice was taken of this wanton act of his tent mate."

There is no mention of any disability or injury in the record of the soldier's service. He seems to have served nearly two years and a half after the injury. He filed an application for a pension in May, 1885, more than twenty-two years thereafter.

Whatever may be the extent of the injury sustained, in regard to which the evidence is apparently quite meager, I can not see that it was such a result of military service as to entitle the applicant to a pension.

The utmost liberality to those who were in our Army hardly justifies a compensation by way of pension for injuries incurred in sport or pastime or as the result of a practical joke.

GROVER CLEVELAND.

EXECUTIVE MANSION, *May 28, 1888.*

To the Senate:

I return without approval Senate bill No. 835, entitled "An act for the relief of Elisha Griswold."

The beneficiary named in this bill, which awards him a pension, enlisted in January, 1864, and was discharged February 12, 1866.

His claim for pension, as developed in the report of the Senate Committee on Pensions, is based upon the allegation that in January, 1866, he fell from a swing which had been put up in the building occupied as a barrack and struck on his head and shoulder.

The committee report in favor of the bill upon the grounds that the soldier was injured "while engaged in recreation" and that "such recreation is a necessary part of a soldier's life."

The beneficiary filed an application in January, 1880, and in support of such application he filed on the 16th day of July, 1886, an affidavit in which he testifies that at the time of the injury he was in prison at San Antonio, Tex., upon charges the character of which he could not ascertain, and that the swing from which he fell was erected by himself and others for pastime and exercise.

It will be seen that the injury complained of is alleged to have been sustained less than a month before his discharge. There is, however, no record of any disability.

His claim based upon this injury was, in my opinion, properly rejected as having no connection with his military service, and I think the facts in his case as herein detailed do not justify the award of a pension to him by special enactment.

On the 23d day of March, 1888, after the introduction of the bill herewith returned, the beneficiary, apparently having abandoned the claim upon which the bill is predicated, filed another application for a pension in the Pension Bureau, alleging that he contracted diarrhea and malarial poisoning in the service. This application is still pending.

GROVER CLEVELAND.

EXECUTIVE MANSION, *May 29, 1888.*

To the House of Representatives:

I return without approval House bill No. 1275, entitled "An act for the erection of a public building at Columbus, Ga., and appropriating money therefor."

The city of Columbus, Ga., is undoubtedly a thriving, growing city. The only present necessity for a public building there is for the accommodation of its post-office. It is stated in the report of the House committee that the gross revenues of the office for the year ending June 30, 1887, were $16,700. The postmaster, in a letter upon the subject, makes the following statement:

I estimate the gross receipts at $17,500 for the fiscal year ending March 31, which will be an increase of nearly 7 per cent over last year's receipts.

There are nine persons employed in the post-office at present, including the postmaster. The present quarters are leased by the Government at an annual rent of $900. The postmaster represents that his accommodations are not adequate or convenient, and that instead of a space of 1,900 square feet, which he now has, he should be provided with 2,500 square feet.

The population of the city in 1880 was 10,123. It is claimed that it is now about 20,000.

In my opinion the facts presented do not exhibit the necessity of the expenditure of $100,000 to afford the increased room for the post-office which may be desirable. I believe a private person would erect a building abundantly sufficient for all our postal needs in that city for many years to come for one-third of that sum.

Business prudence and good judgment seem to dictate that the erection of the proposed building should be delayed until its necessity is more manifest, and so that it can be better determined what expenditure for such a purpose will be justified by the continued growth of the city and the needs of the Government.

GROVER CLEVELAND.

EXECUTIVE MANSION, *June 5, 1888.*

To the House of Representatives:

I return herewith without approval House bill No. 4467, entitled "An act for the erection of a public building at Bar Harbor, in Maine."

The entire town within which Bar Harbor is situated contained in 1880 1,639 inhabitants, as appears by the census of that year.

There is no pretense that there is any need of a public building there except to accommodate the post-office.

This is a third-class office, and the Government does not pay the rent for offices of that class. The gross receipts of the office for the year ended June 30, 1887, are reported by the Postmaster-General at $5,337. The postmaster reports that he employs five clerks in the summer and three in the winter. The fact that Bar Harbor is a place of very extensive summer resort makes its population exceedingly variable, and during a part of the year it is quite likely that the influx of pleasure seekers may make a more commodious post-office desirable, though there does not seem to be much complaint of present inconvenience.

The postmaster pays a rent of $500 per annum for his present quarters.

The amount appropriated by the bill is quite moderate, being only $25,000, but the postmaster expresses the opinion that a proper site alone would cost from twenty to thirty thousand dollars.

I am decidedly of the opinion that if a public building is to be erected at this place, of which at present there appears to be no necessity, it should be done under a system which will not give the post-office and the postmaster there an advantage over others of their class.

GROVER CLEVELAND.

EXECUTIVE MANSION, *June 5, 1888.*

To the House of Representatives:

I return without approval House bill No. 1394, entitled "An act authorizing the Secretary of the Treasury to purchase additional ground for the accommodation of Government offices in Council Bluffs, Iowa."

A new public building at Council Bluffs will be completed in a short time. The ground upon which it is located has a frontage of 192 feet and a depth of 106 feet and 10 inches. The proposition is to add 30 feet to its depth. The act under which this building has been thus far constructed provides that the ground purchased therefor shall be of such dimensions as to leave the building unexposed to fire by an open space of at least 40 feet, including streets and alleys. The building is located on land now belonging to the Government sufficient in size to comply with this provision, and in point of fact more than the open space required is left on all sides of the same. There is no pretense that any enlargement of the building is necessary or contemplated.

The report of the committee to which this bill was referred in the House simply states that "the grounds on which said building is situated are inadequate for its proper accommodation and safety."

If this is so, I can see no reason why additional ground should not be purchased for "the proper accommodation and safety" of a large proportion of the public buildings completed and in process of erection, since the provision that there shall exist 40 feet of open space on all sides is, I think, contained in all the bills authorizing their construction. In this view the proposed legislation would establish a very bad precedent.

It is provided in the bill that the additional 30 feet mentioned shall be purchased for a sum not to exceed $10,000. The adjoining 106 feet and 10 inches, located on the corner of two streets, were purchased in the year 1882 by the Government for $15,000. The permission to purchase this addition at a price per foot greatly in excess of that already owned by the Government seems so unnecessary, except to benefit the owner, that I am of the opinion it should not be granted.

GROVER CLEVELAND.

To the Senate: EXECUTIVE MANSION, *June 5, 1888.*

I return without approval Senate bill No. 739, entitled ''An act granting a pension to Johanna Loewinger.''

The husband of the beneficiary named in this bill enlisted June 28, 1861, and was discharged May 8, 1862, upon a surgeon's certificate of disability. He was pensioned for chronic diarrhea. He died July 17, 1876. A coroner's inquest was held, who found by their verdict that the deceased came to his death ''from suicide by cutting his throat with a razor, caused by long-continued illness.''

This inquest was held immediately after the soldier's death, and it appears that the case was fully investigated, with full opportunities to discover the truth. Upon the verdict found, in the absence of insanity caused by any disability, it can hardly be claimed that his death was caused by his military service. The attempts afterwards to impeach this verdict and introduce another cause of death do not seem to be successful.

GROVER CLEVELAND.

To the Senate: EXECUTIVE MANSION, *June 12, 1888.*

I return without approval Senate bill No. 1772, entitled ''An act for the relief of John H. Marion.''

It is proposed by this bill to relieve the party named therein from an indebtedness to the Government amounting to $1,042.45, arising from the nonfulfillment of a contract made by him in 1884 with the Government, by which he agreed to furnish for the use of the Quartermaster's Department a quantity of grama hay.

The contractor wholly failed to furnish the hay as agreed, and thereupon the Government, pursuant to the terms of the contract, obtained the hay in other quarters, paying therefor a larger sum by $1,042.45 than it would have been obliged to pay the contractor if he had fulfilled his agreement. This amount was charged against the contractor.

It is alleged that the crop of the particular kind of hay which was to be furnished under the contract failed the season in which it was to be supplied on account of drought, and that thus performance became impossible on the part of the contractor.

Between individuals no injustice could be claimed if the contractor in such circumstances should be held to have taken the chances of the crop; and if an equitable adjustment should be suggested in such a case as is here presented it would hardly be asked that the party suffering from the default or failure of the other should sustain all the loss.

It seems that the contractor was the proprietor of a newspaper in Arizona, and that he did some printing for the Government besides agreeing to furnish hay to the Quartermaster's Department. After the ascertainment of the loss to the Government arising out of the hay transactions, certain accounts for printing presented by the contractor were credited against the amount of such loss charged against him. In this way his debt to the Government has been reduced more than $700. The proposed legislation would cause to be paid to the contractor the sums so retained for printing and to relieve him from the remainder of the Government's claims.

Inquiry at the Quartermaster-General's Office fails to substantiate the allegation that there is any understanding when such contracts are made that their performance is to be at all relaxed by the failure of the crop.

There really seems to be no good reason why the contractor should not make good the entire loss consequent upon his default. If, however, strict rights are to be relinquished and the liberality of the Government invoked, it should not be taxed beyond the limit of sharing the loss with the delinquent. This result would be accomplished by discharging the remainder of the contractor's debt after crediting the bills for printing above referred to.

The Government is obliged in the transaction of its business to make numerous contracts with private parties, and if these contracts are to be of any use or protection they should not be lightly set aside on behalf of citizens who are disappointed as to their profitable nature or their ability to perform them.   GROVER CLEVELAND.

EXECUTIVE MANSION, *June 12, 1888.*

To the Senate:

I return without approval Senate bill No. 1017, entitled "An act granting a pension to Stephen Schiedel."

The beneficiary named in this bill served in the First Regiment Missouri Light Artillery from October 24, 1861, to October, 1864. There is no record of any injury or disability while in the service.

In March, 1880, sixteen years after his discharge, he filed an application for a pension, alleging that about June, 1862, while carrying logs to aid in building quarters, a log slipped and fell upon a lever, which flew up and struck him, injuring his back and shoulder.

He furnished the testimony of two witnesses tending to support his statement of the manner in which he was injured, but upon investigation this evidence was found to be unreliable.

Medical examinations failed to disclose any disability from the cause alleged, but do tend to show that he was disabled since his discharge by an injury to his right hand and arm and some rheumatic trouble.

It is not claimed that he incurred any disability from rheumatism while in the Army. It appears distinctly that he was wounded in the right wrist and arm while firing a cannon at the village of Hamburg, Erie County, N. Y., on the 4th day of July, 1866. The doctor who testifies to this injury and who dressed the wound negatives any other illness before the accident.

Even if he has, since his discharge, suffered from rheumatism, he does not claim that this was incurred in the Army. He bases his right to a pension entirely upon an injury which he particularly describes, and which the medical examination does not sustain. It will be observed, too, that he continued his military service for two years and four months after the date of his alleged injury. It seems hardly possible that he could have done this if he had been injured in the manner he alleges.

GROVER CLEVELAND.

EXECUTIVE MANSION, *June 18, 1888.*

To the House of Representatives:

I return without approval House bill No. 3959, entitled "An act granting a pension to Dolly Blazer."

The husband of the beneficiary named in this bill was apparently a good soldier and was confined for a time in a Confederate prison. He was mustered out of the service in June, 1865, and never applied for a pension.

He died in 1878, leaving as survivors his widow and several children, two of whom are alleged to be still under 16 years of age.

The cause of the soldier's death was yellow fever. There is in my mind no doubt of this fact, and the attempt to establish any other cause of death, if successful, would go far toward fixing a precedent for the rejection of all evidence which stood in the way of a claim for pension.

The bill herewith returned is disapproved for the reason that the death of the soldier had no relation to his military service, and I do not think there should be a discrimination in favor of this applicant and against many thousands of widows fully as well entitled.

GROVER CLEVELAND.

EXECUTIVE MANSION, *June 18, 1888.*

To the House of Representatives:

I return without approval House bill No. 5522, entitled "An act for the relief of Elijah Martin."

By this bill it is proposed to increase the pension now paid to the beneficiary therein named, who was a soldier in the War of 1812, from $8 to $20 per month.

Prior to May 22, 1888, an application was made for reimbursement of the expenses attending the last sickness and burial of this pensioner, and on the day mentioned such application was transmitted to the proper auditing officer for adjustment.

I have no other information of the death of this soldier, but as his age is stated in the report of the House committee to be 87 years, and as there can hardly be a mistake as to the identity of the person named in the application mentioned, I am satisfied that the beneficiary has died since the introduction of the bill for his relief.

GROVER CLEVELAND.

EXECUTIVE MANSION, *June 19, 1888.*

To the House of Representatives:

I return without approval House bill No. 488, entitled "An act granting a pension to Elizabeth Burr."

It is proposed by this bill to grant a pension to the beneficiary therein named as the widow of William Burr, who enlisted for one hundred days in 1864 and was discharged on the 3d day of September in that year.

He is reported as present on all roll calls during his service. He died April 7, 1867, of dropsy, never having made any application for a pension.

His widow filed an application for pension in 1880, thirteen years after the soldier's death, alleging that the disease of which he died, claimed to be dropsy, was contracted in the service.

The claim was rejected by the Pension Bureau on the ground that the dropsy causing his death was not due to his military service, but that he was subject to the same before his enlistment.

I am perfectly satisfied that the rejection upon the ground claimed was correct.

GROVER CLEVELAND.

EXECUTIVE MANSION, *June 19, 1888.*

To the Senate:

I return without approval Senate bill No. 1957, entitled "An act granting a pension to Virtue Smith."

The beneficiary named in this bill is the widow of David M. Smith (incorrectly named David W. Smith in the bill), who served as a bugler in a Minnesota regiment from August 22, 1862, to September 28, 1862, in a campaign against the Sioux Indians.

He received a gunshot wound in the right elbow, for which in 1867 he was granted a pension of $6 a month, which was very soon thereafter increased to $8, and in August, 1875, said pension was further increased to $10 a month, which he received to the date of his death.

He died in the city of Washington on the 22d day of January, 1880.

He obtained a position in the Second Auditor's Office of the Treasury Department in 1864, and worked steadily there until about six months before his death.

Medical examinations had from time to time up to 1877 seem to have found him in excellent physical condition except the wound in his right elbow, which caused stiffness, and an injury to his left forearm not received in the Army.

In 1879 he was examined by a physician of this city who stands among the best in the profession, and found in the last stages of consumption, and this physician declares he died from that cause. A female physician certified that the cause of death was "wounds in the Army."

The pensioner was 64 years old at the time of his death.

I am perfectly satisfied from the medical testimony and from other facts connected with this case that the death of the husband of the beneficiary was in no manner related to his military service.

GROVER CLEVELAND.

EXECUTIVE MANSION, *June 22, 1888.*
To the House of Representatives:

I return without approval House bill No. 3016, entitled "An act granting a pension to Mary F. Harkins."

The husband of this beneficiary was discharged from the military service in 1865, and was pensioned for a gunshot wound in the right foot at the rate of $6 per month.

He died in 1882, seventeen years after his discharge, "from rupture of the heart, caused by the bursting and parting of the fibers of the right ventricle."

The claim is now made that the death was the result of the wound in the foot.

An application to the Pension Bureau was rejected on the ground that the death cause was not the result of the wound.

I am satisfied that this was a just conclusion.

GROVER CLEVELAND.

EXECUTIVE MANSION, *June 22, 1888.*
To the House of Representatives:

I return without approval House bill No. 600, entitled "An act increasing the pension of Mary Minor Hoxey."

The husband of the beneficiary named in this bill was, while on military duty, wounded in the left hand and afterwards in the thigh. He was pensioned in 1871 on account of these wounds, and in 1879 was allowed arrearages from time of his discharge. He died in December, 1881, of consumption, being at that time in the receipt of a pension at the rate of $17 per month.

In 1884 his widow was allowed a pension at the same rate, with $2 a month each for two minor children. The children have now attained the age of 16 years, but the widow still receives the pension awarded to her, which is the same as that allowed to all widows of her class.

I discover no reason of any substance why this pension should be increased, and if it should be done it would only be a manifestation of unjust favoritism.

I can not forget the thousands of poor widows with claims superior to this beneficiary, but with no interested friends to push their claims for increase of pension, who would be discriminated against if this proposed bill becomes a law.

It seems to me that there is a chance to do injustice by unfair caprice in fixing the rates of pension, as well as by refusing them altogether when they should be granted.   GROVER CLEVELAND.

EXECUTIVE MANSION, *June 22, 1888.*

To the House of Representatives:

I return without approval House bill No. 8281, entitled "An act for the relief of Lieutenant James G. W. Hardy."

It is proposed by this bill to award a pension to the beneficiary above named.

In the month of January, 1864, he was on recruiting service in the State of Indiana. On the 15th day of that month he was traveling between Indianapolis and Lafayette in a railroad car, and he alleges that he raised a window of the car to obtain air, and placed his arm on the window sill, when it was struck by something from the outside and one of the bones of his arm broken.

In February, 1865, he resigned on account of disability caused by the accident above mentioned, the medical certificate then stating that he had a fracture of the right humerus of ten months' standing which had not been properly adjusted.

He made an application for a pension to the Pension Bureau, which was rejected.

Although it is stated in a general way that he was traveling on business connected with his recruiting service at the time of his injury, he has given no information as to the precise purpose of his journey; and it is conceded that he was guilty of such negligence that he had no right of action against the railroad company.

It also appears by the medical certificate upon which his resignation was permitted that the fracture, not necessarily serious, was never properly treated. It seems, too, that he remained in the service ten months after the injury.

I am unable to discover why a pension should be granted in this case, unless the Government is to be held as an insurer of the safety of every person in the military service in all circumstances and at all times and places.

GROVER CLEVELAND.

EXECUTIVE MANSION, *June 22, 1888.*
To the House of Representatives:

I return without approval House bill No. 8174, entitled "An act granting a pension to Ellen Sexton."

The husband of the beneficiary served in the Union Volunteer Army from October, 1862, to June, 1864, having been during the last seven months of his service in the Veteran Reserve Corps. He was discharged for a disability which, to say the least of it, certainly had no relation to his military service, unless the Government is to be held responsible for injury arising from vicious indulgence.

He died in the city of Cork, Ireland, May 29, 1875, of consumption, certified by the health authorities there to have been of seven years' duration.

GROVER CLEVELAND.

EXECUTIVE MANSION, *June 22, 1888.*
To the House of Representatives:

I return without approval House bill No. 2215, entitled "An act granting a pension to Charles Glamann."

This beneficiary served in an Illinois regiment from September, 1864, to July, 1865, and his record shows no injury or sickness except an attack of remittent fever.

He filed a claim for pension in 1880, alleging that he was struck accidentally with a half brick by a comrade and injured in his left arm.

There is no doubt that whatever disability he thus incurred was the result of a personal altercation between himself and the man who threw the brick.

The extent to which the power to grant pensions by special act has been made to cover all sorts of claims is illustrated by the fact that, in the light of many pensions that have been allowed, this case, though presenting an absurd claim, does not appear to be much out of the way. The effect of precedent as an inducement to increase and expand claims and causes for pensions is also shown by the allegation in the report of the House committee, as follows:

Your committee and Congress have, however, frequently relaxed the rule, and granted pension for injuries and disabilities incurred in such circumstances.

I believe that if the veterans of the war knew all that was going on in the way of granting pensions by private bills they would be more disgusted than any class of our citizens.

GROVER CLEVELAND.

EXECUTIVE MANSION, *June 26, 1888.*

To the Senate:

I return without approval Senate bill No. 845, entitled "An act granting a pension to the widow of John A. Turley."

The husband of this beneficiary belonged to a Kentucky regiment of volunteers, and in 1863, having been in camp and on leave of absence, he and others of the regiment embarked on a steamboat, in charge of a lieutenant, to be taken to Louisville, whither they had been ordered.

While on the steamboat an altercation arose between two of the soldiers, and the deceased interfered to prevent, as is alleged, an affray. By so doing he was pushed or struck by one of the parties quarreling and fell upon the deck of the boat, striking his head against a plank, thus receiving a fatal injury.

It is quite clear to me that the death of this soldier was not the result of his military service. His presence on the boat was in the line of duty, but he had no charge of the rest of the men and was in no degree responsible for them, and whether he should be in any way implicated in the dispute which occurred was a matter entirely within his own control and determined by his own volition. If he had refrained from interference, he would have saved himself and performed to the utmost his military duty.

GROVER CLEVELAND.

EXECUTIVE MANSION, *July 5, 1888.*

To the Senate:

I return without approval Senate bill No. 432, entitled "An act for the relief of Joel B. Morton."

Calvin Morton, the son of the beneficiary named in this bill, enlisted in the volunteer infantry in 1861, and after his discharge again enlisted in the United States cavalry, from which he was discharged in 1867.

It is alleged by his father that he was killed in the battle with the Indians at Little Big Horn, called the "Custer massacre," June 25, 1876.

His name does not appear in any record of the soldiers engaged in that battle. The casualty records of the affair are reported as very complete, but they contain no mention of any soldier of that name.

His father claims in his application before the Pension Bureau to have had a letter from his son in the fall of 1875, dated at some place in the Black Hills, stating that he was a lieutenant in the army under General Custer, but that the letter was lost. He also alleges that he read an account of the massacre in a newspaper, the name of which he has forgotten, and that his son was there mentioned as among the slain.

The report of the House committee states that the only evidence of the death of this soldier is found in a letter of Anderson G. Shaw, who writes that he was present on the field of the battle mentioned when the killed were buried, and that one of the burial party called a corpse found there Morton's. It is further claimed that the description of this body agreed with that given by the father of his son.

Considering the complete list of the casualties attending this battle now in the War Department, it must be conceded that the death of the son of the beneficiary is far from being satisfactorily established.

The claim of the father is still pending in the Pension Bureau, and perhaps with further effort more information on the subject can be obtained.

GROVER CLEVELAND,

To the Senate: EXECUTIVE MANSION, *July 5, 1888.*

I return without approval Senate bill No. 43, entitled "An act granting a pension to Polly H. Smith."

John H. Smith, the husband of the beneficiary named in this bill, enlisted in the Regular Army in 1854 and served until the year 1870.

In 1868 a fistula developed, which was probably the result of quite continuous riding in the saddle. In 1870 he was placed upon the retired list as first lieutenant on account of the incapacity arising from such fistula.

In September, 1885, fifteen years after his retirement, he died suddenly at Portland, Oreg., of heart disease, while attempting to raise a trunk to his shoulder.

I can not see how the cause of death can be connected with his service or with the incapacity for which he was placed upon the retired list.

The application made by the widow for a pension is still pending before the Pension Bureau, and I understand that she or her friends prefer taking the chance of favorable consideration there to the approval of this bill.

GROVER CLEVELAND.

To the Senate: EXECUTIVE MANSION, *July 5, 1888.*

I return without approval Senate bill No. 1547, entitled "An act granting a pension to Mary Ann Dougherty."

A large share of the report of the Senate committee to which this bill was referred, and which report is adopted by the committee of the House, as is usual in such cases, consists of a petition signed by Mary Ann Dougherty, addressed to the Congress, in which she states that she resides in Washington, having removed here with her husband in 1863 from New Jersey; that shortly after their arrival in this city her husband, Daniel Dougherty, returned to New Jersey and enlisted in the Thirty-fourth Regiment New Jersey Volunteers; that she obtained employment in the United States arsenal making cartridges, and that while so engaged she was injured by an explosion.

She also states that she had a young son killed by machinery in the navy-yard, and that at the grand review of the Army after the close of the war another son, 6 years old, was stolen by an officer of the Army and has not been heard of since. She further says that her husband left his home in 1865 and has not been heard of since, and that she believes he deserted her on account of her infirmities.

It is alleged in the report that she received a pension as the widow of Daniel Dougherty until it was discovered that he was alive, when her name was dropped from the rolls.

The petition of this woman is indorsed by the Admiral and several other officers of the Navy and a distinguished clergyman of Washington, certifying that they know Mrs. Dougherty and believe the facts stated to be true.

There is no pretense made now that this beneficiary is a widow, though she at one time claimed to be, and was allowed a pension on that allegation. Her present claim rests entirely upon injuries received by her when she was concededly not employed in the military service. If the pension now proposed is allowed her, it will be a mere act of charity.

Her husband, Daniel Dougherty, is now living in Philadelphia, and is a pensioner in his own right for disability alleged to have been incurred while serving in the Thirty-fourth New Jersey Volunteers. Of this fact this beneficiary has been repeatedly informed; and yet she states in her petition that her husband deserted her in 1865 and has not been heard of since.

It is alleged in the Pension Bureau that in 1878 she succeeded in securing a pension as the widow of Daniel Dougherty through fraudulent testimony and much false swearing on her part.

The police records of the precinct in which she has lived for years show that she is a woman of very bad character, and that she has been under arrest nine times for drunkenness, larceny, creating disturbance, and misdemeanors of that sort.

It happens that this claimant, by reason of her residence here, has been easily traced and her character and untruthfulness discovered. But there is much reason to fear that this case will find its parallel in many that have reached a successful conclusion.

I can not spell out any principle upon which the bounty of the Government is bestowed through the instrumentality of the flood of private pension bills that reach me. The theory seems to have been adopted that no man who served in the Army can be the subject of death or impaired health except they are chargeable to his service. Medical theories are set at naught and the most startling relation is claimed between alleged incidents of military service and disability or death. Fatal apoplexy is admitted as the result of quite insignificant wounds, heart disease is attributed to chronic diarrhea, consumption to hernia, and suicide is traced to army service in a wonderfully devious and curious way.

Adjudications of the Pension Bureau are overruled in the most peremptory fashion by these special acts of Congress, since nearly all the beneficiaries named in these bills have unsuccessfully applied to that Bureau for relief.

This course of special legislation operates very unfairly.

Those with certain influence or friends to push their claims procure pensions, and those who have neither friends nor influence must be content with their fate under general laws. It operates unfairly by increasing in numerous instances the pensions of those already on the rolls, while many other more deserving cases, from the lack of fortunate advocacy, are obliged to be content with the sum provided by general laws.

The apprehension may well be entertained that the freedom with which these private pension bills are passed furnishes an inducement to fraud and imposition, while it certainly teaches the vicious lesson to our people that the Treasury of the National Government invites the approach of private need.

None of us should be in the least wanting in regard for the veteran soldier, and I will yield to no man in a desire to see those who defended the Government when it needed defenders liberally treated. Unfriendliness to our veterans is a charge easily and sometimes dishonestly made.

I insist that the true soldier is a good citizen, and that he will be satisfied with generous, fair, and equal consideration for those who are worthily entitled to help.

I have considered the pension list of the Republic a roll of honor, bearing names inscribed by national gratitude, and not by improvident and indiscriminate almsgiving.

I have conceived the prevention of the complete discredit which must ensue from the unreasonable, unfair, and reckless granting of pensions by special acts to be the best service I can render our veterans.

In the discharge of what has seemed to me my duty as related to legislation, and in the interest of all the veterans of the Union Army, I have attempted to stem the tide of improvident pension enactments, though I confess to a full share of responsibility for some of these laws that should not have been passed.

I am far from denying that there are cases of merit which can not be reached except by special enactment, but I do not believe there is a member of either House of Congress who will not admit that this kind of legislation has been carried too far.

I have now before me more than 100 special pension bills, which can hardly be examined within the time allowed for that purpose.

My aim has been at all times, in dealing with bills of this character, to give the applicant for a pension the benefit of any doubt that might arise, and which balanced the propriety of granting a pension if there seemed any just foundation for the application; but when it seemed entirely outside of every rule in its nature or the proof supporting it, I have supposed I only did my duty in interposing an objection.

It seems to me that it would be well if our general pension laws should be revised with a view of meeting every meritorious case that can arise. Our experience and knowledge of any existing deficiencies ought to make the enactment of a complete pension code possible.

In the absence of such a revision, and if pensions are to be granted upon equitable grounds and without regard to general laws, the present methods would be greatly improved by the establishment of some tribunal to examine the facts in every case and determine upon the merits of the application.　　　GROVER CLEVELAND.

EXECUTIVE MANSION, *July 5, 1888.*
To the House of Representatives:

I return without approval House bill No. 8291, entitled "An act granting a pension to Julia Welch."

The husband of the beneficiary named in this bill served in the Army from December, 1863, to May, 1866.

He never filed an application for pension, and died February 24, 1880 of inflammation of the lungs.

The claim filed by his widow for pension alleged that her husband suffered from chronic diarrhea and disease of the heart and lungs as results of his army service.

The claim was rejected by the Pension Bureau on the ground that the soldier died from an acute disease which bore no relation to any complaint contracted in the Army.

I think the action of the Bureau was correct.

　　　GROVER CLEVELAND.

EXECUTIVE MANSION, *July 5, 1888.*
To the House of Representatives:

I return without approval House bill No. 7907, entitled "An act granting a pension to Mary Ann Lang."

The husband of this beneficiary was wounded in the nose on the 1st day of June, 1864, and was mustered out of the service July 8, 1865. He was pensioned on account of this wound and died February 21, 1881. Prior to his death he had executed a declaration claiming pension also for rheumatism, but the application was not filed before he died.

The cause of his death was dropsy. The widow filed her claim for pension in 1884, which was rejected on the ground that the soldier's fatal disease was not the result of his military service.

A physician of good repute, who appears to have attended him more than any other physician for a number of years prior to his death, gives an account of rheumatic ailments and other troubles, and states that about a year and a half before he died he had a liver trouble which resulted in dropsy, which caused his death. He adds that the soldier was a man who drank beer, and at times to excess, and that he drank harder toward the last of his life. He further states that he is unable to connect the liver trouble with his rheumatism, and could not give any other reason for it except his long use of beer and liquor, and if that was not the cause it greatly aggravated it; that he had cautioned him about drinking, and at times he heeded the advice.

An appeal was taken from the action rejecting the claim and the case was submitted to the medical referee of the Pension Bureau, who decided upon all the testimony that the soldier's fatal disease (dropsy) was due to disease of the liver, which was not a sequence of rheumatism and was the result of excessive use of alcoholic stimulants.

It will be observed that no claim is made that death in any way resulted from the wound for which a pension had been allowed, and that even if rheumatism was connected with the death its incurrence in the Army had never been established.

I am satisfied that this case was properly disposed of by the Pension Bureau.

GROVER CLEVELAND.

EXECUTIVE MANSION, *July 6, 1888.*
To the House of Representatives:

I return without approval House bill No. 9184, entitled "An act granting a pension to William M. Campbell, jr."

This beneficiary was not enrolled in the service of the United States until August 5, 1862. Previous to that time he had been a member of the same regiment in which he was so enrolled, and was in the service of the State of Kentucky.

He alleges that in the month of February, 1862, he was vaccinated with impure virus and in the same month contracted mumps. He claims that as a result of these troubles he has been afflicted with ulcers and other serious consequences.

It is perfectly clear that at the time these disabilities were incurred, if they were incurred, the claimant was not in the military service of the United States.

The records show that he deserted September 16, 1862, a little more than a month after he was mustered into the United States service; that he was arrested April 25, 1864, one year and seven months after his desertion; that he was restored to duty by general court-martial with loss of pay and allowances during absence (the time lost by desertion to be made good), and that he was mustered out July 16, 1865.

This enactment seems neither to have law nor meritorious equity to support it.

GROVER CLEVELAND.

EXECUTIVE MANSION, *July 6, 1888.*

To the House of Representatives:

I return without approval House bill No. 8807, entitled "An act grant-ing a pension to Harriet E. Cooper."

The husband of this beneficiary served as a major in an Illinois regi-ment from September 3, 1862, to April 1, 1863, when his resignation was accepted, it having been tendered on account of business affairs.

He was pensioned for rheumatism from April, 1863, and died October 3, 1883.

It is admitted on all hands that Major Cooper drank a good deal, but the committee allege that they can not arrive at the conclusion that death was attributable to that cause.

There is some medical testimony tending to show that death was caused from rheumatism, but one physician gives it as his opinion that death resulted from rheumatism and chronic alcoholism.

The physician who last attended the soldier testifies that the cause of death was chronic alcoholism. This should be the most reliable of all the medical testimony, and taken in connection with the conceded intem-perate habits of the deceased and the fact that the brain was involved, it satisfies me that the rejection of the widow's claim by the Pension Bureau on the ground that the cause of death was mainly intemperance was correct.

GROVER CLEVELAND.

EXECUTIVE MANSION, *July 6, 1888.*

To the House of Representatives:

I return without approval House bill No. 6431, entitled "An act for the relief of Van Buren Brown."

The beneficiary named in this bill was discharged from the Army Sep-tember 11, 1865.

He filed an application for pension in the Pension Bureau May 19, 1883, alleging chronic diarrhea, rheumatism, spinal disease the result of an injury, and deafness.

His claim was very thoroughly examined and reopened and examined again after rejection, and rejected a second time.

The case is full of uncertainty and contradiction. Without discuss-ing these features, I am entirely satisfied that a pension should not be allowed, for the reason, among others, that three careful medical exam-inations made in 1883, 1884, and 1886 failed to disclose any pensionable disability.

GROVER CLEVELAND.

EXECUTIVE MANSION, *July 6, 1888.*

To the House of Representatives:

I return without approval House bill No. 367, entitled "An act grant-ing a pension to Nathaniel D. Chase."

This beneficiary enlisted September 3, 1863. The records show that he was admitted to a hospital March 3, 1864, with a disease of a discreditable nature and by no means connected with the military service, and that he was discharged from the Army May 20, 1864, upon a certificate of paralysis of left arm, which came on suddenly February 20, 1864, and that the cause was unknown, but believed not to be incident to the service.

He filed an application for a pension in June, 1864, alleging paralysis of the left arm from causes unknown to him.

This claim was not prosecuted at that time, and the claimant reenlisted in January, 1865, and served until September 5, 1865, without any evidence of disability appearing upon the records.

He renewed his claim in 1870, stating that he was first taken with a pain in his left arm about March 1, 1864, and that it became partially paralyzed.

It will be observed that thus far in his application he gives no explanation of the incurrence of his disability which leads to the belief that it was related to his service.

In a letter dated May 31, 1864, his captain states that he can but think that the disability of the claimant was the result of his folly and indiscretion, and that he feels it his duty to decline giving him a certificate.

In 1880 the claimant stated the cause of his disability was an injury to his arm while expelling a soldier from a railroad train at Augusta, Me., he acting as provost guard at the time. Upon this allegation the case was reopened at the Pension Bureau.

In reply to a letter from the Bureau the captain of claimant's company stated that he had no knowledge of such an injury. The same officer, in a letter dated February 25, 1887, expresses the belief that the disability of the applicant, if any existed, was caused by the injudicious use of mercurial medicine self-administered for venereal disease contracted at Augusta, Me., in January, 1864, and that such was the rumor among his comrades when he was sent to the hospital.

I can not believe that an injury was sustained such as was specified by the applicant in 1880 and that nothing was said of it either in the claim made in 1864 or in 1870. In the absence of this or some other definite cause consistent with an honest claim we are left in the face of some contrary evidence to guess that his arm was injured in the service.

The application of this beneficiary is still pending in the Pension Bureau awaiting further information.

GROVER CLEVELAND.

EXECUTIVE MANSION, *July 16, 1888.*
To the House of Representatives:

I return without approval House bill No. 9520, entitled "An act for the relief of Mary Fitzmorris."

It is proposed by this bill to pension the beneficiary named therein, as the widow of Edmund Fitzmorris, under the provisions and limitations of the general pension laws. The name of the beneficiary is already upon the pension roll, and she is now entitled to receive precisely the sum as a pensioner which is allowed her under this bill.

As her application to the Pension Bureau was quite lately favorably acted upon, it is supposed this special bill for her relief was passed by the Congress in ignorance of that fact.

GROVER CLEVELAND.

EXECUTIVE MANSION, *July 16, 1888.*

To the Senate:

I return without approval Senate bill No. 121, entitled "An act granting a pension to Tobias Baney."

This soldier was enrolled on the 28th day of February, 1865, and was discharged on the 31st day of January, 1866.

He filed an application for a pension in 1878, which was supplemented by statements from time to time, not always in exact agreement, but alleging uniformly that during his service, fixing the date at one time as in January, 1866, and at another time as in November, 1865, he was attacked in the city of Washington by palpitation of the heart, which increased after his discharge and resulted in disability. After a careful special examination by the Pension Bureau the claim was rejected upon the ground that origin of disability in the service and line of duty had not been shown, nor that the same existed for some time after discharge.

The beneficiary named in this bill enlisted shortly before the surrender of the Confederate forces, and it appears did little, if anything, more than garrison duty. He does not seem to have suffered any of the exposures usually incident to a soldier's service, and, as I understand his claim, does not himself give any instance of exposure or exertion from which his difficulty arose.

There is no record of any sickness or disability during the time he was in the Army nor any satisfactory proof that he was suffering with any ailment at the time of his discharge. His own statement, which some of the proof taken tends to show is not entirely reliable, goes no further than to claim that during his term of service his difficulty began.

On appeal from the rejection of the beneficiary's claim the case was thoroughly examined at the Interior Department and the rejection affirmed.

I am entirely satisfied that the case was properly determined.

GROVER CLEVELAND.

EXECUTIVE MANSION, *July 16, 1888.*

To the Senate:

I return without approval Senate bill No. 470, entitled "An act granting a pension to Amanda F. Deck."

The husband of this beneficiary was pensioned for a gunshot wound in his right shoulder which he received in 1864 in a battle with Indians.

The report of the committee to which the bill was referred states nothing concerning the death of the soldier and gives no information as to the date or cause of the same, and the recommendation that a pension should be given the widow is based upon the service and injury of the soldier and the circumstances of the beneficiary.

No claim was filed in the Pension Bureau on behalf of the widow. This perhaps is accounted for by the fact that information is lodged in that Bureau to the effect that the deceased soldier died on the 21st day of September, 1883, "from a pistol ball fired by Luther Cultor."

If he was killed in a personal encounter, as the report of his death would seem to indicate, I am unable to see how his death can be in any way attributed to his military service or his widow be justly pensioned therefor.

GROVER CLEVELAND.

To the Senate: EXECUTIVE MANSION, *July 17, 1888.*

I return without approval Senate bill No. 1613, entitled "An act granting an increase of pension to John F. Ballier."

This pensioner is now receiving the full amount of pension allowed for total disability to ex-soldiers of his rank.

Inasmuch as the bill herewith returned limits any increase to the rate fixed by law for cases of total disability, it appears to accomplish nothing of benefit to the beneficiary therein named.

GROVER CLEVELAND.

EXECUTIVE MANSION, *July 17, 1888.*
To the House of Representatives:

I return without approval House bill No. 5913, entitled "An act granting a pension to Thomas Shannon."

This beneficiary enlisted on the 31st day of May, 1870, in the Tenth Regiment of United States Infantry.

On the 4th day of July, 1872, he was upon leave at the city of Rio Grande, in the State of Texas. Some of the citizens were celebrating the day, and one of them had a can of powder in his hand which, according to the report of the accident, "was about to explode." The soldier endeavored to knock the can from the hand of the person who held it, when the powder exploded, severely injuring the soldier and necessitating the amputation of his right forearm.

Though this was a most unfortunate accident, it is quite plain that it had no connection with the military service.

To grant a pension in such a case would establish a precedent in the appropriation of money from the public Treasury which I can hardly think we should be justified in following.

GROVER CLEVELAND.

EXECUTIVE MANSION, *July 17, 1888.*

To the House of Representatives:

I return without approval House bill No. 9174, entitled "An act granting a pension to Woodford M. Houchin."

The beneficiary named in this bill was enrolled September 18, 1861 and discharged December 17, 1864.

He filed a claim for pension in the Pension Bureau December 22, 1876, alleging that he had a sore or ulcer on his left leg "which existed in a small way prior to enlistment," but was aggravated and enlarged by the exposures of the service.

This claim was rejected in 1877 on the ground that the disability existed prior to enlistment.

In September, 1879, he filed another application for pension, alleging a disability arising from an affection of his right eye caused by an attack of measles in September, 1861, and also again alleging ulcerated varicose veins of his left leg.

In October, 1886, the rejection of the claim for ulcerated varicose veins was adhered to and the added claim for disease of the eyes was rejected on the ground that it was not incurred in the service and line of duty.

On appeal from the action of the Pension Bureau to the Secretary of the Interior the rejection of the claim was sustained.

The claimant stated in support of his application that about three months before he enlisted a little yellow blister appeared on his left leg, which made a small sore, which existed when he enlisted; that while he was in Central America with General Walker he received a wound in the temple from a musket ball, and that he had also before enlistment been sick with the dropsy.

The case was very thoroughly examined by officers of the Pension Bureau, and a great mass of testimony was taken from numerous witnesses. Three brothers of the claimant testified to the existence of all the disabilities before his enlistment, and two of them stated facts which go far toward accounting for such disabilities in a way very discreditable to the claimant. Many other witnesses, with good opportunities of knowledge on the subject, testified to the same effect.

While testimony of a different character was also given, tending to establish the theory that the disabilities alleged were at least to some extent attributable to military service, the overwhelming weight of proof seems to establish that whatever disabilities exist are the result of disease contracted by vicious habits, and that such disabilities had their origin prior to enlistment.

GROVER CLEVELAND.

EXECUTIVE MANSION, *July 17, 1888.*

To the House of Representatives:

I return without approval House bill No. 8078, entitled "An act granting a pension to Theresa Herbst, widow of John Herbst, late private Company G, One hundred and fortieth Regiment of New York Volunteers."

John Herbst, the husband of the beneficiary named in this bill, enlisted August 26, 1862. He was wounded in the head at the battle of Gettysburg, July 2, 1863. He recovered from this wound, and on the 19th day of August, 1864, was captured by the enemy.

After his capture he joined the Confederate forces, and in 1865 was captured by General Stoneman while in arms against the United States Government. He was imprisoned and voluntarily made known the fact that he formerly belonged to the Union Army. Upon taking the oath of allegiance and explaining that he deserted to the enemy to escape the hardship and starvation of prison life, he was released and mustered out of the service on the 11th day of October, 1865.

He was regularly borne on the Confederate muster rolls for probably nine or ten months. No record is furnished of the number of battles in which he fought against the soldiers of the Union, and we shall never know the death and the wounds which he inflicted upon his former comrades in arms.

He never applied for a pension, though it is claimed now that at the time of his discharge he was suffering from rheumatism and dropsy, and that he died in 1868 of heart disease. If such disabilities were incurred in military service, they were quite likely the result of exposure in the Confederate army; but it is not improbable that this soldier never asked a pension because he considered that the generosity of his Government had been sufficiently taxed when the full forfeit of his desertion was not exacted.

The greatest possible sympathy and consideration are due to those who bravely fought, and being captured as bravely languished in rebel prisons.

But I will take no part in putting a name upon our pension roll which represents a Union soldier found fighting against the cause he swore he would uphold, nor should it be for a moment admitted that such desertion and treachery are excused when it avoids the rigors of honorable capture and confinement.

It would have been a sad condition of affairs if every captured Union soldier had deemed himself justified in fighting against his Government rather than to undergo the privations of capture.

GROVER CLEVELAND.

To the Senate: EXECUTIVE MANSION, *July 26, 1888.*

I return without approval Senate bill No. 1447, entitled "An act granting a pension to Bridget Foley."

Joseph F. Foley, the husband of the beneficiary named in this bill, enlisted on the 22d day of August, 1862, and was discharged February 13, 1863, for disability which was certified to arise from chronic rheumatism contracted prior to enlistment.

He appears to have been sick with rheumatism a large part of the time he was in the service, and because of that fact never reached a point nearer the front than the city of Washington.

He died May 13, 1873, of consumption.

His widow filed in 1884 a declaration executed by the deceased shortly before his death, in which he alleged that he was first attacked with rheumatism at Capitol Hill, in the District of Columbia, in October, 1862. The soldier never applied for a pension.

It is strenuously disputed that he had this complaint before enlistment. However this may be, it is certain that he died of consumption, and I can find no proof that this disease was contracted in the service or had any relation thereto.

GROVER CLEVELAND.

To the Senate:　　　　　　　　　　EXECUTIVE MANSION, *July 26, 1888.*

I return without approval Senate bill No. 2644, entitled "An act granting the right of way to the Fort Smith, Paris and Dardanelle Railway Company to construct and operate a railroad, telegraph, and telephone line from Fort Smith, Ark., through the Indian Territory, to or near Baxter Springs, in the State of Kansas."

This bill grants a right of way 100 feet in width, with the use of adjoining lands for stations and other purposes, through the eastern part of that portion of the Indian Territory occupied by the Cherokee Indians under a treaty with the United States.

By the terms of the treaty concluded between the Government and the Cherokee Nation in 1866 these Indians expressly granted a right of way through their lands "to any company or corporation which shall be duly authorized by Congress to construct a railroad from any point north to any point south, and from any point east to any point west of, and which may pass through, the Cherokee Nation."

There are excellent reasons why this clause in the treaty should be construed as limiting the railroads which should run through these lands, at least without further permission of the Indians, to only one from north to south and one other from east to west.

It is evident, however, that the Congress has either not so interpreted this provision of the treaty or has determined that it should be disregarded, for there have been six or seven railroads constructed or authorized through these lands by the permission of the Government.

It has become very much the custom to grant these rights of way through Indian lands and reservations merely for the asking. They have been duplicated to such an extent that rival roads are found struggling for the advantage of a prior Congressional grant or for the possession of a contested route through these reservations.

I believe these indiscriminate grants to railroads permitting them to cross the lands occupied by the Indians, if not in absolute violation of their treaty rights, are dangerous to the success of our Indian management.

While maintaining their tribal condition they should not be easily subjected to the disturbance and the irritation of such encroachments. When they have advanced sufficiently for the allotment of their lands in severalty, they should be permitted, as a general rule, to enjoy and cultivate all the land set apart to them, and not discouraged by the forced surrender of a part of it for railroad purposes. In the solution of the problem of their civilization by allotments of land they need the land itself, and not compensation for its appropriation by others. They can not be expected to understand this process in any other way than an indication that their tenure is uncertain and the assurance that they shall hold their allotted land for cultivation a delusion.

It is not necessary in the treatment of this subject to insist that in no case should a railroad be permitted to cross Indian reservations. There may be valid public reasons why in some cases this should be allowed. Important lines of through travel should not be always obstructed or defeated by a refusal of such permission. But I think there should be shown in every case a justification in the public interest or in furtherance of general growth and progress, or at least in a plain local necessity or convenience, before such grants are made.

It seems to me also that the consent of the Indians for the passage of railroads through their land should, as a general rule, be required; that the means of determining the compensation to be made for land taken should be just and definite and easy of application; that the route of the proposed road should be as particularly described as is possible; that a reasonable time should be fixed for the construction of the road, and in default of such construction that the grant should be declared null and void without legislation or judicial action, and that in all cases the rights and interests of the Indians should be carefully considered.

The bill under consideration grants to the railroad company therein named the right to construct its road over substantially the same route described in a law already passed permitting the Kansas City, Fort Scott and Gulf Railway Company to build its road through this reservation. No necessity or good reason is apparent why these two roads should be built upon the same line.

The bill makes no provision for gaining the consent of the Indians occupying these lands. The Cherokee Nation of Indians have their local laws and legislation, and are quite competent to pass upon this question. They have heretofore shown their interest in such subjects, I am informed, by protesting against some of the grants which have been made for the construction of railroads through their lands.

The bill provides for the taking of lands held by individual occupants and the manner of fixing the compensation therefor; but it is declared that when any portion of the land taken by the company shall cease to be used for the purposes for which it is taken the same shall revert to the nation or tribe from which the same shall have been taken. There is no provision that in any case land taken from individual occupants shall revert to them.

In the fifth section of the bill it is provided that the railroad company shall pay to the Secretary of the Interior, for the benefit of the particular nation or tribe through whose lands its line may be located, in addition to other compensation, the sum of $50.

It was, of course, intended to declare that this sum should be paid for every mile of road built through Indian lands, but it is not so expressed. I am by no means certain that the context will aid this omission, which is quite palpable, when that part of the bill is compared with others of the same character. In any event, this is a provision which should be free from all doubt.

There is no time limited in the bill within which the proposed road through the reservation shall be completed, and consequently no forfeiture fixed for noncompletion. The nearest approach to it is found in a clause providing that the company shall build at least 50 miles of its road in the Indian Territory within three years from the passage of the act, or the rights granted shall be forfeited as to that portion not built. The length of the proposed route through the Cherokee lands appears to be considerably over 100 miles, and it is plain that there is no sufficient guaranty in the bill that the entire road will be built within any particular time. There is no forfeiture and no limitation for the completion of the road if 50 miles is built within three years, and there may be some doubt how far the forfeiture would extend in case of a failure to finish the 50 miles within the time specified.

I believe these grants to railroads should be sparingly made; that when made they should present better reasons for their necessity and usefulness than are apparent in this case, and that they should be guarded and limited by provisions which are not found in the bill herewith returned.

GROVER CLEVELAND.

EXECUTIVE MANSION, *August 3, 1888.*

To the House of Representatives:

I return without approval House bill No. 3008, entitled "An act for the relief of P. A. Leatherbury."

This bill provides that the Secretary of the Treasury shall pay to the person above named the sum of $601.27, being the amount paid by him to Lucy Roberts on two pension checks which were afterwards recalled and canceled.

The committee of the House to whom this bill was referred report that—

The Department discovered, after the issuing of the checks, that the claim for pension was fraudulent, but not until after the purchase, in the ordinary course of business, by Mr. Leatherbury paying $601.27 therefor and giving his duebill for the balance, which balance he refused to pay after ascertaining that the check was repudiated by the Government.

Lucy Roberts, a colored woman, filed a claim for pension in 1868, alleging that she was the widow of Nelson Roberts, who died in the military service in 1865.

Her claim was allowed in 1876, and two checks, numbered 6863 and 6864, aggregating $1,301.27, were issued on account of said pension. Before payment of the checks information was received which caused an investigation by the Pension Bureau as to the honesty of the claim for pension. This investigation established its utterly fraudulent character, and thereupon the checks were canceled and the woman's name was dropped from the pension rolls.

Certain important facts are reported to me from the Pension Bureau as having been developed upon the investigation.

It appears that one Thomas had undertaken to act for the claimant in procuring her pension under an agreement that he should have $300 if successful. Mr. Leatherbury was a notary, postmaster, and claim agent, and acted as notary and general assistant to Thomas and the claimant, who was employed at Leatherbury's house. In the month of July, 1876, the same month the claim for pension was allowed, the woman Roberts was indicted for larceny, the complaining witness being Mr. Leatherbury. Shortly after the issue of the checks the woman disappeared, and it is reported that certain indications suggested that both Leatherbury and Thomas were not entirely ignorant of her whereabouts nor completely disconnected with her disappearance. The checks were obtained from Thomas by Leatherbury, he paying, as he alleges, to Thomas the fee of $300 which had been agreed upon. The checks remained in Leatherbury's possession until they were delivered by him to the special agent of the Pension Bureau upon the investigation. He claimed in his deposition that he considered that what money he had let the woman have and the goods she had obtained at his store while she worked for him, and the $300 which he had advanced to Thomas, her agent, justified him in holding her indebted to him in the sum of $600, and that he held the checks as security for the same, admitting that there was still $700 in her favor, written acknowledgment of which he had placed in the hands of his wife. He further stated that rather than gain notoriety in the matter he would return the checks to the special agent, but he trusted that the Government would pay him the $600 which he had sunk in the transaction.

The woman testified that she did take some goods from Leatherbury at his store at his suggestion, after the arrival of the checks and before she left, about August 16, 1876, which purchases amounted to no more than $100, and that he also advanced her $100; that he made no further payment and wrote to her that he had to give up the checks, and that she never indorsed the checks nor authorized anyone to do so.

Both Leatherbury and Thomas disclaimed any knowledge of the fraudulent character of the claim; but the fraudulent claimant lived in the house of one of them and he was assisting in procuring her claim to be allowed, while the other made an unlawful agreement for a liberal compensation for his services if the claim succeeded. The woman was indicted at the instance of Leatherbury at about the time of the issuance of the checks and fled, but if she is to be believed Leatherbury wrote to her during her absence. After her disappearance he ventures to pay to Thomas his illegal fee and takes possession of the checks. He considers that she owes him $600, and the bill under consideration gives him $601.27, the exact amount of the checks less $700.

Someone with more intelligence than this ignorant colored woman concocted the scheme to gain this fraudulent pension; and the circumstances point so suspiciously toward Thomas and Leatherbury, the claim of the latter upon the Government is infected with so much illegality, and the amount of his advances is arrived at so loosely that in my opinion he should not at this late day be relieved.

GROVER CLEVELAND.

EXECUTIVE MANSION, *August 7, 1888.*

To the Senate:

I return without approval Senate bill No. 1870, entitled "An act granting the use of certain lands in Pierce County, Washington Territory, to the city of Tacoma, for the purpose of a public park."

It is proposed by this bill to permit the appropriation for a public park of a certain military reservation containing 635 acres, which was set apart for military and defensive purposes the 22d day of September, 1866.

The establishment of this reservation was strongly recommended by high military authority, and its preservation and maintenance have since that time been also urged by the same authority.

At this time, when the subject of national defense is much discussed, I can not account for the apparent willingness to grant, or permit to be used for other purposes, Government lands reserved for military uses.

I judge from an expression in the letter of the Chief of Engineers, made a part of the report of the committee of the House to which this bill was referred, that its original purpose was to absolutely transfer this reservation to the city of Tacoma. The Chief of Engineers suggested an amendment to the bill providing that the mere permission to use this land for a park should be granted, "and that this permission be given with the full understanding that the United States intends to occupy the lands or any part of them for military or other purposes whenever its proper officials see fit to order the same, and without any claim for compensation or damage on the part of said city of Tacoma.''

Instead of adopting the recommendation of the Chief of Engineers the provision of the bill limiting the extent of the use of this land declares—

That the United States reserves to itself the fee and the right forever to resume possession and occupy any portion of said lands for naval or military purposes whenever in the judgment of the President the exigency arises that should require the use and appropriation of the same for the public defense or for such other disposition as Congress may determine, without any claim for compensation to said city for improvements thereon or damages on account thereof.

The expediency of granting any right to the occupancy of this land is, in my opinion, very doubtful. If it is done, it should be in the form of a mere license, revocable at any time, for the purposes used by the officers to which its use and disposition are now subject.

It seems to me that if any use of this land is given to the city of Tacoma it should be with the proviso suggested by the Chief of Engineers, instead of the indefinite and restricted one incorporated in the bill.

GROVER CLEVELAND.

EXECUTIVE MANSION, *August 9, 1888.*

To the House of Representatives:

I return without approval House bill No. 8761, entitled ''An act granting a pension to Mrs. Anna Butterfield.''

It is proposed by this bill to pension the beneficiary therein named as the ''dependent mother of James A. B. Butterfield, late a sergeant in the Second Illinois Cavalry.''

The records show that the son of this beneficiary enlisted in the regiment mentioned in August, 1861, and was mustered out August 13, 1864. No claim is made in any quarter that he incurred the least disability during this service, and there is no dispute in regard to the date of enlistment or discharge, nor does there seem to be any definite claim that he again entered the military service.

The report of the committee states that his mother is advised that after his discharge her son still remained in the service of the Government and was killed by an explosion on board of the steamer *Sultana*, in April, 1865.

Her claim for pension is now pending in the Pension Bureau awaiting testimony, which seems to be entirely wanting, to support the allegation that at the time of his death the deceased was in the service of the Government in any capacity.

This evidence ought not to be difficult to obtain. Though the mother seems to have saved something, from which she draws a small income, her advanced age and the honorable service of her son would make the allowance of a pension in her case, upon any fair and plausible justification, very gratifying.   GROVER CLEVELAND.

EXECUTIVE MANSION, *August 9, 1888.*

To the House of Representatives:

I return without approval House bill No. 2140, entitled "An act granting a pension to Eliza Smith."

The husband of this beneficiary was a second lieutenant in an Indiana regiment, and was discharged from the service in April, 1864. It is proposed in the bill herewith returned to pension the beneficiary as the widow of a first lieutenant.

The deceased was pensioned for a gunshot wound in his left arm under the general law, and his pension was increased by a special act in 1883.

He died away from home at a hotel in Union City, Ind., on the 18th day of December, 1884, and it was determined at the time, and is still claimed, that his death was the result of an overdose of morphine self-administered.

It is represented that at times the wound of the deceased soldier was very painful and that he was in the habit of taking large doses of morphine to alleviate his suffering.

Two days before his death he was at the house of one Moore, in Union City; he complained of pain, and asked for a dose of morphine, but it does not appear that he obtained it.

On the same day he went to a hotel in the same town and remained there until his death. On the second evening after his arrival there he complained of asthma and pain in his arm, and retired about 9 o'clock p. m. In the afternoon of the next day the door of his room was forced open, and he was found prostrate and helpless, though able to talk. Medicine was administered, but he soon died.

His family physician testified that the deceased did not suffer from asthma; that when his wound was suppurating he had difficulty in breathing, and that at such times he was in the habit of taking morphine in large doses, and that at times he was intemperate, especially when suffering from his wound.

It seems to me it would establish a very bad precedent to allow a pension upon the facts developed in this case.

                                                     GROVER CLEVELAND.

EXECUTIVE MANSION, *August 9, 1888.*

To the House of Representatives:

I return without approval House bill No. 7510, entitled "An act granting a pension to Stephen A. Seavey."

This beneficiary served in a Maine regiment from November 11, 1861, to August 17, 1862, when he was discharged upon a surgeon's certificate of epilepsia and melancholia. The surgeon further stated in his certificate that the soldier had been unfit for duty for sixty days in consequence of epileptic fits, occurring daily, and requiring the constant attendance of two persons during the past thirty days.

In 1879 he applied for a pension, alleging that he incurred a sunstroke on July 20, 1862. This was within the sixty days during which he was unfit for duty and also within the thirty days during which he required the constant attendance of two persons.

He succeeded in securing a pension, and drew the same until December, 1885, when information was received at the Pension Bureau which caused an examination of the merits of the case.

This examination developed such facts as led the Pension Bureau to the conclusion that the condition of the soldier was then identical with that before enlistment and that his disability existed before he entered the service. His name was accordingly dropped from the rolls.

The object of the bill herewith returned is to restore the pensioner to the rolls.

An examination of the facts satisfies me that the act of the Pension Bureau in dropping this name from the pension rolls was entirely correct and should not be reversed.

GROVER CLEVELAND.

EXECUTIVE MANSION, *August 9, 1888.*

To the House of Representatives:

I return without approval House bill No. 6307, entitled "An act granting a pension to Sarah A. Corson."

Joshua Corson, the husband of the beneficiary named in this bill, enlisted in August, 1862, for nine months, was wounded by a ball which passed through the lower part of each buttock, and was discharged June 29, 1863. He was pensioned for his wound, and died December 12, 1885.

The cause of death is stated to have been femoral hernia by a physician who attended him shortly before his death. The official record of his death attributes it to a malignant tumor.

The widow filed a claim for pension in 1886, but furnished no evidence showing when or how the hernia originated. No disability of this description is shown by any service record, nor was it ever claimed by the soldier. It is stated in the report of the committee of the House of Representatives to whom this bill was referred that the hernia first made its appearance about four years prior to the soldier's death.

The claim of this beneficiary for pension was rejected by the Pension Bureau upon the ground that there was no possible connection between the soldier's wounds and the hernia from which he died.

I am forced to the conclusion that the case was properly disposed of, and base my disapproval of the bill herewith returned upon the same ground.

GROVER CLEVELAND.

EXECUTIVE MANSION, *August 9, 1888.*
To the House of Representatives:

I return without approval House bill No. 3521, entitled ·'An act granting a pension to Manuel Garcia."

From the records it appears that the beneficiary named in this bill enlisted as a substitute August 6, 1864, and was transferred to the Eighth New Jersey Volunteers; that he is reported absent sick, and never joined his regiment, and was discharged from a hospital July 2, 1865.

He filed a claim for pension March 4, 1880, alleging that in October, 1864, at Alexandria, Va., he became lame in both legs, and that subsequently his eyes became inflamed. His hospital record shows that he was treated for pneumonia.

The board of examining surgeons in 1883 found no such evidence of varicose veins, which seems to be the disability claimed, as would justify a rating, and there appears to be no proof of the existence of any disability between the date of discharge and the year 1867.

The application of this beneficiary is still pending in the Pension Bureau awaiting any further proof which may be submitted in its support.

GROVER CLEVELAND

EXECUTIVE MANSION, *August 10, 1888.*
To the House of Representatives:

I return without approval House bill No. 149, entitled "An act granting a pension to Rachael Barnes."

The husband of this beneficiary served in the Regular Army of the United States from February 24, 1838, to February 24, 1841.

In 1880 he applied for a pension, alleging that he contracted disease of the eyes during the year 1840 while serving in Florida.

Pending the examination of his application, and on the 24th day of March, 1882, he committed suicide by hanging. His widow filed a claim for pension, alleging that he died of insanity, the result of disease of the head and eyes. Her claim was rejected on the ground that his insanity, forty-one years after discharge from the service, had no connection with his military service.

In July, 1886, a special act was passed granting a pension to the widow, which met with Executive disapproval.

At the time the soldier committed suicide he was 68 years old. Upon the facts I hardly think insanity is claimed. At least there does not appear to be the least evidence of it, unless it be the suicide itself. It is claimed, however, and with good reason, that he had become despondent on account of the delay in determining his application for a pension and because he supposed that important evidence to establish his claim which he expected would not be forthcoming. It is very likely that this despondency existed and that it so affected the mind of this old soldier that it led to his suicide. But the fact remains that he took his own life in a deliberate manner, and that the affection of his eyes, which was the disability claimed, was not in a proper sense even the remote cause of his death.

I confess that I have endeavored to relieve myself from again interposing objections to the granting of a pension to this poor and aged widow. But I can not forget that age and poverty do not themselves justify gifts of public money, and it seems to me that the according of pensions is a serious business which ought to be regulated by principle and reason, though these may well be tempered with much liberality.

I can find no principle or plausible pretext in this case which would not lead to granting a pension in any case of alleged disability arising from military service followed by suicide. It would be an unfair discrimination against many who, though in sad plight, have been refused relief in similar circumstances, and would establish an exceedingly troublesome and dangerous precedent.

GROVER CLEVELAND.

EXECUTIVE MANSION, *August 10, 1888.*

To the House of Representatives:

I return without approval House bill No. 8574, entitled "An act granting a pension to Sallie T. Ward, widow of the late W. T. Ward."

The husband of this beneficiary served about nine months in the Mexican War. He entered the service as a brigadier-general in 1861, and served through the War of the Rebellion with credit, and was wounded in the left arm on the 15th day of May, 1864.

For this wound he was pensioned according to his rank, and received such pension until his death, at the age of 70 years, which occurred October 12, 1878.

The cause of his death was brain disease, and it seems not to be seriously claimed that it had any relation to his wound.

His widow is now in receipt of the pension provided for those of her class by the Mexican pension law.

If this bill becomes a law, I am unable to see why, in fairness and justice, the widow of any officer of the grade of General Ward should not be allowed $50 a month, the amount proposed by this bill to be paid his widow, regardless of any other consideration except widowhood and the rank of the deceased husband.

The bill herewith returned, while fixing the monthly amount to be absolutely paid to the beneficiary, does not make the granting of the pension nor payment of the money subject to any of the provisions of the pension laws nor make any reference to the Mexican service pension she is now receiving. While it is the rule under general laws that two pensions shall not be paid to the same person, inasmuch as the widow is entitled to the pension she is now receiving upon grounds different from those upon which the special bill was passed, and no intention is apparent in the special bill that the other pension should be superseded, it may result that under the peculiar wording of this bill she would be entitled to both pensions.

The beneficiary filed a claim for pension in the Pension Bureau in 1884, which is still pending, awaiting evidence connecting the death of the soldier with his wound.

GROVER CLEVELAND.

EXECUTIVE MANSION, *August 10, 1888.*

To the House of Representatives:

I herewith return without approval House bill No. 490, entitled "An act granting a pension to George W. Pitner."

It appears from the records that the beneficiary named in this bill entered the military service in June, 1863, and was discharged in March, 1866. He was treated while in the Army in the months of December, 1864, and January, 1865, for conjunctivitis.

He filed a claim for pension in 1886, alleging that he had a sunstroke in 1865, and that while at work in a basement in the year 1881 he fell into a well which was open near him and received serious injuries, resulting in the amputation of his right foot and also disability of his left foot. He attributes his fall to vertigo, consequent upon or related to the sunstroke he suffered in the Army.

The claim was rejected on the ground that the evidence taken failed to connect the disabilities for which a pension was claimed with army service.

Whatever may be said of the incurrence of sunstroke in the Army, though he fixes it as after the date of his only medical treatment during his service, and whatever may be said of the continuance of vertigo consequent upon the sunstroke for sixteen years, I find no proof that at the time he fell he was afflicted with vertigo, unless it be his own statement, and whatever disability naturally arose from sunstroke does not appear by him to have been deemed sufficient to induce him to apply for a pension previous to his fall.

In any event there seems to be no satisfactory evidence that anything which occurred in his army service was the cause of his fall and consequent injury.

GROVER CLEVELAND.

EXECUTIVE MANSION, *August 10, 1888.*

To the House of Representatives:

I return without approval House bill No. 9034, entitled "An act granting a pension to Lydia A. Heiny."

The husband of this beneficiary served in an Indiana regiment from August, 1861, to March, 1864, when he reenlisted as a veteran volunteer and served as a private and teamster to July 20, 1865, when he was discharged.

There is no record of any disability, and he never applied for a pension.

On the 12th day of December, 1880, in leaving a barber shop at the place where he resided, he fell downstairs and died the next day from the injuries thus received.

His widow filed an application for a pension in the year 1885, alleging that her husband contracted indigestion, bronchitis, nervous debility, and throat disease in the Army, which were the cause of his death.

The claim was rejected upon the ground that the death of the soldier was not due to an injury connected with his military service.

While there has been considerable evidence presented tending to show that the deceased had a throat difficulty which might have resulted from army exposure, the allegation or the presumption that it caused his fatal fall, it seems to me, is entirely unwarranted.

GROVER CLEVELAND.

EXECUTIVE MANSION, *August 10, 1888.*

To the House of Representatives:

I return without approval House bill No. 9344, entitled "An act granting a pension to James C. White."

The records of the War Department show that this beneficiary enlisted in a Kentucky regiment September 29, 1861. On the muster roll of April 30, 1862, he is reported as absent. On the roll of August 31, 1863, he is mentioned as having deserted July 19, 1862. His name is not borne on subsequent muster rolls until it appears upon those of January and February, 1864, with the remark that he returned February, 1864, and that all pay and allowances were to be stopped from July 19, 1862, to February 5, 1864. It appears that he deserted again on the 18th of December, 1864, and that his name was not borne upon any subsequent rolls.

Naturally enough, there does not appear to be any record of this soldier's honorable discharge.

It seems that this man during the time that he professed to be in the service earned two records of desertion, the first extending over a period of nearly a year and a half and the other terminating his military service.

He filed a claim for pension on the 4th day of August, 1883, alleging that he contracted piles in December, 1861, and a hernia in April, 1862.

A medical examination in 1883 revealed the nonexistence of piles and the presence of hernia.

The fact of the incurrence of any disability at all in the service is not satisfactorily established, and the entire case in all its phases appears to be devoid of merit.

GROVER CLEVELAND.

EXECUTIVE MANSION, *August 10, 1888.*
To the House of Representatives:

I return without approval House bill No. 9183, entitled "An act granting a pension to William P. Riddle."

The records of the War Department show that the beneficiary named in this bill was enrolled October 4, 1861, in the Fifth Kentucky Regiment of Cavalry, and was mustered into the service on the 31st day of March, 1862.

From that time to April 30, 1862, he is reported absent sick. On the rolls for four months thereafter, ending August 31, 1862, he is reported as absent and deserted. His name is not borne on any subsequent rolls.

He did not file an application for pension until April, 1879, when the act granting arrears was in force. He then claimed that he contracted pneumonia February 15, 1862; that about a month after he was sent home, and was under medical treatment for two years; that he returned about May 1, 1864, and was discharged about May 15, 1864, but that his discharge papers were lost.

Though he has furnished some evidence in support of the claim that he was sick at about the time alleged and that he returned to the Army after an absence of two years, no record proof of any kind is furnished of an honorable discharge at any time.

He has been informed that the record of his desertion in the War Department will be investigated with a view to its correction if he will furnish direct proof that it is erroneous. No such proof has been supplied, and the case has not been finally acted upon in the Pension Bureau.

It does not seem to me that this case in its present condition should receive favorable consideration.

GROVER CLEVELAND.

EXECUTIVE MANSION, *August 10, 1888.*
To the House of Representatives:

I return without approval House bill No. 9126, entitled "An act granting a pension to Mrs. Caroline G. Seyfforth."

The husband of this beneficiary served as contract surgeon in the

United States Army from September 12, 1862, to August 17, 1865, and was stationed at Portsmouth Grove Hospital, in Rhode Island.

He never filed a claim for pension, and died July 21, 1874, of congestion of the liver. His widow filed an application for pension in 1882, alleging that her husband's death was caused by blood poisoning contracted while dressing the wound of a patient in January, 1863. There is proof that he suffered from blood poisoning.

The record of death states its cause as congestion of the liver, but the certificate was not signed. A young doctor named Adams, a friend and pupil of the deceased, seems to have been more than any other the attendant physician, but he appeared to think that one of three other doctors had actual charge of the case. These physicians, named, respectively, Sullivan, Dana, and Sargent, agreed that Adams had charge of the case and that they were consulting surgeons in the last illness.

Dr. Adams testified before a special examiner that from intimate association he knew that the deceased was subject to kidney disease and other symptoms of bad health from discharge to his death; that as he had lost a part of one hand from blood poisoning in the Army, he always supposed his subsequent troubles were referable to that cause; that he believed the cause of death was albuminuria, and that his liver was also affected. He further expresses the opinion that the death was the culmination of the disorders which affected him from the time of his discharge from the service.

Dr. Sullivan deposed that he knew the deceased well from about 1869, and never had any reason to think him the subject of blood poisoning or its results. He further says that he was called in consultation at the last illness of the deceased and diagnosed his trouble as liver disease, due to the patient's habits of intemperance.

Dr. Dana testified that he knew the deceased well from the time of his discharge; that he was called to consult in his case with young Dr. Adams a few days before the death occurred; that he took a general view of the case and considered that the trouble was due to habits of intemperance.

Dr. Sargent deposed that he knew the deceased well and knew that he had lost a part of his hand, as alleged, from septic poisoning in the Army, though he was not aware that the poisoning had left any other effect; that the deceased had several spells of alcoholism after the war; that he had heard him complain of his kidneys, but attributed his troubles to his excesses.

Other evidence suggested the same cause for sickness and death spoken of by these physicians, but there seems to be an almost entire absence of evidence connecting the death with service in the Army.

I am of the opinion that a case is not presented in any of its aspects justifying a pension.

GROVER CLEVELAND.

EXECUTIVE MANSION, *August 10, 1888.*

To the House of Representatives:

I return without approval House bill No. 6193, entitled "An act for the relief of Edson Saxberry."

The beneficiary named in this bill filed a declaration for a pension in 1879, alleging that in 1863 he bruised his leg, which became very sore, and when it began to heal his eyes became sore.

The evidence taken upon a careful examination of this application seems to establish, by the admission of the applicant and by other evidence, the correctness of the position taken by the Pension Bureau in rejecting the claim, that whatever disability was incurred existed before enlistment and was in no manner attributable to military service.

GROVER CLEVELAND.

EXECUTIVE MANSION, *August 10, 1888.*

To the House of Representatives:

I return without approval House bill No. 2233, entitled "An act granting a pension to Bernard Carlin."

By this bill it is proposed to pension the beneficiary therein named as of Company A, Fourteenth Regiment of Missouri Volunteer Infantry.

It seems that he served in the company and regiment named, but that he also served in Company A, Sixty-sixth Illinois Regiment, and it is claimed that while in the latter service exclusively he received the injuries for which a pension is claimed.

His application is still pending in the Pension Bureau, and the papers pertaining to the same are now in the hands of an examiner for special examination.

I think this should be completed before a special act is passed, and I understand this to be in accordance with a general rule adopted by Congress and its pension committees. This is certainly the correct course to be pursued in this case, in view of the failure to state in the special bill the regiment and company to which the soldier belonged at the time of the incurrence of disability. This can be corrected by the Pension Bureau if the claim is found meritorious.

GROVER CLEVELAND.

EXECUTIVE MANSION, *August 14, 1888.*

To the Senate:

I return herewith a joint resolution which originated in the Senate, and is numbered 17, providing for the printing of additional copies of the United States map of the edition of 1886, prepared by the Commissioner of Public Lands.

This resolution directs that 7,500 of these maps shall be printed at a rate not exceeding $1.35 each; that 2,000 of said maps shall be for the use of the Senate, 4,000 for the use of the House of Representatives, 500 for the Commissioner of the Land Office, and that 1,000 be mounted and sold at the price of $1.50 each. The sum of $10,125 is appropriated to pay the expense of the publication of said maps.

The propriety and expediency of this appropriation, to be applied so largely by the two branches of Congress, should be left to legislative discretion.

I believe, however, that through inadvertence the duplication of the edition of these maps issued in 1886 has been directed by this joint resolution instead of the edition of 1887.

The map of 1886 was published at a cost of $1.25 per copy.

The map of 1887 will very soon be issued at a cost of $1 per copy, and the publishers have offered to print an enlarged edition at the rate of 95 cents for each map. This map will be later, more correct, more valuable in every way, and cheaper than that issued the previous year.

Upon these facts I return the joint resolution without approval, in the belief that the Congress will prefer to correct the same by directing the publication of the latest, best, and cheapest map, and reducing the amount appropriated therefor.

GROVER CLEVELAND.

To the Senate: EXECUTIVE MANSION, *August 14, 1888.*

I return without approval Senate bill No. 2653, entitled ''An act granting a pension to Mary Curtin.''

The husband of this beneficiary was mustered into the military service October 8, 1862, was wounded in the right arm, and was discharged September 3, 1863.

He was pensioned for his wound to the time of his death, September 17, 1880.

The physician attending him in his last illness testified that the deceased was in the last stages of consumption when pneumonia intervened and caused his death.

I do not understand that this physician gives the least support to the theory that the wound for which this soldier was pensioned was in the slightest degree connected with his death, and there seems to be nothing in the case to justify the conclusion that such was the fact.

GROVER CLEVELAND.

To the Senate: EXECUTIVE MANSION, *August 14, 1888.*

I return without approval Senate bill No. 1076, entitled ''An act granting a pension to the widow of John Leary, deceased.''

This bill does not give the name of the intended beneficiary, but merely directs that the name of the widow of John Leary, late first sergeant in Battery F, Third Artillery, United States Army, be placed upon the pension roll, and that she be paid the sum of $20 per month.

John Leary first enlisted in the Regular Army July 26, 1854, and reenlisted in August, 1859. He was slightly wounded July 1, 1862, and appears to have been discharged March 25, 1863, on account of syphilitic iritis. In April, 1863, he entered the general service and acted as a clerk in the Adjutant-General's Office until April 1, 1864, when he was discharged.

Neither he nor his widow ever filed a claim in the Pension Bureau, but an application on behalf of his minor children was filed in 1882.

The soldier died on the 8th day of December, 1872, of pneumonia, and his widow remarried in 1876.

The application on behalf of the children was denied on the ground that the death of the soldier was not due to any cause arising from his military service. The youngest child will reach the age of 16 in September, 1888.

It is stated in the report of the Senate committee to whom this bill was referred that the second husband, to whom this widow was married in 1876, is now dead, and it is proposed to pension her as the widow of John Leary, her first husband, at the rate of $20 per month.

In the unusual cases when a widow has been pensioned on account of the death of her first husband, notwithstanding her remarriage, which forfeited her claim under the general law, it has been well established that she was again a widow by the death of her second husband, that beyond all controversy the death of the first husband was due to his military service, and such advanced age or disability has been shown on the part of the widow as prevented self-support.

In this case the name of the widow is not in the bill; there is hardly room for the pretense that her first husband's death was due to his military service, her age is given as over 40 years, and $20 a month is allowed her; being considerably more than is generally allowed in cases where a widow's right is clear, with no complications of second marriage, and her necessities great.

GROVER CLEVELAND.

EXECUTIVE MANSION, *August 14, 1888.*

To the Senate:

I return without approval Senate bill No. 1762, entitled "An act granting a pension to Benjamin A. Burtram."

The beneficiary named in this bill was mustered into the military service November 26, 1861; he was reported present until February 28, 1862, and was discharged for disability July 26, 1862.

The medical certificate of the disability of this soldier was made by the senior surgeon of a hospital in Louisville, Ky., and stated that the soldier had been disabled for sixty days; that his lungs were affected with tubercular deposits in both, and that there was some irregularity in the action of the heart; that he was of consumptive family, his mother, brother, and two sisters having died of that disease according to his and his father's account.

It is of course supposed that this certificate was based upon an examination of the patient, though both he and his father seem to have supplemented such an examination with statements establishing a condition and history which operated to bring about a discharge.

I do not find, however, either as the result of examinations or statements, any other trouble or disability alleged than those mentioned above.

But in 1879, seventeen years after the soldier's discharge, and during the period when arrearages of pensions were allowed on such applications, he filed a claim for pension, in which he alleged that about December 1, 1861, while unloading gun boxes, he incurred a rupture, and that in January, 1862, he was taken with violent pains in left arm and side, causing permanent disability.

It will be observed that the time of the incurrence of these disabilities is fixed as quite early in the very short military service of this soldier; and it certainly seems that, though short, his term of service was sufficiently long to develop such disabilities as he claims to have incurred to such an extent that they neither would have escaped in the succeeding July the examination of the surgeon nor the mention of the soldier.

A medical examination which followed the application for pension in 1879 disclosed a large scrotal hernia, but no discoverable trouble of left arm and side.

A special examination of the case was made and a large amount of testimony taken. Without giving it in any detail as it is reported to me, I fail to find in it reasonably satisfactory proof that the disabilities upon which he now bases his claim for a pension were incurred in the military service.

GROVER CLEVELAND.

To the Senate: EXECUTIVE MANSION, *August 22, 1888.*

I return without approval Senate bill No. 3038, entitled "An act for the relief of P. E. Parker."

Mr. Parker was a surety with six other persons upon an official bond given by one Franklin Travis, a collector of internal revenue, which bond was dated on the 9th day of May, 1867. A few years after that the collector became a defaulter to the Government for something over $27,000. Suit was commenced against the sureties upon the bond, and the defense was presented in their behalf that by reason of the imposition of new duties and responsibilities upon the collector after the execution of the bond his sureties were released. Judgment, however, passed against them, and the property of the beneficiary named in this bill was sold upon said judgment for the sum of $2,366.95. But only $1,793.16

THE ANGLO-VENEZUELAN ARBITRATION COMMISSION AT PARIS

VENEZUELA COMMISSION.

For the occasion giving rise to the appointment of the commission shown on the preceding page, consult the Encyclopedic Index, heading *Venezuelan Question* in the article *Venezuela*. Reading from left to right, the persons in the front row of the illustration are: 1—United States Supreme Court Justice Brewer, American arbitrator; 2—Lord Chief-Justice Russell, British arbitrator; 3—His Excellency, Mr. de Maartens, President; 4—United States Supreme Court Chief-Justice Fuller, American arbitrator; 5—Lord Justice Collins, British arbitrator.

of such amount was paid into the United States Treasury, the remainder having been applied to the payment of fees and expenses.

After the application of this sum to the payment of the judgment a bill was passed by the Congress relieving all these sureties from liability upon the bond. It appears that the amount above stated was all the money collected thereupon. The grant of the relief of these sureties by the Congress apparently was the same interposed by them to the suit in which the judgment was recovered.

The present bill directs the Secretary of the Treasury to pay to the surety Parker the sum of $2,336.95, the entire amount for which his property was sold, though the Senate committee to which the bill was referred reported in favor of reducing this sum to $1,793.16, the amount actually received by the United States upon its indebtedness.

It seems to me that the action of Congress in relieving these sureties was generous in the extreme, and if money was to be refunded which was apparently legally recovered and collected it should not exceed the amount the Government actually received. The Government is in no default and should be put to no expense in refunding the small sum recovered on account of the defalcation of its officer whose good conduct this beneficiary guaranteed. I think it would better subserve public interests if no further relief should be granted than that already afforded.

There is another fact reported to me which deprives this surety of any equitable claim for further relief. It appears from an examination of this matter that the man who is now attempting to be reimbursed this money from the Government Treasury commenced a suit against his cosureties for this identical money on the ground of their liability with him, and that he actually collected from two of them in such suit the sum of $1,747.16.

If this is true, it is speaking mildly of the claim he now makes against the Government to say that it should not have been presented.

GROVER CLEVELAND.

EXECUTIVE MANSION, *August 22, 1888.*

To the Senate:

I return without approval Senate bill No. 2616, entitled "An act granting a pension to James E. Kabler."

This beneficiary enlisted August 10, 1862. He is reported as absent sick for November and December, 1862; present for January and February, 1863; on the rolls for March and April he is reported as deserted, and for May and June as under arrest. On the 17th of September, 1863, after having been in the service a little over a year, he was mustered out with his company with the remark "absent without leave and returned to duty with loss of fifty-two days' pay by order of General Boyle." The charge of desertion does not appear to have been removed.

He filed a claim for pension in 1870 on account of quinsy alleged to have been contracted about December 7, 1862, with some evidence to support the claim. Three medical examinations fail to establish the existence of this disease in a pensionable degree, and it is reported to me from the Pension Bureau that in March, 1882, the family physician of the beneficiary stated that though he had practiced in his family for eight or nine years he had no recollection of treating him for quinsy or any other disease.

It seems to me that neither the service nor the alleged disability of this beneficiary are of a meritorious character.

GROVER CLEVELAND.

To the Senate: EXECUTIVE MANSION, *August 22, 1888.*

I return without approval Senate bill No. 2370, entitled "An act granting a pension to Sarah C. Anderson and children under 16 years of age."

William H. Anderson, the husband and the father of the beneficiaries named in this bill, enlisted on the 27th day of August, 1862, and is reported as sick or absent a large part of his short term of service. He was discharged April 23, 1863, to date November 5, 1862, on a surgeon's certificate of disability for "tertiary syphilis, with ulcerated throat and extensive nodes on the tibia of both legs."

He never filed an application for pension. He was admitted to an insane asylum in September, 1883, suffering with epilepsy, chronic diarrhea, and dementia, and died of pneumonia on the 26th day of February, 1884.

His symptoms and troubles after his discharge, so far as they are stated, are entirely consistent with the surgeon's certificate of disability given at the time of his discharge, and there seems to be an entire lack of testimony connecting in any reasonable way his death with any incident of his military service.

GROVER CLEVELAND.

To the Senate: EXECUTIVE MANSION, *August 22, 1888.*

I return without approval Senate bill No. 2206, entitled "An act granting a pension to David H. Lutman."

The beneficiary named in this bill was pensioned in 1885 on account of spinal irritation, the result of measles.

In 1886 he filed a claim for increase of pension, alleging rheumatism, and the board of examining surgeons at Cumberland, Md., upon an examination, found no evidence of spinal irritation or rheumatism, and he was dropped from the pension rolls on the ground that the disability for which he was pensioned had ceased to exist.

He afterwards filed medical and lay testimony tending to show that he suffered from disease of the back, legs, and arms, and he was thereupon, and on the 8th day of October, 1886, again examined by the board of examining surgeons at Hagerstown, Md., who reported as follows:

We have stripped him, and find a splendid specimen, square built from the ground up, muscles well developed, his appearance indicative of perfect health. No curvature of spine, disease or irritation of spinal cord; no atrophy of any muscles or evidence of weakness. No impairment of motion anywhere.

If there is any value to be placed upon the reports of these examining boards, the refusal of the Pension Bureau to restore this beneficiary to the rolls was fully justified; and this is not a proper case, in my opinion, for interference with that determination.

GROVER CLEVELAND.

EXECUTIVE MANSION, *August 22, 1888.*
To the Senate:

I return without approval Senate bill No. 645, entitled ''An act granting a pension to Mrs. Margaret B. Todd.''

This bill does not describe the beneficiary as related to any soldier of the war, but from other data it is found that she is the widow of Frank G. Todd, who served as a private in the One hundred and eighteenth Volunteer Infantry from July, 1863, to May, 1864, when he was transferred to the Navy. It appears that he served in the Navy from May 13, 1864, until April 10, 1866. He died in January, 1878, from exhaustion, as stated by the physicians who attended him.

There is scarcely a particle of satisfactory evidence showing his condition from the time of his discharge to 1871, and there is almost an entire lack of proof showing a connection between his death and any incident of his service. The widow in her application to the Pension Bureau for a pension states that she has children who were born in 1870, 1871, and 1878.

There seems to be no record of any disability during the husband's service in the Army, and the only mention of disability while in the Navy is an entry on the 30th day of May, 1864, showing that he was admitted to treatment for ''syphilis secondary.''

The widow's claim is still pending in the Pension Bureau.

GROVER CLEVELAND.

EXECUTIVE MANSION, *August 22, 1888.*
To the Senate:

I return without approval Senate bill No. 1542, entitled ''An act granting a pension to John W. Reynolds.''

The bill describes this beneficiary as being ''late of the One hundred and fifty-seventh Ohio Volunteer Infantry.''

He filed a claim in 1872 that he was a deputy United States provost-marshal for the Twelfth Ohio district from October, 1864, to March, 1865, and that in December, 1864, while ascending a stairway to arrest two deserters who had been drafted, a barrel of cider was rolled down upon him, by which he was severely injured.

The claim having been rejected on the ground that the claimant was not entitled to a pension as a civil employee of the Government, he afterwards, and in January, 1888, informed the Bureau that he was drafted in November, 1864, while serving as assistant deputy provost-marshal, and was sworn in and reserved for home duty, and was discharged from the One hundred and fifty-first Ohio Volunteers. The records of the War Department show that John W. Reynolds served in the One hundred and fifty-first Ohio Regiment from May 2, 1864, to August 27, 1864.

It is perfectly apparent that this beneficiary was injured while acting as a deputy assistant provost-marshal, arresting deserters for the pay and rewards allowed him, and that his injuries were not at all connected with actual military service.

GROVER CLEVELAND.

EXECUTIVE MANSION, *August 22, 1888.*
To the House of Representatives:

I return without approval House bill No. 2088, entitled "An act for the relief of W. S. Carpenter."

This bill appropriates the sum of $126.26 to be paid to the beneficiary named therein for his salary as an employee in the Railway Mail Service from the 3d day of October until the 20th day of November, 1882.

Mr. Carpenter was employed as a railway postal clerk at a salary of $800 per annum. He abandoned his route about the 2d day of October, 1882, without any leave of absence or explanation at the time, leaving his work in charge of one Jones, another railway postal clerk. He appears to have been paid for all the work he did, unless it be for two or three days in October, for which he apparently makes no claim.

There is nothing in the Post-Office Department showing that the absence of Carpenter was claimed to be on account of sickness, though there are a number of communications relating to the case.

The regulations of the Department permit the performance of the duties of a postal clerk by an associate in case of sickness, but never without the written permission of the division superintendent after an arrangement between the parties in writing, signed by them and filed with the superintendent.

Among a number of communications from Railway Mail Service officials relating to the conduct of Carpenter, all tending in the same direction, there is a letter from the chief clerk of the Railway Mail Service at Peoria, Ill., under whose immediate supervision Mr. Carpenter performed service, written to the superintendent of the sixth division of said service at Chicago, and dated November 16, 1882, containing the following statement:

I desire to call your attention to the case of W. S. Carpenter, Gilman and Springfield R. P. O., as follows: October 10 he was requested to appear at the post-office at

Springfield, Ill., for examination on Illinois scheme. I went to Springfield for the purpose of examining him, but he failed to put in an appearance. Upon my return home I found a letter from him stating that he did not expect to remain in the service, hence his failure to report for examination; and, furthermore, that he would send in his resignation to your office by the first of the following week. This he had not done the 12th instant. He has not been on duty but two days since October 1. He left the run in charge of Mr. Jones, of the same line, telling him he did not know when he would return, and for Jones to keep up the run. He has no leave of absence, either verbally or otherwise. What his motives are for conducting himself in this manner I can not imagine. I have written him on the subject, but can not hear from him. When in Springfield the 3d instant, I requested the postmaster there to not pay Carpenter for October until he received notice to do so. I then notified you of the facts in the matter. I would respectfully recommend that Carpenter be relieved from further duty and a successor be appointed. He is of no account at the best; he has no interest in the work, and should be removed. I would also recommend that he be paid for but the two days' run in the month of October.

Four days after the date of this letter Mr. Carpenter was notified that an order had been issued discontinuing his pay and services.

These facts stated present the case of an employee of the Government abandoning his duties without leave or notice, in direct violation of rules, and claiming compensation for work done in his absence by another employee whose entire services were due the Government.

To allow a claim so lacking in merit would endanger discipline and invite irregularity and loose methods in a very important branch of the public service.

GROVER CLEVELAND.

EXECUTIVE MANSION, *August 27, 1888.*

To the House of Representatives:

I return without approval House bill No. 2524, entitled "An act for the relief of Clement A. Lounsberry."

This bill appropriates the sum of $1,214.51 to reimburse him for clerk hire and fuel and lights in excess of allowances made to him by the Post-Office Department while he was postmaster at Bismarck, in the Territory of Dakota.

Seven hundred and fifty dollars of this sum is appropriated on account of clerk hire paid out from April 1, 1881, to June 30, 1882, and $464.51 for lights and fuel from July 1, 1883, to September 30, 1885.

As a general rule the allowances made by the Post-Office Department in these cases ought not to be interfered with. But sometimes a sudden rush of settlement in a locality, or some other cause, will so increase unexpectedly the need of clerks to distribute and handle the mails that the employment of more than have been provided for is absolutely necessary.

I am inclined to think the item for clerk hire in this bill should be so regarded. This was the only appropriation included in the bill presented in the Forty-eighth Congress in behalf of this postmaster upon which a favorable committee report was made and which was not unfavorably spoken of by the Department.

But it does not follow that the other item for fuel and lights should be allowed. I think it should not, on the grounds that the amount was fixed by the Department upon full examination, that there is no special reason shown why the postmaster should have exceeded the expenditures allowed, and that to give the least encouragement to postmasters that these allowances would be upon their application revised and increased by Congress would lead to demoralization in the service.

It appears that the allowance made to this officer for fuel and lights was increased October 1, 1883, and although the claim now made on this account embraces the period from July 1, 1883, to September, 1885, nothing was asked for fuel or lights in the bill presented to Congress for this beneficiary's relief in 1884.

It should not have been tacked upon the bill now presented.

GROVER CLEVELAND.

EXECUTIVE MANSION, *August 27, 1888.*
To the Senate:

I return without approval Senate bill No. 288, entitled "An act for the erection of a public building at Sioux City, Iowa."

On the 19th day of June, 1886, I was constrained to disapprove a bill embracing the same subject covered by the bill herewith returned. Further investigation on the second presentation of the matter fails to convince me that $150,000 should be expended at present for the erection of a public building at Sioux City.

From all the representations that are made in an effort to show the necessity for this building I gather that the only two purposes for which the Government should furnish quarters at this place are a term of the United States court not specially crowded with business and the post-office, which, though perhaps crowded, I am sure can get on very well for a time without a larger public building.

As far as the court is concerned, it was agreed when a term was located there in 1882 that it might be held in the county building, which from the description furnished me seems to be entirely adequate for the purpose and very well arranged. The term held in October, 1887, was in session for nine days.

I am decidedly of the opinion that if a public building is to be located at Sioux City it had better be delayed until a better judgment can be formed of its future necessity and proper size.

I see some of the parties interested have such confidence in the growth and coming needs of the place that in their opinion the work ought not to be entered upon with a less appropriation than $500,000.

GROVER CLEVELAND.

EXECUTIVE MANSION, *September 1, 1888.*

To the House of Representatives:

I return without approval House bill No. 9363, entitled "An act granting a pension to Edwin J. Godfrey."

The beneficiary named in this bill enlisted on the 27th day of May, 1861, in a New Hampshire regiment, and less than three months thereafter was discharged on a surgeon's certificate of his disability occasioned by "disease of heart existing prior to enlistment."

In 1881, twenty years after discharge, the beneficiary applied to the Pension Bureau for a pension, and alleged that his disease of the heart was the result of fatigue and overheating at Bull Run, Virginia, July 21, 1861.

If the heart disease of which the discharged soldier complained in 1861, and which the claimant of a pension in 1881 alleged still continued, could have been caused by fatigue and overheating in the only battle of his brief service, it seems to me that its manifestations and symptoms a month afterwards could not have been mistaken for such as belonged to a much longer continuance of the disease.

I am fully satisfied that the surgeon was not mistaken who made the certificate upon which the beneficiary was discharged, and that his military service is not properly chargeable with any disability he may have incurred.

GROVER CLEVELAND.

EXECUTIVE MANSION, *September 1, 1888.*

To the House of Representatives:

I return without approval House bill No. 5155, entitled "An act granting a pension to John S. Bryant"

The man for whom this pension is proposed never, so far as I can learn, did a single day's actual military service at the front, nor ever left in such service the State in which he was enlisted.

He enlisted December 7, 1863, in a Maine regiment; on the 16th day of the same month he is marked as a deserter, having failed to report after leave of absence; December 31, 1863, he is reported sick in hospital at Augusta, Me.; January 26, 1864, he is marked as having deserted from Camp Keyes, at Augusta, Me.

He was discharged January 14, 1865, for disability occasioned, as the surgeon's certificate declares, "by a fall from a wagon while at home on a furlough, December 22, 1863." The certificate continues as follows:

Never has done a day's duty. Is utterly worthless and unfit for the Veteran Reserve Corps.

After his discharge the second charge of desertion was removed, and the first charge does not seem to be serious.

But he was injured while home on a furlough, his regiment still being in camp within the State of his residence; and although there are cases in which it seems not improper that pensions should be granted for injuries sustained during furlough and before actual return to duty, this does not appear to me to be one of them.

GROVER CLEVELAND.

EXECUTIVE MANSION, *September 6, 1888.*
To the House of Representatives:

I herewith return without approval House bill No. 2507, entitled ''**An act granting a pension to Russel L. Doane, of Peck, Sanilac County, Mich.**''

It is proposed by this bill to pension the beneficiary therein named as the dependent father of the late Demster Doane, late Company D, Thirty-fifth New York Volunteers.

The only information I have concerning this case is furnished by the report of the committee of the House to whom the bill was referred. There is nothing alleged in the report except that Demster Doane, who was a second lieutenant in the company and regiment named, died at Peck, Mich., on the 22d day of September, 1881, and that the deceased up to the time of his death supported his father, the claimant, who is now over 81 years of age, incapable of manual labor, and destitute of the means of support.

There is no intimation that the death of the son sixteen years after the close of the war was caused or in any way related to his military service. I do not understand that it has ever been claimed that a parent should be pensioned for the death of a son who had been in the Army unless his death could be traced in some way to his army service.

While this case is probably one where the exercise of generosity would be pleasant and most timely to the recipient, I can not think that such a precedent should be established.

GROVER CLEVELAND.

EXECUTIVE MANSION, *September 7, 1888.*
To the House of Representatives:

I return without approval House bill No. 9372, entitled ''An act granting a pension to John Dean.''

The beneficiary named in this bill was mustered into the service of the United States February 25, 1863. He never went to the front, but while in camp at Staten Island, on the 21st day of April, 1863, was granted a pass for forty-eight hours, and on account of sickness did not again rejoin his company or regiment. The charge of desertion made against him has been removed. The Surgeon-General's report shows that he was treated at quarters on Staten Island in April, 1863, for syphilis, rheumatism, and debility.

He was admitted to Charity Hospital, Blackwells Island, New York Harbor, August 5, 1863, and discharged November 18, 1863. He was admitted to the Ladies' General Hospital in New York December 1, 1863, and was discharged from the service for disability April 7, 1864.

The discharge was granted, as stated by the surgeon of volunteers in charge of the hospital, "because of sloughing of both corneas from inflammation contracted while absent without leave, having received a forty-eight-hour pass from his regiment April 15, 1863, then stationed on Staten Island. He lost his sight in August, 1863, while absent without leave. Unfit for Invalid Corps. Admitted to this hospital December 1, 1863. Not a case for pension."

A claim for pension was filed by the beneficiary at the Pension Bureau in March, 1877, alleging that on or about April 1, 1863, he suffered from chronic rheumatism and sore eyes, occasioned by exposure and illness contracted in camp.

It will be observed that no affection of the eyes is mentioned in the record of his treatment in quarters.

The claimant was examined by the New York City board of surgeons in June, 1878, and no rheumatism was found to exist. He is now blind, and while his case is certainly a pitiable one I am forced to the belief that the conclusions reached in 1879 upon his application, that his disease was contracted while absent without leave and that his disability was due to syphilis, were correct.

GROVER CLEVELAND.

EXECUTIVE MANSION, *September 7, 1888.*

To the House of Representatives:

I return without approval House bill No. 217, entitled "An act granting a pension to C. T. Maphet."

This beneficiary enlisted August 1, 1863, and was discharged January 27, 1865, for disability.

The commander of the post certifies:

This soldier says that he was first affected with the present disease, conjunctivitis, in the spring of 1862, since which time his eyes have never been well, and for a great portion of the time since enlistment he has been unfit for duty.

The certificate of the surgeon is as follows:

Incapacitated by reason of long-standing conjunctivitis of both eyes, attended with partial opacity of the cornea. Disability existed prior to enlistment, consequently soldier is ineligible to the Veteran Reserve Corps.

The beneficiary filed no application for pension until April, 1883.

Notwithstanding some evidence of soundness prior to enlistment, it seems to be quite well established that the trouble with his eyes was not the result of his military service, but existed before enlistment.

GROVER CLEVELAND.

EXECUTIVE MANSION *September 7, 1888.*

To the House of Representatives:

I return without approval House bill No. 5503, entitled "An act granting a pension to Charles Walster."

This case has been very exhaustively examined by the Pension Bureau upon the application for a pension filed there by the beneficiary named in this bill. Upon a review of the evidence taken it appears to be well established that any disability of the beneficiary heretofore existing was no attributable to his military service.

In addition to this a board of pension surgeons, as late as July, 1886, determined, after a thorough medical investigation, that no pensionable disability existed.

It thus appears that even if this bill were approved there could be no rating, and the legislation would be of no advantage to the beneficiary named.

GROVER CLEVELAND.

EXECUTIVE MANSION, *September 7, 1888.*

To the House of Representatives:

I return without approval House bill No. 333, entitled "An act granting a pension to Catharine Bussey."

It does not appear that the husband of this beneficiary ever applied for a pension. He was discharged from the Volunteer Army on the 9th day of December, 1864, after a service of more than three years.

He was found dead on a railroad track on the 11th day of June, 1870, apparently having been struck by a passing train.

It is claimed that the deceased suffered a sunstroke while in the Army, which so affected his mind that he wandered upon the railroad track and was killed in a fit of temporary insanity.

Though it would be gratifying to aid his widow, I do not think these facts are proven or can be assumed.

GROVER CLEVELAND.

EXECUTIVE MANSION, *September 7, 1888.*

To the House of Representatives:

I return without approval House bill No. 5525, entitled "An act granting a pension to Mrs. Jane Potts."

The husband of this beneficiary enlisted in 1861 and was mustered out of the service in April, 1865.

He was taken prisoner by the enemy and endured for a long time the hardship of prison life.

He never applied for a pension, though undoubtedly his health suffered to some extent as the result of his imprisonment.

The beneficiary married the soldier in 1871.

He conducted his business affairs, managed his farm, and accumulated property up to the year 1880, when by a decree of court he was adjudged insane, caused by sickness as far as was known, and that his disease was hereditary.

It also appears that his mother and sister had periods of insanity.

He committed suicide in 1882 by drowning.

The beneficiary, his widow, filed a claim for pension in 1885, claiming that the insanity which caused him to commit suicide resulted from the hardships of prison life.

Upon this application the facts of the case have been thoroughly examined. Two witnesses indicate that domestic trouble was the cause of the soldier's suicide. Another says that his wife (the beneficiary) was a pretty rough woman—a hard talker—and that the soldier often consulted him about the matter, and said it was hard to live with her. This witness adds that he does not believe that the soldier would have committed suicide if she had not abused him till he could not longer endure it.

The special examiner, in summing up the proof, says in his report:

The general opinion in the community is to the effect that his wife drove him to commit suicide rather than to live with or to obtain a divorce from her. Her reputation is that of a virago.

This kind of evidence, while not perhaps determining the case, reconciles me to the conclusion, which seems inevitable from other facts developed, that the military service and prison experience of the deceased were in no manner connected with his death.

GROVER CLEVELAND.

EXECUTIVE MANSION, *September 7, 1888.*
To the House of Representatives:

I return without approval House bill No. 7717, entitled "An act granting a pension to Mrs. Catharine Reed."

The husband of this beneficiary served in the Army from July 25, 1862, to October 16, 1862, when he was discharged for disease of the lungs. He was pensioned for hernia and disease of the lungs.

On the 23d day of November, 1880, while working in a sawmill, a piece of board was thrown from a buzz saw and struck him in the groin, causing a wound from which he died two days afterwards.

It is impossible to connect this injury and the resulting death with the disability for which he was pensioned.

GROVER CLEVELAND.

EXECUTIVE MANSION, *September 7, 1888*
To the House of Representatives:

I return without approval House bill No. 4855, entitled "An act granting a pension to Jacob Newhard."

The records show that this beneficiary was mustered into the service

August 20, 1862, as a lieutenant; that on the return for November, 1862, he is reported as "absent without leave—left hospital at Louisville." He was treated for hemorrhoids in the hospital at Nashville from December 12 to December 23, 1862, when, having served a few days more than four months, he tendered his resignation upon the ground of disability and procured the following surgeon's certificate, upon which his resignation was based:

Lieutenant Jacob Newhard having applied for a certificate upon which to ground a resignation, I do hereby certify that I have carefully examined this officer and find him suffering from hemorrhoids, * * * and in consequence thereof is, in my opinion, unfit for duty. I further declare my belief that he will not be fit for the duties of a soldier in any future time, having already been afflicted twelve years, as he asserts.

On the 14th day of February, 1880, nearly eighteen years after his resignation, the beneficiary filed his claim for pension based upon hemorrhoids, the result of diarrhea and fever.

He denied upon this application that he was unsound prior to enlistment, and filed evidence to support his denial. One of the witnesses, a surgeon, who testified to incurrence of disability in the service, on a special examination stated that he so testified, having satisfied himself of the fact by personal interviews with the beneficiary.

I do not think in the circumstances surrounding this case that the beneficiary should at this late day be permitted to impeach and set aside the medical certificate procured by himself and containing his own statements, upon which he secured exemption from further military service.

GROVER CLEVELAND.

EXECUTIVE MANSION, *September 13, 1888.*
To the House of Representatives:

I return without approval House bill No. 6371, entitled "An act granting a pension to Jesse M. Stilwell."

On the 6th day of May, 1885, twenty years after this beneficiary was discharged from the Army, he filed an application in the Pension Bureau for a pension, alleging that in December, 1863, one year and eight months before his discharge, a comrade assaulted him with a stick while he was sitting in front of his tent preparing for bed and injured his back. He alleged that the assault was unprovoked and unexpected.

The claim was rejected upon the facts stated, upon the ground that any injury incurred was not the result of military duty.

Unless the Government is to be held as an insurer against injuries suffered by anyone in the military service, no matter how incurred, and also as guarantor of the good and peaceable behavior toward each other of the soldiers at all times and under all circumstances, this is not a proper case for the allowance of a pension.

GROVER CLEVELAND.

EXECUTIVE MANSION, *September 24, 1888.*

To the House of Representatives:

I return without approval House bill No. 8310, entitled "An act to provide for the disposal of the Fort Wallace Military Reservation, in Kansas."

This bill provides that a portion of this reservation, which is situated in the State of Kansas, shall be set apart for town-site purposes, and may be entered by the corporate authorities of the adjoining city of Wallace.

The second section of the bill permits the Union Pacific Railroad Company to purchase within a limited time a certain part of the military reservation, which is particularly described, at the rate of $30 per acre.

I am informed that this privilege might, by reason of a faulty description of the lands, enable the railroad company to purchase at the price named property in which private parties have interests acquired under our laws.

It is evident that the description of the land which the railroad company is allowed the option of purchasing should be exact and certain for the interest of all concerned.

Section 4 of the bill grants a certain portion of the military reservation heretofore set apart by the military authorities as a cemetery to the city of Wallace for cemetery purposes.

There should, in my opinion, be a provision that no bodies heretofore interred in this ground should be disturbed, and that when the same is no longer used as a cemetery it should revert to the Government.

GROVER CLEVELAND.

EXECUTIVE MANSION, *September 24, 1888.*

To the House of Representatives:

I am unable to give my assent to a joint House resolution No. 14 and entitled "Joint resolution to authorize the Secretary of the Interior to certify lands to the State of Kansas for the benefit of agriculture and the mechanic arts," and I therefore return the same with a statement of my objections thereto.

By an act of Congress passed July 2, 1862, certain public lands were granted to such of the several States as should provide colleges for the benefit of agriculture and the mechanic arts.

Under the terms of this act the State of Kansas was entitled to 90,000 acres of land, subject, however, to the provisions of said statute, which declared that when lands which had been raised to double the minimum price, in consequence of railroad grants, should be selected by a State such lands should be computed at the maximum price and the number of acres proportionately diminished.

Of the lands selected by the State of Kansas, and which have been certified, 7,682.92 acres were within certain limits of a railroad grant, and had therefore been raised to the double minimum in price, so that the number of acres mentioned and thus situated really stood for double that number of acres in filling the grant to which the State of Kansas was entitled.

It is now claimed that after the selection of these lands the route of said railroad was abandoned and another one selected, and that in consequence thereof such lands included within its first location were reduced to the minimum price and restored to public market at that rate. It is supposed upon these allegations that justice and equity require that an additional grant should now be made to the State of Kansas from the public lands equal to the number of acres selected within the limits of the first railroad location.

But an examination discloses that the joint resolution is predicated upon an entire misunderstanding of the facts.

The lands heretofore mentioned as amounting to more than 7,000 acres, selected by the State of Kansas, and charged at double that amount because their price had been raised to the double minimum in consequence of their being within a railroad location, have all except 320 acres remained either in the new or old railroad location up to the present time, and if now vacant would be held by the Government at the double minimum price.

It seems clear to me that the State of Kansas has been granted all the public land to which it can lay any legal or equitable claim under the law of 1862.

GROVER CLEVELAND.

EXECUTIVE MANSION, *October 10, 1888.*

To the Senate:

I herewith return without approval Senate bill No. 2201, entitled "An act for the relief of Laura E. Maddox, widow and executrix, and Robert Morrison, executor, of Joseph H. Maddox, deceased."

An act of Congress approved July 2, 1864, provided among other things that the Secretary of the Treasury, with the approval of the President, might authorize agents "to purchase for the United States any products of States declared in insurrection, at such price as should be agreed on with the seller, not exceeding the market price thereof at the place of delivery."

Under the authority of said act the Secretary of the Treasury, with the approval of the President, prescribed rules and regulations to govern the transactions thus permitted, and appointed one H. A. Risley an agent to act for the United States in making such purchases.

On or about the 13th day of November, 1864, said Risley entered into a written contract with Joseph H. Maddox and two other parties, whereby the latter agreed to sell and deliver to Risley as such agent, at Norfolk or New York, 6,000 boxes of tobacco, 350 barrels of turpentine, and 700 barrels of rosin. It was also agreed that all products transported under the contract should be consigned to said Risley as agent and shipped on a Government transport, or, if not so shipped, should be in the immediate charge of an agent of Risley's, whose compensation and expenses should be paid by the sellers. Said products were to be sold in New York or Baltimore under Risley's direction, and one-fourth of the proceeds, after deducting certain expenses, costs, and charges, were to be retained for the United States and three-fourths paid to Maddox and his associates.

It was expressly provided in said contract as follows:

Nothing in this contract contained shall be construed as incurring any liability on behalf of the United States.

It appears that Maddox, very soon after the contract was made, acquired all the interest of his associates therein.

The President of the United States signed an order or permit for the transportation of the goods, in fulfillment of the contract, and for the passage of the parties selling such goods through the Federal military lines, the permit declaring, however, that such transportation and passage should be "with strict compliance with the regulations of the Secretary of the Treasury, and for the fulfillment of said contract with the agent of the Government."

Maddox and his associates were not at the time the contract was entered into the owners of any of the property they agreed to sell and deliver; but it is alleged that Maddox, as one of the parties to the contract and as assignee of his co-contractors, purchased 4,042 boxes of tobacco, worth at that time more than $735,000, for the purpose of fulfilling this contract.

The tobacco was purchased by him within the rebel lines in the State of Virginia. A part of it, he charges, was forcibly taken by the military forces of the Government and converted to its use or destroyed while being transported to its destination, and the remainder of it, having been detained in storage at Richmond, Va., was afterwards appropriated to the use of the United States or was destroyed in the fires at Richmond upon the capture of the city by the United States forces in 1865.

An action predicated upon the contract with Risley was brought by Maddox in the Court of Claims to recover the value of this property, but it was held by the court that the contract was void.

On appeal to the Supreme Court of the United States the decision of the Court of Claims was affirmed, upon the ground, as had been previously decided by said court, that under the law, the Treasury regulations, and the Executive orders concerning the purchase of products of insurrectionary States a purchasing agent of the Government had no authority to negotiate with anyone in relation to the purchase of such products unless at the time of the negotiation the party either owned or controlled them; that neither the law nor the regulations for its execution protected a speculation wherein the products to be sold were to be procured by the contractor within the rebel lines after the contract was made; that private citizens were prohibited from trading at all in the insurrectionary districts, and that the object of the law and the regulations to carry it into effect was to encourage the insurgents themselves to bring their products to agents of the Government.

With this adverse decision all chance of recovery upon legal grounds or before the courts was dissipated. But recourse to Congress still remained. As appears from a memorandum furnished in support of this bill, the alleged equities of the case were presented to the Forty-second, the Forty-third, the Forty-fourth, the Forty-fifth, the Forty-sixth, the Forty-eighth, and the Forty-ninth Congresses. Two adverse and more than two favorable committee reports have been made upon the claim. No bill for the relief of the claimant has, however, passed Congress until the present session, when a favorable condition seems to have presented itself.

The bill herewith returned empowers and directs the accounting officers of the Treasury to settle and pay to the representatives of Maddox the amount found due him on account of the loss and damage he sustained by the seizure by our military forces of the tobacco purchased by him under the agreement referred to, excluding, however, the tobacco destroyed by fire in the city of Richmond, and provides that said claim shall be determined upon the evidence taken and now on file in the office of the clerk of the United States Court of Claims and the War Department and any other competent evidence.

I fail to appreciate the equities which entitle this claimant to further hearing.

Every intelligent man should be charged with the knowledge that as a general rule commercial intercourse with the enemy is entirely inconsistent with a state of war, and that the law of 1864 had for its object the encouragement of the insurgents themselves to bring their products to us, and not the authorization of persons to roam through the insurrectionary districts and purchase their products on speculation.

Even if the claimant did not understand these conditions, he certainly knew that his contract was based upon a statute; that the agent with whom he was contracting was a creature of statute, and that such statute and certain regulations of the Secretary of the Treasury made thereunder regulated the right and limited the action of all the parties to said contract. These things sufficiently appear from the very terms of the contract and the permit signed by the President. The privileges and liberties contained in this permit are expressly granted "with strict compliance with regulations of the Secretary of the Treasury."

If before or after entering into this contract the claimant had examined these regulations, he would have found that they provided that "commercial intercourse with localities beyond the lines of actual military occupation by the United States forces is absolutely prohibited."

He would have also found that such regulations expressly provided that the power of the agent of the Government to make contracts should be founded upon the statement that the contractor then owned or controlled the products for which he contracted. And yet the permit of the President, which so completely put the claimant upon inquiry as to what he might or might not do, seems now to be relied upon as the source of equities in his favor, and is pressed into his service under the guise of a sanction of his unlawful proceedings.

Besides the general knowledge the claimant should have possessed of the commercial disabilities consequent upon a state of war, and the information afforded him by his contract and permit, a proclamation of the President publicly issued September 24, 1864,* furnished abundant notice of the kind of trading which would be permitted.

The property for which compensation is asked constitutes a part only of that agreed to be furnished. None of it ever reached the possession of the agent of the Government, but, as I understand the case, was at the time of its seizure or destruction still in the territory of the enemy and in rebellious possession. If in the circumstances detailed it was treated by our military forces in like manner as other property in the same situation, there would seem to be no hardship in holding that the contractor assumed this risk as one arising from his unauthorized and, if successful, his profitable venture.

Not being satisfied that there are any especial equities which entitle this claim to more consideration than many others where equities might be claimed in behalf of those who long ago violated our nonintercourse laws, I am unwilling to sanction a precedent which if followed might substantially work a repeal of these laws, regarded necessary and expedient by those charged with legislation during the War of the Rebellion, and who had in full view all the necessities of that period.

GROVER CLEVELAND.

EXECUTIVE MANSION, *October 12, 1888.*

To the Senate:

I return without approval Senate bill No. 3276, entitled "An act granting restoration of pension to Sarah A. Woodbridge."

The first husband of this beneficiary, Anson L. Brewer, was an additional paymaster in the Army, and died February 2, 1866, from injuries received in an explosion of a steamer.

His widow, the beneficiary, was pensioned at the rate of $25 a month from the date of her husband's death until October 21, 1870, when she remarried, becoming the wife of Timothy Woodbridge.

Two children, who were minors at the time she was pensioned, became 16 years of age in April, 1870, and July, 1874, respectively.

*See Executive order of September 24, 1864, pp. 3441-3442.

Upon the remarriage of the beneficiary her pension stopped under the law.

It is now proposed to restore her to the pension roll, notwithstanding the fact that her second husband is still alive.

Many cases have occurred in which pensions have been awarded by special acts to the widows of soldiers who, having remarried, were a second time made widows and rendered destitute by the death of their second husbands. I have not objected to such charitable legislation.

But I think this is the first time that it has been proposed to grant a pension after such remarriage when the second husband still survives.

It seems to me that such a precedent ought not to be established. If in pension legislation we attempt to determine the cases of this description in which the second husband can not or does not properly maintain the soldier's widow whom he has married, we shall open the door to much confusion and uncertainty, as well as unjust discrimination.

I am glad to learn from a statement contained in the committee's report that this beneficiary, though in a condition making the aid of a pension very desirable, has a small income derived from property inherited from her mother.

GROVER CLEVELAND.

To the Senate: EXECUTIVE MANSION, *October 12, 1888.*

I herewith return without approval Senate bill No. 1044, entitled "An act authorizing the Secretary of the Treasury to state and settle the account of James M. Willbur with the United States and to pay said Willbur such sum of money as may be found due him thereon."

The claim mentioned in this bill grows out of alleged extra work done by the claimant in the construction of the post-office and court-house building in the city of New York.

The United States, in September, 1874, entered into a contract with Messrs. Bartlett, Robbins & Co. by which they agreed to furnish and put in place certain wrought and cast iron work and glass for the illuminated tiling required for the said building according to certain specifications and schedules which formed a part of said contract. The work was to be of a specified thickness and the contractors were to be paid for the same at certain rates per superficial foot. The approximate estimate for the entire work was specified at $35,577.56. Samples of the tiling to be put in were submitted to the Supervising Architect and accepted by him.

In August, 1874, the claimant entered into an agreement in writing with Bartlett, Robbins & Co. to do this work as subcontractor for them at certain prices for each superficial foot of said tiling put in place.

In neither contract was the weight of the tiling mentioned.

The work was, under the contract with Messrs. Bartlett, Robbins & Co., completed, and after such completion and the measurement of the work the said firm of Bartlett, Robbins & Co. were paid by the Government the sum of $35,217.57, in full satisfaction of their contract with the United States.

It appears that after the completion of the work the claimant gave notice to the Government that he had a claim against Bartlett, Robbins & Co., growing out of said work, for the sum of $8,744.44, and requested that payment be withheld from said firm until his claim against them was adjusted.

The fact that said claim had been made having been communicated by the Supervising Architect to Bartlett, Robbins & Co., on the 22d day of August, 1876, they responded to the Supervising Architect as follows:

DEAR SIR: We inclose copy of our account against Willbur and the Illuminated Tiling Company and a copy of Willbur's assignment to the Tile Company, which includes a copy of his agreement with us; and when the Department settles the measurement of the work the items in the contract will show just what the amount is, and, as we have repeatedly assured him, he will have all the measurements the Government gives us.

If anyone has cause of complaint in this case it is us. Four times the work came to a stand, or nearly so, and our Mr. B. was compelled to go to New York and stay until it was moving again, charging his expenses, by Willbur's request, and finally it had to be finished by others, etc. We know this does not interest you particularly, as you do not know him in the matter, but there has been so much willful misrepresentation we thought silence might be misconstrued.

It is charitable to think Willbur must be crazy.

Very respectfully, yours,   BARTLETT, ROBBINS & CO.

In an opinion of the Solicitor of the Treasury concerning this claim, dated November 30, 1883, I find a statement that on the 20th day of October, 1876, a paper was filed by the attorneys of the claimant in which his claim for extra work and material in performing his contract was alleged to be $21,857.94. It is further stated that this claim was hastily drawn by one of Willbur's attorneys and without consultation with him.

On or about the 20th day of March, 1877, Mr. Willbur himself filed a statement of such extra work and material, in which he claimed for the same the sum of $42,685.20.

Another statement made by Willbur, in February, 1878, presents a claim on account of the same matters amounting to $47,159.62.

This claim, so variously stated, is based upon the allegation that tiling and frames of greater thickness than were required by the contract were put in the building. Although it is insisted by the claimant that these thicker tiles and frames were directed to be put in, or at least accepted by the person having charge of the construction of the building for the Government, I hardly think it will be seriously contended that the claimant has any legal claim against the United States.

But, with a view of discovering whether, upon equitable grounds, the claimant should be paid anything by the Government for glass and iron of greater thickness than its contract with Bartlett, Robbins & Co.

required, and which had **been put in its building by their** subcontractor, the Secretary of the Treasury in 1884 appointed a committee of three persons to examine and report upon this claim of Willbur's, ''with a view of determining what portion, if any, it is proper for the Government to pay.''

On the 24th day of January, 1885, this committee made a report by which they determined that there should be paid to the claimant on account of the matters alleged the sum of $1,214.90.

This report was based upon the measurements, examinations, and estimates of two experts, one selected by the claimant and the other by the committee. The report was transmitted to the House of Representatives by the Secretary of the Treasury and an appropriation asked to pay the amount awarded.

But Mr. Willbur was not satisfied, and on the 6th day of January, 1885, addressed a communication to the Secretary of the Treasury in which this passage occurs:

I shall insist on a remeasurement of the entire work, as this is vital to my claim. The excess which I furnished can only be ascertained by weight instead of by measuring the thickness of the plates and frames.

At the second session of the Forty-ninth Congress, and early in 1886, this claim was before the Senate Committee on Claims, and at the instance of the committee this work was again examined by experts, who came to the conclusion that the claimant was entitled to the sum of $45,615.67 for the extra work which he had performed and materials furnished.

It is only alleged that the glass tiling and frames actually put in the building were slightly thicker than those required by the contract, and this alleged increased thickness seems to be fairly represented in a general way by the claim that some of the glass and frames which were required to be 1 inch thick were actually put in 1 inch and a quarter thick.

Upon this statement it must be admitted that the sum above stated as the value of this extra thickness is somewhat startling. In the language of the report upon this bill by the Supervising Architect, ''a claim of $47,159.02 for such slight excess on work the price of which was $35,217.57 is hardly entitled to consideration.''

The claim, as well as the award of the experts last named, reach their astonishing proportions by the application of weights to the question in the following manner: A certain area is measured. A square foot of the tiling actually put in is weighed, and a square foot of the tiling required by the contract is also weighed. Both these weights are multiplied by the area. The lesser aggregate weight is deducted from the greater, and the difference is divided by the weight of a square foot of the lightest tiling, thus reducing it to square feet of such lightest tile. These square feet are multiplied by the price agreed to be paid by the contract for each superficial foot, and an item of extra work is determined. Thus additional weight in constructed and finished tiling is converted, as far as price and measurement are concerned, into finished tile, which more than doubles the quantity actually laid down.

This can not be right. And yet the bill herewith returned directs the Secretary of the Treasury to settle this claim for extra work upon the basis of the report of the experts who have adopted this mode of adjustment; or, if not satisfied with their report, he shall within thirty days from the passage of the act cause a reweighing of said material to be made by two sworn experts, one to be appointed by him and one by the claimant, and a third to be appointed by these two in case they can not agree. The bill further provides that he shall then pay to said Willbur the difference of excess in weight and superficial measurement as found by said experts between the illuminated tiling and frames furnished and that contracted for at the contract prices for such work and material.

There are features of this claim which suggest suspicion as to its merit. In any view of the matter, I regard the claimant as seeking equitable relief. He is not entitled to dictate the rule by which his claim is to be adjusted, and he should be quite satisfied if the officers of the Government charged with the settlement of such matters are permitted by the Congress to afford equitable relief according to such rules and methods as are best calculated to reach fair results.

GROVER CLEVELAND.

EXECUTIVE MANSION, *October 15, 1888.*

To the Senate:

I return without approval Senate bill No. 3306, entitled "An act granting a pension to Mary K. Richards."

The beneficiary named in this bill applied for a pension on the 14th day of November, 1878, and the same was rejected in April, 1879. Her claim has lately been reexamined, and since the passage of the bill herewith returned she has been allowed a pension by the Pension Bureau, it having been there determined that the former rejection was a manifest error.

With this action of the Pension Bureau I entirely concur.

I therefore venture, notwithstanding the persistent misrepresentations of my action in similar cases, to disapprove this bill, upon the ground that this deserving beneficiary will receive under the action of the Pension Bureau a much larger sum than she would if such action was superseded by the enactment of the proposed special statute in her behalf.

GROVER CLEVELAND.

EXECUTIVE MANSION, *October 15, 1888.*

To the Senate:

I herewith return without approval Senate bill No. 3208, entitled "An act granting a pension to William S. Bradshaw."

The beneficiary mentioned in this bill was mustered into the military service as first lieutenant on the 28th day of October, 1861.

About eight months afterwards, and in June, 1862, he resigned from the service, his resignation being based upon a surgeon's certificate which he procured, and which is as follows:

William S. Bradshaw having applied for a certificate to accompany his resignation, I do hereby certify that I have carefully examined this officer and find that his disease is of a chronic pleuritic character, contracted (previous to his entering the service) four years since from an injury received in shoeing a fractious horse, in consequence of which he was laid up for a number of weeks with a severe attack of pleuritis; that he has never been able to endure severe labor since; that since entering the service active drilling or marching has invariably developed severe pleuritic pains about his chest and underneath his sternum, rendering him totally unfit for duty.

It is entirely evident that the statements contained in this certificate are of such a nature that they must have almost entirely been communicated to the surgeon by the officer himself. It will be observed that there is an absolute lack of any intimation that his disabilities were attributable in their origin to army service, and he surely can not ask us to believe that a man with the intelligence fitting him to be a commissioned officer in the Army, and having this certificate in his possession, did not know what it contained.

It furnished the reason for his honorable discharge in the dark days of his country's need and operated as an exemption from further military service.

And yet in September, 1883, more than twenty-one years after his discharge, he applied to the Pension Bureau for a pension, alleging lameness of breast and back, contracted in the service.

After an examination of all the facts I can not believe that this is a case in which a pension should be granted.

GROVER CLEVELAND.

EXECUTIVE MANSION, *October 16, 1888.*
To the House of Representatives:

I return without approval House bill No. 7657, entitled "An act granting a pension to Mary Woodworth, widow of Ebenezer F. Woodworth."

The husband of this beneficiary enlisted October 1, 1861. On the rolls of his company for May and June, 1862, he is reported as a deserter, and the report is the same on the muster-out roll of his regiment, dated October 24, 1864.

An effort was made on the application by the beneficiary for pension to the Pension Bureau to attribute the charge of desertion to the unfriendliness and injustice of the soldier's captain, and an unsuccessful effort was made to have the charge removed from the record by the Adjutant-General.

The soldier, therefore, is still recorded as a deserter from camp near Farmington, Miss., since March 12, 1862.

The application of the widow to the Pension Bureau in 1867 states that her husband was missing at Hamburg, Tenn., May 7, 1862, and not having since been heard from is supposed to be dead.

The captain of the company testifies that the soldier was employed with the ambulance corps, and that for misconduct he (the captain) ordered him to his company and censured him; that very soon after that the soldier was absent at roll call and was marked as absent without leave; that in a day or two after that a member of a detail returned to camp from Hamburg Landing and reported that he had seen the soldier there and had been told by him that "he was off and would never go back." Thereupon he was dropped from the roll as a deserter.

Various theories are presented to account for the soldier's absence in other ways than by desertion, some of his comrades going so far as to express the opinion that he was murdered at the instigation of his captain. None of these theories, however, seem to be more than conjectures with various degrees of plausibility.

If the question of desertion could be solved favorably to the beneficiary, another difficulty immediately arises from the fact that there is absolutely no proof of death except the soldier's long absence without knowledge of his whereabouts; and if his death could be presumed the cause of it and whether connected at all with military service are matters regarding which we have no information whatever.

I am unable to see how a case in such a situation can be considered a proper subject for favorable pension legislation.

GROVER CLEVELAND.

EXECUTIVE MANSION, *October 16, 1888.*

To the House of Representatives:

I return without approval House bill No. 10661, entitled "An act granting a pension to Mrs. Sophia Vogelsang."

The husband of this beneficiary was severely wounded in the military service of the United States, and in consequence of said wound his left leg was amputated. This was in 1862. In January, 1863, another amputation was performed higher up above the knee. He appears at that time to have been living, or at least was treated, at Detroit, Mich. He was pensioned at the rate of $30 per month at the time of his death, which occurred at Louisville, Ky., where he appears to have then resided, on the 21st day of July, 1885.

The beneficiary filed a claim for pension in November, 1885, alleging that her husband died of gangrene.

There does not, however, seem to be a particle of evidence establishing that cause of death. On the contrary, the report received at the Pension

Bureau of his death attributes it to sunstroke, and this does not seem to be directly questioned.

The report of the House committee to whom this bill was referred proceeds upon the theory that death was caused from the use of opium to allay the pain of the wound. This theory is presented upon the alleged opinion of the surgeon living in Detroit, who made the second amputation in 1863. He says that the pain of the wound obliged the soldier to take morphine. But it does not appear that he observed the case for a long time preceding death. Instead of his giving an opinion that the disability and morphine produced death, he says, as it is reported to me, after describing the condition of the limb previous to its amputation in 1863 and immediately thereafter:

According to my opinion, said disability and the constant use of morphia in consequence of it may have been the cause of his death.

This and the statement of a druggist in Louisville that he sold him morphine to alleviate pain, and of two different persons with whom he boarded at that city in 1885 to the same effect, is all the evidence that I can discover tending in the least to hint that the death of the pensioner resulted from any cause but sunstroke, which really stands as the undisputed cause of death.

The allegation in the committee's report that the beneficiary's claim was rejected by the Pension Bureau on the ground that her husband's death proceeded from the use of morphine is erroneous. The cause of rejection is stated to be "that the death cause (sunstroke) was not the result of the soldier's military service."

We are not, therefore, left to the consideration of the question whether death from the use of morphine to allay pain can be charged to the disability incurred, for if death resulted from sunstroke it will hardly be claimed that it was in any way related to such disability.

GROVER CLEVELAND.

EXECUTIVE MANSION, *October 16, 1888*
To the House of Representatives:

I return without approval House bill No. 6201, entitled "An act granting a pension to John Robeson."

The beneficiary named in this bill enlisted August 8, 1862, and was discharged for disability on the 21st day of November, 1862, after a service of a little more than three months.

In the certificate of disability upon which his discharge was granted the captain of the beneficiary's company states that "he has been unfit for duty for sixty days; that the soldier represents that he has not done efficient service since enlistment by reason of phthisic, from which he has suffered since childhood, but has grown worse since entering the service."

The surgeon of the regiment states in said certificate that "the soldier has asthma, with which he has been afflicted from his infancy."

Upon this certificate, based necessarily so far as his previous condition is concerned, this man procured his discharge after doing but very slight service.

He filed an application for pension in the Pension Bureau in October, 1879, basing his claim upon the allegation that he contracted asthma in September, 1862, about a month after he entered the service.

Two special examinations were had in his case, and his statement was taken in each.

On the first examination he said he could not account for the statements of his captain and surgeon, unless they arose from a remark he made that he had phthisic when he was small.

On the second he accounted for the statements of the captain and surgeon by saying that he felt very sick and feared that he could not live if he remained in the service; that he was suffering with jaundice as well as asthma; and having been told that he could not be discharged on account of jaundice, but could on account of asthma, he asked the captain to tell the surgeon that he had known him to have asthma before enlistment. He also says that he procured others to tell the same story.

On these examinations there was the usual negative testimony produced of certain parties who knew the claimant before enlistment and did not know that he was afflicted. This is balanced by the evidence of others, who testify that the claimant had asthma before enlistment.

Upon consideration of the character of the ailment, the testimony upon the two examinations, and the conduct of the beneficiary and his own admissions, I can not escape the conviction that whatever disability he had at the date of discharge he had when he enlisted, and that his claim was properly rejected by the Pension Bureau.

GROVER CLEVELAND.

EXECUTIVE MANSION, *October 16, 1888.*

To the House of Representatives:

I return without approval House bill No. 9106, entitled "An act granting a pension to Peter Liner."

The beneficiary named in this bill enlisted as a sergeant in the Regular Army in 1871, and he alleges that he served a previous term of enlistment, commencing in 1866.

While on a march from one post to another on the frontier, in September, 1874, the beneficiary was severely wounded by the bursting of a gun, necessitating the amputation of three of his fingers.

The reports of this occurrence develop the fact that the gun which burst in his hands was a shotgun, and that the accident happened while the beneficiary was hunting "for his own pleasure or benefit."

His wound was a severe one, and the injured man was probably a good and faithful soldier, but it seems quite clear to me that it would be extending the pension theory to an unwarrantable limit to hold the Government responsible for such an accident.

GROVER CLEVELAND.

EXECUTIVE MANSION, *October 16, 1888.*

To the House of Representatives:

I herewith return without approval House bill No. 10563, entitled "An act granting a pension to William S. Latham."

The beneficiary named in this bill enlisted in August, 1862. The rolls for March and April, 1863, report him a deserter, but it having been ascertained that sickness was the cause of his failure to return to his regiment at the end of a furlough granted to him, upon which failure the charge of desertion was based, he was restored to his company and the charge of desertion removed.

All this is stated in the report of the committee to which this bill was referred.

But it is not mentioned in said report that he was again furloughed on the 17th day of August, 1863, and, failing to return at the end of his furlough, one month thereafter, again became a deserter, but was not so reported until October 8, 1863.

He was arrested January 1, 1864, but there appears to be no record of his trial or his restoration.

He filed a claim for pension in the Pension Bureau in January, 1870, and he was informed twice during the year 1888 that no favorable action could be taken until the charge of desertion had been removed.

On application to the Adjutant-General that officer, on the 21st day of February, 1888, declined to remove said charge of desertion.

The claim is still pending before the Pension Bureau.

I do not suppose that the Congress is prepared to go so far in special pension legislation as to grant pensions to those against whom charges of desertion appear of record.

In the belief that the fact of the second desertion above mentioned was overlooked by the Congress, and because the application for pension in this case is still pending in the Pension Bureau, where complete justice can still be done, I am constrained to withhold my approval of this bill.

GROVER CLEVELAND.

EXECUTIVE MANSION, *October 17, 1888.*

To the House of Representatives:

I return without approval House bill No. 2472, entitled "An act granting a pension to Lydia A. Eaton."

The husband of this beneficiary was pensioned for chronic rheumatism, at the rate of $4 a month, up to the date of his death, August 4, 1884.

The beneficiary filed a claim for pension on the 2d day of September, 1884.

The cause of her husband's death was cystitis, which, being interpreted, is inflammation of the bladder.

The claim of the beneficiary was rejected on the ground that the fatal disease was not due to army service, and I fail to discover how any other conclusion can be reached.

GROVER CLEVELAND.

EXECUTIVE MANSION, *October 17, 1888.*
To the House of Representatives:

I return without approval House bill No. 10342, entitled "An act granting a pension to John Dauper."

This beneficiary enlisted April 24, 1861, and was discharged August 28, 1861, four months after enlistment.

He filed a claim for pension in September, 1879, alleging as cause of disability diarrhea and disease of the stomach, liver, kidneys, and bladder.

None of these ailments were established satisfactorily as originating in the soldier's brief service, and as constituting disabilities after discharge.

The claim was therefore rejected by the Pension Bureau, and this action appears to be entirely justified upon the facts presented.

GROVER CLEVELAND.

EXECUTIVE MANSION, *October 17, 1888.*
To the House of Representatives:

I return without approval House bill No. 11005, entitled "An act granting a pension to Ester Gaven."

This act provides that the beneficiary shall be placed upon the pension roll as the widow of Bernard Gaven, and the report of the committee to whom this bill was referred throughout speaks of her as bearing that relation to the soldier.

She filed a claim in the Pension Bureau for a pension on the 31st day of January, 1881, as the mother of Bernard Gaven.

This claim is still pending, and though evidence that the death of the soldier had any relation to his military service is entirely lacking and some other difficulties are apparent, the case may still be made out in the Pension Bureau. If it is, the beneficiary can be put upon the pension roll in her true character as mother of the soldier, instead of widow, as erroneously stated in the bill herewith returned.

Upon the merits as the case now stands, and because of the mistake in describing the relationship of the beneficiary, this bill, I think, should not become a law.

GROVER CLEVELAND.

EXECUTIVE MANSION, *October 17, 1888.*

To the House of Representatives:

I return without approval House bill No. 10504, entitled "An act granting a pension to Mary Hooper."

The husband of this beneficiary was first lieutenant in the volunteer service from December 7, 1861, to February 28, 1862, a little over two months, when he resigned. His resignation was based upon a medical certificate in which it is stated that "this officer is unfit for duty on account of chronic pleuritis and pulmonary consumption, from which he has suffered for the past four months."

This certificate is dated February 14, 1862.

The soldier filed a claim in 1871 alleging typhoid fever resulting in paralysis, and that the fever was contracted in the latter part of February, 1862.

The soldier died January 17, 1884, of paralysis.

The beneficiary filed a claim for pension November 17, 1887, claiming that her husband died of disease contracted in the service.

The claims have been specially and thoroughly examined. The testimony does not establish any disease or disability in the service other than those stated in the certificate procured by him when he resigned, but it does tend to establish that about April 17, 1862, after his resignation, the soldier was sick with typhoid fever, and that afterwards he suffered from partial paralysis, which increased and finally caused his death.

I make no reference to the fact stated in the committee's report suggesting the idea that the courage of the deceased soldier had been questioned further than to correct the allegation of the report that either his or his widow's claim for pension has been rejected for cowardice. It appears from the record furnished to me that they were rejected on the ground that the evidence is insufficient to connect the death cause or disability with the soldier's military service.

I am unable to see what other conclusion could be reached in the face of the soldier's own statements, as contained in the medical certificate furnished him and elsewhere made, and upon consideration of the other facts in the case.

GROVER CLEVELAND.

EXECUTIVE MANSION, *October 17, 1888.*

To the House of Representatives:

I return without approval House bill No. 4820, entitled "An act granting a pension to Ellen Kelley."

The husband of this beneficiary was granted a furlough to go home and vote on the 31st day of October, 1864. On his way there he was severely injured by a railroad collision, and there does not seem to be a particle of doubt that the injuries thus sustained caused his death.

Upon these facts this does not seem to be a proper case for the granting of a pension.

GROVER CLEVELAND.

EXECUTIVE MANSION, *October 17, 1888.*

To the House of Representatives:

I return without approval House bill No. 11222, entitled "An act granting a pension to Elizabeth Heckler."

The husband of this beneficiary was pensioned for asthma, and there is no doubt of the propriety of such pension, nor is there doubt upon the evidence that this affection continued up to the time of his death.

But he died of acute inflammation of the bladder and chronic enlargement of prostate gland. There is no proof that these causes of death were in the least complicated with the difficulty for which the deceased was pensioned, or any other trouble which was the result of military service.

GROVER CLEVELAND.

EXECUTIVE MANSION, *October 17, 1888.*

To the House of Representatives:

I return without approval House bill No. 4102, entitled "An act granting a pension to Mary A. Carr."

The husband of this beneficiary served in the Army from November 5, 1863, to June 15, 1865. He made a claim for pension for injury to his left ankle, caused by being thrown from a horse while in the service, and some time after his death a pension was allowed upon his claim, at the rate of $4 per month, commencing at the date of his discharge and ending at the date of his death.

He died on the 16th day of March, 1877, of apoplexy, and his widow filed a claim for pension on her own behalf in March, 1885, based upon the allegation that the injury for which her husband was pensioned was the cause of his death.

I can not upon the facts of this case arrive at a conclusion different from the Pension Bureau, where it was determined that the death of the soldier could not be accepted as having been caused by the injury to his ankle.

GROVER CLEVELAND.

EXECUTIVE MANSION, *October 17, 1888.*

To the House of Representatives:

I return without approval House bill No. 11332, entitled "An act granting a pension to Eliza S. Glass."

The husband of this beneficiary was in the military service from December 28, 1863, to April 27, 1864, a period of four months. He was discharged at the last-mentioned date for disability, the surgeon stating in the certificate his trouble to be "chronic hemorrhoids and rheumatism, both together producing lameness of back; unfit for Invalid Corps." The captain of the soldier's company in the same certificate states:

During the last two months said soldier has been unfit for duty fifty-four days in consequence of chronic rheumatism, owing to spinal affections and sprains received before entering the service, and made worse by drilling in double quick.

He filed a claim for pension December 24, 1879, more than fifteen years after discharge, in which he claimed that on the 15th day of January, 1864, he received an injury to his back by slipping and falling upon the ground.

After a thorough examination this claim was rejected on the ground that his disability existed prior to enlistment.

The beneficiary filed a claim for pension December 3, 1885, alleging the death of the soldier April 26, 1885. This claim was also rejected, on the ground that the death causes, "nervous prostration and spinal trouble," were not due to the service.

Both of these cases were appealed to the Secretary of the Interior, and in the decision of said appeals it is stated that upon an application for a discharge from the service the soldier first set up an injury to his back from a fall while on drill; that the regimental surgeon refused to entertain this proposition; that the next day the soldier returned, and upon the representations of himself and his captain that his trouble dated back of the alleged accident upon drill and was chronic the certificate for discharge was made out, and pursuant thereto his discharge was granted.

I am of the opinion that, considering the cause of death and all the facts and circumstances surrounding this case, the certificate of discharge which the soldier himself procured to be made out should stand as stating the true origin of his disability; and if the certificate was set aside and all the facts tending to support it were disregarded, the cause of death would still, in my opinion, appear to be disconnected with military service.

GROVER CLEVELAND.

PROCLAMATIONS.

By the President of the United States of America.

A PROCLAMATION.

Whereas the title to all that territory lying between the north and south forks of the Red River and the hundredth degree of longitude and jurisdiction over the same are vested in the United States, it being a part of the Indian Territory, as shown by surveys and investigation made on behalf of the United States, which territory the State of Texas also claims title to and jurisdiction over; and

Whereas said conflicting claim grows out of a controversy existing between the United States and the State of Texas as to the point where the hundredth degree of longitude crosses the Red River, as described in the treaty of February 22, 1819, between the United States and Spain, fixing the boundary line between the two countries; and

Whereas the commissioners appointed on the part of the United States under the act of January 31, 1885, authorizing the appointment of a commission by the President to run and mark the boundary lines between a portion of the Indian Territory and the State of Texas, in connection with a similar commission to be appointed by the State of Texas, have by their report determined that the South Fork is the true Red River designated in the treaty, the commissioners appointed on the part of said State refusing to concur in said report:

Now, therefore, I, Grover Cleveland, President of the United States, do hereby admonish and warn all persons, whether claiming to act as officers of the county of Greer, in the State of Texas, or otherwise, against selling or disposing of, or attempting to sell or dispose of, any of said lands or from exercising or attempting to exercise any authority over said lands.

And I also warn and admonish all persons against purchasing any part of said territory from any person or persons whomsoever.

In witness whereof I have hereunto set my hand and caused the seal of the United States to be affixed.

[*seal.*] Done at the city of Washington, this 30th day of December, A. D. 1887, and of the Independence of the United States the one hundred and twelfth.

GROVER CLEVELAND.

By the President:
T. F. BAYARD,
Secretary of State.

BY THE PRESIDENT OF THE UNITED STATES OF AMERICA.

A PROCLAMATION.

Whereas satisfactory proof has been given to me by the Government of the Empire of Germany that no tonnage or light-house dues, or any equivalent tax or taxes whatever, are imposed upon American vessels entering the ports of the Empire of Germany, either by the Imperial Government or by the governments of the German maritime States, and that vessels belonging to the United States of America and their cargoes are not required in German ports to pay any fee or due of any kind or nature, or any import due higher or other than is payable by German vessels or their cargoes:

Now, therefore, I, Grover Cleveland, President of the United States of America, by virtue of the authority vested in me by section 11 of the act of Congress entitled "An act to abolish certain fees for official services to American vessels, and to amend the laws relating to shipping commissioners, seamen, and owners of vessels, and for other purposes," approved June 19, 1886, do hereby declare and proclaim that from and after the date of this my proclamation shall be suspended the collection of the whole of the duty of 6 cents per ton, not to exceed 30 cents per ton per annum (which is imposed by said section of said act), upon vessels entered in the ports of the United States from any of the ports of the Empire of Germany.

Provided, That there shall be excluded from the benefits of the suspension hereby declared and proclaimed the vessels of any foreign country in whose ports the fees or dues of any kind or nature imposed on vessels of the United States, or the import or export duties on their cargoes, are in excess of the fees, dues, or duties imposed on the vessels of such foreign country or their cargoes, or of the fees, dues, or duties imposed on the vessels of Germany or the cargoes of such vessels.

And the suspension hereby declared and proclaimed shall continue so long as the reciprocal exemption of vessels belonging to citizens of the United States and their cargoes shall be continued in the said ports of the Empire of Germany, and no longer.

In witness whereof I have hereunto set my hand and caused the seal of the United States to be affixed.

[SEAL.]   Done at the city of Washington, this 26th day of January, A. D. 1888, and of the Independence of the United States the one hundred and twelfth.

GROVER CLEVELAND.

By the President:

T. F. BAYARD,
Secretary of State.

BY THE PRESIDENT OF THE UNITED STATES OF AMERICA.

A PROCLAMATION.

Whereas satisfactory proof has been given to me that no light-house and light dues, tonnage dues, beacon and buoy dues, or other equivalent taxes of any kind are imposed upon vessels of the United States in the ports of the island of Guadeloupe, one of the French West India Islands:

Now, therefore, I, Grover Cleveland, President of the United States of America, by virtue of the authority vested in me by section 11 of the act of Congress entitled "An act to abolish certain fees for official services to American vessels, and to amend the laws relating to shipping commissioners, seamen, and owners of vessels, and for other purposes," approved June 19, 1886, do hereby declare and proclaim that from and after the date of this my proclamation shall be suspended the collection of the whole of the tonnage duty which is imposed by said section of said act upon vessels entered in the ports of the United States from any of the ports of the island of Guadeloupe.

Provided, That there shall be excluded from the benefits of the suspension hereby declared and proclaimed the vessels of any foreign country in whose ports the fees or dues of any kind or nature imposed on vessels

CUBAN GUERRILLAS—SPANISH SOLDIERY

CUBAN GUERRILLAS AND SPANISH SOLDIERY

The opening paragraphs of the article, "Spanish-American War," which appears in the Encyclopedic Index, contain Grant's, Cleveland's and McKinley's views of the Cuban Insurrections which occurred during their administrations. Spain's rule was unquestionably despotic and cruel, even to the extent of destroying what little value Cuba had as a colony; but the ragged hordes of ignorant, mongrel natives who harassed the Spanish soldiery bore no resemblance, either mental or physical, to the farmers who fired the shot that rang around the world at Lexington. They too often used the pretext of revolution to cloak brigandage. The group in the upper panel are officers awaiting the arrival of General Garcia, their war-worn old leader, at Siboney.

The conduct of the Spanish soldiers in the war was good. They stood their ground bravely under long-range fire, but retired in confusion whenever hand-to-hand fighting seemed imminent. The intrepid charges of our troops at Las Guasimas and San Juan puzzled them sorely; such methods violated all their notions of civilized warfare. After the affair at Las Guasimas a citizen of Santiago asked one of the participants if the "Yankee pigs" could fight. "Fight!" he exclaimed, with a gesture betokening disgust. "Fight! No! They tried to catch us with their hands."

The article, "Spanish-American War," gives a complete history of the occurrence in brief form. President McKinley's narrative is more detailed, and considers not only the military operations but also the diplomatic and economic questions involved.

of the United States, or the import or export duties on their cargoes, are in excess of the fees, dues, or duties imposed on the vessels of such foreign country or their cargoes, or of the fees, dues, or duties imposed on the vessels of the country in which are the ports mentioned in this proclamation or the cargoes of such vessels.

And the suspension hereby declared and proclaimed shall continue so long as the reciprocal exemption of vessels belonging to citizens of the United States and their cargoes shall be continued in the said ports of the island of Guadeloupe, and no longer.

In witness whereof I have hereunto set my hand and caused the seal of the United States to be affixed.

[SEAL.]   Done at the city of Washington, this 16th day of April, A. D. 1888, and of the Independence of the United States the one hundred and twelfth.   GROVER CLEVELAND.

By the President:
T. F. BAYARD,
Secretary of State.

A PROCLAMATION

BY THE PRESIDENT OF THE UNITED STATES.

Constant thanksgiving and gratitude are due from the American people to Almighty God for His goodness and mercy, which have followed them since the day He made them a nation and vouchsafed to them a free government. With loving kindness He has constantly led us in the way of prosperity and greatness. He has not visited with swift punishment our shortcomings, but with gracious care He has warned us of our dependence upon His forbearance and has taught us that obedience to His holy law is the price of a continuance of His precious gifts.

In acknowledgment of all that God has done for us as a nation, and to the end that on an appointed day the united prayers and praise of a grateful country may reach the throne of grace, I, Grover Cleveland, President of the United States, do hereby designate and set apart Thursday, the 29th day of November instant, as a day of thanksgiving and prayer, to be kept and observed throughout the land.

On that day let all our people suspend their ordinary work and occupations, and in their accustomed places of worship, with prayer and songs of praise, render thanks to God for all His mercies, for the abundant harvests which have rewarded the toil of the husbandman during the year that has passed, and for the rich rewards that have followed the labors of our people in their shops and their marts of trade and traffic. Let us give thanks for peace and for social order and contentment within our borders, and for our advancement in all that adds to national greatness.

And mindful of the afflictive dispensation with which a portion of our land has been visited, let us, while we humble ourselves before the power of God, acknowledge His mercy in setting bounds to the deadly march of pestilence, and let our hearts be chastened by sympathy with our fellow-countrymen who have suffered and who mourn.

And as we return thanks for all the blessings which we have received from the hands of our Heavenly Father, let us not forget that He has enjoined upon us charity; and on this day of thanksgiving let us generously remember the poor and needy, so that our tribute of praise and gratitude may be acceptable in the sight of the Lord.

Done at the city of Washington on the 1st day of November, 1888, and in the year of the Independence of the United States the one hundred and thirteenth.

[SEAL.]

In witness whereof I have hereunto signed my name and caused the seal of the United States to be affixed.

GROVER CLEVELAND.

By the President:

T. F. BAYARD,
Secretary of State.

EXECUTIVE ORDERS.

REVISED CIVIL-SERVICE RULES.

EXECUTIVE MANSION, *February 2, 1888.*

In the exercise of power vested in him by the Constitution and of authority given to him by the seventeen hundred and fifty-third section of the Revised Statutes and by an act to regulate and improve the civil service of the United States, approved January 16, 1883, the President hereby makes and promulgates the following rules and revokes the rules known as "Amended Civil-Service Rules" and "Special Rule No. 1," heretofore promulgated under the power and authority referred to herein: *Provided,* That this revocation shall not be construed as an exclusion from the classified civil service of any now classified customs district or classified post-office.

GENERAL RULES.

GENERAL RULE I.

Any officer in the executive civil service who shall use his official authority or influence for the purpose of interfering with an election or controlling the result thereof; or who shall dismiss, or cause to be dismissed, or use influence of any kind to procure the dismissal of any person from any place in the said service because such person has refused to be coerced in his political action or has refused to contribute money for political purposes, or has refused to render political service; and any officer, clerk, or other employee in the executive civil service who shall wilfully violate any of these rules, or any of the provisions of sections 11, 12, 13, and 14 of the act entitled "An act to regulate and improve the civil service of the United States," approved January 16, 1883, shall be dismissed from office.

GENERAL RULE II.

There shall be three branches of the classified civil service, as follows:

1. The classified departmental service.
2. The classified customs service.
3. The classified postal service.

GENERAL RULE III.

1. No person shall be appointed or employed to enter the civil service, classified in accordance with section 163 of the Revised Statutes and under the "Act to regulate and improve the civil service of the United States," approved January 16, 1883, until he shall have passed an examination or shall have been shown to be specially exempted therefrom by said act or by an exception to this rule set forth in connection with the rules regulating admission to the branch of the service he seeks to enter.

2. No noncompetitive examination shall be held except under the following conditions:

(*a*) The failure of competent persons to be, after due notice, competitively examined, thus making it impracticable to supply to the appointing officer in due time the names of persons who have passed a competitive examination.

(*b*) That a person has been during one year or longer in a place excepted from examination, and the appointing or nominating officer desires the appointment of such person to a place not excepted.

(*c*) That a person has served two years continuously since July 16, 1883, in a place in the departmental service below or outside the classified service, and the appointing officer desires, with the approval of the President, upon the recommendation of the Commission, to promote such person into the classified service because of his faithfulness and efficiency in the position occupied by him, and because of his qualifications for the place to which the appointing officer desires his promotion.

(*d*) That an appointing or nominating officer desires the examination of a person to test his fitness for a classified place which might be filled under exceptions to examination declared in connection with the rules regulating admission to the classified service.

(*e*) That the Commission, with the approval of the President, has decided that such an examination should be held to test fitness for any particular place requiring technical, professional, or scientific knowledge, special skill, or peculiar ability, to test fitness for which place a competitive examination can not, in the opinion of the Commission, be properly provided.

(*f*) That a person who has been appointed from the copyist register wishes to take the clerk examination for promotion to a place the salary of which is not less than $1,000 per annum.

(*g*) To test the fitness of a person for a place to which his transfer has been requested.

(*h*) When the exigencies of the service require such examination for promotion as provided by clause 6 of this rule.

3. All applications for examination must be made in form and manner prescribed by the Commission.

4. No person serving in the Army or Navy shall be examined for admission to the classified service until the written consent of the head of the Department under which he is enlisted shall have been communicated to the Commission.

No person who is an applicant for examination or who is an eligible in one branch of the classified service shall at the same time be an applicant for examination in any other branch of said service.

5. The Commission may refuse to examine an applicant who would be physically unable to perform the duties of the place to which he desires appointment. The reason for any such action must be entered on the minutes of the Commission.

6. For the purpose of establishing in the classified civil service the principle of compulsory competitive examination for promotion, there shall be, so far as practicable and useful, compulsory competitive examinations of a suitable character to test fitness for promotion; but persons in the classified service who were honorably discharged from the military or naval service of the United States, and the widows and orphans of deceased soldiers and sailors, shall be exempt from such examinations.

The Commission may make regulations, applying them to any part of the classified service, under which regulations all examinations for promotion therein shall be conducted and all promotions be made; but until regulations in accordance herewith have been applied to any part of the classified service promotions therein shall be made in the manner provided by the rules applicable thereto. And in any part of the classified service in which promotions are made under examination as herein provided the Commission may in special cases, if the exigencies of the service require such action, provide noncompetitive examinations for promotion.

Persons who were in the classified civil service on July 16, 1883, and persons who have been since that date or may be hereafter put into that service by the inclusion of subordinate places, clerks, and officers, under the provisions of section 6 of the act to regulate and improve the civil service of the United States, approved January 16, 1883, shall be entitled to all rights of promotion possessed by persons of the same class or grade appointed after examination under the act referred to above.

7. No question in any examination shall be so framed as to elicit information concerning the political or religious opinions or affiliations of competitors, and no discrimination in examination, certification, or appointment shall be made by the Commission, the examiners, or the appointing or nominating officer in favor of or against any applicant, competitor, or eligible because of his political or religious opinions or affiliations. The Commission, the examiners, and the appointing or nominating officer shall discountenance all disclosures of such opinions or affiliations by or concerning any applicant, competitor, or eligible; and any appointing or nominating officer who shall make inquiries concerning or in any other way attempt to ascertain the political or religious opinions or affiliations of any eligible, or who shall discriminate in favor of or against any eligible because of the eligible's political or religious opinions or affiliations, shall be dismissed from office.

8. Every applicant must state under oath—

(*a*) His full name.

(*b*) That he is a citizen of the United States.

(*c*) Year and place of his birth.

(*d*) The State, Territory, or District of which he is a *bona fide* resident, and the length of time he has been a resident thereof.

(*e*) His post-office address.

(*f*) His business or employment during the three years immediately preceding the date of his application, and where he has resided each of those years.

(*g*) Condition of his health, and his physical capacity for the public service.

(*h*) His previous employment in the public service.

(*i*) Any right of preference in civil appointments he may claim under section 1754 of the Revised Statutes.

(*j*) The kind of school in which he received his education.

(*k*) That he does not habitually use intoxicating beverages to excess.

(*l*) That he has not within the one year next preceding the date of his application been dismissed from the public service for delinquency or misconduct.

(*m*) Such other facts as the Commission may require.

9. Every applicant for examination for the classified departmental service must support the statements of his application paper by certificates of persons acquainted with him, residents of the State, Territory, or District in which he claims *bona fide* residence; and the Commission shall prescribe the form and number of such certificates.

10. A false statement made by an applicant, or connivance by him with any person to make on his behalf a false statement in any certificate required by the Commission, and deception or fraud practiced by an applicant, or by any person on his behalf with his consent, to influence an examination, shall be good cause for refusal to examine such applicant or for refusing to mark his papers after examination.

11. All examinations shall be prepared and conducted under the supervision of the Commission; and examination papers shall be marked under rules made by the Commission, which shall take care that the marking examiners do not know the name of any competitor in an examination for admission whose papers are intrusted to them.

12. For the purpose of marking examination papers boards of examiners shall be appointed by the Commission, one to be known as the central board, which shall be composed of persons in the classified service, who shall be detailed for constant duty at the office of the Commission. Under supervision of the Commission the central board shall mark the papers of the copyist and of the clerk examinations, and such of the papers of the supplementary, special, and promotion examinations for the departmental service and of examinations for admission to or promotion in the other branches of the classified services as shall be submitted to it by the Commission.

13. No person shall be appointed to membership on any board of examiners until after the Commission shall have consulted with the head of the Department or of the office under whom such person is serving.

14. An examiner shall be allowed time during office hours to perform his duties as examiner, which duties shall be considered part of his official duties.

15. The Commission may change the membership of boards of examiners and—

(*a*) Prescribe the manner of organizing such boards.

(*b*) More particularly define their powers.

(*c*) Specifically determine their duties and the duties of the members thereof.

16. Each board shall keep such records and make such reports as the Commission may require, and such records shall be open to the inspection of any member of this Commission or other person acting under authority of the Commission, which may, for the purposes of investigation, take possession of such records.

GENERAL RULE IV.

1. The names of all competitors who shall successfully pass an examination shall be entered upon a register, and the competitors whose names have been thus registered shall be eligible to any office or place to test fitness for which the examination was held.

2. The Commission may refuse to certify—

(*a*) An eligible who is so defective in sight, speech, or hearing, or who is otherwise so defective physically as to be apparently unfit to perform the duties of the position to which he is seeking appointment.

(*b*) An eligible who has made a false statement in his application, or been guilty of fraud or deceit in any matter connected with his application or examination, or who has been guilty of a crime or of infamous or notoriously disgraceful conduct.

3. If an appointing or nominating officer to whom certification has been made shall object in writing to any eligible named in the certificate, stating that because of physical incapacity or for other good cause particularly specified such eligible is not capable of properly performing the duties of the vacant place, the Commission

may, upon investigation and ascertainment of the fact that the objection made is good and well founded, direct the certification of another eligible in place of the one to whom objection has been made.

GENERAL RULE V.

Executive officers shall in all proper ways facilitate civil-service examinations; and customs officers, postmasters, and custodians of public buildings at places where such examinations are to be held shall for the purposes of such examinations permit and arrange for the use of suitable rooms under their charge, and for heating, lighting, and furnishing the same.

GENERAL RULE VI.

No person dismissed for misconduct, and no probationer who has failed to receive absolute appointment or employment, shall be admitted to any examination within one year after having been thus discharged from the service.

GENERAL RULE VII.

1. Persons who have a *prima facie* claim of preference for appointments to civil offices under section 1754, Revised Statutes, shall be preferred in certifications made under the authority of the Commission to any appointing or nominating officer.

2. In making any reduction of force in any branch of the classified civil service those persons shall be retained who, being equally qualified, have been honorably discharged from the military or naval service of the United States, and also the widows and orphans of deceased soldiers and sailors.

GENERAL RULE VIII.

The Commission shall have authority to prescribe regulations under and in accordance with these general rules and the rules relating specially to each of the several branches of the classified service.

DEPARTMENTAL RULES.

DEPARTMENTAL RULE I.

1. The classified departmental service shall include the several officers, clerks, and other persons in any Department, commission, or bureau at Washington classified under section 163 of the Revised Statutes, or by direction of the President for the purposes of the examinations prescribed by the civil-service act of 1883, or for facilitating the inquiries as to fitness of candidates for admission to the departmental service in respect to age, health, character, knowledge, and ability, as provided for in section 1753 of the Revised Statutes.

2. The word "department," when used in the general or departmental rules, shall be construed to mean any such Department, commission, or bureau classified as above prescribed.

DEPARTMENTAL RULE II.

1. To test the fitness of applicants for admission to the classified departmental service there shall be examinations as follows:

Copyist examination.—For places of $900 per annum and under. This examination shall not include more than the following subjects:

(*a*) Orthography.

(*b*) Copying.

(*c*) Penmanship.

(*d*) Arithmetic—fundamental rules, fractions, and percentage.

Clerk examination.—For places of $1,000 per annum and upward. This examination shall not include more than the following subjects:

(*a*) Orthography.

(*b*) Copying.

(*c*) Penmanship.

(*d*) Arithmetic -fundamental rules, fractions, percentage, interest, and discount.

(*e*) Elements of bookkeeping and of accounts.

(*f*) Elements of the English language.

(*g*) Letter writing.

(*h*) Elements of the geography, history, and government of the United States.

Supplementary examinations.—For places which, in the opinion of the Commission, require, in addition to the knowledge required to pass the copyist or the clerk examination, certain technical, professional, or scientific knowledge, or knowledge of a language other than the English language, or peculiar or special skill.

Special examinations.—For places which, in the opinion of the Commission, require certain technical, professional, or scientific knowledge or skill. Each special examination shall embrace, in addition to the special subject upon which the applicant is to be tested, as many of the subjects of the clerk examination as the Commission may decide to be necessary to test fitness for the place to be filled.

Noncompetitive examinations.—For any place in the departmental service for which the Commission may from time to time (subject to the conditions prescribed by General Rule III, clause 2) determine that such examinations ought to be held.

2. An applicant may take the copyist or the clerk examination and any or all of the supplementary and special examinations provided for the departmental service, subject to such limitations as the Commission may by regulation prescribe; but no person whose name is on a departmental register of eligibles shall during the period of his eligibility be allowed reexamination unless he shall satisfy the Commission that at the time of his examination he was unable, because of illness or other good cause, to do himself justice in said examination; and the rating upon such reexamination shall cancel and be a substitute for the rating of such person upon the previous examination.

3. Exceptions from examination in the classified departmental service are hereby made as follows:

(*a*) One private secretary or one confidential clerk of the head of each classified Department and of each assistant secretary thereof, and also of each head of bureau appointed by the President by and with the advice and consent of the Senate.

(*b*) Direct custodians of money for whose fidelity another officer is under official bond; but this exception shall not include any officer below the grade of assistant cashier or assistant teller.

(*c*) Disbursing officers who give bonds.

(*d*) Persons employed exclusively in the secret service of the Government.

(*e*) Chief clerks.

(*f*) Chiefs of divisions.

4. No person appointed to a place under the exceptions to examination hereby made shall within one year after appointment be transferred from such place to a place not also excepted from examination, but after service of not less than one year in an examination-excepted place he may be transferred in the bureau in which he is serving to a place not excepted from examination: *Provided*, That before any such transfer may be made the Commission must certify that the person whom it is proposed to so transfer has passed an examination to test fitness for the place proposed to be filled by such transfer.

DEPARTMENTAL RULE III.

In compliance with the provisions of section 3 of the civil-service act the Commission shall provide examinations for the classified departmental service at least twice in each year in every State or Territory in which there are a sufficient number of applicants for such examinations; and the places and times of examinations shall, when practicable, be so fixed that each applicant may know at the time of making his application when and where he may be examined; but applicants may be notified to appear at any place at which the Commission may order an examination.

DEPARTMENTAL RULE IV.

1. Any person not under 20 years of age may make application for admission to the classified departmental service, blank forms for which purpose shall be furnished by the Commission.

2. Every application for admission to the classified departmental service should be addressed as follows: "United States Civil Service Commission, Washington, D. C."

3. The date of reception and also of approval by the Commission of each application shall be noted on the application paper.

DEPARTMENTAL RULE V.

1. The papers of all examinations for admission to or promotion in the classified departmental service shall be marked as directed by the Commission.

2. The Commission shall have authority to appoint the following-named boards of examiners, which shall conduct examinations and mark examination papers as follows:

Central board.—As provided for by General Rule III, clause 12.

Special boards.—These boards shall mark such papers of special examinations for the classified departmental service as the Commission may direct, and shall be composed of persons in the public service.

Supplementary boards.—These boards shall mark the papers of such supplementary examinations for the classified departmental service as the Commission may direct, and shall be composed of persons in the public service.

Promotion boards.—One for each Department, of three members, and one auxiliary member for each bureau of the Department for which the board is to act. Unless the Commission shall otherwise direct, these boards shall mark the papers of promotion examinations.

Local boards.—These boards shall be organized at one or more places in each State and Territory where examinations for the classified departmental service are to be held, and shall conduct such examinations; and each shall be composed of persons in the public service residing in the State or Territory in which the board is to act.

Customs and postal boards.—These boards shall conduct such examinations for the classified departmental service as the Commission shall direct.

DEPARTMENTAL RULE VI.

1. The papers of the copyist and of the clerk examinations shall be marked by the central board; the papers of special and supplementary examinations shall be marked as directed by the Commission. Each competitor in any of the examinations mentioned or referred to above shall be graded on a scale of 100, according to the general average determined by the marks made by the examiners on his papers.

2. The papers of an examination having been marked, the Commission shall ascertain—

(a) The name of every competitor who has, under section 1754 of the Revised Statutes, claim of preference in civil appointments, and who has attained a general average of not less than 65 per cent; and all such competitors are hereby declared eligible to the class or place to test fitness for which the examination was held.

(b) The name of every other competitor who has attained a general average of not less than 70 per cent; and all such competitors are hereby declared eligible to the class or place to test fitness for which the examination was held.

3. The names of all preference-claiming competitors whose general average is not less than 65 per cent, together with the names of all other competitors whose general

average is not less than 70 **per cent**, shall be entered upon the register of persons eligible to the class or place to test fitness for which the examination was held.

4. To facilitate the maintenance of the apportionment of appointments among the several States and Territories and the District of Columbia, required by section 2 of the act to regulate and improve the civil service of the United States, approved January 16, 1883, there shall be lists of eligibles for each State and Territory and for the District of Columbia, upon which shall be entered the names of the competitors from that State or Territory or the District of Columbia who have passed the copyist and the clerk examinations, the names of those who have passed the copyist examination and of those who have passed the clerk examination being listed separately; the names of male and of female eligibles in such examinations being also listed separately.

5. But the names of all competitors who have passed a supplementary or a special examination shall be entered, without regard to State residence, upon the register of persons eligible to the class or place to test fitness for which supplementary or special examination was held.

6. The grade of each competitor shall be expressed by the whole number nearest the general average attained by him, and the grade of each eligible shall be noted upon the register of eligibles in connection with his name. When two or more eligibles are of the same grade, preference in certification shall be determined by the order in which their application papers were filed.

7. Immediately after the general averages in an examination shall have been ascertained each competitor shall be notified that he has passed or has failed to pass.

8. If a competitor fail to pass, he may, with the consent of the Commission, be allowed reexamination at any time within six months from the date of failure without filing a new application; but a competitor failing to pass, desiring to take again the same examination, must, if not allowed reexamination within six months from the date of failure, make in due form a new application therefor.

9. No person who has passed an examination shall, while eligible on the register supplied by such examination, be reexamined, unless he shall furnish evidence satisfactory to the Commission that at the time of his examination he was, because of illness or other good cause, incapable of doing himself justice in said examination.

10. The term of eligibility to appointment under the copyist and the clerk examinations shall be one year from the day on which the name of the eligible is entered on the register. The term of eligibility under a supplementary or a special examination shall be determined by the Commission, but shall not be less than one year.

DEPARTMENTAL, RULE VII.

1. Vacancies in the classified departmental service, unless among the places excepted from examination, if not filled by either promotion or transfer, shall be filled in the following manner:

(*a*) The appointing officer shall, in form and manner to be prescribed by the Commission, request the certification to him of the names of either males or females eligible to a certain place then vacant.

(*b*) If fitness for the place to be filled is tested by competitive examination, the Commission shall certify the names of three males or three females, these names to be those of the eligibles who, standing higher in grade than any other three eligibles of the same sex on the list of eligibles from which certification is to be made, have not been certified three times to the officer making the requisition: *Provided*, That if upon any register from which certification is to be made there are the names of eligibles who have, under section 1754 of the Revised Statutes, claim of preference in civil appointments, the names of such eligibles shall be certified before the names of other eligibles higher in grade. The Commission shall make regulations that will secure to each of such preference-claiming eligibles, in the order of his grade among other preference claimants, an opportunity to have his claim of preference considered and determined by the appointing officer.

2. Certifications hereunder sha 1 be made in such manner as to maintain as nearly as possible the apportionment of appointments among the several States and the Territories and the District of Columbia, as required by law.

3. If the three names certified are those of persons eligible on the copyist or the clerk register, the appointing officer shall select one, and one only, and shall notify the person whose name has been selected that he has been designated for appointment: *Provided*, That, for the purpose of maintaining the apportionment of appointments referred to in clause 2 of this rule, the Commission may authorize the appointing officer to select more than one of the three names certified.

When certification is made from a supplementary or a special register, and there are more vacancies than one to be filled, the appointing officer may select from the three names certified more than one.

4. The Commission may certify from the clerk register for appointment to a place the salary of which is less than $1,000 per annum any eligible on said register who has given written notice that he will accept such a place.

5. When a person designated for appointment shall have reported in person to the appointing officer, he shall be appointed for a probational period of six months, at the end of which period, if his conduct and capacity be satisfactory to the appointing officer, he shall receive absolute appointment; but if his conduct and capacity be not satisfactory to said officer he shall be notified that he will not receive absolute appointment, and this notification shall discharge him from the service. The appointing officer shall require the heads of bureaus or divisions under whom probationers are serving to keep a record and to make report of the punctuality, industry, habits, ability, and aptitude of each probationer.

6. All persons appointed to or promoted in the classified departmental service shall be assigned to the duties of the class or place to which they have been appointed or promoted, unless the interests of the service require their assignment to other duties; and when such assignment is made the fact shall be reported to the head of the Department.

DEPARTMENTAL RULE VIII.

1. Transfers will be made as follows:

(*a*) From one Department to another, upon requisition by the head of the Department to which the transfer is to be made.

(*b*) From a bureau of the Treasury Department in which business relating to the customs is transacted to a classified customs district, and from such a district to such a bureau of the Treasury Department, upon requisition by the Secretary of the Treasury.

(*c*) From the Post-Office Department to a classified post-office, and from such an office to the Post-Office Department, upon requisition by the Postmaster-General.

2. No person may be transferred as herein authorized until the Commission shall have certified to the officer making the transfer requisition that the person whom it is proposed to transfer has passed an examination to test fitness for the place to which he is to be transferred, and that such person has during at least six months preceding the date of the certificate been in the classified service of the Department, customs district, or post-office from which the transfer is to be made: *Provided*, That no person who has been appointed from the copyist register shall be transferred to a place the salary of which is more than $900 per annum until one year after appointment.

DEPARTMENTAL RULE IX.

1. A person appointed from the copyist register may, upon any test of fitness determined upon by the promoting officer, be promoted as follows:

(*a*) At any time after probational appointment, to any place the salary of which is not more than $900 per annum.

(*b*) At any time after one year from the date of probational appointment, upon certification by the Commission that he has passed the clerk examination or its equivalent, to any place the salary of which is $1,000 per annum or more.

(*c*) At any time after two years from the date of probational appointment, to any place the salary of which is $1,000 per annum or more.

2. A person appointed from the clerk register or from any supplementary or special register to a place the salary of which is $1,000 per annum or more may, upon any test of fitness determined upon by the promoting officer, be promoted at any time after absolute appointment.

3. A person appointed from the clerk register or from any supplementary or special register to a place the salary of which is $900 or less may, upon any test of fitness determined upon by the promoting officer, be promoted at any time after probational appointment to any place the salary of which is $1,000 per annum.

4. Other promotions may be made upon any tests of fitness determined upon by the promoting officer.

5. The provisions of clauses 1, 2, 3, and 4 of this rule shall become null and void in any part of the classified departmental service as soon as promotion regulations shall have been applied thereto under General Rule III, clause 6.

DEPARTMENTAL RULE X.

Upon requisition of the head of a Department the Commission shall certify for reinstatement in said Department, in a grade requiring no higher examination than the one in which he was formerly employed, any person who within one year next preceding the date of the requisition has, through no delinquency or misconduct, been separated from the classified service of that Department.

DEPARTMENTAL RULE XI.

Each appointing officer in the classified departmental service shall report to the Commission—

(*a*) Every probational and every absolute appointment made by him, and every appointment made by him under any exception to examination authorized by Departmental Rule II, clause 3.

(*b*) Every refusal by him to make an absolute appointment and every refusal or neglect to accept an appointment in the classified service under him.

(*c*) Every transfer within and into the classified service under him.

(*d*) Every assignment of a person to the performance of the duties of a class or place to which such person was not appointed.

(*e*) Every separation from the classified service under him, and whether the separation was caused by dismissal, resignation, or death. Places excepted from examination are within the classified service.

(*f*) Every restoration to the classified service under him of any person who may have been separated therefrom by dismissal or resignation.

CUSTOMS RULES.

CUSTOMS RULE I.

1. The classified customs service shall include the officers, clerks, and other persons in the several customs districts classified under the provisions of section 6 of the act to regulate and improve the civil service of the United States, approved January 16, 1883.

2. Whenever the officers, clerks, and other persons in any customs district number as many as fifty, any existing classification of the customs service made by the Secretary of the Treasury under section 6 of the act of January 16, 1883, shall apply thereto, and thereafter the Commission shall provide examinations to test the fitness

of persons to fill vacancies in said customs district and these rules shall be in force therein. Every revision of the classification of any customs office under section 6 of the act above mentioned, and every inclusion within the classified customs service of a customs district, shall be reported to the President.

CUSTOMS RULE II.

1. To test fitness for admission to the classified customs service, examinations shall be provided as follows:

*Clerk examination.** —This examination shall not include more than the following subjects:

(*a*) Orthography.
(*b*) Copying.
(*c*) Penmanship.
(*d*) Arithmetic—fundamental rules, fractions, percentage, interest, and discount.
(*e*) Elements of bookkeeping and of accounts.
(*f*) Elements of the English language.
(*g*) Letter writing.
(*h*) Elements of the geography, history, and government of the United States.

Law-clerk examination.—This examination shall not include more than the following subjects:

(*a*) Orthography.
(*b*) Copying.
(*c*) Penmanship.
(*d*) Arithmetic—fundamental rules, fractions, percentage, interest, and discount.
(*e*) Elements of the English language.
(*f*) Letter writing.
(*g*) Law questions.

Day-inspector examination.—This examination shall not include more than the following subjects:

(*a*) Orthography.
(*b*) Copying.
(*c*) Penmanship.
(*d*) Arithmetic—fundamental rules, fractions, and percentage.
(*e*) Elements of the English language.
(*f*) Geography of America and Europe.

Inspectress examination.—This examination shall not include more than the following subjects:

(*a*) Orthography.
(*b*) Copying.
(*c*) Penmanship.
(*d*) Arithmetic—fundamental rules.
(*e*) Geography of America and Europe.

Night-inspector, messenger, assistant weigher, and opener and packer examination.—This examination shall not include more than the following subjects:

(*a*) Orthography.
(*b*) Copying.
(*c*) Penmanship.
(*d*) Arithmetic—fundamental rules.

Gauger examination.—This examination shall not include more than the following subjects:

(*a*) Orthography.
(*b*) Copying.
(*c*) Penmanship.
(*d*) Arithmetic—practical questions.
(*e*) Theoretical questions.
(*f*) Practical tests.

*Storekeepers shall be classed as clerks, and vacancies in that class shall be filled by assignment.

Examiner examination.—This examination shall not include more than the following subjects:

(*a*) Orthography.
(*b*) Copying.
(*c*) Penmanship.
(*d*) Arithmetic—fundamental rules, fractions, percentage, and discount.
(*e*) Elements of the English language.
(*f*) Practical questions.
(*g*) Practical tests.

Sampler examination.—This examination shall not include more than the following subjects:

(*a*) Orthography.
(*b*) Copying.
(*c*) Penmanship.
(*d*) Arithmetic—fundamental rules.
(*e*) Practical questions.
(*f*) Practical tests.

Other competitive examinations.—Such other competitive examinations as the Commission may from time to time determine to be necessary in testing fitness for other places in the classified customs service.

Noncompetitive examinations.—Such examinations may, with the approval of the Commission, be held under conditions stated in General Rule III, clause 2.

2. Any person not under 21 years of age may be examined for any place in the customs service to test fitness for which an examination is prescribed, and any person not under 20 years of age may be examined for clerk or messenger.

3. A person desiring examination for admission to the classified customs service must make request, in his own handwriting, for a blank form of application, which request and also his application shall be addressed as directed by the Commission.

4. The date of reception and also of approval by the board of each of such applications shall be noted on the application paper.

5. Exceptions from examination in the classified customs service are hereby made as follows:

(*a*) Deputy collectors, who do not also act as inspectors, examiners, or clerks.
(*b*) Cashier of the collector.
(*c*) Assistant cashier of the collector.
(*d*) Auditor of the collector.
(*e*) Chief acting disbursing officer.
(*f*) Deputy naval officers.
(*g*) Deputy surveyors.
(*h*) One private secretary or one confidential clerk of each nominating officer.

6. No person appointed to a place under any exception to examination hereby made shall within one year after appointment be transferred from such place to another place not also excepted from examination, but a person who has served not less than one year in an examination-excepted place may be transferred in the customs office in which he is serving to a place not excepted from examination: *Provided*, That before any such transfer may be made the Commission must certify that the person whom it is proposed to so transfer has passed an examination to test fitness for the place proposed to be filled by such transfer.

CUSTOMS RULE III.

1. The papers of every examination shall be marked under direction of the Commission, and each competitor shall be graded on a scale of 100, according to the general average determined by the marks made by the examiners on his papers.

2. The Commission shall appoint in each classified customs district a board of examiners, which shall—

(*a*) Conduct all examinations held to test fitness for admission to or promotion in the classified service of the customs district in which the board is located.

(*b*) Mark the papers of such examinations, unless otherwise directed, as provided for by General Rule III, clause 12.

(*c*) Conduct such examinations for the classified departmental service as the Commission may direct.

3. The papers of an examination having been marked, the board of examiners shall ascertain—

(*a*) The name of every competitor who has, under section 1754 of the Revised Statutes, claim of preference in civil appointments, and who has attained a general average of not less than 65 per cent; and all such competitors are hereby declared eligible to the class or place to test fitness for which the examination was held.

(*b*) The name of every other competitor who has attained a general average of not less than 70 per cent; and all such applicants are hereby declared eligible to the class or place to test fitness for which the examination was held.

4. The names of all preference-claiming competitors whose general average is not less than 65 per cent, together with the names of all other competitors whose general average is not less than 70 per cent, shall be entered upon the register of persons eligible to the class or place to test fitness for which the examination was held. The names of male and of female eligibles shall be listed separately.

5. The grade of each competitor shall be expressed by the whole number nearest the general average attained by him, and the grade of each eligible shall be noted upon the register of eligibles in connection with his name. When two or more eligibles are of the same grade, preference in certification shall be determined by the order in which their application papers were filed.

6. Immediately after the general averages in an examination shall have been ascertained each competitor shall be notified that he has passed or has failed to pass.

7. If a competitor fail to pass, he may, with the consent of the board, approved by the Commission, be allowed reexamination at any time within six months from the date of failure without filing a new application; but a competitor failing to pass, desiring to take again the same examination, must, if not allowed reexamination within six months from the date of failure, make in due form a new application therefor.

8. No person who has passed an examination shall while eligible on the register supplied by such examination be reexamined, unless he shall furnish evidence satisfactory to the Commission that at the time of his examination he was, because of illness or for other good cause, incapable of doing himself justice in said examination.

9. The term of eligibility to appointment in the classified customs service shall be one year from the day on which the name of the eligible is entered on the register.

CUSTOMS RULE IV.

1. Vacancies in the lowest class or grade of the classified service of a customs district shall be filled in the following manner:

(*a*) The nominating officer in any office in which a vacancy may exist shall, in form and manner to be prescribed by the Commission, request the board of examiners to certify to him the names of either males or females eligible to the vacant place.

(*b*) If fitness for the place to be filled is tested by competitive examination, the board of examiners shall certify the names of three males or three females, these names to be those of the eligibles who, standing higher in grade than any other three eligibles of the same sex on the register from which certification is to be made, have not been certified three times from said register: *Provided*, That if upon said register there are the names of eligibles who, under section 1754 of the Revised Statutes, have claim of preference in civil appointments, the names of such eligibles shall be certified before the names of other eligibles higher in grade. The Commission shall make regulations that will secure to each of such preference-claiming eligibles, in the order of his grade among other preference claimants, an opportunity to have his claim of preference considered and determined by the appointing officer.

(*c*) Each name on a register of eligibles may be certified only three times: *Provided*, That when a name has been three times certified, if there are not three names on the register of higher grade, it may, upon the written request of a nominating officer to whom it has not been certified, be included in any certification made to said officer.

2. Of the three names certified the nominating officer must select one; and if at the time of making this selection there are more vacancies than one, he may select more than one name. Each person thus designated for appointment shall be notified, and upon reporting in person to the proper officer shall be appointed for a probational period of six months, at the end of which period, if his conduct and capacity be satisfactory to the nominating officer, he shall receive absolute appointment; but if his conduct and capacity be not satisfactory to said officer, he shall be notified that he will not receive absolute appointment, and this notification shall discharge him from the service.

3. Every nominating officer in the classified customs service shall require the officer under whom a probationer may be serving to carefully observe and report in writing the services rendered by and the character and qualifications of such probationer. These reports shall be preserved on file, and the Commission may prescribe the form and manner in which they shall be made.

4. All other vacancies, unless among the places excepted from examination, shall be filled by transfer or promotion.

CUSTOMS RULE V.

1. Until promotion regulations have been applied to a classified customs district, the following promotions may be made therein at any time after absolute appointment:

(*a*) A clerk, upon any test of fitness determined upon by the nominating officer, to any vacant place in the class next above the one in which he may be serving.

(*b*) A day inspector, upon any test of fitness determined upon by the nominating officer, to class 2 in the grade of clerk.

(*c*) A clerk, day inspector, opener and packer, or sampler, after passing the examiner examination, to the grade of examiner.

(*d*) A messenger, after passing the clerk examination, to the lowest class in the grade of clerk.

(*e*) A night inspector, after passing the day-inspector examination, to the grade of day inspector.

2. Other promotions may be made, in the discretion of the promoting officer, upon any test of fitness determined upon by him.

CUSTOMS RULE VI.

1. Transfers may be made as follows:

(*a*) From one office of a classified district to another office in the same district, subject to the provisions of Customs Rule V.

(*b*) From one classified district to another, upon requisition by the Secretary of the Treasury.

(*c*) From any bureau of the Treasury Department in which business relating to customs is transacted to any classified customs district, and from any such district to any such bureau, upon requisition by the Secretary of the Treasury.

2. No person may be transferred as herein authorized until the board of examiners, acting under (*a*) of clause 1, or until the Commission, acting under (*b*) or (*c*) of clause 1 of this rule, shall have certified to the officer making the transfer requisition that the person whom it is proposed to transfer has passed an examination to test fitness

for the place to which he is to be transferred, and that such person has been at least six months preceding the date of the certificate in the classified service of the Department or customs district from which the transfer is to be made.

CUSTOMS RULE VII.

Upon requisition of a nominating officer in any customs district the board of examiners thereof shall certify for reinstatement in any office under his jurisdiction, in a grade requiring no higher examination than the one in which he was formerly employed, any person who within one year next preceding the date of the requisition has, through no delinquency or misconduct, been separated from the classified service of said office.

CUSTOMS RULE VIII.

Each nominating officer of a classified customs district shall report to the board of examiners—

(*a*) Every probational and absolute appointment, and every appointment under any exception to examination authorized by Customs Rule II, clause 5, made within his jurisdiction.

(*b*) Every refusal by him to nominate a probationer for absolute appointment and every refusal or neglect to accept an appointment in the classified service under him.

(*c*) Every transfer into the classified service under him.

(*d*) Every separation from the classified service under him, and whether the separation was caused by dismissal, resignation, or death. Places excepted from examination are within the classified service.

(*e*) Every restoration to the classified service under him of any person who may have been separated therefrom by dismissal or resignation.

POSTAL RULES.

POSTAL RULE I.

1. The classified postal service shall include the officers, clerks, and other persons in the several post-offices classified under the provisions of section 6 of the act to regulate and improve the civil service of the United States, approved January 16, 1883.

2. Whenever the officers, clerks, and other persons in any post-office number as many as fifty, any existing classification of the postal service made by the Postmaster-General under section 6 of the act of January 16, 1883, shall apply thereto, and thereafter the Commission shall provide examinations to test the fitness of persons to fill vacancies in said post-office and these rules shall be in force therein. Every revision of the classification of any post-office under section 6 of the act above mentioned, and every inclusion of a post-office within the classified postal service, shall be reported to the President.

POSTAL RULE II.

1. To test fitness for admission to the classified postal service examinations shall be provided as follows:

Clerk examination.—This examination shall not include more than the following subjects:

(*a*) Orthography.

(*b*) Copying.

(*c*) Penmanship.

(*d*) Arithmetic—fundamental rules, fractions, and percentage.

(*e*) Elements of the English language.

(*f*) Letter writing.

(*g*) Elements of the geography, history, and government of the United States.

Carrier examination.—This examination shall not include more than the following subjects:

(*a*) Orthography.
(*b*) Copying.
(*c*) Penmanship.
(*d*) Arithmetic—fundamental rules.
(*e*) Elements of the geography of the United States.
(*f*) Knowledge of the locality of the post-office delivery.
(*g*) Physical tests.

Messenger examination.—This examination shall not include more than the following subjects:

(*a*) Orthography.
(*b*) Copying.
(*c*) Penmanship.
(*d*) Arithmetic—fundamental rules.
(*e*) Physical tests.

This examination shall also be used to test fitness for the position of piler, stamper, junior clerk, or other places the duties of which are chiefly manual.

Special examinations.—These examinations shall test fitness for positions requiring knowledge of a language other than the English language, or special or technical knowledge or skill. Each special examination shall include, in addition to the special subject upon which the applicant is to be tested, so many of the subjects of the clerk examination as the Commission may determine.

Noncompetitive examinations.—Such examinations may, with the approval of the Commission, be held under conditions stated in General Rule III, clause 2.

2. No person shall be examined for the position of clerk if under 18 years of age; and no person shall be examined for the position of messenger, stamper, or junior clerk if under 16 or over 45 years of age; and no person shall be examined for the position of carrier if under 21 or over 40 years of age. No person shall be examined for any other position in the classified postal service if under 18 or over 45 years of age.

3. Any person desiring examination for admission to the classified postal service must make request, in his own handwriting, for a blank form of application, which request, and also his application, shall be addressed as directed by the Commission.

4. The date of reception and also of approval by the board of each of such applications shall be noted on the application paper.

5. Exceptions from examinations in the classified postal service are hereby made as follows:

(*a*) Assistant postmaster.
(*b*) One private secretary or one confidential clerk of the postmaster.
(*c*) Cashier.
(*d*) Assistant cashier.
(*e*) Superintendents designated by the Post-Office Department and reported as such to the Commission.
(*f*) Custodians of money, stamps, stamped envelopes, or postal cards, designated as such by the Post-Office Department and so reported to the Commission, for whose fidelity the postmaster is under official bond.

6. No person appointed to a place under any exception to examination hereby made shall within one year after appointment be transferred to another place not also excepted from examination; but a person who has served not less than one year in an examination-excepted place may be transferred in the post-office in which he is serving to a place not excepted from examination: *Provided,* That before any such transfer may be made the Commission must certify that the person whom it is proposed to so transfer has passed an examination to test fitness for the place proposed to be filled by such transfer.

POSTAL RULE III.

1. The papers of every examination shall be marked under the direction of the Commission, and each competitor shall be graded on a scale of 100, according to the general average determined by the marks made by the examiners on his papers.

2. The Commission shall appoint in each classified post-office a board of examiners, which shall—

(*a*) Conduct all examinations held to test fitness for entrance to or promotion in the classified service of the post-office in which the board is located.

(*b*) Mark the papers of such examinations, unless otherwise directed, as provided for by General Rule III, clause 12.

(*c*) Conduct such examinations for the classified departmental service as the Commission may direct.

3. The papers of an examination having been marked, the board of examiners shall ascertain—

(*a*) The name of every competitor who has, under section 1754 of the Revised Statutes, claim of preference in civil appointments, and who has attained a general average of not less than 65 per cent; and all such competitors are hereby declared eligible to the class or place to test fitness for which the examination was held.

(*b*) The name of every other competitor who has attained a general average of not less than 70 per cent; and all such applicants are hereby declared eligible to the class or place to test fitness for which the examination was held.

4. The names of all preference-claiming competitors whose general average is not less than 65 per cent, together with the names of all other competitors whose general average is not less than 70 per cent, shall be entered upon the register of persons eligible to the class or place to test fitness for which the examination was held. The names of male and of female eligibles shall be listed separately.

5. The grade of each competitor shall be expressed by the whole number nearest the general average attained by him, and the grade of each eligible shall be noted upon the register of eligibles in connection with his name. When two or more eligibles are of the same grade, preference in certification shall be determined by the order in which their application papers were filed.

6. Immediately after the general averages shall have been ascertained each competitor shall be notified that he has passed or has failed to pass.

7. If a competitor fail to pass, he may, with the consent of the board, approved by the Commission, be allowed reexamination at any time within six months from the date of failure without filing a new application; but a competitor failing to pass, desiring to take again the same examination, must, if not allowed reexamination within six months from the date of failure, make in due form a new application therefor.

8. No person who has passed an examination shall while eligible on the register supplied by such examination be reexamined, unless he shall furnish evidence satisfactory to the Commission that at the time of his examination he was, because of illness or for other good cause, incapable of doing himself justice in said examination.

9. The term of eligibility to appointment in the classified postal service shall be one year from the day on which the name of the eligible is entered on the register.

POSTAL RULE IV.

1. Vacancies in the classified service of a post-office, unless among the places excepted from examination, if not filled by either transfer or promotion, shall be filled in the following manner:

(*a*) The postmaster at a post-office in which a vacancy may exist shall, in form and manner to be prescribed by the Commission, request the board of examiners to certify to him the names of either males or females eligible to the vacant place.

(*b*) If fitness for the place to be filled is tested by competitive examination, the board of examiners shall certify the names of three males or three females, these names to be those of the eligibles who, standing higher in grade than any other three eligibles of the same sex on the register from which certification is to be made, have not been certified three times from said register: *Provided*, That if upon said register there are the names of eligibles who, under section 1754 of the Revised Statutes, have claim of preference in civil appointments, the names of such eligibles shall be certified before the names of other eligibles higher in grade. The Commission shall make regulations that will secure to each of such preference-claiming eligibles, in the order of his grade among other preference claimants, opportunity to have his claim of preference considered and determined by the appointing officer.

(*c*) Each name on any register of eligibles may be certified only three times.

2. Of the three names certified to him the postmaster must select one; and if at the time of making this selection there are more vacancies than one, he may select more than one name. Each person thus designated for appointment shall be notified, and upon reporting in person to the postmaster shall be appointed for a probational period of six months, at the end of which period, if his conduct and capacity be satisfactory to the postmaster, he shall receive absolute appointment; but if his conduct and capacity be not satisfactory to said officer, he shall be notified that he will not receive absolute appointment, and this notification shall discharge him from the service.

3. The postmaster of each classified post-office shall require the superintendent of each division of his office to carefully observe and report in writing the services rendered by and the character and qualifications of each probationer serving under him. These reports shall be preserved on file, and the Commission may prescribe the form and manner in which they shall be made.

POSTAL RULE V.

Until promotion regulations shall have been applied to a classified post-office promotions therein may be made upon any test of fitness determined upon by the postmaster, if not disapproved by the Commission: *Provided*, That no employee shall be promoted to any grade he could not enter by appointment under the minimum age limitation applied thereto by Postal Rule II, clause 2.

POSTAL RULE VI.

1. Transfers may be made as follows:

(*a*) From one classified post-office to another, upon requisition of the Postmaster-General.

(*b*) From any classified post-office to the Post-Office Department, and from the Post-Office Department to any classified post-office, upon requisition of the Postmaster-General.

2. No person may be transferred as herein authorized until the Commission shall have certified to the officer making the transfer requisition that the person whom it is proposed to transfer has passed an examination to test fitness for the place to which he is to be transferred, and that such person has been at least six months next preceding the date of the certificate in the classified service of the Department or post-office from which the transfer is to be made.

POSTAL RULE VII.

Upon the requisition of a postmaster the board of examiners for his office shall certify for reinstatement, in a grade requiring no higher examination than the one in which he was formerly employed, any person who within one year next preceding the date of the requisition has through no delinquency or misconduct been separated from the classified service in said office.

POSTAL RULE VIII.

Each postmaster in the classified postal service shall report to the board of examiners—

(*a*) Every probational and every absolute appointment, and every appointment under any exception to examination authorized by Postal Rule II, clause 5, made in his office.

(*b*) Every refusal to make an absolute appointment in his office and every refusal or neglect to accept an appointment in the classified service under him.

(*c*) Every transfer into the classified service under him.

(*d*) Every separation from the classified service under him, and whether the separation was caused by dismissal, resignation, or death. Places excepted from examination are within the classified service.

(*e*) Every restoration to the classified service under him of any person who may have been separated therefrom by dismissal or resignation.

These rules shall take effect March 1, 1888.

GROVER CLEVELAND.

EXECUTIVE MANSION,
Washington, D. C., March 1, 1888.

In the exercise of authority vested in the President by the seventeen hundred and fifty-third section of the Revised Statutes to prescribe such regulations for the admission of persons into the civil service of the United States as may best promote the efficiency thereof and ascertain the fitness of each applicant in respect to age, health, character, knowledge, and ability for the branch of the service into which he seeks to enter, I hereby direct that the officers, clerks, and other employees of the United States Civil Service Commission, now authorized or that may hereafter be authorized by law, shall be arranged in the following classes, viz:

Class A, including all persons receiving compensation at the rate of less than $1,000 per annum.

Class B, including all persons receiving compensation at the rate of $1,000 or more, but less than $1,200 per annum.

Class 1, including all persons receiving compensation at the rate of $1,200 or more, but less than $1,400 per annum.

Class 2, including all persons receiving compensation at the rate of $1,400 or more, but less than $1,600 per annum.

Class 3, including all persons receiving compensation at the rate of $1,600 or more, but less than $1,800 per annum.

Class 4, including all persons receiving compensation at the rate of $1,800 or more, but less than $2,000 per annum.

Class 5, including all persons receiving compensation at the rate of $2,000 or more per annum.

No person who is appointed to an office by the President by and with the advice and consent of the Senate, or by the President alone, and no person who is to be employed merely as a laborer or workman or as a watchman, shall be considered as within this classification.

And it is ordered, That the United States Civil Service Commission thus classified, as provided by clause 2 of Departmental Rule I of the civil-service rules approved February 2, 1888, and in force on and after the date hereof, shall be considered a part of the classified departmental service, and the rules applicable thereto shall be in force therein.

GROVER CLEVELAND.

EXECUTIVE MANSION,
Washington, March 21, 1888.

To the United States Civil Service Commission.

GENTLEMEN: I desire to make a suggestion regarding subdivision (*c*), General Rule III, of the amended civil-service rules promulgated February 2, 1888. It provides for the promotion of an employee in a Department who is below or outside of the classified service to a place within said classified service in the same Department upon the request of the appointing officer, upon the recommendation of the Commission and the approval of the President, after a noncompetitive examination, in case such person has served continuously for two years in the place from which it is proposed to promote him, and "because of his faithfulness and efficiency in the position occupied by him," and "because of his qualifications for the place to which the appointing officer desires his promotion."

It has occurred to me that this provision must be executed with caution to avoid the application of it to cases not intended and the undue relaxation of the general purposes and restrictions of the civil-service law.

Noncompetitive examinations are the exceptions to the plan of the act, and the rules permitting the same should be strictly construed. The cases arising under the exception above recited should be very few, and when presented they should precisely meet all the requirements specified, and should be supported by facts which will develop the basis and reason of the application of the appointing officer and which will commend them to the judgment of the Commission and the President. The sole purpose of the provision is to benefit the public service, and it should never be permitted to operate as an evasion of the main feature of the law, which is competitive examinations.

As these cases will first be presented to the Commission for recommendation, I have to request that you will formulate a plan by which their merits can be tested. This will naturally involve a statement of all the facts deemed necessary for the determination of such applications, including the kind of work which has been done by the person proposed for promotion and the considerations upon which the allegations of the faithfulness, efficiency, and qualifications mentioned in the rule are predicated.

What has already been written naturally suggests another very important subject, to which I will invite your attention.

The desirability of the rule which I have commented upon would be nearly, if not entirely, removed, and other difficulties which now embarrass the execution of the civil-service law would be obviated, if there was a better and uniform classification of the employees in the different

Departments. The importance of this is entirely obvious. The present imperfect classifications, hastily made, apparently with but little care for uniformity, and promulgated after the last Presidential election and prior to the installation of the present Administration, should not have been permitted to continue to this time.

It appears that in the War Department the employees were divided on the 19th day of November, 1884, into eight classes and subclasses, embracing those earning annual salaries from $900 to $2,000.

The Navy Department was classified November 22, 1884, and its employees were divided into seven classes and subclasses, embracing those who received annual salaries from $720 to $1,800.

In the Interior Department the classification was made on the 6th day of December, 1884. It consists of eight classes and subclasses, and embraces employees receiving annual salaries from $720 to $2,000.

On the 2d day of January, 1885, a classification of the employees in the Treasury Department was made, consisting of six classes and subclasses, including those earning annual salaries from $900 to $1,800.

In the Post-Office Department the employees were classified on February 6, 1885, into nine classes and subclasses, embracing persons earning annual salaries from $720 to $2,000.

On the 12th of December, 1884, the Bureau of Agriculture was classified in a manner different from all the other Departments, and presenting features peculiar to itself.

It seems that the only classification in the Department of State and the Department of Justice is that provided for by section 163 of the Revised Statutes, which directs that the employees in the several Departments shall be divided into four classes. It appears that no more definite classification has been made in these Departments.

I wish the Commission would revise these classifications and submit to me a plan which will as far as possible make them uniform, and which will especially remedy the present condition which permits persons to enter a grade in the service in the one Department without any examination which in another Department can only be entered after passing such examination. This, I think, should be done by extending the limits of the classified service rather than by contracting them.

GROVER CLEVELAND.

EXECUTIVE MANSION, *March 23, 1888.*

To the People of the United States:

The painful duty devolves upon the President to announce the death, at an early hour this morning, at his residence in this city, of Morrison R. Waite, Chief Justice of the United States, which exalted office he had filled since March 4, 1874, with honor to himself and high usefulness to his country.

In testimony of respect to the memory of the honored dead it is ordered that the executive offices in Washington be closed on the day of the funeral and be draped in mourning for thirty days, and that the national flag be displayed at half-mast on the public buildings and on all national vessels on the day of the funeral.

By the President:

T. F. BAYARD, *Secretary*.

EXECUTIVE MANSION,
Washington, May 26, 1888.

Under the provisions of section 4 of the act approved March 3, 1883, it is hereby ordered that the several Executive Departments, the Department of Agriculture, and the Government Printing Office be closed on Wednesday, the 30th instant, to enable the employees to participate in the decoration of the graves of the soldiers who fell during the rebellion.

GROVER CLEVELAND.

UNITED STATES CIVIL SERVICE COMMISSION,
Washington, D. C., June 2, 1888.

The PRESIDENT.

SIR: In the force employed in the office of the collector of customs at the port of New York there are eight tellers who receive and count the money paid in at that office, amounting to $500,000 a day or upward, and who should be persons qualified to handle money with skill and to detect counterfeit coin and bills. One of these places is now vacant, and it is important that it should be filled at the earliest practicable date. The position is not one excepted from examination by Customs Rule II, clause 5; but the collector thinks that it would be imprudent and impracticable for him to be restricted in filling the vacancy to the three names that might be certified to him from the eligible register, and in this opinion the Commission concurs. But whether this class of positions and certain others in the customs service should be filled by noncompetitive examination or by special exception is a matter which the Commission has under consideration, but can not determine until after a visit to New York and perhaps other ports. In view, however, of the necessity for immediately filling the present vacancy—but without establishing a precedent—the Commission aas the honor to recommend that a noncompetitive examination for the purpose be authorized under subdivision (*e*), clause 2 of General Rule III, Civil-Service Rules.

Your obedient servants,

JNO. H. OBERLY,
CHAS. LYMAN,
United States Civil Service Commissioners.

Approved, June 5, 1888.

GROVER CLEVELAND.

CLASSIFIED POSTAL SERVICE, SPECIAL RULE NO. I.

JUNE 16, 1888.

In addition to the exceptions from examination in the classified postal service made by Postal Rule II, clause 5, the following exception to examination in that service is hereby made:

Printers, employed as such.

Provided, That before any person may be employed under this exception to examination the Post-Office Department shall inform the Commission of the authority given to employ printers at any post-office and of the number authorized to be employed at such office.

GROVER CLEVELAND.

Ordered, That noncompetitive examinations to test fitness for the following designated places in the classified departmental service be, and
are hereby, authorized:

1. In all the Departments: Engineers, assistant engineers, pressmen, and com-
positors.

2. In the Department of the Treasury:
In the office of the Secretary: Storekeeper, inspector of electric lights, foreman of
laborers, captain of watch, lieutenants of watch, and locksmith and electrician.
In the office of the Treasurer: Seventeen clerks employed as expert money tellers.
In the office of the Supervising Surgeon-General of Marine-Hospital Service: Hos-
pital steward, employed as chemist.

3. In the Department of the Interior:
In the office of the Secretary: Stenographer (to be confidential clerk to Secretary),
members of the boards of pension appeals, returns-office clerk, and six clerks to act
as assistant disbursing clerks.
In the Bureau of Pensions: Superintendent of buildings and two qualified sur-
geons.
In the Patent Office: Librarian, principal examiners, machinists, and model attend-
ants.
In the office of the Commissioner of Railroads: One bookkeeper.
In the Bureau of Education: Clerk of class 4, as librarian.
In the Geological Survey: In permanent force—Librarian. In temporary force—
Assistant paleontologists, assistant geologists, topographers, and assistant photogra-
phers.

4. In the Department of Agriculture:
In the disbursing office: Four clerks.

5. In the Post-Office Department:
In the office of the Assistant Attorney-General: Stenographer (to be confidential
clerk to the Assistant Attorney-General).

Approved, July 2, 1888.

GROVER CLEVELAND.

SPECIAL DEPARTMENTAL RULE NO. 1.

In addition to the exceptions from examination made by Departmental Rule III, clause 2, the following exceptions to examinations for the
classified departmental service are hereby made, viz:

1. In the Department of State: Lithographer.

2. In the Department of the Treasury:
In the office of the Secretary: Government actuary.
In the office of the Comptroller of the Currency: Bond clerk.
In the office of the Supervising Architect: Supervising Architect, assistant super-
vising architect, confidential clerk to Supervising Architect, and photographer.
In the Bureau of the Mint: Assayer, examiner, computer of bullion, and adjuster
of accounts.
In the Bureau of Navigation: Clerk of class 4, acting as deputy commissioner.
In the office of Construction of Standard Weights and Measures: Adjuster and
mechanician.
In the Bureau of Engraving and Printing: Chief of the Bureau, assistant chief of
Bureau, engravers, and plate printers.
In the Coast and Geodetic Survey: Superintendent, confidential clerk to Superin-

tendent, the normal or field force, general office assistant, confidential clerk to general office assistant, engravers and contract engravers, electrotypist and photographer, electrotypist's helper, apprentice to electrotypist and photographer, copperplate printers, plate-printers' helpers, and mechanicians.

In the office of the Commissioner of Internal Revenue: Superintendent of stamp vault.

3. In the Department of the Interior:

In the office of the Secretary: Superintendent of documents, clerk of class 3 as custodian, clerk to sign land patents, and telephone operator.

In the office of the Assistant Attorney-General: Law clerks—One at $2,750 per annum, one at $2,500 per annum, one at $2,250 per annum, and thirteen at $2,000 per annum.

In the Patent Office: Financial clerk, examiner of interferences, and law clerk.

In the General Land Office: Two law clerks, two law examiners, clerk of class 4 acting as receiving clerk, and ten principal examiners of land claims and contests.

In the Bureau of Pensions: Assistant chief clerk, medical referee, assistant medical referee, and law clerk.

In the Bureau of Indian Affairs: Principal bookkeeper.

In the office of Commissioner of Railroads: Railroad engineer.

In the Bureau of Education: Collector and compiler of statistics and statistician.

In the Geological Survey: In permanent force—General assistant, executive officer, photographer, twelve geologists, two paleontologists, two chemists, chief geographer, three topographers, and three geographers. In temporary force—Six paleontologists, eight geologists, geographer, mechanician, and editor.

4. In the Department of War: Clerk for the General of the Army and clerk for the retired General of the Army.

In the office of the Chief Signal Officer: Lithographer.

5. In the Department of the Navy:

In the Hydrographic Office: Engravers, copperplate printers, printers' apprentices.

6. In the Department of Justice: Pardon clerk and two law clerks.

7. In the Department of Agriculture:

In the office of the Commissioner: Private secretary to the chief clerk, superintendent of grounds, and assistant chief of each of the following divisions: Of botany, of chemistry, of entomology, of forestry, and of statistics.

In the Bureau of Animal Industry: Chief of the Bureau, assistant chief, private secretary to chief, and chief clerk.

8. In the Post-Office Department: Assistant Attorney-General, law clerk, and agents and employees at postal-note, postage-stamp, postal-card, and envelope agencies.

9. In the Department of Labor: Statistical experts and temporary experts.

Approved, July 2, 1888.   GROVER CLEVELAND.

SPECIAL DEPARTMENTAL RULE NO. 2.

No substitute shall hereafter be employed in any Department; and the head of any Department in which substitutes are now employed may appoint any of such substitutes to take the place of his principal, or to any place of lower grade: *Provided*, That no substitute shall be appointed as herein authorized until he shall have passed an appropriate examination by the Civil Service Commission and his eligibility shall have been certified by said Commission to the head of the Department in which he is employed.

Approved, August 3, 1888.   GROVER CLEVELAND.

EXECUTIVE MANSION, *August 9, 1888.*

The Heads of Departments:

As a mark of respect to the memory of General Sheridan, the President directs that the several Executive Departments in the city of Washington be closed and all public business at the national capital suspended on Saturday, August 11 instant, the day of the funeral.

By direction of the President:

DANIEL S. LAMONT,
Private Secretary.

SPECIAL CUSTOMS RULE NO. I.

In addition to exceptions from examination in the classified customs service made under Customs Rule II, clause 5, the following special exceptions are made:

In the Boston customs district, office of the naval officer: Assistant deputy naval officer.

Approved, August 10, 1888.

GROVER CLEVELAND.

WAR DEPARTMENT,
Washington City, August 14, 1888.

By direction of the President, Major-General John M. Schofield is assigned to the command of the Army of the United States.

WM. C. ENDICOTT,
Secretary of War.

UNITED STATES CIVIL SERVICE COMMISSION,
Washington, D. C., August 25, 1888.

The PRESIDENT.

SIR: The Commission respectfully submits for your consideration the following extract from the minutes of its proceedings of August 23, 1888:

"Navy Department, August 23. Harmony, Acting Secretary of the Navy, refers, with a request that the examination asked for therein be held at the earliest possible moment, a communication of the same date of G. S. Dyer, lieutenant, United States Navy, in charge of the Hydrographic Office, Navy Department, requesting that Francis A. Lewis, at New York City, and Joseph T. McMillan, of San Francisco, may be noncompetitively examined for the positions of assistants at the branch hydrographic offices at those places, respectively, under General Rule III, paragraph 2 (*e*), stating that the positions of assistants at those offices require men specially fitted by a technical nautical education, and therefore such as is only obtained in the Navy, and that the young men referred to are recent graduates of the Naval Academy and have been honorably discharged from the service.

"The positions named in this communication, and similar positions at other branch hydrographic offices, being regarded as in the classified departmental service in the Department of the Navy, and subject to examination, and in view of the qualifications required in such positions and of the fact that the service is to be rendered at points remote from the city of Washington, it is deemed impracticable to fill these places by competitive examination. It is therefore ordered that they be included among the places to be filled by noncompetitive examination under the provision of General Rule III, clause 2 (*e*), and that the President be asked to approve this order.''

The Commission respectfully requests that you indorse this communication with your approval of the action above quoted and return it as the authority of the Commission for including the places mentioned among the noncompetitive examination places under General Rule III, clause 2 (*e*).

Very respectfully,

> A. P. EDGERTON,
> JOHN H. OBERLY,
> CHAS. LYMAN,
> *United States Civil Service Commissioners.*

Approved:

GROVER CLEVELAND.

UNITED STATES CIVIL SERVICE COMMISSION,
Washington, D. C., October 17, 1888.

The PRESIDENT.

SIR: This Commission has been informed by the Treasury Department that an additional teller has been authorized to be appointed at the custom-house in the city of New York, and that his immediate employment is desired.

This position is not one excepted from examination by Customs Rule II, clause 5, but the collector thinks, in view of its fiduciary character, that it ought to be filled by noncompetitive instead of by competitive examination, and in this view the Commission concurs. It is therefore respectfully recommended that a noncompetitive examination for the purpose be authorized under subdivision (*e*) of clause 2 of General Rule III, Revised Civil-Service Rules.

I have the honor to be, sir, your obedient servant,

> CHAS. LYMAN,
> *Commissioner, in Charge.*

Approved, October 17, 1888.

GROVER CLEVELAND.

UNITED STATES CIVIL SERVICE COMMISSION,
Washington, D. C., October 31, 1888.

The PRESIDENT.

SIR: Approval of the following order for noncompetitive examinations under the provisions of General Rule III, section 2, clause (*e*), of Revised Civil-Service Rules, is respectfully recommended:

Ordered, That noncompetitive examinations to test fitness for the following-designated places in the classified customs service are hereby authorized:

1. In the customs distr.ct of New York, collector's office: The tellers employed in the cashier's office; three stenographers employed under the immediate supervision of the collector.

2. In the customs district of San Francisco: Chinese interpreter.

I have the honor to be, sir, your obedient servant,

> CHAS. LYMAN,
> *Commissioner, in Charge.*

Approved, November 1, 1888.

GROVER CLEVELAND.

UNITED STATES CIVIL SERVICE COMMISSION,
Washington, D. C., October 31, 1888.

The PRESIDENT.

SIR: Approval of the following order for noncompetitive examinations under the provisions of General Rule III, section 2, clause (*e*), of Revised Civil-Service Rules, is respectfully recommended:

Ordered, That noncompetitive examinations to test fitness for the following-designated places in the classified departmental service are hereby authorized:

1. In the Department of the Interior, Geological Survey, permanent force: Assistant photographers.

2. In the Department of Labor: Special agents.

I have the honor to be, sir, your obedient servant,

CHAS. LYMAN,
Commissioner, in Charge.

Approved, November 1, 1888.

GROVER CLEVELAND.

Clause (*e*) of section 2 of General Rule III is amended by adding thereto the following, and as thus amended is hereby promulgated:

But no person appointed to such a place upon noncompetitive examination shall within one year after appointment be transferred or appointed to any place not excepted from examination; but after having served in such noncompetitive place not less than one year he may be transferred or appointed in the bureau or office in which he is serving to a place not excepted from examination upon the certificate of the Commission or the proper board of examiners that he has passed an examination to test fitness for the place to which his transfer or appointment is proposed.

Approved, November 1, 1888.

GROVER CLEVELAND.

SPECIAL DEPARTMENTAL RULE NO. 1.

So much of Special Departmental Rule No. 1, approved July 2, 1888, as applies to the Department of Agriculture is hereby amended and promulgated as follows:

7. In the Department of Agriculture:

In the office of the Commissioner: Private secretary to the chief clerk, superintendent of grounds, and assistant chief of each of the following divisions: Of botany, of chemistry, of entomology, of forestry, and of statistics, and the director of experiment stations and the assistant director.

In the Bureau of Animal Industry: Chief of the Bureau, assistant chief, private secretary to the chief, and chief clerk.

Approved, November 1, 1888.

GROVER CLEVELAND.

SPECIAL CUSTOMS RULE NO. 1.

Special Customs Rule No. 1, specially excepting from examination certain places in the customs service, is hereby amended by including among those places the following:

At the port of New York, office of the collector: Bookbinder.

EXECUTIVE MANSION,
Washington, November 1, 1888.

The foregoing amendment is hereby approved.

GROVER CLEVELAND.

Departmental Rule VII is hereby amended by inserting at the end of the first sentence of section 1 the following:

Provided, That no certification shall be made from the clerk or any supplementary register to any Department to which promotion regulations have been applied under General Rule III, section 6, to fill a vacancy above the grade of class 1.

So that as amended the first paragraph of section 1 will read:

1. Vacancies in the classified departmental service, unless among the places excepted from examination, if not filled by either promotion or transfer, shall be filled in the following manner: *Provided,* That no certification shall be made from the clerk or any supplementary register to any Department to which promotion regulations have been applied under General Rule III, section 6, to fill a vacancy above the grade of class 1.

Approved and promulgated.

EXECUTIVE MANSION, *November 1, 1888.*

The foregoing amendment is hereby approved.

GROVER CLEVELAND.

The following amendments to departmental rules are hereby made and promulgated:

To Departmental Rule IV: After the word "service," in section 1 of said rule, insert the following:

Provided, That any person may apply for the position of printer's assistant in the Bureau of Engraving and Printing who is not under 18 nor over 35 years of age.

And after the word "for," in the same section, strike out the words "which purpose" and insert in lieu thereof the words "such application," so that as amended section 1 will read:

1. Any person not under 20 years of age may make application for admission to the classified departmental service: *Provided,* That any person may apply for the position of printer's assistant in the Bureau of Engraving and Printing who is not under 18 nor over 35 years of age; and blank forms for such application shall be furnished by the Commission.

To Departmental Rule VI: After the word "examination," where it first occurs in section 5 of said rule, insert the words "or an examination for printer's assistant in the Bureau of Engraving and Printing." After the word "which" strike out the words "supplementary or special," where they last occur in said section, and insert in lieu thereof "the," so that as amended section 5 will read:

5. But the names of all competitors who have passed a supplementary or a special examination, or an examination for printer's assistant in the Bureau of Engraving

and Printing, shall be entered, without regard to State residence, upon the register of persons eligible to the class or place to test fitness for which the examination was held.

To Departmental Rule VII: After the word "or," in the second paragraph of section 3 of said rule, strike out the article "a," and after the word "register" in said paragraph insert the words "or the printer's-assistant register," so that as amended said second paragraph of section 3 will read:

When certification is made from a supplementary or special register, or the printer's-assistant register, and there are more vacancies than one to be filled, the appointing officer may select from the three names certified more than one.

EXECUTIVE MANSION,
Washington, November 5, 1888.

The foregoing amendments are hereby approved.

GROVER CLEVELAND.

UNITED STATES CIVIL SERVICE COMMISSION,
Washington, D. C., October 31, 1888.

The PRESIDENT.

SIR: The order heretofore approved by you authorizing noncompetitive examinations under General Rule III, section 2, clause (*e*), to test fitness for certain designated places in the classified departmental service, included among such places the following:

In the office of the Treasurer of the United States, seventeen clerks employed as expert money tellers.

The attempts thus far made to make appointments to these places under this order have fully satisfied the Commission and the Treasury Department of the impracticability of this method of procedure, not because of any difficulty of applying suitable tests to determine the expertness required, but because there are really no experts to be tested. The duties of these positions can not be learned elsewhere than in the positions themselves, and therefore the only experts are those now occupying them and the very few who have left them for one cause or another, but who are not seeking to return. Therefore, since experts are not available, and persons will have to be appointed who must learn the duties of the positions in the actual performance of those duties, there would seem to be no good reason why such persons should not be selected from the eligible registers of this Commission, which are at all times abundantly supplied with the names of persons who are both competent and worthy. And besides, so long as these tempting places are in the noncompetitive list, the Department will be subjected to solicitation and pressure concerning them which it would rather avoid.

In view of these considerations it is respectfully recommended that you approve the revocation of so much of the order above referred to as provides for the appointment upon noncompetitive examination of seventeen clerks in the office of the Treasurer of the United States employed as expert money tellers.

I have the honor to be, sir, your obedient servant,

CHAS. LYMAN,
Commissioner, in Charge.

Approved, November 13, 1888.

GROVER CLEVELAND.

FOURTH ANNUAL MESSAGE.

WASHINGTON, *December 3, 1888.*

To the Congress of the United States:

As you assemble for the discharge of the duties you have assumed as the representatives of a free and generous people, your meeting is marked by an interesting and impressive incident. With the expiration of the present session of the Congress the first century of our constitutional existence as a nation will be completed.

Our survival for one hundred years is not sufficient to assure us that we no longer have dangers to fear in the maintenance, with all its promised blessings, of a government founded upon the freedom of the people. The time rather admonishes us to soberly inquire whether in the past we have always closely kept in the course of safety, and whether we have before us a way plain and clear which leads to happiness and perpetuity.

When the experiment of our Government was undertaken, the chart adopted for our guidance was the Constitution. Departure from the lines there laid down is failure. It is only by a strict adherence to the direction they indicate and by restraint within the limitations they fix that we can furnish proof to the world of the fitness of the American people for self-government.

The equal and exact justice of which we boast as the underlying principle of our institutions should not be confined to the relations of our citizens to each other. The Government itself is under bond to the American people that in the exercise of its functions and powers it will deal with the body of our citizens in a manner scrupulously honest and fair and absolutely just. It has agreed that American citizenship shall be the only credential necessary to justify the claim of equality before the law, and that no condition in life shall give rise to discrimination in the treatment of the people by their Government.

The citizen of our Republic in its early days rigidly insisted upon full compliance with the letter of this bond, and saw stretching out before him a clear field for individual endeavor. His tribute to the support of his Government was measured by the cost of its economical maintenance, and he was secure in the enjoyment of the remaining recompense of his steady and contented toil. In those days the frugality of the people was stamped upon their Government, and was enforced by the free, thoughtful, and intelligent suffrage of the citizen. Combinations, monopolies, and aggregations of capital were either avoided or sternly regulated and restrained. The pomp and glitter of governments less free offered no temptation and presented no delusion to the plain people who, side by side, in friendly competition, wrought for the ennoblement and dignity of man, for the solution of the problem of free government, and for the achievement of the grand destiny awaiting the land which God had given them.

A century has passed. Our cities are the abiding places of wealth and luxury; our manufactories yield fortunes never dreamed of by the fathers of the Republic; our business men are madly striving in the race for riches, and immense aggregations of capital outrun the imagination in the magnitude of their undertakings.

We view with pride and satisfaction this bright picture of our country's growth and prosperity, while only a closer scrutiny develops a somber shading. Upon more careful inspection we find the wealth and luxury of our cities mingled with poverty and wretchedness and unremunerative toil. A crowded and constantly increasing urban population suggests the impoverishment of rural sections and discontent with agricultural pursuits. The farmer's son, not satisfied with his father's simple and laborious life, joins the eager chase for easily acquired wealth.

We discover that the fortunes realized by our manufacturers are no longer solely the reward of sturdy industry and enlightened foresight, but that they result from the discriminating favor of the Government and are largely built upon undue exactions from the masses of our people. The gulf between employers and the employed is constantly widening, and classes are rapidly forming, one comprising the very rich and powerful, while in another are found the toiling poor.

As we view the achievements of aggregated capital, we discover the existence of trusts, combinations, and monopolies, while the citizen is struggling far in the rear or is trampled to death beneath an iron heel. Corporations, which should be the carefully restrained creatures of the law and the servants of the people, are fast becoming the people's masters.

Still congratulating ourselves upon the wealth and prosperity of our country and complacently contemplating every incident of change inseparable from these conditions, it is our duty as patriotic citizens to inquire at the present stage of our progress how the bond of the Government made with the people has been kept and performed.

Instead of limiting the tribute drawn from our citizens to the necessities of its economical administration, the Government persists in exacting from the substance of the people millions which, unapplied and useless, lie dormant in its Treasury. This flagrant injustice and this breach of faith and obligation add to extortion the danger attending the diversion of the currency of the country from the legitimate channels of business.

Under the same laws by which these results are produced the Government permits many millions more to be added to the cost of the living of our people and to be taken from our consumers, which unreasonably swell the profits of a small but powerful minority.

The people must still be taxed for the support of the Government under the operation of tariff laws. But to the extent that the mass of our citizens are inordinately burdened beyond any useful public purpose and for the benefit of a favored few, the Government, under pretext of an exercise of its taxing power, enters gratuitously into partnership with these favorites, to their advantage and to the injury of a vast majority of our people.

This is not equality before the law.

The existing situation is injurious to the health of our entire body politic. It stifles in those for whose benefit it is permitted all patriotic love of country, and substitutes in its place selfish greed and grasping avarice. Devotion to American citizenship for its own sake and for what it should accomplish as a motive to our nation's advancement and the happiness of all our people is displaced by the assumption that the Government, instead of being the embodiment of equality, is but an instrumentality through which especial and individual advantages are to be gained.

The arrogance of this assumption is unconcealed. It appears in the sordid disregard of all but personal interests, in the refusal to abate for the benefit of others one iota of selfish advantage, and in combinations to perpetuate such advantages through efforts to control legislation and improperly influence the suffrages of the people.

The grievances of those not included within the circle of these beneficiaries, when fully realized, will surely arouse irritation and discontent. Our farmers, long suffering and patient, struggling in the race of life with the hardest and most unremitting toil, will not fail to see, in spite of misrepresentations and misleading fallacies, that they are obliged to accept such prices for their products as are fixed in foreign markets where they compete with the farmers of the world; that their lands are declining in value while their debts increase, and that without compensating favor they are forced by the action of the Government to pay for the benefit of others such enhanced prices for the things they need that the scanty returns of their labor fail to furnish their support or leave no margin for accumulation.

Our workingmen, enfranchised from all delusions and no longer frightened by the cry that their wages are endangered by a just revision of our tariff laws, will reasonably demand through such revision steadier employment, cheaper means of living in their homes, freedom for themselves and their children from the doom of perpetual servitude, and an open door to their advancement beyond the limits of a laboring class. Others of our citizens, whose comforts and expenditures are measured by moderate salaries and fixed incomes, will insist upon the fairness and justice of cheapening the cost of necessaries for themselves and their families.

When to the selfishness of the beneficiaries of unjust discrimination under our laws there shall be added the discontent of those who suffer from such discrimination, we will realize the fact that the beneficent purposes of our Government, dependent upon the patriotism and contentment of our people, are endangered.

171

Communism is a hateful thing and a menace to peace and organized government; but the communism of combined wealth and capital, the outgrowth of overweening cupidity and selfishness, which insidiously undermines the justice and integrity of free institutions, is not less dangerous than the communism of oppressed poverty and toil, which, exasperated by injustice and discontent, attacks with wild disorder the citadel of rule.

He mocks the people who proposes that the Government shall protect the rich and that they in turn will care for the laboring poor. Any intermediary between the people and their Government or the least delegation of the care and protection the Government owes to the humblest citizen in the land makes the boast of free institutions a glittering delusion and the pretended boon of American citizenship a shameless imposition.

A just and sensible revision of our tariff laws should be made for the relief of those of our countrymen who suffer under present conditions. Such a revision should receive the support of all who love that justice and equality due to American citizenship; of all who realize that in this justice and equality our Government finds its strength and its power to protect the citizen and his property; of all who believe that the contented competence and comfort of many accord better with the spirit of our institutions than colossal fortunes unfairly gathered in the hands of a few; of all who appreciate that the forbearance and fraternity among our people, which recognize the value of every American interest, are the surest guaranty of our national progress, and of all who desire to see the products of American skill and ingenuity in every market of the world, with a resulting restoration of American commerce.

The necessity of the reduction of our revenues is so apparent as to be generally conceded, but the means by which this end shall be accomplished and the sum of direct benefit which shall result to our citizens present a controversy of the utmost importance. There should be no scheme accepted as satisfactory by which the burdens of the people are only apparently removed. Extravagant appropriations of public money, with all their demoralizing consequences, should not be tolerated, either as a means of relieving the Treasury of its present surplus or as furnishing pretext for resisting a proper reduction in tariff rates. Existing evils and injustice should be honestly recognized, boldly met, and effectively remedied. There should be no cessation of the struggle until a plan is perfected, fair and conservative toward existing industries, but which will reduce the cost to consumers of the necessaries of life, while it provides for our manufacturers the advantage of freer raw materials and permits no injury to the interests of American labor.

The cause for which the battle is waged is comprised within lines clearly and distinctly defined. It should never be compromised. It is the people's cause.

It can not be denied that the selfish and private interests which are so persistently heard when efforts are made to deal in a just and comprehensive manner with our tariff laws are related to, if they are not responsible for, the sentiment largely prevailing among the people that the General Government is the fountain of individual and private aid; that it may be expected to relieve with paternal care the distress of citizens and communities, and that from the fullness of its Treasury it should, upon the slightest possible pretext of promoting the general good, apply public funds to the benefit of localities and individuals. Nor can it be denied that there is a growing assumption that, as against the Government and in favor of private claims and interests, the usual rules and limitations of business principles and just dealing should be waived.

These ideas have been unhappily much encouraged by legislative acquiescence. Relief from contracts made with the Government is too easily accorded in favor of the citizen; the failure to support claims against the Government by proof is often supplied by no better consideration than the wealth of the Government and the poverty of the claimant; gratuities in the form of pensions are granted upon no other real ground than the needy condition of the applicant, or for reasons less valid; and large sums are expended for public buildings and other improvements upon representations scarcely claimed to be related to public needs and necessities.

The extent to which the consideration of such matters subordinate and postpone action upon subjects of great public importance, but involving no special private or partisan interest, should arrest attention and lead to reformation.

A few of the numerous illustrations of this condition may be stated.

The crowded condition of the calendar of the Supreme Court, and the delay to suitors and denial of justice resulting therefrom, has been strongly urged upon the attention of the Congress, with a plan for the relief of the situation approved by those well able to judge of its merits. While this subject remains without effective consideration, many laws have been passed providing for the holding of terms of inferior courts at places to suit the convenience of localities, or to lay the foundation of an application for the erection of a new public building.

Repeated recommendations have been submitted for the amendment and change of the laws relating to our public lands so that their spoliation and diversion to other uses than as homes for honest settlers might be prevented. While a measure to meet this conceded necessity of reform remains awaiting the action of the Congress, many claims to the public lands and applications for their donation, in favor of States and individuals, have been allowed.

A plan in aid of Indian management, recommended by those well informed as containing valuable features in furtherance of the solution of the Indian problem, has thus far failed of legislative sanction, while grants of doubtful expediency to railroad corporations, permitting them to pass through Indian reservations, have greatly multiplied.

The propriety and necessity of the erection of one or more prisons for the confinement of United States convicts, and a post-office building in the national capital, are not disputed. But these needs yet remain unanswered, while scores of public buildings have been erected where their necessity for public purposes is not apparent.

A revision of our pension laws could easily be made which would rest upon just principles and provide for every worthy applicant. But while our general pension laws remain confused and imperfect, hundreds of private pension laws are annually passed, which are the sources of unjust discrimination and popular demoralization.

Appropriation bills for the support of the Government are defaced by items and provisions to meet private ends, and it is freely asserted by responsible and experienced parties that a bill appropriating money for public internal improvement would fail to meet with favor unless it contained items more for local and private advantage than for public benefit.

These statements can be much emphasized by an ascertainment of the proportion of Federal legislation which either bears upon its face its private character or which upon examination develops such a motive power.

And yet the people wait and expect from their chosen representatives such patriotic action as will advance the welfare of the entire country; and this expectation can only be answered by the performance of public duty with unselfish purpose. Our mission among the nations of the earth and our success in accomplishing the work God has given the American people to do require of those intrusted with the making and execution of our laws perfect devotion, above all other things, to the public good.

This devotion will lead us to strongly resist all impatience of constitutional limitations of Federal power and to persistently check the increasing tendency to extend the scope of Federal legislation into the domain of State and local jurisdiction upon the plea of subserving the public welfare. The preservation of the partitions between proper subjects of Federal and local care and regulation is of such importance under the Constitution, which is the law of our very existence, that no consideration of expediency or sentiment should tempt us to enter upon doubtful ground. We have undertaken to discover and proclaim the richest blessings of a free government, with the Constitution as our guide. Let us follow the way it points out; it will not mislead us. And surely no one who has taken upon himself the solemn obligation to support and preserve the Constitution can find justification or solace for disloyalty in the excuse that he wandered and disobeyed in search of a better way to reach the public welfare than the Constitution offers.

What has been said is deemed not inappropriate at a time when, from a century's height, we view the way already trod by the American people and attempt to discover their future path.

The seventh President of the United States—the soldier and statesman and at all times the firm and brave friend of the people—in vindication of his course as the protector of popular rights and the champion of true American citizenship, declared:

The ambition which leads me on is an anxious desire and a fixed determination to restore to the people unimpaired the sacred trust they have confided to my charge; to heal the wounds of the Constitution and to preserve it from further violation; to persuade my countrymen, so far as I may, that it is not in a splendid government supported by powerful monopolies and aristocratical establishments that they will find happiness or their liberties protection, but in a plain system, void of pomp, protecting all and granting favors to none, dispensing its blessings like the dews of heaven, unseen and unfelt save in the freshness and beauty they contribute to produce. It is such a government that the genius of our people requires—such an one only under which our States may remain for ages to come united, prosperous, and free.

In pursuance of a constitutional provision requiring the President from time to time to give to the Congress information of the state of the Union, I have the satisfaction to announce that the close of the year finds the United States in the enjoyment of domestic tranquillity and at peace with all the nations.

Since my last annual message our foreign relations have been strengthened and improved by performance of international good offices and by new and renewed treaties of amity, commerce, and reciprocal extradition of criminals.

Those international questions which still await settlement are all reasonably within the domain of amicable negotiation, and there is no existing subject of dispute between the United States and any foreign power that is not susceptible of satisfactory adjustment by frank diplomatic treatment.

The questions between Great Britain and the United States relating to the rights of American fishermen, under treaty and international comity, in the territorial waters of Canada and Newfoundland, I regret to say, are not yet satisfactorily adjusted.

These matters were fully treated in my message to the Senate of February 20, 1888,* together with which a convention, concluded under my authority with Her Majesty's Government on the 15th of February last, for the removal of all causes of misunderstanding, was submitted by me for the approval of the Senate.

This treaty having been rejected by the Senate, I transmitted a message to the Congress on the 23d of August last† reviewing the transactions and submitting for consideration certain recommendations for legislation concerning the important questions involved.

Afterwards, on the 12th of September,‡ in response to a resolution of the Senate, I again communicated fully all the information in my possession as to the action of the government of Canada affecting the commercial relations between the Dominion and the United States, including

*See pp. 5188-5192.   †See pp. 5205-5212.   ‡See pp. 5213-5215.

the treatment of American fishing vessels in the ports and waters of British North America.

These communications have all been published, and therefore opened to the knowledge of both Houses of Congress, although two were addressed to the Senate alone.

Comment upon or repetition of their contents would be superfluous, and I am not aware that anything has since occurred which should be added to the facts therein stated. Therefore I merely repeat, as applicable to the present time, the statement which will be found in my message to the Senate of September 12 last, that—

Since March 3, 1887, no case has been reported to the Department of State wherein complaint was made of unfriendly or unlawful treatment of American fishing vessels on the part of the Canadian authorities in which reparation was not promptly and satisfactorily obtained by the United States consul-general at Halifax.

Having essayed in the discharge of my duty to procure by negotiation the settlement of a long-standing cause of dispute and to remove a constant menace to the good relations of the two countries, and continuing to be of opinion that the treaty of February last, which failed to receive the approval of the Senate, did supply "a satisfactory, practical, and final adjustment, upon a basis honorable and just to both parties, of the difficult and vexed question to which it related," and having subsequently and unavailingly recommended other legislation to Congress which I hoped would suffice to meet the exigency created by the rejection of the treaty, I now again invoke the earnest and immediate attention of the Congress to the condition of this important question as it now stands before them and the country, and for the settlement of which I am deeply solicitous.

Near the close of the month of October last occurrences of a deeply regrettable nature were brought to my knowledge, which made it my painful but imperative duty to obtain with as little delay as possible a new personal channel of diplomatic intercourse in this country with the Government of Great Britain.

The correspondence in relation to this incident will in due course be laid before you, and will disclose the unpardonable conduct of the official referred to in his interference by advice and counsel with the suffrages of American citizens in the very crisis of the Presidential election then near at hand, and also in his subsequent public declarations to justify his action, superadding impugnment of the Executive and Senate of the United States in connection with important questions now pending in controversy between the two Governments.

The offense thus committed was most grave, involving disastrous possibilities to the good relations of the United States and Great Britain, constituting a gross breach of diplomatic privilege and an invasion of the purely domestic affairs and essential sovereignty of the Government to which the envoy was accredited.

Having first fulfilled the just demands of international comity by affording full opportunity for Her Majesty's Government to act in relief of the situation, I considered prolongation of discussion to be unwarranted, and thereupon declined to further recognize the diplomatic character of the person whose continuance in such function would destroy that mutual confidence which is essential to the good understanding of the two Governments and was inconsistent with the welfare and self-respect of the Government of the United States.

The usual interchange of communication has since continued through Her Majesty's legation in this city.

My endeavors to establish by international cooperation measures for the prevention of the extermination of fur seals in Bering Sea have not been relaxed, and I have hopes of being enabled shortly to submit an effective and satisfactory conventional projet with the maritime powers for the approval of the Senate.

The coastal boundary between our Alaskan possessions and British Columbia, I regret to say, has not received the attention demanded by its importance, and which on several occasions heretofore I have had the honor to recommend to the Congress.

The admitted impracticability, if not impossibility, of making an accurate and precise survey and demarcation of the boundary line as it is recited in the treaty with Russia under which Alaska was ceded to the United States renders it absolutely requisite for the prevention of international jurisdictional complications that adequate appropriation for a reconnoissance and survey to obtain proper knowledge of the locality and the geographical features of the boundary should be authorized by Congress with as little delay as possible.

Knowledge to be only thus obtained is an essential prerequisite for negotiation for ascertaining a common boundary, or as preliminary to any other mode of settlement.

It is much to be desired that some agreement should be reached with Her Majesty's Government by which the damages to life and property on the Great Lakes may be alleviated by removing or humanely regulating the obstacles to reciprocal assistance to wrecked or stranded vessels.

The act of June 19, 1878, which offers to Canadian vessels free access to our inland waters in aid of wrecked or disabled vessels, has not yet become effective through concurrent action by Canada.

The due protection of our citizens of French origin or descent from claim of military service in the event of their returning to or visiting France has called forth correspondence which was laid before you at the last session.

In the absence of conventional agreement as to naturalization, which is greatly to be desired, this Government sees no occasion to recede from the sound position it has maintained not only with regard to France, but as to all countries with which the United States have not concluded special treaties.

Twice within the last year has the imperial household of Germany been visited by death; and I have hastened to express the sorrow of this people, and their appreciation of the lofty character of the late aged Emperor William, and their sympathy with the heroism under suffering of his son the late Emperor Frederick.

I renew my recommendation of two years ago for the passage of a bill for the refunding to certain German steamship lines of the interest upon tonnage dues illegally exacted.

On the 12th [2d] of April last* I laid before the House of Representatives full information respecting our interests in Samoa; and in the subsequent correspondence on the same subject, which will be laid before you in due course, the history of events in those islands will be found.

In a message accompanying my approval, on the 1st day of October last, of a bill for the exclusion of Chinese laborers, I laid before Congress full information and all correspondence touching the negotiation of the treaty with China concluded at this capital on the 12th day of March, 1888, and which, having been confirmed by the Senate with certain amendments, was rejected by the Chinese Government. This message contained a recommendation that a sum of money be appropriated as compensation to Chinese subjects who had suffered injuries at the hands of lawless men within our jurisdiction. Such appropriation having been duly made, the fund awaits reception by the Chinese Government.

It is sincerely hoped that by the cessation of the influx of this class of Chinese subjects, in accordance with the expressed wish of both Governments, a cause of unkind feeling has been permanently removed.

On the 9th of August, 1887, notification was given by the Japanese minister at this capital of the adjournment of the conference for the revision of the treaties of Japan with foreign powers, owing to the objection of his Government to the provision in the draft jurisdictional convention which required the submission of the criminal code of the Empire to the powers in advance of its becoming operative. This notification was, however, accompanied with an assurance of Japan's intention to continue the work of revision.

Notwithstanding this temporary interruption of negotiations, it is hoped that improvements may soon be secured in the jurisdictional system as respects foreigners in Japan, and relief afforded to that country from the present undue and oppressive foreign control in matters of commerce.

I earnestly recommend that relief be provided for the injuries accidentally caused to Japanese subjects in the island Ikisima by the target practice of one of our vessels.

A diplomatic mission from Korea has been received, and the formal intercourse between the two countries contemplated by the treaty of 1882 is now established.

* See p. 5107.

Legislative provision is hereby recommended to organize and equip consular courts in Korea.

Persia has established diplomatic representation at this capital, and has evinced very great interest in the enterprise and achievements of our citizens. I am therefore hopeful that beneficial commercial relations between the two countries may be brought about.

I announce with sincere regret that Hayti has again become the theater of insurrection, disorder, and bloodshed. The titular government of President Saloman has been forcibly overthrown and he driven out of the country to France, where he has since died.

The tenure of power has been so unstable amid the war of factions that has ensued since the expulsion of President Saloman that no government constituted by the will of the Haytian people has been recognized as administering responsibly the affairs of that country. Our representative has been instructed to abstain from interference between the warring factions, and a vessel of our Navy has been sent to Haytian waters to sustain our minister and for the protection of the persons and property of American citizens.

Due precautions have been taken to enforce our neutrality laws and prevent our territory from becoming the base of military supplies for either of the warring factions.

Under color of a blockade, of which no reasonable notice had been given, and which does not appear to have been efficiently maintained, a seizure of vessels under the American flag has been reported, and in consequence measures to prevent and redress any molestation of our innocent merchantmen have been adopted.

Proclamation was duly made on the 9th day of November, 1887, of the conventional extensions of the treaty of June 3, 1875, with Hawaii, under which relations of such special and beneficent intercourse have been created.

In the vast field of Oriental commerce now unfolded from our Pacific borders no feature presents stronger recommendations for Congressional action than the establishment of communication by submarine telegraph with Honolulu.

The geographical position of the Hawaiian group in relation to our Pacific States creates a natural interdependency and mutuality of interest which our present treaties were intended to foster, and which make close communication a logical and commercial necessity.

The wisdom of concluding a treaty of commercial reciprocity with Mexico has been heretofore stated in my messages to Congress, and the lapse of time and growth of commerce with that close neighbor and sister Republic confirm the judgment so expressed.

The precise relocation of our boundary line is needful, and adequate appropriation is now recommended.

It is with sincere satisfaction that I am enabled to advert to the spirit of good neighborhood and friendly cooperation and conciliation that has marked the correspondence and action of the Mexican authorities in their share of the task of maintaining law and order about the line of our common boundary.

The long-pending boundary dispute between Costa Rica and Nicaragua was referred to my arbitration, and by an award made on the 22d of March last the question has been finally settled to the expressed satisfaction of both of the parties in interest.

The Empire of Brazil, in abolishing the last vestige of slavery among Christian nations, called forth the earnest congratulations of this Government in expression of the cordial sympathies of our people.

The claims of nearly all other countries against Chile growing out of her late war with Bolivia and Peru have been disposed of, either by arbitration or by a lump settlement. Similar claims of our citizens will continue to be urged upon the Chilean Government, and it is hoped will not be subject to further delays.

A comprehensive treaty of amity and commerce with Peru was proclaimed on November 7 last, and it is expected that under its operation mutual prosperity and good understanding will be promoted.

In pursuance of the policy of arbitration, a treaty to settle the claim of Santos, an American citizen, against Ecuador has been concluded under my authority, and will be duly submitted for the approval of the Senate.

Like disposition of the claim of Carlos Butterfield against Denmark and of Van Bokkelen against Hayti will probably be made, and I trust the principle of such settlements may be extended in practice under the approval of the Senate.

Through unforeseen causes, foreign to the will of both Governments, the ratification of the convention of December 5, 1885, with Venezuela, for the rehearing of claims of citizens of the United States under the treaty of 1866, failed of exchange within the term provided, and a supplementary convention, further extending the time for exchange of ratifications and explanatory of an ambiguous provision of the prior convention, now awaits the advice and consent of the Senate.

Although this matter, in the stage referred to, concerns only the concurrent treaty-making power of one branch of Congress, I advert to it in view of the interest repeatedly and conspicuously shown by you in your legislative capacity in favor of a speedy and equitable adjustment of the questions growing out of the discredited judgments of the previous mixed commission of Caracas. With every desire to do justice to the representations of Venezuela in this regard, the time seems to have come to end this matter, and I trust the prompt confirmation by both parties of the supplementary action referred to will avert the need of legislative or other action to prevent the longer withholding of such rights of actual claimants as may be shown to exist.

As authorized by the Congress, preliminary steps have been taken for the assemblage at this capital during the coming year of the representatives of South and Central American States, together with those of

Mexico, Hayti, and San Domingo, to discuss sundry important monetary and commercial topics.

Excepting in those cases where, from reasons of contiguity of territory and the existence of a common border line incapable of being guarded, reciprocal commercial treaties may be found expedient, it is believed that commercial policies inducing freer mutual exchange of products can be most advantageously arranged by independent but cooperative legislation.

In the mode last mentioned the control of our taxation for revenue will be always retained in our own hands unrestricted by conventional agreements with other governments.

In conformity also with Congressional authority, the maritime powers have been invited to confer in Washington in April next upon the practicability of devising uniform rules and measures for the greater security of life and property at sea. A disposition to accept on the part of a number of the powers has already been manifested, and if the cooperation of the nations chiefly interested shall be secured important results may be confidently anticipated.

The act of June 26, 1884, and the acts amendatory thereof, in relation to tonnage duties, have given rise to extended correspondence with foreign nations with whom we have existing treaties of navigation and commerce, and have caused wide and regrettable divergence of opinion in relation to the imposition of the duties referred to. These questions are important, and I shall make them the subject of a special and more detailed communication at the present session.

With the rapid increase of immigration to our shores and the facilities of modern travel, abuses of the generous privileges afforded by our naturalization laws call for their careful revision.

The easy and unguarded manner in which certificates of American citizenship can now be obtained has induced a class, unfortunately large, to avail themselves of the opportunity to become absolved from allegiance to their native land, and yet by a foreign residence to escape any just duty and contribution of service to the country of their proposed adoption. Thus, while evading the duties of citizenship to the United States, they may make prompt claim for its national protection and demand its intervention in their behalf. International complications of a serious nature arise, and the correspondence of the State Department discloses the great number and complexity of the questions which have been raised.

Our laws regulating the issue of passports should be carefully revised, and the institution of a central bureau of registration at the capital is again strongly recommended. By this means full particulars of each case of naturalization in the United States would be secured and properly indexed and recorded, and thus many cases of spurious citizenship would be detected and unjust responsibilities would be avoided.

The reorganization of the consular service is a matter of serious importance to our national interests. The number of existing principal consular offices is believed to be greater than is at all necessary for the conduct of the public business. It need not be our policy to maintain more than a moderate number of principal offices, each supported by a salary sufficient to enable the incumbent to live in comfort, and so distributed as to secure the convenient supervision, through subordinate agencies, of affairs over a considerable district.

I repeat the recommendations heretofore made by me that the appropriations for the maintenance of our diplomatic and consular service should be recast; that the so-called notarial or unofficial fees, which our representatives abroad are now permitted to treat as personal perquisites, should be forbidden; that a system of consular inspection should be instituted, and that a limited number of secretaries of legation at large should be authorized.

Preparations for the centennial celebration, on April 30, 1889, of the inauguration of George Washington as President of the United States, at the city of New York, have been made by a voluntary organization of the citizens of that locality, and believing that an opportunity should be afforded for the expression of the interest felt throughout the country in this event, I respectfully recommend fitting and cooperative action by Congress on behalf of the people of the United States.

The report of the Secretary of the Treasury exhibits in detail the condition of our national finances and the operations of the several branches of the Government related to his Department.

The total ordinary revenues of the Government for the fiscal year ended June 30, 1888, amounted to $379,266,074.76, of which $219,091,173.63 was received from customs duties and $124,296,871.98 from internal-revenue taxes.

The total receipts from all sources exceeded those for the fiscal year ended June 30, 1887, by $7,862,797.10.

The ordinary expenditures of the Government for the fiscal year ending June 30, 1888, were $259,653,958.67, leaving a surplus of $119,612,116.09.

The decrease in these expenditures as compared with the fiscal year ended June 30, 1887, was $8,278,221.30, notwithstanding the payment of more than $5,000,000 for pensions in excess of what was paid for that purpose in the latter-mentioned year.

The revenues of the Government for the year ending June 30, 1889, ascertained for the quarter ended September 30, 1888, and estimated for the remainder of the time, amount to $377,000,000, and the actual and estimated ordinary expenditures for the same year are $273,000,000, leaving an estimated surplus of $104,000,000.

The estimated receipts for the year ending June 30, 1890, are $377,000,000, and the estimated ordinary expenditures for the same time are $275,767,488.34, showing a surplus of $101,232,511.66.

The foregoing statements of surplus do not take into account the sum necessary to be expended to meet the requirements of the sinking-fund act, amounting to more than $47,000,000 annually.

The cost of collecting the customs revenues for the last fiscal year was 2.44 per cent; for the year 1885 it was 3.77 per cent.

The excess of internal-revenue taxes collected during the last fiscal year over those collected for the year ended June 30, 1887, was $5,489,-174.26, and the cost of collecting this revenue decreased from 3.4 per cent in 1887 to less than 3.2 per cent for the last year. The tax collected on oleomargarine was $723,948.04 for the year ending June 30, 1887, and $864,139.88 for the following year.

The requirements of the sinking-fund act have been met for the year ended June 30, 1888, and for the current year also, by the purchase of bonds. After complying with this law as positively required, and bonds sufficient for that purpose had been bought at a premium, it was not deemed prudent to further expend the surplus in such purchases until the authority to do so should be more explicit. A resolution, however, having been passed by both Houses of Congress removing all doubt as to Executive authority, daily purchases of bonds were commenced on the 23d day of April, 1888, and have continued until the present time. By this plan bonds of the Government not yet due have been purchased up to and including the 30th day of November, 1888, amounting to $94,-700,400, the premium paid thereon amounting to $17,508,613.08.

The premium added to the principal of these bonds represents an investment yielding about 2 per cent interest for the time they still had to run, and the saving to the Government represented by the difference between the amount of interest at 2 per cent upon the sum paid for principal and premium and what it would have paid for interest at the rate specified in the bonds if they had run to their maturity is about $27,165,000.

At first sight this would seem to be a profitable and sensible transaction on the part of the Government, but, as suggested by the Secretary of the Treasury, the surplus thus expended for the purchase of bonds was money drawn from the people in excess of any actual need of the Government and was so expended rather than allow it to remain idle in the Treasury. If this surplus, under the operation of just and equitable laws, had been left in the hands of the people, it would have been worth in their business at least 6 per cent per annum. Deducting from the amount of interest upon the principal and premium of these bonds for the time they had to run at the rate of 6 per cent the saving of 2 per cent made for the people by the purchase of such bonds, the loss will appear to be $55,760,000.

This calculation would seem to demonstrate that if excessive and unnecessary taxation is continued and the Government is forced to pursue this policy of purchasing its own bonds at the premiums which it will be necessary to pay, the loss to the people will be hundreds of millions of dollars.

Since the purchase of bonds was undertaken as mentioned nearly all that have been offered were at last accepted. It has been made quite apparent that the Government was in danger of being subjected to combinations to raise their price, as appears by the instance cited by the Secretary of the offering of bonds of the par value of only $326,000 so often that the aggregate of the sums demanded for their purchase amounted to more than $19,700,000.

Notwithstanding the large sums paid out in the purchase of bonds, the surplus in the Treasury on the 30th day of November, 1888, was $52,234,610.01, after deducting about $20,000,000 just drawn out for the payment of pensions.

At the close of the fiscal year ended June 30, 1887, there had been coined under the compulsory silver-coinage act $266,988,280 in silver dollars, $55,504,310 of which were in the hands of the people.

On the 30th day of June, 1888, there had been coined $299,708,790; and of this $55,829,303 was in circulation in coin, and $200,387,376 in silver certificates, for the redemption of which silver dollars to that amount were held by the Government.

On the 30th day of November, 1888, $312,570,990 had been coined, $60,970,990 of the silver dollars were actually in circulation, and $237,418,346 in certificates.

The Secretary recommends the suspension of the further coinage of silver, and in such recommendation I earnestly concur.

For further valuable information and timely recommendations I ask the careful attention of the Congress to the Secretary's report.

The Secretary of War reports that the Army at the date of the last consolidated returns consisted of 2,189 officers and 24,549 enlisted men.

The actual expenditures of the War Department for the fiscal year ended June 30, 1888, amounted to $41,165,107.07, of which sum $9,158,516.63 was expended for public works, including river and harbor improvements.

"The Board of Ordnance and Fortifications" provided for under the act approved September 22 last was convened October 30, 1888, and plans and specifications for procuring forgings for 8, 10, and 12 inch guns, under provisions of section 4, and also for procuring 12-inch breech-loading mortars, cast iron, hooped with steel, under the provisions of section 5 of the said act, were submitted to the Secretary of War for reference to the board, by the Ordnance Department, on the same date.

These plans and specifications having been promptly approved by the board and the Secretary of War, the necessary authority to publish advertisements inviting proposals in the newspapers throughout the country was granted by the Secretary on November 12, and on November 13 the advertisements were sent out to the different newspapers designated. The bids for the steel forgings are to be opened on December 20, 1888, and for the mortars on December 15, 1888.

A board of ordnance officers was convened at the Watervliet Arsenal on October 4, 1888, to prepare the necessary plans and specifications for the establishment of an army gun factory at that point. The preliminary report of this board, with estimates for shop buildings and officers' quarters, was approved by the Board of Ordnance and Fortifications November 6 and 8. The specifications and form of advertisement and instructions to bidders have been prepared, and advertisements inviting proposals for the excavations for the shop building and for erecting the two sets of officers' quarters have been published. The detailed drawings and specifications for the gun-factory building are well in hand, and will be finished within three or four months, when bids will be invited for the erection of the building. The list of machines, etc., is made out, and it is expected that the plans for the large lathes, etc., will be completed within about four months, and after approval by the Board of Ordnance and Fortifications bids for furnishing the same will be invited. The machines and other fixtures will be completed as soon as the shop is in readiness to receive them, probably about July, 1890.

Under the provisions of the Army bill for the procurement of pneumatic dynamite guns, the necessary specifications are now being prepared, and advertisements for proposals will issue early in December. The guns will probably be of 15 inches caliber and fire a projectile that will carry a charge each of about 500 pounds of explosive gelatine with full-caliber projectiles. The guns will probably be delivered in from six to ten months from the date of the contract, so that all the guns of this class that can be procured under the provisions of the law will be purchased during the year 1889.

I earnestly request that the recommendations contained in the Secretary's report, all of which are, in my opinion, calculated to increase the usefulness and discipline of the Army, may receive the consideration of the Congress. Among these the proposal that there should be provided a plan for the examination of officers to test their fitness for promotion is of the utmost importance. This reform has been before recommended in the reports of the Secretary, and its expediency is so fully demonstrated by the argument he presents in its favor that its adoption should no longer be neglected.

The death of General Sheridan in August last was a national affliction. The Army then lost the grandest of its chiefs. The country lost a brave and experienced soldier, a wise and discreet counselor, and a modest and sensible man. Those who in any manner came within the range of his personal association will never fail to pay deserved and willing homage to his greatness and the glory of his career, but they will cherish with more tender sensibility the loving memory of his simple, generous, and considerate nature.

The Apache Indians, whose removal from their reservation in Arizona followed the capture of those of their number who engaged in a bloody and murderous raid during a part of the years 1885 and 1886, are now held as prisoners of war at Mount Vernon Barracks, in the State of Alabama. They numbered on the 31st day of October, the date of the last report, 83 men, 170 women, 70 boys, and 59 girls; in all, 382 persons. The commanding officer states that they are in good health and contented, and that they are kept employed as fully as is possible in the circumstances. The children, as they arrive at a suitable age, are sent to the Indian schools at Carlisle and Hampton.

Last summer some charitable and kind people asked permission to send two teachers to these Indians for the purpose of instructing the adults as well as such children as should be found there. Such permission was readily granted, accommodations were provided for the teachers, and some portions of the buildings at the barracks were made available for school purposes. The good work contemplated has been commenced, and the teachers engaged are paid by the ladies with whom the plan originated.

I am not at all in sympathy with those benevolent but injudicious people who are constantly insisting that these Indians should be returned to their reservation. Their removal was an absolute necessity if the lives and property of citizens upon the frontier are to be at all regarded by the Government. Their continued restraint at a distance from the scene of their repeated and cruel murders and outrages is still necessary. It is a mistaken philanthropy, every way injurious, which prompts the desire to see these savages returned to their old haunts. They are in their present location as the result of the best judgment of those having official responsibility in the matter, and who are by no means lacking in kind consideration for the Indians. A number of these prisoners have forfeited their lives to outraged law and humanity. Experience has proved that they are dangerous and can not be trusted. This is true not only of those who on the warpath have heretofore actually been guilty of atrocious murder, but of their kindred and friends, who, while they remained upon their reservation, furnished aid and comfort to those absent with bloody intent.

These prisoners should be treated kindly and kept in restraint far from the locality of their former reservation; they should be subjected to efforts calculated to lead to their improvement and the softening of their savage and cruel instincts, but their return to their old home should be persistently resisted.

The Secretary in his report gives a graphic history of these Indians, and recites with painful vividness their bloody deeds and the unhappy failure of the Government to manage them by peaceful means. It will be amazing if a perusal of this history will allow the survival of a desire for the return of these prisoners to their reservation upon sentimental or any other grounds.

The report of the Secretary of the Navy demonstrates very intelligent

management in that important department, and discloses the most satisfactory progress in the work of reconstructing the Navy made during the
past year. Of the ships in course of construction five, viz, the *Charles-
ton*, *Baltimore*, *Yorktown*, *Vesuvius*, and the *Petrel*, have in that time
been launched and are rapidly approaching completion; and in addition
to the above, the *Philadelphia*, the *San Francisco*, the *Newark*, the *Ben-
nington*, the *Concord*, and the Herreshoff torpedo boat are all under contract for delivery to the Department during the next year. The progress
already made and being made gives good ground for the expectation that
these eleven vessels will be incorporated as part of the American Navy
within the next twelve months.

The report shows that notwithstanding the large expenditures for new
construction and the additional labor they involve the total ordinary or
current expenditures of the Department for the three years ending June
30, 1888, are less by more than 20 per cent than such expenditures for
the three years ending June 30, 1884.

The various steps which have been taken to improve the business
methods of the Department are reviewed by the Secretary. The purchasing of supplies has been consolidated and placed under a responsible
bureau head. This has resulted in the curtailment of open purchases,
which in the years 1884 and 1885 amounted to over 50 per cent of all
the purchases of the Department, to less than 11 per cent; so that at the
present time about 90 per cent of the total departmental purchases are
made by contract and after competition. As the expenditures on this
account exceed an average of $2,000,000 annually, it is evident that an
important improvement in the system has been inaugurated and substantial economies introduced.

The report of the Postmaster-General shows a marked increase of business in every branch of the postal service.

The number of post-offices on July 1, 1888, was 57,376, an increase of
6,124 in three years and of 2,219 for the last fiscal year. The latter-
mentioned increase is classified as follows:

New England States	
Middle States	181
Southern States and Indian Territory (41)	1,406
The States and Territories of the Pacific Coast	190
The ten States and Territories of the West and Northwest	435
District of Columbia	2
Total	2,219

Free-delivery offices have increased from 189 in the fiscal year ended
June 30, 1887, to 358 in the year ended June 30, 1888.

In the Railway Mail Service there has been an increase in one year of
168 routes, and in the number of miles traveled per annum an increase
of 15,795,917.48. The estimated increase of railroad service for the year
was 6,000 miles, but the amount of new railroad service actually put on
was 12,764.50 miles.

The volume of business in the Money-Order Division, including trans-actions in postal notes, reached the sum of upward of $143,000,000 for the year.

During the past year parcel-post conventions have been concluded with Barbados, the Bahamas, British Honduras, and Mexico, and are now under negotiation with all the Central and South American States. The increase of correspondence with foreign countries during the past three years is gratifying, and is especially notable and exceptional with the Central and South American States and with Mexico. As the greater part of mail matter exchanged with these countries is commercial in its character, this increase is evidence of the improved business relations with them. The practical operation of the parcel-post conventions, so far as negotiated, has served to fulfill the most favorable predictions as to their benefits. In January last a general postal convention was nego-tiated with the Dominion of Canada, which went into operation on March 1, and which practically makes one postal territory of the United States and Canada. Under it merchandise parcels may now be trans-mitted through the mails at fourth-class rates of postage.

It is not possible here to touch even the leading heads of the great postal establishment to illustrate the enormous and rapid growth of its business and the needs for legislative readjustment of much of its machin-ery that it has outgrown. For these and valuable recommendations of the Postmaster-General attention is earnestly invited to his report.

A Department whose revenues have increased from $19,772,000 in 1870 to $52,700,000 in 1888, despite reductions of postage which have enor-mously reduced rates of revenue while greatly increasing its business, demands the careful consideration of the Congress as to all matters sug-gested by those familiar with its operations, and which are calculated to increase its efficiency and usefulness.

A bill proposed by the Postmaster-General was introduced at the last session of the Congress by which a uniform standard in the amount of gross receipts would fix the right of a community to a public building to be erected by the Government for post-office purposes. It was demon-strated that, aside from the public convenience and the promotion of har-mony among citizens, invariably disturbed by change of leasings and of site, it was a measure of the highest economy and of sound business judgment. It was found that the Government was paying in rents at the rate of from 7 to 10 per cent per annum on what the cost of such public buildings would be. A very great advantage resulting from such a law would be the prevention of a large number of bills constantly intro-duced for the erection of public buildings at places, and involving expend-itures not justified by public necessity. I trust that this measure will become a law at the present session of Congress.

Of the total number of postmasters 54,874 are of the fourth class. These, of course, receive no allowances whatever for expenses in the service, and their compensation is fixed by percentages on receipts at their respective offices. This rate of compensation may have been, and probably was, at some time just, but the standard has remained unchanged through the several reductions in the rates of postage. Such reductions have necessarily cut down the compensation of these officials, while it undoubtedly increased the business performed by them. Simple justice requires attention to this subject, to the end that fourth-class postmasters may receive at least an equivalent to that which the law itself, fixing the rate, intended for them.

Another class of postal employees whose condition seems to demand legislation is that of clerks in post-offices, and I call especial attention to the repeated recommendations of the Postmaster-General for their classification. Proper legislation of this character for the relief of carriers in the free-delivery service has been frequent. Provision is made for their promotion; for substitutes for them on vacation; for substitutes for holidays, and limiting their hours of labor. Seven million dollars has been appropriated for the current year to provide for them, though the total number of offices where they are employed is but 358 for the past fiscal year, with an estimated increase for the current year of but 40, while the total appropriation for all clerks in offices throughout the United States is $5,950,00 .

The legislation affecting the relations of the Government with railroads is in need of revision. While for the most part the railroad companies throughout the country have cordially cooperated with the Post-Office Department in rendering excellent service, yet under the law as it stands, while the compensation to them for carrying the mail is limited and regulated, and although railroads are made post-roads by law, there is no authority reposed anywhere to compel the owner of a railroad to take and carry the United States mails. The only alternative provided by act of Congress in case of refusal is for the Postmaster-General to send mail forward by pony express. This is but an illustration of ill-fitting legislation, reasonable and proper at the time of its enactment, but long since outgrown and requiring readjustment.

It is gratifying to note from the carefully prepared statistics accompanying the Postmaster-General's report that notwithstanding the great expansion of the service the rate of expenditure has been lessened and efficiency has been improved in every branch; that fraud and crime have decreased; that losses from the mails have been reduced, and that the number of complaints of the service made to postmasters and to the Department are far less than ever before.

The transactions of the Department of Justice for the fiscal year ended June 30, 1888, are contained in the report of the Attorney-General, as well as a number of valuable recommendations, the most part of which are repetitions of those previously made, and ought to receive consideration. It is stated in this report that though judgments in civil suits amounting to $552,021.08 were recovered in favor of the Government during the year, only the sum of $132,934 was collected thereon; and that though fines, penalties, and forfeitures were imposed amounting to $541,808.43, only $109,648.42 of that sum was paid on account thereof. These facts may furnish an illustration of the sentiment which extensively prevails that a debt due the Government should cause no inconvenience to the citizen.

It also appears from this report that though prior to March, 1885, there had been but 6 convictions in the Territories of Utah and Idaho under the laws of 1862 and 1882, punishing polygamy and unlawful cohabitation as crimes, there have been since that date nearly 600 convictions under these laws and the statutes of 1887; and the opinion is expressed that under such a firm and vigilant execution of these laws and the advance of ideas opposed to the forbidden practices polygamy within the United States is virtually at an end.

Suits instituted by the Government under the provisions of the act of March 3, 1887, for the termination of the corporations known as the Perpetual Emigrating Fund Company and the Church of Jesus Christ of Latter-day Saints have resulted in a decree favorable to the Government, declaring the charters of these corporations forfeited and escheating their property. Such property, amounting in value to more than $800,000, is in the hands of a receiver pending further proceedings, an appeal having been taken to the Supreme Court of the United States.

In the report of the Secretary of the Interior, which will be laid before you, the condition of the various branches of our domestic affairs connected with that Department and its operations during the past year are fully exhibited. But a brief reference to some of the subjects discussed in this able and interesting report can here be made; but I commend the entire report to the attention of the Congress, and trust that the sensible and valuable recommendations it contains will secure careful consideration.

I can not too strenuously insist upon the importance of proper measures to insure a right disposition of our public lands, not only as a matter of present justice, but in forecast of the consequences to future generations. The broad, rich acres of our agricultural plains have been long preserved by nature to become her untrammeled gift to a people civilized and free, upon which should rest in well-distributed ownership the numerous homes of enlightened, equal, and fraternal citizens. They came to national possession with the warning example in our eyes of the entail of iniquities in landed proprietorship which other countries have permitted and still suffer. We have no excuse for the violation of principles cogently taught by reason and example, nor for the allowance of pretexts which have sometimes exposed our lands to colossal greed. Laws which open a door to fraudulent acquisition, or administration which permits favor to rapacious seizure by a favored few of expanded areas that many should enjoy, are accessory to offenses against our national welfare and humanity not to be too severely condemned or punished.

It is gratifying to know that something has been done at last to redress the injuries to our people and check the perilous tendency of the reckless waste of the national domain. That over 80,000,000 acres have been arrested from illegal usurpation, improvident grants, and fraudulent entries and claims, to be taken for the homesteads of honest industry—although less than the greater areas thus unjustly lost—must afford a profound gratification to right-feeling citizens, as it is a recompense for the labors and struggles of the recovery. Our dear experience ought sufficiently to urge the speedy enactment of measures of legislation which will confine the future disposition of our remaining agricultural lands to the uses of actual husbandry and genuine homes.

Nor should our vast tracts of so-called desert lands be yielded up to the monopoly of corporations or grasping individuals, as appears to be much the tendency under the existing statute. These lands require but the supply of water to become fertile and productive. It is a problem of great moment how most wisely for the public good that factor shall be furnished. I can not but think it perilous to suffer either these lands or the sources of their irrigation to fall into the hands of monopolies, which by such means may exercise lordship over the areas dependent on their treatment for productiveness. Already steps have been taken to secure accurate and scientific information of the conditions, which is the prime basis of intelligent action. Until this shall be gained the course of wisdom appears clearly to lie in a suspension of further disposal, which only promises to create rights antagonistic to the common interest. No harm can follow this cautionary conduct. The land will remain, and the public good presents no demand for hasty dispossession of national ownership and control.

I commend also the recommendations that appropriate measures be taken to complete the adjustment of the various grants made to the States for internal improvements and of swamp and overflowed lands, as well as to adjudicate and finally determine the validity and extent of the numerous private land claims. All these are elements of great injustice and peril to the settlers upon the localities affected; and now that their existence can not be avoided, no duty is more pressing than to fix as soon as possible their bounds and terminate the threats of trouble which arise from uncertainty.

The condition of our Indian population continues to improve and the proofs multiply that the transforming change, so much to be desired, which shall substitute for barbarism enlightenment and civilizing education, is in favorable progress. Our relations with these people during the year have been disturbed by no serious disorders, but rather marked by a better realization of their true interests and increasing confidence and good will. These conditions testify to the value of the higher tone of consideration and humanity which has governed the later methods of dealing with them, and commend its continued observance.

Allotments in severalty have been made on some reservations until all those entitled to land thereon have had their shares assigned, and the work is still continued. In directing the execution of this duty I have not aimed so much at rapid dispatch as to secure just and fair arrangements which shall best conduce to the objects of the law by producing satisfaction with the results of the allotments made. No measure of general effect has ever been entered on from which more may be fairly hoped if it shall be discreetly administered. It proffers opportunity and inducement to that independence of spirit and life which the Indian peculiarly needs, while at the same time the inalienability of title affords security against the risks his inexperience of affairs or weakness of character may expose him to in dealing with others. Whenever begun upon any reservation it should be made complete, so that all are brought to the same condition, and as soon as possible community in lands should cease by opening such as remain unallotted to settlement. Contact with the ways of industrious and successful farmers will perhaps add a healthy emulation which will both instruct and stimulate.

But no agency for the amelioration of this people appears to me so promising as the extension, urged by the Secretary, of such complete facilities of education as shall at the earliest possible day embrace all teachable Indian youth, of both sexes, and retain them with a kindly and beneficent hold until their characters are formed and their faculties and dispositions trained to the sure pursuit of some form of useful industry. Capacity of the Indian no longer needs demonstration. It is established. It remains to make the most of it, and when that shall be done the curse will be lifted, the Indian race saved, and the sin of their oppression redeemed. The time of its accomplishment depends upon the spirit and justice with which it shall be prosecuted. It can not be too soon for the Indian nor for the interests and good name of the nation.

The average attendance of Indian pupils on the schools increased by over 900 during the year, and the total enrollment reached 15,212. The cost of maintenance was not materially raised. The number of teachable Indian youth is now estimated at 40,000, or nearly three times the enrollment of the schools. It is believed the obstacles in the way of instructing are all surmountable, and that the necessary expenditure would be a measure of economy.

The Sioux tribes on the great reservation of Dakota refused to assent to the act passed by the Congress at its last session for opening a portion of their lands to settlement, notwithstanding modification of the terms was suggested which met most of their objections. Their demand is for immediate payment of the full price of $1.25 per acre for the entire body of land the occupancy of which they are asked to relinquish.

The manner of submission insured their fair understanding of the law, and their action was undoubtedly as thoroughly intelligent as their capacity admitted. It is at least gratifying that no reproach of over-reaching can in any manner lie against the Government, however advisable the favorable completion of the negotiation may have been esteemed.

I concur in the suggestions of the Secretary regarding the Turtle Mountain Indians, the two reservations in California, and the Crees. They should, in my opinion, receive immediate attention.

The number of pensioners added to the rolls during the fiscal year ended June 30, 1888, is 60,252, and increase of pensions was granted in 45,716 cases. The names of 15,730 pensioners were dropped from the rolls during the year from various causes, and at the close of the year the number of persons of all classes receiving pensions was 452,557. Of these there were 806 survivors of the War of 1812, 10,787 widows of those who served in that war, 16,060 soldiers of the Mexican War, and 5,104 widows of said soldiers.

One hundred and two different rates of pensions are paid to these beneficiaries, ranging from $2 to $416.66 per month.

The amount paid for pensions during the fiscal year was $78,775,861.92, being an increase over the preceding year of $5,308,280.22. The expenses attending the maintenance and operation of the Pension Bureau during that period was $3,262,524.67, making the entire expenditures of the Bureau $82,038,386.57, being 21½ per cent of the gross income and nearly 31 per cent of the total expenditures of the Government during the year.

I am thoroughly convinced that our general pension laws should be revised and adjusted to meet as far as possible, in the light of our experience, all meritorious cases. The fact that 102 different rates of pensions are paid can not, in my opinion, be made consistent with justice to the pensioners or to the Government; and the numerous private pension bills that are passed, predicated upon the imperfection of general laws, while they increase in many cases existing inequality and injustice, lend additional force to the recommendation for a revision of the general laws on this subject.

The laxity of ideas prevailing among a large number of our people regarding pensions is becoming every day more marked. The principles upon which they should be granted are in danger of being altogether ignored, and already pensions are often claimed because the applicants are as much entitled as other successful applicants, rather than upon any disability reasonably attributable to military service. If the establishment of vicious precedents be continued, if the granting of pensions be not divorced from partisan and other unworthy and irrelevant considerations, and if the honorable name of veteran unfairly becomes by these means but another term for one who constantly clamors for the aid of the Government, there is danger that injury will be done to the fame and patriotism of many whom our citizens all delight to honor, and that a prejudice will be aroused unjust to meritorious applicants for pensions.

The Department of Agriculture has continued, with a good measure of success, its efforts to develop the processes, enlarge the results, and augment the profits of American husbandry. It has collected and distributed practical information, introduced and tested new plants, checked the spread of contagious diseases of farm animals, resisted the advance of noxious insects and destructive fungous growths, and sought to secure to agricultural labor the highest reward of effort and the fullest immunity from loss. Its records of the year show that the season of 1888 has been one of medium production. A generous supply of the demands of consumption has been assured, and a surplus for exportation, moderate in certain products and bountiful in others, will prove a benefaction alike to buyer and grower.

Four years ago it was found that the great cattle industry of the country was endangered, and those engaged in it were alarmed at the rapid extension of the European lung plague of pleuro-pneumonia. Serious outbreaks existed in Illinois, Missouri, and Kentucky, and in Tennessee animals affected were held in quarantine. Five counties in New York and from one to four counties in each of the States of New Jersey, Pennsylvania, Delaware, and Maryland were almost equally affected.

With this great danger upon us and with the contagion already in the channels of commerce, with the enormous direct and indirect losses already being caused by it, and when only prompt and energetic action could be successful, there were in none of these States any laws authorizing this Department to eradicate the malady or giving the State officials power to cooperate with it for this purpose. The Department even lacked both the requisite appropriation and authority.

By securing State cooperation in connection with authority from Congress the work of eradication has been pressed successfully, and this dreaded disease has been extirpated from the Western States and also from the Eastern States, with the exception of a few restricted areas, which are still under supervision. The danger has thus been removed, and trade and commerce have been freed from the vexatious State restrictions which were deemed necessary for a time.

During the past four years the process of diffusion, as applied to the manufacture of sugar from sorghum and sugar cane, has been introduced into this country and fully perfected by the experiments carried on by the Department of Agriculture. This process is now universally considered to be the most economical one, and it is through it that the sorghum-sugar industry has been established upon a firm basis and the road to its future success opened. The adoption of this diffusion process is also extending in Louisiana and other sugar-producing parts of the country, and will doubtless soon be the only method employed for the extraction of sugar from the cane.

An exhaustive study has also within the same period been undertaken of the subject of food adulteration and the best analytical methods for detecting it. A part of the results of this work has already been published by the Department, which, with the matter in course of preparation, will make the most complete treatise on that subject that has ever been published in any country.

The Department seeks a progressive development. It would combine the discoveries of science with the economics and amelioration of rural practice. A supervision of the endowed experimental-station system recently provided for is a proper function of the Department, and is now in operation. This supervision is very important, and should be wisely and vigilantly directed, to the end that the pecuniary aid of the Government in favor of intelligent agriculture should be so applied as to result in the general good and to the benefit of all our people, thus justifying the appropriations made from the public Treasury.

The adjustment of the relations between the Government and the railroad companies which have received land grants and the guaranty of the public credit in aid of the construction of their roads should receive early attention. The report of a majority of the commissioners appointed to examine the affairs and indebtedness of these roads, in which they favor an extension of the time for the payment of such indebtedness in at least one case where the corporation appears to be able to comply with well-guarded and exact terms of such extension, and the reenforcement of their opinion by gentlemen of undoubted business judgment and experience, appointed to protect the interests of the Government as directors of said corporation, may well lead to the belief that such an extension would be to the advantage of the Government.

The subject should be treated as a business proposition with a view to a final realization of its indebtedness by the Government, rather than as a question to be decided upon prejudice or by way of punishment for previous wrongdoing.

The report of the Commissioners of the District of Columbia, with its accompanying documents, gives in detail the operations of the several departments of the District government, and furnishes evidence that the financial affairs of the District are at present in such satisfactory condition as to justify the Commissioners in submitting to the Congress estimates for desirable and needed improvements.

The Commissioners recommend certain legislation which in their opinion is necessary to advance the interests of the District.

I invite your special attention to their request for such legislation as will enable the Commissioners without delay to collect, digest, and properly arrange the laws by which the District is governed, and which are now embraced in several collections, making them available only with great difficulty and labor. The suggestions they make touching desirable amendments to the laws relating to licenses granted for carrying on the retail traffic in spirituous liquors, to the observance of Sunday, to the proper assessment and collection of taxes, to the speedy punishment of minor offenders, and to the management and control of the reformatory and charitable institutions supported by Congressional appropriations are commended to careful consideration.

I again call attention to the present inconvenience and the danger to life and property attending the operation of steam railroads through and across the public streets and roads of the District. The propriety of such legislation as will properly guard the use of these railroads and better secure the convenience and safety of citizens is manifest.

The consciousness that I have presented but an imperfect statement of the condition of our country and its wants occasions no fear that anything omitted is not known and appreciated by the Congress, upon whom rests the responsibility of intelligent legislation in behalf of a great nation and a confiding people.

As public servants we shall do our duty well if we constantly guard the rectitude of our intentions, maintain unsullied our love of country, and with unselfish purpose strive for the public good.

GROVER CLEVELAND.

SPECIAL MESSAGES

To the Congress: EXECUTIVE MANSION, *December 21, 1888.*

On the 2d of April last I transmitted to the House of Representatives, in response to its resolution of the 8th of the preceding March, a report of the Secretary of State, with accompanying correspondence, relative to affairs in Samoa.* On the same day I answered a resolution of the Senate of the 21st of the preceding December to the same effect, but adopted in executive session, and, in order to avoid duplication of the numerous documents involved, referred to the correspondence which accompanied my public response to the resolution of the House of Representatives, and which was duly printed and published by order of that body (House Executive Document No. 238, Fiftieth Congress, first session).

In my annual message of the 3d instant I announced my intention in due course to lay before Congress further correspondence on Samoan affairs. Accordingly, I now transmit a report of the Secretary of State, with accompanying correspondence, on that subject.

GROVER CLEVELAND.

*See p. 5199.

To the Senate:

On or about the 25th day of September, 1888, I received a copy of a resolution adopted on that day by the Senate in executive session, requesting the transmission to that body by the President of all communications and correspondence (not heretofore sent to the Senate) under his control on the subject of the proposed convention with China, transmitted by him to the Senate by message dated 16th March, 1888,* and on the subject of the reported failure of the Government of China to finally agree to the same.

A few days after the copy of said resolution was received by me, and on the 1st day of October, 1888, I sent a communication to the Congress,† accompanying my approval of a bill prohibiting the return of Chinese laborers to the United States, in which I supposed all the information sought under the terms of the Senate resolution above recited was fully supplied.

I beg to refer in this connection to Senate Executive Document No. 273, first session of the Fiftieth Congress, and especially to page 3 thereof.

Believing the information contained in said document answered the purposes of said Senate resolution, no separate and explicit answer was made thereto.

But in my message of October 1, 1888, the tenor and purport of a cipher dispatch from our minister in China to the Secretary of State, dated September 21, 1888, was given instead of attempting to transmit a copy of the same.

For greater precision, however, and with the object of answering in more exact terms the resolution of the Senate, I transmit with this, in paraphrase of the cipher, a copy of the said dispatch. I also transmit copies of two notes which accompanied my message of October 1, 1888, one from Mr. Shu Cheon Pon, chargé d'affaires of the Chinese legation in this city, dated September 25, 1888, to the Secretary of State, and the other being the reply thereto by the Secretary of State, dated September 26, 1888, both of which will be found in Senate Executive Document No. 273.

The dispatch and notes above referred to comprise, in the language of the Senate resolution, "all communications and correspondence" the transmission of which is therein requested.

GROVER CLEVELAND.

EXECUTIVE MANSION, *January 3, 1889.*

To the Senate and House of Representatives:

I transmit herewith for the consideration of the Congress a report of the Secretary of State, with accompanying papers, recommending an appropriation for the relief of Japanese subjects injured and of the families of Japanese subjects killed on the island of Ikisima in consequence of target practice directed against the shore by the United States man-of-war *Omaha* in March, 1887.

GROVER CLEVELAND.

EXECUTIVE MANSION, *January 3, 1889.*

To the Senate:

I desire to supplement the message yesterday sent to your honorable body in response to a Senate executive resolution dated September 25, 1888, asking the transmission of certain communications and correspondence on the subject of the recent proposed convention with China and the reported failure of the Government of China to finally agree to the same, by adding to said response two telegrams I omitted therefrom, which were sent in cipher by the Secretary of State to our minister at Peking, and which may be considered by the Senate relevant to the subject of its inquiry.

One of said dispatches is as follows:

WASHINGTON, *September 4, 1888.*

DENBY,
   Minister, Peking:

Rejection of treaty is reported here.   What information have you?

BAYARD.

Two replies to this dispatch were made by our minister to China, dated, respectively, September 5 and September 6, 1888.   They were heretofore, and on September 7, 1888,* sent to the Senate, and are printed in Senate Executive Document No. 271.

The other of said dispatches is as follows:

WASHINGTON, *September 18, 1888.*

DENBY,
   Minister, Peking:

The bill has passed both Houses of Congress for total exclusion of Chinese and awaits President's approval.   Public feeling on the Pacific Coast excited in favor of it, and situation is critical.   Impress upon Government of China necessity for instant decision in the interest of treaty relations and amity.

BAYARD.

The answer of our minister at Peking to this dispatch, dated September 21, 1888, was yesterday sent to the Senate with the message to which this is a supplement.

The matters herein contained are now transmitted, to the end that they may, if deemed pertinent, be added to the response already made to the Senate resolution of inquiry, and with the intent that in any view of the subject the answer to said resolution may be full and complete.

GROVER CLEVELAND.

* See p. 5212.

EXECUTIVE MANSION,
Washington, January 7, 1889.

To the Senate:

I transmit, with a view to its ratification, an agreement signed by the plenipotentiaries of the United States and Denmark on the 6th ultimo, submitting to arbitration the claim of Carlos Butterfield & Co. against the Government of Denmark for indemnity for the seizure and detention of the steamer *Ben Franklin* and the bark *Catherine Augusta* by the authorities of the island of St. Thomas, of the Danish West India Islands, in the years 1854 and 1855; for the refusal of the ordinary right to land cargo for the purpose of making repairs; for the injuries resulting from a shot fired into one of the vessels, and for other wrongs. I also transmit a report from the Secretary of State inclosing the recent correspondence between the two Governments in regard to the claim.

GROVER CLEVELAND.

EXECUTIVE MANSION, *January 14, 1889.*

To the Senate and House of Representatives:

Whereas, by virtue of the provisions of the act of Congress approved June 22, 1860 (12 U. S. Statutes at Large, p. 73), entitled "An act to carry into effect provisions of the treaties between the United States, China, Japan, Siam, Persia, and other countries giving certain judicial powers to ministers and consuls or other functionaries of the United States in those countries, and for other purposes," Charles Denby, minister of the United States at Peking, has formally promulgated, under date of August 18, 1888, additional regulations governing the rendition of judgments by confession in the consular courts of the United States in China, the same having been previously assented to by all the consular officers of this Government in that Empire:

Now, therefore, in accordance with section 4119 of the Revised Statutes of the United States, being the sixth section of the act above mentioned, and which directs that all such regulations shall be transmitted to the Secretary of State, "to be laid before Congress for revision," I do herewith transmit to Congress a copy of Mr. Denby's dispatch No. 754, of November 5, 1888, containing the regulations so decreed.

GROVER CLEVELAND.

EXECUTIVE MANSION, *January 14, 1889.*

To the Senate and House of Representatives:

I transmit herewith, for the consideration of Congress and such legislation in respect of the matters therein presented as may seem necessary and proper, a report of the Secretary of State, with accompanying explanatory correspondence, in reference to the international questions arising from the imposition of differential rates of tonnage dues upon vessels entering ports of the United States from foreign countries under the provisions of the fourteenth section of the act of June 26, 1884, and the later amendatory provisions of the act of June 19, 1886, as set forth in said report.

GROVER CLEVELAND.

To the Congress: EXECUTIVE MANSION, *January 15, 1889.*

On the 2d day of April, 1888, I transmitted to the House of Representatives, in response to a resolution passed by that body, a report from the Secretary of State, relating to the condition of affairs in the Samoan Islands, together with numerous letters, dispatches, and documents connected with the subject, which gave a history of all disorders in that locality up to that date.[*]

On the 21st day of December, 1888, this information was supplemented by the transmission to the Congress of such further correspondence and documents as extended this history to that time.[†]

I now submit a report from the Secretary of State, with later correspondence and dispatches, exhibiting the progress of the disturbances in Samoa up to the present date.

The information thus laid before the Congress is of much importance, since it has relation to the preservation of American interests and the protection of American citizens and their property in a distant locality and under an unstable and unsatisfactory government.

In the midst of the disturbances which have arisen at Samoa such powers have been exercised as seemed to be within Executive control under our Constitution and laws, and which appear to accord with our national policy and traditions, to restore tranquillity and secure the safety of our citizens.

Through negotiation and agreement with Great Britain and Germany, which, with our own Government, constitute the treaty powers interested in Samoan peace and quiet, the attempt has been made to define more clearly the part which these powers should assume in the Government of that country, while at the same time its autonomy has been insisted upon.

These negotiations were at one time interrupted by such action on the part of the German Government as appeared to be inconsistent with their further continuance.

Germany, however, still asserts, as from the first she has done, that she has no desire or intention to overturn the native Samoan Government or to ignore our treaty rights, and she still invites our Government to join her in restoring peace and quiet. But thus far her propositions on this subject seem to lead to such a preponderance of German power in Samoa as was never contemplated by us and is inconsistent with every prior

[*] See p. 5197. [†] See p. 5385.

agreement or understanding, while her recent conduct as between native warring factions gives rise to the suspicion that she is not content with a neutral position.

Acting within the restraints which our Constitution and laws have placed upon Executive power, I have insisted that the autonomy and independence of Samoa should be scrupulously preserved according to the treaties made with Samoa by the powers named and their agreements and understanding with each other. I have protested against every act apparently tending in an opposite direction, and during the existence of internal disturbance one or more vessels of war have been kept in Samoan waters to protect American citizens and property.

These things will abundantly appear from the correspondence and papers which have been submitted to the Congress.

A recent collision between the forces from a German man-of-war stationed in Samoan waters and a body of natives rendered the situation so delicate and critical that the war ship *Trenton*, under the immediate command of Admiral Kimberly, was ordered to join the *Nipsic*, already at Samoa, for the better protection of the persons and property of our citizens and in furtherance of efforts to restore order and safety.

The attention of the Congress is especially called to the instructions given to Admiral Kimberly dated on the 11th instant and the letter of the Secretary of State to the German minister dated the 12th instant, which will be found among the papers herewith submitted.

By means of the papers and documents heretofore submitted and those which accompany this communication the precise situation of affairs in Samoa is laid before the Congress, and such Executive action as has been taken is fully exhibited.

The views of the Executive in respect of the just policy to be pursued with regard to this group of islands, which lie in the direct highway of a growing and important commerce between Australia and the United States, have found expression in the correspondence and documents which have thus been fully communicated to the Congress, and the subject in its present stage is submitted to the wider discretion conferred by the Constitution upon the legislative branch of the Government.

GROVER CLEVELAND.

EXECUTIVE MANSION, *January 15, 1889.*
To the Senate of the United States:

I transmit herewith, in response to the resolution of the Senate of the 4th instant, a report of the Secretary of State, with accompanying copies of correspondence, touching recent occurrences in the island of Hayti, both as relates to the state of the Government there and to the seizure and delivery up of the American vessel *Haytien Republic.*

GROVER CLEVELAND.

EXECUTIVE MANSION, *January 16, 1889.*

To the Senate and House of Representatives:

I have the honor to lay before you a report from the Secretary of State, with accompanying correspondence, in relation to the possible disturbances on the Isthmus of Panama in the event of the stoppage of work on the proposed interoceanic canal.   GROVER CLEVELAND.

EXECUTIVE MANSION, *January 21, 1889.*

To the Senate of the United States:

I transmit herewith, in response to a resolution of the Senate of the 5th instant, a report of the Secretary of State, touching correspondence with Venezuela in regard to the exchange of ratifications of the claims convention of December 5, 1885, between the United States and Venezuela and to the suspension by Venezuela of the monthly quotas of indebtedness under the convention between the two countries of April 25, 1866, together with copies of sundry correspondence between the Department of State and owners of Venezuelan certificates of award or their attorneys on the same subject, as requested in said resolution.

GROVER CLEVELAND.

EXECUTIVE MANSION, *January 30, 1889.*

To the Senate and the House of Representatives:

For the information of Congress I herewith transmit a report of the Secretary of State, with accompanying correspondence, relating to the execution of an agreement made between the representatives of certain foreign powers and the Korean Government in 1884 in respect to a foreign settlement at Chemulpo.   GROVER CLEVELAND.

EXECUTIVE MANSION, *January 30, 1889.*

To the Congress:

I had the honor on the 15th instant to communicate to your honorable body certain correspondence and documents in relation to affairs in the Samoan Islands;* and having since that date received further dispatches from the vice-consul at Apia and the commander of the United States naval vessel *Nipsic* in those waters, I lose no time in laying them before you.

I also transmit herewith the full text of an instruction from Prince von Bismarck to the German minister at this capital, which was communicated to the Secretary of State on the afternoon of the 28th instant.

This appears to be an amplification of a prior telegraphic instruction on the same subject communicated through the same channel, and, being set forth in the note of the Secretary of State to Count von Arco-Valley,

* See pp. 5389-5390.

the German minister, of the 12th instant, was duly laid before Congress with my last message in relation to Samoan affairs.

It is also proper to inform you that on Monday, the 28th instant, the occasion of the communication of the note of the Prince Chancellor, the Secretary of State was given to understand by the German minister that a proposition from his Government to that of the United States for a conference on the Samoan subject was on its way by mail, having left Berlin on the 20th instant, so that its arrival here in due course of mail could be looked for in a very short time.

In reply to an inquiry from the Secretary of State whether the proposition referred to was for a renewal of the joint conference between the United States, Germany, and Great Britain which was suspended in July, 1887, or for a consideration of Samoan affairs *ab novo*, the German minister stated his inability to answer until the proposition which left Berlin on the 20th instant should have been received.

I shall hereafter communicate to the Congress all information received by me in relation to the Samoan status.

GROVER CLEVELAND.

EXECUTIVE MANSION,
Washington, February 1, 1889.

To the Senate and House of Representatives:

As supplementary to my previous messages on the subject, I have now the honor to transmit a report from the Secretary of State relating to affairs in Samoa.

GROVER CLEVELAND.

EXECUTIVE MANSION, *February 5, 1889.*

To the Congress:

I transmit herewith, for approval and ratification, a provisional agreement lately entered into between the Government of the United States and the Creek Nation of Indians, through their duly authorized representatives, and which has been approved by the National Council of said nation, by which agreement the title and interest of the said Creek Nation of Indians in and to all lands in the Indian Territory or elsewhere, except such as are held and occupied as the homes of said nation, are ceded to the United States.

The eighth section of the Indian appropriation bill approved March 3, 1885, authorized the President "to open negotiations with the Creeks, Seminoles, and Cherokees for the purpose of opening to settlement under the homestead laws the unassigned lands in the Indian Territory ceded by them respectively to the United States by the several treaties of August 11, 1866, March 21, 1866, and July 19, 1866." This section also contains an appropriation in furtherance of its purpose, and requires that the action of the President thereunder should be reported to Congress.

The "unassigned" lands thus referred to should be construed to be those which have not been transferred by the United States in pursuance of the treaties mentioned in the section quoted.

The treaty with the Creeks is dated June 14, 1866. It was confirmed by a Senate resolution passed July 19, 1866, and was proclaimed August 11, 1866 (14 U. S. Statutes at Large, p. 785).

The third article of the treaty makes a cession of lands in the following words:

In compliance with the desire of the United States to locate other Indians and freedmen thereon, the Creeks hereby cede and convey to the United States, to be sold to and used as homes for such other civilized Indians as the United States may choose to settle thereon, the west half of their entire domain, to be divided by a line running north and south; the eastern half of said Creek lands, being retained by them, shall, except as herein otherwise stipulated, be forever set apart as a home for said Creek Nation; and in consideration of said cession of the west half of their lands, estimated to contain 3,250,560 acres, the United States agree to pay the sum of 30 cents per acre, amounting to $975,168.

The provision that the lands conveyed were "*to be sold to* and used as homes for such other civilized Indians," etc., has been steadily regarded as a limitation upon the grant made to the United States. Such a construction is admitted to be the true one in many ways, especially by the continual reservation of the ceded lands from settlement by the whites, by the sale of a portion of the same to Indians, by the use of other portions as the home of Indians, and also by various provisions in proposed legislation in Congress. Thus the bill now pending for the organization of Oklahoma provides for the payment to the Creeks and Seminoles of the ordinary Government price of $1.25 per acre, less the amount heretofore paid.

The section of the law of 1885 first above quoted appears also to have been passed in contemplation not only of the existence of a claim on the part of the Creeks, but of the substantial foundation of that claim in equity, if not in law, and in acknowledgment of the duty of the Government to satisfactorily discharge the claim of the Indian people before putting the land to the free uses of settlement and territorial occupation by whites.

But it seems to have been considered that so far as the lands had been assigned they may fairly be taken to be such as under the treaty were "to be sold," As to these, they having been assigned or "sold" in accordance with said treaty, the claim of the Creeks thereto has been entirely discharged, and the title from the United States passed unburdened with any condition or limitation to the grantees. This seems to be an entirely clear proposition.

The unassigned lands must be those which are unsold, because not only is that the fair significance of the term, as used technically in conveyancing, but because the limiting condition in the Creek treaty was that the lands should be sold to, as well as used as homes for, other Indians.

The total quantity of lands in the western half of the Creek Nation, and which were ceded in 1866, is.. 3,402,428.88 Acres.

The assigned lands as above defined are in three bodies:

1. The Seminole country, by the treaty of 1866 .... 200,000.00 Acres.
2. The Sac and Fox Reservation, sold and conveyed by article 6 of the treaty of February 18, 1867 (15 U. S. Statutes at Large, p. 495), amounting to............................... 479,668.05
3. The Pawnee Reservation, granted by section 4 of the act of Congress of April 10, 1876 (19 U. S. Statutes at Large, p. 29), for which the Government received the price allowed the Creeks, 30 cents per acre.................................... 53,005.94

Making a total of assigned or sold lands of............................. 732,673.99

And leaving as the total unassigned lands 2,669,754.89

Of this total quantity of unassigned land which is subject to the negotiations provided for under the law of 1885 there should be a further division made in considering the sum which ought fairly to be paid in discharge of the Creek claim thereto.

I. In that part of these lands called the Oklahoma country no Indians have been allowed to reside by any action of the Government, nor has any execution been attempted of the limiting condition of the cession of 1866.

The quantity of these lands carefully computed from the surveys is 1,392,704.70 acres.

II. The remainder of these unassigned lands has been appropriated in some degree to Indian uses, although still within the control of the Government.

Thus by three Executive orders the following Indian reservations have been created:

1. By President Grant, August 10, 1869, the reservation of the Cheyennes and Arapahoes, which embraces of this land............................... 619,450.59 Acres.
2. By President Arthur, August 15, 1883, the reservation for the Iowas, containing.. 228,417.67
3. By President Arthur, August 15, 1883, the Kickapoo Reservation, embracing.. 206,465.61
4. A tract set apart for the Pottawatomies by the treaty of February 27, 1867 (15 U. S. Statutes at Large, p. 531), followed by the act of May 23, 1872 (17 U. S. Statutes at Large, p. 159), by which individual allotments were authorized upon the tract, though but very few Indians have selected and paid for such allotments according to the provisions of that law. The entire quantity of the Pottawatomie Reservation is.................... 222,716.32

This shows the quantity of lands unassigned, but to some extent appropriated to Indian uses by the Government, amounting to....... 1,277,050.19

For the lands which are not only unassigned, but are unoccupied, and which have been in no way appropriated, it appears clearly just and right that a price of at least $1.25 should be allowed to the Creeks. They held more than the ordinary Indian title, for they had a patent in fee from the Government. The Osages of Kansas were allowed $1.25 per acre upon giving up their reservation, and this land of the Creeks is reported by those familiar with it to be equal to any land in the country. Without regard to the present enhanced value of this land, and if reference be only had to the conditions when the cession was made, no less price ought to be paid for it than the ordinary Government price. Therefore in this provisional agreement which has been made with the Creeks the price of $1.25 has been settled upon for such land, with the deduction of the 30 cents per acre which has already been paid by the Government therefor.

As to the remainder of the unassigned lands, in view of the fact that some use has been made of them of the general character indicated by the treaty of 1866, and because some portion of them should be allotted to Indians under the general allotment act, and to cover the expenses of surveys and adjustments, a diminishment of 20 cents per acre has been acceded to. There is no difference in the character of the lands.

Thus, computing the unassigned and entirely unappropriated land, being the Oklahoma country, containing 1,392,704.70 acres, at 95 cents per acre, and the remainder which has been appropriated to the extent above stated, being 1,277,050.19 acres, at 75 cents per acre, the total price stipulated in the agreement has been reached—$2,280,857.10.

But as it was desirable that the Indian title should be beyond all question extinguished to all parts of the land ceded by the Creeks in 1866, with their full consent and understanding, the agreement of cession has been made to embrace a complete surrender of all claim to the western half of their domain, including the assigned as well as the unassigned lands, for the price named. So the agreement takes the form in the first article of such a cession, and in the second article is stipulated the price in gross of all the lands and interests ceded, with no detailed reference to the manner of its ascertainment.

The overtures which led to this agreement were made by representatives of the Creek Nation, who came here for that purpose. They were intelligent and evidently loyal to the interests of their people. The terms of the agreement were fully discussed and concessions were made by both parties. It was promptly confirmed by the National Council of the Creek Indians, and its complete consummation only waits the approval of the Congress of the United States.

I am convinced that such ratification will be of decided benefit to the Government, and that the agreement is entirely free from any suspicion of unfairness or injustice toward the Indians.

I desire to call especial attention to the fact that to become effective the agreement must be ratified by the Congress prior to the 1st day of July, 1889.

The draft of an act of ratification is herewith submitted.

GROVER CLEVELAND.

EXECUTIVE MANSION, *February 8, 1889.*
To the Senate and House of Representatives:

I transmit herewith a further report of the Secretary of State, with accompanying correspondence, relating to Samoa, and the joint protocols of the conferences held in this city in the summer of 1887, to the publication of which the Governments of Germany and Great Britain have consented.

GROVER CLEVELAND.

EXECUTIVE MANSION, *February 8, 1889.*

To the Senate:

In response to the resolution of the Senate of the 23d ultimo, directing the Secretary of State to transmit to that body copies of all correspondence on the files of his Department relative to the case of the ship *Bridgewater*, I transmit herewith, being of the opinion that it is not incompatible with the public interest to do so, a report from the Secretary of State, accompanying which is the correspondence referred to.

GROVER CLEVELAND.

EXECUTIVE MANSION, *February 12, 1889.*

To the Senate:

I herewith transmit, in reply to the resolution of the Senate of the 2d ultimo, a report from the Secretary of State, with the accompanying documents, in relation to the seal fisheries in Bering Sea.

GROVER CLEVELAND.

EXECUTIVE MANSION, *February 19, 1889.*

To the Congress:

I herewith submit, for your consideration, a communication from the Secretary of the Interior, transmitting a proposition made on behalf of the Seminole Nation of Indians for the relinquishment to the Government of the United States of their right to certain lands in the Indian Territory.

GROVER CLEVELAND.

EXECUTIVE MANSION, *February 19, 1889.*

To the Senate of the United States:

In compliance with a resolution of the Senate of the 18th instant, I return herewith the bill (S. 3640) entitled "An act to amend the laws relating to the selection and service of jurors in the supreme court of the District of Columbia."

GROVER CLEVELAND.

EXECUTIVE MANSION, *February 20, 1889.*

To the Senate and House of Representatives:

I transmit herewith a report of the Secretary of State of this day's date, with accompanying correspondence, touching the case of Lord Sackville.*

GROVER CLEVELAND.

* The British minister at Washington, who was given his passports for writing an indiscreet letter on American politics.

EXECUTIVE MANSION,
Washington, February 22, 1889.

To the Senate:

I transmit herewith, with a view to its ratification, a convention signed on the 2d day of June, 1887, between the United States and the Netherlands, for the extradition of criminals; also a report from the Secretary of State, and accompanying papers, relating to the said convention.

GROVER CLEVELAND.

EXECUTIVE MANSION,
Washington, February 27, 1889.

To the Senate:

I herewith transmit, for the consideration of the Senate with a view to its ratification, a convention signed at Washington the 18th instant, between the United States and Mexico, to revive the provisions of the convention of July 29, 1882, to survey and relocate the existing boundary line between the two countries west of the Rio Grande, and to extend the time fixed in Article VIII of the said convention for the completion of the work in question.

Although the present convention fully explains the reasons for its negotiation, it may not be improper here to add that Article VII of the convention of July 29, 1882, stipulated that the said convention should continue in force until the completion of the work, "provided that such time does not exceed four years and four months from the date of the exchange of ratifications hereof."

The exchange of ratifications took place March 3, 1883, and the period within which the convention was in force ended July 3, 1887.

In order, therefore, to continue the provisions of the said convention of July 29, 1882, an additional article concluded at Washington December 5, 1885, further extended the time for the completion of the work for "eighteen months from the expiration of the term fixed in Article VIII of the said treaty of July 29, 1882," or until January 3, 1889.

As there was no further provision extending the said treaty of July 29, 1882, beyond that date, it expired by limitation. Hence the necessity for the convention of the 18th instant in its present form.

GROVER CLEVELAND.

EXECUTIVE MANSION,
Washington, February 27, 1889.

To the Senate:

I transmit herewith, in confidence, for the information of the Senate, a report from the Secretary of State, showing the progress of the correspondence in relation to the conference to be held at Berlin between the Governments of the United States, Germany, and Great Britain to settle the affairs of the Samoan Islands.

The nature of this information and the stage of the negotiations thus agreed upon and about to commence at Berlin make it proper that such report should be communicated to the Senate in the confidence of execu‧tive session.

As the conference has been proposed and accepted and the definitive bases of its proceedings agreed upon by all three Governments and on the lines with which the Senate has heretofore been made fully acquainted, nothing remains to be done but to select and appoint the commissioners to represent the United States, and the performance of this duty, in view of the few days that now remain of my term of office, can be most prop‧erly left to my successor.

In response to the inquiry of the German minister at this capital whether the names of the proposed representatives of the United States at the conference in Berlin could at once be given to him, he has been informed that the appointments in question would be made by my suc‧cessor and not by me, and that in coming to this decision the expedition desired by Germany in the work of the conference would in my judgment be promoted.

GROVER CLEVELAND.

EXECUTIVE MANSION,
Washington, February 27, 1889.

To the Senate:

I transmit, with a view to its ratification, a convention for the extradi‧tion of criminals, signed by the plenipotentiaries of the United States and Russia on the 28th day of March, 1887, also a report from the Secretary of State and accompanying papers relating to the negotiations which terminated in the conclusion of the treaty in question.

GROVER CLEVELAND.

EXECUTIVE MANSION,
Washington, February 27, 1889.

To the Senate:

I herewith transmit a report of the Secretary of State and accompa‧nying documents, relative to a naturalization treaty between the United States and Turkey signed the 11th day of August, 1874, as to the proc‧lamation of which the advice of the Senate is desired. The advice and consent of the Senate were given to the ratification of the convention on the 22d of January, 1875, but with certain amendments which were not fully accepted by the Ottoman Porte. Because of such nonacceptance the treaty has never been proclaimed. Finally the Turkish Government, after the passage of fourteen years, has accepted the amendments as ten‧dered. But in view of the long period that has elapsed since the Senate formerly considered the treaty I have deemed it wiser that before pro‧claiming it the Senate should have an opportunity to act upon the matter again, my own views being wholly favorable to the proclamation.

GROVER CLEVELAND.

EXECUTIVE MANSION,
Washington, February 27, 1889.

To the House of Representatives:

I transmit herewith, in response to the resolution of the House of Representatives of the 21st of December last, a report of the Secretary of State and accompanying documents, touching affairs in Madagascar.

GROVER CLEVELAND.

EXECUTIVE MANSION, *February 28, 1889.*

To the Senate of the United States:

I have the honor to transmit herewith a report of the Secretary of State, concerning the expenses of the representation of the United States at the Brussels Exhibition of 1888.

GROVER CLEVELAND.

[The same message was sent to the House of Representatives.]

EXECUTIVE MANSION, *February 28, 1889.*

To the Senate of the United States:

I have the honor to transmit herewith a report of the Secretary of State, respecting the representation of the United States at the Barcelona Exposition of 1888.

GROVER CLEVELAND.

[The same message was sent to the House of Representatives.]

EXECUTIVE MANSION, *March 2, 1889.*

To the Congress:

I herewith transmit the fifth report of the Civil Service Commission, covering the year which ended June 30, 1888.

The cause of civil-service reform, which in a great degree is intrusted to the Commission, I regard as so firmly established and its value so fully demonstrated that I should deem it more gratifying than useful if at this late day in the session of Congress I was permitted to enlarge upon its importance and present condition.

A perusal of the report herewith submitted will furnish information of the progress which has been made during the year to which it relates in the extension of the operations of this reform and in the improvement of its methods and rules.

It is cause for congratulation that watchfulness and care and fidelity to its purposes are all that are necessary to insure to the Government and our people all the benefits which its inauguration promised.

GROVER CLEVELAND.

EXECUTIVE MANSION,
Washington, March 2, 1889.

To the Senate of the United States:

I transmit herewith, for the consideration of the Senate with a view of giving its advice and consent to the ratification thereof, a convention signed in Washington on March 1, 1889, by duly authorized representatives of the United States and Mexico, providing for the institution of an international commission to determine questions between the United States and Mexico arising under the convention of November 12, 1884, by reason of changes in the river bed of the Rio Grande and the Colorado River when forming the boundary between the two countries.

A report of the Secretary of State, with the accompanying correspondence therein described, is also communicated for the information of the Senate. GROVER CLEVELAND.

EXECUTIVE MANSION, *March 2, 1889.*

To the Senate and House of Representatives:

I herewith transmit a report of the Secretary of State and accompanying documents, relative to the undetermined boundary line between Alaska and British Columbia. GROVER CLEVELAND.

EXECUTIVE MANSION, *March 2, 1889.*

To the House of Representatives:

I herewith transmit a report from the Secretary of State, in further response to the resolution of the House of Representatives of the 22d [21st] of December last, touching affairs in Madagascar.

GROVER CLEVELAND.

EXECUTIVE MANSION, *March 2, 1889.*

To the Senate:

I herewith transmit, for the information of Congress, a report from the Secretary of State, with its accompanying correspondence, in regard to the construction of certain dams or wing facings in the Rio Grande at Paso del Norte (Ciudad Juarez), opposite the city of El Paso, Tex.

GROVER CLEVELAND.

EXECUTIVE MANSION, *March 2, 1889.*

To the Senate of the United States:

I have the honor to transmit herewith a communication from the Secretary of State, covering the report of the commissioner of the United States to the Brussels Exhibition of 1888.

GROVER CLEVELAND.

VETO MESSAGES.

EXECUTIVE MANSION, *December 19, 1888.*

To the House of Representatives:

I return without approval House bill No. 5080, entitled "An act for the relief of C. B. Wilson."

This bill directs the Postmaster-General to credit to the beneficiary therein named, who is the postmaster at Buena Vista, in the State of Colorado, the sum of $225, being post-office funds forwarded by him to the deposit office at Denver, but which were lost in transmission.

A general law was passed on the 9th day of May, 1888, authorizing the Postmaster-General to make allowances and credits to postmasters in precisely such cases.

On the 8th day of September, 1888, under the sanction of that law, the credit directed by this bill was made.

It is plain, therefore, that the bill herewith returned ought not to become a law unless it is proposed to duplicate the credit therein mentioned.

GROVER CLEVELAND.

EXECUTIVE MANSION, *January 16, 1889.*

To the House of Representatives:

I return without approval House bill No. 8469, entitled "An act for the relief of Michael Pigott."

This bill appropriates the sum of $48 to the beneficiary therein named, formerly the postmaster at Quincy, Ill., which was paid by him for the use of a telephone for the year ending June 30, 1873.

There is evidently a mistake made in the statement of the period covered by the use of this telephone, for the official term of the beneficiary extended from May 16, 1881, to June 18, 1885.

Assuming, however, that it was intended to describe the period ending June 30, 1883, it appears that the use of a telephone during that time was wholly unauthorized by the Post-Office Department, and that the only authority given for any expenditure for that purpose covered the period of one year from the 1st day of January, 1884.

The following letter, dated July 16, 1884, was sent to the beneficiary from the salary and allowance division of the Post-Office Department:

In reply to your letter relative to amounts disallowed for use of telephone for your office, you are informed that the said expenditures were made without the authority of this office, and it is therefore deemed advisable not to approve the same.

Your authority for a telephone was for one year beginning January 1, 1884. At the expiration of the time named, if you desire to continue the telephone service, you should make application to the First Assistant Postmaster-General for a renewal of the same.

The multitude of claims of the same kind which the legislation proposed would breed and encourage, and the absolute necessity, in the interest of good administration, of limiting all public officers to authorized expenditures, constrain me to withhold my approval from this bill.

GROVER CLEVELAND.

EXECUTIVE MANSION, *January 16, 1889.*

To the House of Representatives:

I return without approval House bill No. 7, entitled "An act granting a pension to Thomas B. Walsh."

This beneficiary enlisted January 1, 1864, and was discharged August 1, 1865.

He is reported absent without leave in April, 1864, and further recorded as having deserted November 24, 1864. He was restored to duty in May, 1865, by the President's proclamation.

He filed an application for pension in December, 1881, alleging that he contracted rheumatism in May, 1865.

This statement of the claimant and nearly, if not all, the evidence in the case which tends to show the incurrence of the disability complained of appear to fix its appearance at a date very near the return of the beneficiary after his desertion.

In these circumstances the proof of disability, such as it is, is as consistent with its incurrence during desertion as it is with the theory that the beneficiary suffered therefrom as the result of honorable military service.

GROVER CLEVELAND.

EXECUTIVE MANSION *January 16, 1889.*

To the House of Representatives:

I return without approval House bill No. 2236, entitled "An act granting a pension to Eli. J. Yamgheim."

The beneficiary named in this bill filed an application for pension in the Pension Bureau April 15, 1875, basing his claim upon an alleged wound of his left leg from a spent ball about October 15, 1861.

There is no record of his incurring any wound or injury during his service, and it does not appear that the company to which he belonged was in action nearer to the date he specifies than September 17, 1861, and his captain testifies that the beneficiary was not injured in the engagement of that day, which lasted only about fifteen minutes.

The proof taken in the case establishes that before enlistment the beneficiary had a sore on his leg which was quite troublesome, which suppurated, and after healing would break out again.

In the medical examinations made during the pendency of the claim the diseased leg was always found, but no mention is made of any other injury and no other injury seems to have been discoverable.

I can not avoid the conviction upon the facts presented that whatever disability has existed since the discharge of the beneficiary arose from causes which were present before enlistment, and that the same is not chargeable to his military service.

GROVER CLEVELAND.

EXECUTIVE MANSION, *January 16, 1889.*

To the House of Representatives:

I return without approval House bill No. 4887, entitled "An act granting a pension to Charles E. Scott."

This beneficiary entered the volunteer service nearly at the close of the War of the Rebellion and served from the 8th day of March, 1865, to July 24, in the same year, a period of four months and sixteen days.

He filed a claim for pension in 1884, alleging that he incurred camp itch in July, 1865, which resulted in partial blindness.

Upon the proof presented, and after examination, the claim was rejected upon the ground that it did not appear that the impairment of his vision was the result of any incident of his army service.

I am entirely satisfied that this was a correct disposition of the case, and that upon the same ground the bill herewith returned should not be approved.

GROVER CLEVELAND.

EXECUTIVE MANSION, *January 17, 1889.*

To the Senate:

I return without approval Senate bill No. 3646, entitled "An act for the relief of William R. Wheaton and Charles H. Chamberlain, of California."

These parties were, respectively, for a number of years prior to 1879, the register and receiver of the land office at San Francisco, in the State of California.

Prior to July, 1877, they had collected and retained, apparently without question, certain fees allowed by law for reducing to writing the testimony heard by them in establishing the rights of claimants to public lands.

On the 9th day of July, 1877, these officials were notified by the Acting Commissioner of the General Land Office that monthly thereafter, and dating from July 1, 1877, such fees should be reported with other fees to the General Land Office.

This notification furnished clear information that, whatever may have been the justification for their retention of these fees in the past, the parties notified must thereafter account to the Government for the same.

On the 8th day of February, 1879, the beneficiaries were peremptorily required by the Commissioner of the General Land Office to deposit in the Treasury of the United States the sums which they had received for the services mentioned since July 1, 1877, and which, though reported, had not been paid over. Soon thereafter, and pursuant to this demand, the sum of $5,330.76, being the aggregate of such fees for the nineteen months between July 1, 1877, and February 1, 1879, was paid over to the Government.

On the 19th day of February, 1879, these officers were authorized to employ two clerks, each upon a salary of $100 per month.

The purpose of the bill now under consideration is to restore to the beneficiaries from the money paid over to the Government, as above stated, the sum of $3,800. This is proposed upon the theory that clerks were employed by the register and receiver to do the work for which the fees were received, and that these officials having paid them for their services they should be reimbursed from the fund.

It will be observed that whatever services were performed by clerks in the way of writing down testimony, and paid for by the beneficiaries, were performed and paid for after July, 1877, and after they had in effect received notice that such employment and payment would not be approved by the Government.

Upon this statement the claim covered by the bill can hardly be urged on legal grounds, whatever the Government may have allowed prior to such notice.

I am decidedly of the opinion that the relations, the duties, and the obligations of subordinates in public employment should be clearly defined and strictly limited. They should not be permitted to judge of the propriety or necessity of incurring expenses on behalf of the Government without authority, much less in disregard of orders. And yet there are cases when in an emergency money is paid for the benefit of the public service by an official which, though not strictly authorized, ought in equity to be reimbursed.

If there is any equity existing in favor of the beneficiaries named in the bill herewith returned, it is found in the fact that during the nineteen months from the 1st day of July, 1877, to the 1st day of February, 1879, they paid out certain moneys for which the Government, in the receipt of the fees which they paid over, received the benefit. Manifestly such equity in this case, if it can be claimed at all in view of the facts recited, is measured by the sum actually paid by these officials to the persons, if such there were, who did the work from which the fees arose which were paid over to the Government.

In other words, if certain clerks were paid by the beneficiaries from their private funds for doing this work, there should be a distinct statement of the sum so paid, and their claim should rest upon indemnity and reimbursement alone. But no such statement appears, so far as I can see from an examination of papers presented to me by the Interior Department and from the report of the Senate committee who reported this bill, except as it may be gathered from the rather indirect allegations contained in a paper prepared by counsel.

No vouchers have ever been received at the General Land Office for money paid for clerical services rendered during the period for which reimbursement is sought. The verified statement of the claimants annexed to the committee's report contains only the allegation that they paid for the necessary clerical services, and the affidavits of the clerks themselves furnish no clew to the amount they received. Such an omission, in my opinion, discredits the claim made, and the allowance of the sum of $100 per month for two clerks during the period of nineteen months covered by this claim, because that was the sum authorized to be paid thereafter for clerks' services, is, it seems to me, adopting a standard entirely inapplicable to the subject.

In any event these beneficiaries should be required to establish the sum necessary for such indemnification, and the amount appropriated for their relief should be limited to that sum.

GROVER CLEVELAND.

EXECUTIVE MANSION, *January 18, 1889.*
To the House of Representatives:

I return without approval House bill No. 9173, entitled "An act granting a pension to Mary J. Drake."

It is proposed by this bill to pension the beneficiary therein named as the widow of Newton E. Drake, who served as a soldier from August 1, 1863, to January 18, 1865.

The records do not show that he suffered from any disability during his term of service.

He filed an application for pension September 23, 1879, claiming that he contracted rheumatism about October, 1864.

He died June 7, 1881, and there does not appear to have been any evidence produced as to the cause of his death or establishing, except by the allegations of his own application, that he contracted any disease or disability in the service.

GROVER CLEVELAND.

EXECUTIVE MANSION, *January 18, 1889.*
To the House of Representatives:

I return without approval House bill No. 9791, entitled "An act for the relief of Charles W. Geddes."

This bill directs the Secretary of the Interior to include the name of the beneficiary mentioned, late assistant engineer in the United States Navy, among those who served in the Mexican War, and issue to him a land warrant for his services as assistant engineer on the United States steamer *General Taylor* during said war.

On an application made by this beneficiary for bounty land under general laws the Secretary of the Navy reported that the vessel to which he was attached was not considered as having been engaged in the war with Mexico, and thereupon his application was rejected. Upon appeal to the Secretary of the Interior he states the settled doctrine of such cases to be that "service must have been *in*, not simply *during*, a war to give title to bounty land."

The only claim made by the beneficiary is that the vessel upon which he was employed was engaged for a time in transporting seamen from New Orleans, where they were enlisted, to Pensacola, and that he was informed and believed that they were enlisted to serve on board vessels composing the Gulf Squadron, then cooperating with the land forces in the Mexican War.

It seems to me that it is establishing a bad precedent, tending to the breaking down of all distinctions between civil and military employment and service, to hold that a man engaged on a vessel transporting recruits to a rendezvous from which they may be sent to the scene of hostilities should be allowed the same advantages which are bestowed upon those actually engaged in or more directly related to the dangers and chances of military operations.

GROVER CLEVELAND.

EXECUTIVE MANSION, *January 18, 1889.*

To the House of Representatives:

I return without approval House bill No. 9252, entitled "An act granting a pension to Mrs. Catherine Barberick, of Watertown."

The beneficiary named in this bill is the mother of William Barberick, who enlisted February 19, 1862, and died of smallpox August 2, 1864, at his home while on veteran furlough.

It is not claimed that the soldier contracted the fatal disease while in the Army. On the contrary, the testimony taken upon his mother's application for pension to the Pension Bureau shows that he was taken sick after his arrival at his home on furlough, and that several of his family had died of the contagious disease to which he fell a victim before he was taken sick with it.

In these circumstances, unless there is to be a complete departure from the principle that pensions are to be granted for death or disability in some way related to the military service, this bill should not become a law.

GROVER CLEVELAND.

EXECUTIVE MANSION, *January 18, 1889.*

To the House of Representatives:

I return without approval House bill No. 7877, entitled "An act to place Mary Karstetter on the pension roll."

The beneficiary named in this bill is the widow of Jacob Karstetter, who enlisted in June, 1864, and was discharged in June, 1865, on account of a wound in his left hand received in action. He died in August, 1874, of gastritis, or inflammation of the stomach, and congestion of the liver. He was granted a pension for his gunshot wound and was in receipt of such pension at the time of his death.

I was constrained to return without approval a bill identical with the one herewith returned, and which was passed by the last Congress, and stated my objections to the same in a communication addressed to the House of Representatives, dated July 6, 1886.*

It seemed to me at that time that the soldier's death could not be held to be the result of his wound or any other cause chargeable to his military service.

Upon reexamination I am still of the same opinion, which leads me to again return the bill under consideration without approval.

GROVER CLEVELAND.

EXECUTIVE MANSION, *January 18, 1889.*

To the House of Representatives:

I return without approval House bill No. 9296, entitled "An act granting a pension to Bridget Carroll."

This bill proposes to pension the beneficiary therein named as the dependent mother of Patrick Carroll, who was enrolled as a sergeant in the Regular Army in 1881, this being, as it is stated, his second term of enlistment.

In September, 1886, being absent from his command at Fort Warren, Mass., he was drowned while sailing in a small boat with two companions.

The beneficiary is aged and in need of assistance, but there is no pretense that the soldier's death was in the least degree related to his military service.

I am sure no one could fail to be gratified by an opportunity to join in according aid to this dependent old mother of a faithful soldier, but I can not believe that such a departure as is proposed should be made from the just principles upon which pension legislation ought to be predicated.

GROVER CLEVELAND.

EXECUTIVE MANSION, *January 18, 1889.*

To the House of Representatives:

I return without approval House bill No. 9175, entitled "An act granting a pension to George Wallen."

---

* See pp. 5054–5055.

The beneficiary named in this bill filed an application for pension in June, 1873, alleging as his disability a fracture of his right arm.

In a subsequent affidavit filed in 1883 he alleged deafness, which appears to be the disability upon which the special act proposed for his relief is based.

The records establish that he enlisted July 27, 1861, that he deserted April 25, 1862, and returned February 20, 1863, after an absence of about ten months, and that he deserted again April 30, 1864, and returned prior to August 31, 1864. I am informed that his record shows two enlistments and desertion during each. He was discharged December 31, 1864.

An application to remove the charge of desertion against him was denied.

Without especially discussing the question of disability chargeable to military service, it seems to me that a soldier with such a record should not be pensioned. GROVER CLEVELAND.

EXECUTIVE MANSION, *January 31, 1889.*
To the Senate:

I return without approval Senate bill No. 3264, entitled "An act granting a pension to Mrs. Ellen Hand."

The husband of the beneficiary named in this bill enlisted August 22, 1862, and was mustered out with his company July 10, 1865.

He filed a claim for pension in 1881, sixteen years after his discharge, alleging that he contracted rheumatism about December, 1862.

He died in February, 1883, the cause of death being, as then certified, typhoid fever.

His claim for pension on account of rheumatism seems to have been favorably determined after his death, for it was made payable to his widow and was allowed from the time of filing his petition to February 25, 1883, the day of his death.

The facts of the case as now presented appear to me to lead in the most satisfactory manner to the conclusion that the soldier's death was in no way related to any incident of his military service.

GROVER CLEVELAND

EXECUTIVE MANSION, *February 12, 1889.*
To the House of Representatives:

I return without approval House bill No. 9163, entitled "An act granting a pension to Eli Garrett."

This beneficiary enlisted in the Confederate Army December 1, 1862. He was captured by the United States forces on the 26th of November, 1863, and enlisted in the Union Navy January 22, 1864.

He was discharged from the Navy for disability September 8, 1864, upon the certificate of a naval surgeon, which states that he had valvular cardiac disease (disease of the heart), and that there was no evidence that it originated in the line of duty.

His claim for pension was rejected in 1882 upon the ground that the act which permits pensions to Confederate soldiers who joined the Union Army did not extend to such soldiers who enlisted in the Navy.

I can see no reason why such a distinction should exist, and the recommendation of the Commissioner of Pensions, made in 1887, that this discrimination be removed should be adopted by the enactment of a law for that purpose.

In this case, however, I am unable to discover any evidence that the trouble with which this beneficiary appears to be afflicted is related to his naval service which should overcome the plain statement of the surgeon upon whose certificate he was discharged to the effect that there was no evidence that his disability originated in the line of naval duty.

GROVER CLEVELAND.

EXECUTIVE MANSION, February 12, 1889.

To the House of Representatives:

I return without approval House bill No. 11052, entitled "An act granting a pension to Clara M. Owen."

The husband of this beneficiary was pensioned for a gunshot wound in the left chest and lung, received in action on the 30th day of September, 1864.

He was drowned August 31, 1884.

It appears that he was found in a stream where he frequently bathed, in a depth of water variously given from 5 to 8 feet. He had undressed and apparently gone into the water as usual.

Medical opinions are produced tending to show that drowning was not the cause of death.

No *post mortem* examination was had, and it seems to me it must be conceded that a conclusion that death was in any degree the result of wounds received in military service rests upon the most unsatisfactory conjecture.

GROVER CLEVELAND.

EXECUTIVE MANSION, February 12, 1889.

To the House of Representatives:

I return without approval House bill No. 5752, entitled "An act for the relief of Julia Triggs."

This beneficiary filed an application for pension in 1882, claiming that her son, William Triggs, died in 1875 from the effects of poison taken during his military service in water which had been poisoned by the rebels and in food eaten in rebel houses, which had also been poisoned.

He was discharged from the Army with his company July 24, 1865, after a service of more than four years.

The cause of his death is reported to have been an abscess of the lung.

The case was specially examined, and the evidence elicited to support the claim of poisoning appears to have been anything but satisfactory.

The mother herself testified that her son was absent from Chicago, where she lived, and in the South from 1868 to 1869, and that he was in Indiana from 1869 to 1874.

The claim was rejected on the 12th day of February, 1887, on the ground that evidence could not be obtained upon special examination showing that the soldier's death was due to any disability contracted in the military service.

While I am unable to see how any other conclusion could have been reached upon the facts in this case, there is reason to believe that a favorable determination upon its merits would be of no avail, since, on the 17th day of April, 1888, a letter was filed in the Pension Office from a citizen of Chicago in which it is stated that the beneficiary named in this bill died on the 27th day of February, 1888, and an application is therein made on behalf of her daughter for reimbursement of money expended for her mother in her last illness and for her burial.

GROVER CLEVELAND.

EXECUTIVE MANSION, *February 13, 1889.*

To the Senate:

I return without approval Senate bill No. 2514, entitled "An act granting a pension to Michael Shong."

It appears that the beneficiary named in this bill, under the name of John M. Johns, enlisted in Company I, Fourteenth New York Volunteers, on the 17th day of May, 1861, and was discharged May 24, 1863.

In November, 1876, more than thirteen years after his discharge, under the same name of John M. Johns, he filed an application for pension, alleging a fever sore on his right leg contracted July 1, 1862, which resulted in the loss of the leg.

His claim was rejected in November, 1882, after a thorough special examination, on the ground that the disease of the leg resulting in amputation was contracted after the soldier's discharge from the service.

The leg was amputated in February, 1865.

While there is some evidence tending to show lameness in the service and following discharge, and while one witness swears to lameness and fever sores in the service, evidence was also produced showing that the soldier returned home from the Army in good physical condition and that the disease of his leg first manifested itself in the latter part of 1864.

It will be observed that he served in the Army nearly a year after it is alleged he contracted his disability, and that though his leg was amputated in February, 1865, he did not apply for a pension until 1876.

Moreover, the surgeon who amputated his leg testified that the soldier and his parents stated that he came out of the Army without a scratch; that on New Year's night in 1865 he became very warm at a dance; that he went outdoors and was taken with a chill and pain in his side, which subsequently settled in the leg and caused a gangrenous condition, and that upon amputating the leg the artery below the knee was found plugged by a blood clot, which caused the diseased condition of the leg and foot.

This testimony and the other facts established and the presumptions arising therefrom clearly indicate, in my opinion, that the claim made for a pension by this beneficiary is without merit.

GROVER CLEVELAND.

To the Senate: EXECUTIVE MANSION, *February 13, 1889.*

I return without approval Senate bill No. 3451, entitled "An act granting a pension to Frank D. Worcester."

The beneficiary named in this bill served in the Volunteer Army from February 4, 1863, to January 27, 1864, a period of less than one year, when he was discharged upon the certificate of a surgeon, alleging as his disability "manifest mental imbecility and incontinence of urine. Disease originated previous to enlistment."

In 1880, sixteen years after his discharge, a claim for pension was filed in his behalf by his father as his guardian, in which it was alleged that his mind, naturally not strong, became diseased in the Army by reason of excitement and exposure.

He was adjudged insane in 1872 and sent to an insane hospital, where he remained about six years, when he was discharged as a harmless incurable. His mental condition has remained about the same since that time.

Upon the declared inability to furnish testimony to rebut the record of mental disease prior to enlistment, the claim for pension was rejected in 1883.

In 1887 the case was reopened and a thorough examination was made as to soundness prior to enlistment and the origin and continuance of mental unsoundness.

Upon this examination evidence was taken showing that he was deficient intellectually when he joined the Army; that he was stationed where he was not much exposed, and that his duties were comparatively light; that he never was considered a boy of solid intelligence, and that he had epileptiform seizures prior to enlistment.

On the other hand, no disinterested and unbiased evidence was secured tending to rebut these conditions.

The claim was thereupon again rejected. This was a proper disposition of the case unless the Government is held liable for every disability which may afflict those who served in the Union Army.

GROVER CLEVELAND.

EXECUTIVE MANSION, *February 14, 1889.*

To the Senate:

I return without approval Senate bill No. 2665, entitled "An act granting a pension to Charles J. Esty."

A bill in precisely the same words as the bill herewith returned was approved on the 8th day of July, 1886, and under its provisions the beneficiary is now upon the pension rolls.

It is supposed that the bill now under consideration was passed by the Congress in ignorance of the previous statute. A duplication of the act would manifestly be entirely useless.

GROVER CLEVELAND.

EXECUTIVE MANSION, *February 21, 1889.*

To the House of Representatives:

I herewith return without approval House bill No. 1368, entitled "An act to quiet title of settlers on the Des Moines River lands, in the State of Iowa, and for other purposes."

This bill is to all intents and purposes identical with Senate bill No. 150, passed in the first session of the Forty-ninth Congress, which failed to receive Executive approval. My objections to that bill are set forth in a message transmitted to the Senate on the 11th day of March, 1886.* They are all applicable to the bill herewith returned, and a careful reexamination of the matters embraced in this proposed legislation has further satisfied me of their validity and strength.

The trouble proposed to be cured by this bill grew out of the indefiniteness and consequent contradictory construction by the officers of the Government of a grant of land made in 1846 by Congress to the State of Iowa (then a Territory) for the purpose of aiding in the improvement of the Des Moines River. This grant was accepted on the 9th day of January, 1847, by the State of Iowa, as required by the act of Congress, and soon thereafter the question arose whether the lands granted were limited to those which adjoined the river in its course northwesterly from the southerly line of the State to a point called the Raccoon Fork, or whether such grant covered lands so adjoining the river through its entire course through the Territory, and both below and above the Raccoon Fork.

The Acting Commissioner of the General Land Office, on the 17th day of October, 1846, instructed the officers of the land office in Iowa that the grant extended only to the Raccoon Fork.

On the 23d day of February, 1848, the Commissioner of the General Land Office held that the grant extended along the entire course of the river.

Notwithstanding this opinion, the President, in June, 1848, proclaimed

* See pp. 4996-4998.

the lands upon the river above the Raccoon Fork to be open for sale and settlement under the land laws, and about 25,000 acres were sold to and preempted by settlers under said proclamation.

In 1849, and before the organization of the Department of the Interior, the Secretary of the Treasury decided, upon a protest against opening said lands for sale and settlement, that the grant extended along the entire course of the river.

Pursuant to this decision, and on the 1st day of June, 1849, the Commissioner of the General Land Office directed the reservation or the withholding from sale of all lands on the odd-numbered sections along the Des Moines River above the Raccoon Fork.

This reservation from entry and sale under the general land laws seems to have continued until a deed of the lands so reserved was made by the State of Iowa and until the said deed was supplemented and confirmed by the action of the Congress in 1861 and 1862.

In April, 1850, the Secretary of the Interior, that Department having then been created, determined that the grant extended no farther than the Raccoon Fork; but in view of the fact that Congress was in session and might take steps in the matter, the Commissioner of the General Land Office expressly continued the reservation.

In October, 1851, another Secretary of the Interior, while expressing the opinion that the grant only extended to the Raccoon Fork, declared that he would approve the selections made by the State of Iowa of lands above that point, "leaving the question as to the construction of the statute entirely open to the action of the judiciary."

In this condition of affairs selections were made by Iowa of a large quantity of land lying above the Raccoon Fork, which selections were approved and the land certified to the State. In the meantime the State had entered upon the improvement of the river and it appears had disposed of some of the land in furtherance of said improvement. But in 1854 the State of Iowa made a contract with the Des Moines Navigation and Railroad Company for the continuance of said work at a cost of $1,300,000, the State agreeing in payment thereof to convey to the company all the land which had been or should thereafter be certified to the State of Iowa under the grant of 1846.

In November, 1856, further certification of lands above the Raccoon Fork under the grant to the State of Iowa was refused by the Interior Department. This led to a dispute and settlement between the State of Iowa and the Des Moines Navigation and Railroad Company, by which the State conveyed by deed to said company—

All lands granted by an act of Congress approved August 8, 1846, to the then Territory of Iowa to aid in the improvement of the Des Moines River which have been approved and certified to the State of Iowa by the General Government, saving and excepting all lands sold and conveyed, or agreed to be sold and conveyed, by the State, by its officers and agents, prior to the 23d day of December, 1853, under said grant.

This exception was declared in the deed to cover the lands above the Raccoon Fork disposed of to settlers by the Government in 1848 under the proclamation of the President opening said lands to sale and settlement, which has been referred to; and it is conceded that neither these lands nor the rights of any settlers thereto are affected by the terms of the bill now under consideration.

The amount of land embraced in this deed located above the Raccoon Fork appears to be more than 271,000 acres.

It is alleged that the company in winding up its affairs distributed this land among the parties interested, and that said land, or a large part of it, has been sold to numerous parties now claiming the same under titles derived from said company.

In December, 1859, the Supreme Court of the United States decided that the grant to the Territory of Iowa under the law of 1846 conveyed no land above the Raccoon Fork, and that all selections and certifications of lands above that point were unauthorized and void, and passed no title or interest in said lands to the State of Iowa. In other words, it was determined that these lands were, in the language of the bill under consideration, "improperly certified to Iowa by the Department of the Interior under the act of August 8, 1846."

This adjudication would seem to conclusively determine that the title to these lands was, as the law then stood, and notwithstanding all that had taken place, still in the United States. And for the purpose of granting all claim or right of the Government to said lands for the benefit of the grantees of the State of Iowa, Congress, on the 2d day of March, 1861, passed a joint resolution providing that all the title still retained by the United States in the lands above the Raccoon Fork, in the State of Iowa, "which have been certified to said State improperly by the Department of the Interior as part of the grant by act of Congress approved August 8, 1846, and which is now held by *bona fide* purchasers under the State of Iowa, be, and the same is hereby, relinquished to the State of Iowa."

Afterwards, and on the 12th day of July, 1862, an act of Congress was passed extending the grant of 1846 so as to include lands lying above the Raccoon Fork.

The joint resolution and act of Congress here mentioned have been repeatedly held by the Supreme Court of the United States to supply a title to the lands mentioned in the deed from the State of Iowa to the Navigation and Railroad Company, which inured to the benefit of said company or its grantees.

No less than ten cases have been decided in that court more or less directly establishing this proposition, as well as the further proposition that no title to these lands could prior to said Congressional action be gained by settlers, for the reason that it had been withdrawn and reserved from entry and sale under the general land laws. It seems to be perfectly well settled also, if an adjudication was necessary upon that question, that all interest of the United States in these lands was entirely and completely granted by the resolution of 1861 and the act of 1862.

The act of 1862 provides for the setting apart of other lands in lieu of such as were covered by the act, but had been before its passage sold and disposed of by the United States, excepting such as had been released to the State of Iowa under the joint resolution of 1861.

It is claimed, I believe, that in a settlement of land grants thereafter had between the United States and the State of Iowa lands were allowed to the State in lieu or indemnity for some of the lands which it had conveyed to the Des Moines Navigation and Railroad Company. But if the title of the company is valid to lands along the river and above the Raccoon Fork, under the deed from Iowa and the joint resolution and act of Congress, it can not be in the least affected by the fact that the State afterwards, justly or unjustly, received other lands as indemnity.

The bill under consideration provides that all the lands "improperly certified to Iowa" under the grant of 1846, as referred to in the joint resolution of 1861, and for which indemnity lands were selected and received by the State, as provided in the act of 1862, "are, and are hereby, declared to be public lands of the United States."

The claims of persons and their heirs who, with intent in good faith to obtain title under the preemption and homestead laws of the United States, have entered and remained upon any tract of said land prior to 1880 are confirmed and made valid to them and their heirs, not exceeding 160 acres; and upon due proof and payment of the usual price or fees it is directed that such claims shall be carried to patent.

It is further provided that the claims of settlers and claimants which do not come in conflict with the claims of the parties above mentioned are confirmed and made valid. By the second section of the bill it is made the duty of the Attorney-General, as soon as practicable, and within three years after the passage of the act, to institute legal proceedings to assert and protect the title of the United States to said lands and to remove all clouds from its title thereto.

One result of this legislation, if consummated and if effectual, would be to restore to the United States, as a part of the public domain, lands which more than twenty-five years ago the Government expressly granted and surrendered, and which repeated decisions of the Supreme Court have adjudged to belong by virtue of this action of the Government to other parties.

Another result would be not only to validate claims to this land which our highest judicial tribunal have solemnly declared to be invalid, but to actually direct the issue of patents in confirmation of said claims.

Still another result would be to oblige the Government of the United States to enter the courts ostensibly to assert and protect its title to said land, while in point of fact it would be used to enforce private claims to the same and unsettle private ownership.

It is by no means certain that this proposed legislation, relating to a subject peculiarly within the judicial function, and which attempts to disturb rights and interests thoroughly intrenched in the solemn adjudications of our courts, would be upheld. In any event, it seems to me that it is an improper exercise of legislative power, an interference with the determinations of a coordinate branch of the Government, an arbitrary annulment of a public grant made more than twenty-five years ago, an attempted destruction of vested rights, and a threatened impairment of lawful contracts.

The advocates of this measure insist that a point in favor of the settlers upon these lands and important in the consideration of this bill is found in the following language of the constitution of the State of Iowa, which was adopted in 1857:

> The general assembly shall not locate any of the public lands which have been or may be granted by Congress to this State, and the location of which may be given to the general assembly, upon lands actually settled, without the consent of the occupant.

The State under its constitution was perfectly competent to take the grants of 1861 and 1862. The clause of the constitution above quoted deals expressly with "lands which have been or may be granted by Congress to the State," and thus of necessity recognizes its right to take such grants. This competency in the State as a grantee was all that was needed to create, under the joint resolution of 1861 and the act of 1862, a complete divestiture of the interests of the United States in these lands. It must be borne in mind, too, that prior to this time these lands had been conveyed by the State of Iowa in furtherance of the purposes of the original Congressional grants, and that the joint resolution of 1861 and the act of 1862 were really made for the benefit of those who held under grants from the State. After these grants by the Government it had no concern with these lands. If in any stage of the proceedings the general assembly of Iowa was guilty of any neglect of duty or failed to act in accordance with the constitution of the State of Iowa, the remedy should be found in the courts of that State; and it is difficult to see how the situation in this aspect can be changed or improved by the bill under consideration.

I am not unmindful of the fact that there may be persons who have suffered or who are threatened with loss through a reliance upon the erroneous decisions of Government officials as to the extent of the original grant from the United States to the Territory of Iowa. I believe cases of this kind should be treated in accordance with the broadest sentiments of equity, and that where loss is apparent arising from a real or fairly supposed invitation of the Government to settle upon the lands mentioned in the bill under consideration such loss should be made good. But I do not believe that the condition of these settlers will be aided by encouraging them in such further litigation as the terms of this bill invite, nor do I believe that in attempting to right the wrongs of which they complain legislation should be sanctioned mischievous in principle, and in its practical operation doing injustice to others as innocent as they and as much entitled to consideration.

GROVER CLEVELAND.

EXECUTIVE MANSION, *February 23, 1889.*
To the House of Representatives:

I herewith return without approval House bill No. 220, entitled "An act granting a pension to John J. Lockrey."

It is stated that this beneficiary enlisted April 11, 1865, but it appears from the muster roll of his company for May and June, 1865, that he was a recruit assigned, but who had not joined. There is nothing appearing on the record which positively shows that he ever reached his regiment.

It is conceded that his real and nominal connection with the Army extended only from April 11, 1865, when he was mustered in, until August, 1865, when he was discharged for disability, consisting of a disease of the eye, called in the surgeon's certificate "iritis with conjunctivitis."

It seems that this claimant enlisted just at the close of the war, and was connected in a manner with the Army for four months. It is not probable that he ever saw any actual service, for none is stated in the papers before me; and it does appear that he spent a large part of his short term of enlistment in hospitals and under treatment for a trouble with his eye. As early as May 23, 1865, he was admitted to hospital with gonorrheal ophthalmia. His claim was rejected by the Pension Bureau on the ground that this was the cause of his disability, and the inferences from the proof presented make this extremely probable.

One of the witnesses who testified that the beneficiary caught cold in his eye in April, 1865, on the Mississippi River is shown to have been at that time with his regiment and company at Danville, Va.

The circumstances surrounding this case and the facts proved satisfy me that the determination of the Pension Bureau was correct, and there is certainly no sentiment in favor of the claimant which justifies the indulgence of violent presumptions for the purpose of overriding such determination.

GROVER CLEVELAND.

EXECUTIVE MANSION, *February 23, 1889.*
To the House of Representatives:

I return without approval House bill No. 5807, entitled "An act granting a pension to John McCool."

This beneficiary served in an Iowa regiment of volunteers from May 27, 1861, to July 12, 1865.

He filed a petition for pension, alleging an accidental wound in the right thumb while extracting a cartridge from a pistol in August, 1861.

There is no record of any such disability, though it appears that he was on a furlough about the date of his alleged injury. It appears that he served nearly four years after the time he fixed as the date of his injury.

No evidence was filed in support of the claim he filed, and he refused to appear for examination, though twice notified to do so.

His claim was rejected in May, 1888, no suggestion having been made of any other disability than the wound in the thumb, upon which his claim before the Bureau was based.

The report of the committee in the House of Representatives recommending the passage of this bill contains no intimation that there exists any disability contracted in the military service, but distinctly declares the pension recommended a service pension, and states that the beneficiary is blind.

As long as the policy of granting pensions for disability traceable to the incidents of army service is adhered to, the allowance of pensions by special acts based upon service only gives rise to unjust and unfair discriminations among those equally entitled, and makes precedents which will eventually result in an entire departure from the principle upon which pensions are now awarded. GROVER CLEVELAND.

EXECUTIVE MANSION, *February 23, 1889.*

To the House of Representatives:

I return without approval House bill No. 11803, entitled "An act granting a pension to Henry V. Bass."

This beneficiary enlisted September 9, 1862, and was mustered out August 15, 1865. The records show no disability during his service.

It is now alleged that the soldier was sitting on the ground near his tent while two comrades were wrestling near him, and that in the course of the scuffle one of the parties engaged in it was thrown or fell upon the beneficiary, injuring his right knee and ankle.

Upon these facts the claim was rejected by the Pension Bureau on the ground that the injury was not received in the line of duty.

I do not think that the Government should be held as an insurer against injuries of this kind, which are in no manner related to the performance of military service. GROVER CLEVELAND.

EXECUTIVE MANSION, *February 23, 1889.*

To the House of Representatives:

I herewith return without approval House bill No. 11999, entitled "An act granting a pension to William Barnes."

The beneficiary named in this bill served in a Kentucky regiment from August 9, 1861, to December 6, 1864.

He made claim for pension in the Pension Bureau in September, 1882, alleging that in October, 1862, he was accidentally injured by a pistol shot in the thigh while in the line of duty.

It is conceded that he was wounded by the discharge of a pistol which he was carrying while he was absent from his command with permission on a visit to his home, and that the discharge of the pistol was accidental.

The circumstances of the injury are neither given in the report of the committee to whom the claim was referred by the House of Representatives nor in the report of the case furnished to me from the Pension Bureau, but on the conceded facts the granting of a pension in this case can be predicated upon no other theory except the liability of the Government for any injury by accident to a person in the military service, whether in the line of duty or not.

I think the adoption of the principle that the Government is an insurer against accidents under any circumstances befalling those enlisted in its military service when visiting at home is an unwarrantable stretch of pension legislation.

GROVER CLEVELAND.

EXECUTIVE MANSION, *February 25, 1889.*

To the House of Representatives:

I herewith return without approval House bill No. 10448, entitled ''An act granting a pension to Squire Walter.''

The son of the beneficiary named in this bill enlisted in a West Virginia regiment on the 28th day of June, 1861.

On the 15th day of September, 1862, while bathing in the Potomac River near the Chain Bridge, with the knowledge and consent of his commanding officer, he was drowned.

It is perfectly clear that he lost his life while in the enjoyment of a privilege and when at his request military discipline was relaxed and its restraints removed for his comfort and pleasure. His death resulted from his voluntary and perfectly proper personal indulgence, and can not be in the least attributed to military service.

The father does not appear to be so needy and dependent as is often exhibited in cases of this class.

GROVER CLEVELAND.

To the Senate: EXECUTIVE MANSION, *February 25, 1889.*

I herewith return without approval Senate bill No. 3561, entitled ''An act granting a pension to Edwin W. Warner.''

A claim for pension on behalf of the beneficiary named in this bill was filed in the Pension Bureau May 6, 1867. It has been examined and reexamined and always rejected, until, on the 29th day of December, 1888, as the result of a personal and thorough investigation by the Commissioner, a pension was allowed and a certificate issued under which the claimant will be paid $18 a month hereafter and arrearages amounting to something near $2,000.

As the special act for the benefit of this claimant was passed by the Congress upon the supposition that nothing had been done for the beneficiary therein named, I deem it best, in his interest, and probably consistent with the intent of the Congress, that the bill herewith returned should not become a law.

GROVER CLEVELAND.

EXECUTIVE MANSION, *February 26, 1889.*

To the House of Representatives:

I return without approval House bill No. 12047, entitled "An act granting an increase of pension to George Colwell."

The record shows that this beneficiary was enrolled in the military service August 10, 1862, and was mustered out June 1, 1865.

There is no record of any disability during his service.

He was pensioned at the rate of $2 a month for a dog bite just above the ankle.

In September, 1865, three months after his discharge, he strained the knee of the leg which had been bitten.

In 1887 he applied for an increase of pension, alleging increased disability. This increased disability appears plainly to be the result of the strain or injury to the knee, and in no way connected with the bite for which he was pensioned.

GROVER CLEVELAND.

EXECUTIVE MANSION, *February 26, 1889.*

To the House of Representatives:

I herewith return without approval House bill No. 10791, entitled "An act granting a pension to Marinda Wakefield Reed."

This beneficiary filed an application for pension in November, 1876, alleging that her husband, William A. Reed, died in September of that year of consumption contracted in the line of military duty.

The records show that the soldier was in hospital in the year 1864 for chronic diarrhea and intermittent fever.

On the 5th day of November, 1864, he was injured in a railroad accident while on his way home to vote at the Presidential election of that year.

The beneficiary claimed in August, 1885, in support of her application for pension that those injuries resulted in consumption, from which the soldier died, and the favorable report of the House committee to which the bill herewith returned was referred seems to proceed upon the same theory.

Nothing appears which satisfactorily connects this injury, which was received in November, 1864, with death from consumption in 1876.

Another difficulty in the case is found in the fact that when the soldier was injured he was clearly not engaged in any military duty nor was his injury in any degree attributable to military service.

GROVER CLEVELAND.

EXECUTIVE MANSION, *February 26, 1889.*

To the House of Representatives:

I return without approval House bill 11466, entitled "An act granting a pension to Mary A. Selbach."

This bill does not give the name of any soldier to whom the beneficiary was related or in what capacity the pension provided for is to be paid to her, but it appears from the report of the committee accompanying the bill that she is the widow of Gustavus Selbach, a volunteer in the Ninth Regiment of Ohio Volunteers.

This soldier drew a pension from January, 1882, to January 16, 1886, when he died. He claimed disability for disease of the ears and a resulting deafness of his left ear. There appears to be no evidence in his record of any disability or medical treatment while in the service, and the medical examination upon his application for pension shows no rating for any disability other than that alleged by him and for which he was pensioned—disease of the ears and resulting deafness.

It is conceded that the soldier died January 16, 1886, of pneumonia.

The widow filed a claim for pension in May, 1887.

The testimony of physicians upon her claim covered seven years prior to his death, thus dating back to the year 1879, and they speak of the disease of the ear and of the kidneys, which, in their opinion, undermined his health, so that "he succumbed to an attack of pneumonia, which to a person of ordinary good health would not have been considered serious."

It can hardly be supposed that the trouble with his ears caused the soldier to fall a victim to pneumonia; and so far as the kidney disease tended in that direction, it is to be observed that it apparently did not make its appearance until fourteen years after the soldier's discharge.

GROVER CLEVELAND.

EXECUTIVE MANSION, *February 26, 1889.*

To the House of Representatives:

I return without approval House bill No. 11586, entitled "An act for the relief of Stephen Williams."

It appears from the records that the beneficiary for whom a pension is provided in this bill served as a volunteer in an Illinois regiment from October, 1862, to October, 1864, at which date he is reported as a deserter.

He filed a claim for pension in 1881, in which he alleged that he was struck with a gunstock upon his head and injured in October, 1864.

The evidence shows that a drunken comrade struck the claimant with the stock of his gun because he would not buy whisky for him.

This, upon all the facts, does not appear to be a proper case for allowing a pension for an injury suffered in the line of military duty.

GROVER CLEVELAND.

To the Senate: EXECUTIVE MANSION, *March 2, 1889.*

I herewith return without approval Senate bill No. 139, entitled "An act to credit and pay to the several States and Territories and the District of Columbia all moneys collected under the direct tax levied by the act of Congress approved August 5, 1861."

The object of this bill is quite clearly indicated in its title. Its provisions have been much discussed in both branches of Congress and have received emphatic legislative sanction. I fully appreciate the interest which it has excited and have by no means failed to recognize the persuasive presentation made in its favor. I know, too, that the interposition of Executive disapproval in this case is likely to arouse irritation and cause complaint and earnest criticism. Since, however, my judgment will not permit me to assent to the legislation proposed, I can find no way of turning aside from what appears to be the plain course of official duty.

On the 5th day of August, 1861, a Federal statute was passed entitled "An act to provide increased revenue from imports, to pay interest on the public debt, and for other purposes."

This law was passed at a time when immense sums of money were needed by the Government for the prosecution of a war for the Union, and the purpose of the law was to increase in almost every possible way the Federal revenues. The first seven sections of the statute were devoted to advancing very largely the rates of duties on imports, and to supplement this the eighth section provided that a direct tax of $20,000,000 should be annually laid and that certain amounts therein specified should be apportioned to the respective States. The remainder of the law, consisting of fifty sections, contained the most particular and detailed provisions for the collection of the tax through Federal machinery.

It was declared, among other things, that the tax should be assessed and laid on all lands and lots of ground, with their improvements and dwelling houses; that the annual amount of said taxes should be a lien upon all lands and real estate of the individuals assessed for the same, and that in default of payment the said taxes might be collected by distraint and sale of the goods, chattels, and effects of the delinquent persons.

This tax was laid in execution of the power conferred upon the General Government for that purpose by the Constitution. It was an exercise of the right of the Government to tax its citizens. If dealt with individuals, and the strong arm of Federal power was stretched out to exact from those who owed it support and allegiance their just share of the sum it had decreed should be raised by direct taxation for the general good. The lien created by this tax was upon the land and real estate of the "individuals" assessed for the same, and for its collection the distraint and sale of personal property of the "persons delinquent" were permitted.

But while the direct relationship and responsibility between the individuals taxed and the Federal Government were thus created by the exercise of the highest attribute of sovereignty, it was provided in the statute that any State or Territory and the District of Columbia might lawfully "assume, assess, collect, and pay into the Treasury of the United States" its quota of said tax in its own way and manner and by and through its own officers, assessors, and collectors; and it was further provided that such States or Territories as should give notice of their intention to thus assume and pay or to assess, collect, and pay into the Treasury of the United States such direct tax, should be entitled, in lieu of the compensation, pay, per diem, and percentage in said act prescribed and allowed to assessors, assistant assessors, and collectors of the United States, to a deduction of 15 per cent of the quota of direct tax apportioned to such States or Territories and levied and collected through their officers.

It was also provided by this law and another passed the next year that certain claims of the States and Territories against the United States might be applied in payment of such quotas. Whatever may be said as to the effect of these provisions of the law, it can hardly be claimed that by virtue thereof or any proceedings under them the apportioned quotas of this tax became debts against the several States and Territories, or that they were liable to the General Government therefor in every event, and as principal debtors bound by an enforceable obligation.

In the forty-sixth section of the law it is provided that in case any State, Territory, or the District of Columbia, after notice given of its intention to assume and pay or to levy, collect, and pay said direct tax apportioned to it, should fail to pay the amount of said direct tax, or any part thereof, it should be lawful for the Secretary of the Treasury to appoint United States officers as in the act provided, whose duty it should be to proceed forthwith to collect all or any part of said direct tax "the same as though said State, Territory, or District had not given notice nor assumed to levy, collect, and pay said taxes or any part thereof."

A majority of the States undertook the collection of their quotas and accounted for the amount thereof to the General Government by the payment of money or by setting off claims in their favor against the tax. Fifteen per cent of the amount of their respective quotas was retained as the allowance for collection and payment. In the Northern, or such as were then called the loyal States, nearly the entire quotas were collected and paid through State agencies. The money necessary for this purpose was generally collected from the citizens of the States with their other taxes, and in whatever manner their quotas may have been canceled, whether by the payment of money or setting off claims against the Government, it is safe to say, as a general proposition, that the people of these States have individually been obliged to pay the assessments made upon them on account of this direct tax and have intrusted it to their several States to be transmitted to the Federal Treasury.

In the Southern States, then in insurrection, whatever was actually realized in money upon this tax was collected directly by Federal officers without the interposition of State machinery, and a part of its quota has been credited to each of these States.

The entire amount applied upon this tax, including the 15 per cent for collection, was credited to the several States and Territories upon the books of the Treasury, whether collected through their instrumentalities or by Federal officers.

The sum credited to all the States was $17,359,685.51, which includes more than $2,000,000 on account of the 15 per cent allowed for collecting. Of the amount credited only about $2,300,000 is credited to the insurrectionary States. The amount uncollected of the twenty millions directed to be raised by this tax was $2,646,314.49, and nearly this entire sum remained due upon the quotas apportioned to these States.

In this condition of affairs the bill under consideration directs the Secretary of the Treasury " to credit to each State and Territory of the United States and the District of Columbia a sum equal to all collections, by setoff or otherwise, made from said States and Territories and the District of Columbia, or from any of the citizens or inhabitants thereof, or other persons, under the act of Congress approved August 5, 1861, and the amendatory acts thereto." An appropriation is also made of such a sum as may be necessary to reimburse each State, Territory, and the District of Columbia for all money found due to it under the provisions of the bill, and it is provided that all money still due to the United States on said direct tax shall be remitted and relinquished.

The conceded effect of this bill is to take from the money now in the Treasury the sum of more than $17,000,000, or, if the percentage allowed is not included, more than $15,000,000, and pay back to the respective States and Territories the sums they or their citizens paid more than twenty-five years ago upon a direct tax levied by the Government of the United States for its defense and safety.

It is my belief that this appropriation of the public funds is not within the constitutional power of the Congress. Under the limited and delegated authority conferred by the Constitution upon the General Government the statement of the purposes for which money may be lawfully raised by taxation in any form declares also the limit of the objects for which it may be expended.

All must agree that the direct tax was lawfully and constitutionally laid and that it was rightfully and correctly collected. It can not be claimed, therefore, nor is it pretended, that any debt arose against the Government and in favor of any State or individual by the exaction of this tax. Surely, then, the appropriation directed by this bill can not be justified as a payment of a debt of the United States.

The disbursement of this money clearly has no relation to the common defense. On the contrary, it is the repayment of money raised and long ago expended by the Government to provide for the common defense.

The expenditure can not properly be advocated on the ground that the general welfare of the United States is thereby provided for or promoted. This "general welfare of the United States," as used in the Constitution, can only justify appropriations for national objects and for purposes which have to do with the prosperity, the growth, the honor, or the peace and dignity of the nation.

A sheer, bald gratuity bestowed either upon States or individuals, based upon no better reason than supports the gift proposed in this bill, has never been claimed to be a provision for the general welfare. More than fifty years ago a surplus of public money in the Treasury was distributed among the States; but the unconstitutionality of such distribution, considered as a gift of money, appears to have been conceded, for it was put · into the State treasuries under the guise of a deposit or loan, subject to the demand of the Government.

If it was proposed to raise by assessment upon the people the sum necessary to refund the money collected upon this direct tax, I am sure many who are now silent would insist upon the limitations of the Constitution in opposition to such a scheme. A large surplus in the Treasury is the parent of many ills, and among them is found a tendency to an extremely liberal, if not loose, construction of the Constitution. It also attracts the gaze of States and individuals with a kind of fascination, and gives rise to plans and pretensions that an uncongested Treasury never could excite.

But if the constitutional question involved in the consideration of this bill should be determined in its favor, there are other objections remaining which prevent my assent to its provisions.

There should be a certainty and stability about the enforcement of taxation which should teach the citizen that the Government will only use the power to tax in cases where its necessity and justice are not doubtful, and which should also discourage the disturbing idea that the exercise of this power may be revoked by reimbursement of taxes once collected. Any other theory cheapens and in a measure discredits a process which more than any other is a manifestation of sovereign authority.

A government is not only kind, but performs its highest duty when it restores to the citizen taxes unlawfully collected or which have been erroneously or oppressively extorted by its agents or officers; but aside from these incidents, the people should not be familiarized with the

THE WEDDING OF GROVER CLEVELAND

THE WEDDING OF PRESIDENT CLEVELAND.

On June 2, 1886, occurred the first occasion on which a President of the United States was married in the White House. On that day, Miss Frances Folsom married the bosom friend and former law partner of her father, and forever afterwards was known as the "Bride of the White House." The marriage was performed in the Blue Room of the Executive Mansion, which for the occasion had been transformed into a veritable fairyland of flowers and plants. From Miss Holloway's "Ladies of the White House," we learn that the bride was attired in a "gown of ivory satin, with trimmings of India silk, arranged in Grecian folds over the front of the high corsage, and fastened in the folds of satin at the side. Orange blossoms and buds and leaves outlined this drapery and adorned the edge of the skirt. . . . A veil of silk tulle . . . fell over the entire length of the long court train. . . . She carried no flowers and wore no jewels except her engagement ring. . . . The President's gift to his bride was a diamond necklace." The honeymoon was spent quietly in Deer Park, Md., on the crest of the Blue Ridge.

spectacle of their Government repenting the collection of taxes and restoring them.

The direct tax levied in 1861 is not even suspected of invalidity. There never was a tax levied which was more needed, and its justice can not be questioned. Why, then, should it be returned?

The fact that the entire tax was not paid furnishes no reason that would not apply to nearly every case where taxes are laid. There are always delinquents, and while the more thorough and complete collection of taxes is a troublesome problem of government, the failure to solve the problem has never been held to call for the return of taxes actually collected.

The deficiency in the collection of this tax is found almost entirely in the insurrectionary States, while the quotas apportioned to the other States were, as a general rule, fully paid; and three-fourths or four-fifths of the money which it is proposed in this bill to return would be paid into the treasuries of the loyal States. But no valid reason for such payment is found in the fact that the Government at first could not, and afterwards, for reasons probably perfectly valid, did not, enforce collection in the other States.

There were many Federal taxes which were not paid by the people in the rebellious States; and if the nonpayment by them of this direct tax entitles the other States to a donation of the share of said taxes paid by their citizens, why should not the income tax and many other internal taxes paid entirely by the citizens of loyal States be also paid into the treasuries of these States? Considerations which recognize sectional divisions or the loyalty of the different States at the time this tax was laid should not enter into the discussion of the merits of this measure.

The loyal States should not be paid the large sums of money promised them by this bill because they were loyal and other States were not, nor should the States which rebelled against the Government be paid the smaller sum promised them because they were in rebellion and thus prevented the collection of their entire quotas, nor because this concession to them is necessary to justify the proposed larger gifts to the other States.

The people of the loyal States paid this direct tax as they bore other burdens in support of the Government, and I believe the taxpayers themselves are content. In the light of these considerations I am opposed to the payment of money from the Federal Treasury to enrich the treasuries of the States. Their funds should be furnished by their own citizens, and thus should be fostered the taxpayer's watchfulness of State expenditures and the taxpayer's jealous insistence upon the strict accountability of State officials. These elements of purity and strength in a State are not safely exchanged for the threatened demoralization and carelessness attending the custody and management of large gifts from the Federal Treasury.

The baneful effect of a surplus in the Treasury of the General Government is daily seen and felt. I do not think, however, that this surplus should be reduced or its contagion spread throughout the States by methods such as are provided in this bill.

There is still another objection to the bill, arising from what seems to me its unfairness and unjust discrimination.

In the case of proposed legislation of at least doubtful constitutionality and based upon no legal right, the equities which recommend it should always be definite and clear.

The money appropriated by this bill is to be paid to the governors of the respective States and Territories in which it was collected, whether the same was derived through said States and Territories, or directly "from any of the citizens or inhabitants thereof or other persons;" and it is further provided that such sums as were collected in payment of this Federal tax through the instrumentality of the State or Territorial officials, and accounted for to the General Government by such States and Territories, are to be paid unconditionally to their governors, while the same collected in payment of said tax by the United States, or, in other words, by the Federal machinery created for that purpose, are to be held in trust by said States or Territories for the benefit of those paying the same.

I am unable to understand how this discrimination in favor of those who have made payment of this tax directly to the officers of the Federal Government, and against those who made such payments through State or Territorial agencies, can be defended upon fair and equitable principles. It was the General Government in every case which exacted this tax from its citizens and people in the different States and Territories, and to provide for reimbursement to a part of its citizens by the creation of a trust for their benefit, while the money exacted in payment of this tax from a far greater number is paid unconditionally into the State and Territorial treasuries, is an unjust and unfair proceeding, in which the Government should not be implicated.

It will hardly do to say that the States and Territories who are the recipients of these large gifts may be trusted to do justice to its citizens who originally paid the money. This can not be relied upon; nor should the Government lose sight of the equality of which it boasts, and, having entered upon the plan of reimbursement, abandon to other agencies the duty of just distribution, and thus incur the risk of becoming accessory to actual inequality and injustice.

If in defense of the plan proposed it is claimed that exact equality can not be reached in the premises, this may be readily conceded. The money raised by this direct tax was collected and expended twenty-seven years ago. Nearly a generation has passed away since that time. Even if distribution should be attempted by the States and Territories, as well as by the Government, the taxpayers in many cases are neither alive nor represented, and in many other cases if alive they can not be found. Fraudulent claims would often outrun honest applications and innumerable and bitter contests would arise between claimants.

Another difficulty in the way of doing perfect justice in the operation of this plan of reimbursement is found in the fact that the money to be appropriated therefor was contributed to the Federal Treasury for entirely different purposes by a generation many of whom were not born when the direct tax was levied and paid, who have no relation to said tax and can not share in its distribution. While they stand by and see the money they have been obliged to pay into the public Treasury professedly to meet present necessities expended to reimburse taxation long ago fairly, legally, and justly collected from others, they can not fail to see the unfairness of the transaction.

The existence of a surplus in the Treasury is no answer to these objections. It is still the people's money, and better use can be found for it than the distribution of it upon the plea of the reimbursement of ancient taxation. A more desirable plan to reduce and prevent the recurrence of a large surplus can easily be adopted—one that, instead of creating injustice and inequality, promotes justice and equality by leaving in the hands of the people and for their use the money not needed by the Government "to pay the debts and provide for the common defense and general welfare of the United States."

The difficulties in the way of making a just reimbursement of this direct tax, instead of excusing the imperfections of the bill under consideration, furnish reasons why the scheme it proposes should not be entered upon.

I am constrained, upon the considerations herein presented, to withhold my assent from the bill herewith returned, because I believe it to be without constitutional warrant, because I am of the opinion that there exists no adequate reasons either in right or equity for the return of the tax in said bill mentioned, and because I believe its execution would cause actual injustice and unfairness. GROVER CLEVELAND.

PROCLAMATION.

BY THE PRESIDENT OF THE UNITED STATES OF AMERICA.

A PROCLAMATION.

Whereas public interests require that the Senate should be convened at 12 o'clock on the 4th day of March next to receive such communications as may be made by the Executive:

Now, therefore, I, Grover Cleveland, President of the United States, do hereby proclaim and declare that an extraordi, try occasion requires the Senate of the United States to convene at the Capitol, in the city of Washington, on the 4th day of March next, at 1 'clock noon, of which all persons who shall at that time be entitled to a t as members of that body are hereby required to take notice.

Given under my hand and the seal of the Unite l States, at Washington, the 26th day of February, A. D. 89, and of the Independence of the United States of Ame ica the one hundred and thirteenth.

[SEAL.]

GROV R CLEVELAND.

By the President:

T. F. BAYARD,
Secretary of State.

EXECUTIVE ORDER\ l

EXECU TIVE MANSION,
Washingto   December 5, 1888.

To the Civil Service Commission.

GENTLEMEN: The efficiency of the public servi t, in my opinion, renders it necessary to include in the classified servic and subject to examination the employees in the railway mail servic The difficulties in the way of this movement can, I believe, be over me by carefully prepared rules and regulations.

I have this day directed the Postmaster-General o so revise the classification of his Department as to include these employees in one or more classes; and in furtherance of my purpose I have to request that, after conference with the Postmaster-General, you will prepare the necessary modifications of the present rules and regulations to meet the proposed extension.

Yours, very truly,

GROVER CLEVELAND.

UNITED STATES CIVIL SERVICE COMMISSION,
Washington, D. C., December 5, 1888.

The PRESIDENT.

SIR: The Commission recommends that Special Departmental Rule No. 1 be amended by adding to the exceptions from examination therein declared the following:

"10. In all the Departments: Bookbinders."

Very respectfully,

A. P. EDGERTON,
CHAS. LYMAN,
United States Civil Service Commissioners.

EXECUTIVE MANSION,
Washington, December 6, 1888.

The above proposed amendment is hereby approved.

GROVER CLEVELAND.

Amendments to General Rules II, III, IV, Departmental Rules V, VIII, Customs Rule III, and Postal Rules II, VI, are hereby made and promulgated as follows:

GENERAL RULE II.

In line 1 strike out the word "three" and insert in place thereof the word "four." At the end of the rule insert the following: "4. The classified railway mail service." The rule as thus amended will read:

There shall be four branches of the classified civil service, as follows:
1. The classified departmental service.
2. The classified customs service.
3. The classified postal service.
4. The classified railway mail service.

GENERAL RULE III.

In section 9, line 2, after the word "service," insert the words "and the classified railway mail service." The section as thus amended will read:

9. Every applicant for examination for the classified departmental service and the classified railway mail service must support the statements of his application paper by certificates of persons acquainted with him, residents of the State, Territory, or district in which he claims *bona fide* residence; and the Commission shall prescribe the form and number of such certificates.

In section 10, line 1, after the word "or," insert the words "procured by his;" strike out all after the word "connivance" in line 1 to and including the word "and" in line 3, and in place of the words stricken out insert the words "or any;" strike out all after the word "consent" in line 4 to and including the word "examination" in line 5; strike out the words "for refusing" in line 6; change the period to a comma at the end of line 6 and insert after the comma the words "or to certify him for appointment, or for his removal after appointment." The section as thus amended will read:

10. A false statement made by an applicant, or procured by his connivance, or any deception or fraud practiced by an applicant, or by any person on his behalf with his consent, shall be good cause for refusal to examine such applicant, or to mark his papers after examination, or to certify him for appointment, or for his removal after appointment.

GENERAL RULE IV.

In section 2 strike out the letter "*a*," in brackets, in line 2; change the period to a semicolon at the end of line 4; in line 5 strike out the letter "*b*," in brackets, and strike out all after the word "has" to and including the word "has" in line 7, and write the section as one paragraph. The section as thus amended will read:

2. The Commission may refuse to certify an eligible who is so defective in sight, speech, or hearing, or who is otherwise so defective physically as to be apparently unfit to perform the duties of the position to which he is seeking appointment, or an eligible who has been guilty of crime or of infamous or of notoriously disgraceful conduct.

DEPARTMENTAL RULE V.

In section 2, paragraph 6, after the word "service" in line 3, insert the words "or the classified railway mail service;" in paragraph 7, line 1, strike out the word "and," and after the word "postal" in the same line insert the words "and railway mail." The section as thus amended will read:

Local boards.—These boards shall be organized at one or more places in each State and Territory where examinations for the classified departmental service or the classified railway mail service are to be held, and shall conduct such examinations; and each shall be composed of persons in the public service residing in the State or Territory in which the board is to act.

Customs, postal, and railway mail boards.—These boards shall conduct such examinations for the classified departmental service as the Commission may direct.

DEPARTMENTAL RULE VIII.

In section 1, clause (*c*), line 1, after the word "post-office," insert "or to the classified railway mail service;" in line 2, after the word "from," strike out the words "such an office" and insert "a classified post-office or the classified railway mail service." The clause as thus amended will read:

(*c*) From the Post-Office Department to a classified post-office or to the classified railway mail service, and from a classified post-office or the classified railway mail service to the Post-Office Department, upon requisition by the Postmaster-General.

In section 2, line 6, after the word "been," insert "in the classified railway mail service or." The section as thus amended will read:

2. No person may be transferred as herein authorized until the Commission shall have certified to the officer making the transfer requisition that the person whom it is proposed to transfer has passed an examination to test fitness for the place to which he is to be transferred, and that such person has during at least six months preceding the date of the certificate been in the classified railway mail service or in the classified service of the Department, customs district, or post-office from which the transfer is to be made: *Provided*, That no person who has been appointed from the copyist register shall be transferred to a place the salary of which is more than $900 per annum until one year after appointment.

CUSTOMS RULE III.

In section 2, clause (*c*), at the end of line 1, insert "and the classified railway mail service." The clause as thus amended will read:

(*c*) Conduct such examinations for the classified departmental service and the classified railway mail service as the Commission may direct.

POSTAL RULE II.

In section 5, at the end of clause (*e*) of that section, strike out the period and insert a comma, and after the comma the following:

Provided, That superintendents of mails shall be selected from among the employees of the railway mail service.

The clause as thus amended will read:

Superintendents designated by the Post-Office Department, and reported as such to the Commission, *Provided*, That superintendents of mails shall be selected from among .he employees of the railway mail service.

POSTAL RULE VI.

In section 1, clause (*a*), after the word "another" in line 1 of that clause, strike out the comma and insert a semicolon, and after the semicolon the following:

From any classified post-office to the classified railway mail service, and from the classified railway mail service to any classified post-office.

In clause (*b*), after the word "post-office" in line 1, insert "or from the classified railway mail service," and in line 2, after the word "post-office," insert "or to the classified railway mail service."

In section 2, line 6, after the word "certificate" insert "in the classified railway mail service or." The rule as thus amended will read:

1. Transfers may be made as follows:

(*a*) From one classified post-office to another, from any classified post-office to the classified railway mail service, and from the classified railway mail service to any classified post-office, upon requisition of the Postmaster-General.

(*b*) From any classified post-office or from the classified railway mail service to the Post-Office Department, and from the Post-Office Department to any classified post-office, or to the classified railway mail service, upon requisition of the Postmaster-General.

2. No person may be transferred as herein authorized until the Commission shall have certified to the officer making the transfer requisition that the person whom it is proposed to transfer has passed an examination to test fitness for the place to which he is to be transferred, and that such person has been at least six months next preceding the date of the certificate in the classified railway mail service or in the classified service of the Department or post-office from which the transfer is to be made.

Approved, January 4, 1889. **GROVER CLEVELAND.**

RAILWAY MAIL RULES.

RAILWAY MAIL RULE I.

The classified railway mail service shall include all the officers, clerks, and other persons in that service classified under the provisions of section 6 of the act to regulate and improve the civil service of the United States, approved January 16, 1883.

RAILWAY MAIL RULE II.

1. To test fitness for admission to the classified railway mail service the following examinations shall be provided:

Clerk examination.—This examination shall include not more than the following subjects:

(*a*) Orthography.

(*b*) Copying.

5433 Messages and Papers of the Presidents

(*c*) Penmanship.

(*d*) Arithmetic—fundamental rules, fractions, and percentage.

(*e*) Letter writing.

(*f*) The geography of the United States, and especially of the State or railway mail division in which the applicant resides.

(*g*) The railway systems of the State or railway mail division in which the applicant resides.

(*h*) Reading addresses.

Other competitive examinations.—Such other competitive examinations as the Commission may from time to time deem necessary.

Noncompetitive examinations.—Such examinations may, with the approval of the Commission, be held under conditions stated in General Rule III, clause 2.

2. No person shall be examined for the railway mail service if under 18 or over 35 years of age, except that any person honorably discharged from the military or naval service of the United States by reason of disability resulting from wounds or sickness incurred in the line of duty, and whose claim of preference under section 1754 of the Revised Statutes has been allowed by the Commission, may be examined without regard to his age.

3. Any person desiring examination for admission to the classified railway mail service must, in his own handwriting, make request for a blank form of application, which request, and also his application, shall be addressed as follows: "United States Civil Service Commission, Washington, D. C."

4. The date of reception, and also of approval, by the Commission of each application shall be noted on the application paper.

5. Exceptions from examination in the classified railway mail service are hereby made as follows:

(*a*) General superintendent.

(*b*) Assistant general superintendent.

6. No person appointed to a place under any exception to examination hereby made shall within one year after appointment be transferred to another place not also excepted from examination; but after service of not less than one year in an examination-excepted place he may be transferred to a place not excepted from examination upon the certificate of the Commission that he has passed an examination to test fitness for the place to which his transfer is proposed.

RAILWAY MAIL RULE III.

1. The papers of every examination shall be marked under the direction of the Commission, and each competitor shall be graded on a scale of 100, according to the general average determined by the marks made by the examiners on his papers.

2. The Commission shall appoint in each railway mail division as many boards of examiners as it may deem necessary for the good of the service and the convenience of applicants: *Provided,* That there shall be at least one such board in each Territory and not less than two in each State, except that the number may be limited to one each in the States of Rhode Island and Delaware.

3. These boards shall conduct such examinations for admission to and promotions in the classified railway mail service and such examinations for the other branches of the classified service as the Commission may direct. They shall also mark such examination papers as the Commission may direct.

4. Unless otherwise directed by the Commission, the papers of examination for admission to the classified railway mail service shall be marked by the central board.

5. The papers of an examination having been marked, the Commission shall ascertain—

(*a*) The name of every competitor who has, under section 1754 of the Revised Statutes, claim of preference in civil appointments, and who has attained a general average of not less than 65 per cent; and all such competitors are hereby declared eligible to the class or place to test fitness for which the examination was held.

(*b*) The name of every other competitor who has attained a general average of not less than 70 per cent; and all such applicants are hereby declared eligible to the class or place to test fitness for which the examination was held.

6. The names of all preference-claiming competitors whose general average is not less than 65 per cent, together with the names of all other competitors whose general average is not less than 70 per cent, shall be entered upon the register of persons eligible to the class or place to test fitness for which the examination was held.

7. The grade of each competitor shall be expressed by the whole number nearest the general average attained by him, and the grade of each eligible shall be noted upon the register of eligibles in connection with his name. When two or more eligibles are of the same grade, preference in certification shall be determined by the order in which their application papers were filed.

8. There shall be a register of eligibles for each State and Territory, and the names of all the eligibles of any State or Territory shall be entered upon the register for that State or Territory. The eligibles of the District of Columbia shall be entered, according to their election, upon the register of the State of Maryland or upon that of the State of Virginia.

9. Immediately after the general averages shall have been ascertained each competitor shall be notified that he has passed or has failed to pass.

10. If a competitor fail to pass, he may, with the consent of the Commission, be allowed a reexamination at any time within six months from the date of failure without filing a new application; but if such reexamination be not allowed within that time he shall not be again examined without making in due form a new application.

11. No eligible shall be allowed reexamination during the term of his eligibility unless he shall furnish evidence satisfactory to the Commission that at the time of his examination, because of illness or other good cause, he was incapable of doing himself justice in said examination.

12. The term of eligibility shall be such as the Commission may by regulation determine, but shall not be less than one year from the day on which the name of the eligible is entered upon the register: *Provided*, That for public and sufficient reasons the Commission shall have authority to extend the term of eligibility of the eligibles on the register of any State or Territory for such period, not exceeding one year, as it may deem necessary, without correspondingly extending the term of the eligibles on the registers of the other States and Territories as to which the same reasons do not exist.

RAILWAY MAIL RULE IV.

1. All vacancies in the classified railway mail service above class 1, unless among the places excepted from examination, shall be filled by promotion, upon such tests of fitness as the Postmaster-General, with the approval of the Commission, may prescribe: *Provided*, That a vacancy occurring in a State or railway mail division in any grade may be filled by the transfer of a clerk of the same grade from another State or division, under such regulations as the Postmaster-General, with the approval of the Commission, may prescribe, or by reappointment under the provisions of Railway Mail Rule VI.

2. All vacancies in class 1, unless filled by transfer or reappointment under Railway Mail Rule VI, shall be filled in the following manner:

(*a*) The general superintendent shall, in form and manner to be prescribed by the Commission, request the certification to him of eligibles from a State or Territory in which a vacancy then exists.

(*b*) The Commission shall certify from the register of the State or Territory in which the vacancy exists the names of the three eligibles thereon having the highest averages who have not been three times certified: *Provided*, That if upon said register there are the names of eligibles having a claim of preference under section 1754, Revised Statutes, the names of such eligibles shall be certified before the names of other elig bles of higher grade: *Provided further*, That if there are not three eligibles upon the register of the State or Territory in which the vacancy exists eligibles may be certified from the register of any adjoining State or Territory.

(*c*) The name of an eligible shall not be certified more than three times.

3. Of the three names certified to the general superintendent one shall be selected and designated for appointment, and more than one may be if there be more than one vacancy existing at the time.

4. Each person designated for appointment shall be notified, and upon reporting to the proper officer shall be appointed for a probational period of six months, at the end of which period, if his conduct and capacity be satisfactory, he shall be absolutely appointed; but if his conduct and capacity be not satisfactory he shall be so notified, and such notice shall be his discharge from the service.

5. The general superintendent, with the approval of the Postmaster-Genera' shall prescribe regulations under which each probationer shall be observed and tested and a record kept of his conduct and capacity, and such record shall determine his fitness for the service and whether he shall be dropped during or at the end of pro bation or be absolutely appointed.

6. There may be certified and appointed in each State and Territory, in the manner provided for in this rule, such number of substitute clerks, not exceeding the ratio of one substitute to twenty regular clerks, in such State or Territory as the Postmaster-General may authorize, and any vacancies occurring in class I in any State or Territory in which substitutes have been appointed shall be filled by the appointment thereto of those substitutes in the order of their appointment as substitutes without further certification. The time during which any substitute is actually employed in the service shall be counted as a part of his probation.

RAILWAY MAIL RULE V.

1. Transfers may be made as follows:

(*a*) From the classified railway mail service to any classified post-office, and from any classified post-office to the classified railway mail service, upon requisition of the Postmaster-General.

(*b*) From the classified railway mail service to the Post-Office Department, and from the Post-Office Department to the classified railway mail service, upon requisition of the Postmaster-General.

2. No person shall be transferred as herein authorized until the Commission shall have certified to the Postmaster-General that the person whom it is proposed to transfer has passed an examination to test fitness for the place to which he is to be transferred, and that such person has been at least six months next preceding the date of the certificate in the classified railway mail service or in the classified service of the post-office or Department from which the transfer is to be made: *Provided*, That no employee shall be transferred to any grade which he could not enter by original appointment by reason of any age limitation prescribed by the civil-service rules.

RAILWAY MAIL RULE VI.

1. Upon requisition of the Postmaster-General the Commission shall certify for reinstatement in a grade or class no higher than that in which he was formerly employed any person who within one year next preceding the date of the requisition has, through no delinquency or misconduct, been separated from the classified railway mail service.

RAILWAY MAIL RULE VII.

1. The general superintendent of the railway mail service shall report to the Commission—

(*a*) Every probational (whether substitute or regular) and every absolute appointment in the railway mail service in each State or Territory; every appointment under any exception to examination authorized by Railway Mail Rule II, clause 5; every reappointment under Railway Mail Rule VI, and every appointment of a substitute to a regular place.

(*b*) Every refusal to make an absolute appointment and the reason therefor, and every refusal or neglect to accept an appointment in the classified railway mail service.

(*c*) Every transfer into the classified railway mail service.

(*d*) Every separation from the classified railway mail service and the cause of such separation.

(*e*) Every promotion or degradation in the classified railway mail service, if such promotion or degradation be from one class to another class.

(*f*) Once in every six months, namely, on the 30th of June and the 31st of December of each year, the whole number of employees in each railway mail division, arranged by States and classes, showing the number of substitutes and the number of regular employees in each class in each State or Territory.

EXECUTIVE MANSION,
Washington, January 4, 1889.

The above rules are hereby approved, to take effect March 15, 1889: *Provided*, That such rules shall become operative and take effect in any State or Territory as soon as an eligible register for such State or Territory shall be prepared, if it shall be prior to the date above fixed.

GROVER CLEVELAND.

UNITED STATES CIVIL SERVICE COMMISSION,
Washington, D. C., February 8, 1889.

The PRESIDENT.

SIR: The Commission recommends that Special Departmental Rule No. 1 be amended by adding to the exceptions from examination therein declared the following:

"11. In the Department of Justice: Assistant attorneys.

"12. In the Department of Agriculture, Bureau of Experiment Stations: Private secretary to the Director."

Very respectfully,

CHAS. LYMAN,
United States Civil Service Commissioner.

Approved, February 11, 1889.　　　　GROVER CLEVELAND.

UNITED STATES CIVIL SERVICE COMMISSION,
Washington, D. C., February 9, 1889.

The PRESIDENT.

SIR: This Commission has the honor to recommend that the order of the President fixing the places to which appointments may be made upon noncompetitive examination under General Rule III, section 2, clause (*f*), may be amended by including among such places the following:

"In the Post-Office Department: Captain of the watch."

This recommendation is based upon the letter of the Postmaster-General dated December 19, 1888, in which he says :

" I would request that places in the Post-Office Department subject to noncompetitive examination be increased by including the position of captain of the watch, as the duties of the position are of such a nature that the head of the Department should be permitted to recommend for examination such person as would possess such other qualifications in addition to the merely clerical ones as would commend him to the head of he Department to fill satisfactorily such position."

Very respectfully,

CHAS. LYMAN,
United States Civil Service Commissioner.

Approved, February 11, 1889.

GROVER CLEVELAND.

UNITED STATES CIVIL SERVICE COMMISSION,
Washington, D. C., February 9, 1889.

The PRESIDENT.

SIR : This Commission has the honor to recommend that the order heretofore approved by you authorizing noncompetitive examination under General Rule III, section 2, clause (*e*), to test fitness for certain designated places in the classified departmental service, may be amended by the revocation of so much of the order above referred to as provides for the appointment upon noncompetitive examination of "inspector of electric lights" in the office of the Secretary in the Treasury Department.

Very respectfully,

CHAS. LYMAN,
United States Civil Service Commissioner.

Approved, February 11, 1889.

GROVER CLEVELAND.

EXECUTIVE MANSION, *February 26, 1889.*

Whereas by an act of Congress entitled "An act to enable the President to protect the interests of the United States in Panama," approved February 25, 1889, it was enacted as follows :

That there be, and is hereby, appropriated, out of any money in the Treasury not otherwise appropriated, the sum of $250,000 to enable the President to protect the interests of the United States and to provide for the security of persons and property of citizens of the United States at the Isthmus of Panama in such manner as he may deem expedient.

And whereas satisfactory information has been received by me that a number of citizens of the United States have been thrown out of employment and left destitute in the Republic of Colombia by the stoppage of work on the Panama Canal:

It is therefore ordered, That so much as is necessary of the fund appropriated by the said act be expended, under the direction and control of the Secretary of State, in furnishing transportation to the United States to any citizen or citizens of the United States who may be found destitute within the National Department of Panama, in the Republic of Colombia.

GROVER CLEVELAND.

QUESTIONS.

1. If an epidemic should break out, has the President authority to spend Government money to check it? Page 4898.

2. What was Cleveland's recommendation as to the basis for revenue for Government Buildings? Page 5377.

3. What was Cleveland's attitude toward the development of our Navy? Page 4936.

4. Can a person be a citizen of a State and not of the United States? Page 4921.

5. Cite the nature of the benefits and the obligations as well as of the frauds under naturalization laws. Pages 4921, 5090, 5366, 5370.

6. Are there any means of expatriation for a native or naturalized citizen of the United States? Page 4921.

7. What was the "Presidential Succession Act"? (See Presidential Succession, Encyclopedic Index.)

8. What was Cleveland's view as to the discretionary power of Presidents over nominations? Page 4960.

9. What were Cleveland's views on Chinese Immigration? Pages 4914, 4968, 4975, 5083, 5194, 5215.

10. On what ground did Cleveland dismiss a British ambassador? Pages 5365, 5396. (See also Sackville-West Affair, Encyclopedic Index.)

SUGGESTIONS.

Civil Service attracted the particular attention of Cleveland. Pages 4948, 4974, 5112, 5201, 5348, 5399, 5429.

Read Cleveland's Foreign Policy. Page 4912.

NOTE.

For further suggestions on Cleveland's administration see Cleveland, Grover, Encyclopedic Index.

By reading the Foreign Policy of each President, and by scanning the messages as to the state of the nation, a thorough knowledge of the history of the United States will be acquired from the most authentic sources; because, as has been said, "Each President reviews the past, depicts the present and forecasts the future of the nation."

Benjamin Harrison

March 4, 1889, to March 4, 1893

HOME, VILLA, INDIANAPOLIS, INDIANA; OF BENJAMIN HARRISON.

With reproduction of official portrait by Johnson, from the "White House Collection"

HOME, AT INDIANAPOLIS, INDIANA, OF BENJAMIN HARRISON
With reproduction of official portrait, by Johnson, from the White House Collection

HARRISON

It is easy to write of a friend. The reader willingly makes generous allowance for the partialities of personal friendship. But to write discriminatingly of a living public man, correctly estimating and fairly presenting his character, attainments, and achievements, is a delicate and difficult task. Somebody has well said that there is nothing more inspiring than the story of a triumphant life. Men never tire of it and it cannot be too often told. There are grades in greatness. Some men are born great; upon their shoulders God has dropped the mantle of genius, giving them moral worth and intellectual power, and unfolding to their keen conceptions, the wonderful mysteries of life. There are other men less richly endowed by nature's partial hands, who by will and work, animated and guided by noble purposes and lofty virtues, have climbed to the highest peaks of power and fame, and calmly trod the dizzy heights, admired and honored by all the world.

Benjamin Harrison was a self-made and a well-made man. Though coming from a distinguished ancestry, he was in youth poor and comparatively obscure. Yet by the power of his intellect and the nobility of his character, he rose to the highest rank among the rulers of the world, the Presidency of the United States of America.

As a man and citizen Benjamin Harrison presents a model of our best manhood and citizenship—industrious, frugal, sincere and unpretending. As a public official he was ever able, painstaking and courageous. Not many men had a life more remarkable or attained dignity and honor more striking. He won his own illustrious way by his great abilities, his splendid accomplishments and the heroic virtue and manliness of his character. The higher he rose, the more strikingly were displayed his remarkable abilities and sterling virtues. He put brains and conscience into all his work, and the more prodigious the tasks that confronted him, the more brilliancy and bravery he displayed in their accomplishment. It is a long road from the office of a country lawyer to the White House. It is full of struggles and beset with temptations. It takes keen eyes, steady nerves and fearless feet to safely find the way. Benjamin Harrison trod this dangerous road in hope, honor and bravery. He rarely faltered or stumbled. He moved upward with the sturdy tread of conscious strength and honesty. He made politics statesmanship, and showed that the successful office-seeker may be the dignified and Christian gentleman.

It may be safely said that no man who ever occupied the Presidential chair was more familiar with all the details of Government than was President Harrison. He knew the functions and was informed as to

5437-C

the duties of every department and bureau. He could have taken any cabinet portfolio or any bureau or commissionership and discharged the duties of the positions without hesitation. His accurate knowledge as to departmental matters was a constant surprise to those who had occasion to consult him with reference to any branch of the public service. He not only knew all about the business of the Government, but he insisted that it be transacted with intelligence and fidelity. He had little toleration for carelessness or incapacity in public officials and employes. He conscientiously believed in the motto that, "public office is a public trust." He often in private and public utterances emphasized the fact that stronger and better men were needed in the public service. He believed that in the affairs of Government as in private business, the rule of the survival of the fittest should ever hold absolute and inexorable sway. He was eminently practical in directing the administration of public affairs. He realized that facts and not theories must be the moving forces in Government—that in the logic of events there is the highest wisdom.

Benjamin Harrison was not only able, intelligent and practical in the discharge of his duties as a local and State official, and United States Senator and President, but was thoroughly conscientious and always showed the courage of his convictions. He never hesitated to say or do what he thought ought to be said or done. He was a deeply religious man and believed that religion is for everyday use in all the duties of life. In his private life and in his public acts and utterances he exhibited the virtues of the Christian as conspicuously as he displayed those of the statesman and patriot.

The people of the United States honor and respect Benjamin Harrison. They believe in him. They admire his great talents and sterling virtues. They know he was honest, wise and brave. His Administration will go into history as one of the wisest and best that the country has ever enjoyed.

Benjamin Harrison as a citizen, as a soldier and as the Nation's Highest Official, filled the measure of his duty full. American history can furnish few parallels to his useful and exalted record. As has been well said of another illustrious American—the immortal Lincoln: "None but himself can be his parallel."

Horace A. Taylor

CAROLINE SCOTT HARRISON

Caroline Lavinia Scott, daughter of Prof. Scott, President of Oxford Seminary, was born in Oxford, Ohio. She married Benjamin Harrison in 1853, before he attained his majority. Nearly forty years passed in congenial companionship, before death deprived him of a faithful and devoted wife. She was talented in music and painting and had decided literary taste. She was also an earnest and truly charitable church worker. Her social bearing in her high station was dignified, womanly and hospitable, and her death during her husband's term cast a heavy shadow over its closing months. They had two children, Russell and Mary. The latter, Mrs. McKee, made her home at the Executive Mansion, assisting her mother most graciously in her many and varied social duties. After Mrs. Harrison's death, she assumed entire charge as mistress of the White House, until the close of her father's administration in 1893.

Benjamin Harrison

BENJAMIN HARRISON, twenty-third President of the United States, was born at North Bend, Ohio, August 20, 1833. His father, John Scott Harrison, was the third son of General William Henry Harrison, ninth President of the United States, who was the third and youngest son of Benjamin Harrison, one of the signers of the Declaration of Independence. John Scott Harrison was twice married, his second wife being Elizabeth, daughter of Archibald Irwin, of Mercersburg, Pa. Benjamin was the second son of this marriage. His parents were resolutely determined upon the education of their children, and early in childhood Benjamin was placed under private instruction at home. In 1847 he and his elder brother were sent to a school on what was known as College Hill, a few miles from Cincinnati. After remaining there two years entered the junior class at Miami University, at Oxford, Ohio, where he was graduated in 1852. Was married October 20, 1853, to Caroline Scott, daughter of Dr. John W. Scott, who was then president of Oxford Female Seminary, from which Mrs. Harrison was graduated in 1852. After studying law under Storer & Gwynne in Cincinnati, Mr. Harrison was admitted to the bar in 1854, and began the practice of his profession at Indianapolis, Ind., which has since been his home. Was appointed crier of the Federal court, at a salary of $2.50 per day. This was the first money he had ever earned. Jonathan W. Gordon, one of the leaders of the Indianapolis bar, called young Harrison to his assistance in the prosecution of a criminal tried for burglary, and intrusted to him the plea for the State. He had taken ample notes of the evidence, but the case was closed at night, and the court-house being dimly lighted by tallow candles, he was unable to read them when he arose to address the court and jury. Laying them aside, he depended entirely upon his memory and found it perfect. He made an eloquent plea, produced a marked impression, and won the case. Since then he has always been an impromptu speaker. Formed a partnership later with William Wallace, but in 1860 the latter became clerk of Marion County, and the firm was changed to Harrison & Fishback, which was terminated by the entry of the senior partner into the Army in 1862. Was

5438

chosen reporter of the supreme court of Indiana in 1860 on the Republican ticket. This was his first active appearance in the political field. When the Civil War began assisted in raising the Seventieth Indiana Regiment of Volunteers, taking a second lieutenant's commission and raising Company A of that regiment. Governor Morton tendered him the command of the regiment and he was commissioned its colonel. Mr. Harrison appointed a deputy reporter for the supreme court. In the ensuing autumn the Democratic State committee, considering his position as a civil officer vacated by this military appointment, nominated and elected a successor, although his term of office had not expired. Their view was sustained by the State supreme court; but in 1864, while Colonel Harrison was in the Army, the people of Indiana gave their judgment by reelecting him to the position of supreme-court reporter by an overwhelming majority. In 1862 the Seventieth Indiana went into the field with Harrison as its colonel, their objective point being Bowling Green, Ky. It was brigaded with the Seventy-ninth Ohio and the One hundred and second, One hundred and fifth, and One hundred and twenty-ninth Illinois regiments, under Brigadier-General Ward, of Kentucky, and this organization was kept unchanged until the close of the war. Colonel Harrison had the right of the brigade, and his command was occupied at first in guarding railroads and hunting guerrillas, his energies being largely spent in drilling his men. When General Rosecrans set out for Chattanooga General Ward was sent on duty to Nashville, and on January 2, 1864, his command was called to the front. Later this brigade became the First Brigade of the Third Division of the Twentieth Army Corps, under General Hooker, General Ward resuming its command. The campaign under General Sherman, upon which his regiment with its associate forces entered, was directed, as is now known, against the Confederate army of General Joseph E. Johnston, and not against any particular place. In the Federal advance one of the severest actions was fought at Resaca, Ga., May 14 and 15, 1864, and the Seventieth Indiana led the assault. His regiment participated in the fights at New Hope Church and at Golgotha Church, Kenesaw Mountain, and Peach Tree Creek. When Atlanta was taken by Sherman, September 2, 1864, Colonel Harrison received his first furlough to visit home, being assigned to special duty in a canvass of the State to recruit for the forces in the field. Returning to Chattanooga and then to Nashville, he was placed in command of a provisional brigade held in reserve at the battle at the latter place (December 15 and 16, 1864), and was but little engaged. When the fight was over he was sent in pursuit of the Confederate general Hood. Recalled from that pursuit, was next ordered to report to General Sherman at Savannah. While passing through New York he succumbed to an attack of scarlet fever, but in a few weeks was able to proceed on his way. Joining Sherman at Goldsboro, N. C., resumed command of his old brigade, and at the close of the war went with it to Washington to take part in the grand review of the armies. Was duly mustered out of the service June 8, 1865, not, however, until he had received a commission as brevet brigadier-general, dated January 23, 1865. Returning to Indianapolis after the war, resumed his office of reporter of the supreme court, but in 1867 declined a renomination, preferring to devote himself exclusively to the practice of law. Became a member of the firm of Porter, Harrison & Fishback, and, after subsequent changes, of that of Harrison, Miller & Elam. Took part in 1868 and 1872 in the Presidential campaigns in support of General Grant, traveling over Indiana and speaking to large audiences. In 1876 at first declined a nomination for governor on the Republican ticket, consenting to run only after the regular nominee had withdrawn. In this contest he received almost 2,000 more votes than his associates, but was defeated. Was a member of the Mississippi River Commission in 1879. In 1880, as chairman of the Indiana delegation in the Republican national convention, he cast nearly the entire vote of the State for James A. Garfield for President. President Garfield offered him a place in his Cabinet, but he declined it, preferring the United States Senatorship from Indiana, to which he had just been chosen, and which he held from 1881 to 1887. In the Senate he advocated the tariff views of his party, opposed President Cleveland's vetoes of pension bills, urged the reconstruction and upbuilding of the Navy, and labored and voted for civil-service reform. Was a delegate at large to the Republican national convention in 1884, and in 1888 at Chicago was nominated for the Presidency on the eighth ballot. The nomination was made unanimous, and in November he was elected, receiving 233 electoral votes to 168 for Grover Cleveland. Was inaugurated March 4, 1889. Was again nominated for the Presidency at the national Republican convention which met at Minneapolis in 1892, but was defeated at the November election, receiving 145 electoral votes, against 276 votes for Grover Cleveland. Upon his retiring from office located at Indianapolis, Ind., where he now resides.

INAUGURAL ADDRESS.

FELLOW-CITIZENS: There is no constitutional or legal requirement that the President shall take the oath of office in the presence of the people, but there is so manifest an appropriateness in the public induction to office of the chief executive officer of the nation that from the beginning of the Government the people, to whose service the official oath consecrates the officer, have been called to witness the solemn ceremonial. The oath taken in the presence of the people becomes a mutual covenant. The officer covenants to serve the whole body of the people by a faithful execution of the laws, so that they may be the unfailing defense and security of those who respect and observe them, and that neither wealth, station, nor the power of combinations shall be able to evade their just penalties or to wrest them from a beneficent public purpose to serve the ends of cruelty or selfishness.

My promise is spoken; yours unspoken, but not the less real and solemn. The people of every State have here their representatives. Surely I do not misinterpret the spirit of the occasion when I assume that the whole body of the people covenant with me and with each other to-day to support and defend the Constitution and the Union of the States, to yield willing obedience to all the laws and each to every other citizen his equal civil and political rights. Entering thus solemnly into covenant with each other, we may reverently invoke and confidently expect the favor and help of Almighty God—that He will give to me wisdom, strength, and fidelity, and to our people a spirit of fraternity and a love of righteousness and peace.

This occasion derives peculiar interest from the fact that the Presidential term which begins this day is the twenty-sixth under our Constitution. The first inauguration of President Washington took place in New York, where Congress was then sitting, on the 30th day of April, 1789, having been deferred by reason of delays attending the organization of the Congress and the canvass of the electoral vote. Our people have already worthily observed the centennials of the Declaration of Independence, of the battle of Yorktown, and of the adoption of the Constitution, and will shortly celebrate in New York the institution of the second great department of our constitutional scheme of government. When the centennial of the institution of the judicial department, by the organization of the Supreme Court, shall have been suitably observed, as I trust it will be, our nation will have fully entered its second century.

I will not attempt to note the marvelous and in great part happy contrasts between our country as it steps over the threshold into its second century of organized existence under the Constitution and that weak but wisely ordered young nation that looked undauntedly down the first century, when all its years stretched out before it.

Our people will not fail at this time to recall the incidents which accompanied the institution of government under the Constitution, or to find inspiration and guidance in the teachings and example of Washington and his great associates, and hope and courage in the contrast which thirty-eight populous and prosperous States offer to the thirteen States, weak in everything except courage and the love of liberty, that then fringed our Atlantic seaboard.

The Territory of Dakota has now a population greater than any of the original States (except Virginia) and greater than the aggregate of five of the smaller States in 1790. The center of population when our national capital was located was east of Baltimore, and it was argued by many well-informed persons that it would move eastward rather than westward; yet in 1880 it was found to be near Cincinnati, and the new census about to be taken will show another stride to the westward. That which was the body has come to be only the rich fringe of the nation's robe. But our growth has not been limited to territory, population, and aggregate wealth, marvelous as it has been in each of those directions. The masses of our people are better fed, clothed, and housed than their fathers were. The facilities for popular education have been vastly enlarged and more generally diffused.

The virtues of courage and patriotism have given recent proof of their continued presence and increasing power in the hearts and over the lives of our people. The influences of religion have been multiplied and strengthened. The sweet offices of charity have greatly increased. The virtue of temperance is held in higher estimation. We have not attained an ideal condition. Not all of our people are happy and prosperous; not all of them are virtuous and law-abiding. But on the whole the opportunities offered to the individual to secure the comforts of life are better than are found elsewhere and largely better than they were here one hundred years ago.

The surrender of a large measure of sovereignty to the General Government, effected by the adoption of the Constitution, was not accomplished until the suggestions of reason were strongly reenforced by the more imperative voice of experience. The divergent interests of peace speedily demanded a "more perfect union." The merchant, the shipmaster, and the manufacturer discovered and disclosed to our statesmen and to the people that commercial emancipation must be added to the political freedom which had been so bravely won. The commercial policy of the mother country had not relaxed any of its hard and oppressive features. To hold in check the development of our commercial marine, to prevent or retard the establishment and growth of manufactures in the States, and so to secure the American market for their shops and the carrying trade for their ships, was the policy of European statesmen, and was pursued with the most selfish vigor.

Petitions poured in upon Congress urging the imposition of discriminating duties that should encourage the production of needed things at home. The patriotism of the people, which no longer found a field of exercise in war, was energetically directed to the duty of equipping the young Republic for the defense of its independence by making its people self-dependent. Societies for the promotion of home manufactures and for encouraging the use of domestics in the dress of the people were organized in many of the States. The revival at the end of the century of the same patriotic interest in the preservation and development of domestic industries and the defense of our working people against injurious foreign competition is an incident worthy of attention. It is not a departure but a return that we have witnessed. The protective policy had then its opponents. The argument was made, as now, that its benefits inured to particular classes or sections.

If the question became in any sense or at any time sectional, it was only because slavery existed in some of the States. But for this there was no reason why the cotton-producing States should not have led or walked abreast with the New England States in the production of cotton fabrics. There was this reason only why the States that divide with Pennsylvania the mineral treasures of the great southeastern and central mountain ranges should have been so tardy in bringing to the smelting furnace and to the mill the coal and iron from their near opposing hillsides. Mill fires were lighted at the funeral pile of slavery. The emancipation proclamation was heard in the depths of the earth as well as in the sky; men were made free, and material things became our better servants.

The sectional element has happily been eliminated from the tariff discussion. We have no longer States that are necessarily only planting States. None are excluded from achieving that diversification of pursuits among the people which brings wealth and contentment. The cotton plantation will not be less valuable when the product is spun in the country town by operatives whose necessities call for diversified crops and create a home demand for garden and agricultural products. Every new mine, furnace, and factory is an extension of the productive capacity of the State more real and valuable than added territory.

Shall the prejudices and paralysis of slavery continue to hang upon the skirts of progress? How long will those who rejoice that slavery no longer exists cherish or tolerate the incapacities it put upon their communities? I look hopefully to the continuance of our protective system and to the consequent development of manufacturing and mining enterprises in the States hitherto wholly given to agriculture as a potent influence in the perfect unification of our people. The men who have invested their capital in these enterprises, the farmers who have felt the benefit of their neighborhood, and the men who work in shop or field will not fail to find and to defend a community of interest.

Is it not quite possible that the farmers and the promoters of the great mining and manufacturing enterprises which have recently been established in the South may yet find that the free ballot of the workingman, without distinction of race, is needed for their defense as well as for his own? I do not doubt that if those men in the South who now accept the tariff views of Clay and the constitutional expositions of Webster would courageously avow and defend their real convictions they would not find it difficult, by friendly instruction and cooperation, to make the black man their efficient and safe ally, not only in establishing correct principles in our national administration, but in preserving for their local communities the benefits of social order and economical and honest government. At least until the good offices of kindness and education have been fairly tried the contrary conclusion can not be plausibly urged.

I have altogether rejected the suggestion of a special Executive policy for any section of our country. It is the duty of the Executive to administer and enforce in the methods and by the instrumentalities pointed out and provided by the Constitution all the laws enacted by Congress. These laws are general and their administration should be uniform and equal. As a citizen may not elect what laws he will obey, neither may the Executive elect which he will enforce. The duty to obey and to execute embraces the Constitution in its entirety and the whole code of laws enacted under it. The evil example of permitting individuals, corporations, or communities to nullify the laws because they cross some selfish or local interest or prejudices is full of danger, not only to the nation at large, but much more to those who use this pernicious expedient to escape their just obligations or to obtain an unjust advantage over others. They will presently themselves be compelled to appeal to the law for protection, and those who would use the law as a defense must not deny that use of it to others.

If our great corporations would more scrupulously observe their legal limitations and duties, they would have less cause to complain of the unlawful limitations of their rights or of violent interference with their operations. The community that by concert, open or secret, among its citizens denies to a portion of its members their plain rights under the law has severed the only safe bond of social order and prosperity. The evil works from a bad center both ways. It demoralizes those who practice it and destroys the faith of those who suffer by it in the efficiency of the law as a safe protector. The man in whose breast that faith has been darkened is naturally the subject of dangerous and uncanny suggestions. Those who use unlawful methods, if moved by no higher motive than the selfishness that prompted them, may well stop and inquire what is to be the end of this.

An unlawful expedient can not become a permanent condition of government. If the educated and influential classes in a community either practice or connive at the systematic violation of laws that seem to them to cross their convenience, what can they expect when the lesson that convenience or a supposed class interest is a sufficient cause for lawlessness has been well learned by the ignorant classes? A community where law is the rule of conduct and where courts, not mobs, execute its penalties is the only attractive field for business investments and honest labor.

Our naturalization laws should be so amended as to make the inquiry into the character and good disposition of persons applying for citizenship more careful and searching. Our existing laws have been in their administration an unimpressive and often an unintelligible form. We accept the man as a citizen without any knowledge of his fitness, and he assumes the duties of citizenship without any knowledge as to what they are. The privileges of American citizenship are so great and its duties so grave that we may well insist upon a good knowledge of every person applying for citizenship and a good knowledge by him of our institutions. We should not cease to be hospitable to immigration, but we should cease to be careless as to the character of it. There are men of all races, even the best, whose coming is necessarily a burden upon our public revenues or a threat to social order. These should be identified and excluded.

We have happily maintained a policy of avoiding all interference with European affairs. We have been only interested spectators of their contentions in diplomacy and in war, ready to use our friendly offices to promote peace, but never obtruding our advice and never attempting unfairly to coin the distresses of other powers into commercial advantage to ourselves. We have a just right to expect that our European policy will be the American policy of European courts.

It is so manifestly incompatible with those precautions for our peace and safety which all the great powers habitually observe and enforce in matters affecting them that a shorter waterway between our eastern and western seaboards should be dominated by any European Government that we may confidently expect that such a purpose will not be entertained by any friendly power.

We shall in the future, as in the past, use every endeavor to maintain and enlarge our friendly relations with all the great powers, but they will not expect us to look kindly upon any project that would leave us subject to the dangers of a hostile observation or environment. We have not sought to dominate or to absorb any of our weaker neighbors, but rather to aid and encourage them to establish free and stable governments resting upon the consent of their own people. We have a clear right to expect, therefore, that no European Government will seek to establish colonial dependencies upon the territory of these independent American States. That which a sense of justice restrains us from seeking they may be reasonably expected willingly to forego.

It must not be assumed, however, that our interests are so exclusively American that our entire inattention to any events that may transpire elsewhere can be taken for granted. Our citizens domiciled for purposes of trade in all countries and in many of the islands of the sea demand and will have our adequate care in their personal and commercial rights. The necessities of our Navy require convenient coaling stations and dock and harbor privileges. These and other trading privileges we will feel free to obtain only by means that do not in any degree partake of coercion, however feeble the government from which we ask such concessions. But having fairly obtained them by methods and for purposes entirely consistent with the most friendly disposition toward all other powers, our consent will be necessary to any modification or impairment of the concession.

We shall neither fail to respect the flag of any friendly nation or the just rights of its citizens, nor to exact the like treatment for our own. Calmness, justice, and consideration should characterize our diplomacy. The offices of an intelligent diplomacy or of friendly arbitration in proper cases should be adequate to the peaceful adjustment of all international difficulties. By such methods we will make our contribution to the world's peace, which no nation values more highly, and avoid the opprobrium which must fall upon the nation that ruthlessly breaks it.

The duty devolved by law upon the President to nominate and, by and with the advice and consent of the Senate, to appoint all public officers whose appointment is not otherwise provided for in the Constitution or by act of Congress has become very burdensome and its wise and efficient discharge full of difficulty. The civil list is so large that a personal knowledge of any large number of the applicants is impossible. The President must rely upon the representations of others, and these are often made inconsiderately and without any just sense of responsibility. I have a right, I think, to insist that those who volunteer or are invited to give advice as to appointments shall exercise consideration and fidelity. A high sense of duty and an ambition to improve the service should characterize all public officers.

There are many ways in which the convenience and comfort of those who have business with our public offices may be promoted by a thoughtful and obliging officer, and I shall expect those whom I may appoint to justify their selection by a conspicuous efficiency in the discharge of their duties. Honorable party service will certainly not be esteemed by me a disqualification for public office, but it will in no case be allowed to serve as a shield of official negligence, incompetency, or delinquency. It is entirely creditable to seek public office by proper methods and with proper motives, and all applicants will be treated with consideration; but I shall need, and the heads of Departments will need, time for inquiry and deliberation. Persistent importunity will not, therefore, be the best support of an application for office. Heads of Departments, bureaus, and all other public officers having any duty connected therewith will be expected to enforce the civil-service law fully and without evasion. Beyond this obvious duty I hope to do something more to advance the reform of the civil service. The ideal, or even my own ideal, I shall probably not attain. Retrospect will be a safer basis of judgment than promises. We shall not, however, I am sure, be able to put our civil service upon a nonpartisan basis until we have secured an incumbency that fair-minded men of the opposition will approve for impartiality and integrity. As the number of such in the civil list is increased removals from office will diminish.

While a Treasury surplus is not the greatest evil, it is a serious evil. Our revenue should be ample to meet the ordinary annual demands upon our Treasury, with a sufficient margin for those extraordinary but scarcely less imperative demands which arise now and then. Expenditure should always be made with economy and only upon public necessity. Wastefulness, profligacy, or favoritism in public expenditures is criminal. But there is nothing in the condition of our country or of our people to suggest that anything presently necessary to the public prosperity, security, or honor should be unduly postponed.

It will be the duty of Congress wisely to forecast and estimate these extraordinary demands, and, having added them to our ordinary expenditures, to so adjust our revenue laws that no considerable annual surplus will remain. We will fortunately be able to apply to the redemption of the public debt any small and unforeseen excess of revenue. This is better than to reduce our income below our necessary expenditures, with the resulting choice between another change of our revenue laws and an increase of the public debt. It is quite possible, I am sure, to effect the necessary reduction in our revenues without breaking down our protective tariff or seriously injuring any domestic industry.

The construction of a sufficient number of modern war ships and of their necessary armament should progress as rapidly as is consistent with care and perfection in plans and workmanship. The spirit, courage, and skill of our naval officers and seamen have many times in our history given to weak ships and inefficient guns a rating greatly beyond that of the naval list. That they will again do so upon occasion I do not doubt; but they ought not, by premeditation or neglect, to be left to the risks and exigencies of an unequal combat. We should encourage the establishment of American steamship lines. The exchanges of commerce demand stated, reliable, and rapid means of communication, and until these are provided the development of our trade with the States lying south of us is impossible.

Our pension laws should give more adequate and discriminating relief to the Union soldiers and sailors and to their widows and orphans. Such occasions as this should remind us that we owe everything to their valor and sacrifice.

It is a subject of congratulation that there is a near prospect of the admission into the Union of the Dakotas and Montana and Washington Territories. This act of justice has been unreasonably delayed in the case of some of them. The people who have settled these Territories are intelligent, enterprising, and patriotic, and the accession of these new States will add strength to the nation. It is due to the settlers in the Territories who have availed themselves of the invitations of our land laws to make homes upon the public domain that their titles should be speedily adjusted and their honest entries confirmed by patent.

It is very gratifying to observe the general interest now being manifested in the reform of our election laws. Those who have been for years calling attention to the pressing necessity of throwing about the ballot box and about the elector further safeguards, in order that our elections might not only be free and pure, but might clearly appear to be so, will welcome the accession of any who did not so soon discover the need of reform. The National Congress has not as yet taken control of elections in that case over which the Constitution gives it jurisdiction, but has accepted and adopted the election laws of the several States, provided penalties for their violation and a method of supervision. Only the inefficiency of the State laws or an unfair partisan administration of them could suggest a departure from this policy.

It was clearly, however, in the contemplation of the framers of the Constitution that such an exigency might arise, and provision was wisely made for it. The freedom of the ballot is a condition of our national life, and no power vested in Congress or in the Executive to secure or perpetuate it should remain unused upon occasion. The people of all the Congressional districts have an equal interest that the election in each shall truly express the views and wishes of a majority of the qualified electors residing within it. The results of such elections are not local, and the insistence of electors residing in other districts that they shall be pure and free does not savor at all of impertinence.

If in any of the States the public security is thought to be threatened by ignorance among the electors, the obvious remedy is education. The sympathy and help of our people will not be withheld from any community struggling with special embarrassments or difficulties connected with the suffrage if the remedies proposed proceed upon lawful lines and are promoted by just and honorable methods. How shall those who practice election frauds recover that respect for the sanctity of the ballot which is the first condition and obligation of good citizenship? The man who has come to regard the ballot box as a juggler's hat has renounced his allegiance.

Let us exalt patriotism and moderate our party contentions. Let those who would die for the flag on the field of battle give a better proof of their patriotism and a higher glory to their country by promoting fraternity and justice. A party success that is achieved by unfair methods or by practices that partake of revolution is hurtful and evanescent even from a party standpoint. We should hold our differing opinions in mutual respect, and, having submitted them to the arbitrament of the ballot, should accept an adverse judgment with the same respect that we would have demanded of our opponents if the decision had been in our favor.

No other people have a government more worthy of their respect and love or a land so magnificent in extent, so pleasant to look upon, and so full of generous suggestion to enterprise and labor. God has placed upon our head a diadem and has laid at our feet power and wealth beyond definition or calculation. But we must not forget that we take these gifts upon the condition that justice and mercy shall hold the reins of power and that the upward avenues of hope shall be free to all the people.

I do not mistrust the future. Dangers have been in frequent ambush

along our path, but we have uncovered and vanquished them all. Passion has swept some of our communities, but only to give us a new demonstration that the great body of our people are stable, patriotic, and law-abiding. No political party can long pursue advantage at the expense of public honor or by rude and indecent methods without protest and fatal disaffection in its own body. The peaceful agencies of commerce are more fully revealing the necessary unity of all our communities, and the increasing intercourse of our people is promoting mutual respect. We shall find unalloyed pleasure in the revelation which our next census will make of the swift development of the great resources of some of the States. Each State will bring its generous contribution to the great aggregate of the nation's increase. And when the harvests from the fields, the cattle from the hills, and the ores of the earth shall have been weighed, counted, and valued, we will turn from them all to crown with the highest honor the State that has most promoted education, virtue, justice, and patriotism among its people.

MARCH 4, 1889.

SPECIAL MESSAGE.

EXECUTIVE MANSION, *March 11, 1889.*

To the Senate of the United States:

I transmit herewith, in answer to the Senate resolution of the 11th ultimo, a report of the Secretary of State, with accompanying papers, in regard to the case of Louis Riel, otherwise known as Louis David Riel.*

BENJ. HARRISON.

PROCLAMATIONS.

BY THE PRESIDENT OF THE UNITED STATES OF AMERICA.

A PROCLAMATION.

The following provisions of the laws of the United States are hereby published for the information of all concerned:

Section 1956, Revised Statutes, chapter 3, Title XXIII, enacts that—

No person shall kill any otter, mink, marten, sable, or fur seal, or other fur-bearing animal within the limits of Alaska Territory or in the waters thereof; and every person guilty thereof shall for each offense be fined not less than $200 nor more than $1,000, or imprisoned not more than six months, or both; and all vessels, their tackle, apparel, furniture, and cargo, found engaged in violation of this section shall be forfeited; but the Secretary of the Treasury shall have power to authorize the killing ot

---

*Tried and executed by the authorities of British North America for complicity in the rebellion in the Northwest Territory.

any such mink, **marten, sable,** or other fur-bearing animal, except fur **seals,** under such regulations as he may prescribe; and it shall be the duty of the Secretary to prevent the killing of any fur seal and to provide for the execution of the provisions of this section until it is otherwise provided by law, nor shall he grant any special privileges under this section.

*   *   *   *   *   *   *

Section 3 of the act entitled "An act to provide for the protection of the salmon fisheries of Alaska," approved March 2, 1889, provides that—

SEC. 3. That section 1956 of the Revised Statutes of the United States is hereby declared to include and apply to all the dominion of the United States in the waters of Bering Sea, and it shall be the duty of the President at a timely season in each year to issue his proclamation, and cause the same to be published for one month in at least one newspaper (if any such there be) published at each United States port of entry on the Pacific coast, warning all persons against entering such waters for the purpose of violating the provisions of said section, and he shall also cause one or more vessels of the United States to diligently cruise said waters and arrest all persons and seize all vessels found to be or to have been engaged in any violation of the laws of the United States therein.

Now, therefore, I, Benjamin Harrison, President of the United States, pursuant to the above-recited statutes, hereby warn all persons against entering the waters of Bering Sea within the dominion of the United States for the purpose of violating the provisions of said section 1956, Revised Statutes; and I hereby proclaim that all persons found to be or have been engaged in any violation of the laws of the United States in said waters will be arrested and punished as above provided, and that all vessels so employed, their tackle, apparel, furniture, and cargoes, will be seized and forfeited.

In testimony whereof I have hereunto set my hand and caused the seal of the United States to be affixed.

[SEAL.]   Done at the city of Washington, this 21st day of March, 1889, and of the Independence of the United States the one hundred and thirteenth.   BENJ. HARRISON.

By the President:

JAMES G. BLAINE, *Secretary of State.*

BY THE PRESIDENT OF THE UNITED STATES OF AMERICA.

A PROCLAMATION.

Whereas, pursuant to section 8 of the act of Congress approved March 3, 1885, entitled "An act making appropriations for the current and contingent expenses of the Indian Department and for fulfilling treaty stipulations with various Indian tribes for the year ending June 30, 1886, and for other purposes," certain articles of cession and agreement were made and concluded at the city of Washington on the 19th day of January, A. D. 1889, by and between the United States of America and the

Muscogee (or Creek) Nation of Indians, whereby the said Muscogee (or Creek) Nation of Indians, for the consideration therein mentioned, ceded and granted to the United States, without reservation or condition, full and complete title to the entire western half of the domain of the said Muscogee (or Creek) Nation in the Indian Territory, lying west of the division line surveyed and established under the treaty with said nation dated the 14th day of June, 1866, and also granted and released to the United States all and every claim, estate, right, or interest of any and every description in and to any and all land and territory whatever, except so much of the former domain of said Muscogee (or Creek) Nation as lies east of said line of division surveyed and established as aforesaid, and then used and occupied as the home cf said nation, and which articles of cession and agreement were duly accepted, ratified, and confirmed by said Muscogee (or Creek) Nation of Indians by act of its council approved on the 31st day of January, 1889, and by the United States by act of Congress approved March 1, 1889; and

Whereas by section 12 of the act entitled "An act making appropriations for the current and contingent expenses of the Indian Department and for fulfilling treaty stipulations with various Indian tribes for the year ending June 30, 1890, and for other purposes," approved March 2, 1889, a sum of money was appropriated to pay in full the Seminole Nation of Indians for all the right, title, interest, and claim which said nation of Indians might have in and to certain lands ceded by article 3 of the treaty between the United States and said nation of Indians concluded June 14, 1866, and proclaimed August 16, 1866, said appropriation to become operative upon the execution by the duly appointed delegates of said nation specially empowered to do so of a release and conveyance to the United States of all right, title, interest, and claim of said nation of Indians in and to said lands in manner and form satisfactory to the President of the United States; and

Whereas said release and conveyance, bearing date the 16th day of March, 1889, has been duly and fully executed, approved, and delivered; and

Whereas section 13 of the act last aforesaid, relating to said lands, provides as follows:

SEC. 13. That the lands acquired by the United States under said agreement shall be a part of the public domain, to be disposed of only as herein provided; and sections 16 and 36 of each township, whether surveyed or unsurveyed, are hereby reserved for the use and benefit of the public schools to be established within the limits of said land under such conditions and regulations as may be hereafter enacted by Congress.

That the lands acquired by conveyance from the Seminole Indians hereunder, except the sixteenth and thirty-sixth sections, shall be disposed of to actual settlers under the homestead laws only, except as herein otherwise provided (except that section 2301 of the Revised Statutes shall not apply): *And provided further*, That any person who, having attempted to but for any cause failed to secure a title in fee to a homestead under existing law, or who made entry under what is known as the

By the President of the United States of America.

A Proclamation.

Whereas the Congress of the United States did by an act approved on the twenty-second day of February, one thousand eight hundred and eighty-nine, provide that the inhabitants of the Territory of Washington might, upon the conditions prescribed in said act, become the State of Washington;

And whereas it was provided by said act that delegates elected as therein provided, to a Constitutional convention in the Territory of Washington, should meet at the seat of government of said Territory; and that, after they had met and organized they should declare on behalf of the people of Washington that they adopt the Constitution of the United States; whereupon the said convention should be authorized to form a State Government for the proposed State of Washington;

And whereas it was provided by said act that the Constitution so adopted should be republican in form and make no distinction in civil or political rights on account of race or color, except as to Indians not taxed, and not be repugnant to the Constitution of the United States and

BENJAMIN HARRISON'S PROCLAMATION ADMITTING
WASHINGTON TO STATEHOOD.

is now complete.

In Testimony Whereof, I have hereunto set my hand and caused the seal of the United States to be affixed.

Done at the City of Washington this eleventh (11th) day of November, in the year of our Lord one thousand eight hundred and eighty-nine, and of the Independence of the United States of America the one hundred and fourteenth.

Benj Harrison

By the President:

James G. Blaine
Secretary of State

LAST PAGE OF PROCLAMATION ADMITTING WASHINGTON TO STATEHOOD WITH SIGNATURES OF HARRISON AND SECRETARY BLAINE.

commuted provision of the homestead law, shall be qualified to make a homestead entry upon said lands: *And provided further*, That the rights of honorably discharged Union soldiers and sailors in the late Civil War as defined and described in sections 2304 and 2305 of the Revised Statutes shall not be abridged: *And provided further*, That each entry shall be in square form as nearly as practicable, and no person be permitted to enter more than one quarter section thereof, but until said lands are opened for settlement by proclamation of the President no person shall be permitted to enter upon and occupy the same, and no person violating this provision shall ever be permitted to enter any of said lands or acquire any right thereto.

The Secretary of the Interior may, after said proclamation and not before, permit entry of said lands for town sites, under sections 2387 and 2388 of the Revised Statutes, but no such entry shall embrace more than one half section of land.

That all the foregoing provisions with reference to lands to be acquired from the Seminole Indians, including the provisions pertaining to forfeiture, shall apply to and regulate the disposal of the lands acquired from the Muscogee (or Creek) Indians by articles of cession and agreement made and concluded at the city of Washington on the 19th day of January, A. D. 1889.

Now, therefore, I, Benjamin Harrison, President of the United States, by virtue of the power in me vested by said act of Congress approved March 2, 1889, aforesaid, do hereby declare and make known that so much of the lands as aforesaid acquired from or conveyed by the Muscogee (or Creek) Nation of Indians and from or by the Seminole Nation of Indians, respectively, as is contained within the following-described boundaries, viz:

Beginning at a point where the degree of longitude 98 west from Greenwich, as surveyed in the years 1858 and 1871, intersects the Canadian River; thence north along and with the said degree to a point where the same intersects the Cimarron River; thence up said river, along the right bank thereof, to a point where the same is intersected by the south line of what is known as the Cherokee lands lying west of the Arkansas River, or as the "Cherokee Outlet," said line being the north line of the lands ceded by the Muscogee (or Creek) Nation of Indians to the United States by the treaty of June 14, 1866; thence east along said line to a point where the same intersects the west line of the lands set apart as a reservation for the Pawnee Indians by act of Congress approved April 10, 1876, being the range line between ranges 4 and 5 east of the Indian meridian; thence south on said line to a point where the same intersects the middle of the main channel of the Cimarron River; thence up said river, along the middle of the main channel thereof, to a point where the same intersects the range line between range 1 east and range 1 west (being the Indian meridian), which line forms the western boundary of the reservations set apart, respectively, for the Iowa and Kickapoo Indians by Executive orders dated, respectively, August 15, 1883; thence south along said range line or meridian to a point where the same intersects the right bank of the North Fork of the Canadian River; thence up said river, along the right bank thereof, to a point where the same is intersected by the west line of the reservation occupied by the Citizen band of Pottawatomies and the Absentee Shawnee Indians, set apart under the provisions of the treaty of February 27, 1867, between the United States and the Pottawatomie tribe of Indians, and referred to in the act of Congress approved May 23, 1872; thence south along the said west line of the aforesaid reservation to a point where the same intersects the middle of the main channel of the Canadian River; thence up the said river, along the middle of the main channel thereof, to a point opposite to the place of beginning, and thence north to the place of beginning (saving and excepting 1 acre of land in square form in the northwest corner of section 9, in township 16 north, range 2 west of the Indian meridian in Indian Territory, and also 1 acre of land in the southeast corner of the northwest quarter of section 15, township 16 north, range 7 west of the Indian meridian in the Indian Territory, which last-described 2 acres are hereby reserved for Government use and control), will, at and after the hour of 12 o'clock noon of the 22d day of April next, and not before, be open for settlement, under the terms of and subject to all the conditions, limitations, and restrictions contained in said act of Congress approved March 2, 1889, and the laws of the United States applicable thereto.

And it is hereby expressly declared and made known that no other parts or portions of the lands embraced within the Indian Territory than those herein specifically described and declared to be open to settlement at the time above named and fixed are to be considered as open to settlement under this proclamation or the act of March 2, 1889, aforesaid.

And warning is hereby again expressly given that no person entering upon and occupying said lands before said hour of 12 o'clock noon of the 22d day of April, A. D. 1889, hereinbefore fixed, will ever be permitted to enter any of said lands or acquire any rights thereto, and that the officers of the United States will be required to strictly enforce the provision of the act of Congress to the above effect.

In witness whereof I have hereunto set my hand and caused the seal of the United States to be affixed.

[SEAL.] Done at the city of Washington, this 23d day of March, A. D. 1889, and of the Independence of the United States the one hundred and thirteenth.

BENJ. HARRISON.

By the President:
  JAMES G. BLAINE,
      Secretary of State.

BY THE PRESIDENT OF THE UNITED STATES OF AMERICA.

. A PROCLAMATION.

A hundred years have passed since the Government which our forefathers founded was formally organized. At noon on the 30th day of April, 1789, in the city of New York, and in the presence of an assemblage of the heroic men whose patriotic devotion had led the colonies to

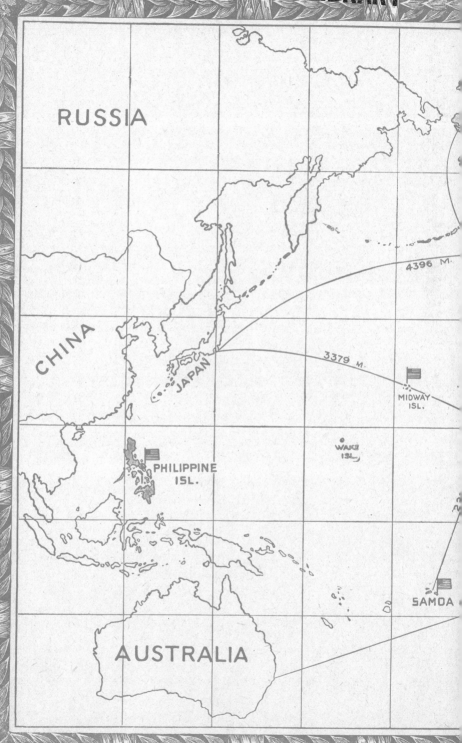